THE AMAZONS

THE
AMAZONS

LIVES AND LEGENDS OF WARRIOR
WOMEN ACROSS THE ANCIENT WORLD

ADRIENNE MAYOR

PRINCETON UNIVERSITY PRESS   PRINCETON & OXFORD

Requests for permission to reproduce material from this work should be sent
to Permissions, Princeton University Press
Published by Princeton University Press,
41 William Street, Princeton, New Jersey 08540
In the United Kingdom: Princeton University Press,
6 Oxford Street, Woodstock, Oxfordshire OX20 1TW
press.princeton.edu
Jacket image: Saikal, the Kalmyk warrior-heroine of the
Central Asian *Manas* epic, illustration by Teodor Gercen
featured on postage stamp, Kyrgyz Republic, 1995.
Library of Congress Cataloging-in-Publication Data
Mayor, Adrienne, 1946–
The Amazons : lives and legends of warrior women across the ancient world /
Adrienne Mayor.
pages cm
Includes bibliographical references and index.
ISBN 978-0-691-14720-8 (hardcover : alk. paper) 1. Amazons. 2. Amazons in
literature. 3. Mythology, Greek. 4. Women soldiers—History. 5. Women,
Prehistoric. 6. Women, Prehistoric—Social conditions. I. Title.
BL820.A6M39 2014
398'.352—dc23
2014004926
British Library Cataloging-in-Publication Data is available
This book has been composed in Sabon Next LT Pro
Printed on acid-free paper. ∞
Printed in the United States of America
1 3 5 7 9 10 8 6 4 2

FOR SAGE ADRIENNE

═══════════

AND IN MEMORY OF
SUNNY LYNN BOCK
1952–1995
AMAZON SPIRIT

CONTENTS

ILLUSTRATIONS

MAPS

ACKNOWLEDGMENTS

COMPILING THIS *ENCYCLOPEDIA AMAZONICA* HAS entailed a long journey from classical Greece across vast, unexplored territories. The task was at once daunting and delightful, and, like any compendium of ancient myths and realities, the book is also unfinished and subject to revision. The excitement of discovering the lives and legends of Amazons and Amazon-like women in so many unexpected places is tempered by the realization that one has only skimmed the surface. Many branching trails beckon future investigators to forge deeper into the ancient histories of warrior women.

A host of people made this book possible. I began this project at the Getty Villa Scholars Program, where I was welcomed as a resident guest researcher in August–September 2010, thanks to Peter Bonfitto, Mary Louise Hart, Kenneth Lapatin, Claire Lyons, David Saunders, and Karol Wight. I'm indebted to my peerless and visionary editor, Rob Tempio, the anonymous readers for the Press, illustration manager Dimitri Karetnikov, and my favorite copyeditor, Lauren Lepow. My sincere appreciation goes to Sandy Dijkstra, Andrea Cavallaro, and everyone at Sandra Dijkstra Literary Agency. To my dear friends who read and commented on early drafts—Kris Ellingsen, Deborah Gordon, Marcia Ober, and Barry Strauss—your help was crucial. I'm grateful for Betchen Barber's thoughtful suggestions for revision. I treasure the honest and insightful critiques of Michelle Maskiell and Josh Ober who read the entire manuscript twice. Special thanks go to Richard Martin and John Oakley, who over the decades have cheerfully endured a barrage of queries about classical myth and art. Henryk Jaronowski, Carla Nappi,

Sarah Pines, and Fred Porta provided translations. I thank Paul Alexander for fact checking and David Luljak for indexing. I am fortunate to benefit from Michele Angel's creative maps and illustration skills, and from Barbara Mayor's keen proofreading.

Many scholars and experts in many disciplines generously shared their specialized knowledge and helped with illustations: Farid Alakbarli, Mustafa Bashir, Roberta Beene, John Boardman, Larissa Bonfante, Kathleen Braden, John Colarusso, Jeannine Davis-Kimball, Dan Diffendale, Ertekin M. Doksanalti, Piotr Dyczek, Lowell Edmunds, Jack Farrell, Debbie Felton, Michael Anthony Fowler, Matthew Funk, Laura Gill, N. S. Gill, Hans Goette, Mazen Haddad, Irene Hahn, William Hansen, Jenny Lando Herdman, Rebecca Hickman, Nino Kalandadze, Robin Lane Fox, Martin Lemke, Terrence Lockyer, Rossella Lorenzi, John Ma, Ruel Macaraeg, Kent Madin, Victor Mair, Justin Mansfield, Jody Maxmin, David Mazierski, David Meadows, Mete Mimiroglu, Maya Muratov, Michael Padgett, Svetlana Pankova, Michel Prieur, Richard Rawles, Ian Rutherford, David Salo, Uli Schamiloglu, Arthur Shippee, Stuart Tyson Smith, Ed Snible, Matthew Sommer, Helen South, Katie Stearns, Tatjana Stepanowa, Bob Sutton, Linda Svendsen, Jean Turfa, Peter van Alfen, James Vedder, Claudia Wagner, Christine Walter, Kirsten Wellman, and Dianna Wuagneux. Heartfelt thanks go to myriad erudite allies and friends of Mithradates Eupator on Facebook for crowd-sourced research on a multitude of Amazon-related topics.

This book is dedicated to my goddaughter Sage, maker of beautiful knives, and to the memory of Sunny, another blonde, tattooed Amazon spirit. Josiah Ober, steadfast companion, this description of an ideal nomadic pair from antiquity expresses what's in my heart: "Wherever they roamed, they were always at home when they were together."

THE AMAZONS

PROLOGUE

ATALANTA, THE GREEK AMAZON

KING IASOS WANTED ONLY SONS. HE LEFT HIS INFANT daughter to die on a mountainside in Arcadia, the rugged highlands of southern Greece. A mother bear nursed the abandoned baby. Hunters found the feral girl and named her Atalanta. Like a female Tarzan, Atalanta was a natural athlete and hunter. Self-reliant, with a "fiery, masculine gaze," she wrestled like a bear and could outrun any animal or man. Atalanta loved wrestling and she was strong enough to defeat the hero Peleus in a grappling contest. This bold tomboy of Greek myth was happiest roaming alone in the forest with her bow and spear. Life in the wilderness held dangers. But when a pair of malicious Centaurs tried to rape Atalanta, she killed them with her arrows.

Because of her bravery and prowess, Atalanta was the only woman invited to join the mythic expedition to destroy the terrible Calydonian Boar. In the myth, a monstrous boar had been sent by the goddess Artemis to ravage southern Greece. To slay the rampaging beast, Meleager gathered more than a dozen prominent Greek heroes, including Jason and Telemon of the Argonauts, Athens's founding king Theseus, Atalanta's wrestling partner Peleus, and Atalanta herself. Whoever killed the giant boar would win its head and hide. As the sole female, Atalanta, by her very presence, ignited strong emotions among the male heroes. Some of the men refused to participate if Atalanta came along. But Meleager, who was in love with Atalanta, compelled them all to set out together.

The hunters ran into trouble from the start. The ferocious boar gored and killed several of the men and hounds. In the mayhem, some hunters were accidentally slain by their fellows. Atalanta proved to be more courageous and skilled than any of the men; only Meleager was her equal. Atalanta was the first to wound the boar. Then Meleager rushed up and dispatched it with his spear. He presented the boar's hide and head to Atalanta, since she had drawn the first blood.

The hunting party was still in turmoil after the kill. Meleager's uncles shouted that it was a disgrace for a woman to have the prize. They seized the boar's hide from Atalanta. A fight erupted. In the uproar Meleager killed his own kinsmen and again presented the boar trophies to Atalanta. She dedicated the boar's huge tusks, head, and hide in the temple at Tegea, her birthplace. Meanwhile, her lover Meleager died as a result of the family feud that raged on after the expedition. Atalanta gave Jason a special "far-flying" spear and volunteered to sail with the Argonauts across the Black Sea on the quest for the Golden Fleece. But Jason denied her request for fear of discord among the male crew.[1]

After proving her heroism in the great boar hunt, Atalanta was reunited with her biological parents. Her father, the king, was now very proud of her but could not tolerate his daughter's unwed state. He insisted that she marry. Aghast at the idea of giving up her freedom, Atalanta demanded a high-stakes contest. She would wed only the man who could defeat her in a footrace. She would give each suitor a head start. But she would kill with her spear every man who lost the race. The headstrong huntress designed the race as a hunt for human prey, but it is significant that the contest also held out the enticing possibility of finding a man who was worthy of her. True to her name, ancient Greek for "balance, equal," Atalanta desired an egalitarian relationship—and so did her hopeful suitors.

The athletic, radiant Atalanta was so desirable that even though the penalty was instant death, many young men eagerly lined up to race her. Many lost their lives. Finally a youth named Hippomenes, realizing he could never outrun Atalanta in a fair race, asked Aphrodite to help him win by trickery. The goddess of love gave him three golden apples, magically irresistible. During their race, Hippomenes dropped the apples one by one to distract Atalanta. She stopped to pick up the first two apples but was able to recover her pace. The third apple and a great burst of speed gave the youth his victory. Atalanta was a man-killer but she was not a man-hater. She consented to be Hippomenes's mate.[2]

Theirs was not a typical Greek marriage, however. Atalanta and Hippomenes spent their days as hunting companions and impetuous lovers. One day while out chasing game, they impulsively had sex in a sacred precinct. In the midst of their passionate lovemaking, they were transformed into a pair of lions. From that moment and for all time, Atalanta and Hippomenes would live as lioness and lion.

Atalanta's fabled racetrack became a well-known landmark in Arcadia; it was still proudly pointed out to tourists in the time of the Roman Empire. At Tegea, Atalanta's birthplace, the gigantic tusks of the Calydonian Boar were displayed in the temple (until the emperor Augustus took them to Rome). The Greek traveler Pausanias visited the temple in about AD 180 and marveled at its monumental frieze depicting the Calydonian Boar Hunt (by the great sculptor Skopas, 350 BC). In the 1880s, French archaeologists discovered those temple ruins. They unearthed fragments of the grand pediment sculptures admired by Pausanias: hunting hounds, heroes, the head of the Calydonian Boar, and Atalanta. The altar was strewn with boars' tusks dedicated by generations of hunters in memory of Atalanta. The archaeologists also found marble reliefs of a lion and a lioness representing the transformation of Atalanta and Hippomenes.[3]

Greek myths were illustrated in thousands of paintings on vases, sculptures, and other artworks in antiquity, and Atalanta's story was no exception. The great boar hunt was extremely popular, appearing in frescoes, statues, and vase paintings from the sixth century BC through the Roman period. In Greek art, Atalanta was often depicted as a huntress with her bow, spear, and dog—and the boar's head. Several vases capture the moment when Meleager presents this trophy. Presenting the spoils of a hunt to one's beloved was an erotic gesture in ancient Greek poetry and art, so the incident tells us that Meleager and Atalanta were lovers.[4]

But the artistic evidence only deepens some mysteries in Atalanta's complicated, paradoxical story. In some boar-hunting scenes, for example,

MAP P.1. Ancient Greek world. Map © Michele Angel.

Atalanta wears a belted tunic with zigzag patterns, a soft pointed cap, and high cuffed boots. These are typical elements of the attire worn by foreign male and female archers from the lands the Greeks called "Scythia." This clothing began to appear in art after the Greeks' first contacts with peoples of the Black Sea and Eurasian steppes in the seventh century BC. Classical art experts struggle to explain why Atalanta, a Greek heroine, was shown wearing Scythian-style outfits like those worn by Amazons.[5]

More riddles arise in the earliest image of the Calydonian Boar Hunt, on the magnificent François Vase discovered in 1844. The spectacular two-foot-high wine krater signed by the painter Kleitias (ca. 570 BC) depicts more than two hundred people, many with identifying inscriptions. (Unfortunately, in 1902, the precious vase was smashed into 638 shards when a guard in the Florence museum hurled a stool at it; it was fully restored in 1973.) The giant boar is being attacked by Meleager, Peleus, Atalanta, and other Greek heroes. But three archers in the

FIG. P.1. Atalanta in athletic outfit (her name is inscribed above). Red-figure kylix (drinking cup), Euaion Painter, fifth century BC, Inv. CA2259, Musée de Louvre, Paris. © Musée de Louvre, Dist. RMN-Grand Palais/Les frères Chuzeville/Art Resource, NY.

scene present an enigma. One draws a Scythian bow; their quivers are at their waists in Scythian style; and they wear the distinctive pointed caps of Scythians. One bears the name "Kimerios," which associates him with the Cimmerians, a tribe of Scythia; another archer's name, "Toxamis," combines Greek "arrow" with the Iranian suffix -mis. Why would Atalanta be accompanied by bowmen dressed like Scythians in this quintessential Greek myth?[6]

Atalanta was the only wrestling heroine in Greek myth and art, and her grappling contest with Peleus was also very popular in artworks. In these athletic scenes, Atalanta is shown in a belted loincloth (*perizoma*, typically worn by barbarian male athletes). She goes topless or wears a kind of sports bra (*strophion*, often worn by female acrobats) and an exercise cap. Sexy details in the wrestling images hint that there might have been more to her match with Peleus than just sport. In one vase painting, a small lion figure is embroidered on the seat of Atalanta's wrestling trunks, an allusion to her character and to her mythic fate.[7]

FIG. P.2. Atalanta wrestling Peleus. Attic black-figure amphora from Nola, Diosphos Painter, sixth–fifth centuries BC, INV: F1837, bpk, Berlin/Antikensammlung, Staatliche Museen/ photo by Johannes Laurentius/Art Resource, NY.

Atalanta's transformation into a lioness also mystifies. Later Latin and medieval commentators tried to explain the conversion as a divine punishment—by making the perverse claim that lions could never mate with their own species.[8] This peculiar notion is accepted by modern scholars who portray Atalanta as "sentenced to hunt forever" as a solitary lioness, "never permitted to have sex again." But both she *and* her lover were changed into lions. And there is no evidence for the odd belief about the love life of lions in classical Greek literature. The Roman naturalist Pliny (first century AD) is commonly cited for this erroneous idea about lions, but in fact what Pliny says is that lions are extremely passionate, jealous mates with each other and they some- times interbreed with other large cats. The lovers' transformation into a lion and a lioness at a moment of sexual bliss seems uniquely gratifying, less a punishment and more like a sympathetic divine intervention for a couple who refused to conform to traditional Greek marriage roles.[9] In the form of lions, the most noble of wild animals—creatures known to stalk and kill prey together—the hunting companions/lovers Ata- lanta and Hippomenes could continue to hunt and mate in mythic eternity.

That Atalanta was changed into a lioness does drive home a power- ful message, though. There was no place in ordinary Greek society for a woman like Atalanta who loved to chase game, fight men, and wander at will. She would be an outsider, bereft of community, for rejecting the life of Greek wives who were confined to a domestic sphere of children and kinfolk. The myth expresses the powerful mixed emotions that At- alanta's independence and physical vigor aroused among Greek males. Some men, like Meleager's uncles, reacted with anger and violence. But other men, like Meleager and Hippomenes, thought Atalanta deserved to live as she wished, and a great many men found her sexually desir- able and might risk their lives to be her lifelong partner. As the ancient writer Aelian declared, no timid man would ever be attracted to Atalanta—and only the most courageous could even meet her chal- lenging gaze.[10]

But Greek men who yearned for a self-reliant mate like Atalanta would not find her in Greece. Such women dwelled among barbarians around the Black Sea. Several myths told of Greek heroes who were paired with formidable women of those regions. One was the Argo- nauts' leader, Jason, who fell for the fiercely independent Medea on the far shore of the Black Sea and brought her back to Greece (where she was labeled "a lioness"). Odysseus became the enchantress Circe's pris- oner of love; her name appears to be Circassian, a language of the Cau- casus.[11] The Greek hero Theseus kidnapped a warrior princess—the

Amazon Antiope—from the southern Black Sea coast and brought her back to Athens (chapter 16).

Perhaps some Greek girls longed to be like Atalanta, the intrepid huntress who went her own way. But their hopes were dashed at puberty when they were expected to marry and obey their husbands. Young Athenian girls participated in an initiation ritual called the Arkteia ("She-Bear"), in which they pretended to be wild bear cubs in sanctuaries of Artemis. In her myth, Atalanta had been a "cub" raised by a she-bear. The cult is mysterious, but we know the girls' activities included footraces, which also evokes Atalanta. Archaeological artifacts from the Arkteia sanctuary at Brauron include images of bears and young girls running, and numerous toys and dolls that were dedicated to Artemis at the conclusion of the girls' ritual entry into womanhood.[12]

Scholars believe that the She-Bear rites stressed the suppression of the young girls' untamed Atalantean nature as a preparation for marriage. Greek male writers often characterized pubescent girls as wild animals who desired to lead the unrestrained life of an Atalanta. Instead of lionesses, Greek maidens were supposed to be transformed into docile matrons. As one classicist expresses this concept, "the Amazon in them had to die."[13]

Another intriguing question concerns the ownership of the erotically charged artworks featuring the huntress heroine who defied Greek sexual norms. It turns out that many of the vases decorated with images of Atalanta, like the François Vase, were special shapes specifically designed as wedding gifts. Atalanta also appears on women's perfume flasks. Why would illustrations of *Atalanta* be considered appropriate gifts for newlyweds and women? Atalanta—an icon of "social and sexual perversity" who escaped the yoke of marriage—seems to be a particularly "troubling" image to give to a bride, remarks one classical scholar. Were pictures of Atalanta really negative examples to warn the bride and groom of the dangers of both excessive lust and chastity, as some argue? Did such gifts really symbolize the "taming of the wild by the civilized Greek male"?[14]

As everyone knew, Atalanta was never tamed. The popularity of her image in public and private art—and especially on wedding vases and women's personal objects—raises some tantalizing questions about

Greek private life.[15] Perhaps the stories and illustrations of Atalanta encouraged a Greek woman, inside her own home and in the secluded bedchamber with her husband, to imagine herself as an Atalanta or even a lioness.

Atalanta was also pictured on Greek vases used at male-only symposiums. So *both* men and women chose to surround themselves with vibrant images of this strong, independent woman; contemplating these images provided pleasure and food for thought for both sexes. The popularity of the myth of Atalanta shows that Greek men and women could delight in the tale of a vigorous young woman free of social constraints and traditional marriage. Despite the dissonance and ambivalence ignited by the idea of women as men's equals, Greeks enjoyed the stories of heroes and heroines as partners in a dangerous hunt and other adventures filled with peril and glory.

Puzzles about Atalanta multiply the closer one looks. There is even something curious about Atalanta's name. The sounds of the ancient Greek for "balance, equal," *Atalanta*, closely resemble a phrase in an ancient Caucasian language spoken in Abkhazia (northeastern coast of the Black Sea), meaning "He gave or set something down before her." Could this phrase allude to the presentation of the trophy boar and/or throwing down the golden apples? The Greeks were notoriously fond of making up Greek etymologies for borrowed foreign words (chapters 1 and 5). The two names, Abkhazian and Greek, are semantically complementary; each fits features of Atalanta's myth. Some scholars speculate that the Calydonian Boar Hunt could contain traces of Scythian folklore, a fascinating possibility.

Remarkably, another Abkhazian-sounding phrase appears in the non-Greek inscription on the vase painting of Atalanta wrestling Peleus, describing her as "curly-haired" (fig. P.2). A recently translated ancient Abkhazian saga tells of a strong young woman, Gunda the Beautiful (also called Lady Hero), who vowed she would marry only the man who could defeat her in wrestling. Ninety-nine eager young suitors failed—she cut off their ears and branded the losers. Finally she grappled with a burly young man from a faraway land who managed to win the match, which lasted all day and shook the earth. They lived happily ever after.[16] Atalanta's wedding challenge was shocking in a Greek context, but vigorous young women setting athletic contests for potential suitors is a ubiquitous theme in Caucasian, Persian, and steppe nomad traditions (chapters 22 and 24).

No wonder Atalanta's story creates "befuddlement" among classicists pondering the meanings of her myth. In an attempt to capture her elusive significance, scholars argue that Atalanta embodied a chain of contradictions. She is said to represent both nonsexual virginity *and* wild, animal sex; she rejects motherhood *but* she bears a son who becomes a hero; she stands for nubile girls *and* young boys; she is *both* hunter and hunted; a threat to male order *but* a desired love object; a man-killer *but* a man-lover. Atalanta is "a study in ambiguity," a "mélange of discordant behaviors." Most scholars conclude that Atalanta's myth must have been part of a ritual initiation for Greek *boys*, while serving as a negative role model for *girls*. The great French classicist Jean-Pierre Vernant admitted, "Everything with Atalanta gets so confused."[17]

Atalanta is unique in Greek myth, and her story is extraordinary and complex, a magnetic focus for the push-pull of anxiety and desire disturbing the Greeks who repressed their own daughters and wives. She is a most untypical Greek female. Her life is idyllic; she rambles around the countryside engaged in hunting and sports, pastimes ordinarily enjoyed by men. Atalanta is bold, armed and dangerous; she defends herself with bow and spear; she challenges and kills men and wins heroic honors in a male-dominated expedition. She rejects traditional marriage and enjoys sex with lovers of her own choosing.[18]

Atalanta was an outlier, a lone, isolated figure. A Greek girl like Atalanta remained a mythic dream. But the Greeks had heard about a place where Atalanta would have fit in perfectly, a land where someone like Atalanta could find sisterhood, social acceptance, and male companionship. That place was among the Amazons.

Who were the Amazons?

In Greek myth, Amazons were fierce warrior women of exotic Eastern lands, as courageous and skilled in battle as the mightiest Greek heroes. Amazons were major characters not only in the legendary Trojan War but also in the chronicles of the greatest Greek city-state, Athens.

Every great champion of myth—Heracles, Theseus, Achilles—proved his valor by overcoming powerful warrior queens and their armies of women. Those glorious struggles against foreign man-killers were recounted in oral tales and written epics and illustrated in countless artworks throughout the Greco-Roman world. Famous historical figures, among them King Cyrus of Persia, Alexander the Great, and the Roman general Pompey, also tangled with Amazons. Greek and Latin authors never doubted that Amazons had existed in the remote past, and many reported that women living the life of Amazons still dwelled in lands around the Black Sea and beyond.[19] Modern scholars, on the other hand, usually consign Amazons to the realm of the Greek imagination.

But were Amazons real? Though they were long believed to be purely imaginary, overwhelming evidence now shows that the Amazon traditions of the Greeks and other ancient societies derived in large part from historical facts.[20] Among the nomad horse-riding peoples of the steppes known to the Greeks as "Scythians," women lived the same rugged outdoor life as the men. These "warlike tribes have no cities, no fixed abodes," wrote one ancient historian; "they live free and unconquered, so savage that even the women take part in war."[21] Archaeology reveals that about one out of three or four nomad women of the steppes was an active warrior buried with her weapons. Their lifestyle—so different from the domestic seclusion of Greek women—captured the imagination of the Greeks. The only real-life parallels in Greece were rare instances of wives forced to defend their families and towns against invaders in the absence of their husbands.

The myth of Atalanta seems to suggest that a girl raised in a natural state would grow up to be something like an Amazon. In reality, "going Amazon" was an option for girls who had been raised since childhood to ride horses and shoot arrows on the steppes. The "equalizing" combination of horseback riding and archery meant that women could be as fast and as deadly as men. Whether by choice or compelled by circumstances, ordinary women of Scythia could be hunters and warriors without giving up femininity, male companionship, sex, and motherhood.

The universal quest to find balance and harmony between men and women, beings who are at once so alike and so different, lies at the heart of all Amazon tales. That timeless tension helps to explain why there were as many love stories about warrior women as there were war stories.

In a nutshell: Amazons, the women warriors who fought Heracles and other heroes in Greek myth, were long assumed to be an imaginative Greek invention. But Amazon-like women were real—although of course the myths were made up. Archaeological discoveries of battle-scarred female skeletons buried with weapons prove that warlike women really did exist among nomads of the Scythian steppes of Eurasia. So Amazons were Scythian women—and the Greeks understood this long before modern archaeology. And the Greeks were not the only ones to spin tales about Amazons. Thrilling adventures of warrior heroines of the steppes were told in many ancient cultures besides Greece.

Our mission is to sort myth from fact. As the first full compendium of the lives and legends of Amazons across the ancient world, this study explores the realities behind the stories, digging deep and ranging far afield to unearth hidden knowledge and surprising recent discoveries about the women warriors mythologized as Amazons. How do we know for certain that Amazon-like women actually existed in antiquity? Did Amazons really cut off one breast? Were Amazons tattooed? What about their sex life? Why would Amazons prefer trousers instead of skirts? Which intoxicants did they favor? How did they train their horses? What were the Amazons' most deadly weapons and what kind of injuries did they inflict? The answers to all these questions and more, drawing on ancient sources and the latest advances in archaeology, history, ethnology, linguistics, and scientific knowledge, are found in these pages.

Once we know what genuine warrior women's lives were like, the famous Amazons of classical myth and legend spring to life with remarkable new clarity. Why did Heracles kill Hippolyte, queen of the Amazons, instead of becoming her lover? What was the fate of Antiope, the only Amazon to marry a Greek hero? Why did the Amazons invade Athens—and who won that war? Could Achilles and the Amazon Penthesilea have been friends in an alternative world? How did a band of Amazons happen to sail to Rome? Who was the beautiful Amazon queen who stalked Alexander the Great across Asia?

The final section presents Amazons as they have never been seen before, from a non-Greek perspective. Instead of peering out with Greek eyes toward the barbarian East, we travel beyond the Mediterranean world, around the Black and Caspian seas, and across the steppes, forests, mountains, and deserts to discover stories told by the ancient Scythians themselves and their neighbors, in Persia and Egypt, the Caucasus, Central Asia, India. At last we find ourselves in China looking west toward the "Great Wilderness" of the Xiongnu, a Chinese name for nomads whose women were as fierce as the men.

A comprehensive *Encyclopedia Amazonica* ranging from the Mediterranean to the Great Wall of China necessarily contains a great many unfamiliar proper names of people and places, testament to the far-flung, sweeping popularity of warrior women tales in antiquity. Anticipating that some readers might skip ahead and turn directly to chapters of greatest personal curiosity or interest, I have included plentiful cross-references to relevant discussions.

PART 1

WHO WERE THE AMAZONS?

I

ANCIENT PUZZLES AND MODERN MYTHS

In olden times, the earth thundered with the pounding of horses' hooves. In that long ago age, women would saddle their horses, grab their lances, and ride forth with their men folk to meet the enemy in battle on the steppes. The women of that time could cut out an enemy's heart with their swift, sharp swords. Yet they also comforted their men and harbored great love in their hearts. . . . After the frenzied battle, Queen Amezan leaned down from her saddle and realized in despair that the warrior she had killed was her beloved. A choking cry filled her throat: My sun has set forever!

—*Caucasus tradition, Nart Saga 26*

Achilles removed the brilliant helmet from the lifeless Amazon queen. Penthesilea had fought like a raging leopard in their duel at Troy. Her valor and beauty were undimmed by dust and blood. Achilles' heart lurched with remorse and desire. . . . All the Greeks on the battlefield crowded around and marveled, wishing with all their hearts that their wives at home could be just like her.

—*Quintus of Smyrna*, The Fall of Troy

IF QUEEN AMEZAN AND QUEEN PENTHESILEA COULD somehow meet in real life, they would recognize each other as sister Amazons. Two tales, two storytellers, two sites far apart in time and place, and yet one common tradition of women who made love and war. The first tale arose *outside* the classical Greek world, in the northern Black Sea–Caucasus region among the descendants of the steppe nomads of Scythia. The other tale originated *within* the ancient Greek world, in epic poems about the legendary Trojan War. In the two traditions the male and female roles are reversed, yet the stories resonate in striking ways—sharing similar characters, dramatic battle situations, emotions, tragic themes—and even the word "Amazon."

Recently translated from the Circassian language, the first story tells of the mythic leader of a band of women warriors, Amezan. It is one of many "Nart" sagas, oral traditions about heroes and heroines of the heart of ancient Scythian—and Amazon—territory (now southern Russia). The Caucasus tales preserve ancient Indo-European myths combined with the folk legends of Eurasian nomads, first encountered by Greeks who sailed the Black Sea in the seventh century BC. The sagas not only describe strong horsewomen who match the descriptions of Amazons in Greek myth, but they also suggest a possible Caucasian etymology for the ancient Greek loanword "amazon."[1]

The second vignette, about Achilles and Penthesilea, is an episode from the archaic Trojan War epic cycles, one of which was the *Iliad*. Many oral traditions about Amazons were already circulating before Homer's day, the eighth/seventh century BC, around the time when the first recognizable images of Amazons appeared in Greek art. The *Iliad* covered only two months of the great ten-year war with Troy. At least six other epic poems preceded or continued the events in the *Iliad*, but they survive only as fragments. Many other lost oral traditions about the Trojan War are alluded to the *Iliad* and other works, and they are illustrated in ancient art depicting Greeks fighting Amazons. The lost poem *Arimaspea* by the Greek traveler Aristeas (ca. 670 BC) contained Amazon stories. Another wandering poet, Magnes from Smyrna (said to be Homer's birthplace), recited tales in Lydian about an Amazon invasion of Lydia in western Anatolia in the early seventh century BC. Some scholars suggest that there was once a freestanding epic poem about Amazons, along the lines of the *Iliad*, a tantalizing possibility.[2]

One of the lost Trojan War epics, the *Aethiopis* (attributed to Arctinos of Miletos, eighth/seventh century BC), was a sequel to the *Iliad*, taking up the action where Homer left off. The *Aethiopis* described the arrival of Queen Penthesilea and her band of Amazon mercenaries who came to help the Trojans fight the Greeks. Scenes from this poem were very popular in Greek vase paintings. In the third century AD, the Greek poet Quintus of Smyrna drew on the *Aethiopis* to retell the story of Penthesilea's duel with the Greek champion Achilles, in his *Fall of Troy*, quoted in this chapter's second epigraph.

Both of the tales quoted above—one from Scythia and the other from the Greek homeland—feature women whose fighting skills matched those of men. Their heroic exploits were imaginary, but their characters and actions arose from a common historical source: warrior cultures of the steppes where nomad horsemen and -women could experience parity at a level almost unimaginable for ancient Hellenes.

Myth and reality commingled in the Greek imagination, and as more and more details came to light about Scythian culture, the women of Scythia were explicitly identified as "Amazons." Today's archaeological and linguistic discoveries point to the core of reality that lay behind Greek Amazon myths. But in fact, the newfound archaeological evidence allows us to finally catch up with the ancient Greeks themselves. The Amazons of myth and the independent women of Scythia were *already* deeply intertwined in Greek thinking more than twenty-five hundred years *before* modern archaeologists and classicists began to realize that women warriors really did exist and influenced Greek traditions.

Amazons of classical literature and art arose from hazy facts elaborated by Greek mythographers and then came into sharper focus as knowledge increased. Rumors of warlike nomad societies—where a *woman* might win fame and glory through "manly" prowess with weapons—fascinated the Greeks. The idea of bold, resourceful women warriors, the equals of men, dwelling at the edges of the known world, inspired an outpouring of mythic stories, pitting the greatest Greek heroes against Amazon heroines from the East. Every Greek man, woman, boy, and girl knew these adventure stories by heart, stories illustrated in public and private artworks. The details of the "Amazon" lifestyle aroused speculation and debate. Many classical Greco-Roman historians, philosophers, geographers, and other writers described Amazonian-Scythian history and customs.

The early Greeks received their information about northeastern peoples from many different sources, including travelers, traders, and explorers, and from the indigenous, migrating tribes around the Black Sea, Caucasus Mountains, Caspian Sea, and Central Asia. The tribes' accounts of themselves and culturally similar groups were transmitted (and garbled) by layers of translations over thousands of miles. Another probable source was the high population of household slaves in Greece who hailed from Thrace and the Black Sea region.[3] Selection bias was a factor. Accounts of "barbarian" customs that piqued Greek curiosity or matched Greek expectations might have been chosen over others. Yet a surprising number of accurate details, confirmed by archaeology, managed to sneak through all these obstacles.

The Scythians themselves left no written records. Much of our knowledge about them comes from the art and literature of Greece and Rome. But the Scythians did leave spectacular physical evidence of their way of life for archaeologists to uncover. Dramatic excavations of tombs, bodies, and artifacts illuminate the links between the women called Amazons and the warlike horsewomen archers of the Scythian steppes. According to one leading archaeologist, "All of the legends about Amazons find their visible archaeological reflection within the grave goods" of the ancient Scythians.[4] That is an overstatement, yet recent and ongoing discoveries do offer astonishing evidence of the existence of authentic women warriors whose lives matched the descriptions of Amazons in Greek myths, art, and classical histories, geographies, ethnographies, and other writings. Scythian graves do contain battle-scarred skeletons of women buried with their weapons, horses, and other possessions. Scientific bone analysis proves that women rode, hunted, and engaged in combat in the very regions where Greco-Roman mythographers and historians once located "Amazons."

Archaeology shows that Amazons were not simply symbolic figments of the Greek imagination, as many scholars claim. Nor are Amazons unique to Greek culture, another common claim. In fact, Greeks were not the only people to spin tales about Amazon-like figures and warrior women ranging over the vast regions east of the Mediterranean. Other literate cultures, such as Persia, Egypt, India, and China, encountered warlike nomads in antiquity, and their narratives drew on their own knowledge of steppe nomads through alliances, exploration, trade, and warfare. Their heroes also fought and fell in love with Amazon-like heroines. Moreover, vestiges of the tales told in antiquity by Scythian peoples about themselves are preserved in traditional oral legends, epic poems, and stories of Central Asia, some only recently committed to writing.

Who were the Amazons? Their complex identity is enmeshed in history and imagination. To see them clearly, we first need to cast away murky symbolic interpretations and spurious popular beliefs.

POPULAR MISCONCEPTIONS

The single most notorious "fact" often used to describe Amazons is wrong. The idea that each Amazon removed one breast so that she could shoot arrows with ease is based on zero evidence. It was refuted in antiquity. Yet this bizarre belief, unique to the ancient Greeks, has persisted for more than twenty-five hundred years since it was first proposed in the fifth century BC by a Greek historian dabbling in etymology. The origins of the "single-breasted" Amazon and the controversies that still surround this false notion are so complex and fascinating that Amazon bosoms have their own chapter.

Some fallacies about Amazons can be traced to inconsistencies, gaps—and wild speculations—in the ancient Greek and Latin sources. Other modern misconceptions originate in attempts to explain Amazons solely in terms of their symbolic meaning for the Greeks, especially male Athenians.[5] Conflicting claims in antiquity are still debated today, like the single-breast story. Were the Amazons a true gynocracy, a society of self-governing women living apart from men? Some pictured a tribe of man-hating virgins or domineering women who enslaved weak men and mutilated baby boys, a vision that led to speculations on how Amazon society reproduced.

AMAZONS, A TRIBE KNOWN FOR STRONG WOMEN

The notion that Amazons were hostile toward men was controversial even in antiquity. The confusion begins with their name. Linguistic evidence suggests that the earliest Greek form of the non-Greek name *Amazon* designated an ethnic group distinguished by a high level of equality between men and women. Rumors of such parity would have startled the Greeks, who lived according to strictly divided male and female roles. Long before the word "Scythian" or specific tribal names appeared in Greek literature, "Amazons" may have been a name for a people notorious for strong, free women.[6]

The earliest reference to the Amazons in Greek literature appears in Homer's *Iliad* in the formulaic phrase *Amazones antianeirai*. Modern scholars are unanimous that the plural noun *Amazones* was not originally a Greek word. But it is unclear which language it was borrowed from and what its original meaning was. What is known for certain is that *Amazon* does not have anything to do with breasts (chapter 5 for probable origins of the name).

There is something remarkable about Homer's earliest use of *Amazones* in the *Iliad*. The form of the name falls into the linguistic category of ethnic designations in epic poetry (another Homeric example is *Myrmidones*, the warriors led by Achilles at Troy). This important clue tells us that *Amazones* was originally a Hellenized name for "a plurality, a people," as in *Hellenes* for Greeks and *Trooes* for the Trojans. The Greeks used distinctive feminine endings (typically -*ai*) for associations made up exclusively of women, such as *Nymphai* (Nymphs) or *Trooiai* for Trojan women. But *Amazones* does not have the feminine ending that one would expect if the group consisted only of women. Therefore, the name *Amazones* would originally have been "understood as . . . a people consisting of men and women." As classicist Josine Blok points out in her discussion of this puzzle, without the addition of the feminine epithet *antianeirai* "there is no way of telling that this was a people of female warriors."[7] The inescapable conclusion is that *Amazones* was not a name for a women-only entity, as many have assumed. Instead *Amazones* once indicated an entire ethnic group.

So the earliest literary references to Amazons identified them as a nation or people, followed by *antianeirai*, a descriptive tag along the lines of "the Saka, Pointed Hat Wearers," or "the Budini, Eaters of Lice." Indeed, many ancient Greek writers do treat Amazons as a tribe of men and women. They credit the tribe with innovations such as ironworking and domestication of horses. Some early vase paintings show men fighting alongside Amazons.[8]

But what about the meaning of the epithet attached to *Amazones*? That word is slippery and complex. *Antianeirai* is often translated in modern times as "opposites of men," "against men," "opposing men," "antagonistic to men," or "man-hating." In fact, however, in ancient Greek epic diction the prefix *anti-* did not ordinarily suggest opposition or antagonism as the English prefix "anti-" does today. Instead *anti-* meant "equivalent" or "matching." Accordingly, *antianeirai* is best translated as "equals of men."

Such ethnonyms, names of tribes, are typically masculine, with the understanding that the female members are included in the collective name (as in "man" for all humans or "les Indiens d'Amérique" for an entire ethnic group). But the curious formation *aneirai* is a unique feminine plural compound that included the Greek masculine noun "man," *aner*. A parallel formation occurs in the Amazon name Deianeira, "Man-Destroyer," in which *aner* is the object of the verb stem *dei* (destroy) with the suffix *-ia*. If there had been a group of women named thus, the plural would be the *Deianeirai*.[9]

Amazones antianeirai is "unmistakably an ethnic designation," yet the epithet is feminine, a reversal of expectations that puzzles scholars.[10] The odd semantic effect of "men," in the sense of a whole people or nation, combined with a feminine description brings to mind the popular tendency among English speakers to refer to cats as "she" and dogs as "he," even though it is understood that tomcats and bitches are also members of the respective species.

The adaptation of the original, unknown barbarian name to the Greek epic formula for a whole people produced "a proper noun riddled with ambiguity." Some scholars interpret this peculiarity as evidence that Homer's *Amazones antianeirai* must have been a purely mythic construction created by the Greeks for a fictional "race" of women warriors. The assumption is that the idea of women behaving like men was so difficult to grasp, so "confusing and menacing" and disruptive for Greeks, that the name was "only conceivable in the imaginary world of myth." But should we underestimate the ancient Greeks' ability to conceive of and name a real people whose gender relations were different from their own? In fact, it was common for the Greeks to describe and *name foreigners by reference to their exotic, disturbing customs*, such as lice eating, head-hunting, polyandry (multiple husbands), and cannibalism.[11]

The linguistic evidence points to a reasonable explanation for the unusual semantics of the name "Amazons, equals of men." The fact that the earliest nomenclature for Amazons took the form of a name for an ethnic group is highly significant. Real ethnic groups, of course, are made up of men, women, and children, and in early antiquity the word *Amazones* would have been "understood as a group of people consisting of men and women," as Blok points out. Homer and other archaic writers could have used the phrase *Amazones andres*, "the Amazon people," but their choice of *Amazones antianeirai* clearly highlighted this group's most outstanding quality. Because *aner/andres* could also mean "man/men" in the sense of a whole people, a tribe, or a nation, the phrase also carries the connotation of "equal humans." The Greeks first identified the Amazons ethnographically, as a nation of men and women distinguished by something outstanding in their gender relations. Later, any ambivalence or anxiety that knowledge of this alternative gender-neutral culture evoked among Greeks was played out in their mythic narratives about martial women.

Here is a plausible sequence: Archaic Greeks had heard about peoples ranging over the Black Sea–steppes region, a warrior society that exhibited a remarkable degree of sexual equality. Their non-Greek name, sounding something like "amazon," was adapted to the epic form of ethnonyms, thus *Amazones*. The descriptive epithet *antianeirai* was added to call out the most notable feature of this group: gender equality. The epithet was feminine to emphasize the extraordinary status of women among this particular people, relative to the status of women in Greek culture. Unlike most other ethnic groups familiar to the Greeks, in which the men were the most significant members, among *Amazones* it was the women who stood out. *Amazones antianeirai* could originally have meant something like "Amazons, the tribe whose women are equals," or simply "Amazons, the equals." A race of warlike men *and women* piqued the curiosity of the Greeks and led to stories about heroic women of faraway lands who were worthy opponents of male warriors.

Gradually, as more travel and information allowed the Greeks to differentiate among the numerous individual ethnolinguistic tribes of Scythia, the old concept of "Amazons" as a collective name to designate an exotic "race" of equal sexes evolved to refer to a related but novel idea: a long-ago tribe of warlike women who fought men, dominated men, or lived entirely without men. The meaning of *anti-* in the epithet began to shift from "equals of" to "opponents of" to suggest hostility to males, and the atypical feminine form of what was once a proper name for an entire people now encouraged visions of a mythic gynocracy.[12]

The earliest name for Amazons preserved in literature is strong evidence that it first entered Greek culture as a term for hazily understood "Scythian" peoples; then over time Amazons became a mythic construct, while still retaining and accumulating kernels of truth. The linguistic evidence gives us a practical approach to understanding Amazons as members of real nomad tribes. This perspective, in turn, helps us make sense of many other striking and ambiguous features of the mythic and later historical accounts of Amazons.

MAN-HATING VIRGINS?

The Greek playwright Aeschylus (fifth century BC) called Amazons "maidens fearless in battle." *Maiden*, often conflated with *virgin*, meant "unmarried." The notion that Amazons were lifelong virgins who resisted sex with men might have arisen from comparisons with the virginal Greek goddesses of war and hunting, Athena and Artemis. "Mankillers" (*androktones*) was another ancient label for Amazons too. Herodotus (ca. 450 BC) remarked that some Amazons of Scythia did not marry unless they had slain (or fought) a man in battle, and he commented that a few never married. Pomponius Mela (ca. AD 43) wrote that "to kill the enemy is a woman's military duty [and] virginity was the punishment for those who fail." But that did not mean that the women remained technical virgins, since Herodotus and other ancient authors describe plenty of Amazon sex with men outside of traditional marriage as understood by the Greeks. Some, like Diodorus and Hippocrates, reported that it was the custom for younger women to practice martial arts and serve as active soldiers, while older women with children would ride to war only in emergencies.[13]

A strong bond of sisterhood was another famous Amazon trait, sometimes interpreted today as a sexual preference for women. The image of Amazons as man-hating lesbians is a twentieth-century twist, however. No ancient account mentions this possibility—and the Greeks and Romans were certainly never shy about discussing male or female homosexuality. Hellanikos, a contemporary of Herodotus, described Amazons as "man-loving." Numerous other Greek and Roman writers agreed that Amazons were eager sexual partners with chosen male lovers and that they sometimes formed long-term relationships with men (chapter 8). The Amazons' sexual activity with men is underscored by the fact that only three Amazons—Alkippe, Sinope, and Orithyia—were singled out as remarkable because of their vows of virginity.[14]

Verdict: man-killers on the battlefield but not man-haters, Amazons were modeled on stories of self-confident women of the steppe cultures who fought for glory and survival and enjoyed male companionship, but on terms that seemed extraordinary to the ancient Greeks.

SYMBOLIC FIGURES?

Archaeological evidence shows that Eurasian women fitting the description of mythic Amazons were contemporaries of the ancient Greeks. Warlike women of the steppes also appear in the traditions of non-Hellenic cultures. Yet the idea that Amazons were fantasy figures conjured up by Greek men to reflect anxiety-fraught aspects of their own Hellenic culture still holds sway. Amazons in Greek art are interpreted as illustrations of myth, not reality. This view is expressed in a recent off-the-cuff comment by a leading art historian: "It is useless to say anything about what the Amazons really were, because they were not *really* anything."[15]

So many diverse meanings are projected onto Amazons that it is impossible to do them all justice here. Amazons have been interpreted as negative role models for Greek women; as repulsive monsters or "Others" who threatened the Greek masculine ego; as figures justifying gender inequality or expressing fears of female rebellion against male oppression; as enemies of civilization; as symbols of wild, animal-like sexuality; as women who refuse to grow up and accept marriage and childbirth; as asexual "un-women"; as political stand-ins for inferior barbarians, "effeminate" Persians, or foreign wives of Athenian citizens; as representations of pubescent Greek girls or teenage Greek boys; and as an inside-out, upside-down mirror of Hellenic culture.[16]

Some interpretations are incompatible with ancient and modern evidence. For example, Amazons have been paired with Centaurs as unruly forces of uncivilized Nature. But unlike the drunken, priapic half-horse–half-men of myth whose crude weapons were boulders and uprooted trees, Amazons were said to tame horses, form orderly warrior societies, use iron weapons, wear tailored clothing, control their own sexuality, manifest historical progress, carry out strategic warfare, and found important cities. Amazons as loathsome "Others" is hard to reconcile with the positive ways they were actually portrayed in antiquity. Greeks imagined many truly repugnant female monsters—Medusa, Echidna, Scylla, Harpies—but Amazons were consistently depicted as admirable, athletic, beautiful, sexually desirable, valiant women who embodied the same traits that distinguished heroic Greek males. Seeking unconscious metaphors in mythological stories can spark insights about ancient Greek psychology. But explaining Amazons as wholly make-believe figures created by Greeks for Greeks has resulted in a logjam of competing theories. Thanks to archaeology, the tide is beginning to turn and Amazons are at last achieving "historical respectability."[17]

Yet many still believe that the Greek psyche summoned mythic Amazons into existence so they could be killed off. Amazons "exist [only] in order . . . to be defeated"; they have no history, "no future," and the heroic warrior status to which they aspire is "impossible."[18] It's true that Amazons do end up killed by Greek heroes in the major myths. But is it any wonder that Greek national myths would show their own heroes triumphing over powerful foreign enemies? Greek heroes crush foes, male and female alike, from Medusa to the Trojans. More significant is that the myths invariably feature equally matched Greek and Amazon antagonists. Akin to the noble heroes of Troy bested by Greek champions in the *Iliad*, each Amazon fighter is just as brave as the hero she confronts. In Greek vase paintings, the outcome is often suspenseful: Amazons are shown fighting and dying courageously, and some are even shown killing Greek warriors. Amazons in Greek art are always depicted running *toward* danger, never fleeing (as Persians sometimes were). Out of more than 550 vase paintings of fighting Amazons, fewer than 10 show Amazons gesturing for mercy. Combat with an Amazon foe requires a fair match; otherwise there can be no honor for the ultimate Greek victor.[19]

AMAZON AS HEROES

In the Greek myths Amazons always die young and beautiful. But a short, splendid life and violent death in battle was the perfect *heroic* ideal in myth. Indeed, this destiny (*kleos aphthiton*, "imperishable glory") was what every great Greek hero craved for himself—the "beautiful death" was supposed to guarantee eternal fame and glory. The heroic spirit—"If our lives be short, let our fame be great"—was also the choice of the heroes and heroines in the Nart sagas of the Caucasus. The many wounded and dead Amazons depicted in classical Greek art are invariably beautiful and brave (the only difference is that they are not shown "heroically nude" like male heroes; see chapter 7).[20] One cannot help but notice that in the Greek myths *and* in semihistorical accounts, nearly every Amazon we know by name displays exemplary heroic attributes and achieves honor by dying heroically in battle.

In fact, what is truly surprising about Amazons is the realization that these non-Greek women actually *surpass* the Greek mythic heroes in the manner of their deaths. Despite their vaunted courage and might, not one great Greek hero manages to achieve a glorious death on the battlefield.[21] Perseus, the slayer of Medusa, dies of old age. Bellerophon, thrown by his flying horse, Pegasus, into a thornbush, ends up a blind, lame hermit. Theseus, Athens's founding hero? Shoved off a cliff by an elderly king. Odysseus? Accidentally done in by his son, stabbed with a stingray spine. The superhero Heracles perishes ignominiously, wrapped in a poisoned tunic, a gift from his wife. The mighty Achilles is felled by an arrow in the heel, shot from behind. Jason, leader of the Argonauts—crushed in his sleep by a rotten beam from his old ship, the *Argo*.

The quintessentially heroic credentials of Amazons make it difficult to see them as objects of contempt or victims in a tragedy of ancient misogyny. Instead, Amazons of myth represented worthy human adversaries for Greek heroes. The heroic status of Amazons is evident in a striking painting of the Trojan War on an Etruscan vase (ca. 330 BC). The Etruscans, a mysterious Italian civilization that flourished from about 700 BC until they were absorbed by the Romans in what is now Tuscany, were very familiar with Greek myths, but they also had their own tales. Etruscan women enjoyed relatively liberated lives compared to Greek women. On one side of the vase Achilles is killing a Trojan.

The other side shows an Amazon mourning as the ghosts of two bandaged and cloaked Amazons enter the Underworld as heroes. They are labeled "Pentasila" (Penthesilea) and "hinthi (A)turmucas." *Hinthi* is Etruscan for "soul or shade"; *(A)turmuca* is the Etruscan version of either Andromache ("Manly Fighter") or Dorymache ("Spear Fighter"). The Amazons' bandages are artistic shorthand for their having died violently and honorably in battle. Andromache is a known Amazon name, but this would be the only instance of an Amazon named Aturmuca/Dorymache (although there is an Amazon named Enchesimargos, "Spear Mad").[22] Was there once a popular Greek or Etruscan story, now lost, that associated this heroine with Penthesilea's band of Amazons at Troy?

A stunning discovery in 2013 suggests that warrior women existed among the Etruscans. Inside a rock-cut tomb in ancient Tarquinia (ca. 620 BC), archaeologists found a skeleton holding a spear; the burned remains of another person lay nearby. Jewelry, a bronze sewing box, and a painted Corinthian perfume/oil flask accompanied the pair. The spear led the archaeologists to identify the skeleton as a warrior prince buried with his cremated wife. But DNA bone analysis soon revealed that the lance belonged to a woman aged 35–40 and the ashes belonged to a man of 20–30. (Preconceptions about "masculine" and "feminine" grave goods have led archaeologists to make a host of similar errors; scientific osteological testing is overturning these biases; see chapter 4).[23]

Amazons in classical literature were *human*, with desires, flaws, virtues, ambitions, and vulnerabilities similar to those attributed to mortal Greek heroes. Moreover—like the greatest Greek heroes—each famous Amazon queen was the protagonist of her own mythic biography, which generated multiple alternative versions. Like the tales of Theseus, Heracles, Achilles, and Atalanta, the many different stories of individual Amazons were filled with great challenges, adventures, victories, and loss.

A PURELY GREEK INVENTION?

Western scholars often take it for granted that Amazons were the exclusive creative property of the ancient Greeks. "It is important to stress that these foreign heroes existed only in Greek myth and not in native mythic traditions," is how one classicist expresses the claim. Another states that "Amazons are not represented in cultures based on non-Greek emblems and norms." But this unexamined assumption turns out to be false.[24] The belief that Amazons existed only in Greek culture has led classicists to maintain that all Amazon figures in Greek art and literature were doomed cardboard figures created to fill conceptual, symbolic niches for the Greeks. Such a Hellenocentric claim is disproved by literary, historical, artistic, linguistic, and archaeological evidence for warlike women of ancient Scythia in a wide range of other ancient cultures. Even the tendency to view Amazon figures as purely symbolic is not confined to classical Greek scholarship. The classicists' interpretation of Amazons as symbols unknowingly recapitulates the interpretations of some modern religious Islamicist scholars, who make similar claims about Amazon-like women in ancient Persian literature (chapter 23).[25]

So the Greeks did *not* invent the idea of Amazons. But a stark difference *does* distinguish the main Greek *mythic script* from other Amazon traditions in antiquity. In the Greek myths, Greek heroes always destroy Amazons. Psychosocial explanations focus on the drastic scenes of violence toward strong foreign women in Greek myth and art.[26] Greek myths are unique in their insistence on death to Amazons, but this focus misses a bigger story. The mythic formula is radically at odds with the more realistic, evenhanded descriptions of Amazon warrior women by Greco-Roman historians, geographers, and ethnographers, and their accounts share much in common with the tales of non-Greek cultures that met Scythian horse archers on the battlefield. In these more realistic scenarios, warlike women can forge alliances with former enemies, have male companions, fall in love, have children, and sometimes win and sometimes lose in love and war.

Surprisingly, even in the dark archaic Greek myths one can detect glimmers of other options. Traces of alternative story lines in vase paintings and fragments of Greek literature hint that peaceful interactions, even romance, might have been possible outcomes. In the Greek myths about Amazons that have come down to us, war always triumphs over love. But *outside* Greek mythology, and *beyond the Greek world*, women warriors and male warriors might make love and war together as equals—and even live happily ever after.

THREE CATEGORIES OF AMAZONS

In untangling the myths and realities of warrior women of antiquity, at least three categories of "Amazons" emerge (and sometimes converge). In the contexts of history, Greek mythology, and non-Greek settings, the women we call Amazons fall into the following groups.

1. *Real nomadic horsewomen archers of the steppes.* The historical reality of Amazon-like women contemporary with the ancient Greeks is now fully documented by archaeological evidence. The lives of these once-living counterparts of mythic and legendary Amazons are accessible to us through excavations of burials, scientific analysis of bodily remains and grave goods, comparative ethnological studies, linguistics, and historical sources both ancient and modern.

2. *Amazon queens Hippolyte, Antiope, and Penthesilea and other Amazons of classical mythology.* The adventures and biographies of warrior women who battled Greeks took shape in the storytelling imagination interwoven with strands of reality from the domain of steppe nomads. In the major myths about Greeks versus Amazons, despite their bravery, erotic appeal, and prowess the women are almost always killed or captured.

3. *Women warriors in non-Greek traditions from the Black Sea to China.* Amazon-like heroines appear in Egyptian romances, Persian legends, epic traditions of the Caucasus and Central Asia, and Chinese chronicles. These non-Greek stories diverge from the grim Greek mythic script that doomed Amazons to defeat and death. Among the cultures the Greeks designated as "barbarian," myths, legends, and historical accounts express great pride in their own heroic warrior women who won victories over men and survived to fight again. When non-Greek societies faced female fighters among their enemies, many tales recount how they eagerly sought to have these Amazons as lovers, companions, and allies instead of killing them.

After Heracles, Amazons were the single most popular subjects in Greek vase paintings. Amazons appeared in city murals and monumental civic sculptures in Athens and other Greek cities; tombs and places

FIG. 1.1. Left, Amazon doll with helmet, articulated arms and legs, terra-cotta, fifth century BC, Greek, Aegina, Inv. CA955, Musée de Louvre, Paris. Photo: Gerard Blot. © RMN-Grand Palais/ Art Resource, NY. Right, Amazon doll with articulated legs, dressed as a hoplite, terra-cotta, signed MAECIUS, Asia Minor, Inv. CA1493, Musée de Louvre, Paris. © Musée de Louvre, Dist. RMN-Grand Palais/Les frères Chuzeville/Art Resource, NY.

linked to Amazons were revered in the Greek and Anatolian landscape. Some of the most poignant and little-known ancient artifacts are dolls representing Amazons, discovered in the graves of young girls in Greece and Asia Minor. Had the little girls lived to be married, they would have dedicated these dolls to the goddess Artemis. Clay dolls in the Louvre and other collections are identified as Amazons by their pointed Scythian-style caps with lappets (earflaps), like the caps of many Amazons in Greek art, and by their armor and weapons. The doll on the left in figure 1.1 was made Athens in 450–400 BC. She is six inches tall, and her molded hair and helmet were once brightly painted. (Early artistic images of Amazons have helmets like those of Greek hoplites; the goddess Athena often wears a similar helmet, but a nude Athena doll is unlikely.) Movable arms and legs allowed the owner to dress this doll in miniature Amazon-style clothing. The doll on the right was discovered in a young girl's grave in Roman-era Asia Minor. About ten inches tall, she wears an imposing helmet, with long hair curling over her shoulder. She is dressed as a classical Amazon, in a belted tunic that exposes one breast, with a studded belt around her waist and across her chest. Articulated legs allow her to "walk." Her broken arm held a bow, spear, or shield. This doll is a remarkable find, for it bears the signature of its maker, Maecius.[27] Whether these dolls were treasured toys or ritual figures, the fact that Amazon figurines belonged to girls is striking. They suggest that Amazons were female models available to young women in the classical world.

Did men, women, or both tell the earliest tales—oral traditions— about Amazons and their living counterparts on the steppes? It does not really matter, since the stories spread throughout Hellenic society and every listener—men and women, boys and girls—could understand the message of equality extended to barbarians and even women. Amazon myths and legends offered a vision impossible in Greek society but rumored to exist in a faraway land called Scythia, the Amazon homeland.

2

SCYTHIA, AMAZON HOMELAND

SCYTHIANS! SOMEWHERE TO THE NORTH AND EAST, beyond the world familiar to the Greeks, restless nomads crisscrossed a landscape of immense emptiness. Expert horse riders, the men and women spent their lives astride tough ponies and nourished their babies with mare's milk. They perfected their deadly aim by shooting at turquoise gems embedded in high rocky crags. They dipped their arrows in the venom of steppe vipers, scalped their foes, and drank from the gilded skulls of their enemies and ancestors. Under the influence of intoxicating clouds of burning hemp, they buried dead companions with their favorite horses and fabulous golden treasures under earthen mounds scattered across the featureless steppes. In Far Scythia, nomadic prospectors braved the desert wilderness to reach secret gold sands guarded by fantastic beaked monsters called griffins. Men and women wore trousers and tattooed themselves with strange designs and stags with towering antlers. The peoples of Scythia were wide-ranging: traversing vast seas of grass and sand, trekking over forbidding mountain passes, and crossing frozen straits. From time to time, waves of these aggressive mounted archers advanced inexorably westward, only to recede back into the steppes.

Evidence exists for all of these attributes ascribed to steppe nomads in Greek literature and art (with the exceptions of target practice with embedded gems and the use of poisoned arrows).[1] For the Greeks, who mostly farmed small plots or lived in towns, the idea of a boundless,

MAP 2.1. Nomadic cultures, Eurasia to China. Map © Michele Angel.

uncultivated sweep of land inhabited by wild "Scythians" was an intimidating notion, arousing respect laced with shivers of anxiety. The earliest Greek vision of "Scythia" emerged from travelers' tales; curious rumors; folklore from Thrace, the Black Sea, and beyond; traders' gossip; and dimly understood facts and garbled descriptions.

"Scythia" was a fluid term in antiquity. For the Greeks, "Scythia" stood for an extensive cultural zone of a great many loosely connected nomadic and seminomadic ethnic and language groups that ranged over the great swath of territory extending from Thrace (another fluid geographic term in antiquity), the Black Sea, and northern Anatolia across the Caucasus Mountains to the Caspian Sea and eastward to Central and Inner Asia (it is more than four thousand miles from Thrace to the Great Wall of China). "The Greeks call them Scythians," wrote Herodotus; the Persians called them Saka (Chinese names included Xiongnu, Yuezhi, Xianbei, and Sai). "Although each people has a separate name of its own," remarked the geographer Strabo, the Scythians, Massagetae, Saka, and other nomadic tribes "are given the general name of Scythians." Pliny named twenty of the "countless tribes of Scythia." As Gocha Tsetskhladze, a historian of Scythia, points out, "We call them Scythians because the Greeks did." There are more restrictive modern descriptions for "Scythians" based on ethnographic, geographic, and linguistic parameters, but the terms *Scythia* and *Scythians*, the names used by the ancient Greeks, are convenient catchall terms to refer to the diverse yet culturally similar nomadic and seminomadic groups of Eurasia to western China. Modern historians and archaeologists use "Scythian" to refer to the vast territory characterized in antiquity by the horse-centered nomad warrior lifestyle marked by similar warfare and weapons, artistic motifs, gender relations, burial practices, and other cultural features.[2]

Scythia's forests, grassy steppes, desert oases, and mountains were home to a multitude of individual tribes with their own names, histories, customs, and dialects but sharing a migratory life centered on horses, archery, hunting, herding, trading, raiding, and guerrilla-style warfare. Endless journeys over waterless prairies, invasions, plunder, wars, alliances, agreements, quarrels, more wars: "such is the life of nomads," commented Strabo. Lucian of Samosata (Syria) concurred: "Scythians live in a state of perpetual warfare, now invading, now receding, now contending for pasturage or booty." Going by myriad names, waxing and waning in population over the centuries, continually on the move, the Scythian nomads, as described in ancient texts, had a history "inseparable from that of the nomadic and semi-nomadic tribes of the Eurasian steppes." Their common material culture, the "Scythian Triad" of distinctive weapons, horses, and artistic "animal-style" motifs, is evident in archaeological artifacts in burials from the Carpathian Mountains to northern China. Grave goods demonstrate far-reaching trade among these groups.[3]

Not all of these peoples wandered the ocean of grass under infinite skies, however. By the fifth century BC, seminomadic clans known as the "Royal Scythians" had come to reside in wagons or settlements clustered around the northeastern Black Sea–Don area, taking up agriculture and trade, facilitating exchange between Greece and points along the Silk Routes to Asia. It was mainly through the coastal trading colonies that the Greeks first came to hear of the many different tribes of greater Scythia.

No aspect of Scythian culture unsettled the Greeks more than the status of women. Hellenes expected strict division of male and female roles.[4] But among nomadic people, girls and boys wore the same practical clothing and learned to ride and shoot together. In small hunting and raiding groups where everyone was a stakeholder and each was expected to contribute to survival in an unforgiving environment, this way of life made good sense. It meant that a girl could challenge a boy in a race or archery contest, and a woman could ride her horse to hunt or care for herds alone, with other women, or with men. Women were as able as men to skirmish with enemies and defend their tribe from attackers. Self-sufficient women were valued and could achieve high status and renown. It is easy to see how these commonsense, routine features of nomad life could lead outsiders like the Greeks—who kept females dependent on males—to glamorize steppe women as mythic Amazons. The opportunity for an especially strong, ambitious woman to head women-only or mixed-sex raiding parties or even armies was exaggerated in Greek myths into a kind of war of the sexes, pitting powerful Amazon queens against great Greek heroes.

THE GAME OF AMAZONS

For the Greeks, tantalizing scraps of information and legends about women of Scythia—especially the idea of "rogue" groups of female roughriders roaming on their own without men—inspired countless "what if" scenarios. A mythic "alternative world" of Amazons was created from pieces of evidence about the real-world Scythians, who posed a theoretical question of vital interest to a male-centered warrior society like Greece. The sequence might have gone something like this:

- Amazons were warlike women of Scythia or closely associated with Scythians. Scythians were fearsome opponents on the battlefield.
- Unlike docile, sequestered Greek wives, Scythian women lived much like the men. Horse riders, archers, fighters, they were sexually free and *always* armed and dangerous. Imagine facing a hundred Atalantas in battle!
- Thought experiment: What would happen if our Greek heroes encountered a band of Amazons? Sparks would fly!

The Greek thought experiment resulted in an outpouring of thrilling Amazon stories, typically set around the Black Sea. Bards regaled eager listeners with the romantic and military adventures of fictional

Amazons. Myths gave birth to many alternative tales for characters and events, taking details from a core of reality, stoked by curiosity, and embroidered by creative storytelling. The stories were lavishly illustrated in paintings and sculpture. More than a thousand Greek vases depicting Amazons exist today. Even though only a fraction of the Amazon-related art and literature that existed in antiquity has come down to us, what survives still retains the power to enchant.

How did the ancient Greeks come by their imperfect but surprisingly detailed knowledge of Scythia? And how did Amazons fit into the picture?

WHO WERE THE SCYTHIANS?

Despite their rich culture (which flourished from the seventh century BC to about AD 500), the Saka-Scythians, Thracians, Sarmatians, and kindred groups left no written histories. What we know about them must be gleaned from other oral, written, or artistic materials, chiefly from Greece and Rome but also non-Greek sources from what is now Iran, Armenia, Azerbaijan, Kazakhstan, India, China. The lifestyles of Eurasian nomads in later times can also contribute to our understanding of ancient life on the steppes. Excavations of grave mounds (kurgans) began in the 1870s, and every year since then numerous archaeological teams are uncovering more and more evidence, much of it confirming ancient Greek reports and also revealing that Scythian culture was more sophisticated and complex than previously realized (chapter 4).[5]

By the seventh century BC, powerful Scythian forces were attacking, plundering, and exacting tribute in Thrace, the Caucasus, and Anatolia, penetrating south as far as Syria and Media, even advancing toward Egypt and moving eastward toward China. The Scythians' reach contracted again after defeats in the Near and Far East in the sixth century BC, but Scythians continued to dominate the Caucasus and Central Asian steppes.[6]

Scythians were horse people. They traveled extremely long distances by land, much of it harsh going. To reach Thrace or the mouth of the Danube or northern Greece, for example, they would follow a long

MAP 2.2. The Black Sea region. Map © Michele Angel.

southwestern arc down from the steppes. To reach Colchis, Armenia, Anatolia, and Persia from the north, they took one of two major migration routes used by nomads, traders, and invaders from time immemorial. These routes, first described by Herodotus, involved arduous journeys over or around the snow-clad Caucasus range. The Scythian Gates (or Keyhole) was a precipitous, winding mountain trail over the central Caucasus: the journey from the Sea of Azov to the Phasis River in Colchis took about thirty days. The ancient Persians called this narrow defile *Dar-e Alan*, "Gate of the Alans" (Daryal Pass), after one of the nomadic tribes of Scythia. The other difficult and longer passage, sometimes called the "Caspian Gates" or the Marpesian Rock, was between the steep eastern end of the mountains and the Caspian Sea (Persian, *Darband*, "Closed Gates," modern Derbent, Dagestan). From Pontus (northeastern Turkey) Scythians could cross west into Europe (Thrace) in wintertime over the frozen Bosporus Strait between the Black Sea and the Sea of Marmara (maps 2.2 and 2.4).[7]

In about 1000–700 BC, Greeks began establishing colonies along the Aegean coast of Anatolia, where they became aware of local histories and legends about Amazons. Many towns in Anatolia claimed Amazons as their founders; grave mounds and other shrines were local landmarks linked with Amazons.[8] By the eighth and seventh centuries BC, Greek adventurers began exploring the rim of the Black Sea, which they called the Euxine or simply Pontus ("the Sea"). At some later point "Pontus" came to specify the wedge of land between the Phasis River of Colchis and the Thermodon River of northeastern Anatolia. By the sixth century, Greek colonies were sprinkled around the Black Sea, and by 450 BC more than a dozen Greek colonies were established on the northern Black Sea, from Tyras on the Dniester River to Gorgippia (ancient Sinda), south of the Taman Peninsula, and Tanais, a Scythian trading post at the mouth of the Don River on the Sea of Azov.

Descriptions of barbarian societies of the north and east, many distinguished by a degree of gender role blurring unknown in Hellenic society, began to filter back to Greece as a few traders and travelers journeyed beyond the colonies on the Black Sea, venturing deeper into the lands of nomadic groups, on the steppes, the Caucasus Mountains, around the Caspian Sea, and eastward along the trade routes to the distant Altai Mountains, India, and China. As travelers pushed farther, the stories got stranger, but meanwhile the Royal Scythians who had settled near the Black Sea colonies were becoming more familiar to the Greeks.[9]

Literary and archaeological evidence points to an uneasy relationship between Greeks and Scythians in the Black Sea region in the sixth and fifth centuries BC, followed by a period of lively trade and mutual integration in the fourth century BC. Many slaves in Athens came from Thracian and Scythian tribes, purchased at Black Sea emporiums such as Tanais on the Don (see chapter 6 on Thrace-Scythia links). Meanwhile Greek merchants and travelers carried out commerce and made marriage alliances with Scythian clans. In the fifth century BC, Scythian soldiers and policemen were employed in Athens, but numerous vase paintings and inscriptions about Scythians and Thracians attest to Greek familiarity with their clothing, tattoos, and weapons by the mid-sixth century BC. Male archers and Amazons wearing Scythian-style costumes became favorite subjects on Athenian vases by 575 BC. Some archaic black-figure paintings (575–550 BC) show men fighting on the Amazons' side against Greeks; scholars suggest that these could be either Scythians or Trojans. Around 490 BC, the time of the Persian Wars, the popularity of male Scythian archers in art faded, perhaps because of their association with Persians (although Scythians were also enemies of the Persians). But female Scythian archers—"Amazons"—never lost their popular appeal in Greek vase paintings and other art forms.[10]

Archaeologists now know that "legends about Amazons are reflected in the grave goods of excavated Scythian tombs." The accumulating evidence of female warriors buried with their weapons is leading classical scholars to acknowledge that some Greek beliefs about Amazons were influenced by women who shared the same activities as men in the nomadic cultures of Eurasia.[11] But this "novel" insight from modern archaeology—that Amazons were Scythian women—was *already* obvious to the Greeks in classical times. Whatever psychological meanings the Amazon myths may have held in antiquity, a wealth of little-studied literary evidence shows that Greco-Roman authors clearly associated the Amazons with historical, nomadic Scythians at an early date.

AMAZONS: HIGH PLAINS DRIFTERS

Greek writings about Amazons indicated several different Amazon "habitats" and zones of activity in Scythia. Some sources located Amazons in Thrace and western Anatolia; some placed them in Pontus on the southern shore of the Black Sea; still others put them in the northern Black Sea–Sea of Azov–Caucasus regions; and many writers mentioned more than one locale. Modern scholars have taken this apparent inconsistency as proof that the Greeks were simply making up ecological niches for imaginary beings. In fact, however, this mobile "sphere of influence" for Amazons makes sense. Whether or not the ancient mythographers and historians realized it, the depiction of shifting environments around the Black Sea for the Amazons' home bases, strongholds, migrations, and battle campaigns accurately captured the realities of nomadic life. There is no doubt that at various times in historical antiquity groups of Scythians were present in the various regions designated in classical texts as occupied by Amazons (map 2.3).[12]

In Homer's *Iliad*, for example, King Priam of Troy recalls seeing Amazons in northern Anatolia as a youth. At the beginning of the war with the Greeks, Priam musters his army at a man-made mound near Troy

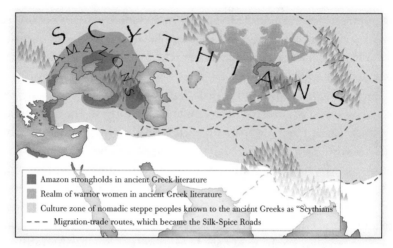

MAP 2.3. Amazons and warrior women in ancient Greek literature within the context of nomadic steppe peoples of "Scythia" and migration and trade routes. Map © Michele Angel.

said to be the grave of the Amazon queen Myrina. Mound tumuli are scattered across Phrygia, Mysia, and Thrace, and Scythian tomb mounds (*kurgans*) of the seventh–sixth centuries BC exist near Sinope, Pontus. Priam's ally Queen Penthesilea was a Thracian, but she led a band of Amazons from Pontus. The mythic quest of Jason and Argonauts for

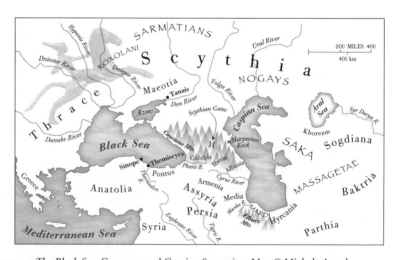

MAP 2.4. The Black Sea, Caucasus, and Caspian Sea region. Map © Michele Angel.

the Golden Fleece is at least as ancient in its origins as the Trojan War cycle. According to the *Argonautica* (the version of the myth composed by Apollonius of Rhodes, ca. 280 BC), Pontus and Colchis were occupied by three different tribes famed for women warriors (chapter 10).[13]

In the mid-seventh century BC, the adventurer Aristeas (from an island in the Sea of Marmara) wrote about his journey east across Scythia to Issedonia and the Altai Mountains. His epic, *Arimaspea* (a Scythian word meaning something like "people rich in horses"), preserved only in fragments, was very influential in forming the early Greek picture of Scythia and Amazons. Aristeas said that Amazons wandered the iron-rich territory around the Maeotis (Sea of Azov) and the River Tanais (Don). Another lost work, by Skylax of Caryanda (sixth century BC), described the Maeotians, the Sinti (Sinds), and the Sarmatians as "people ruled by women." Several authors referred to Amazons as Maeotides, "people of the Maeotis." (Scythian tribes around the Sea of Azov included the Sinds, Dandarii, Doschi, Ixomatae, and many others.) Other ancient historians placed Amazons and their allied forces among the nomads beyond the Borysthenes (Dnieper) River on the steppes north of the Black Sea.[14]

Pontus was the Amazon headquarters in another lost epic, the *Theseis*, about the Athenian hero Theseus, probably composed in the sixth century BC. In the fifth century BC the playwright Euripides located the Amazons in Pontus; so did the poet Pindar, who described Amazons "armed with spears with broad iron points." The play *Prometheus Bound* (Aeschylus, ca. 480 BC) speaks of the "fearless maidens" of Colchis and the Caucasus and the "Scythian multitudes" to the north; it foretells that this Amazon host will "one day settle at Themiscyra by the Thermodon" in Pontus. The fourth-century BC Greek historian Ephorus (from Cyme, named for an Amazon) reported that a faction of Scythians had once left the northern Black Sea and settled in Pontus, becoming the Amazons. The geographer Strabo (first century BC) located various Amazon tribes in the valleys and mountains of Pontus, Colchis, the Don region, and the Caucasus.[15] Instead of evidence for Greek confusion about where to locate imaginary Amazons, these examples represented Amazons as people who roved around the Black Sea. Scythian culture was consistently recognized as the wellspring of the women warriors known as Amazons.

AMAZONS AND SCYTHIANS

A millennium of detailed descriptions of Amazons presented as history began with Herodotus (fifth century BC) and continued through the late antique authors Orosius and Jordanes (fifth–sixth centuries AD). Between the lifetimes of these men, many other Greek and Roman historians also chronicled the origins, rise, and fall of the legendary Amazon "empire." Each of these writers had access to texts and unwritten traditions that no longer exist today. Their accounts commingle fact and fancy, legend and history, but all identify the women called Amazons as Scythians.

Herodotus, the inquisitive Greek historian from Halicarnassus (Caria, part of the Persian Empire), preserved a treasury of information about the many tribes of Near and Far Scythia, based on personal observations, local histories and legends, and interviews. Admiration for resourceful, self-reliant Amazons is evident in Herodotus's "historical" account of the origin of the Sarmatians. That story (recounted in the next chapter) tells how a gang of Amazons from Pontus joined a band of young Scythian men from the northern Black Sea and relocated to form a new ethnolinguistic group, a realistic option in the nomadic context of flexibility, alliances, and constant movement around the Black Sea and steppes.[16]

About a century after Herodotus, in 380 BC, the Athenian orator Isocrates named the three most dangerous enemies of Athens: the Thracians, "the Scythians led by the Amazons," and the Persians. Isocrates was harking back to glorious victories when "Hellas was still insignificant." He reminded his audience that the first Athenians had repelled an "invasion of the Scythians, led by the Amazons." Isocrates was alluding to the mythic Battle for Athens, which the Athenians treated as a historical event (chapter 17). After their defeat, Isocrates recalls, the army of women did not return to Pontus but went to live with their Scythian allies in the north.[17]

The Greek historian Diodorus of Sicily (65–50 BC) also wrote about Amazons, associating them with Saka-Scythian women who were as brave and aggressive in battle as the men. He pointed to the historical example of Zarina, who led a Saka-Parthian coalition to victories against tribes who wanted to enslave them (her story appears in chapter 23).[18]

For his research on Amazon history, Diodorus consulted works by Ctesias (a Greek physician who settled in Persia around 400 BC) and Megasthenes (a Greek ethnographer who traveled to India ca. 350–290 BC). According to Diodorus's sources, after a series of "revolutions" in Scythia, the Scythians were often ruled by strong women "endowed with exceptional valor"; they "train for war just like the men and in acts of manly courage they are in no way inferior to the men." Many of these women accomplished "many great deeds, not just in Scythia, but in the lands bordering Scythia."

At some point in the past, Pontus became home to a Scythian group governed by women who rode to war beside their men. One woman (Diodorus does not give her name) possessed extraordinary authority, superb intelligence, physical strength, and battle prowess. This brilliant leader trained a handpicked force of fighting women and began subduing neighboring lands. She founded Themiscyra at the mouth of the Thermodon in Pontus. Filled with pride "as the tide of her fortunes" rose, she began calling herself "Daughter of Ares," the war god. Under this "kindly ruler beloved by her subjects, young girls were taught to hunt and they drilled daily in the arts of war." She continued to lead her special army on wars of further conquest, advancing as far north as the Don River.

So far there is nothing incredible in Diodorus's account of a group of Scythians led by a successful female commander at some point in the distant past. But in the following passage we can glimpse mythography in process, as the plausible is transformed into something more sensational. Ordinary Scythian society is twisted into an ominous "rule of hubristic women" scenario, a reversal of what was normal in the Mediterranean world, bound to titillate Diodorus's audience. This powerful "queen," declares Diodorus, enacted new laws that created a true gynocracy in Pontus, in which the women would *always* be sovereign and trained for warfare. She assigned men to domestic tasks, spinning wool and caring for children. She ordered that baby boys' legs were to be maimed and girls would have one breast seared. From then on, Diodorus tells us, this Scythian tribe ruled exclusively by women was known as the Amazons and their queens were called "Daughters of Ares."

This first great Amazon queen died heroically in battle. Her daughter (also unnamed) surpassed her mother's great accomplishments, relates

Diodorus, conquering lands around the Black Sea from the Don to Thrace, and she even made forays south into Syria. For many generations, these queens' descendants continued to advance the Amazon nation in power and fame. Their decline began when the Greek hero Heracles killed their queen, Hippolyte. Then Theseus abducted Antiope and made her his wife in Athens. In retaliation, the Amazons, aided by other Scythians, invaded Greece and besieged the Acropolis. But meanwhile, the native Anatolians they had conquered saw a chance to exploit the Amazons' absence. They united to make war against the few Amazons guarding Pontus. These wars were so successful, says Diodorus, that the great race of Amazons of Pontus was essentially erased from history. Soon the Amazons were so diminished that only a few scattered bands remained. One of these small vestigial bands, led by Penthesilea, helped to defend Troy in the legendary Trojan War.

People "in my day wrongly consider the ancient stories about the Amazons to be fictitious tales," declares Diodorus. He explains why. After the Amazons lost the great Battle for Athens, the surviving Amazons gave up the idea of returning to Pontus, because it was ravaged by wars while they were away. Echoing Isocrates, above, Diodorus says the defeated Amazons accompanied their allies "the Scythians, into Scythia." Thus the great Amazon empire vanished—absorbed back into the steppes of Scythia.[19]

Strabo, a well-traveled native of Pontus, also speaks of the Amazons as an ethnic group consisting of both men and women. These people had once lived on the coast of Pontus, "the plain of the Amazons," but were driven out. Strabo reports that some say they still live in the mountains of Caucasian Albania (eastern Georgia and Azerbaijan), while others place them in the northern foothills of the Caucasus. According to Strabo, the Amazon tribe was seminomadic and not all female. "When they were at home, they planted crops . . . and raised and trained horses, but the bravest among them spent most of their time away, hunting on horseback and making war." Strabo's account is another realistic description of a typical pastoral, seminomadic lifestyle, in which men and women could choose to hunt and campaign together or in segregated groups.[20]

Scythians and Amazons received special attention in a work of the first century BC by Pompeius Trogus, a historian of Celtic roots with encyclopedic knowledge. His lost history was summarized and elaborated by Justin, who probably lived in the second century AD. The Scythians are described as battle-hardened warriors who prized independence and repelled all would-be conquerors. Trogus and Justin are clear that Amazons were *Scythian women*, capable of making war when they chose to. Scythian men and women were equals in heroic exploits, remarks Justin, making it "difficult to decide which of the two sexes had the more distinguished history." Scythian men founded the Baktrian and Parthian empires, he reports, while Scythian women founded the Amazonian empire.[21]

Once when the Scythian men were away for fifteen years making war in Asia, the women sent their husbands a message: If you don't return home we will have sex with the neighboring tribe and the resulting children will carry on the Scythian race. This story appears to refer to the seventh–sixth centuries BC during the Scythians' conquests across western Asia, when there would have been long spans of years when most of the men were away. This theme of Scythian women taking up with other men of their own choosing recurs in many nomadic and Amazon traditions. Herodotus, for example, relates that while the Scythians from the Don region were away for nearly thirty years campaigning against the Cimmerians and Medes, their women "consorted with the male slaves." The women and their new consorts not only raised a whole generation of children to adulthood, but together they created an army to oppose the male warriors when they came home.[22]

In Justin's account, the men returned home after receiving their women's message. But in his detailed story of the origin of the Amazons of Pontus we hear about yet another group of resourceful Scythian women whose men had been killed in battle. On the northern Black Sea, wrote Justin, two young Scythians named Plynus and Skolopitus were forced out of their homeland by a faction. They assembled a large band of young men and traveled south over the Caucasus Mountains and occupied Pontus. "From their new base in Pontus, they plundered the nearby lands for a long time." At last, the native peoples rose up. They ambushed and slaughtered most of the Scythian men. "The Scythians' wives now perceived that they were widows as well as outsiders. They took up arms and defended their territory. And then the women went on the attack. They refused to marry, calling it slavery." These women, says Justin, "embarked on an enterprise unparalleled in all history," creating and defending a state without men. They even killed the husbands who had survived by remaining at home, so that no woman would seem more fortunate than those who had lost their men. Next they avenged their husbands' deaths by destroying the guilty local tribes. In the peace that followed, they had sex with neighboring peoples so that their bloodline would not die out. The Amazons of Pontus killed baby boys and raised the girls to ride horses, kill game, and train for combat "instead of keeping them in idleness or working with wool" like Greek wives.[23]

An earlier fragmentary version of this Amazon origin tale comes from the geographer Skymnos of Chios (ca. 185 BC). In his account, a group of Maeotians led by two young men named Ilinus and Skolopitus journeyed from the Sea of Azov over the Caucasus and settled in Pontus. After the men were killed by an uprising of the natives, the women took up arms and became successful warriors in their own right. The warrior women were later conquered by the Greeks and dispersed back to the north. These "Amazons and their husbands" migrated back to the land west of the Don and continued to be known as Maeotians. Skymnos clearly identifies Amazons as women of Scythian origins.[24] (See chapter 22 for a historical warrior queen of the Maeotians, Tirgatao.)

The geographer Pomponius Mela, writing in about AD 43, located Amazons on the steppes around the Don, the Sea of Azov, and the Caspian Sea, and also in the vast expanse eastward toward the land of the Seres ("Silk People," China). In Pontus, on the Thermodon plain, a place called "Amazonius" had long ago been an encampment of Amazons when they dominated Anatolia. They had worshipped Artemis at Ephesus and named the town of Cyme on the Aegean coast after the Amazon leader who drove out the native inhabitants (Cyme issued coins showing an Amazon and a prancing horse). The steppes, he wrote, are rich in pastures and they are occupied by the Amazons. The Maeotians around the Sea of Azov are called *Gynaecocratumenoe* ("Ruled by Women"). The men are archers on foot, while the women ride on horseback and lasso enemies with lariats. There is no predictable age for women to marry, noted Pomponius Mela, because the women remain single until they prove themselves in battle.[25]

Pliny the Elder, the Roman natural historian writing in about AD 70, uses words and names similar to those used by Skymnos and Pomponius Mela. Pliny calls the Sarmatians *Gynaecocratumenoe* ("Ruled by Women") and also refers to the "Amazons and their husbands." A century later, during the Roman defeat of the Goths in Thrace (AD 270–275), the Romans referred to the captive Gothic women as "Amazons."[26]

Orosius, a learned and well-traveled Christian historian of the early fifth century AD, consulted numerous classical sources, such as Livy, Tacitus, Diodorus, and Justin, as well as Trogus and other texts that no longer survive, including traditional foundation tales of cities that claimed Amazons in their past. In his *History Against the Pagans*, Orosius tells how the Amazons came to rule in long-ago Pontus. Orosius's history recaps Diodorus's account, above, but supplies proper names and details from Justin's account. Orosius also inserts his own views.[27]

One of Orosius's important sources was Justin, who reported that the ancient Amazons of Pontus were ruled by a pair of queens named Martesia (Marpesia, "Snatcher or Seizer") and Lampeto (Lampedo, "Burning Torch"). Justin says the corulers divided their all-women forces and took turns leading conquering armies and defending Pontus (Orosius says they drew lots). According to Orosius, Lampedo led the invading Amazon army to subdue most of Thrace and captured some cities of Anatolia, founding Ephesus and other towns. Her victorious army, "laden with rich booty, returned to Pontus. But she found that the other half of the forces that had remained with Queen Marpesia to protect their empire had been cut to pieces in a battle."

Marpesia's daughter, Sinope, succeeded her mother, giving her name to Sinope in Pontus. As a "crowning achievement to her matchless reputation for courage," says Orosius, Sinope remained a virgin to the end of her life." So great was the "admiration and fear spread by her fame" that when Heracles was ordered to bring the weapons of the Amazon queen to his master, he was "certain that he would face inevitable peril." Orosius expected his Christian audience to be shocked and outraged by the "shame and human error" of powerful women of antiquity willfully dominating men, choosing foreign lovers, killing baby boys, building cities, and marching out to conquer. Unlike Justin, who plainly admired the "unparalleled enterprise" of the women, Orosius is the first ancient writer to explicitly express disapproval of the "unnatural" state of independent Scythian women who behaved as the equals of men. Yet even Orosius cannot suppress his admiration for the Amazons of yore. In a surprising conclusion, Orosius *praises* the sublime courage of the four greatest Amazon queens, Hippolyte, Melanippe, Antiope, and Penthesilea.

Notably, in 2006, archaeologists discovered magnificent life-size portraits of the famous quartet of Amazon queens, Hippolyte, Antiope, Melanippe, and Penthesilea, in a mosaic floor of the ruins of a villa under a parking lot in ancient Edessa (Sanliurfa, Turkey) (plate 1). The action-packed scenes are unusual because they show the queens hunting lions and leopards instead of making war. The spectacular mosaics at the Villa of the Amazons were made in the fifth or sixth century AD, in the period when Orosius was writing his history of the pagans.[28] The power of ancient Amazon stories to thrill had not faded after four centuries of Christianity.

Another author of later antiquity, an Alan-Goth from the northern Caucasus named Jordanes, wrote a fascinating history of the Goths—laced with heaping doses of fiction—in AD 551. Jordanes, who had access to ancient Gothic and Alan traditions, portrayed the Goths, who migrated from Europe to the steppes, as the heirs of the Scythians "whom ancient tradition asserts to have been the *husbands of the Amazons* [my italics]." Here is yet another succinct expression of the ancient understanding of Amazons as Scythian women. Jordanes says that the Amazons once dwelled around the Sea of Azov, from the Borysthenes to the Don—and he claims the Amazon queens Marpesia and Lampeto as the ancient "ancestors" of the Goths.

In Jordanes's Gothocentric version of the old legends told by Justin and Orosius, long ago while the Goth men were away on an expedition, an enemy tribe attempted to carry off the Goth women. But "they made a brave resistance, as they had been taught to do by their husbands." After routing the attackers, the Goth women "were inspired with great daring." They took up arms and chose as their leaders the two boldest women, Marpesia and Lampeto. In this Gothic rendition, it was Marpesia who led an army of conquest while Lampeto stayed to guard their native land.

On her campaigns Marpesia and her Amazon army encamped for a long time at the eastern tip of the Caucasus range where it meets the

Caspian Sea (ancient Caucasian Albania, now Dagestan), one of the major nomad migration routes described earlier. This place, says Jordanes, was thereafter called the "Rock of Marpesia." This legend was already known in the first century BC to Virgil, who calls it the "Marpesian Cliff." Jordanes lists the glorious conquests across Anatolia and Armenia by the "Scythian-born women who had by chance gained control over the tribes of Asia and held them for almost a hundred years, before returning to their kinsfolk at the Marpesian Rock." Amazons retained "power in that region up to the time of Alexander the Great" (here Jordanes alludes to Alexander's meeting with Amazons on the southern shore of the Caspian; chapter 20). By Jordanes's time—more than a thousand years after Homer and Herodotus—the fame of the warlike Scythian women, called Amazons, evoked such respect and awe that the legendary Amazon queens were claimed as ancestors of the powerful Goths.[29]

3

SARMATIANS, A LOVE STORY

I N Greek myth, Heracles and other heroes set
out on an expedition to win the war belt of the Amazon queen Hippolyte. After their victory the Greek
ships sailed away loaded with many captive Amazons (including Antiope, destined to become Theseus's wife in Athens). What became of
the other Amazon prisoners on the ships? The myth does not tell.

But Herodotus does. Long ago, he relates, a Greek expedition force
defeated Amazons at the Thermodon River in Pontus. The Greeks captured as many of the women as they could and sailed off in three ships.
The captive Amazons knew they were bound for a life of enslavement and
humiliation. Their battle-axes, spears, bows, and arrows, taken as booty,
were stowed in the holds of the vessels bearing them away from their
ravaged homeland. As the Greek sailors steered toward sunset on the
Black Sea, making for the Hellespont and the Aegean, the Amazons secretly got possession of their weapons. Suddenly, the women rose up and
lunged at the men. They murdered every Greek and took over the ships.[1]

But now what? Amazons were horsewomen, not sailors. At sea, on
their own "with no knowledge of boats and unable to handle rudder,
sails, or oars, the women were at the mercy of wind and wave." The ships
were blown more than five hundred miles north to Kremnoi—the
"Cliffs"—a small trading settlement in Maeotia on the Sea of Azov.
Since the prevailing winds on the Black Sea in winter are northeasterly,
we know it would have been summer when the winds blow from the

southeast (from Pontus it would take about four days to sail there). The Amazons landed in part of the territory of the Royal Scythians.[2]

The Amazons managed to get ashore with their weapons. They set off on foot, traveling inland. Before long, they came upon a herd of horses grazing. These were apparently semiwild and domesticated horses, left to pasture on their own and rounded up as needed by the local Scythians. Some of the horses had been trained to respond to a rider's knee and heel pressure. We can imagine the experienced horsewomen of Pontus cautiously approaching the horses, the patient process of gentling them, and the happy result. The Amazons "seized these mounts and rode off in search of loot."[3]

Now the stranded Amazons had fully recovered their accustomed mode of transport—and their freedom. They began pillaging the new territory, resuming their familiar way of life.

The marauding gang on horseback soon caught the attention of the Scythians. The intruders' clothing and speech were not local. Defending their property from what they assumed were boys too young to have beards, the Scythians charged out and killed a few of the raiders. When they retrieved the bodies, however, they realized that the strangers were young women warriors, *Oiorpata* ("man-killers," the Scythian word for Amazons; chapter 14). This startling discovery led the Scythians to change their plans. The elders decided to send out a detachment of young men, as many as they estimated were in the Amazon party. How many? Herodotus does not say, so we must guess how many prisoners could have been aboard the Greek ships. Perhaps two dozen, fifty?

The Scythians' orders were not to kill the Amazons but to try to approach them, make friends, and convince them to join the Scythian clan. The young men were to take their cue from the Amazons' actions. If the Amazons pursued them, the men would retreat without a fight. When the Amazons stopped chasing them and set up camp, the men would encamp nearby.

The motive was a desire to have children with these robust, capable women warriors and thereby improve their own stock. The lifestyle of the Royal Scythians around the Black Sea coast had become more settled and their women were soft and weak—they no longer rode out to hunt and fight on their own or with the menfolk, as in the olden days on the steppes.[4] In their deliberations, the elders saw an opportunity to rejuvenate their people and recapture lost vigor by bringing the Amazons into the tribe as wives for their young men. But the plan was more than simple nostalgia for old ways. Passionate voluntary sex, among gods, mythic warriors, and superior mortals, was believed to ensure a good time and magnificent offspring (see chapters 8 and 20).

The young men followed their elders' instructions. The Amazons, realizing that they meant no harm, stopped chasing the youths away. Each day, the Scythians bivouacked a little closer to the Amazons, almost as though they were stalking wild creatures that they hoped to befriend, much as the women had acquired their horses earlier.

Each group owned nothing but their weapons and horses, and the men and women lived the same sort of life, hunting rabbits and deer and stealing horses from other groups at will. The Scythian men noticed that around midday, the Amazons would stroll out from their camp, alone or in pairs. The young men followed suit. One day, a Scythian youth came upon a single Amazon by herself. Wordlessly, he made advances and she responded. They made love in the grass. Afterward, the Amazon gestured to indicate that he should return the next day to the same spot—and to bring a friend. She made it clear that she would bring a friend too.

The Scythian returned to his camp and regaled the others with what had happened. Next day, he and a comrade came to the same place and found his Amazon and her friend. After the success of this double date, the rest of the young Scythians and Amazons arranged to meet for sexual trysts. Each man and woman formed special ties with their original partners. After the couples had pair-bonded, says Herodotus, the camps were united and the Amazons and Scythians continued to live together as equals and companions, enjoying riding, hunting, and raiding other groups on the steppes.

The men failed to learn the women's language. But the women quickly picked up the men's and after some time together they were able to understand each other (chapter 14). How long did this idyllic companionship last? Several months? A year? At any rate, when they were able to communicate with one another, the young men made their proposal. "We have parents and property. Let us give up this way of life and return to live with our people. We promise to keep you as our wives and we will not take up with any other women."

The Amazons' response? "Impossible! We cannot live among your women because we have different customs. We live to shoot arrows, throw javelins, and ride horses, and have no knowledge of women's chores." They knew that the young men's families had settled near the trading centers on the Black Sea coast; their wives stayed in wagons doing domestic work. "Your women never leave home to hunt or explore or for any other reason. We would never be able to live like that."

Rejecting the sorry lot of the Royal Scythian wives, the Amazons of Pontus presented a counterproposal. "If you really want to keep our relationship, and if you wish to do what would be fair and just, then go back to your parents and get your share of belongings and return to us. Then, let us go off by ourselves, and live just as we have been doing."

Significantly, the Amazons were not averse to marriage per se. They proposed a different sort of union based on partnership and parity. The young men were persuaded by their lovers' argument. When they returned with their inherited possessions, the Amazons made another proposal. "We are uneasy about staying in this region. The land is too ravaged from our raids. And we have taken you away from your parents—they might carry out reprisals against us. If you really are resolved to make a new life with us, let us leave this country and head north across the Tanais [Don] River." Their mates consented to this plan.

The band crossed the Don and rode east for three days. Then they turned north, traveling away from the Sea of Azov for another three days. Here on the steppes the new coalition decided to stay. They became known as the Sarmatians. They spoke a hybrid form of Scythian and raised their girls and boys alike. To this day, remarked Herodotus, Sarmatian women and men wear the same clothing; all ride horses at an early age and master the bow and spear. Sarmatian women practice their old way of life, regularly riding out to hunt and skirmish, sometimes alongside the men and other times on their own. Girls do not marry until they have killed a male enemy.[5]

What is especially delicious about Herodotus's account is his sly twist on the concept of "taming." By having sex with the Amazons, says Herodotus, the Scythians "tamed" Amazons. But he uses an unusual, charged word to capture the attention of his ancient listeners. The Greek term *ektilosanto* is rare and archaic, originally used by Homer and Pindar to mean to make "tractable, tame, docile, or domesticated," usually applied to animals, especially pets or the lead animal of a flock. Herodotus often deliberately selected rare words in order to call particular attention to a point or message. Here his word choice evokes old poetic traditions, emphasizing the epic aspect of the Sarmatian story. This unique term from archaic epic poetry could be a clue that one of Herodotus's sources for this love story was actually a written epic, perhaps the *Arimaspea*, the famous lost poem about Scythia by the early Greek traveler Aristeas (650 BC). We know that Herodotus had read the *Arimaspea* because he cites it in other descriptions of Scythia.[6]

But Herodotus's use of the word "tame" is also ironic and subversive. As we saw, the Amazons tamed the horses, but do the Scythian men really tame the Amazons? The Scythian men deliberate, devise plans, and advance proposals, and the Amazons are proactive too. The women invade and raid the Scythians' property, suggest meeting for sex, learn the men's language, refuse traditional marriage, urge the men to leave their clan and move to new territory, and raise their children alike. Significantly, the women convince the men that the relationship they propose is "fair and just."

Herodotus's Greek audience could not help but notice that these decisions were negotiated among equals, bringing to mind democratic deliberations enjoyed by Athenian males who agree to rule and be ruled in turn. But Greek listeners were also accustomed to zero-sum contests of winners and losers, and in their culture the males dominated females. They tended to assume that if men are strong, then women must be weak, and vice versa.[7] In this story, however, the surprise answer to the question of who will be dominated and tamed is *no one*. In some barbarian societies with certain admirable qualities, Herodotus suggests, egalitarianism and respect can include women. As classics scholar Carolyn Dewald has pointed out, the story demonstrates "complementarity and mutual adjustments between the sexes." These practical customs of nomad culture persisted among many descendants of the Sarmatians and other steppe peoples into modern times.[8]

Fewer than a hundred years after Herodotus, in about 380 BC, the philosopher Plato cited the examples of the Amazons and the real

Sarmatian women to justify his belief that in the ideal Republic both women and men should serve as soldiers. The philosopher's challenge to his fellow Athenians was this: if barbarian women can fight like men, why not Greek women too? How radical ideas of gender equality might play out in Greek society was also being explored in the theater, for example in Aristophanes's plays *Lysistrata* (411 BC) and *The Assembly Women* (392 BC).[9]

Herodotus's purpose, clearly stated in the first sentence of his *Histories*, was to record the "astonishing achievements of both our own [Greek] people and those of other peoples." Some criticized Herodotus as a "barbarian-lover" for focusing on the histories of non-Greek cultures instead of glorious Greek deeds. Herodotus preserved traditions circulating among the Greek colonists, Greek-Scythians, and Scythians in Olbia, Borysthenes, Tyras, and other colonies and outposts that he visited in the fifth century BC; his information about more distant tribes came from his reading and through local contacts, traders, and chains of translators. The narratives were filtered through Greek perspectives, but modern archaeology confirms that Herodotus gathered a lot of genuine information about Scythians.[10]

The Sarmatian story was not a Greek myth. It was a Scythian "history," a foundation legend that Herodotus thought would be novel and interesting to transmit to his Greek audience, in keeping with his stated goals above. Yet many classical scholars interpret the Sarmatian legend as a coded account of Greek rites of passage for boys and girls before they entered into traditional Greek marriage, in which males "tame" females through sex. According to William Blake Tyrrell and Frieda Brown, for example, the Amazons of Pontus really represented Greek girls who refuse to become ideal Greek wives and mothers, and the Scythians symbolized both "Greek boys" on the cusp of manhood and "Greek *women*." In this view, the Sarmatians of Herodotus's story have no historical basis but simply hold up a distorting mirror to Greek culture.[11]

Such reasoning might make sense if Herodotus had made up the tale or if he were recounting a fantastic fiction *created by the Greeks* about imaginary people and places. But ancient Greek historians, including Herodotus, identified Amazons as real people of Scythia. "Lured on by pastures," wrote Pomponius Mela, the Sarmatians "live in camps and carry all their possessions and wealth with them. Archery, horseback riding, and hunting are a girl's pursuits." As Herodotus, Mela, and many other writers knew, conquests and defeats within the vast Scythian territories often resulted in the relocation of many different tribes to new lands. The Sarmatians, according to Diodorus's sources, were formed by people transplanted from south of the Black Sea to the northern Black Sea along the Don River.[12] Modern ethnography and recent archaeology provide substantial evidence to indicate that Herodotus and his Black Sea informants were talking about actual nomads who had migrated north to what is now Ukraine and the northern Caucasus, and that the women were freer than Greek women, participating in activities reserved, in Hellenic cultures, for men.

Nomadic groups of various sizes and makeup continually arose, migrated, fought, merged, allied, expanded and diminished, dispersed, and disappeared or were absorbed into other groups in antiquity. The Sarmatians, a loosely related group of tribes, emerged as a force on the steppes between the Don and the Urals around the time that the Greeks were beginning to travel and trade in the northern Black Sea area. Sarmatians spoke an Iranian dialect, related to Saka-Scythic, which evolved into Ossetian, still spoken by people in the north Caucasus. The oral tradition explaining an alliance of a dislocated band of women warriors and Scythian men that Herodotus recorded in about 450 BC could have arisen a century or two earlier, when the Sarmatians first coalesced on the northern steppes. One of Herodotus's known ancient sources, Aristeas, was traveling across this region during that time. Aristeas was the first Greek writer to identify the Amazons with the Sarmatians, so Herodotus's account may well have derived from Aristeas's *Arimaspea*, as suggested above. Some twenty-five hundred years after Herodotus visited the Black Sea and reported the Sarmatian origin story, European travelers in the north Caucasus, once part of ancient Sarmatia, heard Circassian bards recite traditional folklore with striking similarities to Herodotus's story (chapter 22).

There was nothing inherently impossible about two roaming bands, local males and women from afar, who agreed to unite to form a new group. What else was plausible, perceptive, accurate, or imagined in the incredibly detailed classical descriptions of Amazon and Scythian life?

The next section sorts out the colorful, intricate, tangled threads of fact and fiction about Amazons, beginning with the reality of Saka-Scythian-Sarmatian women, bowlegged from riding since childhood and scarred by battle, buried with their weapons and horses in the vast landscape of Scythia.

PART 2

HISTORICAL WOMEN
WARRIORS AND CLASSICAL
TRADITIONS

4

BONES: ARCHAEOLOGY OF AMAZONS

WOUNDS FROM A BATTLE-AXE IN THE SKULL AND A bent bronze arrowhead embedded in the knee. Obviously this warrior had died in battle. Two iron lances were plunged into the ground at the grave's entrance and two more spears lay beside the skeleton inside. A massive armored leather belt with iron plaques lay next to a quiver and twenty bronze-tipped arrows with red-striped wooden shafts. Other grave goods included glass beads, pearls, bracelets of silver and bronze, a bronze mirror, a lead spindle-whorl, a needle, an iron knife, and a wooden tray of food.

A typical Scythian warrior's grave of the fourth century BC. Except that this particular warrior was a young woman. She was buried in a *kurgan* (mound) on the northern Black Sea, near ancient Tyras on the Dniester River. Tyras was a Greek colony (founded ca. 600 BC) in the territory of the Tyragetae ("Getae/Thracians of the Tyras"). This tribe had migrated to Thrace from Sarmatia, another Amazonian homeland. We can guess that the woman in the burial mound was one of their best warriors.[1]

This remarkable tomb of a woman who hunted and fought like men—a true Amazon—is not an anomaly or unique to just one time and place. More than a thousand tombs of ancient Scythians and related tribes have been excavated across the Eurasian steppes from Bulgaria to Mongolia. Now that modern bioarchaeological methods can determine the sex of skeletons, we know that in some cemetery populations on the steppes armed females represent as many as 37 percent of the burials.[2] In the Thracian-Scythian region alone, between the Danube and Don rivers, archaeologists have discovered more than 112 graves of women warriors of the fifth and fourth centuries BC, most of them between 16 and 30 years old. Farther east, between the Don and the Caspian Sea, where Herodotus located Sarmatians, archaeologist Renate Rolle reported the discovery of 40 additional women warrior burials. In the northern Black Sea–Don–Volga region, about 20 percent of the fifth- and fourth-century BC graves that contain weapons turn out to belong to women. According to Elena Fialko, about 130 graves of that era in southern Ukraine contained women buried with arrows and lances. In eastern Scythia, on the steppes of southwestern Siberia, Natalia Berseneva excavated Sargat Culture kurgans (580 BC to AD 350) and found that 20 percent of the female graves contained bows and arrowheads.[3]

This chapter surveys the archaeological and osteological (skeletal) evidence for women who hunted, used tools, rode, and engaged in battle in antiquity. The archaeological record proves beyond a doubt that hunter-warrior horsewomen were a historical reality across a great expanse of geography and chronology, from the western Black Sea to northern China, for more than a thousand years. The persistence and range of this "unisex" nomadic lifestyle throughout the Scythian world means that the ancient Greeks (and many other cultures) were bound to encounter examples of foreign females who did not shirk combat.

The greatest number of known warrior women's graves are found around the northern Black Sea, the region closest to Greece and strongly associated with Amazons. The archaeological discoveries there and farther east are radically changing scholars' views of the accounts by Herodotus and other classical writers. The ancient descriptions of Amazons as fighting horsewomen of Scythia are now "verified by the proof of rich female graves containing full sets of weapons and horse trappings." Diodorus, for example, had reported that warrior queens were buried in splendid tombs, and although Herodotus did not specifically mention graves of warrior women, archaeologists marvel at the accuracy of his descriptions of Scythian burial practices and customs.[4]

In the not-too-distant past, archaeologists routinely identified Scythian burials as "male" or "female" based on preconceived notions about the types of grave goods expected for each gender. Weapons and tools were assumed to belong to men, while spindles, jewelry, and mirrors were supposed to be feminine. Now, however, the scientific determination of the sex of skeletons proves that not only were a substantial number of women of all social classes buried with a wide range of tools, weapons, and armor, but their bones sometimes bear battle scars identical to those of male warriors. The armed women were buried exactly as the armed males were, with similarly constructed graves, sacrificed horses, funeral feasts, food offerings, weaponry, and valuable local and imported grave goods. This chapter discusses some sensational reversals of sex assignments for skeletons once identified as male simply because weapons were found in the tombs.[5]

Arrows, used for hunting and battle, are the most common weapons buried with women, but swords, daggers, spears, armor, shields, and sling stones are also found. Some female warriors buried in Ukraine owned heavily armored war belts with bronze or iron plates like the one found at Tyras, above. Farther east, in Central Asia and southern Siberia, numerous female graves contain gold, bronze, and iron belt plaques and fancy buckles embossed with animals. One cannot fail to be impressed by the sheer weight of the heavily armored belts, iron bracelets, and bronze and iron weapons that male and female warriors donned for battle.

Tools—knives, awls, whetstones, spindle-whorls—are typically found in the graves of women, men, and youngsters. There is evidence that leatherworking was done by women, using awls and pigments (often assumed to be women's cosmetics); needles and ink were used for tattooing. We now know that Scythian men wore earrings and owned fancy combs, as did the women. Once assumed to be purely feminine tools, spindle-whorls (discs of stone or other materials with central holes) could be used with a flywheel to make fire, and they may also have held symbolic meanings. Whetstones had magical and practical functions in Nart sagas. Mirrors, once believed to belong to priestesses, turn out to be ubiquitous in the graves of Scythian men, women, and children. Like spindle-whorls and whetstones, mirrors could have been both symbolic in death and practical in life—a mirror could send flashing signals on the steppes.[6]

Besides sex and age at death, osteological remains reveal everyday wear and tear on bones, chronic diseases, and healed or fatal fractures. A lifetime on horseback is evident in bowed legs (some women were buried in riding position). Male and female skeletons across Scythia exhibit the signs of strenuous physical lifestyles, and many display combat injuries. Some scholars have suggested that the weapons in women's graves

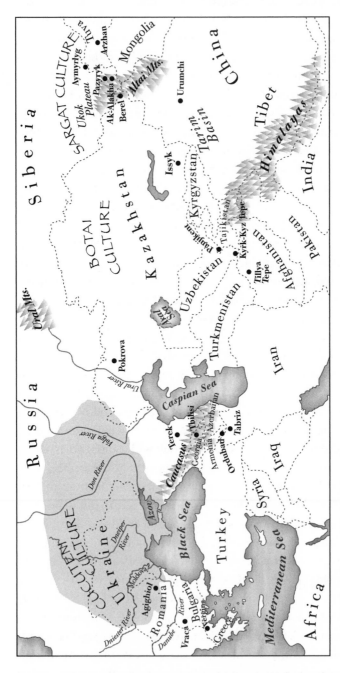

MAP 4.1. Archaeological sites with warrior women's graves; modern borders are shown. Map © Michele Angel.

- Archaeological sites associated with warrior women

▨ Sites in shaded area: Akkermen, Bobrica, Bobrytsia, Borysthenes, Chertomlyk, Cholodny Yar, Elizavetovsky, Kobiakov, Mamaj Gora, Ordzhonikidze, Repiakhouvata Mohyla, Rostov-on-Don, Ternovoye, Tyras, Želenoje.

Not shown: Etruscan armed female burial and remains of warrior women in Cumbria, United Kingdom were placed there only for ritual reasons, perhaps for symbolic protection in the afterlife. But archaeologists point out that the presence of war wounds is a strong argument that women buried with weapons were genuine warriors. Sometimes arrowheads are still embedded in bones, as with the woman warrior of Tyras, above. A number of female and male warriors' bones and skulls show injuries inflicted by pointed battle-axes (*sagareis*), slashes from swords, stab wounds from daggers and spears, and punctures from projectiles. In many cases, the direction of the attack is obvious, and some bones can even tell us whether wounds were sustained during hand-to-hand combat, while in motion, on horseback, while fleeing, or after death. The descriptions of the injuries conjure up scenes of violent battle and duels. For example, in a study of Scythian male and female skeletons with head wounds from battle-axes (detailed below), most of the blows were dealt by a right-handed opponent in face-to-face combat. Other evidence comes from cutting wounds or "nightstick" fractures of left forearm bones. Forensic analysis suggests that these individuals warded off blows with their left arms while attacking with their right.[7]

Graves of armed women have been excavated over the entire expanse of the ancient territories once identified with Amazons. The following gazetteer of representative female hunter-warrior burials begins in the west, in ancient Thrace, and moves east across the steppes and the Caucasus to Central Asia, concluding with a surprising outlier in Roman Britain. Reading scattered archaeological reports about old bones and objects buried in the ground for millennia might seem an arid exercise, since the biographies of these individual women are lost to us. But it is in these spare details of their deaths and possessions that we can recover the incontrovertible evidence for the existence of women who were the historical counterparts of legendary Amazons.

NORTHERN BLACK SEA, MACEDONIA, THRACE, SARMATIAN STEPPES, CAUCASUS

In the fourth-century BC royal Macedonian tombs at Vergina (northern Greece) mystery still surrounds the identities of the male and female skeletal remains wrapped in purple and gold cloth and accompanied by luxurious grave goods, jewelry, armor, and weapons in Tomb II. They are thought to have been members of Alexander's family, and several candidates have been proposed since their discovery in 1977, including Philip II, Alexander's father. The bones in the antechamber of Tomb II, buried with a Scythian-style *gorytos* quiver (see chapter 13) containing seventy-four arrows of three different types and part of a bow, two iron spears, an Illyrian pin, a linen corselet, and gilded greaves, have been identified as a young "warrior woman." The bow was not a Macedonian war weapon; the quiver and arrows match those found in Scythian graves, leading some to suggest that she was one of Philip I's Scythian wives, Meda (a Getae princess of Thrace). Others propose that she is Cynna (Cynnane), Alexander's half sister, who was trained as a warrior huntress by her Illyrian mother, the warrior princess Audata, daughter of the Dardanian king Bardyllis of Illyria. (Audata married Philip II of Macedon in 359 BC to seal a treaty.) Cynna commanded a Macedonian army against other Illyrians and died in 323 BC in a battle against Alexander's successors (chapter 20). Another possibility is that the remains belong to Cynna's daughter, Adea (later called Eurydice), who was also raised to be a traditional Illyrian warrior woman, killed during the wars of Alexander's successors. Whoever she was, the young woman was clearly buried as an "Amazonian" heroine, "literally and figuratively."[8]

In ancient Thrace, two mounds filled with magnificent treasure, weapons, armor, and richly equipped horses were discovered at Agighiol (eastern Romania, in 1931) and Vratsa (Vraca, Bulgaria, in 1965). These fourth-century BC graves held ornate gilded silver Thracian helmets and greaves, silver cups, Greek pottery, trilobate arrowheads (the shape used for war), and other precious objects decorated with tattooed human faces and fantastic animals. The remains found in these two "princely" burials were originally identified as those of warrior chieftains and their wives. In 2010, however, analysis of the skeletons revealed that *all* of the bodies were actually female. These were women warriors of high status buried with their arsenals and horses. Both mounds contained silver cups inscribed with the name "Kotys" in Greek.[9] King Kotys I (382–359 BC), an ally of Athens, ruled a confederation of Thracian tribes. Did he present the silver cups to the Amazon leaders to seal an alliance?

In northern Thrace, a few miles east of the battle-scarred Amazon's grave at Tyras (described above), a fifth-century BC kurgan on the north-

ern Black Sea at the mouth of the Borysthenes (Dnieper) River contained the body of another "man-killer." She was accompanied by a
quiver of bronze arrowheads and an iron dagger. Her bronze mirror and
golden earrings are decorated with the goddess Cybele on her lion
throne. Identical earrings were found in two other female warriors'
graves nearby. These women had lived and died around the time when
Herodotus was visiting the Greek trading ports in this region, interviewing Scythians about their lifestyles and describing Amazons. A century
later (ca. 330 BC), Alexander the Great's general Zopyrion would be
defeated by the local Thracian-Scythian tribes here.[10]

A sixth-century BC burial farther north on the Dnieper River belonged to a warrior woman with a bracelet of fox teeth and gold earrings, a bronze mirror, a quiver with 92 arrows, and an iron spearhead.
Next to her was a child. A similar burial near Bobrytsia (Ukraine) held
a warrior woman, a child, and a horse; a necklace of pearls, agate, topaz,
amber, and glass beads; and 21 arrows in a leather and wood quiver.
Another female warrior's skeleton (fourth century BC, Kurgan 20,
Cholodny Yar) on the west bank of the Tyasmin River, Ukraine, wore
silver earrings, a necklace of bone and glass beads, and a bronze arm-
ring. Two iron lance points about 20 inches long were placed by her
head; next to her left arm was a brightly painted leather and wooden
quiver with 47 trilobate bronze arrows, 2 iron knives, a whetstone, pebble missiles for a sling, a spindle-whorl, and a bronze mirror. At her feet
lay the skeleton of a younger man (perhaps her groom or servant; his
only grave goods were 2 bronze bells and an iron bracelet).[11]

Four female warriors' burials were identified among the 50 warrior
burials at Chertomlyk (Ukraine) of the fourth century BC. An arrowhead was embedded in the spine of the woman in Kurgan 9; she owned
a long iron lance head, 18 arrowheads of different types, knives, jewelry,
and a mirror. Another woman (Kurgan 30) had a large shield, sling
pebbles, a mirror, pearls, and red and white pigments. In Kurgan 11,
jewelry and a number of arrowheads accompanied a young woman
whose 2 finger bones on the right hand indicated heavy usage of a bow.
Kurgan 16 contained another young woman of about 20, buried with
13 arrowheads and an infant. West of these graves lay another large
group of mounds (near Ordzhonikidze). One kurgan held the remains
of a man, woman, and child, laid to rest with sacrificed horses, weapons,

and opulent artifacts in the fourth century BC. All three were clad in tunics and boots covered with gold-scaled armor, made from hundreds of overlapping half-moon plates engraved with fantastic animals similar to the artifacts and tattoos on frozen mummies of Pazyryk (chapter 6). Another grave contained a woman's skeleton with an arrowhead at the left knee, indicating a battle wound. A bronze mirror, an iron awl, jewelry, 7 bronze arrowheads, and an iron spearhead were found with her, along with the remains of 2 children. As Russian archaeologist V. I. Guliaev points out, "The presence of children suggests that the Amazons were not just young virgins but that their group included child-bearing women." Another burial in the same region, a girl about 10 years old, stands out because of her military grave goods. She was buried with iron armor and 2 spearheads, evidence for the early training of Scythian children in the use of weapons for hunting and battle.[12]

Elena Fialko describes numerous "Amazon" burials in the Dnieper-Don region, Ukraine. One exceptional burial, Zelenoje Kurgan 5, contained 3 young girls between 10 and 15 years old, with scaled armor, a helmet, a javelin, a spear, and a shield (heavy cavalry items), plus arrows, pebbles for slings, necklaces, and mirrors. In Bobrica Kurgan 35, a woman warrior was buried with her horse in the seventh/sixth century BC. Of the Mamaj Gora cemetery's 317 graves, Fialko found that 12 belonged to women warriors. The oldest was about 60 and the youngest about 16. Six of the armed women were between 25 and 35, and infants were found with 4 of them.[13]

In the heart of Amazon/Sarmatian territory described by Herodotus, north of the Sea of Azov along the Don River, archaeologists excavated numerous Scythian kurgans, many containing women with weapons. For example, at the Elizavetovsky cemetery, a group of 7 female warriors were buried in the fifth century BC, and 24 female warriors were interred here in the fourth century. One of the women in the first group (Kurgan 30), about 40 years old, was surrounded by a rich assemblage: an iron sword and spearhead, bronze and iron arrowheads, a bronze mirror, a clay spindle-whorl, and a chunk of meat with an iron knife. She wore bronze bracelets and a necklace of gold and glass beads. She was buried with a Greek amphora. Another large Greek amphora belonged to the warrior woman in Kurgan 4. She wore earrings and a gold necklace and was accompanied by a long iron sword, a spear point, arrowheads of iron and bronze, a bronze mirror, and the typical last meal of meat with an iron knife.[14]

In 1993–2001, 5 more female warrior burials of the same era were discovered in this same region. These Amazon graves near Ternovoye were very large and rich, judging by what remained after the most valuable treasures had been looted in antiquity. All 5 women were between 20 and 30 years old. In Kurgan 6 lay the skeleton of a young woman wearing gold earrings and large gold and glass pendants. Next to her were 2 iron darts, more than 30 bronze trilobate arrowheads, and a mirror. The second female warrior was in a large tomb (Kurgan 5) surrounded by a moat. Inside her chamber were arrowheads and gold belt plaques, the plate of meat with an iron knife, and pottery. The youngest woman was buried in Kurgan 8 with several golden ornaments in the shape of griffins, an iron arrowhead, and a fine bone comb with the figure of a spotted leopard. She too owned a painted Greek vase. The fourth woman had an iron knife and an iron arrowhead, golden griffin belt plaques, a spindle-whorl, and pottery. The oldest woman (Kurgan 12) was laid to rest with an iron arrowhead, 2 gold belt plaques, and a Greek wine bowl. The presence of Greek vases indicates active trade relations with Greece. Perhaps the number of arrows in the graves signaled archery prowess or military status; if so, the young woman in Kurgan 6 may have been a champion bow-woman or leader in battle.[15]

Near Rostov-on-Don, Russia, in 1987 a kurgan (Kobiakov 10) was excavated to make way for a highway. Inside lay a Sarmatian woman warrior about 20 years old, buried with an iron battle-axe, horse harnesses, and a Chinese mirror. She wore a diadem of golden stags and birds and a magnificent pectoral collar of gold and turquoise, decorated with dragons fighting monkeys around a seated man. The artifacts, dated to the second century AD, combine Scythian and Asian motifs. She had been killed by an arrow.[16]

Moving east, to the northern Caucasus Mountains on the Terek River, which flows through Dagestan and into the Caspian Sea, archaeologists excavated a woman's skeleton with armor, arrowheads, an iron knife, and "a slate discus." Some ancient discuses were made of stone; if the slate item really is a discus (and not a plate or altar), it seems unlikely that she was adept at this ancient Greek Olympic sport. Instead, the item

FIG. 4.1. The earliest known "Amazon" graves, about 1000 BC, contained three women with their weapons and jewelry, excavated by G. Niordze at Sema Awtschala, north of Tbilisi, Georgia. Photos of the original 1927 excavation report, one woman's skull with wound made by a pointed battle-axe, her bronze sword and agate necklace, courtesy of Nino Kalandadze, Georgian National Museum. Collage by Michele Angel.

could represent a fighting discus, as described in ancient Ubykh Nart sagas of the Caucasus, in which a discus is a traditional weapon.[17]

An extraordinary discovery in the southern Caucasus, ancient Colchis (now Georgia), a land strongly associated with Amazons in antiquity, occurred in 1927. Believed to be the oldest known "Amazon" graves, 3 armed women's skeletons were excavated at Semo Awtschala near Tbilisi, Georgia. One warrior, just under 5 feet tall, was about 30–40 years old when she died, around 1000 BC. She was buried in a sitting position, with her bronze sword on her knees and an iron dagger and lance at her feet. Under the lance point lay the jawbone of her horse. Her grave goods included rings, an awl, and 2 clay pots. She wore a necklace of red and white cloud jasp-agate beads with an angular pointed pendant. The left side of her skull has a pointed axe wound that had begun to heal before she died. Nearby was another young woman with an arrowhead embedded in her skull. Not far away was the grave of yet another warrior woman; several lion or leopard claws lay next to her right hand, hunting trophies, or perhaps part of a spotted skin cape like those worn by many Amazons in vase paintings.[18]

MIDDLE EAST AND CENTRAL ASIA

In Ordubad on the ancient Silk Route through Media (now the Nakh-chivan Autonomous Region of Azerbaijan, a landlocked "island" terri-tory inside Armenia), Soviet archaeologists excavated ancient settle-ments of the Bronze Age to the fourth century BC, including a necropolis with many warriors' graves. In 1926, the skeletons were all assumed to be male. But new studies conducted by the Archaeological and Ethnological Institute of the Azerbaijan National Academy of Sci-ences in 2004 discovered that at least one of the skeletons buried in Kurgan 6 of the Plovdagh II cemetery belonged to a woman warrior, accompanied by her quiver, arrows, and a helmet.[19]

Due south of Ordubad, in northwestern Iran near Tabriz (also an-cient Media), archaeologist Alireza Hejabri-Nobari reported the discov-ery of 109 graves containing skeletons and weapons. In 2004, a DNA test revealed that one "broad-framed skeleton" buried with a sword was a female warrior who lived about two thousand years ago. According to Iranian media reports, "other ancient tombs believed to belong to women warriors have been unearthed close to the Caspian Sea." Further DNA testing of the other skeletons was planned, but results have not been released. This region, west of ancient Hyrcania, was associated with the Amazon queen Thalestris, who was said to have met Alexander the Great during his campaign, ca. 330 BC (chapter 20; see chapter 23 for Median and Persian stories of women warriors).[20]

Farther east, on the steppes between the Caspian Sea and the Ural Mountains near Pokrova, Russia, on the Kazakhstan border, a Russian-American expedition led by Jeannine Davis-Kimball in 1992–95 excavated the graves of 150 ancient Saka-Scythian-Sauro/Sarmatians of the sixth to second centuries BC. These people were tall and robust, the women averaging 5 ft., 6 in., while the men averaged 5 ft., 10 in. Of the 40 burials containing weaponry, 7 proved to be of females. Their graves held quivers, bronze arrowheads, daggers, and swords, along with earrings, jewelry decorated with lions, beads, knives, whetstones, and spindle-whorls, signs of multitasking lifestyles. One of the women buried with weapons apparently died of a battle wound: a bent bronze arrowhead lay under her ribs. Most of the men were buried with weapons, but 4 men were buried with small children and no weapons.

All of the weapons showed signs of wear. Davis-Kimball noticed that the women's blades were the same size as the men's—one was unusually long, over 3 feet, for fighting on horseback. However, the decorated handles of the women's swords and daggers were smaller. Chemical analysis revealed that the bronze came from 4 different regions, the Caucasus, the Volga basin, the Urals, and Central Asia, signifying active long-distance trade (and plunder) among nomads across Scythia. Other signs of far-reaching exchange are amber from the Baltic; bronze and gold artifacts from northwest China; fossil *Gryphaea* oyster shells; and camel bones from the Tarim Basin and Turkestan. One of the most impressive discoveries was the grave of a young girl, 13–14 years old. She was buried (ca. 300 BC) with 40 bronze arrowheads and a quiver. She owned 2 fossilized seashells and a translucent pink shell-shaped stone containing a white paste. Two other amulets suggested her hunting and battle prowess. She wore a 6-inch-long boar's tusk and a single bronze arrowhead in a leather bag around her neck. Another warrior woman was found with a large iron dagger in her right hand and 2 arrowheads (plate 3).[21]

Issyk, in southern Kazakhstan near the border of Kyrgyzstan (ancient Sogdiana), is the site of one of the most magnificent Saka-Scythian burials ever found (fifth to third centuries BC). Dazzling golden artifacts and weapons surrounded the body in a fir coffin. The skull was crushed, but the skeleton is that of a young person about 18 years old. It was clad in leather trousers and a leather tunic of scaled armor, reminiscent of the armor in Kurgan 13, above. There were more than 2,000 arrow-shaped solid gold plaques, trimmed with larger gold plates of lions, and a golden belt decorated with deer, elk, and griffins, all in the twisted, typical Scythian animal style. High boots were covered with the same triangular golden scales. A pointed headdress of wool felt was covered with gold-foil birds, snow tigers, and rams. A dagger and a long sword—the blades and scabbards embellished with golden horses and elk—hung from the belt. There were gold and turquoise earrings, carnelian beads, vessels of silver and bronze, a whip bound in gold, a silver spoon, a utensil for *koumiss* (fermented mare's milk), and a bronze mirror. The rich artifacts demonstrate close contacts with Pazyryk nomads whose tattooed mummies were found northeast of Issyk. A silver bowl inscribed with a mysterious script surprised archaeologists who had assumed Scythian cultures to be illiterate (see chapter 14 on language).[22]

When the spectacular armored skeleton was discovered in 1969, it was dubbed the "Golden Man of Issyk." In 1997, Davis-Kimball published her theory that the occupant of the tomb should be renamed the "Golden Woman." Nomad men and women were often equipped and dressed alike in burials. High pointed hats and other objects were similar to those found in the grave of the Pazyryk "Ice Princess" of the Ukok Plateau (conical hats are also worn by female mummies of the Tarim Basin). The Issyk skeleton was slight, about 5 ft., 3 in., and the physical anthropologist who examined the bones in 1969 stated that "the bones were very small and could have been female." It was the "prestigious artifacts, particularly the sword and dagger," that led the Soviet archaeologists to conclude that the tomb belonged to a man.

We now have the scientific methods to determine the sex of the Golden Warrior of Issyk by analysis of the skeleton. But the identity of this body must remain a frustrating "mystery of the steppes." All the bones from the Issyk grave are missing, apparently discarded. Although it cannot be proven by osteological evidence, Davis-Kimball's point is generally accepted by scholars today. We can no longer accept the reasoning of the archaeologists who, in 1969, published their opinion that the glorious Golden Warrior was male; it is just as likely that the remains were those of a female.[23]

In 2010, archaeologists in northern Kazakhstan announced the discovery of a similarly opulent "Golden Warrior." This tomb (seventh to fourth centuries BC) contained a figure clad in gold and a hoard of treasure, more than a hundred gold objects including a "tiger-griffin," a cache of bronze arrowheads, and sword belts. Although the skeleton was at first hailed as a middle-aged male, some reports say it could be a woman chieftain of the Saka tribe. Some Kazakh nationalists suggested that the tomb might even be that of Tomyris, the historical warrior queen of the Saka-Massagetae who fought Cyrus the Great of Persia (ca. 530 BC), described by Herodotus (see chapter 9, fig. 24.3). As of this writing, the gender of the second "Golden Warrior" of Kazakhstan is still unknown. A third rich Saka grave (fourth century BC) was discovered in 2013 containing a tall (5 ft., 5 in.) female skeleton wearing a high pointed hat covered with gold animals, as well as golden jewelry and green and blue clothing.[24]

Confusion about the sex of a skeleton, but with a more satisfying ending than the case of the Golden Warrior, arose in northern China in 1976 upon the discovery of a sumptuous Shang Dynasty burial (ca. 1200 BC). The grave was filled with such extravagant treasures, including 130 weapons, that the archaeologists at first thought that the occupant must be male. But bronze inscriptions identified the tomb to be that of the renowned warrior queen Fu Hao. A princess from a tribe in the "Western Regions" who married the emperor, Fu Hao ended up leading imperial armies to protect China's western frontier from her own people. (Her story is told in chapter 25.)

In northern Afghanistan in 1978, along the Amu Darya River, Afghan-Russian archaeologists excavated six fantastically rich graves from a cemetery mound, Tillya Tepe, in the ruins of a citadel in ancient Baktria. Alexander the Great had passed through here on his way to India in about 328 BC. Two hundred years later, under pressure from the Xiongnu (Hsiung-nu) nomad empire, the Yuezhi (the Chinese name for the nomads of the Tien Shan area) would arrive in this region, dispersing the Saka (Sai in Chinese). The ethnicity of the five women and one man buried at Tillya Tepe ("Golden Mound") are unknown, but their skulls and grave goods tell us that that this was a group of multicultural nomads living along the Silk Route in the first century AD. Their bodies were covered in gold, accompanied by more than twenty thousand pieces of exquisitely crafted gold and turquoise ornaments. The objects display a staggering kaleidoscope of influences and long-distance trade:

fine Roman glass, Indian ivory, Buddhist images, depictions of Greek gods with Greek inscriptions, Xiongnu-style golden crowns, Pazyryk-style boots, Han Chinese mirrors, Siberian daggers, Saka-Scythian-Sarmatian artifacts, and coins from Rome, Persia, Parthia, and India. This magnificent Baktrian treasure, excavated under difficult circumstances, was stored in the Kabul Museum just before the Soviets invaded Afghanistan. It disappeared during the war, thought to have been destroyed by the Taliban. But the hoard was rediscovered by chance in 2003, hidden away in supply containers by heroic museum workers.

The woman (aged 30–40) in Grave 2 at Tillya Tepe was buried with a pointed battle-axe and 2 "Siberian"-style daggers. The woman in Grave 3 (aged 15–25) had a gold and iron dagger and a double golden belt clasp showing 2 facing warriors, and ivory, and mirrors from China and India. The man in Grave 4 (aged 20–30) had a full weapon set: 4 daggers, a sword, 2 bows, and 2 quivers with arrows; his war belt had 9 golden medallions depicting a woman riding a lion. The woman in Grave 6 (aged 20–30) had iron knives. The relationship of the individuals and manner and order of death are mysteries, but the weapons of the oldest woman in Grave 2 appear to mark her as a warrior, perhaps from the northeastern steppes.[25]

ALTAI, UKOK PLATEAU, SOUTH SIBERIA, TUVA, NORTHWESTERN CHINA

The incredibly preserved tattooed mummies of the Taklamakan Desert (Tarim Basin, northwest China) were horse-riding men and women dressed in colorful, skillfully constructed wardrobes of wool, felt, fur, and leather garments. Buried with their bows and arrows and many other artifacts, these mysterious people of mixed ethnicity (Tocharians?) flourished between about 2000 and 200 BC (chapters 6 and 12).[26]

The two bodies in the Pazyryk culture burial at Ak-Alakha (Ukok Plateau, Altai region) were not mummified, but it was obvious they had both been warriors. Nine caparisoned horses accompanied them in death. The pair were equipped and dressed exactly alike. Their felt caps with earflaps, parts of their leather boots, and red woolen trousers had survived in the ice for more than two millennia. Each individual had a complete set of battle weapons at hand—pointed battle-axes, bows,

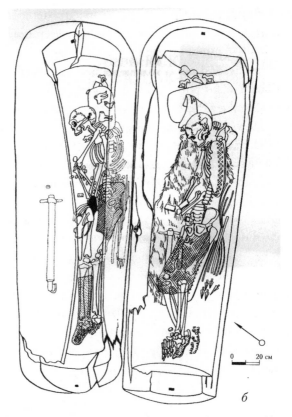

FIG. 4.2. Young woman and man dressed alike in felt caps, wool trousers, and boots, each buried with their battle-axes, arrows, and shields, accompanied by nine horses, Pazyryk culture,
fifth century BC, Ak-Alakha, mound 1, Ukok Plateau, Altai region, excavated by Natalya Polosmak in 1990. Drawing courtesy of Svetlana Pankova, from N. Polosmak, *Ukok Riders* (Novosibirsk, 2001).

quivers, arrows, shields—and their collars and hats were decorated with
golden leopards, stags, horses, and wolves. The woman had a mirror and
cowrie shells from India or China. The man was about 45 at death; his
companion was 16 or 17, a robust young woman "unusually tall and
strong, well built." Both showed signs of hereditary arthritis. The evidence suggests that they rode to war together. This "Amazon" burial
(fig. 4.2) was excavated by Natalya Polosmak, in 1990, three years before
her famous discovery of the "Ice Princess" (below).[27]

In 2009, forensic examination of the skeletons of 7 males (aged 16–65) and 1 female (aged 25–30) in Pazyryk culture graves of the fifth century BC revealed that they had each died violently in a fight or ambush, with injuries inflicted by weapons just like the bronze arrows, daggers, and battle-axes they were buried with. Each had been buried with a horse; one of the men had been scalped. The young woman's rib cage showed deep V-shaped cuts from a double-edged Scythian dagger slicing upwards from left to right (fig. 4.3).[28]

East of the Ukok Plateau, archaeologists excavated the Aymyrlyg cemetery complex in the Autonomous Republic of Tuva (south Siberia) in 1968–84. This area covered the easternmost reaches of the "Scythian World" once explored by the Greek traveler Aristeas (ca. 650 BC). The team unearthed more than 800 skeletal remains of men, women, and children of nomadic-pastoral groups of the eighth to second centuries BC. Most of the burials are from the third and second centuries BC, and the grave goods show evidence of combined cultures of the shifting "Scythian," "Sarmatian," and Inner Asian nomad populations, including those identified in ancient Chinese texts as the Xiongnu (chapter 25).[29] Numerous graves held quivers of leather and birch bark, bows, and several different kinds of arrows for hunting and warfare. Although many of the tombs had been ransacked by looters who took weapons, archaeologists recovered pointed battle-axes, daggers, and swords in leather scabbards painted with geometric, curvilinear, and zigzag designs, like those that Scythians and Amazons carry in Greek vase paintings. Conical golden headdresses, gold and bronze earrings, pins, and other jewelry, and leather, wool, silk, and fur clothing were also found. A great number of gold, bronze, and iron belt buckles were decorated with animals in a variety of shapes. Examples of armed women from Tuva include 2 females aged 35–45. One was buried with arrowheads, a broken birch shaft, a bronze mirror, and an ivory spike; the other woman's grave goods were a bronze earring, 3 boar's tusk pendants, a cowrie seashell from India or China, an iron awl, and a bronze arrowhead.[30]

The most lavish graves excavated in Tuva are also the oldest. The burials in one huge (361-ft. diameter) mound (Arzhan 1, eighth century BC) had been badly damaged by looters, but contained a "royal couple" (although not enough bones remained to determine gender) and a number of attendants, all dressed in sable fur and richly ornamented woolen clothing woven in four colors with rhomboid and triangle shapes reminiscent of exotic Scythian-Amazon costumes on Greek vase paintings. Six horses were sacrificed; another 160 horses had been buried around their kurgan. The artifacts and weapons (bronze daggers, several pointed battle-axes, gold belts, many bronze and bone arrowheads, and pendants of horn and boar tusks) and exquisite horse trappings of bronze and gold were decorated with Scythian-style figures of leopards, tigers, and boars, similar to the grave goods in the Black Sea region.

Another grave in this complex (Arzhan 2, burial 5, seventh century BC; excavated in 2000–2004) is a spectacular double burial of the complete skeletons of a man (aged about 50) and a woman (about 30) with their weapons and an opulent inventory of more than 5,000 golden artifacts, making it the richest Scythian grave found in Siberia. The couple (buried in 650–600 BC) wore sumptuous clothing studded with hundreds of gold animal plaques and thousands of gold beads; there were also arrowheads, a pointed battle-axe, and a gold quiver cover. Fourteen horses, buried with beautiful golden equipment, were found as well. The woman wore a tall pointed cap adorned with golden animals and a belt with a gold-encrusted iron dagger. The weapons and horses of this couple, buried as equals, suggest that they were companions in hunting and battle.[31]

The Tuva skeletons were scientifically analyzed in 1994–98 by Eileen Murphy to determine sex, age, and evidence of violent injuries from accidents or warfare. Several women had healed fractures consistent with falls from horses. Battle wounds were mostly to the upper body, indicating combat on equal ground or on horseback. At least 4 females had suffered left forearm fractures, most likely from combat, as noted above. One of them, aged about 45 at death, also had a fractured rib and "boxer's fractures" of the right hand, probably from "dealing a blow" during a fight. A broken nose and other facial fractures of a 25- to 35-year-old woman were also attributed to "interpersonal or intergroup violence." About 24 percent of the head fractures with blunt weapons had been sustained by women. Typically the damage was on the left side of the skull, indicating "hand-to-hand combat when facing a right-handed opponent."

Of a dozen skeletons displaying evidence of lethal trauma inflicted by a pointed battle-axe, one was female. Another dozen skeletons showed

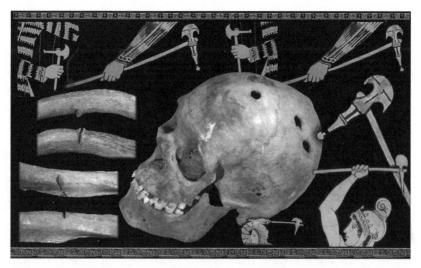

FIG. 4.3. Combat injuries of female warriors from ancient Scythian graves in the Altai region. Center, woman's skull punctured by a pointed battle-axe. Left, woman's ribs slashed by sword. Collage by Michele Angel, after images in Jordana 2009, fig. 12, and *Amazonen* 2010.

evidence of multiple slashing-sword wounds while in motion and facing an opponent; two were female. One warrior woman sustained several nicks and cuts "indicative of free-moving combat," that is, sword fighting with a foe. The location and direction of the slashes suggest that she "was actively engaged in the combat, . . . wielding a weapon making it difficult for her opponent to make a clean fatal stroke." The other woman had a single sword slash to the thigh and had been beheaded. As Murphy remarks, the battle scars and weapon trauma displayed by female skeletons show that "warfare was not an exclusive male activity," although we cannot know in every case whether the individual was a fighter or a victim.[32]

SARMATIAN AMAZONS IN ROMAN BRITAIN

In 2004, British archaeologists led by Hilary Cool were astonished by the discovery of a pair of ancient "Amazon" companions who fought far from their traditional homeland. The women's remains were found among the more than 120 sets of partially cremated bodies recovered from an ancient Roman cemetery at the Roman fort Brocavum (AD 200–300), Brougham, Cumbria, near Hadrian's Wall (northeastern England). The cemetery had been excavated in 1966 to make way for a highway, but the sex of the skeletal remains was not revealed until more than 30 years later. The female soldiers, aged 20–45 when they died, had been burned on individual, high-status funeral pyres along with their horses, sword scabbards, objects of silver, glass, and ivory, and a hunk of meat in a dish.

Many of the artifacts in the fort's cemetery came from the Sarmatian Danube region (ancient Thrace/Illyria). Cremation of horses was highly unusual in Roman funerals, but as we have seen, Scythian male and female warrior burials typically included sacrificed horses—and a last meal of meat. We know that under the Roman emperor Marcus Aurelius, the Sarmatian Iazyges tribe agreed to provide 8,000 cavalry from the Danube area; 5,500 of these served with the Roman legion in northern Britain to guard Hadrian's Wall. Cool's exciting discovery means that able-bodied horsewomen could join the imperial Roman army, previously thought to be exclusively masculine. The expensive grave goods and the horses suggest that these two women were cavalry officers recruited "from the area where the ancient Greeks placed the origin of the female warriors called Amazons."[33]

BONES OF AMAZONS

Archaeologists used to identify skeletons buried with weapons as male, but modern DNA testing now allows determination of sex and age with a high degree of accuracy. Scientific analysis reveals that at least a quarter of the female burials in Scythia are classified as warriors. This means that skeletons that were assumed to be male before sexing methods became standard should be reassessed. No archaeological evidence points to societies of women only. Instead, the findings confirm the ancient Greek accounts that described Amazons as living in tribes consisting of males, females, and children; some small bands of women warriors killed in battle were buried together by their people. In the words of Eileen Murphy, the archaeologist who examined remains from Tuva, the "existence of female warriors in the steppes during the

Iron Age is heavily supported by evidence from the archaeological re-cord." "These women were, according to all indications, the true Ama-zons of the classical written tradition," concludes archaeologist V. I. Guliaev. "These women were warriors," agrees Davis-Kimball, but "they were not necessarily fighting battles all the time like Genghis Khan."[34]

Children started their training at an early age; as among steppe no-mads today, toddlers would have ridden horses with their parents and been able to ride alone by age five. Youths of the tribe were capable of defending themselves, herds, property, and territory. The ratio of female to male graves with weaponry suggests that the most proficient and courageous young women could choose to remain hunters and war-riors when they were adults. Guliaev and Elena Fialko reason that cer-tain "social and age groups of Scythian women and girls" took on mili-tary obligations, serving as light-armed mounted skirmishers who could ride out to war whenever needed alongside the men or could repel attackers when men were away. This parallels the statements of Herodotus and Hippocrates, that it was customary for young women to prove themselves in battle, and that older women fought by choice or whenever necessary.[35]

The details of the condition of the women's skeletons and their grave goods, meticulously recorded by modern archaeologists, throw open an extraordinary window into how warlike women of the cultur-ally related tribes of Eurasia lived, died, and were laid to rest by their kin and companions. Skeletons and grave goods can reveal an amazing amount of information about the life and death of a person, even some-one who lived and died thousands of years ago. But bare bones cannot provide the answer to one of the most burning questions about Ama-zons' bodies. One breast or two?

5

BREASTS: ONE OR TWO?

A BEAUTIFUL COURTESAN OF ATHENS NAMED PHRYNE was a sensational celebrity in the time of Alexander the Great for exposing her breasts in public. In myth, the irresistible Helen of Troy saved her life by suddenly flashing her breasts to distract her murderous husband. In antiquity, Roman tourists visited the temple of Rhodes to gaze at a silver and gold chalice said to have been molded from one of Helen's perfect breasts. That cup is lost and forgotten, and Phryne's fame has long since faded from memory.[1]

The most notorious breasts in all classical antiquity, still raising eyebrows today, are those of Amazons. The warlike women were said to remove one (usually the right) breast in order to draw a bow and hurl javelins. The idea was so startling and graphic that it has a kept a powerful grip on the popular imagination for more than two thousand years. It is the one thing everybody "knows" about Amazons.

Unlike Helen and Phryne, Amazons were barbarians, outside the classical Greek ideal of womanhood.[2] Theirs was an aggressive, fierce beauty. Perhaps it is no surprise that an ancient Greek claim—a libel, really—arose about Amazons' breasts. Where did this physiologically illogical notion come from? Anyone familiar with archery and spear throwing, as the Greeks certainly were (after all, their own goddess of the hunt, Artemis, was a double-breasted archer), would know better. A stationary archer normally draws the string of a bow back against the cheek, level with the bottom of the nose or side of the mouth, with the body turned to the side. When throwing a javelin, the arm is raised and the action of hurling it occurs nowhere near the chest. Different bow sizes and shapes involved modifications of stance and position.

Most Greek vase paintings and Scythian artifacts show the more compact recurve bows that were used by steppe nomads. These archers hold their smaller bows out in front of the body, and the shorter draw brings the bowstring to just in front of the chest, posing even less threat to breasts (see figs. 12.3, 13.1, 13.7, 16.1). Scythian and Amazon mounted archers in art were depicted holding the bow away from the chest as they twist this way and that. Modern-day archers who shoot replica Scythian bows hold them out from the chest too. Archery on horseback requires an instinctive technique called a "floating anchor," which means that the archer does not draw the string to a fixed position on the body or face and the string never touches the body. To avoid hitting the upper arm with the bowstring as one shoots ambidextrously, skilled archers learn to relax rather than lock the elbow (chapter 13, plates 4 and 5). The point is that female archers and javelin throwers are not ordinarily inhibited by their breasts.[3]

WHAT DOES THE WORD "AMAZON" MEAN?

The mistaken claim that Amazons must have received their name because they were single-breasted was widely repeated by Greek and Roman writers, and every author thereafter is obliged to grapple with the paradoxical image. A fiction invented in the fifth century BC was behind the notion. This fake "fact" surfaced at least two centuries after the tribal name "Amazon" for an ethnic group of men and women was used by the Greeks (chapter 1). The historian Hellanikos of Lesbos (b. 490 BC) described Amazons as "a host of golden-shielded, silver-axed, man-loving, boy-killing females." Then Hellanikos attempted to make their foreign name "Amazon" into a Greek word. The Greeks were fond of this sort of etymological exercise of forcing Greek meanings onto loanwords from other languages, based on similarities to sounds in Greek. The strong tendency of ancient writers to create and accept crude, "patently absurd" word derivations is well known. In this case, Hellanikos maintained that *Amazones* must mean "breastless" or "lacking breast" because *a-* means "without" in Greek and *mazos* sounded to Greek ears a bit like *mastos*, the Greek word for "breast." A rival folk etymology suggested that the name meant "without grain," because *maza* was Greek for "barley." The Scythian nomads were in fact meat-eaters, not vegetarians, but this dietary label was much too dull to compete with the lurid image of women who sacrificed their breasts to become warriors.[4] Hellanikos's false etymology demanded a story to explain the Amazon's missing breast. Various dreadful scenarios were proposed for the method of this alleged self-mutilation, which was based solely on specious wordplay.

Airs, Waters, Places, a treatise attributed to the physician Hippocrates (fourth century BC), stated that Sarmatian women seared the right breast of baby girls with a red-hot bronze tool, so that the right arm would be stronger. The idea here was that the potential power of the breast would be displaced to the corresponding arm. It is physiologically true that handedness often corresponds to slightly larger hands and feet on the dominant side of the body, and that habitual exercise of one limb or hand can result in development of larger bones and musculature. (As noted in the previous chapter, bioarchaeological signs of right-handedness and larger finger bones among archers have been observed in the skeletal remains of warriors of both sexes in burial sites across Scythia.)[5]

Hellanikos and Hippocrates were contemporaries of Herodotus, our earliest and most accurate Greek source of detailed information about Sarmatians, Scythians, and Amazons based on his firsthand observations and interviews around the Black Sea in the fifth century BC. Significantly, however, even though Herodotus describes many gruesome and extraordinary Scythian customs, he never mentions this self-inflicted breast deformity. Nevertheless, the idea took hold. Diodorus, Strabo, Pomponius Mela, Justin, and Orosius repeated the tale that Amazons used an iron tool to cauterize the breast at infancy or before puberty so that it would not hinder their use of the bow and spear. Pomponius Mela said that removal of the right breast made them "ready for action, able to withstand blows to the chest like men." According to

Apollodorus and Curtius, Amazons "pinched off" the right breast but retained the left for nursing their babies. Arrian described Amazons who came to join Alexander's campaign in Persia (330 BC); to him, the right exposed breast appeared to be smaller than the covered left breast (see chapter 20).[6]

We know that at least three later writers disagreed with the one-breast notion. John Tzetzes, the Byzantine commentator on Hellanikos, pointed out that the etymology was untrue because cutting off a breast would cause fatal bleeding. Another author, Philostratus (third century AD), rejected Hellanikos's claim and proposed a more logical—and more humane—explanation, that *amazon* actually meant "not breast-fed." Philostratus argued that real-life Amazons love their children but do not nurse them because the practice results in mollycoddled children and saggy breasts, undesirable traits in their warrior culture. Instead, the nomadic horsewomen nourish their babies with mare's milk, honey, and dew. Tryphiodorus, a Greek poet of the fifth century AD, also defined *amazon* as "unsuckled." Such a concept was far removed from Greek culture, with its stay-at-home nursing mothers, but seemed reasonable for nomadic hunter-warrior women. A similar practice appears in a sixth-century AD Roman description of a northern nomad tribe called the Scrithiphini (probably the Sami people of the western Arctic region) whose women and men hunted together. According to Procopius, their infants were not nursed but fed with bone marrow and swaddled in cradle boards hung on trees while the mother and father pursued game.[7]

The original meaning of the name *Amazon* is uncertain, but it is clear that it was not originally a Greek word and had nothing to do with breasts. The fictional meaning that stuck like superglue to the non-Greek ethnonym *Amazon* "illustrates how language was used to fill in the picture of Amazons" for the Greeks, notes scholar Josine Blok. The Hellenized name *Amazones* may have had multiple sources from Eurasian languages. One modern theory proposes that it derived from ancient Iranian *ha-mazon*, "warriors." An Indo-European linguist suggests that the word meant "husbandless." Another potential source with similar sounds would be the Circassian name *a-mez-a-ne*, "Forest (or Moon) Mother." *Amezan* was the name of the heroic horsewoman warrior queen of the Nart sagas, oral traditions of the Caucasus region that combine ancient Indo-European myths and Caucasian folklore (chapters 1 and 22). Yet another scholar suggests *ama-zonais*, "wearing (armored) belts." Whatever its original source or sources, the foreign word in its many forms apparently entered the Greek language, along with early stories about heroic fighting women of Scythia, through the Black Sea trading colonies where Caucasian, Iranian, and early Indo-European languages were spoken. The timing is appropriate: female warriors first appeared in Greek art in the eighth century BC, based on oral traditions, and the first mention of *Amazones* in Greek literature is in Homer's *Iliad*.[8]

Once the sensational "factoid" of one breast became embedded in the catalog of Amazon attributes, each successive writer routinely included it in his description of the women warriors. Perhaps the concept seemed appropriate because Amazons represented the opposite of Greek wives and mothers, and their "terrifying asymmetry" signaled their barbarism. Some modern scholars suggest that deliberately removing one breast was intended to symbolize the Amazons' willful destruction of their own femininity and so resonated with Greek men who feared women who behaved like men. For Greek women, the removal of one breast would signify the terrible sacrifice Amazons made to become more like men. For other scholars "one-breastedness" signified Amazons' freedom from nursing and maternal attachments: Amazons "don't need breasts because they will never raise children." But many ancient Greek texts described Amazon mothers, and some referred to nursing babies (not to mention the archaeological discoveries of female warriors buried with children; chapter 4). According to another theory, Amazon "breastlessness" stood for the "sexual unripeness of the nubile adolescent" Greek maiden. Some scholars point out that Greeks associated the right side of the body with masculinity and the left with femininity. Most classical writers described removal of the right breast while the left was exposed, but some reversed the sides. And Greek artists were inconsistent about which of the two breasts was exposed in Amazon battle scenes.[9]

If the concept of removing a breast was such an important symbolic attribute for the Greeks, then one must wonder why no single-breasted Amazons appear in classical art.

DOUBLE-BREASTED AMAZONS IN ANCIENT ART

Despite the popularity into modern times of "just-so stories" about how the Amazon "lost her breast," ancient Greek painters and sculptors invariably depicted the mythic Amazons double-breasted. As noted, symmetry was an essential quality of the Greek ideal of beauty. Amazons of myth and art were always portrayed as beautiful heroic women, the equals of the handsome aristocratic Greek heroes. Perhaps physical asymmetry in artistic scenes would be jarring to Greek aesthetic sensibilities. (Ugly or deformed people appear in artistic illustrations of ancient comedies or scenes of daily life but are rare in heroic situations.)[10] Moreover, artistic portrayals of Amazons are often erotic—showing mutilated women could interfere with sexual appeal.

Vase painters and sculptors often emphasized Amazons' bosoms with diaphanous drapery or body-hugging garments. Another artistic "convention" was to show fighting and wounded Amazons in chitons (loose, short, belted tunics fastened at the shoulder—also worn by Greek males) worn in *exomis* style, with one breast and shoulder exposed. Art historians have interpreted this typical Amazonian pose in many different ways. Was revealing a breast an erotic gesture? Was the "one breast exposed" intended as a subtle, less graphic stand-in for the "one breast missing" literary motif? Was a bared breast meant to evoke sympathy, in the case of wounded Amazons? Was flaunting the breast in the midst of battle a way of taunting or distracting the male heroes, or was it to make sure the men (and the viewer) understood that they were being attacked by women?[11] In fact, one exposed breast reflected practical active attire (fig. 20.1, plate 1). The archer goddess Artemis and the huntress Atalanta were dressed for action this way, and so were many Greek male archers, workers, warriors, and heroes. In Greece and other ancient cultures, the dominant shoulder of active figures was often left unclothed for freedom of movement.

Apparently Greek artists and their audiences were not persuaded by the literary trope that female archers were hindered by their breasts. But if artists never depicted one-breasted Amazons, why did the idea catch on and persist so stubbornly in Greek literature? Did some ancient cultures really practice breast removal or suppression? Was there some exotic custom or mode of dress that could have been misunderstood in

FIG. 5.1. Greeks battling Amazons. The vase painter emphasizes that Amazons are double-breasted; some of the women (far left and center) wear breast-molded corselets, while others are dressed as hoplites and in Scythian attire. Attic red-figure krater, Painter of Bologna 279, ca. 475 BC, Antikenmuseum Basel und Sammlung Ludwig, Inv. BS 486. Photo: Andreas F. Vogelin.

antiquity, leading Greeks to believe reports of "breastless" or "single-breasted" women warriors?

BREAST SUPPRESSION CUSTOMS

An atrocious practice in West and Central Africa today results in the maiming of millions of young girls by their mothers who hope to prevent rape. "Breast ironing" involves cauterizing budding breasts with a heated metal tool to inhibit breast development. Is it possible that travelers' tales of similar African "breast-searing" customs were known to the writers of the Hippocratic texts and projected onto Sarmatian women and Amazons of Scythia? There is no way of knowing how ancient this "secret" ritual of Central Africa really is, and in the absence of any other evidence the likelihood of a similar practice in ancient Eurasia seems slight. Nonetheless, the coincidence is striking, given that several ancient Greek sources mention the use of a heated metal tool. A fictional romance written in Egypt by Dionysius Skytobrachion, about Amazons transported to a Libyan setting, included ethnological details from North Africa to give local flavor to his tale (see chapter 23). When girls were born to the Amazons, he wrote, "both their breasts were seared so that they would not develop into maturity, for they thought that projecting breasts were a hindrance in warfare [and] this is why they are called by the Greeks *Amazons*."[12] He is the only ancient author to say *both* breasts were cauterized, as in modern reports of breast ironing. Did the author know of an African breast-searing custom? The answer is unknown.

A less violent, practical ethnological tradition of "breast suppression" for the comfort of horsewomen existed much closer to home—in the heart of ancient Amazon territory. Since antiquity girls and women of the Black Sea–Caucasus were trained to be expert archers and riders who hunted and fought. Ethnographic evidence among Circassians, Ossetians, Adigeans, Karbardians, Abkhazians, and other groups points to a long tradition of "flattening the breasts during maidenhood." When girls were seven to ten years of age, their mothers laced a leather vest or corset around their chests, to suppress movement when the girls were riding and shooting. The leather corset was worn until marriage. On the wedding night, the groom slowly, patiently unlaced the fifty-some ties to demonstrate his love, respect, and self-control. Early European travelers in the Caucasus described this traditional article of young women's attire, which later became known (and modified) as the "Circassian corset." In the Caucasus, commented the German historian Julius von Klaproth in 1807, "young unmarried females compress their breasts with a close leather jacket, in such a manner that they are scarcely perceptible." Archaeologist John Abercromby remarked in 1891, "There is nothing improbable in believing that the Caucasian custom has a long row of centuries behind it."[13]

One of the Nart sagas refers indirectly to the custom of enclosing the torso of girls in leather corsets. In one saga the hero Warzameg mocks a young woman for having "breasts like old bouncing pumpkins." The simile reveals Caucasian cultural values, notes the Nart saga translator John Colarusso. Ridiculing large, unrestrained, bobbling breasts was meant as a great insult. Among horse peoples of the Caucasus, swinging,

pendulous breasts were considered unsightly and awkward "for one simple reason." Colarusso explains: "If a woman were to go galloping on her
horse across the steppes with large breasts unconstrained, she would be
uncomfortable and in pain from their bouncing. So there was a pre-
mium on small, firm breasts" for active outdoorswomen. Notably, in the
1920s, European and American women's new liberated, active lifestyle
coincided with tight bandeaus to minimize the chest and flatten the
breasts into a boyish silhouette.

Athletic women of most body types tend to favor some sort of
bosom support, and modern mounted archers wear tight bodices. It's
reasonable to guess that in antiquity, most female riders, archers, fighters, and athletes bound or supported their breasts in some fashion.
"Support, binding, or restraint, or some form of sports bra for riding"
was probably used by mounted nomad women. Greek artists often depicted Amazons with tight-fitting tunics and diagonal chest bands that
may have functioned something like a modern "cross-your-heart" bras-
siere, notes one art historian (figs. 15.1, 18.1, plates 7 and 13).[14]

AMAZON ARMOR

Was there any other special attire that could have been misunderstood
by the Greeks as "breastlessness" in antiquity? In vase paintings, many
Amazons are clad in cuirasses (rigid bronze breastplates), scaled armored tunics, laced corselets, and upper garments and straps, much like
those worn by men and all of which had a "flattening effect" (figs. 8.1,
12.1, 15.2, 16.3). These artistic depictions reflected the chest armor of
padded or rigid materials and scaled armor worn by real nomad warriors of both sexes in antiquity. Archaeological discoveries in Saka-
Scythian-Sarmatian lands have turned up a variety of armored tunics
fashioned from horn, hooves, bone, and small gold plates or scales in
the graves of both men and women (chapters 4, 12, and 13). Baldrics
(diagonal chest straps) and wide belts of leather with gold, bronze, and
iron plates were also common in male and female burials. If the Greeks
observed fighting women clad in protective chest armor that looked
just like male armor, the flat-chested effect would help explain descriptions of "breastless" Amazons.

Modern "Amazon" fantasies often picture women wearing curvaceous metallic chest armor molded in the shape of breasts, à la Wonder Woman and Xena, Warrior Princess (fig. 16.4). An ancient version seems to be depicted in figure 5.1. But such erotic "breasted" armor is impractical and dangerous. Experienced female soldiers of any era know that breast-shaped metal chest armor would be life-threatening. Why? Because cone- or dome-shaped projections would direct the force of blows of weapons *toward* the sternum and heart. Even a fall could be fatal, causing the sharp metal separating the breast hollows to injure or even fracture the breastbone. Therefore, armored fighting women in antiquity would have worn padding under chest plates shaped exactly like the men's, presenting a flat surface or a ridge down the center to deflect blows *away* from the heart.[15]

In antiquity, some male and female warriors wore heavier armor on one side of their bodies, leaving the other side less protected or exposed, which could give an impression of single-breastedness. As we saw in the archaeology of Scythians (chapter 4), the skeletons of warrior men and women indicated that most battle injuries were on the left side of the body, dealt by right-handed opponents. Heavy armor for a gladiator's sword arm and shoulder was used in Roman times, especially for the gladiator known as the "Thracian." Suits of armor with pauldrons, heavy plates protecting one shoulder and arm, were often used in mounted combat. One-sided armor or shoulder padding unfamiliar to the Greeks could have been mistaken for single-breastedness and could account for Arrian's report of the asymmetrical chests of the Amazons encountered by Alexander.[16]

The notion of single-breasted Amazons—which seems to signal something about a warrior women's sexuality, willpower, and masculine strength achieved by sacrificing a feminine attribute—has clung to the standard literary description of Amazons for more than two millennia. It seizes the imagination because it is gruesome, just as the tale of African mothers who cauterize their daughters' breasts grabs attention today. A seductive false "logic" still clings to the ancient image. To people who have never drawn a Scythian-style bow or observed women archers competing in Mongolia, it seems to make sense that womanly breasts might present an encumbrance in archery. But drawing the bowstring back along the cheek or holding the bow out from the body while turning to the side means that breasts are no hindrance and there is no danger of injury to them. Instead, a real concern is that loose clothing might interfere with the bowstring. Therefore archers wear body-hugging upper garments, like those shown on many Amazons in ancient art. For beginning longbow archers, the most vulnerable area is the inner forearm, which can be struck by the bowstring. Yet the notion of protecting the chest persists in archery. Women—and men too—are often encouraged, even required, to wear chest-guards, even though expert male and female archers find that close-fitting shirts and a forearm guard are the only safety requirements. An analogy exists in modern boxing. Unsubstantiated safety concerns were long used to justify excluding women from boxing. Women won the right to box in the 1970s in the United States but were required to wear an unwieldy plastic chest shield, which caused more cuts and bruises and made the chest a much bigger target. In 2008, medical experts convinced the boxing commission to lift the regulation.[17]

Like Helen's bared breasts in Greek myth, Amazon breasts were often exposed in scenes tinged with eroticism. This was not the only feature that Helen and the Amazons shared. Poets liked to portray the young Helen as an athletic Spartan girl, much like the Greek "Amazon" Atalanta, hunting topless with her brothers: "With naked breasts she carried her weapons, they say, and did not blush."[18] In the Greek myths, Amazons were presented as physically attractive. The literary topos that they removed one breast was ignored by artists. No vase painter or sculptor depicted lopsided Amazons. Going by the images in classical art, if an ordinary Greek were to find himself in the company of an Amazon, he would expect her bosom to be as symmetrical and enticing as Helen's. Countless paintings and statues invited the Greeks and Romans to admire Amazons' exposed breasts and to imagine what was barely concealed by their skintight bodysuits.

of their customs merged. Several mixed Thracian-Scythian tribes, such as the Tyragetai and Agathyrsi, were discussed by Herodotus and Strabo. According to Strabo, the Bithynians, Phrygians, Mysians, Mygdonians, and Trojans were all of Thracian origin, and one Thracian tribe, the Saraparai ("Beheaders"), was said to have migrated far east beyond Armenia and onto the Scythian steppes.[3]

Thracians, Scythians, and Amazons shared a guerrilla style of fighting, as light infantry (peltasts), archers, and cavalry, and their clothing, weapons, equipment, and artistic motifs were similar. Greek colonists skirmished with indigenous Thracians in the seventh to sixth centuries BC. A black-figure painted cup (ca. 560 BC, believed to be from a Thracian tomb) juxtaposes Greeks, Thracians, and Amazons in an interesting way. The cup's exterior shows a "quasi-historical" battle between Greeks and Thracians, while on the inside the Greek hero Heracles battles an Amazon. The mythic scene seems to equate the Amazon with Thracians.[4]

By about 550 BC, Greek vase painters began to depict Amazons with a combination of Thracian and Scythian clothing and equipment, coinciding with increasing Greek familiarity with those two warrior races and the ongoing intermingling of the two peoples at the margins of their territories. (In earlier art, Amazons had been imagined as female Greek hoplites, with short chiton, armor, helmet, round shield, and spear.) As the popularity of Amazon scenes rose and familiarity increased, artists began to show Hippolyte, Antiope, Penthesilea, and other Amazons with quivers, bows, and javelins, clothed in patterned tunics and trousers, boots, and pointed soft caps, typical attire of Thracians and Scythians (and, later, Persians). By 525 BC, many Amazons were being shown with the Thracian *pelta*, a half-moon-shaped wicker shield, and some wear the distinctive Thracian cloak (*zeira*). Vase paintings also portray Amazons wearing spotted leopard skins, the signature accessory of Thracian maenads (violent female followers of Dionysus; in some myths it was they who killed Orpheus).[5]

Thracians, Scythians, and Amazons were horse people. An Amazon rider on a vase painting by Polygnotus is named Dolope, the name of a Thracian tribe. Thracians were described by the Greeks as tall, with straight reddish hair and pale tattooed skin. Thracians, Scythians, and Persians were frequently depicted as red-haired on vases. The artistic pairing of Amazons with Thracians leads some scholars to assume that the vase painters and their viewers knew of genuinely ancient oral traditions that located Amazons in Thrace. Indeed, one of the earliest mentions of Amazons in Greek writing places them in Thrace. According to the *Aethiopis* epic (seventh century BC) Amazons were a Thracian race, and Penthesilea, the Amazon queen with a starring role in the legendary Trojan War, was born in Thrace. In Homer's *Iliad*, the Thracians and Amazons were both allies of Troy. (See fig. 8.2 for a vase painting of a Thracian huntress offering a gift to Penthesilea.)

According to the Greek historian Hecataeus of Miletus (550–476 BC), the Amazons of Pontus spoke a Thracian dialect. Strabo recounts an old story about some Thracians joining the Gargarians of the northern Caucasus to make war on the Amazons (chapter 8). Diodorus describes a war against the Amazons waged by a Thracian-Scythian army led by Mopsus the Thracian and Sipylus the Scythian. Several ancient sources state that various groups in Anatolia were originally from Thrace. The strong cultural ties and geographic proximity of Thracians and Scythians and Amazons suggests that these groups shared many customs, including tattooing.[6]

TATTOOS IN GREEK VASE PAINTING

Many other Athenian vase painters besides the "Trustworthy Foreigner" (above) delighted in representing attractive, tattooed Thracian women attacking Orpheus, and they also depicted tattooed foreign slave women, young and old, in domestic scenes. The arms and legs (and sometimes faces and necks) of the slave women are decorated with zigzags, chevrons, "ladders," "fences," wavy lines, sunbursts, circles, spirals, rosettes, and deer.

A red-figure vase of 500–450 BC shows two robust, running women with heavily tattooed arms and legs. Their flowing red hair associates them with Thracians or Scythians (Orpheus does not appear on the vase). One woman has wavy lines on her ankles and outstretched arms. The other woman strides forth with a sword. Deer are tattooed on each shoulder and on her legs, along with zigzags, sunbursts, and dots, which continue onto her hands and feet (fig. 6.2). Another fine fragmentary krater (fourth century BC) depicts a gang of ferocious barefoot and

FIG. 6.2. Red-haired Thracian woman running with sword and scabbard; her arms and legs are tattooed with deer, sunbursts, dots, and wavy lines. Red-figure column-krater, Pan Painter, Attic, Greek, ca. 480–450 BC, inv. 2378. Photograph by Renate Kühling, Staatliche Antikensammlungen und Glyptothek, Munich.

booted women dressed in Thracian-Scythian-Amazon-style patterns (fig. 6.3). Their arms and legs are completely covered with sunbursts, geometric lines, and snake and deer figures.[7]

Another elegant example of tattooed Thracian women appears on an engraved silver drinking cup discovered in 2007 in a fifth-century BC royal Thracian tomb in southeastern Bulgaria. The cup was made around the same time as the Athenian vase paintings of tattooed

FIG. 6.3. Gang of Thracian women heavily tattooed with deer, snakes, and geometric designs. Red-figure kylix krater, Black Fury Group, ca. 470 BC, Courtesy of the Allard Pierson Museum, Amsterdam, Inv. APM 02581.

FIG. 6.4. Thracian woman attacking Orpheus with an axe; her arms (and legs, one shown) are tattooed with stars and bracelet/anklet designs. Silver cup (katharos), fifth century BC, Vassil Bojkov Collection, Bulgaria. Courtesy of Ivan Marazov.

Thracian women. The sternly beautiful Thracian woman attacking Orpheus with an axe has tattoos encircling her wrists and ankles, and seven-pointed stars adorn her upper arms (fig. 6.4).[8]

Geometric patterns and animal motifs similar to the Thracian and other foreign women's tattoos began to appear on the Scythian-style (sometimes called "Eastern" or "Oriental") clothing of Amazons in vase paintings in the mid-sixth century BC. An early example of animal figures embroidered or appliquéd on the front of a tunic appears on a black-figure amphora (570–560 BC) showing an Amazon named Andromache fighting Heracles. Andromache's outfit is sumptuously ornamented with fantastic griffins, birds, and felines. An Amazon named Kydoime on a vase by Euphronios (520–40 BC) wears a lion device on the shoulder flap of her corselet.[9] In other vase images Amazons wear close-fitting, richly decorated long sleeves and leggings. On the Thracian women and foreign slaves, designs are clearly depicted as etched on bare skin, whereas the wildly patterned arms and legs of Amazons represent body-hugging garments with designs resembling tattoos. Like tattoos on living people, the dynamic tattoos on the Thracians' bodies and the lively patterns on the clothed limbs of the Amazons accentuate their muscles and movement, drawing attention to the women's strength, athleticism, and sexuality.

With some vase paintings, one must look closely to tell whether the wavy lines, zigzags, circles, and animals are on skin or clothing. The Thracian women's tattoos stop at the ankles and wrists, giving the appearance of long sleeves and leggings. On most Amazon figures, painted lines at the wrist and ankle indicate cuffs or bands of sleeves or pants. But some patterns on the Amazons' arms and legs are so tattoo-like that the viewer does a double-take (plate 12, figs. 6.5, 13.6, 13.8).

The Thracian women's arms and legs in figures 6.2, 6.3, and 6.4 are tattooed with deer, snakes, and geometric designs; the lines at the wrists and ankles give the appearance of bracelets or cuffs. The visual effect oscillates between a sort of body stocking printed with designs and marks printed on skin. Optical illusions, teasing visual effects, and allusions to other well-known artistic images were common tricks of the Athenian vase painters' trade. Modern tattoo cultures often play with this same ambiguity: full-body and "sleeve" tattoos resemble clothing, and some formfitting tops and tights deliberately imitate tattoos.

Tattooed sleeves, collars, bracelets, and anklets that mimic the edges of garments are traditional designs in many tattooing cultures. In the Balkans, for example, early ethnographers observed that rural women still tattooed their arms with traditional designs reminiscent of Thracian tattoos in Greek art—sunbursts, half-moons with rays, rosettes, spirals, and cross-hatched ladders and fences. What were once seen as long, elaborately embroidered gloves on images of women of Daunia, carved on ancient stone steles in southern Italy, are now thought to represent forearm tattoos. Daunia was settled by Illyrians of western Thrace who were known to practice tattooing.[10]

Many vase paintings are impressionistic, and the "ambiguity" of some lines on Amazons' wrists and ankles could result from hasty or sloppy painting. The similarity of tattoo and clothing patterns might reflect the standard artistic repertoire of wild designs to indicate barbarian "Others." Perhaps some artists deliberately painted lines that could be either collars, sleeves, and cuffs—or tattoos, encouraging viewers to compare the patterns on Amazon figures to Thracian and other tattoos.

FIG. 6.5. Amazon, barefoot in tattoo-like sleeves and leggings, with bow, quiver, and sword. Attic red-figure olpe (pitcher), Louvre Painter, sixth century BC, Inv. G443, Musée de Louvre, Paris. Photo: Hervé Lewandowski. © RMN-Grand Palais/Art Resource, NY.

Vase painters often teased viewers by intertwining myth and current social realities. By the sixth century BC, Athenians were very familiar with the sight of tattooed foreigners in their city and homes. Sharpening the edge of the artistic ambiguity about tattoos was the idea that the Amazons of myth were bold, free women, not slaves.

TATTOOS IN ANCIENT GREEK, LATIN, AND CHINESE TEXTS

Besides Thracians, Greeks encountered many other tattooed people among their neighbors around the Black Sea and in Pontus, major Amazon strongholds. Numerous authors reported tattooing among Scythians. Hippocrates, for example, remarked that the Scythian nomads "branded" figures on their shoulders, arms, chests, and thighs to "instill strength and courage," suggesting a magical function of tattoos. Herodotus wrote that the Thracians thought plain skin signaled a lack of identity. Elaborate tattoos were considered beauty marks of nobility for both men and women in Thrace; even ordinary folk had a few small tattoos. Some four hundred years after Herodotus, the Greek orator Dio Chrysostom remarked that the women of Thrace were still covering themselves with tattoos as marks of high social standing. Herodotus also described the tattoos of the Iranian-speaking Scythian-Thracian people called the Agathyrsi. According to a story he heard in Pontus, the Agathyrsi claimed descent from a Scythian woman and Heracles. The Agathyrsi were one of the tribes that had repelled Darius I of Persia (sixth century BC). Later (fourth century BC) they would migrate north to the Sarmatian steppes. Agathyrsi women especially favored tattoos, noted Herodotus. The higher their status, the larger, more richly detailed and colorful were their skin designs. Ammianus Marcellinus (fourth century AD) reported that Agathyrsi tattoos were checkered designs in blue-black ink.[11]

When the Greek general and historian Xenophon led his army across Pontus (ca. 400 BC), the land of the Amazons, he observed that the skin of the men and women and children of the Mossynoeci tribe was covered with colorful tattoos of flowers. Pomponius Mela also reported that these people completely marked their entire bodies with tattoos. The Sarmatians, strongly associated with Amazons, received their first tattoos as children, according to Sextus Empiricus and Pliny; Pliny also reported that among Sarmatians, Dacians, and Britons, the women "wrote on their own bodies."[12]

Clearchus of Soli explicitly stated that Scythian women—the historical counterparts of Amazons—taught the art of tattooing to Thracian women who lived on the northwestern frontiers of Scythia. A Greek philosopher who traveled widely and wrote extensively about Thrace and Scythia (ca. 320 BC), Clearchus reported that Scythian women "used to decorate the Thracian women all over their bodies, using the tongues of their belt buckles (or pins of brooches) as needles." After several generations, Thracian women began to add their own embellishments and other designs to the Scythian motifs. Ancient accounts of tattooing by the Thracians, Scythians, Sarmatians, Agathyrsi, Mossynoecians of Pontus, Illyrians, Dacians, Geloni, and Iaopodes are compelling evidence that many of the women known as Amazons also practiced tattooing.[13]

Because the Greeks thought of tattoos as marks of degradation instead of signs of nobility, courage, and beauty, they sought to explain why women would *choose* to endure pain to decorate their bodies with indelible designs. Clearchus implied that tattoos were initially inflicted violently by Scythian women and then later embraced by Thracian women, who cleverly transformed "shameful" tattoos into lovely body ornaments. Scythians did invade parts of Thrace, intermarried with Thracians, and influenced Thracian culture. Forcible tattooing of captives is certainly attested in ancient and modern times. But sharing tattoo motifs and techniques among cultures is also well known.[14] What was the historical context of Clearchus's report? Did some Scythian women once tattoo captive Thracian women? Or did they simply teach their Thracian neighbors how to tattoo?[15]

Other literary evidence for tattooing customs among steppe cultures comes from sources far removed from Greece. The confederation of nomads of far eastern Scythia (Inner Asia) were known to the Chinese as Xiongnu. Several ancient Chinese sources described tattoos as adornment among the "barbarian" nomads of the north and west. For example, the *Liji* ("Record of Rites") of the Warring States period and early Han Dynasty (ca. 475–87 BC) said that these "wild" tribes ate meat and wore animal skins, and some tattooed their foreheads. The *Zhan Guo Ce* ("Intrigues of the Warring States," third to first centuries BC) says that the western nomads engraved their left shoulders with tattoos. The *Nan Shih* ("History of the Southern Dynasties," ca. AD 630) tells of the "Land of the Tattooed" where "uncivilized" people marked themselves with stripes and spots like wild beasts; Siberian peoples of "giant" stature wore tattoos signifying courage and marital status. Many artistic representations in archaeological sites of the Shang to Han dynasties

(1500 BC–AD 220) confirm that people living north and west of China practiced tattooing.[16]

A Han history (*Shiji*, "Records of the Historian" by Sima Qian, ca. 147–85 BC) recounts the emperor's negotiations with the powerful Xiongnu tribes who exerted constant pressure on China's western frontier. The nomads held the upper hand in the fifth to third centuries BC, receiving precious gifts and Han princesses as wives to seal treaties (see chapter 25). The nomad leaders demanded that the Chinese envoys be tattooed (*me [mo] ch'ing*, "tattoo in black ink") before they could meet the *Shan-yu* ("Greatest," chieftain). The Chinese, like the Greeks, generally considered tattooing a form of punishment. However, as in ancient Greece, lines were blurred between shameful, heroic, and beautiful tattoos for the Chinese, especially those dealing with the powerful warlike nomads of the west. Some Chinese envoys, such as Wang Wu, a northerner familiar with Xiongnu customs, had no qualms in complying with the nomads' conditions.[17]

WOMEN AND TATTOOS

Tattooing is often associated with women in many of the ancient and modern examples. Tattooed Thracian men are not represented in Greek art, although Herodotus, Xenophon, Cicero, and others included men in their descriptions of tattooing.[18] Archaeological evidence hints that female tattooing may have an extremely ancient history across Thrace and western Scythia. Neolithic sites of Cucuteni culture (4800–3000 BC) in the forest steppes of Romania and southwestern Ukraine have yielded hundreds of clay female figurines inscribed with lines and spirals; some scholars believe they represent tattoos. Along with the clay figurines, archaeologists also unearth caches of inscribed horse phalanges (toe bones). The bones' natural shape suggests a nude female torso; the distal condyles resemble breasts or shoulders. The four-inch-long bones were smoothed and polished and then incised with geometric designs (sometimes nipples were indicated). One obvious interpretation of the decorations is that they signified tattoos. Similar incised figurines have been discovered at sites of the same date near Lykastia, Pontus (a region known for women warriors, according to Apollonius

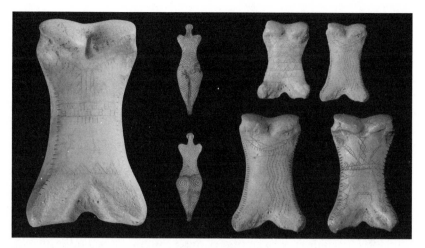

FIG. 6.6. Neolithic female forms, incised with tattoo-like designs. Left and right, horse toe bone figures, Botai culture, Kazakhstan; center, Cucuteni culture clay figure, Ukraine. Photos courtesy of Sandra Olsen, collage by Michele Angel.

of Rhodes; chapter 10). Painted spiral patterns also decorate similar figures of the same time frame in Turkmenistan. Yet another region long associated with Amazons, Gobustan in Azerbaijan, has about seven thousand ancient petroglyphs (Neolithic-Bronze Age) depicting symbols, animals, and people armed with bows, axes, and spears, some riding horses. One composition shows eight females (carrying bows?) whose body markings could indicate tattoos.[19]

The curious practice of creating decorated female torsos from horse bones was very widespread, from Romania and Pontus to Kazakhstan, the heart of ancient Scythia. Troves of these incised female forms, along with vast collections of horse remains, were recently excavated from sites of the Botai culture of northern Kazakhstan (ca. 3700–3100 BC). These seminomadic people were among the first to domesticate horses. The archaeological evidence shows that they also made human skulls into bowls, drank fermented mare's milk (*koumiss*; chapter 9), and apparently enjoyed a high level of gender equality, prominent features of Scythian-Amazon life reported by Herodotus and others.[20]

The archaeologists interpret the geometric markings on the Botai horse-bone figures as some of the earliest representations of ancient clothing construction. Based on their assumption that the marks on the torsos indicate stitching, belts, and necklines of clothing, the archaeologists suggest that Botai horsewomen wore stiff, loose-fitting, ankle-length dresses of homespun hemp. If the incisions on the torsos do represent clothing, a close-fitting tunic might be indicated, since nothing below the hips is shown. (Wide skirts could be modified into trouser-like garments for riding; see below and chapter 12).

An alternative possibility, not mentioned by the archaeologists, is that the lines on some of the female torso shapes represent tattoos. As we have seen, it can be difficult to distinguish tattoos or body paintings from garments in ancient artifacts. The Botai patterns that the archaeologists interpret as stitched seams call to mind the ladder/fence tattoo designs that mimic the seams of sleeves along the edges of the bare arms of Thracian women on Greek vases. Similar stitching/seam patterns appear on nude female clay figures from Turkmenistan (2600–2100 BC); they also appear on Bosnian and Kurdish women's arm tattoos.[21] The deliberately smoothed surface of the horse bone to make it look more like a shapely female torso—sometimes with dots around the pubic region or nipples—conveys an impression of nudity. If these objects had some ritual purpose, as argued by the archaeologists, a naked female form seems more appropriate and powerful than a clothed one. It is interesting that the dashes, zigzags, cross-hatchings, ladders, triangles, and chevrons prefigure some of the patterns on both the exotic attire of Amazons and Thracian tattoos in vase paintings. At any rate, the mysterious female forms created from horse bones point to a strong, very ancient relationship between horses and women in Thracian-Scythian lands.

Tattooing traditions among women persist in many locales associated with ancient Amazons, both mythic and historical. As in the Balkans, in Dagestan between the Caucasus and Caspian Sea (where the Amazon queen Marpesia was active) women still tattoo their arms with geometric symbols. Their traditional marks include dots (coded love messages), moons (for happiness and luck), and bird-tracks (thought to make a girl a fast runner). Ornamental tattooing is also practiced by Aghach Eris women, Turki-Persian-speaking nomads of Iran, and by Turkmen people. Kurdish women of northern Iraq and the southern Caucasus, thought to be descendants of Bronze Age Hurrians who spoke a Caucasian language, still tattoo themselves with rayed circles

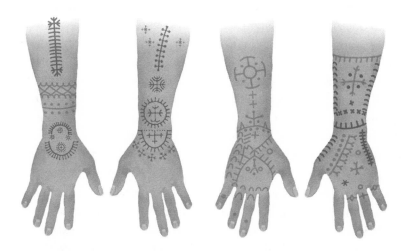

FIG. 6.7. Traditional forearm and hand tattoos of Bosnian women (left) and Kurdish women (right). Drawing by Michele Angel.

and half-circles, dots, chevrons, and stitch, fence, and comb shapes. On his journey across Central Asia in the thirteenth century Marco Polo described how women and men used needles and ink to engrave the "strange likenesses" of raptors, lions, and dragons on their bodies. In many cultures, tattoo designs are repeated in clothing, textiles, and other objects, which helps explain the similarity of motifs on barbarian clothing and the skin of Thracians, Scythians, and Amazons in ancient Greek art.[22]

Some modern scholars argue that Athenian vase painters drew tattoos on Thracian women to brand them as savage "barbarians" who failed to conform to the classical Greek feminine ideal. Likewise, the exuberantly patterned clothing worn by Amazons and Scythians in Greek art is thought to be an artistic convention for signaling "Otherness." But the artfully rendered tattoos of the Thracian women on Greek vases were grounded in fact: such tattoos were a daily sight in Athens. The specific forms of the Thracian tattoos—repeated in the patterns worn by Amazons—were not simply invented by Greek artists in pottery workshops. The same abstract and animal designs appear on leather, wood, and golden objects and textiles excavated from tombs of Thrace and Scythia, ca. 550–100 BC, and they also match traditional tattoo motifs on once-living inhabitants of ancient Amazonian territories.[23]

Tattooing methods, like tattoo motifs, are extraordinarily conservative, unchanged over millennia (needles, pigments, and stencils have been recovered from Scythian graves). First the design was drawn or traced on the skin. A bundle of three to seven needles punctured the design into the skin and then pigment was rubbed in (carbon paste from charcoal ash). The paste was variously mixed with other substances, such as tallow, honey, wild berry juice or indigo (for blue pigment), sap, ox bile (to set the dye), saliva, or the breast milk of a woman nursing an infant girl or, in the Balkans, a son. The colorful flower tattoos of the Mossynoeci of Pontus suggest that colored pigments were known in antiquity.[24]

Tattooing equipment was recently excavated in 2013, next to a skeleton dressed in a richly decorated tunic and trousers, buried with lavish grave goods in a Sarmatian-Scythian kurgan on the steppes between the Ural Mountains and the Caspian Sea. The tattoo kit consisted of pigments and spoons for mixing them on two stone palettes, gilded iron needles, and other tools. Many Scythian burials contain similar items, which had been mistaken for women's cosmetics by earlier archaeologists.[25]

Plentiful evidence makes it safe to assume that Greeks were familiar with tattooing practices of Scythian and related Eurasian tribes, and that they would expect the women they called Amazons to wear inked designs. The most powerful proof is frozen in time—inscribed on the skin of mummified bodies recovered from icy graves in the Altai. Thanks to some extraordinary recent discoveries, we now know precisely what sort of tattoos were worn by real horsewomen of the steppes.

TATTOOED ICE MUMMIES OF ANCIENT SCYTHIA

In 2003, in the scientific laboratory of the Hermitage Museum in St. Petersburg, the archaeologists watched intently as infrared rays played over the mummified bodies of women and men of Scythia from the time of Herodotus. Invisible to the naked eye until this moment, swirling images of deer and other animal designs seemed to magically appear on their skin. The faded charcoal pigment of the exceptionally fine, elaborate tattoos became visible under the infrared light, allowing the Russian archaeologists L. L. Barkova and Svetlana Pankova to photograph for the first time a stunning number of previously hidden tattoos. Characteristic of ancient Scythian "animal-style" art, the newly discovered skin pictures include deer, elk, horses, mountain sheep (*argali*), tigers, leopards, birds, and imaginary creatures with beaks, wings, and fantastic antlers. The drawings had been pricked into the skin with needles and then rubbed with soot. The Scythian tattoo artists are thought to have been the first to use transfer stencils—a cutout leather stencil of one mummy's ram tattoo was actually found in his grave. Many of the animal figures were carefully placed on the body to give a rippling effect when the person moved or flexed his or her muscles.

The Altai steppes span parts of Russia, Kazakhstan, China, Mongolia, and the Altai Republic. The vast Altai region is dotted with the kurgans of nomadic people closely related to the Saka, Sarmatian, and Scythian groups who used to range over the vast high plains between the Black Sea and Mongolia.[26] The bodies of the two women and two men stored in the Hermitage had been buried with golden treasures and sacrificed horses in the fifth to third centuries BC. Their bodies had been preserved entirely intact by permafrost in the Pazyryk ("mound") Valley, Russia. When graves of the Pazyryk culture were first excavated in 1947–49 by Sergei Rudenko, the extensive animal tattoos of only one male warrior (the famous "tattooed chieftain of Pazyryk" in mound 2) were visible. The infrared camera picked up a new tattoo of a rooster on his finger. Another frozen mummy of the later Tashtyk culture, first century AD, had been excavated in 1969 Khakasia to the north. He too turned out to be heavily tattooed with half-circles, rosettes, a bow and arrow, and large, unidentifiable figures.[27]

One of the Pazyryk women was in her early forties when she was buried next to the tattooed chieftain in mound 2. More than two millennia after her death, the infrared camera revealed that she was also intricately tattooed. On her shoulder is a fantastic twisting stag. It has a griffin's beak and black antlers with prongs shaped like griffin heads (a motif seen in Thracian and Scythian artifacts). On her other shoulder is a contorted mountain sheep. A realistic deer-antler design encircles her wrist.

The other woman, about fifty at death, was buried in mound 5 with a man of about fifty-five. Thanks to technology, we can now admire their finely drawn tattoos. The man's body is heavily inked with birds, two horses with expressive faces, five deer, three mountain sheep, and a very large, ferocious tiger wrapped around his left shoulder and chest. The woman's arms and hands are covered in tattoos. On her left forearm, a large bird of prey attacks a struggling deer. On her right forearm, an elegant tattoo depicts a snow leopard and two Caspian tigers attacking a stag and a spotted elk or fallow deer with broad antlers (Caspian tiger habitat once extended from the Caucasus to the Altai). The archaeologists believe that this complex "cartouche" composition shows Chinese influence. Chinese silk and artifacts have been found in several Altai kurgans, demonstrating trade and perhaps marriage alliances with China; grave goods in the Pazyryk tombs came from China, India, and Iran.[28]

The archaeologists at the Hermitage were delighted to find that these women of the steppes were tattooed. They were following a hunch based on Rudenko's 1947 excavation of the tattooed chieftain and another remarkable body recovered in 1993 in the Altai region. That year, the Russian archaeologist Natalya Polosmak had unearthed a thrilling discovery, an unlooted, luxurious tomb of a sixth mummy, frozen for twenty-five hundred years.

With the help of some Russian soldiers stationed at the lonely outpost on the high Ukok Plateau (7,500 ft.), Polosmak and her team excavated a large kurgan just ten yards from the barbed-wire fence marking the no-man's-land on the border with China. After two weeks of digging deep into the mound that snowy spring, they came upon a larchwood log coffin decorated with large leather cutouts of deer. Prying off the four copper nails securing the lid, they found a block of ice inside. The team carefully drizzled cups of hot water over the coffin. At last, a shoulder covered with marten (sable) fur emerged. Polosmak lifted the fur and saw "a brilliant blue tattoo of a magnificent griffin-like creature" on the woman's skin. Polosmak identified the "Ice Princess" as "one of the Amazon women mummies" of the Pazyryk culture.[29]

A tall (5 ft., 6 in.) horsewoman, she was about twenty-five years old when she died in about 500 BC. Her six chestnut horses with dazzling gold bridles had been sacrificed and buried around her. She wore elaborate earrings, a yellow and maroon silk tunic, a towering headdress bedecked with deer and swans, thigh-high boots of embroidered felt and fur, and a wide red wool skirt that could be hiked up for riding by

FIG. 6.8. "Cartouche" tattoo of leopard and two tigers attacking a stag and an elk on female frozen mummy's arm, revealed by infrared camera, mound 5, Pazyryk, fifth to third centuries BC. Drawing used with permission, courtesy of Svetlana Pankova; from Barkova and Pankova 2005, fig. 14.

a red braided belt. Analysis of her clothing showed that her Chinese-style tunic was of wild silk from India, and that the dyes came from the eastern Mediterranean or Iran. The exotic grave goods show that the Pazyryk culture "had extraordinarily wide connections to China, India, Iran, and the Mediterranean." For her journey to the afterlife, she was accompanied by a bowl of fermented mare's milk (*koumiss*), a wooden platter of meat with a bronze knife, and her everyday possessions, including a small mirror with a deer engraved on the back.[30]

Horses, deer, and large felines were extremely important animals for the peoples of Scythia. Their unique artistic style often featured deer with contorted bodies and exaggerated branching antlers. (They even fitted their horses with antlers.) The Ice Princess's shoulder was decorated with a large, twisting deer with a griffin's beak and stylized extravagant antlers, each point ending in the head of a griffin (very similar to one of the Pazyryk woman's tattoos). Her arms were decorated with a mountain sheep and a spotted panther or snow leopard. Another deer head with ornate antlers encircles her wrist, like the "antler bracelet" on the Pazyryk woman, above. Two males buried nearby had similar deer tattoos across their shoulders and chests. Antlered deer are also prominent in petroglyphs and carved "deer stones" found from Mongolia to the Black Sea (chapter 14).[31]

For oral societies such as the Scythians, tattoos may have encoded mythological ideas and traditional stories. The beautifully rendered, stylized animals are decorative, to be sure, but probably held deep meanings for individuals and the tribe. Tattoos could be seen as a living language written on the body, a form of inscribed communication. Each inked animal and scene existed within a repertoire of commonly held stories, while specific details might have referred to personal experiences (such as hunting success, vision quests, dreams) of the tattooed individual. Perhaps heavily tattooed individuals were storytellers or shamans whose body art served as illustrations for cultural narratives. Greek accounts describe Scythians as fully clothed, never nude or even seminude in public (unlike the Greeks). Many vase painters stress this by depicting Amazons clothed in long sleeves and leggings pitted against nude Greek warriors. Because their dramatic tattoos would not ordinarily be observed by enemies or strangers, Russian archaeologist Sergey Yatsenko suggests that Scythian tattoos were private "spiritual weapons" and magical protectors.[32]

Evidence for even earlier tattooing customs came to light in northwest China. In the Taklamakan Desert and other sites in the Tarim Basin along the Silk Route, numerous male and female mummies were naturally dehydrated in desert sand for about three thousand years. Their culture and origins are mysterious, but their extremely well-preserved

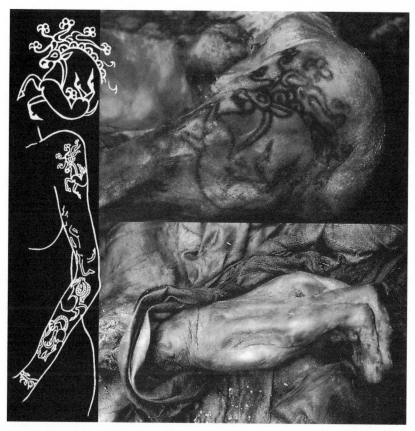

FIG. 6.9. Tattoos of the "Ice Princess," discovered by Natalya Polosmak, Ukok Plateau, fourth century BC. Images courtesy of Svetlana Pankova, Hermitage Museum, St. Petersburg.

bodies are tattooed with geometric shapes that recur in their patterned woolen clothing, still bright and colorful these many centuries later.[33]

Mummies are rare; they depend on very special conditions maintained within burial chambers over millennia.[34] The more typical occupants of nomads' tombs on the steppes are mere skeletons. Yet even bare bones can reveal evidence of tattooing among Scythians. The most startling example is a snake figure imprinted on the shin bone of a Bronze Age nomad who was buried near the Sea of Azov. The charcoal tattoo pricked into the skin was transferred onto the shin bone during decomposition of the body. A more gruesome example comes from an ancient

Chinese text stating that traces of tattoos could be discerned on the skulls or shin bones of the dead. Indeed, Sergei Rudenko's examination of the tattooed Pazyryk mummy showed that the tattoo needles had penetrated very deep into the muscle.[35]

The Altai and Tarim mummies are tangible proof of tattooing among nomadic peoples closely related to the groups identified as Scythians and Amazons by their contemporaries, the ancient Greeks. The common motifs of deer in Thracian women's tattoos and on Amazons' sleeves and leggings in so many Greek vase paintings is striking. The vase painters accurately reproduced geometric designs and animals preferred by real Scythians to decorate their skin, textiles, and other possessions. If the Ice Princess and her companions could view the vase paintings of Thracian women and Amazons, they would recognize the deer tattoos and decorations as miniature images of their own. Greek observers of the vases, meanwhile, might wonder whether the exotic marks on an Amazon's arms and legs were part of her skintight garment or actually inscribed on her naked skin. They could even entertain *both* options, imagining that the patterned fabric concealed patterned flesh.

7

NAKED AMAZONS

EXCEPT FOR A STRAY BARE BREAST AND OCCASIONAL bare feet, Amazons in ancient Greek art were usually modestly dressed compared to their male opponents. Greek heroes typically fought in a "costume of heroic nudity" against clothed Amazons. An Amazon's garment often left one breast exposed or slipped off her shoulder in the frenzy of battle. Despite the sex appeal of the warrior women's lithe bodies in action, however, it is a challenge to find any scantily clad or naked Amazons in archaic and classical sculpture and painting.

Some unclothed Amazons do appear in later Hellenistic art, after the death of Alexander in 323 BC and into the Roman era. For example, a nude Achilles supports a nude Penthesilea on a sculpted relief on a Roman temple of the first century AD at Aphrodisias (Turkey), a scene copied on a fourth-century AD sarcophagus (fig. 18.4). Privately owned erotic art is another story. There are hints that pornographic paintings of naked Amazons were commissioned by connoisseurs in classical antiquity. Parrhasius, the celebrated trompe l'oeil artist of fifth-century Athens, enjoyed making highly realistic obscene paintings of mythic subjects for special customers. One of his works featured the Greek "Amazon" Atalanta "pleasuring Meleager with her lips." That painting was last seen hanging in the emperor Tiberius's bedchamber in the first century AD. Similar erotic scenes featuring Amazons may well have been painted by Parrhasius and other classical artists for private owners, although none exist today.[1]

Rare scenes of nude Amazons from classical antiquity survive on two sixth-century BC vases, one from Athens and one from Corinth, and on an Etruscan painted tomb of about 400 BC.

HEROICALLY NUDE AMAZON WARRIORS

Three Amazon warriors battle four Greek hoplites on a black-figure vase made in Corinth, 575–550 BC. The scene is quite unusual.[2] Not only are the Greek males nude (except for helmets and greaves), but the Amazons are also "heroically nude," wearing the same pieces of armor. All combatants carry round shields and spears. The conventional white skin of the women stands out even more thanks to the heavy black outlines around their bodies. The Greek on the left plunges his spear into the thigh of a falling Amazon; she is viewed from the rear (fig. 7.1). Behind her is a Greek hurling his spear. To his right are two Greeks with spears, over the body of a wounded or dead Amazon who has fallen face down. On the right is a kneeling Amazon archer shooting an arrow; her quiver is slung over her back.

Even though the outcome seems to favor the Greeks, the striking thing about the composition is the impression of equality. The artistic details of perfectly matched arms and armor even extend to the heroic nudity of the female warriors, underscoring their status as noble heroines worthy of noble heroes (on Amazons as heroes, see chapter 1).

BATHING BEAUTIES

A unique scene of naked women swimming appears on an extraordinary amphora (ca. 520 BC) by the Andokides Painter (fig.7.2). Several features make this vase remarkable. The painting is experimental, unique in combining the new white-ground and red-figure techniques. And the subject matter was (and is) startling, exotic, and erotic for its time.[3] These bathing women were apparently intended to be taken for Amazons—even though Amazons were expected to expose only their

FIG. 7.1. Heroically nude Amazons battling heroically nude Greek hoplites. A Greek warrior plunges a spear into an Amazon's thigh while his companion hurls a spear; the battle continues on the other side, with a fallen Amazon and an Amazon archer, also nude. Black-figure lekythos (oil flask), Corinthian, ca. 575–550 BC, inv. 1884,0804.8, British Museum. © The Trustees of the British Museum/Art Resource, NY.

upper bodies in battle. (And even in the unusual vase discussed above, the heroically nude Amazons are discreetly shown from the back.) This vase is among the very first scenes of nude female bathers in Greek art. In archaic and early classical paintings, full female nudity usually implied some kind of sexual activity. Naked courtesans, prostitutes, and female entertainers, for example, were shown in brazen poses on pornographic vase paintings. Bathing scenes of proper Greek maidens and wives—including Helen of Troy—typically showed women washing in modest poses, amid perfume flasks, sponges, mirrors, basins, and fountains in the women's quarters. Women bathing or swimming outdoors was a rare subject. The Andokides Painter's innovative and intimate vignette of a group of Amazons—unself-conscious, athletic, and stark naked—is unparalleled in Greek art.[4]

The Andokides Painter's pairing of related scenes on this wine amphora was, like many of his other paired paintings, visually playful, intended to stimulate conversation at a Greek symposium, a drinking party where aristocratic men enjoyed solving riddles and making racy jokes that turn on ambiguous wordplay and imagery. Many vases painted with provocative scenes for symposiasts to ponder have survived. A sexy novelty cup (in the Athens National Museum) created for a drinking party, for example, shows a young man and woman engaged in lively sex while surrounded by scenes of Greeks battling Amazons. One can imagine the lascivious speculations sparked by the pair of images on another wine amphora (Karkinos Painter) from the same era as the Andokides vase. On one side, five Greek men recline on cushions, conversing and gesturing. On the other side are five attractive Amazons armed with spears, one woman for each man, evoking a quintuple blind date.[5]

The Andokides vase also has two scenes back-to-back: Amazons in battle gear on one side and Amazons relaxing on the other. The unexpected juxtaposition of women arming themselves for war and peaceful nude women bathing causes the viewer to do a double take.

In the bathing scene the woman in the center is about to dive, to join her companion who is already swimming. The artist brushed the swimmer's body with a light wash of diluted paint to suggest submersion in the sea. The fish painted below, a clever touch, turn the glossy black background into open water. On the left, a third woman oils her skin after her swim, from a small aryballos, a jar normally used by male athletes. (Perhaps she is applying invigorating *halinda* oil, used by Amazon bathers; chapter 10.) On the right, a fourth woman is stepping out of the scene past a column, turning back to look and gesture toward her friends. Her figure is partially damaged, so we cannot be certain whether she is nude—she appears to wear a soft cap with the flaps tucked up.[6]

On the other side of the vase, we see three typical Amazons with their arms and armor. On the left, an Amazon stands next to her shield and is tying—or is she untying?—the red laces of her patterned linen corselet over a short red tunic. In the center, an archer wearing a pointed, red Scythian-style cap with earflaps and holding a bow and quiver sits astride a spirited white horse with a red mane. Her Corinthian-style helmet (with bull's horns and ears) is on the ground. On the far right an Amazon in a patterned outfit and cap carries a spear and turns back toward her friends in the same pose as the Amazon on the other side of the vase.

How do we know that the women frolicking in the sea are Amazons? The artist planted several hints to seduce his viewers into playing voyeurs peeping at naked Amazons. First, notice the two (poorly pre-served) spotted objects hanging above the bathing scene. They are not sponges, as proposed in 2007 by a French vase scholar, although sponges would be appropriate in washing scenes. A closer look reveals a pair of soft, pointed caps with a diamond pattern and long ties, set aside by the diver and the swimmer. Some scholars note that at first glance these more closely resemble some soft caps worn by Scythians and Amazons than they do ordinary *sakkoi* (Greek women's head coverings). Indeed, the swimmers' caps resemble the headgear of the right-hand Amazon on the other side of the vase.[7]

The Andokides Painter encourages the viewer to keep turning the vase and comparing the details to find more links and relationships between the two images. Are the Amazons on one side disrobing to go swimming or are they putting on their clothes and armor after a swim? Turning the amphora (if one were the ancient owner and his friends) or walking around it (if one is a modern visitor to the Louvre Museum, where the vase is now displayed) creates a captivating narrative se-quence, like a filmstrip loop: Amazons removing their armor, plunging into the sea, and then dressing again.

The key figure linking the two sides is the woman on the right. The viewer soon realizes that she is repeated in the same pose on both sides, looking back while stepping into the next scene. In fact, this woman is one of the Andokides Painter's *stock Amazon figures*. She reappears on another Andokides vase, an early red-figure amphora from Orvieto. Four Amazons battle Heracles, and on the far right, the familiar backward-turning Amazon wears the same outfit and cap (now with the flaps down). She carries a bow instead of a spear. The very same

FIG. 7.2. Above, Amazons swimming. Below, Amazons arming. Greek red-figure/white-figure amphora, Andokides Painter, ca. 525 BC. Inv. F203, Musée de Louvre, Paris. Top photo, Erich Lessing/Art Resource, NY; bottom photo, Hervé Lewandowski. © RMN-Grand Palais/Art Resource, NY.

Corinthian helmet with bulls' horns and ears also appears on one of these Amazons. Earrings and zigzag necklaces are other accoutrements linking the swimming women with the armed Amazons on both vases.[8]

The matching details and deliberate artistic clues strongly suggest that the artist was urging his viewers to relate the women warriors on the front of the Louvre vase to the naked bathers on the back. The surprising and titillating meaning comes into focus: we are watching Amazons at work and at play. Fully clothed and armed, the women are dangerous, but a peek at the unarmed Amazons relaxing at the seaside reveals a seldom-seen sensual, vulnerable side. Notably, many miniature paintings illustrating the Persian legend of the nomad archer horsewoman Shirin show her bathing; her tunic, bow case, and quiver of arrows hang on the branches of a tree (fig. 22.1).[9]

A BEAUTIFUL DEATH

The beautiful paintings in glorious color on an alabaster sarcophagus (ca. 400–340 BC) stunned the archaeologists who excavated the Etruscan tomb in Tarquinia, Italy. Some of the paintings were already damaged when the tomb was opened in 1869, and exposure to air caused them to fade and flake (an artist's colored sketches were published in 1883). The painted "Amazon" sarcophagus can now be viewed in Florence. The sides of the coffin illustrate several dynamic scenes of battling Greeks and Amazons. Some Amazons are winning, while others succumb. In one panel, an Amazon in a short belted tunic and trousers, described by archaeologists as young, bold, and powerful with a typical "pathetic-indignant" expression, rides a white horse with blue eyes (plate 6). She turns to slash with her sword at an armored Greek with a spear. Another mounted Amazon wears a tunic, a Phrygian cap, trousers, boots, and a leopard skin. Two pairs of Amazons in chariots drawn by four white, blue-eyed horses attack two Greeks on foot, while another two Amazons prepare to slay a Greek on his knees between them.

Two scenes of fallen Amazons, painted with particular tenderness and empathy, stand out because the women are nude. One has sunk to her knees, blood pouring from a spear wound, "pain and despair" in her face. The other nude warrior has fallen onto her shield, while her attacker

FIG. 7.3. Nude dying Amazon on Etruscan tomb painting, ca. 400–340 BC, Tarquinia. Drawing of the "Amazon Sarcophagus" (marble original in Florence), by A. Baumeister in *Denkmaler des klassischen altertums* (Munich, 1888).

drags her up by the arm and is about to deal a death blow with his sword (fig. 7.3). Vulnerability and pathos are evoked by these images of Amazons bereft of clothing and armor. No "parallel instance of such nudity in a combatant Amazon" is known in Greek sculpture or vase painting. Scholars note that Etruscan painters were especially sympathetic toward Amazons, depicted here as strong but lightly armed and dressed compared to the heavily armored Greek warriors. Was this because Etruscan women were freer than Greek women? (Chapter 1 discusses an Etruscan vase showing Amazon heroines, and a female skeleton buried with a spear was discovered in Tarquinia.)[10]

The Etruscan tomb paintings use frontal nudity to evoke compassion for the dying heroines. The battle scene on the Corinthian vase portrays unclothed Amazons in action displaying heroic nudity that made them the equals of the nude Greek hoplites. The lighthearted scene of Amazons swimming depicts the women cavorting naked, but from the side, leaving something to the imagination.

Vase painters and sculptors often depicted fighting or wounded Amazons' upper bodies exposed either deliberately or accidentally during exertion. The revealing disarray of clothing or its complete absence could have an erotic dimension. But did classical Greek artists ever create more flagrantly sexual images of an Amazon's naked lower body?

EROTIC CAMEOS AND PERSONAL OBJECTS

Mythological stories and erotic scenes were favorite subjects on small carved gemstones, precious cameos set in gold finger rings. These incredibly detailed miniature reliefs, owned by both men and women in antiquity, were tiny personal adornments that could be enjoyed privately and shared with friends. We are used to viewing Greek and Roman art as dominated by painted vases and sarcophagi and marble and bronze sculpture. This lesser-known genre of ancient art was much more private and intimate than vases, paintings, and large-scale statues.

Gems and other objets d'art featuring partially nude and nude Amazons were made in the Hellenistic and Roman periods. They also appear on antique neoclassical cameos in early modern European collections, illustrating mythic stories in imitation of ancient examples. The later ancient and antique gems frequently show Greek heroes brutally victorious over Amazons, grabbing them by the hair, pulling them from their horses, and delivering death blows. A small silver box (230 BC) with a gold-relief lid from Sicily, for example, has a violent scene of Achilles pulling Penthesilea's head back to cut her throat; her clothing has fallen away. A Roman gem (ca. 27 BC–AD 14) shows a naked Greek male warrior dragging a naked Amazon from her horse by her hair. A more humane scene appears on a sardonyx cameo of the first century BC/AD. An Amazon supports the nude body of her dying companion, whose dress has slipped down to her thigh (fig. 7.4).[11]

An exquisite naked Amazon appears on a much earlier gemstone of about 500 BC. The beautiful deep-coral carnelian illustrates a romantic climax in the Trojan War. In the myth, Achilles kills the Amazon queen, Penthesilea. As she dies, Achilles is overcome and falls in love, too late (chapter 18). Less than an inch across, the remarkable miniature scene shows the heroically nude Achilles piercing her side with his spear. The dying Penthesilea's eyes are wide open, and she still holds her spear and bow. She wears a pointed cap, a necklace, a bracelet, and an earring. As she swoons, her short tunic hikes up, revealing her pubic area. Achilles's curly hair and sideburns and the Amazon's hair under her helmet are indicated by tiny pellets. The same technique is used to render their pubic hair. Greek women depilated their "uncouth" body hair by

FIG. 7.4. Amazon supporting dying nude companion still holding her bow, with sympathetic horse. Carved red and white sardonyx gem, first century BC/AD. Marlborough Gems, Beazley no. 507, formerly at Blenheim Palace, 2009. Photo by John Boardman. Bottom: antique engraving of the gem.

FIG. 7.5. Achilles spearing partially nude Penthesilea. Carnelian gem, Greek, early fifth century BC, Museum of Fine Arts, Boston, Francis Bartlett Donation of 1912, 27.682. Photograph © 2014 Museum of Fine Arts, Boston. Right, cast of gem, photo by John Boardman.

singeing or plucking.[12] This titillating glimpse of Penthesilea's pubic hair signals that she is a wild barbarian woman (fig. 7.5).

The carnelian, displayed in Boston's Museum of Fine Arts, is one of nine intaglios carved by the Semon Master, thought to be a Greek engraver who worked in Anatolia, known for his intricate anatomical details. This graphic illustration of Achilles's erotic attraction to Penthesilea adorned the hand of a man or woman who lived in Cyprus twenty-five hundred years ago.

AMAZONS WITHOUT ARMOR

Inspired by myths, artists revealed more of Amazons' bodies than ancient mythographers did. In the written versions of the myth, for example, Achilles falls in love as he removes the dead Penthesilea's helmet; her naked form is not described. But the historian Herodotus provides one remarkably intimate detail about the bodies of Scythian women. To cleanse themselves, writes Herodotus, the nomad men and women take vapor baths inside felt tipis constructed over red-hot stones (to which is added a special ingredient; see chapter 9). After their sauna, the Scythian women indulge in a unique beauty treatment. The women pound cypress, cedar, frankincense, and a little water into a paste on a rough stone palette. "Applying this thick substance all over their bodies and faces," they retire for the night. When the women remove the paste the next morning, "their bodies are steeped in the sweet fragrance and their skin is clean and glossy."[13]

All three ingredients are used in perfumes, cosmetics, and pharmaceuticals today. Cedar and cypress oils have antiseptic, astringent qualities, and the trees grow at high altitudes, easily available in Scythia. Frankincense, the aromatic resin of *Boswellia* trees of the Arabian desert, appears in ancient Egyptian beauty mask recipes for toning and smoothing scars; it has antiseptic, anti-inflammatory, rejuvenating properties. Frankincense would have been a precious trade commodity available from merchants on the Silk Routes across Central Asia. Herodotus's recipe and the details would have fascinated Greek men and women alike, since they too applied exotic unguents and perfumes to their bodies. And as we know, images of Amazons were popular decorations on the jars that held Greek women's precious oils and cosmetics.

ΜΕΛΛΝΙΤΠΗ

. Amazon queen Melanippe, mosaic at ancient Edessa
Sanliurfa, Turkey). Photo © Pasquale Sorrentino.

4. Modern mounted female archer Katie Stearns (riding Tasha) of the Flying Duchess Ranch, Arlington, Washington. Photo by Richard Beard.

5. Modern mounted female archer Roberta Beene of Rogue

5. Amazon on blue-eyed palomino horse, battling a Greek warrior. She wears a belted tunic and red-brown trousers. Detail from the Sarcophagus of the Amazons, Etruscan, Tarquinia, 375 BC, Museo Archeologico, Florence, Italy. Photo: Scala/Art Resource, NY.

. Amazon huntress spearing a fallow deer, with her horse, dog, and trained eagle. Gold ing, Greek, 425–400 BC, Francis Bartlett Donation of 1912, 21.1204, Museum of Fine Arts, oston. Photograph © 2014 Museum of Fine Arts, Boston.

1. Amazons battling Greeks, red-figure pitcher (oinochoe), Helios Group, 320–310 BC, Greek, from Apulia, Italy, Museum of Fine Arts, Boston, Gift of H. J. Bigelow, 89.260. Photograph © 2014 Museum of Fine Arts, Boston.

2. Amazon in belted tunic, patterned sleeves and leggings, and soft decorated cap, with a pelta and wielding a battle-axe. Louvre Painter, Lucanian pelike (jug), ca. 350 BC, inv. K544,

13. Pair of Amazons, red hair, blue caps and boots with red laces, fuchsia skirts with red belts and chest straps. South Italian, Canosan, ca. 300–280 BC, painted terra-cotta, eight–nine inches high, Princeton University Art Museum, Carl Otto von Kienbusch Jr., Memorial Collection Fund 1995–110. Photo: Bruce M. White/ Art Resource, NY.

14. Treasures from Teuta's pirate empire: bronze coin hoard, gold ring with carved agate depicting Artemis, from Rhizon, ancient Illyria (Bay of Kotor, Montenegro). Courtesy of Professor Piotr Dyczek, Antiquity of Southeastern Europe Research Centre, University of Warsaw, photos by Janusz Recław, collage by Michele Angel.

8

SEX AND LOVE

NEMIES OF WEDDED LIFE, SELF-SUFFICIENT outdoorswomen, belonging to no man, free to make love on their own terms. A host of questions surround Amazon sex and love, in the Greek imagination and in reality. Did Amazons remain virgins until they had proved themselves in war? Did Amazons enjoy sex? Or did they mate only to reproduce their special society? What sort of partners did Amazons prefer—and what sort of men would consort with Amazons? Could Amazons form bonds of friendship, love, and companionship with men? Is there evidence for long-term relationships for the warrior women of myth and legend—and of history?

Gossip and rumor ran rife about Amazon sexuality: the ancient Greek and Latin authors tended to "dwell on the exceptional, the scandalous."[1] Like Atalanta, the Amazons of myth and historical legend had little in common with Greek women—the Amazons and Scythian women behaved more like free Greek men. Several ancient historians reported that warrior women of Eurasia arranged trysts with men of neighboring tribes to have sex without marriage or any emotional strings. For those Greeks who believed that the Amazons were a society of women hostile to men, this custom explained how they could reproduce. In other accounts, in which Scythian women had lost their men to war, the practical widows were said to seek intercourse with outsiders in order to perpetuate their tribe.

Amazon sex was robust, promiscuous. It took place outdoors, outside of marriage, in the summer season, with any man an Amazon cared to mate with. Some modern scholars interpret these details in ancient Greek sources as imaginary reversals of proper Hellenic women's confined, indoor life, a distorted mirror image invented by Greek men to equate autonomous women with wild animals. Other scholars declare that Amazons were "not only asexual but antisexual." But still others raise the possibility of underlying ethnographic facts.[2] Might some ancient Greek descriptions of legendary Amazons' sex life parallel real-life experiences of fighting women of Scythia? Could some Greek sources have preserved nuggets of accurate knowledge about some nomad customs?

Seasonal patterns are typical of nomad life. The pastoralists of ancient Scythia migrated from high summer pastures to winter camps. Each spring, bands came together to bury their preserved dead in kurgan cemeteries. In spring they took purifying saunas; met with other tribes annually for trade fairs; and competed in riding and shooting contests. Warfare and raiding may have been seasonal too, with bands of mostly males away for much of a year, returning each summer to the women with small children. For the Greeks these unfamiliar patterns could have given rise to the idea that the men and women lived separately, coming together once a year to mate.[3] Another factor is that small, isolated, close-knit tribes can avoid incest and inbreeding by mating with outsiders. (Whether or not they had an embryonic grasp of the scientific rationale, these breeders of horses and other animals would have noticed inbreeding effects.) Exogamous sexual unions among culturally related groups may well have taken place at certain times of the year. It was common practice to forge alliances by intermarriage.

In some nomad groups polyamory or "free love" practices—multiple sexual partners for males and females, and polyandry (many "husbands" or men) and polygamy (many "wives" or women)—were accepted. Xenophon, for example, remarked on the indiscriminate, public sexual intercourse of the tattooed Mossynoeci tribe of Pontus. Herodotus reported that the Agathyrsi, the nomadic Thracian-Scythian tribe, mated freely in order to "foster sibling-like relationships and to eliminate jealousy and hatred." According to Strabo, among the Siginni of the northwest Caucasus the most accomplished women charioteers could "cohabit with whomever they chose." Strabo also described the sexual mores of the mountain tribes of Media (northwestern Iran): the men have up to five women and "likewise the women believe it honorable to have as many men as possible and consider less than five a calamity." Polyandry was practiced by the women of another nomad group near the Caspian Sea, the Tapyri, who had children by several men. The Massagetae, a Saka-Scythian tribe of Central Asia, formed companionate couples with an "open marriage" option, according to Herodotus and Strabo. The men and women were free to initiate discreet sexual relations with others. The sign for sex in progress was a quiver hung outside a woman's wagon. (In the Caucasian Nart sagas, the signal that a woman had a sexual guest was his lance stuck in the ground outside her abode.) Ancient Chinese sources also described polyandry and polyamory among the nomad tribes of Inner Asia (chapter 25).[4]

Ancient notions of virginal Amazons seem to be at odds with reports of Amazons as sexually active; some scholars argue that Amazons were imaginary figures intended to represent Greek girls out of male control.[5] Yet many features of the seemingly contradictory Greek descriptions of legendary Amazons may reflect misunderstood nomad customs.

AMAZON MAIDENS

Greek girls were usually married by age eighteen, when they passed from the guardianship of their male relatives into their husband's household. Greek men controlled their wives' and daughters' sexual activities. In contrast, there was no set "marriageable" age for girls in Scythia. Herodotus and other writers said that Saka-Scytho-Sarmatian girls did not marry until they had fought and/or killed at least one enemy. In antiquity "virgin" and "maiden" were not always technical terms meaning "intact hymen" or "lacking sexual experience"; the words could mean a sexually active woman who was "unmarried/unattached" to one man. As noted in chapter 1, only three Amazons were renowned for their lifelong vows of virginity. In some nomad cultures, unattached young women enjoyed liberties shocking to Greeks. In Thrace, for example, where "to live by war and plunder is most glorious," Herodotus marveled that "they keep no watch over maidens and leave them altogether free."[6]

Girls and boys in nomadic societies were trained alike in the arts of war. In the steppe nomad context, it would be reasonable to expect youths of both sexes to prove their worth before marrying and/or having children. A ritualized duel with a suitor, often from another tribe, could be one way of proving one's mettle. The natural historian Aelian described courtship and marriage among the Saka (Massagetae) as a mock battle for dominance. "If a man wants to marry a maiden, he must fight a duel with her. They fight to win but not to the death. If the girl wins, she carries him off as captive and has power and control over him, but if she is defeated then she is under his control."[7] Aelian may have exaggerated the actual outcome based on the Greco-Roman difficulty in imagining a relationship grounded in equality. Similarly, the notion that only one partner could be dominant led classical writers to insist that any man who loved an Amazon had to either assert his power or submit to hers (see chapter 10). And yet Aelian's description turns out to have a basis in reality. Among the nomads of Central Asia, serious and mock duels between heroes and heroines in epic poems often end in love. The traditional courtship customs of nomadic Kyrgyz people and others of ancient Saka lands entail arduous physical contests, such as racing and wrestling, to win a maiden's love. The contests are sometimes said to determine which marriage partner wins (symbolic) dominance in the relationship (chapters 22–24).

NATURAL LOVERS OF MEN

As in Atalanta's lusty relationship with Meleager, Amazons were enthusiastic lovers of men of their own choosing. Herodotus's story of the Sarmatians (chapter 3) told how Amazons and young Scythian men had sex, fell in love, and eloped to create a new tribe. The strangers shared sexual attraction and took mutual pleasure in intercourse, repeated over time and, in this case, with the same partners. The couples bonded and decided as a group to spend their lifetimes together, promising to raise their children free of imposed gender roles.

Random sex among multiple partners, agreed upon among equals, appears in Strabo's description of the seasonal mating of Amazons with their neighbors, the Gargarians. It is not clear whether the Gargarians of the Caucasus were believed to be an all-male tribe. (Their name comes from *gargar*, ancient Georgian for apricot, native to Colchis.) In Strabo's account, the Gargarians had originally "lived with" the Amazons in Pontus and migrated with them over the Caucasus Mountains to the northern Black Sea region. At some point, the Gargarians "revolted" and a war ensued. The Gargarians and Amazons finally made peace. They agreed to "a compact that they would live independently but still have dealings with each other in the matter of children." The clear understanding is that each tribe would benefit from this arrangement.

And so, continues Strabo, following this ancient compact, each summer the Gargarian men go up to a mountain on the border with the Amazon territory to meet Amazonian women. First the men and women offer sacrifices together, signifying the religious propriety of what was to follow. Then, for two months, the Amazons and the Gargarians enjoy casual sex after dark with whoever is handy. The men return to their land and many of the women go home pregnant. Strabo goes on to say that baby girls born of these unions are raised by the Amazons, but "they take the boys to the Gargarians, who adopt and raise them as their own sons, despite uncertain paternity."[8]

Strabo's account was drawn from two ancient historians of the Amazons, Metrodorus and Hypsicrates, both of Pontus (their works are unfortunately lost). Might his description reflect a garbled ethnological history of divisions and alliances within a tribe or confederation of tribes in which women were fighters and leaders? Scythian bands continually waxed and waned, united and divided, fought and allied. Modern scholars assume that Strabo intended his story to portray Amazons mating like wild animals solely for reproduction. But his account is complex and may well contain incomplete information about genuine past practices. The treaty between Amazons and the Gargarian men who were once closely associated with the Amazons specified that they would come together each summer to worship and procreate.

Annual gatherings would have involved reunions of friends and relations from past years. Ritualized sacrifice and consensual sex with multiple partners within a sacred precinct is not implausible. Seasonal rendezvous customs fostered exogamy and provided other important social and economic opportunities for scattered nomad groups. One ancient Greek writer clearly associated Amazon sexual activity with nomadic trade fairs: "Whenever the Amazons need children they go to the marketplace on the River Halys (western Pontus) and have intercourse with men." Strabo reported that as many as seventy tribes of Sarmatia and the Caucasus region came together each year at Dioscurias on the coast of Colchis to socialize and trade. It is interesting that many Central Asian epics tell of heroes who travel long distances to find brides, and many non-Greek Amazon tales feature marriage to husbands from other tribes, practices that avoid incest and seal alliances.[9]

In antiquity, Amazons were assumed to be strongly heterosexual. The women warriors were, as Plutarch put it, "natural lovers of men." Indeed, some ancient beliefs about physiognomy maintained that it would be natural for "manly" Amazons to be especially attracted to "manly" men. According to this theory, it was overly feminine women who would be attracted to loving other women. Virile women, like Amazons—who could overcome the weak, "effeminate" traits in themselves—were assumed to desire virile men.[10]

COURTING AMAZONS

Amazons were very popular images on white-ground alabastra in the late sixth–fifth centuries BC. These tall, slender jars for exotic perfume and unguents are believed to have been used exclusively by Greek women. Two fascinating alabastra (ca. 510–500 BC) by the same painter combine courtship and sexual fantasy themes about Amazons. Each shows a draped Greek youth and an Amazon in trousers with her weapons (fig. 8.1). Between one couple stands a heron, a favorite pet in women's quarters; between the other couple is the Amazon's helmet on a stool. The pose of the cloaked male youths, leaning on a staff and one foot on tiptoe, is an artistic hallmark of courting scenes (compare Heracles's stance in plate 7). The vase inscriptions *o pais kalos* ("the boy is pretty/hot") also take us into the realm of sexual desire. Who purchased and who owned these erotic jars? Some scholars even wonder whether there was a fad among young Athenian men for alabastra with Amazon images. Did men give these vases to female lovers as hints about their own sexual fantasies? Did they belong to women who imagined themselves in the role of the Amazon? Whatever the

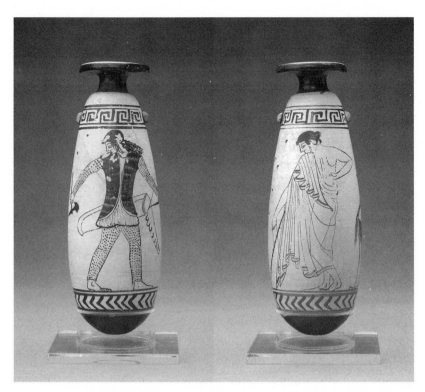

FIG. 8.1. Amazon and Greek male lover, white-ground women's perfume jar (alabastron), ca. 510–500 BC, Antikenmuseum und Sammlung Ludwig, Basel, Inv. KA403.

answers, there is no doubt that the Amazons were being depicted in an overtly sexual context.[11]

Same-sex desire among Amazons is not in evidence in ancient Greco-Roman art or literature—and these were cultures with few qualms about public discussion or depictions of homosexual activities. And yet, what should we make of a painting on another alabastron showing an encounter between a Thracian woman and an Amazon?

The white-ground alabastron is signed by the Pasiades Painter, 525–500 BC. As noted, women's pottery often featured Amazons, but this vase is highly unusual. On one side, a ponytailed Thracian woman steps forward, clad in high boots and a leopard skin, with a large snake coiled around one arm. A poorly preserved inscription appears to give her name

FIG. 8.2. Thracian huntress courting the Amazon Penthesilea. White-ground alabastron, Pasia-des Painter, ca. 525–500 BC, drawing after original in National Archaeological Museum, Athens 15002.

as Theraichme, "Huntress." She is gallantly presenting a rabbit to an Amazon on the other side of the vase, clearly labeled "Penthesilea." Penthesilea wears a zigzag-patterned tunic and leggings, a quiver, and a helmet, and is armed with a bow, arrows, and a battle-axe. Unlike most Amazons in art, however, she wears sandals. A heron stands between them. A rabbit is a very common gift depicted in many Athenian vase paintings, but it carries a specific meaning: male homosexual seduction.[12]

So this scene is a startling reversal of a common *male* courtship theme, in which a suitor presents a rabbit as a love-token to his beloved. This unique scene is not known from any myth or literary text about Penthesilea. We can guess that the image is a provocative twist on the expected theme of rabbit love-gifts and hunting trophies as a courtship metaphor among homosexual men. The gesture also reminds us of Meleager presenting his lover Atalanta with the trophy of the Calydonian Boar Hunt (prologue). Possibly this painting illustrates a lost story about a Thracian woman and Penthesilea, who was a Thracian by birth. A "sister" alabastron by the same artist shows a Thracian woman (or maenad) in a spotted fawn skin and pointed cap. She is in exactly the same pose as Penthesilea on the first vase (and she wears the same sandals). She holds out a leafy branch toward a woman in a long saffron chiton, and a heron appears between them.

The meanings that these audacious "wild" women held for the painters and the presumably female vase owners remain mysterious, especially the erotic pairing of the Greek youths and Amazons and the Thracian woman seemingly courting Penthesilea. Scholarly claims that Greek men "propagandized women's place by commissioning vases whose paintings depicted them at home at their chores" cannot explain why so many scenes on vases used by women featured Thracian women and maenads, Atalanta, and Amazons, all defiant icons of female sexual autonomy.[13]

AMAZON LOVE AND DEVOTION

"Amazon unions are one-shot affairs" with random men and "no constancy" or attachment, maintains William Tyrrell in his study of Amazon myths.[14] In fact many ancient writers describe Amazons' bonds of friendship, empathy, love, devotion, and companionship, as Herodotus does in his Sarmatian history. In a story about Antiope, for another example, the Amazon treats a young Greek sailor with gentle compassion, and several traditions describe Antiope's devotion to Theseus (chapter 16). Some versions of the myth of Heracles and Queen Hippolyte begin with the promise of love (chapter 15). Another story, recounted by Philostratus, tells how Amazons captured and planned to kill shipwrecked sailors. One young Amazon felt pity and sexual desire for the youngest sailor. When she pleaded for his freedom, the Amazons decided to release all the men. The sailors chose to stay and "formed close relationships with the women." (The men also taught the Amazons to sail; chapter 19.)[15]

Pairs of Amazons frequently appear in Greek vase paintings in scenes intended to show their sisterhood and devotion to their comrades in arms. In many images, the Amazons set off to hunt, fight, or ride together (plate 13, fig. 7.2). In Amazonomachies, we see Amazons rushing to the aid of beleaguered comrades battling Greek warriors or pairing up to attack the enemy. Several artworks show Amazons supporting wounded companions (fig. 7.4) or carrying a dead Amazon from the battlefield (the earliest examples are on a vase by Kleitias,

570–560 BC). A frenzied battle between Greeks and Amazons on a frieze from the Temple of Apollo at Bassae shows an Amazon trying to lift her fallen comrade while the fighting surges around them.[16] These tableaux parallel scenes depicting Greek warriors aiding companions or carrying their dead, evocations of the pathos of war. Similar images of Amazons in the act of caring for their war dead are striking because they illustrate the profound feelings of comradeship in warfare that were usually reserved for Greek male warriors. It shows that the Greeks could imagine Amazons, "unnatural" women, experiencing deep human emotional attachments.

EQUALITY, THE WAY TO AN AMAZON'S HEART

In Greek mythology, confronting a beautiful, passionately resisting, powerful Amazon aroused the Greek heroes to dominate, harm, rape, humiliate, and/or murder such threatening women (chapters 15–18). Yet *outside* the world of myth, in the Amazonian sexual encounters described by ancient historians and other authors, a consistent theme emerges of mutual sexual attraction, pleasurable consensual sex—plenty of it—and a sense of equality with male lovers. Sexual relations between equal men and women developed into long-term relationships in Herodotus's story of the Sarmatians, who decided that gender equality was "fair and honorable." Herodotus also reported that among the "*civilized and righteous* Issedonians the women share power equally with their men" (italics added; Issedonia was a Silk Route crossroads between the Altai region and northwest China).[17]

Companionable relationships characterized by equality and a sense of interdependence, like those the Greeks reported among Scythians in antiquity, are traditional and practical ways of life in many nomadic and seminomadic cultures. The ancient Nart sagas of the Caucasus, for example, frequently allude to the shared authority, responsibility, interdependence, love, and affection of male and female "soul mates." Mutual respect was seen as a necessary condition for a husband and wife. Early modern European travelers in the Caucasus remarked on the "great freedom and respect accorded to women" and the "humanity and affection" and friendship of husbands and wives. Klaproth remarked, for example, that in the Caucasus "the wife is the companion, and not the menial servant, of the husband." "Easy camaraderie" and "blurred lines between sex roles" are phrases used to describe the egalitarian lifestyle of some nomads living today in Kazakhstan and other ancient Scythian lands. Among the polytheistic Kalash tribe of northwest Pakistan the women have a remarkable degree of sexual freedom (some Kalash claim descent from Alexander's Greeks and local women). While modern ethnography does not prove the antiquity of specific lifestyles, it does suggest the persistence of practical egalitarian attitudes over time.[18]

Archaeological evidence from ancient Scythian graves seems to support the reality of male and female partnership ties. Chapter 4 described the remains of girls and women buried with the same honors as men. Armed females were typically dressed in the same clothing as male warriors, with equivalent weapons, sacrificed horses, riding equipment, and grave goods. Companionship with a life partner is evident in the examples of the Pazyryk culture's couple placed together in a grave with weapons and nine horses, and of the elderly Tuva man and woman wrapped in furs and buried with their horses, weapons, and costly possessions.

Did the Greeks ever suspect what they might have been missing by suppressing women? Greeks also held a belief that sex between equals— especially gods and heroes but also mortals—could be exciting and fulfilling. That idea anticipates some modern scientific studies correlating gender equality with more frequent sex and happier coupling. Perhaps the popularity of Amazon stories among the Greeks served as a kind of "what if/if only" compensation.[19]

The Greek historian Xenophon wrote an oft-quoted dialogue in which a man instructs his young bride on the proper duties of an ideal Greek wife. Yet, like Herodotus, Xenophon also expressed admiration for other societies in which women, like men, were encouraged to engage in vigorous sports like "running and feats of strength" and outdoor activities. Xenophon remarked that "if both mothers and fathers were physically fit their children would be much stronger."[20]

A pair of lesser-known passages by Xenophon illustrate fascinating real-life situations suggesting that Greeks could enjoy envisioning men and women on more equal terms.[21] In Xenophon's *Symposium* (380 BC) we witness the growing excitement of Greek men at a banquet as they observe a steamy sexual encounter of two passionate, willing partners.

A handsome young man and woman—noncitizen slaves of equal status—have already entertained the men with choreographed, sinuous gymnastics and a dangerous sword dance–duel. Now they act out a sex scene, taking the roles of the mythic lovers Dionysus and Ariadne. As the two kiss and caress one another, the men, says Xenophon, suddenly realize that the actors are not simply reciting a typical "burlesque" script. The two people are really in love and lust. Watching genuine lovers of equal status on the verge of satisfying their obvious mutual desire arouses the men to a high pitch, says Xenophon. As the pair discreetly withdraw from view, the bachelors in the audience vow to get married and the married men rush home to their wives, eager to replicate what they have just seen.

Xenophon includes another remarkable account of gender equality in his historical memoir of leading his army of ten thousand Greek soldiers back to Greece after a failed campaign in Babylonia (400 BC). Their long march took them north from Persia through Armenia to Pontus, the fabled Amazon homeland on the Black Sea. Along the way, Xenophon says, the Greek soldiers took "some boys and many women captive, depending on their sexual preferences." Like the boys, the "beautiful and tall" women and girls of local villages were at first exploited as sexual objects and made to perform daily chores for the men. But during the months of shared hardships and dangers crossing the Armenian mountains in winter, Xenophon explains that a new relationship began to develop between the individual men and the foreign women. They were gradually becoming trusted companions dependent on each other for survival. Several times the men risked their lives to save the women. The women took up the army's war cry at crucial moments. Camping together in the cold, hostile land, fending off deadly attacks from natives, and learning each other's languages and personalities, the Greek soldiers and the barbarian women forged bonds that made them essentially equals. Xenophon's Greek army had taken on some of the attributes that made Scythian bands so formidable: everyone, male and female, was a potential fighter.

Xenophon illustrates this new relationship in his account of the banquet that he, as general, gave for the local Paphlagonian chiefs, because his army needed safe passage through their territory west of Pontus. To entertain their guests, the Greek men performed their traditional

FIG. 8.3. Female armed war dancer with shield and spear. She wears a Greek helmet (and a *perizoma* much like Atalanta's wrestling outfit). Red-figure lekythos (oil flask), Athens, ca. 475–425 BC, inscribed *Zephyria kale* ("Zephyria is beautiful"). Iziko Museums, Cape Town, South Africa, 207942 Cape Town 18, SACHM134.

pyrrhic war dances. The choreographed military moves in full armor with weapons and shields was also a not-so-subtle display of martial prowess. Then one of the foreign women at the banquet donned some Greek armor and took up a light shield to "perform a pyrrhic dance with grace." The amazed Paphlagonian chieftains asked whether these women fought alongside the Greeks. The Greeks assured their guests, "These very women drove off the King of Persia!" In this extraordinary reply, the Greek soldiers were claiming—boasting!—that they had Amazons as their companions in love and war.[22]

DRUGS, DANCE, AND MUSIC

A HARD-DRINKING AMAZON? OUTSIDE OF COMEDY, women who overindulge in alcohol were rare in ancient Greek literature. But this was the reputation of the Amazon who gave her name to Sinope, one of several towns in Anatolia that claimed Amazons in their mythic past. The Greek tradition about the drinking Amazon appears in an ancient commentary on the epic voyage of the Argonauts to Pontus. The commentator cites lost histories of the Black Sea by Hecataeus (fifth century BC) and Andron of Teos (ca. 350 BC). According to the story, an Amazon named Sanape, a "Daughter of Ares," had "fled to Pontus and married a local king," presumably during some conflict in her homeland. "Because she drank too much wine she was called Sanape." The commentator explains, "Those with a liking for drink were called *sanapai* by the Thracians, whose dialect the Amazons also use." So, he concludes, the town where she and the king lived "was called Sanape, later corrupted to Sinope." In keeping with the restless Amazonian nature, "This hard-drinking Amazon later left this place for Lytidas." (No one knows whether Lytidas was a place or a person.)[1]

Ancient Greek etymological claims are notoriously spurious. Some modern scholars have interpreted *Sinope* to mean "to seize or carry off." But in this case, the ancient etymology of *Sanape* appears to have an accurate core. In the heroic Nart sagas of Caucasia, the Circassian word *sana* means "wine" and *sanapai* means "the one from/of the place of *sana*." The Amazon who came to Pontus may not have been a hard drinker but simply a woman from a wine-growing region. Colchis was known in antiquity for its fine vineyards; Sinope was also known for its wine. The Amazon's name, derived from a Circassian word for wine, was explained with a colorful story. The Sinopeans celebrated their Amazonian history by issuing coins with Sanape's image and an annual procession on the city walls of women dressed as armed warriors.[2]

The tale of the tipsy Amazon brings up a question. Did intoxicants have a place in Amazonian-Scythian culture? In antiquity, wine and opium were the chief drugs known to the Greeks. The Greeks often portrayed "inferior" barbarians as especially susceptible to liquor. In Greek thinking, extreme passion for warfare went hand in hand with compulsive drinking. So, since at least the sixth century BC, the bellicose Scythians were stereotyped as unrestrained wine drinkers seeking "maenadic" alcoholic frenzy. This belief would have made Sanape's name seem appropriate for a war-loving Amazon. According to the Greeks, Scythians preferred to drink wine straight, unlike the Greeks who liked to water their wine. Hence the proverbial saying in Athens, "to drink in Scythian style."[3]

The stereotype of Scythians' wild drinking bouts was applied to the seminomadic Scythians whom Greeks met in Black Sea trading colonies. These Scythians imported wine from Greece or from vineyards in Black Sea agricultural regions. The Nart sagas of the northwest Caucasus describe the introduction of *sana* (wine) from the south. According to an Abaza tradition of Abkhazia, *sana* was a gift of the gods, a sweet, strong drink that made one feel powerful and "pleased with the world." Many Greek wine amphoras—some with stamps from Aegean islands and some even containing red wine deposits—have been found in several archaeological sites in the northern Black Sea–Don River region. Some real-life warrior women of that region were buried with their painted Greek wine amphoras (chapter 4), bringing to mind the story of the Amazon Sanape's liking for wine.[4]

QUEEN TOMYRIS OF THE MASSAGETAE

The nomadic Saka-Scythian groups of Central Asia were less familiar with wine, as we can gather from accounts about Queen Tomyris told by Herodotus, Strabo, and Justin. In the sixth century BC, King Cyrus of Persia invaded the land of the Massagetae, a confederation of Saka-Scythian nomads east of the Caspian Sea. Warlike horse people, like their neighbors the Issedonians, the Massagetae were distinguished by gender equality and the sexual freedom of their women. They sacrificed horses to the Sun. Armored in helmets and wide war belts of brass and gold, they fought with bows, lances, and battle-axes. The ruler of the Massagetae at this time was a powerful woman named Tomyris.

Like other Scythian tribes, the Massagetae were milk drinkers unused to wine. This fact was exploited by Cyrus. Retreating after losing a battle with Tomyris (ca. 530 BC), he resorted to treachery. According to Herodotus's account, he set out a fancy banquet with large quantities of wine under his Persian tents and withdrew. The pursuing nomads, led by Tomyris's son, came upon the abandoned feast. They drank the wine and fell into a stupor. The Persians came back and slaughtered the Massagetae; they captured Tomyris's son, who killed himself as soon as he regained his senses. Enraged, Tomyris sent a message castigating Cyrus. "Glutton for blood! Your weapon was red wine, which you Persians drink until you are so crazy that shameful words float on the liquor's fumes. This was the poison you used to destroy my army and my son. Leave my land now, or I swear by the Sun I will give you more blood than you can drink."

The mayhem was horrendous in the next battle. Tomyris's army destroyed the Persians and Cyrus was killed. According to the legend, Tomyris found the king's corpse, hacked off his head, and plunged it into a wine jug filled with blood drained from Cyrus's men, crying, "Drink your fill of blood!"[5]

The chief intoxicants known to the Massagetae, Saka, Scythians, and other nomads on the steppes would have been fermented mare's milk and cannabis/hashish, both readily available. Their herds of horses were of paramount importance to the peoples of the Eurasian steppes, providing transport, leather, horsehair, hooves, meat, and milk. The vitamin-rich mare's milk was a vital supplement to the nomadic diet of mostly meat. Low in fat but very rich in sugar, and harboring organisms that trigger fermentation, mare's milk "is ideal for the preparation of an alcoholic drink called *koumiss*."[6]

FERMENTED MARE'S MILK

The horse people of the steppes were known as *hippomolgoi galakto-phagoi*, "mare-milking milk-drinking Scythians," since Homeric times. The Amazons nourished their babies with mare's milk, according to Philostratus. He was right, but that milk would have been fermented first. Because of its high lactose content mare's milk is a strong laxative; it requires fermentation to be a viable source of nutrition. During fermentation, lactobacilli bacteria acidify the milk and yeasts create carbonated ethanol. While the milk is fermenting, it must be agitated or churned like butter. The result is mildly alcoholic koumiss, high in calories and vitamins, that can be stored longer than fresh milk. The alcoholic content can be enriched by a process developed by the nomads called "freeze distillation"—freezing, thawing, removing the ice crystals, and refreezing, and repeating the process until the desired potency is reached.[7]

Herodotus described the ancient Scythian milk-fermenting process on a large scale, probably observed among the settled Scythians around the Black Sea. "The milk is poured into deep wooden casks, then stirred vigorously until it ferments." The early traveler William of Rubruck, who trekked across the steppes in about AD 1250, offered more details. "As the nomads churn and beat the milk it begins to ferment and bubble up like new wine." He described the effervescent koumiss as pungent tasting and intoxicating. It "makes the inner man most joyful!" Smaller batches of koumiss would have been fermented in leather bags by nomad families on the move. In Inner Asia, it was the custom to hang the sack where passersby would periodically punch the bag to agitate the koumiss. Koumiss is still prepared by steppe peoples from the Black Sea to western China.[8]

How ancient is koumiss? Very ancient indeed. Evidence for the great antiquity of koumiss (*kumys, kumiss, qimiz*) comes from historical linguistics and from archaeology. Three very ancient alcoholic beverages are mead (fermented honey), kvass (beer), and koumiss. *Kvass* and *mead* have cognates in Proto-Indo-European, while *koumiss* derives from the ancient Central Asian Turkic language family. Koumiss drinking originated along with the domestication of the horse in Central Asia. Milking mares is easier than milking cows, and mares produce almost as much milk. About forty-five hundred years ago Eurasian nomads perfected the special technique required for milking mares. The mares graze on their own during the day and return to their foals in camp. The foal starts the flow and then is held close to the mare's side while the milker kneels on one knee with the container propped on the other, and with arms wrapped around the mare's hind leg. The lipids from horse milk can now be identified on artifacts from very ancient burials. Archaeologists have discovered bowls containing residue of mare's milk in Botai culture sites, ca. 3500 BC, in northern Kazakhstan.[9] (The Botai, early domesticators of horses, engraved horse bones with tattoo-like patterns; chapter 6.)

Koumiss is prominent in Scythian burials from the Black Sea to the Altai. Special utensils for beating or stirring koumiss and drinking vessels with traces of horse milk are very common grave goods of both men and women. For example, the Golden Warrior of Issyk (chapter 4) was accompanied by koumiss beaters and bowls that held mare's milk. Archaeologists excavating the rich cemetery at Chertomlyk (Ukraine), where several warrior women were buried with their weapons, recovered a magnificent silver vase elaborately decorated with birds, lions, and griffins and a frieze of Scythians training their horses. The famous Chertomlyk Vase was "evidently meant for *kumys*, as it has a sieve in the neck" and three spouts shaped like lions and a horse at the base. If so, it was probably ceremonial or used for serving, since wooden and leather vessels would be more suited to the fermentation process. In the grave of the tattooed Ice Princess of the Ukok Plateau the Russian archaeologists discovered a wooden stirring stick in a cup with a handle carved in the shape of two snow leopards. Inside the cup was the residue of the koumiss that would sustain her in the Other World. The remains of koumiss and chunks of horse meat from the departed's last meals and mourners' feasts confirm the ancient Greek descriptions of the milk-and-meat diet of steppe nomads, many of whom who depend on these same staples today.[10]

HAOMA AND HONEY

The horsewomen of the steppes, contemporaries of the ancient Greeks and known as Amazons, certainly prepared and drank fermented milk on a daily basis. What other intoxicating substances were known to the peoples of Scythia? Saka-Scythian groups in Central Asia used *haoma/soma*, a mysterious plant-based Persian/Indian intoxicant. Persian inscriptions from the time of Darius refer to as *Saka haumavarga*, "haoma-drinking Saka-Scythians" (the Amyrgioi tribe of Sogdiana-Bakria, led by Amorges in the time of Cyrus; see chapter 23). The identities of the sacred plants *haoma* and *soma* are unknown; candidates include mead, cannabis, *Amanita muscaria* (fly agaric) mushroom, ephedra, and opium.[11]

There is ancient literary evidence that some Scythians may have fermented honey into alcoholic mead. According to Pliny, in Pontus a very special wild honey of the Black Sea area was made into mead. The bees of Pontus collect neurotoxic nectar from the poisonous rhododendrons that grow in profusion there. The dangers of Pontic honey were recognized in antiquity. On their march through Pontus in 400 BC, for example, Xenophon's army of ten thousand Greeks feasted on the honeycombs and suffered the dire effects of "mad honey." In the first century BC during the Mithradatic Wars, a tribe of Pontus used the toxic honey as a bait to ambush and decimate Pompey's Roman army. Tiny doses were (and still are) traditionally used by local people as an intoxicant and tonic. Some nomadic pastoralists even feed small quantities to their herds to strengthen them. Although the women warriors of Pontus surely were aware of the effects of their local wild rhododendron honey, no ancient source links them to it, and so far no archaeological evidence of toxic honey use has come to light.[12]

INTOXICATING HEMP

Another natural intoxicant of the steppes was easily accessible to Scythians. Hemp (*Cannabis sativa*, *Cannabis indica*; hashish) originated in Central Asia. Wild hemp was gathered for millennia and the plant was one of the first to be domesticated. Hemp pollen, fiber, and textiles are found in ancient sites from the Black Sea to China. Hemp was prized for the strong flax-like fiber that can be made into twine or rope and woven into textiles for clothing. Cannabis contains psychoactive agents, making the herb valuable for spiritual and recreational purposes.[13]

Herodotus described both uses of hemp in Thrace and Scythia. "A plant called *kannabis* grows in Scythia, similar to flax but much thicker and taller. It grows wild in Scythia. The Thracians cultivate this *kannabis* and weave garments from it that are just like linen—unless you are very familiar with hemp you would think the cloth to be linen." Herodotus speaks with authority, apparently having seen and touched hemp clothing.[14]

But when he tells about the mind-altering aspects of *kannabis*, Herodotus relies on accounts he heard from his Scythian informants and translators around the Black Sea. In his descriptions of the way of life of the Scythian tribes who dwell beyond the Black Sea, his phrases "it is said" and "they report" signal that he is relying on oral sources. Herodotus is not sure whether *kannabis* is a shrub or a tree or whether it is the seeds or fruit that were burned to create a bewitching effect on the senses. In a passage about the people living between the Black Sea and the Caspian (Turkey, Armenia, Azerbaijan, Iran), Herodotus describes their custom of gathering an intoxicating "fruit" from a tree to use when they assemble in large groups. They sit in a circle around a fire and throw this "fruit" onto the embers. "As it burns, the people inhale the fumes and become intoxicated, just as Greeks become inebriated with wine." Herodotus continues, "They keep adding more fruit to the fire and become even more intoxicated—they get so drunk on the smoke that they jump up and dance and sing around the fire."[15]

Herodotus describes the same intoxicating effect from the inhaled smoke of *kannabis* in another passage about Scythian customs. As we saw in chapter 7, the Scythians constructed felt tipis over braziers filled with red-hot rocks. They creep into the little tents and "throw *kannabis* seeds onto the heated stones. These seeds smoulder and smoke and send forth great clouds of steam. The Scythians," declares Herodotus, "howl with joy, awed and elated by their vapor-bath."

One archaeologist chides Herodotus as "naïve," claiming that he was ignorant of the psychotropic effects of the "pure hemp seeds." But Herodotus's other description of socializing Scythians inhaling the inebriating smoke of burning "fruits" demonstrates that he understood the *kannabis* smoke to be an intoxicant. Some modern scholars seem as confused as Herodotus about the technique of inhaling hemp smoke, however, since many accept his statement that the hemp "seeds" were the part of the plant to be thrown on the fire. This notion appears to be supported by the fact that hemp seeds have been discovered in Scythian graves, along with hemp-burning equipment just like the paraphernalia described twenty-five hundred years ago by Herodotus.[16]

Herodotus's uncertainty about what was thrown on the fire is explicable: the clustered flower buds (which produce seeds) are essentially the "fruit" of cannabis. The Scythians, like all sophisticated hemp smokers, would have known that the prime buds produce the strongest high. The buds, of course, contain seeds, but hemp seeds are the least desirable component if the goal is intoxication. The charred seeds found by archaeologists were most likely what remained after the flowering buds had been burned at the funeral ceremony.

Personal hemp-burning kits were discovered in all of the graves of the Pazyryk culture males and females in the Altai region excavated by Sergei Rudenko. The frozen mummies of the men and women in mounds 2 and 5 (described in chapters 4 and 6), whose skin was heavily tattooed with pictures of fantastic stags, griffins, and tigers, were alive in the time of Herodotus. Because their individual hemp kits—which showed definite use and wear—were included with other possessions of daily life, such as tools, weapons, and koumiss utensils, the archaeologists conclude that cannabis inhalation was not restricted to ritual use but was a part of everyday Scythian life.

Hemp-burning equipment consisted of decorated felt and leather mats that were stretched over frames of six poles, tied at the top, to make miniature tipis about four feet high (Herodotus reported three poles). The hexapod pole set belonging to the tattooed chieftain in mound 2 lay next to a leather blanket decorated with winged lion-griffins seizing elk and a small bronze cauldron with heat cracks. The cauldron was filled with stones, with a few charred hemp seeds. The cauldron had a felt base and its handles were wrapped in birch-bark "pot holders." The man's tattooed female companion owned a pole stand covered with birch bark over a square bronze brazier on four legs. Her brazier also contained rocks and hemp seeds. The charred hemp seeds among the stones show that these "incense" burners had been left smouldering inside the grave so that the dead entered oblivion wreathed in cannabis smoke.

The archaeologists have also recovered leather bags containing unburned hemp seeds, probably intended to sustain the departed in the afterlife. Other fragrant seeds, melilot (yellow clover) and coriander,

FIG. 9.1. Scythian cannabis burning equipment, Berel Kurgan 9, fourth century BC. Photo by Viktor Kharchenko, Margulan Institute of Archaeology, Almaty, Kazakhstan, Z. Samashev 2011, p. 26, fig. 26.

and ephedra twigs have also been found in Pazyryk and Altai graves, burned as incense and as supplies for the dead. A vessel recently excavated from a Scythian kurgan in Kazakhstan contained hemp buds and eight stones for heating. Traces of hashish (resin from cannabis buds) and opium have been found in Sarmatian (Alan) tombs of the northern Caucasus and as far west as Romania. Numerous portable stone "altars" with rims and legs decorated in Scythian animal style and lumps of charcoal were discovered in Sarmatian graves of armed females in the Ural Mountains of Russia and Kazakhstan. The shapes of these portable incense "altars" recall the small bronze braziers for burning hemp in the frozen Pazyryk graves.[17]

No ancient Greek source claimed that Scythians (or Amazons) went to battle under the influence of cannabis. One modern historian of steppe cultures suggests that the drug would surely interfere with shooting arrows accurately while riding a galloping horse. But an archaeologist of Scythian graves maintains that cannabis was likely used before battle. It also occurs to scholars to wonder whether hallucinogens played a role in the fantastic Scythian animal-style art that decorates their artifacts and their skin.[18] Might drug-induced visionary experiences have inspired some of the phantasmagoric creatures with infinitely proliferating antlers tipped with griffin heads and the twisting forms of deer and tigers transmogrifying into flying birds and beaked griffins?

Ancient Greek sources and modern archaeological discoveries confirm that two intoxicants, fermented mare's milk and hallucinogenic cannabis, were part of everyday life in Scythia. The Greeks were unaware that the mare's milk that nourished the Scythians and the Amazon babies was mildly alcoholic, but the psychoactive effects of *kannabis* were very clear in Herodotus's account. Since the Greeks understood that Amazons were Scythian women, and since Scythians inhaled the intoxicating smoke of prime cannabis buds, any Greek with a knowledge of Herodotus's histories would be justified in imagining euphoric, naked, glistening Amazons inside their steamy sauna tents, inhaling billowing clouds of hemp smoke, and then languorously applying lotion redolent of cedar and frankincense before retiring to their beds of soft furs.

DANCE AND MUSIC

Herodotus remarked that the Scythians were moved to dance and sing around the *kannabis* fire circle. Dance and music were associated with ecstatic states in antiquity. Abundant literary and artistic evidence describes Amazons—the "Daughters of Ares" and worshippers of Artemis—performing dances and playing musical instruments, usually associated with battle. For example, an Amazon labeled "Antiope" and many other Amazons arming for battle blow trumpets on vase paintings. The names of two Amazons, Melo and Molpadia, are associated with singing. Some puzzling, non-Greek inscriptions on vase paintings showing Amazons in the midst of battle may be efforts to convey the sounds of the foreign women's war cries. One Amazon name, Kydoime, means "Din of Battle."[19]

The previous chapter told how the captive foreign women of Xenophon's army of ten thousand became the tough companions of the soldiers, so respected and trusted that the Greeks liked to think of them as Amazons. They took up the war cries of the men, and at least one woman knew how to execute a martial dance wearing armor and flourishing a sword and shield. Xenophon details the leaping, whirling, fancy footwork, and tricky swordplay of several traditional war dances performed by Thracians, Persians, Mysians, Mantineans, Arcadians, and others (chapter 8). These moves, generically called pyrrhic (war) dances, were excellent military training drills for strength, flexibility, and martial arts maneuvers.[20]

Several ancient Greek vase paintings illustrate women in armor dancing with swords and shields. Are these women Amazons? Some images of solo dancers in armor with weapons might show foreign female entertainers at Greek symposia, recalling the female war dancers at the two different banquets described by Xenophon (fig. 8.3). But some vases showing armed dances performed by groups of women do appear to depict Amazons. On a fragmentary red-figure cup (attributed to Makron, ca. 490 BC) four women, presumably Amazons, brandish swords and execute a choreographed pyrrhic-type dance by a palm tree and altar. Each dancer wears a *chitoniskos* (short tunic), a cloak, and a baldric strap across the chest. Pyrrhic dances and palm trees are associated with Artemis, and palms often appear with Amazons on other vases. Two black-figure vases show Amazons in short belted tunics and Scythian caps with earflaps dancing with shields and spears to flute music played by a figure next to an altar. Another enigmatic vase, a red-figure pyxis, shows a helmeted girl in trousers with a spear and a shield decorated with a snake. She is dancing a pyrrhic dance before an altar and a life-size statue of Artemis with a quiver and bow.[21]

These vase paintings illustrate the sort of war dances performed by the Amazons to honor Artemis at Ephesus, as described in ancient Greek literature. Some classical scholarship interprets the female pyrrhic dancers on the vases as *Greek* maidens undergoing initiation rites at Greek Artemis sanctuaries, modeled on Amazon dances. It is not clear why all these dancers with Scythian clothing and gear must be interpreted as *Greek* girls and not Amazons, however. At any rate, the evocation of the Amazon war dances at Ephesus by the vase painters is unmistakable.[22]

Ephesus, like Sinope, claimed Amazon founders. The great Temple of Artemis there, one of the Seven Wonders of the World, was built upon a sanctuary believed to have been established long ago by the Amazons. In Greek myth, the god Dionysus fought and killed many Amazons at Ephesus and on the nearby island of Samos (chapter 19). In the fifth century BC, a group of bronze statues of beautiful Amazons in different poses was dedicated in the temple, the results of a competition among the best Greek artists of the day. The originals no longer exist, but they provided the models for numerous Roman marble copies. The marble Amazons are typically clad in short chitons that expose one breast, with quivers, bows, battle-axes, and crescent shields, leaning on spears with one arm raised; sometimes the Amazon is wounded. The women's expressions evoke paradoxical adjectives: austere, beautiful, heroic, merciless, vulnerable, androgynous.[23]

One of these original bronze Amazon statues, a masterpiece by the sculptor Strongylion, was plundered from Ephesus and brought to Rome. From small copies found by archaeologists, we know that Strongylion portrayed the Amazon as an agile maiden riding a spirited, rearing horse, about to throw her spear. Her short dress exposed her sensuous limbs, inspiring her nickname *Euknemon*, "Lovely Legs." An Amazon named Knemis fought at Troy, according to a late Roman scholar—her name could mean either "greaves" or "knees." Could she be associated with Strongylion's famous Amazon? The emperor Nero became enamored with that bronze statue and confiscated it from the private owner. Thereafter the Amazon known as "Lovely Legs" was always carried along in Nero's retinue.[24]

The Greek poet Callimachus (third century BC) created a vivid picture of the Amazons honoring Artemis with a war dance at Ephesus. Each year "the Amazons, their minds set on war, set up an image of Artemis under a great oak tree. Their queen, Hippo, led the Amazons in a clamorous war dance, called the *prylis*, around the statue. The women wore armor and shields and rattled their quivers and stamped their feet loudly to the shrill music of pipes." In another verse, Callimachus alludes to a tradition that Queen Hippo (perhaps short for Hippolyte) was punished by the goddess for refusing to join the annual dance at Ephesus. A fragment of Callimachus names seven daughters of the queen of the Amazons as "the first to establish the dance and the nocturnal maiden's festival." Their names were Glaukia, Protis, Parthenia, Lampado, Maia, Stonychia, and Kokkymo.[25]

An Athenian comedy of the fifth century BC, lost but quoted by Aelian, described the movements of the Amazonian war dance in humorous terms: "At the temple of Artemis at Ephesus, the [Amazon] girls lightly leap up, shaking their hair and clapping their hands, now sinking down upon their haunches and again springing up, like the hopping wagtail." The comparison is to a bird with a habit of constantly shaking its tail. Amusing pyrrhic dances were sometimes performed by men and women entertainers in Athens.[26]

Can the archaeology of Scythian burials tell us anything about the sort of music associated with historical Amazons who lived in ancient Scythia? Besides the vase paintings showing armed women dancing to pipes and flutes, there are ancient artistic representations of Scythian musicians playing lyres (small harps). Callimachus's poem says that the Amazons at Ephesus had not yet learned to make bone flutes, so they danced to the music of pipes. In Greek myth, Pan's pipes produced eerie, haunting notes. A remarkable set of panpipes (*syrinx*) made from the foot bones of a bird of prey was excavated from a Scythian kurgan at Skatovka on the Volga northeast of the Sea of Azov (south Russia). Bird bones make ideal flutes because they are strong, lightweight, and hollow like reeds. Traditional Bulgarian folk flutes made from raptor bones are said to have a "gentle, but rich and intense" tone.

In the Hermitage Museum, St. Petersburg, one can see other examples of musical instruments once played by the steppe nomads. The collection includes those unearthed from the frozen tombs of the couples in Pazyryk mounds 2 and 5. These were the tattooed mummies of men and women who had been buried with their personal hemp-burning tents and braziers. Perhaps in shamanistic rites, or maybe to accompany cannabis-inspired dancing and singing, these men's and women's hands had once beat rhythms on a horn drum shaped like an hourglass and played melodies on a "Pazyryk harp," a horsehair-stringed instrument. Similar harps have been found in Scythian graves in Olbia, Ukraine, and most recently in nomad tombs (some of women) of 1000–450 BC in ancient Issedonia (northwest China).[27]

Potent smoke and drink, music and dancing: these were important features of the Scythian way of life. How many other aspects of the Scythian/Amazonian lifestyle can be gleaned from ancient literature and art, and clarified by archaeology?

10

THE AMAZON WAY

N Pontus, wrote Diodorus in the first century BC, there lived a tribe called the Amazons, in which the women went to war like the men. One woman's intelligence, courage, and physical strength made her their warrior queen. Leading an army of women, she subdued lands as far as the Don River. This self-styled "Daughter of Ares" established new laws. The Amazon women would make war while the men stayed home spinning wool and minding children. "To incapacitate the men from the demands of war, she ordered that boys' arms and legs should be maimed." Other historians went further, presenting the Amazons as a group of Scythian war widows who had murdered their surviving men. The self-sufficient women had children by men of adjacent tribes. They taught their girls to be warriors. Newborn boys were killed.[1]

MISTREATED BOYS?

Like the rumor that Amazons cut or burned off one breast of girls, claims of their maiming, abandoning, or even killing baby boys became a mainstay of Amazon lore. Where did these grim ideas come from?

A possible source might be a seventh-century BC poem by Mimnermus of Smyrna (a city named for an Amazon), famous for pithy erotic poetry recited for entertainment at drinking parties. In a verse riffing on the proverb "A lame man makes the best lover" the poet joked that the Amazon queen Antianeira crippled her male attendants. Another possible origin of the maiming theme could be the Hippocratic surgical treatise *On Joints* (dated to the late fifth–early fourth centuries BC). It stated, "Amazon women dislocate the hip or knee joint of male infants, to ensure that they will not conspire to overthrow the females." Yet no harm to boys was ever mentioned by Herodotus, the earliest "anthropologist" of Saka-Scythian-Sarmatian ways of life, writing in the mid-fifth century BC. Herodotus never passed up juicy details about barbarians. Yet he simply said that nomad girls and boys were brought up alike. Could the Greek idea about injured boys and men have stemmed from some Scythians' ill-treatment of captives? Herodotus claimed that the Royal Scythians blinded their slaves. Perhaps a now-lost ancient account described a cruel practice, among the Kyrgyz of Central Asia, of crippling captives by inserting a stiff horsehair into a cut on the sole of the foot.[2]

That infant boys were injured or killed persists as a cliché about Amazons. It was at odds with other historical accounts of Scythian men as tough warriors. And the notion that only weak, lame, or unwarlike men lived side by side with women warriors is not supported by archaeological evidence of hundreds of skeletons of men, women, and children in ancient Scythian kurgans from the Black Sea to the Altai. Equivalent honors, horse sacrifices, grave goods, and last meals are evident in the burials of males and females. Most but not all men were accompanied by weapons and a smaller percentage of women had weapons (chapter 4). Careful scientific analysis of the skeletons for bone trauma reveals an extremely harsh and violent lifestyle, with numerous healed broken limbs and dislocations that likely resulted in lifelong pain and lameness, along with fatal war injuries suffered by both men and women. Men received the most injuries from weapons, but many of the armed women sustained such injuries too.

But no forensic bioarchaeological evidence points to systematic, deliberate maiming of young males in the cultures of the Eurasian steppes. Could cliché have a medical source? It is striking that Scythian boys' lameness first appeared in the Hippocratic treatise about joints. In other works in the Hippocratic corpus certain medical conditions are attributed to Scythian males and females, with variable plausibility and in accounts rife with contradictions. One Hippocratic text explains that a lifetime of horse riding causes Scythians to develop lameness and hip-joint problems. One wonders whether a high incidence of healed broken bones, traumatic joint dislocations, or even congenital hip dysplasia (dislocation) of infants in Scythia might have been observed by the Hippocratic medical writers, leading to misunderstandings. Scythian nomads practiced swaddling of infants and spent much of their lives on horses. Dislocated arm and leg joints and broken bones were common injuries suffered in falls from horses. Hip dysplasia can be hereditary or it can develop in infancy owing to swaddling. In the modern world this childhood condition is prevalent in two ethnic groups: the nomadic Sami people (the Scythian-like Scrithiphini tribe of antiquity described in chapter 5) and the nomads of Mongolia. In fact, bioarchaeologists studying ancient Scythian skeletons describe a number of congenital hip and spinal abnormalities, including hip dysplasias.[3] A higher-than-expected incidence of limping or lame Scythian boys and men could have been misinterpreted in antiquity to fit the Greek image of Amazon women bent on subjugating males.

AMAZON FAMILIES

Strabo, a native of Pontus, reported that Amazons sent boys away to be raised by their fathers, the Gargarians. This practice has been misinterpreted by some modern scholars who assume that the story was fabricated by the Greeks to show how Amazons "negate the value of boys by banishing them." But Strabo's account had a basis in fact. What Strabo describes is the premodern, widespread custom known as *fosterage*. Sending children, especially boys but sometimes girls, to be raised apart from the clan or tribe was common among Caucasian, Circassian, Scythian, Central Asian, and Persian-influenced cultures in antiquity, and it was still in evidence in early modern times in the Caucasus (it was also traditional among Welsh, Irish, and Scottish clans). Fosterage was a kind of guest-hostage exchange of sons, similar in purpose to marriage alliances. Raising each other's children ensured trust and friendly political relations among groups that might otherwise be in conflict. Homer and Hesiod allude to the practice, and many other ancient sources describe fosterage relationships for sons of powerful families in Macedonia, Armenia, Media, and Persia.[4] The Amazon queen who invited Alexander the Great to her bed promised him fosterage of their son (chapter 20). Among many groups in the Caucasus and Central Asia, sexual relations within a clan or tribe were forbidden as incest; fosterage was another way to encourage exogamy.

Jordanes, the historian of the Goths, said that Amazons' sons were either given to their fathers or else "killed with a hatred like that of wicked stepmothers." He added another detail: "Among the Amazons childbearing was detested although everywhere else it is desired." But Philostratus disagreed, declaring that the Amazons "loved their baby girls immediately upon birth and cared for them as is the nature of mothers, regarding them as belonging to the race of Amazons. The boys they take to the borders to allow their fathers to claim them."[5]

In Greek myth, two Amazon mothers raised their sons to young adulthood. Both boys came to bad ends. Hippolytus was the son of Antiope and Theseus, and Tanais was the son of Lysippe and Berossus, a mystery man with a Babylonian/Akkadian name. Both young men died because of their vows to reject sex, love, and marriage, which angered the goddess Aphrodite. The goddess caused Hippolytus to be destroyed by his own horses. Tanais was compelled to drown himself in the Amazon River (so called because the Amazons used to bathe there). His mother, Lysippe, renamed the river "Tanais." The mythic message seems to be that headstrong, powerful foreign women raise sons who refuse to take on the traditonal male roles of Greek men.[6]

As fascinated as the Greeks were by the heroic valor and erotic appeal of Amazons of myth, their own male-dominant perspective made it a challenge to envision an actual society in which women could be the equals of men in so many ways. As Strabo exclaimed, "One would have to believe that women were men and men were women!"[7] Greeks would expect able-bodied Greek men to revolt and take their rightful place as the masters of women. So it is easy to see how the rumor of Amazons' breaking boys' legs—and spirits—might have appeared plausible to the Greeks. As travelers' and historians' tales began to multiply about tribes in Scythia in which women really did ride and fight, Greeks strove to understand why Scythian men would agree to share power and glory with their women. One popular conclusion was that if women went to war, then the men must have been disabled and forced to do domestic work.

Archaeological findings help us to visualize many features of nomad life and tease out which aspects were known to the Greeks and which support or conflict with their image of Scythian Amazons. For example, signs of maternal attachment despite a woman's warrior status might have surprised ancient Greeks. Yet as we saw in chapter 4, archaeologists have discovered infants and children buried with armed women and children interred with armed male and female couples, indicating family groups (on the Dnieper River, and near Bobrytsia, Chertomlyk, Ordzhonikidze, and other Ukrainian sites). Notably, at Pokrova (Kazakhstan) some children were buried with single adult men. In some cemeteries, in fact, all the children's skeletons found by archaeologists had been interred with men.[8] This intriguing evidence from the grave suggests that some men associated with warrior women helped to raise children, recalling Diodorus's description, above. Moreover, awls, knives, hemp-burning kits, spindle-whorls, whetstones, jewelry, and mirrors appeared in men's as well as women's graves.

In Greek families, sons were highly valued, while daughters were less well fed and educated, confined indoors working wool, and considered a drain on resources to be "transferred by marriage to another house as soon as possible."[9] In contrast, within nomad bands on the harsh steppes each individual was crucial to the survival of the tribe. Children dressed and ate alike, and all learned to tame and ride fast horses, shoot deadly arrows, bring home game, defend the tribe, and attack foes. Many of the shared duties attributed to Scythians and Amazons in antiquity are mirrored among some present-day nomadic peoples of Caucasia and Central Asia.

In Kazakhstan today, for example, women and men alike still participate in the traditional singing contests called *aites*, long question-and-response sessions that test the people's knowledge of their traditional history. Girls and boys are expected to learn by heart at least ten generations of their family trees. Within living memory in the Caucasus, another heartland of the ancient Amazons, female and male bards would recount old legends and heroic tales (Nart sagas) in many different languages whenever the scattered tribes converged for seasonal socializing and rituals. Egalitarianism is reflected in the celebrations and festivals that bring far-flung groups together for communal feasts, games, and contests in Central Asia. For instance, it is common for girls and boys aged six to nine compete in horse races as equals, riding their ponies a grueling twenty miles or so over the steppes.[10]

LIFE ON THE STEPPES

It seems reasonable to suppose that the historical counterparts of Amazons and their male companions on the steppes spent the majority of their time much as did their descendants described in eighteenth- and nineteenth-century ethnographic literature. They followed age-old patterns of herding, raising horses, attending festivals, telling stories, trading, and hunting, punctuated by skirmishing and small-scale marauding.

In the glimpses of Amazon life we can glean from ancient Greek literature and art, the women warriors were passionately devoted to riding horses and perfecting guerrilla-style combat skills for defense, raiding, and conquest; wielding swords, bows, and spears; and fighting and dying valiantly. But the independent women of the Black Sea–Caucasus–steppe region are also portrayed by Greek writers as taking time out for such peaceful activities as capturing, training, and milking their horses; chasing game; harvesting fruit; having sex; getting tattooed; raising tomboys and delivering sons to their fathers; fashioning leather into helmets, clothing, boots, and belts; swimming and grooming; inhaling hemp smoke; dancing, playing music, and performing sacrifices and religious rites. In short, the picture of Amazon daily life imagined by the Greeks conforms in large part to the glimpses of the flexible, fluid nomad life on the steppes that we can gather from history, archaeology, and anthropology.[11]

Scythians were known in antiquity for their endurance and ability to withstand wintry temperatures, ice, and snow. The distinctive leggings and tunics, cloaks, leather boots, hats with earflaps, and animals skins worn by Amazon and Scythian archers in ancient Greek vase paintings were obviously designed for cold weather. Similar articles of clothing and furs have been recovered from ancient burials, along with the supplies for hemp-vapor sweat-bath saunas.

Another secret weapon against freezing temperatures known to Amazons and Scythians was mentioned in an obscure ancient treatise, *On Rivers*, by Pseudo-Plutarch (third century AD). This is the same author who explained that the Tanais (Don) River was once known as the Amazon River because the Amazons used to bathe there. "Along the Amazon River grows a plant called *halinda*, like a colewort. Bruising this plant and anointing their bodies with the juice makes them better able to endure the extreme cold.[12] Perhaps the Amazons depicted on the unique Greek vase painting in figure 7.2 were meant to be swimming in the Amazon River; one of the women is applying oil from an aryballos.

What was this mysterious Amazon folk remedy for warming the body? Luckily, Pseudo-Plutarch gives us a clue for identifying the ancient Scythian word *halinda* by comparing it to colewort, cabbage. Botanical detective work reveals that the *halinda* plant was probably *Brassica napus*, a hardy wild cabbage of Russia and Siberia, related to *Brassica oleracea*. Wild coleworts were the ancestors of today's edible cabbages, kale, collards, Brussels sprouts, broccoli, cauliflower, and rapeseed/canola oil. The cruciferous plants were first cultivated between twenty-five hundred and four thousand years ago and were bred to reduce the amount of toxic mustard oils, sulfur-containing glucosinolates, which give plants of this species their pungent, bitter taste. Wild cabbage contains a lot of the mustard oil, an irritant. Rubbed on the body as a massage oil, it is a strong stimulant of circulation, bringing blood to the skin surface, causing an invigorating, warm sensation and alleviating the aches of arthritis. Archaeological studies of female and male skeletons reveal that arthritis pain dogged the rugged horse riders of the steppes. The analgesic action of *halinda* oil salve would be similar to the medical uses of capsaicin, the irritant oil of hot chili peppers from the New World, applied as a topical ointment to relieve arthritic pain.

Halinda oil also had antibacterial, antifungal properties and repelled insects, and the oil's propensity to cling to metal and repel water would make it valuable for rustproofing the iron knives and tools unearthed in the graves of warrior women and men. In Pseudo-Plutarch's day, the local people along the Amazon River called *halinda* oil "Berossus oil." Berossus was the husband of the Amazon Lysippe and the father of

Tanais, who drowned in the Don River. It seems that a fuller story about this Amazon family was once current, lost except for this intriguing fragment.

Someday tests of substances in "cosmetic jars" preserved in Scythian burials might turn up traces of the Amazons' *halinda* oil or their après-sauna cedar-frankincense unguent described by Herodotus. Residues of koumiss, pigments, pollens, hemp, and other seeds have been already been discovered among the grave goods of women warriors, and analysis of cosmetics shows that Pazyryk women used "the natural blue pigment vivanite and made complicated fat-based masques to protect the skin from extreme climates."[13]

AMAZON GEOGRAPHY

It was a matter of pride for many cities of western Asia Minor to claim Amazons as "founders." Diodorus stated that Amazons established a *polis* at Themiscyra; Apollonius of Rhodes's *Argonautica* epic mentions three Amazon territories in Pontus. The only ancient image showing Amazons defending a city wall appears on a large black-figure amphora by the Castellani Painter (sixth century BC); some scholars guess that it represents Themiscyra, but Troy seems more likely. The Amazons of myth and in legendary-historical accounts were never homebodies tied to one place for long. They crisscrossed the steppes east and west, from Thrace to the Altai, or shuttled north and south over the Caucasus range, establishing general territories that shifted over time. Herodotus spoke of the Amazons, Scythians, Sarmatians, and others encamping with their horses; he explained how some tribes constructed felt tents for winter abodes. He and other writers also described migrations of whole peoples over long distances and portrayed nomad bands as mobile communities on horseback and/or horse-drawn wagons. Clay models of nomad wagons have been found in many Scythian burials. Other archaeological evidence shows that the ancient steppe people erected tents of felt and hides, and some even built log structures.[14]

Landmarks associated with Amazons have a very ancient history. Beginning with Homer, grave mounds in northern Anatolia were said to belong to long-ago Amazons. It was the Scythian custom to raise kurgans over their burials, and ancient Phrygians and Lydians also built conspicuous grave mounds. In Greece, Plutarch and Pausanias visited memorials to fallen Amazons who had died during the legendary Battle for Athens (chapter 17). The Amazon foundation stories of various cities in Anatolia may have arisen from oral traditions that linked Amazons with features of the landscape, such as mounds, campsites, altars, or battlefields, perhaps some dating to early conquests by Scythian forces in which women warriors may have participated. Some scholars suggest that Amazon traditions in Anatolia might even hark back to Hittite times. Still other ancient sites associated with Amazons may have been, like Ephesus, gathering places where women performed military dances with weapons and other sacred rites.[15]

AMAZON GOVERNMENT

The Greek myths and historians speak of Amazon "queens" and "princesses." Some famous Amazon leaders were said to have inherited their role from their mothers, but they usually achieved acclaim and leadership because of personal qualities, then declared wars and established laws. In nomad groups described in ancient and modern historical times, leaders—some male, some female—sometimes inherited leadership from parents or spouses, but they also arose by popular agreement and group decisions were often by consensus. In other situations, an especially strong leader (male or female) acquired more autocratic power over a group or confederation. Several ancient sources described warrior queens and independent female rulers. Strabo, for example, reported that in his day the traditional Amazon lands of Pontus and Colchis were ruled by "a wise and qualified woman" named Pythodoris (30 BC–AD 38). A Circassian Nart saga about ancient heroes and heroines of the Caucasus describes a "council of the women in the olden days" made up of "wise and far-sighted older women" who discussed daily issues and established laws and customs based "on their long experience and perspicacity." In the accounts and stories of women warriors in Central Asia (chapters 22–24), widows, wives, or daughters of slain chieftains (or leaders incapacitated by drink) often become the head of a tribe or clan, reflecting the practices of many nomadic steppe groups.[16]

Greek literature and history is rife with deadly rivalries of male rulers and war champions. Rival Amazon queens or wars between groups of Amazons are rare (except for the myth of Antiope and the historical duel between Cynna and Caeria; chapters 16 and 20). The ancient sources that mention Amazonian decision making suggest discussion and consensus. For example, Herodotus recounted the give-and-take between the Amazons and Scythian men as they negotiated their future as the new Sarmatian tribe (chapter 3). In chapter 19's story of the shipwrecked sailors who joined the Amazons, the Amazon leader acquiesced in a young Amazon's request to free them. An Amazon Assembly is described in the Greek *Alexander Romance* (chapter 20). The Roman historian Ammianus Marcellinus claimed that steppe nomads held their assemblies on horseback.[17]

In *auls* (villages of yurts) of northern Kazakhstan in the present day, women's crucial responsibilities give them a say in local government by consensus. Women gain extra clout by being known as an *ana* or *hewana* ("mother of the tribe"), a title bestowed on widows raising children alone or mothers of seven sons), or as a *kelen*, a woman originally from outside the village whose exceptional abilities allow her to become a leader and organizer of the *aul*. Some communities are led by women because they have been recognized as "the most adept." Women's roles and status are determined "by pragmatism, not sexual politics."[18]

AMAZON RELIGION

The historical Scythians whose women were the models for the Amazons of legend did not worship the gods and goddesses of the Greek pantheon. But some similar attributes of deities and rituals reported and/or observed by early Greek travelers in the Black Sea–Caucasus region led the Greeks to compare or assimilate them to Hellenic beliefs and gods. For example, Greeks referred to Amazons as "Daughters of Ares" who worshipped the god of war and Artemis the Huntress with armed dances at Ephesus. This was a Greek way of explaining the women's warlike nature, their ardent resistance to male control, their preference for outdoor pursuits, and their expertise as archers.

A picture of Amazon religion emerges from the myths of Jason and the Argonauts, a collection of early Bronze Age oral traditions. The first full written account that survives is the *Argonautia* by Apollonius of Rhodes. On the way to Colchis to obtain the Golden Fleece, the *Argo* sailed east along the southern Black Sea coast. The Argonauts moored in a harbor at Lyra and met the lonely ghost of Sthenelus, a Greek warrior who had died of an arrow wound inflicted by an Amazon archer during Heracles's great expedition against Queen Hippolyte at Themiscyra (chapter 15). The Argonauts stopped again at Sinope and at the mouth of the Thermodon, with the "Amazonian Mountains" in the distance. Here they spotted a band of Themiscyrian Amazons, descendants of survivors of the war with Heracles. Jason and his men prepared to fight the Amazon women assembling on the beach, but strong winds drove their ship on, past the land of the Mossynoeci, the tattooed "free love" neighbors of the Amazons described by Xenophon (chapter 6).

Apollonius remarked that the "Daughters of Ares are scattered over the land in three tribes." Besides the Themiscyrian Amazons, there were also women warriors among the Chadesians of Chadesia and the Lykastians of Lykastia ("Wolf-Land"). According to Hecataeus, "Chadesiai" was another name for Amazons. Lykastia, near Amisus according to ancient geographers, has been identified as the ancient archaeological site of Dündartepe, ca. 2000 BC; among the finds there are spearheads; animal figures similar to those of the same date found around the Sea of Azov; and clay female figurines with incised tattoos similar to those found in the Neolithic Cucuteni culture of Ukraine's forest steppes (chapter 6).[19]

The Argonauts dropped anchor at Aretias, a small desert island less than a mile from the coast, also known as Ares or Amazon Island. Here Jason and his men found "an old stone temple to Ares built by the Amazon queens Otrera and Antiope." They also discovered the altar "where the Amazons sacrificed before going to war." But the description of the Amazons' altar and sacred rites makes it clear that this was not a typical Greek temple to Ares. The archaic "temple," already very old when the Argonauts arrived, had no roof. Inside the open-air enclosure "was fixed a black stone, to which of yore the Amazons used to pray."

Veneration for a sacred black stone was a prominent feature of ancient Anatolian worship of the great "mountain mother" Cybele of Asia

Minor, a goddess associated with rock, wild animals (especially lions), and birds of prey such as eagles. Her attributes recall the divine warrior horsewoman Lady Amezan of the Caucasus Nart sagas, whose name means "Forest Mother." At Cybele's sanctuary at Pessinus in central Anatolia, the goddess was worshipped in the form of "a black stone that fell from the sky." (That sacred meteorite was transported to Rome in 215 BC.) Moreover, Cybele's rites included ecstatic music and frenzied dancing featuring clashing shields and spears, calling to mind the Amazonian war dances at Ephesus described in Greek literature. Golden earrings with images of Cybele were found in the graves of women warriors of the northern Black Sea area (chapter 4). According to Diodorus, the Amazon queen Myrine set up altars and sacrificed to Cybele on another desert island, Samothrace.[20]

Many of the Argonauts' adventures are fantasies, but "Amazon Island" and the sacred black stone happen to be real. The tiny (four-acre) rocky islet was clearly described by later ancient writers who also referred to the old temple of Ares and gave the island's exact location. Now called Giresun Island, it is the only island off the southern Black Sea coast (opposite the sixth-century BC Greek colony of Pharnacia/Kerasus, now Giresun, Turkey).[21]

The large, round black rock, about twelve feet in diameter, believed to have been worshipped by the Amazons thousands of years ago, can be seen today on the island. During traditional spring rituals on Amazon Island each May, the mystical "Hamza Stone" is venerated as a magical "wishing stone" by women seeking fertility. In the local Turkish folklore, the ancient Amazons used to meet here with men from other tribes to make sacrifices and procreate.[22]

According to Apollonius of Rhodes, Jason and his Argonauts observed the "altar made of pebbles where the Amazons once sacrificed burnt offerings." The Greeks assumed that the warlike women they called "Daughters of Ares" must have made sacrifices to Ares here. But we now know that the black rock and archaeological features of the open-air "temple" point to Cybele worship. Turkish archaeologists began to investigate the antiquities on Amazon Island in 2010. The oldest structures include steps cut into the bedrock to a level platform "altar" in the middle of the island. Attic black-glaze pottery sherds were found in the lowest excavation levels, and there are ancient rock

FIG. 10.1. Sacred black rock venerated by the Amazons, on Amazon (Giresun) Island, Black Sea, Turkey. Photo courtesy of Ertekin M. Doksanalti.

cuttings for mooring ships in the harbor at the southern end of the island. Two deep holes cut into the great boulder indicate that ropes were used to place the sacred stone on the rocky promontory. Square and round "offering holes" for Cybele worship were cut into the bedrock near the rock. Not far away, the archaeologists discovered another, smaller, spherical black rock next to more rock-cut niches (the round stones are not meteorites, but they may have been brought to the island in antiquity). Stepped altars and rock-cut niches in open-air sacred precincts are typical of other ancient Cybele cult sites in Anatolia.[23]

Apollonius described the burned offerings of the Amazons. Unlike the Greeks who "sacrifice sheep and oxen to the gods, the Amazons sacrificed horses from their great herds on the mainland." Here again, we are on familiar ground, given what we know about horse cultures of Scythia. Apollonius described the three tribes of Amazons in Pontus as nomadic people, like the Saka-Scythians, who did not own oxen for plowing or flocks of sheep and instead sacrificed their most prized

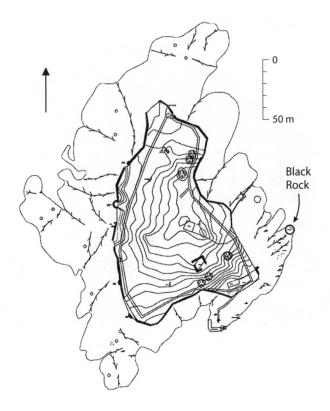

FIG. 10.2. Plan of the archaeological ruins on Amazon Island showing the large black rock described in the *Argonautica* epic as sacred to the Amazons. The ancient mooring cuttings are at the bottom right. Drawings courtesy of Mete Mimiroglu.

possessions, horses.[24] A few Greek vase paintings show Amazons sacrificing at altars before departing for battle: one shows an Amazon in tunic, trousers, and pointed cap standing before an altar, her battle-axe and shield on the ground behind her. Another shows an Amazon with her weapons running with her dog, looking back at an altar with a flame. A third vase depicts an Amazon wearing an animal-skin sash on her knees before an altar; her quiver and bow are hung up behind her.[25]

Horses, a god of war, and a mother goddess probably held deep meanings for the real warrior women who were mythologized as Amazons by the Greeks. Since the peoples of ancient Scythia did not leave writings, however, we can only speculate about the religious ideas of the myriad, culturally related groups of the steppes and mountains, drawing on what Greeks and others reported and guessed, and on clues in modern archaeology and ethnographic comparisons. The richest ancient source for nomad belief systems is Herodotus, who gathered detailed descriptions of the religious rites, sorcery, fortune-telling, hemp smoking, methods of sacrifice, and embalming and funeral practices of Scythians, Issedonians, Massagetae, Saka, and others from the Black Sea to Central Asia. Many of his minute details are now confirmed by archaeological excavations of kurgans from Ukraine to the Altai. Herodotus said that the Scythians sacrificed horses to "Ares," represented by an iron sword, and that Persian magi and the Massagetae-Saka-Scythians sacrificed horses to the Sun. A Chinese eunuch who joined the steppe tribes of the Xiongnu (second century BC) related that the nomads "set out from camp at dawn to worship the rising sun and at nightfall to worship the moon." Another ancient Chinese source tells how the nomads sealed a treaty by dipping a sword in wine and sacrificing a white horse. Chapter 4 surveyed numerous ancient burials of armed women and men from the Black Sea to the Altai, all distinguished by the physical remains of huge numbers of horses that were sacrificed at the funerals of males and females. The mourners ate great quantities of horse meat and prepared a portion for the journey of their dead. A belief in a kind of afterlife seems evident in the typical grave goods of food, weapons, clothing, supplies, tools, personal amulets, items of daily use, and golden treasures.[26]

In the end, all we can have is an impressionistic sense of the beliefs of the women archers of Scythian lands known as Amazons, an intangible mosaic of animism, totemism, magic, of sacred fire and gold, of reverence for Sun, Moon, sky, earth, nature, wild animals, fantastic creatures. And horses.[27]

II

HORSES, DOGS, AND EAGLES

AMAZONS WERE THE FIRST PEOPLE TO RIDE HORSES," the orator Lysias reminded the Athenians in his *Funeral Oration* (395 BC). Across the Black Sea, an ancient Abkhaz saga claimed that the nomads of the northern Caucasus were the first to tame and ride horses. It is said that the boundless steppes seem incomplete without a horse and rider, and the ancient Scythians—and Amazons—are indeed unthinkable without the horse. Horses were first domesticated, probably for milk and meat and pulling carts, and then for riding, around 4000 BC by nomadic men and women of the northern Black Sea–Caspian grasslands, legendary Amazon territory. Horses were ideally suited to the northern steppes. They can tolerate freezing temperatures better than cattle, and horses can reach grass under more than a foot of snow; horses can pull wagons and carry riders and loads; they provide nutritious food and drink; and they do not need full-time herders. The Amazonian lifestyle, remarked Strabo, revolved around raising and training horses whose speed and grace gave the Amazons the nickname "far-bounding." The strongest women, Strabo noted, spent their lives hunting on horseback and honing their skills for mounted warfare. The celebrated equestrian expertise of steppe people, the centrality of horses in their lives, the nomads' own oral traditions, and perhaps a belief in a special relationship between independent women and wild horses led the ancient Greeks to believe that the Amazons must have been the earliest horse people.[1]

The horse was the great equalizer of males and females on the steppes, probably one of the chief reasons for the nomads' noteworthy gender equality. A skilled archer horsewoman could hold her own against men in battle. Riding horses liberated women, bestowing freedom of movement and an exhilarating, challenging life outdoors. Among the Greeks, only men enjoyed such physical independence in the open air; women were, ideally, confined indoors at home. On the steppes, men and women alike could travel vast distances with changes of horses bred for endurance. Three experienced riders of either sex could control large herds of semiwild horses. Horses leveled out differences in male and female strength, providing the mobility and muscle to transport riders and heavy gear, weapons, armor, household goods, plunder, and large game. Horse riding also demanded comfortable, convenient unisex clothing (see chapter 12). Because girls could learn to ride, tame, and control horses, and shoot arrows just as well as boys, the steppe culture was the perfect environment for women to become mounted hunters and fighters (plates 4 and 5).[2]

What might lie behind the long-standing notion that some mystical synergy, psychic harmony, or "mind meld" exists between women and horses? Archaeologists of Botai and other early horse-riding cultures suggest that such beliefs might explain prehistoric horse/female artifacts (chapter 6). Herodotus's story of the stranded Amazons and young Scythian men who "tamed" each other seems to allude to Greek assumptions about wild and domesticated women and horses (chapter 3). Some modern writers account for the long-standing impression of women's unique rapport with horses by pointing out differences in typically "masculine" and "feminine" training styles. Horses naturally resist or fight when threatened but respond positively to nonconfrontational training based on trust and patience rather than brute force. Part of the fascination with Amazons since antiquity seems to arise from the deep historical evidence of nomad women's special prowess when mounted on horseback.[3]

A fascinating historical account involving Scythian women and horses was related by Justin. He describes how in 339 BC Alexander's father, Philip II, overcame a great Scythian confederation led by King Ateas, whose peoples extended from the Danube in Thrace to the Sea of Azov. After his defeat of Ateas, Philip tried to bring twenty thousand purebred Scythian mares back to Macedon in the hope of improving the Greek horse stock. Philip also brought back twenty thousand Scythian women and children. The figures may be exaggerated, but they give an indication of the population of Scythians in that region and their vast herds. Some of the Scythian captives were probably horsewomen, and they would have tended their own horses on the long march to Macedon. On the way, Philip was attacked by another powerful Thracian-Scythian tribe, the Triballi. In the battle, a spear pierced Philip's thigh and killed his horse. All of the captive mares and the women were freed and escaped back into Scythia.[4]

HORSE-CENTERED CULTURE

Nomadic Eurasian tribes maintained large herds of mares, stallions, geldings, and foals, which were allowed to pasture semiwild until needed. Horses are easily stolen by experienced horse people. Steppe nomads, like Plains Indians of North America, habitually raided horses even of friendly tribes as a kind of aggressive sport. (See chapter 20 for the theft of Alexander's horse by nomads.) The stranded Amazons from Pontus, in Herodotus's tale, were able to quickly ride horses from a herd they came across in northern Scythian territory. Each warrior on the steppes owned several horses and developed strong attachments to favorites. In nomad cultures, horses had individual names, even their own legends; owners were sometimes known by their horse's name. Indeed, horse and nomad were inseparable companions even in eternity, since even the humblest steppe rider was buried with his or her horse.[5]

It has been noted that Scythian, Saka, Thracian, Sarmatian, Massagetae, and other steppe cultures were strongly influenced by horse behavior, and the horses they developed were, in turn, influenced by nomad practices. For example, the power of mares in herds was obvious to the earliest horse people. Mares can be as strong and fast as stallions, and they can fight ferociously. An alpha female horse dominates the other members of the herd and physically disciplines the young male horses, while the stallions help defend the herd and await the mares' sexual interest. Other equine-nomad parallels include seasonal migrations, seasonal mating, sexual activity and reproduction regulated by female acquiescence, styles of fighting and escaping danger, and sensitivity to minute shifts in body language of horse and rider.[6]

Vase paintings of Amazons show the women riding both male and female horses. According to Strabo, the Sarmatian men and women preferred to ride geldings. They "castrate their horses to make them easy to manage," he wrote, "for although the horses are small they are exceedingly quick and difficult to control." This practice is mentioned in northern Caucasian sagas about mythic Nart heroes of the steppes; they also knew how to break wild stallions by riding them into rivers with strong currents. On the other hand, Pliny tells us that the "Scythians favored mares for battle because they can urinate while galloping." Pausanias wrote that the Sarmatians "breed herds of mares, which they ride to war, sacrifice, eat, and use the hooves to make armor." It was also said that the Scythians employed "controlled incest" to "cross particularly fine mares with their stallion sons." A modern historian of Scythia believes that images on Scythian artifacts "suggest that Scythians preferred to ride stallions." But it is likely that the nomadic horsewomen known to the Greeks as Amazons rode both mares and stallions, and that they gelded some of their horses for selective breeding and to make the males more tractable, quiet, and sociable in herds.[7]

Training horses for the complex maneuvers of hunting large and small game and the rigors of mounted battle would have started when the horse was about two years old. The very naturalistic scene on the painted cup in figure 11.1 shows a barefoot Amazon wearing a spotted body stocking and a pointed Scythian hat, training a colt or filly. (Behind the tree on the Amazon's left, under the cup handle, is her small white dog.) She is urging the young, wild-eyed horse to walk forward, but it is pulling back and bucking up a bit with its hind legs, resisting the pressure of the lead rope. Colts and fillies can develop deep rapport with riders, responding to spoken commands but especially to cues of touch, without reins—which explains how the Amazons could easily mount and control the horses they stole from the Scythians. It is interesting to compare the similarly skilled equestrian techniques of Libyan nomads of North Africa, described by Strabo and the Roman historian Arrian. Young children rode bareback on small swift horses with no reins, expertly guiding their horses with body shifts and little rods as they sped after and lassoed wild asses.[8]

FIG. 11.1. Amazon training a horse (out of sight under handle, her small white dog). Black-figure skyphos (drinking cup), Durand Painter, Greek, ca. 510–500 BC, Museum of Fine Arts, Boston, Henry Lillie Pierce Fund, 99.524. Photograph © 2014 Museum of Fine Arts, Boston.

Nomad horses on the steppes were ridden with felt blankets and perhaps a cushion-saddle, no stirrups or spurs, and simple bridles with very loose reins, or bareback with no reins, guided by the rider's shifting weight and pressure from thighs, knees, and heels. Young girls and boys learned to balance, relax, and move with the horse, guiding it with voice and body movements, without reins. Riding bareback involves intimate communication and rhythm between horse and rider; horses can "read" heart rate, breathing, and body language. For example, a horse can sense the rider turning her head in a desired direction and anticipates confirmation by her subtle balance shift. The children also learned how to handle long spears and aim bow and arrows at a gallop. The Turkic word *dzhigit* or *jigit* in ballads and legends of Central Asia describes a daring rider warrior who has mastered the kinds of dangerous acrobatic moves that were perfected in antiquity—such as the notorious "Parthian shot" that so awed the Greeks and Romans. This feat involved turning backward on one's horse while racing away and continuing to shoot arrows at pursuing enemies on both sides (see chapter 5). The technique of riding forward while shooting backward with the wind appears in many ancient paintings and sculptures of Amazons (plate 5, figs. 12.3, 16.1). The earliest artistic representation of a mounted Penthesilea is a Chalcidian vase (550 BC) showing her on a galloping horse with the reins slung around her waist as she twists around to shoot arrows at Achilles who pursues on foot. One arrow has already punctured his shield; she is about to let fly another.[9]

HORSE TYPES ON THE STEPPES

It is impossible to determine ancient horse "breeds" from painted or sculpted images of antiquity, and some images probably depict horses from populations that no longer exist. But one can point to certain characteristics of horse types associated with Scythians and Amazons, including probable ancestors of the modern breeds that were developed after the introduction of the Arabian horse (sixth–seventh centuries AD).

Horse remains found in Scythian tombs indicate that the Eurasian nomads were familiar with several different horse types. The artistic, historical, literary, and bioarchaeological evidence suggests the prevalence of at least two kinds of horses, one stocky and small, the other tall and lean. Steppe horses, descendants of the extinct Tarpan (Eurasian wild horses), were similar to the rugged little Caspian, Altai, and Mongol horses living today. Herodotus and Strabo attributed their small size to the freezing weather of the steppes.[10] From Central Asia, Scythians of the northern steppes obtained larger, slender, long-legged ancestors of the Turanian/Turkoman horses, comparable to the magnificent Akhal Teke horses of today.

Both equine types are known for endurance in different harsh environments. The sturdy, shaggy little horses with strong backs and short forelimbs and necks were suited to a cold climate; they evolved the ability to take evasive action to dodge predators. The tall, angular Turkoman-type horses evolved on the hot, dry Turan Plains, surviving by running very fast and very far on very little water. Their pastures were the legendary Ferghana Valley of what is now Kazakhstan, Uzbekistan, Turkmenistan. Both types are described in ancient literature and represented in ancient art.

AMAZONS' HORSES IN ART AND LITERATURE

The earliest picture of Amazons on horseback in Greek art are the four Amazon riders on a vase of 575–550 BC (Marmaro Painter). As Greeks became more familiar with Scythians and their horses, many Amazonomachy scenes began to depict mounted Amazons fighting Greek warriors on foot. The Amazons ride bareback with light, short reins and simple bridles with no throat-latch, and their horses' manes are roached (trimmed), often with long or knotted forelocks. Many of these details of equipment and turnout can be seen in Central Asian horse riding today. The Amazons in ancient art ride mares and stallions; some of these animals are stocky with short necks and others tall with arched necks. Amazons ride light-colored and dark horses. In steppe customs, the color of one's horse could reflect deliberate psychological warfare or bravado. Some warriors chose black, red, or bay horses so that blood from wounds would not encourage the enemy; others felt that white, dun, or gray showed off honorable bloodshed.[11]

Greek writers do not describe the steeds of the Amazons except to say that they, like the Scythians, owned many fine herds. Herodotus mentioned large herds of "wild white horses grazing around the mouth of the Hypanis (Bug) River on the northern Black Sea." These could be the "snow-white horses" belonging to the Thracian allies of Troy mentioned in Homer's *Iliad*. According to Strabo, the large, heavy Nisaean (Parthian) horse originated in the fertile high pastures of Armenia; during the Persian Empire as many as fifty thousand Nisaean mares grazed there and twenty thousand foals were sent to the Persian king each year. A large, colorful knotted pile carpet from Pazyryk Kurgan 5 (fifth century BC) has a border of heavy gray stallions with bodies similar to the Persian horses depicted in reliefs at Persepolis.[12]

The beautiful Etruscan sarcophagus painted with scenes of battle between Amazons and Greeks, described in chapter 7 (fig. 7.3), is re-

markable for its depiction of a nude Amazon. It is also remarkable for
the Amazons' special white horses and because it shows Amazons driving war chariots. On one side of the sarcophagus, two pairs of Amazons
in chariots drawn by four white horses attack two Greek warriors on
foot. In ancient art, Amazons driving two-horse chariots are quite rare,
and four-horse chariots even rarer. The other examples of Amazon four-
horse chariots appear in Italo-Greek vase paintings, leading one scholar
to conjecture that Italian artists might have been influenced by ancient
Greek coinage from Sicily decorated with a four-horse chariot crowned
by Victory.[13]

But two ethnographic influences for the Italian paintings of Amazon charioteers might be more likely. According to Herodotus, the
Greeks learned to yoke four horses to chariots from nomad tribes in
Libya "whose women served as charioteers in war." Another influence
could have been the charioteer horsewomen of a tribe across the Adriatic, described by Herodotus and Strabo. The Siginni people, who
"dressed like Medes" in trousers and tunics and claimed to be their descendants, dwelled north of the Danube in Thrace in the fifth century
BC. Herodotus says that their land extended west to the Adriatic; by
Strabo's time in the first century BC the Siginni had migrated back east
to the northern Caucasus. Too small to carry adult riders, their ponies
were "extremely swift when yoked four abreast to chariots." As we saw
in chapter 8, the girls of this Amazon-like tribe learned to drive these
unique four-horse chariots at a young age, and the best female charioteers enjoyed their pick of male sexual partners.[14]

These chariot women may well have inspired the idea of representing Amazons fighting from four-horse chariots. According to Herodotus and Strabo, the Siginni ponies were diminutive, snub-nosed, and
covered in long, shaggy hair, something like a modern Shetland pony.
Examples of small, plump, sturdy ponies with small heads and long,
thick manes and tails appear in Greek art; one pulls a four-horse chariot
on a late seventh-century vase by the Nettos Painter. But the painter of
the Etruscan Amazon sarcophagus chose to depict horses very different
from those of the Siginni women charioteers.[15]

Instead of small stocky ponies, all ten of the horses belonging to the
Amazons on the painted sarcophagus are large, silvery-white steeds

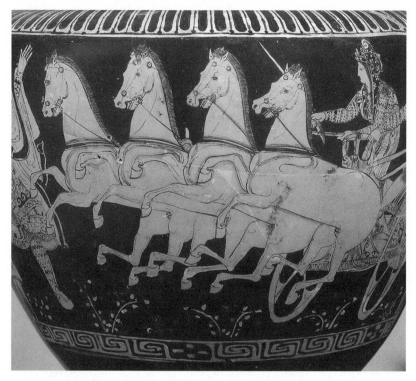

FIG. 11.2. A four-horse chariot driven by a barbarian who appears to be an Amazon, with a male barbarian rider, far right, and a similarly attired Amazon with battle-axe in front, far left (out of sight). Attic Greek, red-figure column-krater, Suessula Painter, ca. 400 BC, Princeton University Art Museum, Fowler McCormick, Class of 1921 Fund, Carl Otto von Kienbusch Jr. Memorial Collection Fund and Classical Purchase Fund, 2007–98. Photo: Bruce M. White/ Art Resource, NY.

with blonde manes and tails and startling light-blue eyes (plate 6). A similarly colored horse appears on a beautiful Greek painted terra-cotta cup molded in the shape of a mounted Amazon huntress (found in Meroe, Sudan, ca. 440 BC). Her white steed has blue eyes, blonde roached mane, and light-red nostrils and mouth (see plate 2).[16]

The coloring of these luminous horses calls to mind the legendary "Golden Horses" raised by the Saka peoples of the Ferghana Valley region (Kazakhstan, Uzbekistan, Kyrgyzstan, Turkmenistan, Tajikistan) so coveted by Persian kings and Chinese emperors in antiquity. These steeds were the ancestors of the elegant breed known today as Akhal Teke. Blue eyes can show up in many horse breeds, but the combination of very light blue eyes with a lustrous light coat suggests that the artists were depicting "double dilute creams" (a gene expression responsible for cream-colored coats and extremely light blue eyes) of an "oriental" horse type from Central Asia perhaps related to the Akhal Tekes. Many Greek vase paintings depict Amazons with long-legged, light-colored horses with arched necks (see figs. 7.2, 11.3, 16.3, 18.1).

AKHAL TEKE HORSES

The horses from which today's Akhal Teke horses are derived first appeared thousands of years ago on the deserts and grasslands of Central Asia. Tall and elegant with high-set necks, long legs with visible tendons, and relatively small, hard hooves (Akhal Tekes are rarely shod), these svelte creatures are the greyhounds of the horse world. Prized for speed, endurance, power, and beauty, Akhal Tekes have a "floating stride" and thin coats with a shimmering metallic sheen. These features inspired their nicknames, "Heavenly," "Celestial," "Golden." The Turkoman nomads who raised Akhal Teke–type horses used layers of felt blankets for warmth and to promote sweating, keeping the horses lean. For the horses bred for racing, the diet would have been supplemented with high-protein legumes, grains, even fat and eggs.

Copying the earlier efforts of his father, Philip, to acquire Scythian horses (above), after his conquests in Persia and Asia, Alexander successfully imported five thousand horses of the Akhal Teke type to Macedonia to interbreed with the shorter-legged Greek horses. About a century later, the Chinese emperor Wu-Ti waged wars against the nomads of the Ferghana Valley in an attempt to obtain their fabulous horses. Later trade agreements arranged for Chinese silk to be exchanged for Celestial horses (chapter 25).[17]

Horses resembling Akhal Tekes appear in Scythian artifacts, and some were sacrificed and buried with Pazyryk warriors of the Altai, indicating that these desirable desert horses of great stamina and speed (also called Sogdian, Hyrcanian, Median, Baktrian) were actively traded along the Silk Routes. The evidence from art and archaeology leaves little doubt that at least some real women warriors of Scythia rode horses that were ancestors of Akhal Tekes.

DID AMAZONS AND SCYTHIANS BRAND HORSES?

Ptolemy, in his *Geographia*, called the northernmost Caucasus Mountains the "Hippe (Horse) Mountains" because of the region's famous herds. In the early 1800s, Julius von Klaproth remarked on the herds of fine Circassian and Abassian horses he saw there, grazing in the high mountains in summer and in winter pastures along the Terek River flowing into the Caspian Sea. The most highly valued horses, called "Shalokh," were branded on the haunches with a special symbol, facing S's meeting at the top. The brand that Klaproth reproduced is a recognizable *tamga*. Tamgas were abstract emblems used by ancient Eurasian nomad tribes, clans, and individuals to mark their possessions, including horses (chapter 14). Tamgas appear on ancient jewelry, vessels, figurines, textiles, tattoos, inscriptions, and rock art in Sarmatian-Saka-Scythian lands. Several examples of tamga brands on Vandal and Alan horses can be seen in late Roman-era mosaics in North Africa. Horses of the steppes still bear tamga brands.[18]

There is plenty of ancient literary and artistic evidence for the Greeks branding horses. A large archive of lead plates unearthed in Athens lists the colors, brands, and owners' names of Athenian cavalry horses of the fourth century BC. A notable artistic example of branding is the famous Hellenistic bronze equestrian statue known as the Jockey of Artemision. The boy is riding a purebred-type racehorse; its haunch is engraved with a brand of Nike (Victory) holding a wreath. Brands appear on the flanks of horses in Greek vase paintings beginning in about 550 BC.

Were Amazon horses branded? No survey of all the horses belonging to Scythians and Amazons on vase paintings has been done to see how many bear brands. But a few examples show that Greek artists did portray Amazons riding horses displaying brands. The most remarkable instance is the Amazonomachy scene on a large krater for mixing wine (ca. 460 BC). It shows an Amazon mounted on a horse with a roached mane and forelock knot, and branded on the haunch with a victory wreath–like mark (fig. 11.3). She is spearing a dying Greek warrior whose own shield is decorated with a horse's rump branded with a *kerykeion* (caduceus, herald's wand).[19]

Tamga brands on horses' flanks and shoulders are depicted on funeral stelai in Sarmatia, ancient Amazon territory.[20] It is likely that real women warriors who were contemporary with the ancient Greeks

FIG. 11.3. Amazon on branded horse spearing a Greek warrior whose shield is decorated with a branded horse. Volute krater, Woolly Satyrs Painter, ca. 450 BC, detail, Metropolitan Museum, Rogers Fund, 1907, 07286.84. Image © The Metropolitan Museum of Art/Art Resource, NY.

branded some horses with tamgas. Perhaps one day archaeological evidence of branding will be found on the actual mummified bodies of horses preserved in ice in ancient Pazyryk kurgans (discussed below).

HORSES IN ARCHAEOLOGY

It is impossible to conjure up an image of Amazons or women warriors without their horses nearby. A wealth of physical evidence shows the importance of horses in Scythian cultures. Thousands of pieces of horse equipment, blankets, harnesses, bridles, bits, frontlets, false antlers and masks, light saddles, and other trappings made of wood, iron, leather, felt, silver, and gold have been recovered from Scythian kurgans. Many exquisitely detailed artistic representations of horse culture appear on Scythian artifacts. The most famous example is the relief frieze around the elaborate gilded silver amphora from a queen's burial in Chertomlyk, Ukraine, the site of numerous women warrior burials (chapters 4 and 9).

The naturalistic frieze shows eight Scythians carrying out various activities with two types of horses. The people are dressed alike in tunics and trousers and have shoulder-length hair; six are bearded males and the other two are women or beardless youths. A man and a woman (or youth) are shown catching two fine wild horses with flowing manes, while two semiwild horses with roached manes graze peaceably, representing the tribe's herd. Another scene shows a man hobbling a stout, short-necked horse with a trimmed mane, bridle, and blanket/cushion with loosened girth strap. Beside them, a man pours *koumiss* from a skin bag into a cup. Two men and a woman (or youth) are training a wild horse to kneel. Next to them, a fine bridled stallion obeys a man's command to kneel.

Kneeling horses appear in many other Scythian artworks. Teaching horses to kneel for mounting was unique to Scythians. Kneeling was crucial in battle to allow a fallen warrior carrying weapons to swiftly remount (stirrups were unknown at this time). The Greeks, in contrast, mounted their horses by clutching the mane or vaulting with the help of a staff—except in the case of Alexander's faithful horse companion Bucephalus, who had been taught to kneel. (Some suggest that Bucephalus was a Scythian-trained Akhal Teke–type horse.) Herodotus remarked that nomad horses were "trained to crouch on their bellies." This practice was also mentioned by Aelian, who wrote that among the Saka, if a horse loses its rider it is trained to wait for her to mount again. Kneeling horses are not depicted in Greek vase paintings of Amazons, however. In Greek art, Amazons "dismount by sliding down the right side of the horse." Amazons standing on the horse's right side are thought to have just dismounted, while Amazons on the left side are about to mount.[21]

Among nomads, wealth in gold could not be stored but was worn by riders and their horses and buried with them in death. Unlike the plainer equipment of Greek and Persian cavalry horses, the mounts of Amazons and Scythians would have been decked out in dazzling finery.

Herodotus and many other Greek writers remark on the nomads' gold, silver, and bronze weapons, jewelry, and horse decorations. The opulence of nomads' horse gear can be imagined from the heaps of golden and gilded horse equipment recovered from kurgans all across the steppes.[22]

Archaeologists have discovered vast numbers of horse remains (mostly skeletons but some well-preserved frozen bodies) buried with female and male warriors in Scythian kurgans from the Black Sea to the Altai (chapter 4).[23] The evidence of the horse sacrifices confirms numerous details of Herodotus's ancient descriptions of Scythian funerals. Two kinds of horses, stocky and tall, have been found in Scythian kurgans. Both kinds were decorated with costly ornaments and both are depicted in Scythian artwork. Small steppe horses stood about 11–14 hands high at the shoulder (hand = 4 inches); larger desert-type horses were 15–16 hands. The most perfectly preserved mare of Pazyryk culture was 12–15 years old and 13 hands high. She was wearing elaborate regalia, including a stag mask with huge, branching antlers and a beautiful red felt blanket with leather cutouts. She had suffered years of severe arthritis in her hind leg, suggesting to the archaeologists that she had been a favorite, cared for despite her lameness until the death of her owner. Notably, the smaller steppe horses found in kurgans appear to be of all ages and health conditions, whereas the larger, slender purebred types, perhaps more prized and rare, are old or lame. Ongoing skeletal and DNA testing of the equine remains will reveal much more about ancient horse types and relations to modern breeds.[24]

One extraordinary discovery by a French-Italian-Kazakh team in 1999, at the Berel kurgan complex, Bukhtarma Valley (northern Kazakhstan), was a great mound (330–270 BC) containing the coffin of a woman and man clad in furs accompanied by the bodies of thirteen perfectly frozen horses. This was the first Scythian grave to yield such a massive trove of sacrificed horses, all preserved intact in blocks of ice with their equipment and finery in place. Each horse had been sacrificed on an autumn day more than 2,300 years ago by a single blow of a pointed battle-axe to the forehead. The horses were "past their prime" at 9–18 years old, leading these archaeologists to guess that the nomads "were unwilling to part with their younger horses for the sake of ceremony."

Arranged in two layers separated by twigs and sheets of birch bark, the horses were fitted with extravagant regalia, pendants, garlands, harnesses, and wooden ornaments covered in gold leaf depicting elk, griffins, lions, and stags, ornaments that would have shown brilliantly against the red felt blankets when they were ridden by the woman and man. The designs combined Persian, Scythian, and Chinese motifs, an amazing integration of diverse styles indicating extensive travels and trade activities. Several horses wore leather and wood masks of horned ibexes, elk, and tiger-griffins, similar to the many towering antler masks worn by other horses in Pazyryk culture graves. Some DNA testing in 2005 showed genetic diversity and relationships to modern equines.[25]

GRIFFINS AND AMAZONS

The semiwild horse herds grazing on their own in mountain pastures and grassy steppes had to defend themselves from predators and other herds. Caspian and Siberian tigers, snow leopards, Asiatic lions, Eurasian bears, and wolves were dangerous predators, and many Scythian artworks depict these wild animals taking down horses as well as stags and rams. As one ancient writer remarked, the land around the Caspian Sea was known for fine Nisaean horses and for "thousands of tigers and other wild beasts." Scythian horses were capable of fighting off predators; perhaps some of the animal decorations and masks on sacrificed horses honored such encounters.[26]

But the Scythian imagination also pictured monsters preying on their horses. Examples of such imaginary scenes appear on numerous artifacts recovered from kurgans, including the Chertomlyk vase, showing griffins, fantastic four-legged creatures with talons and cruel beaks, leaping onto the backs of struggling horses and tearing open their necks. Did images of griffins and similar creatures illustrate oral legends that no longer survive? Ancient Scythian folklore was recorded by the Greek traveler Aristeas. Fragments of his epic about Central Asian nomad life, preserved by Herodotus, tell of nomads battling terrifying gold-guarding griffins beyond the Altai Mountains. According to the Issedonians (who dwelled between the Tien Shan and Altai mountains), a neighboring

FIG. 11.4. Mounted Amazon with pointed axe fighting a griffin in a barren landscape. Red-figure kylix (drinking cup), Greek, fourth century BC, Jena Painter, Museum of Fine Arts, Boston, Henry Lillie Pierce Fund, 01.8092. Photograph © 2014 Museum of Fine Arts, Boston.

tribe called the Arimaspi ("Owners of Many Horses") prospected for gold in deserts guarded by griffins. The griffins were said to have bodies like wolves, lions, and tigers but with beaks like eagles. Artists in Greece were familiar with some of these exotic Scythian stories, since numerous vase paintings show scenes of Amazons on horseback and on foot fighting griffins in rocky landscapes with dead trees. The Amazon in fig. 11.4, for example, wears flamboyantly patterned leggings and tunic, a soft pointed cap with earflaps, and short laced boots. Her thick-necked stallion has a short bridle with a kind of halter under the neck (his hooves are very pointed, an impractical aesthetic detail). She keeps the reins tight as he lunges forward past the rock outcrop, rolling his eyes as she turns and raises a pointed battle-axe against the attacking griffin behind them.[27]

AMAZONS' DOGS

In vase paintings of Amazons and Scythian archers, dogs are frequently shown trotting along. A vase (discussed further in chapter 14) depicts a pair of Amazons with a dog sporting a red collar. Non-Greek words inscribed above the women's heads seem to indicate their conversation, which appears to refer to their dog. On the other side of the vase shown in fig. 11.1 a little white dog accompanies the Amazon training her mare. The dog imagery associated with Amazons and Scythians in art parallels pictures of Greek male hunters and warriors accompanied by their hounds. Xenophon, who had traveled in Persia and Anatolia, and commented about gender equality in other works (chapters 8 and 9), wrote a treatise about hunting with hounds. Xenophon concluded his book by declaring that both men and women can be excellent hunters, "as the examples of Atalanta and many other female huntresses prove."[28]

Archaeological evidence of domestic dogs appears alongside evidence of the first domesticated horses in the archaeological sites of Botai and other very early Eurasian cultures, and artifacts from Scythian kurgans depict dogs; one example is a fine silver beaker from Ukraine showing a dog in a hunting scene. The Amazon mosaics at Sanliurfa show Hippolyte and her hound hunting a leopard (chapter 2). Herodotus described nomads of Central Asia hunting with horses and dogs. He remarked that among the tribes near the Caspian Sea, the hunters' horses and dogs were trained to lie under a tree until the prey had been shot with an arrow; then the rider, horse, and dog set off in hot pursuit.[29] Strabo wrote about the dogs owned by the Iberians and Albanians between the southern Caucasus and the Caspian Sea (eastern Georgia, Dagestan, and Azerbaijan), an area traditionally associated with Amazons. It was here that a Roman army led by Pompey encountered women warriors during the Third Mithradatic War (chapter 21). "These people and their dogs are surpassingly fond of hunting," wrote Strabo. In the Nart sagas, the heroic traditions of the Caucasus, dogs were the constant companions of nomadic horse people, along with trained birds of prey. There is no doubt that the living counterparts of Amazons owned dogs for hunting, battle, and protecting their property and horse herds.[30]

AMAZONS AND LIONS

Both lions and birds of prey were creatures sacred to Cybele, the goddess associated with Amazons and real women warriors (chapter 10). Cybele is often depicted in a lion-drawn chariot or riding a lion. For example, on a red-figure vase fragment Cybele is dressed in patterned Scythian-Amazon attire and mounted on a male lion; similar images appear in gold from Tillya Tepe (chapter 4). An ancient Greek vase painting also shows an Amazon astride a lion; many vases show Amazons wearing spotted pelts. Did real-life women warriors occasionally capture lion or leopard cubs and raise them as pets or hunting companions? Archaeological evidence shows that the ancient Egyptians and Nubians tamed cheetahs, and Aelian wrote that Indian royalty trained leopards and lions to hunt deer. The great warrior queen Semiramis of Assyria was a skilled huntress. Ctesias, the Greek physician residing in Persia in about 470 BC, viewed a colorful glazed brick frieze in Babylon showing Semiramis on horseback throwing a javelin at a leopard. But according to Aelian, "What raised Semiramis's spirits most was not to *kill* a lion or leopard but to *capture* a live lioness."[31]

A great many vase paintings depict Amazons with shields decorated with animals, including snakes, foxes, dogs, rabbits, horses, bulls, panthers, and lions. Several Amazon shields display bird images that could represent raptors.

AMAZON EAGLE HUNTERS

Falconry, using large birds of prey such as hawks and even eagles to hunt one's quarry, is particularly suited to the open grasslands and snow-covered steppes, especially in combination with horses and dogs. One of the earliest artistic depictions of falconry is an Assyrian hunting scene relief showing a man with a hawk on his right wrist (eighth century BC). Falconry was practiced by the natives of Thrace, Persia, and Central Asia, according to Aristotle, Xenophon, Pliny, Aelian, and others. Ctesias explained how the nomads of Central Asia trained raptors (and yellow-bellied martens) to hunt hares and foxes. Many ancient

Caucasian legends, Nart sagas, and Kazakh and Kyrgyz oral epics describe falconry with hawks and especially eagles. Hunting with the trio of horse, dog, and raptor is a common motif of these stories, lovingly detailed in long descriptions of arming and setting out on fine steeds accompanied by one's trained hounds and eagles.[32]

An extraordinary ancient image of an Amazon doing exactly that appears on a Greek artifact of the fifth century BC. The exquisitely detailed scene on a gold ring shows an Amazon huntress on horseback with her dog and her eagle. Wearing a belted chiton and cloak, she has the reins choked up tight to control her large, spirited horse, in anticipation of spearing the deer. The deer is so minutely detailed that we can tell the species: it is a spotted fallow buck with broad palmate antlers, and it has a broken leg. Her hunting dog attacks the deer from the rear. Art historians have ignored the significance of the "flying bird" in the scene. But the bird hovering above the deer's head is no random detail. It is obviously an eagle with spread wings and hooked beak, trained to help the huntress. All four—Amazon, dog, horse, and eagle—are focused on the prize. The scene is compelling evidence that the classical Greeks had heard about or observed horsewomen of eastern barbarian lands who trained eagles to hunt (plate 8).[33]

Mongolian and other nomads of Central Asia traditionally hunted on horseback with raptors—falcons, hawks, and especially golden eagles—as detailed by Marco Polo in 1276. Today Kazakh *berkutchi* (eagle hunters) still hunt hares, foxes, and even wolves with golden eagles, assisted by a special breed of hunting hound (Asiatic sighthounds, *tazy* in Kazakh; *taigan* in Kyrgyz). The Kyrgyz people are also avid hunters in winter with horses, *taigan* hounds, and eagles. It takes great strength to hold an eagle on one's arm, even with support. Up to 3 feet tall, the eagles weigh 15–20 pounds; they have a 7-foot wingspan and a diving speed of 190 miles per hour.[34]

Female eagle hunters on the steppes are rare today. But in antiquity some physically strong nomad horsewomen were falconers, like the men of their tribes. Archaeological evidence comes from the mummies of Urumchi, interred for more than twenty-five hundred years in the extremely dry Tarim Basin of northwest China. The tall, lavishly dressed, and tattooed bodies were perfectly preserved in the salt sand, along with weapons and other grave goods. The archaeologists noted that the left hand of one of the women (buried near Turfan in about 700 BC) was "encased in a gigantic leather mitten" just like those worn by falconers.[35]

A similar large, thick leather mitt protects the right hand and arm of a young Kazakh horsewoman named Makpal Abdrazakova. It is the perch of her magnificent golden eagle named Akzhelke (plate 9). Makpal's father began to teach her to handle hunting eagles when she was thirteen. Beginning in 2003, Makpal and her eagle won numerous eagle hunting contests, reported in international media. Eagles are captured young; the laborious training is based on mutual trust. Female eagles, larger and stronger than the males, are preferred. Makpal recalls that the Kazakh elders allowed her to compete as a *berkutchi* "because they remembered that a long time ago women used to hunt with dogs and eagles."[36] Now more girls are apprentice eagle hunters.

The horse, the dog, and the eagle: by training these three animals the nomads made the rugged, relentless steppes into a land rich with accessible game. In antiquity some horsewomen of Thrace, Caucasia, and Central Asia certainly hunted with raptors, even eagles. Reports of this activity filtered back to the Greek world, resulting in the beautiful golden ring engraved with an Amazon eagle hunter.

Women of Scythian tribes, known as Amazons to the Greeks, hunted animals for food and fur and to defend their herds. They mastered the art of throwing javelins and spearing their quarry while on horseback. Rabbits, marmots, ground squirrels, martens, wolves, foxes, leopards, mountain sheep, boars, ibex, deer, and elk: a wide array of pelts, horns, bones, claws, and teeth has been recovered from Scythian burials. Sable (marten) and other furs are common in Pazyryk frozen tombs. Boar's tusks and lion's claws were personal hunting amulets or trophies often buried with women warriors (chapter 4).[37]

The horse defined the world of steppe nomads, and horses were deeply embedded in Amazon life. As the great equalizer of women and men on the steppes, horseback riding meant that both sexes learned the same hunting and war skills. Riding horses meant that women and men were armed with the same weapons and often dressed alike. One particular article of clothing, mocked by the bare-legged skirt-wearing Greeks, was absolutely essential to those who lived on horseback: a strong pair of trousers.

1 2

WHO INVENTED TROUSERS?

ORE THAN A THOUSAND AMAZONS ARE DEPICTED on Greek vase paintings, and most of the warrior women are clad in tunics and trousers or leggings, like those worn by their fellow Scythians. Standard Greek attire was a rectangle of cloth draped and fastened with pins and belts, as it was for many other ancient cultures (such as the Roman toga, Egyptian wrap-around skirt, and Asian sari). But trousers were more complex. Trousers and tunics required piecing together wool, leather, or cloth and sewing strong seams to construct shaped garments; the seams were frequently decorated with contrasting thread. The earliest preserved trousers have been excavated in burials of horse-riding men and women in the Tarim Basin, dating to 1200 to 900 BC. The most recent discoveries are two pairs of trousers fashioned more than three thousand years ago from three pieces of wool with complicated zigzag and other woven patterns and featuring an inset crotch gusset for freer movement. The design was an innovation that facilitated riding on horseback. In other words, trousers were the world's first "tailored" clothing. Trousers did not just happen but had to be invented.[1]

Who invented trousers? According to the Greeks, it was powerful barbarian women. Ancient Greek traditions traced the origin of this exotic attire to various warrior queens of the East. One legend claimed that trousers and long sleeves were first introduced by Medea, the mythic sorceress-princess of Colchis who became the lover of the

FIG. 12.1. Amazon in trousers and corselet, with Thracian cloak. Attic, Greek, white-ground alabastron (perfume jar), Syriskos Painter, ca. 480–470 BC. Princeton University Art Museum, Carl Otto von Kienbusch Jr. Memorial Collection Fund, y1984–12. Photo: Bruce M. White/ Art Resource, NY.

Argonaut Jason. According to this ancient folklore preserved by Strabo of Pontus, Medea wore trousers and a tunic when she and Jason ruled the mountainous territory on the Caspian Sea (now Azerbaijan and Armenia), home of the Nisaean horse herds. Some fifth-century BC Greek vase paintings show Medea in this Amazon-like attire. Medea's garb was so suitable for archers on horseback that her style was taken up by nomads and later adopted by the Medes and Persians.[2]

According to the lost history of Hellanikos (fifth century BC), a great Assyrian or Persian queen of the misty past named Atossa was the first to wear trousers. She had been raised as a boy by her father, King Ariaspes. After she inherited his kingdom, Atossa created a new kind of dress to be worn by her male *and* female subjects: long-sleeved shirts and trousers that obscured gender differences. Thus "disguising her feminine nature, Atossa ruled over many tribes and was most warlike and brave in every deed." The name "Atossa" is known in Persian royal histories, but this Atossa is an enigmatic figure. So is another fabled Persian warrior queen named Rhodogyne ("Woman in Red") who rode a black Nisaean mare with white blazes to her many victories over the Armenian tribes. This queen refused to marry and delighted in killing men. "Resplendent in a scarlet belted tunic and trousers woven with charming designs," Rhodogyne rushed off to battle before she could finish braiding her hair. Some scholars wonder whether Atossa and Rhodogyne might have been conflated with another more famous Assyrian warrior queen, Semiramis, renowned for her impressive conquests, new cities, innovations, and stupendous building programs.[3]

Semiramis (Akkadian, *Sammuramat*; Persian and Armenian, *Shamiram*) was a historical queen of the late ninth century BC. A large body of legends grew up about her reign (ca. 810–805 BC; see chapter 22). It was said that she disguised herself as a boy and revealed her sex only after illustrious victories on the battlefield. According to legend, Semiramis designed a new style of clothing for herself and her subjects: long sleeves and trousers that were deliberately intended to blur the physical differences between men and women. The outfit was streamlined, offered protection from the elements, minimized chafing on horseback, and allowed Semiramis to attend to all her personal needs modestly. In this "comfortable, practical garb," Semiramis rode her horse to conquer Baktria (Afghanistan). She personally led a special group of rock-climbing soldiers to attack the enemy's citadel on a high cliff. In another legendary exploit, she waged war against an Indian army, riding a swift horse and surviving arrow and javelin wounds. Like the Amazons, Semiramis rejected marriage as a threat to her power. She chose the most handsome of her soldiers for sex. (After their dalliances with the queen it was said that they were never seen again.) Semiramis's tunic and trousers were so convenient and attractive that, as Strabo had claimed about Medea's clothing, the Medes and Persians adopted them ever after.[4]

The ancient Greeks considered their short, draped, sleeveless chiton the proper attire for men; women wore layers of similar, ankle-length garments. Arms and legs were bare; cloaks and capes provided warmth in mild Mediterranean winters. In contrast, snug or loose trousers (*anaxyrides* and *sarabara*, Greek words of probable Persian origins) and long sleeves were the mode of dress favored by barbarians from the Black Sea to the Xiongnu territories on the western border of China. By the sixth century BC, trousers had become emblematic of foreign archers—especially Scythians, Persians, and Amazons—in Greek art. Greek writers described Scythians, Saka, Sarmatians, Dacians, Getae, Celts, Siginni, Medes, Persians, Phrygians, Parthians, Hyrcanians, Baktrians, Armenians—and Amazons—as clothed in *anaxyrides*. The Greeks were literally surrounded by trouser-wearing peoples.[5]

What did all these trousered folk have in common? They were horse people par excellence, and—no coincidence—many of these groups were also distinguished by relative gender equality, compared to the Greeks. The nomads, reported Hippocrates, "always wear trousers and spend all their time on horseback." Leg and seat coverings are essential for serious—all day, day in and day out—horseback riding, to prevent chafing. As we saw in the previous chapter, the Greeks believed that the Amazons had been the first people to ride horses. So it comes as no surprise that the Greeks assumed that trousers must also have originated with women warriors.[6]

Trousers and long sleeves were especially required in cold northerly climates, but Strabo explained that the Medes and Persians had decided to adopt this "feminine" Scythian style because it seemed so "august and ceremonial" compared to "going lightly clad." We know from ancient writings and art that the Greeks themselves adopted some distinctive articles of Thracian, Scythian, and Persian dress as practical or fashionable "foreign accents." Vase paintings, for example, show Greek men flaunting geometrically patterned Thracian cloaks (*zeira*) of thick wool, and some even sport Scythian-style caps at symposia. Greek men and women also wore Persian-style sleeved tunics with patterns and decorative borders. Some modern scholars suggest that some Greek appropriations of foreigners' dress in artworks should be viewed as "politically motivated mythologizations" of certain attire. (Others maintain that ethnicity has nothing to do with Scythian-style clothing worn by males in vase paintings—instead the non-Greek attire is thought to signal low-status Greeks, either pubescent boys or archers. However, this argument explicitly excludes Amazons in Scythian-style attire.) As the Greeks became more familiar with peoples of Thrace, Anatolia, Persia, and Scythia, they began to depict foreign figures such as Medea, King

Priam of Troy, and Amazons in the typical garb of contemporary ethnic groups. Even Atalanta, the Greek "Amazon," was sometimes portrayed in Scythian-style dress (prologue).[7]

OUTLANDISH BARBARIAN TROUSERS

Despite the Greek acceptance of some barbarian styles, however, one garment stands out as "completely inadmissible": trousers. Practical and warm, trousers were de rigueur for protecting the loins and legs of horse riders and others who lived their lives out in the elements—a fact that even some Greek writers acknowledged. By the later Roman era, we hear that the descendants of Greek colonists on the chilly northern Black Sea coast had adopted Scythian trousers, and Roman soldiers adopted the breeches of Gallia Bracata ("Trousered Gaul") in northern Europe. But in his essential manual on horsemanship, Xenophon, who was personally familiar with Persian riding clothes, did not advise Greek riders to wear trousers. Instead, Xenophon says that upon straddling his horse a rider should "rearrange his skirts or mantle" under his buttocks. For the classical Greeks the very idea of trousers evoked anxiety and ambivalence—they were just "too foreign." Even Alexander the Great, who irritated his soldiers by enthusiastically adopting Persian-style dress after his conquests, never took up trousers. The Greeks derided the barbarians' trousers as "effeminate," a sign of weakness, mocking them as ridiculous "multicolored bags or sacks" (*thulakoi*) for the lower limbs. Nevertheless, many ancient Greek descriptions of barbarians' leather trousers also portray the wearers as tough and masculine.[8]

Why were trousers so disturbing for Greeks? Among modern explanations, a structuralist theory maintains that the "verticality" of a tunic and trousers worn by eastern "Others" was in opposition to "the horizontally agglutinative grammar of Greek clothes." (In other words, the Greeks preferred layering and were distressed by bisected tops and bottoms.)[9] Trousers seemed to represent everything alien and transgressive about barbarian—and Amazon—culture. Several Greek writers described the barbarian practice of covering up arms and legs, normally left naked in the warm Mediterranean climate, as somehow unseemly. Civilized Greeks appreciated athletic nudity, while the primitive barbarians concealed their bodies. Moreover, the gaudy, colorful patterns and rough textures of Amazon and Scythian leggings and trousers clashed with elegantly draped Greek garments.

But perhaps even more worrying was the fact that barbarian males and females often wore *exactly the same costume*: hat, tunic, belt, boots, and trousers. This fact was emphasized by Herodotus in his account of the Amazons from Pontus and the Scythian men from the northern Black Sea area who joined forces to become the Sarmatians (chapter 3). He makes it clear that nomad males and females dressed alike. Many features of this unisex outfit disquieted the Greeks. First, it signified that the two sexes behaved the same way and engaged in the same physical activities. Like the horse, trousers were equalizers, permitting women to move freely and be as athletically active as men while preserving modesty, as bloomers did for nineteenth-century female bicyclists. (The two-hundred-year-old French ban forbidding a woman to wear trousers in public, unless she was riding a bicycle or a horse, was lifted in 2013.) Trousers also allowed the wearer to control visual—and sexual—access to their bodies in a way that skirts worn by Greek men and women did not. This may be one reason trousers have appealed to independent women and confounded repressive men in various cultures over the ages.

Next, the belief that *women* had invented the barbarian ensemble of tunic and trousers made the outfit unsuitable for "real" (Greek) men. Because trousers were worn by Scythian women and because Greeks liked to portray barbarians as "womanish," trousers were seen as "feminine attire," in stark contrast to modern Western attitudes. Greek males firmly rejected the idea of covering their own lower bodies with trousers. Compared to skirts, trousers may have been perceived as inhibiting natural functions. Moreover, Greek men were accustomed to glimpsing male genitals exposed by miniskirted chitons in daily life (undergarments were not worn). Two literary examples suffice: In *The Assemblywomen*, an Athenian comedy by Aristophanes, the women appropriate their husbands' clothing in order to take over the Assembly, but they caution each other to be careful when clambering over the men to take their seats or striding up to the podium, lest their female sex be revealed. Amusingly, Xenophon warns Greek men to be sure to remain upright when mounting a horse "lest they present an indecent spectacle from behind." Trousers would, of course, prevent such "awkward" exposures—but perhaps such male modesty was undesirable among Greek men.[10]

Finally, for Greek men the most anxiety-producing feature of trousers was probably the garment's androgynous nature. It was damnably difficult to know whether someone in trousers was a man or a woman. Some vase painters appear to trade on this sexual ambiguity in their many depictions of undifferentiated Amazons and Scythians. Indeed, deliberate gender ambiguity was exactly the motivation that the Greeks attributed to Atossa and Semiramis, two of the female "inventors" of trousers.

But if the outlandish trousers the Greeks derided were really so ugly and ridiculous, then why did so many vase painters devote so much effort to depicting Amazon attire in such loving detail and with such seeming admiration? The details of Amazon-Scythian fashions suggest keen curiosity about and awareness of the wardrobes of these "Others." The attractive, sometimes sexually charged images of Amazons astride horses and leaping and whirling in battle scenes appealed to Greek male and female vase owners alike. The warrior women's beauty and freedom of movement in their dashing action-wear, which followed the contours of their limbs like a second skin, demonstrated how natural trousers were for physical activities revolving around horses and warfare. It is a fascinating fact that in antiquity so many perfume flasks and other objects used by Greek women were decorated with images of audacious Amazons clad in trousers (figs. 8.1, 8.2, 12.1, 13.1, 13.5).

PRACTICAL TROUSERS

Associating warrior women with the invention of trousers was not irrational. Trousers were a practical innovation of men and women who domesticated horses on the steppes, optimally designed for riding long distances and engaging in activities on horseback. Early European travelers remarked on the trousers worn by the women of the Caucasus (white for young girls, red for married women, and blue for widows and older women). The efficiency of trousers is vividly illustrated in

Indian accounts of the Rani Lakshmi Bai of Jhansi, the heroine of the 1857 Indian Rebellion against the British. After her husband was killed, the rani immediately drew the front of her sari between her legs and tucked it into a belt to create loose trousers so that she could ride into battle. This style was called *veeragacche*, "soldier's tuck" or "hero's girdle." The traditional saris of the Mahratta (Maratha) tribeswomen and others were worn "kasata"-style, tucked up at the back of the waist to create baggy breeches, much like a man's dhoti. This style was said to have originated "in the old days" when the women were "expert horsewomen and rode to war side-by-side with the men." Likewise, wide skirts preserved in steppe nomad women's burials could easily be adjusted for riding.[11]

Another striking illustration of trousers as a crucial military technology occurred in China during the Warring States period (fifth through third centuries BC), when Chinese rulers struggled against the powerful horse nomads of Inner Asia known as the Xiongnu. These male (and female) mounted archers naturally wore pants, while the Chinese at that time wore robes. The *Zhan Guo Ce* ("Chronicles of the Warring States") describes how King Wuling of the Zhao State (northwest China, 325–299 BC) realized that his infantry was no match for the mounted archers. He also saw that his commanders on horseback were impeded by their long robes. Wuling ordered his people to adopt the barbarians' uniform of trousers, boots, and fur caps and to practice horsemanship. But his officers resisted. Acknowledging that it might take generations before his Chinese soldiers stopped laughing and accepted "such strange and perverse attire," Wuling set the example by donning trousers himself to promote his reforms. Eventually it was the semibarbarian state of Qin (western China) that fully adopted the winning combination of Xiongnu-style cavalry and trousers, conquered the nomads, and unified the Warring States (221 BC; see chapter 25).[12]

Over time, as cavalry became more and more important in warfare, trousers became prestigious attire for noble horsemen of the Roman Empire and for medieval European knights. The practicality and high social status of trousers spread to other males in the Western world, and the strong historical correlation between horse riding and unisex nomad attire, once understood by the Greeks, was forgotten.

AMAZON AND SCYTHIAN DRESS IN ANCIENT LITERATURE AND ART

Strabo, Justin, and Plutarch mentioned that the Amazons of the Caucasus "make their helmets, clothing, and belts from the skins of wild animals." The Roman historian Ammianus Marcellinus claimed that once a steppe nomad donned his or her "hideous" hemp tunic and leggings of rodent and goatskins, that outfit was worn until the rags fell away. He also declared that the nomads "lived glued to their horses" because their boots were too ill-fitting for walking. The Scythians "wear skins and stitched trousers as protection from the cold," remarked the Roman poet Ovid with distaste, "and the only part of their body one can see is their face." Other writers, however, wrote more admiringly of nomad dress. Strabo, for example, praised the soft woolen trousers and tunics dyed with many bright colors and lavish golden belts and headdresses of the Saka (Massagetae).[13]

Herodotus provides the fullest ancient descriptions of the dress of the myriad Eurasian tribes allied with the Persians in the fifth century BC. Thracians, he noted, wore fox-skin caps, tunics, colorful woven cloaks (*zeirai*), and high fawn-skin boots. Various tribes of Anatolia were clothed in animal skins, brightly dyed tunics, belted robes or *zeirai* fastened with brooches, high boots, linen breastplates, and flexible helmets of plaited leather strips or of bronze decorated with bulls' ears and horns (like those on Amazons' helmets in sixth-century BC vase paintings; see below). The Medes, Persians, Hyrcanians (southern Caspian region), and other Central Asians wore soft felt or woven caps, multicolored long-sleeved, belted woolen or leather tunics, trousers, and great quantities of gold. The Saka-Scythians, reported Herodotus, dressed in similar outfits but with "stiff, pointed turbans." Many of these costumes are depicted in ancient Assyrian and Mesopotamian reliefs.[14]

The earliest Amazon scenes suddenly appeared with unprecedented force on black-figure vase paintings in 575–550 BC. More than five hundred vases depicting Amazons survive from this period. In black-figure vase painting, women were distinguished by white skin, a feature that arose because proper Greek women stayed indoors, while the men were out bronzing in the sun, exercising, hunting, and fighting. Ironically, the logic of pale skin for women was inappropriate for Amazons (and

Atalanta), who carried out the same outdoor activities as men, but the artistic convention is helpful for us moderns, allowing us to tell Amazons apart from Scythian men in black-figure paintings, since they often wear similar costumes (figs. 7.1, 11.1, 18.2, 18.5). A few painters chose to leave Amazons' skin black, probably to emphasize the women's manly nature. In this earliest period, Amazons were kitted out like Greek hoplites, in short belted chiton, peplos, or exomis (exposing one breast), greaves (shin-guards), cuirasses (breastplates), crested helmets, round shields, and spears, and they fought on foot. A vase painted by the imaginative and detail-oriented painter Exekias (550–525 BC) shows Penthesilea in a Greek helmet decorated with a tiny griffin ornament; she also wears a belted tunic and full leopard skin.[15]

The first Amazon archer to wear long sleeves and trousers in a vase painting appears on a black-figure amphora of 575–550 BC. By the end of the sixth century BC, Athenian vase painters began to show Amazons wearing Scythian-Sarmatian-Thracian patterned attire, and several vases depict Amazons with the Thracian *zeira* (fig. 12.1). Through trade and travel, the Greeks were becoming increasingly familiar with the diverse but culturally related nomad groups around the Black Sea and beyond whose women and men rode horses and dressed alike. This growing knowledge was reflected in stage plays featuring foreign characters in exotic, richly decorated finery. Notably, the fifth-century BC playwright Euripides remarked that "Amazons' garments woven with many designs were dedicated by Herakles in the temple of Apollo at Delphi." After the Persian Wars (480 BC), Amazons, Scythians, and Persians in Greek art wore similar articles of clothing (chapter 17).[16]

Innovations of red-figure and colored white-ground vase painting allowed extremely detailed decorative possibilities. By 525–500 BC, vase painters were becoming adept in reproducing the flamboyant patterns and textures of Amazon and Scythian wardrobes (figs. 11.3, 11.4). Amazons appear in a surprising variety of individualized nomad outfits, a result of Greek perceptions of the women's origins combined with the artists' and their customers' enthusiasm for eclectic, unusual fashions. Antiope's ensemble on a vase painted by Myson (500–480 BC; see fig. 16.2) is visually stunning: a short chiton under a jacket complemented by trousers sewn from two materials, a woven fabric with leopard skin on the inner thighs. She also wears an earring and a large quiver on a shoulder strap, topped off with a round cap decorated with a palmette. Often several Amazons on a single vase are dressed in different costumes but with recognizable elements of Thracian, Scythian, Persian, and Greek attire (figs. 5.1, 13.6, 13.7, 18.2).[17]

A striking Amazonomachy attributed to the Andokides Painter (530 BC; he created the remarkable vase showing Amazons swimming and arming) is filled with unusual details of costume. Some of the Amazons are dressed as archers, others as hoplites with helmets. (One Amazon helmet has bull's ears and horns like the one in fig. 7.2 and like those Herodotus would describe on nomad warriors about a hundred years later; see chapter 23 for Egyptian examples.) All wear necklaces and some wear earrings. The fringed tunic of a fallen Amazon is richly ornamented with woven bands of animals and geometric designs; her cap has lozenges and dots; her shield bears an eagle device. The Amazon hoplite's corselet is decorated with rosettes, while her archer companion wears a short chiton with dots and crosses. One Amazon wears a pointed cap of spotted fur; another has a dotted turban.[18]

A medley of Scythian, Persian, and Greek details appears on the extraordinary drinking cup in the shape of an Amazon huntress riding a white horse with blue eyes (signed by Sotades, mid-fifth century BC, found in Meroe, Sudan; see chapters 11 and 23). The Amazon once held a metal hunting spear. Her quarry, a boar and a lion, crouch in the green grass under her horse. Traces of paint show that her eyes were violet and her white shoes had purple laces and red soles. She wore red trousers, a purple shirt with red dots, and a yellow-and-black leopard skin around her waist. A red quiver with a wave design and a red and violet Greek-style helmet with white crest completed her outfit. The drinking cup portion was decorated with red-figure scenes showing a bearded Persian rider and either a Scythian or an Amazon on foot attacking two Greek hoplites (plate 2).[19]

Traces of paint on marble sculptures of Scythians and Amazons reveal that their clothing was exuberantly colorful and patterned, as were the warrior women's costumes in the large paintings of Amazonomachies that once adorned public and private walls in Athens. Those murals no longer exist, but we have descriptions of the most impressive ones by several ancient Greek writers. Their details provide evidence of the popularity of scenes from famous Amazonomachy wall paintings, copied by vase painters onto their pots featuring Amazons.[20]

The artists' pleasure in representing the sheer variety of Amazons' athletic poses and eye-catching attire is evident, and the erotic appeal is obvious. In contrast to the ancient writers who disapproved of the way the barbarians' attire covered up the body, the vase painters seemed to take sensual delight in the ways Scythian-style outfits could reveal the bodies of physically fit, desirable foreign women. In the words of one vase scholar, the Amazons' thin, transparent chitons and close-fitting tops and trousers "invite [and] tease the male viewer to caress the Amazons' trim, lithe bodies [with] the eye's hand." Whether or not real Scythian clothing was as variegated and sexy as depicted in art, the vase painters seized on the possibilities of fitted Scythian couture to express individuality and sexuality without nudity.[21]

In effect, the vase painters of Amazons became the first fashion designers. The vast popularity of Amazons in vase paintings means that we have a veritable catalog of sumptuous barbarian women's fashions as imagined by artists. They dressed the warrior women in body-hugging "unitards" or tunics, short chitons or belted dresses, sometimes over leggings and trousers, often profusely decorated with animals, stars, cross-hatching, dots, circles, stripes, checks, waves, zigzags, and other designs. Some Amazons have patterned *zeirai* or animal skins, and their hair could be either short or long, either loose or tied back with bands. In paintings and sculpture, pointed or soft Scythian caps with earflaps or ties (*kidaris*) soon replaced the Greek helmets, and the women wear a variety of belts, baldrics (diagonal straps), corselets, shoulder cords or bands, and crisscrossing leather straps attached to belt loops like those worn by the archer huntress Artemis. (As noted in chapter 5, these may have served as bosom support.)[22]

Amazon footgear included soft leather moccasin-like shoes, calf-high boots (*endromides*), or taller laced boots (*embades*) with scallops or flaps and lined with felt or fur. But there are many artistic examples of barefoot Amazon riders too. According to early travelers, the women of hunting and marauding tribes in the Caucasus and steppes went barefoot in the summer and wore boots in winter; we might imagine that this was the custom in antiquity too. A barefoot long-distance bareback

FIG. 12.2. Barefoot Amazon tying on heel/ankle guards or spurs; her shield, quiver, and bow are suspended above left. Athenian white-ground lekythos (oil flask) from Cyprus, ca. 475–425 BC, Inv. A256, Musée de Louvre, Paris. Photo: Hervé Lewandowski. © RMN-Grand Palais/ Art Resource, NY.

rider, however, would risk chafing on the ankles. This might help explain the curious ankle and heel straps with a "stirrup" band under the instep, shown on some Amazons in paintings and sculptures. A vase painting in the Louvre, for example, shows a barefoot Amazon putting on a pair of ankle guards, and other vases depict Amazons with similar heel straps (fig. 12.2). Some scholars have wondered whether the straps were intended as "spurs" of some sort, but ankle guards are also worn by acrobats and athletes. The straps were most likely worn to support and protect the bare ankle and heel from abrasion injuries or sprains. Their inclusion in Amazon statues and paintings suggests that Greek artists drew on detailed knowledge of gear used by real Scythian horsewomen to equip their imagined Amazons.[23]

ARCHAEOLOGY

Archaeological discoveries of well-preserved sets of clothing confirm that real horsewomen of ancient Scythian lands dressed much as did those described in Greek texts and illustrated in Scythian and Greek artworks. Nomads wearing tunics, trousers, and pointed caps appear on numerous ancient gold reliefs, terra-cotta figures, and vases made in the northern Black Sea region, and on artifacts depicting the daily life and horse culture of Scythia. One famous example is the exquisite Chertomlyk vase showing trousered men and women or youths training horses. Other fine examples are the gold beaker from Kul Oba Kurgan (Kerch, fourth century BC), showing scenes from Scythian life, and the detailed relief on the fine silver and gilt bowl from Gaymanova Kurgan, showing several Scythian men (and possibly one woman) in typical dress, with weapons, at a banquet (all fourth century BC).[24]

The oral *Manas* epic of the nomadic Kyrgyz describes the hero's wife sewing a pair of strong *kandagai*, "trousers." Trousers and tunics fashioned from leather, wool, hemp, flax, and silk have been found in Scythian burials. In some cases, inner layers of wool or silk were worn under heavier clothes of leather and fur. Pieces of material of different sizes and thickness were stitched with decorative seams. As noted above, the earliest preserved trousers were part of the full wardrobes of the desiccated Tarim mummies, ca. 1200–900 BC, along with fur-trimmed coats with cuffs and wide skirts with colorful leggings of wrapped wool (the leggings in Greek vase paintings may reflect similar garments). The Golden Warrior of Issyk (fifth–third centuries BC) wore leather trousers with spangled seams, a cloth shirt under a leather tunic, and boots, all covered with golden scales. The Pazyryk man and young woman buried together with their weapons and horses at Ak-Alakha in the Altai both wore trousers of wool (fifth century BC; fig. 4.2). Preserved pieces of trousers from Ak-Alakha 1, mound 1, indicate that the pants legs were about eleven inches wide, probably similar to loose Turkish trousers gathered at the ankle, and perhaps tied under the instep as shown in some Scythian artifacts and Greek vases. The archaeologists who analyzed the clothing in Pazyryk women's tombs suggest that "the girls, being warriors, wore trousers," while older women wore robes or skirts over leggings. This would fit several ancient Greek accounts of young Amazon warriors as active-duty soldiers and older women as reserves, fighting only when required.[25]

In 1984 in the Tarim Basin archaeologists at Sampula discovered an extraordinary pair of trousers in a mass grave containing the jumbled skeletons of about 133 male and female nomads killed in a Xiongnu attack (third to first centuries BC). The bones were buried with textiles, tools, mirrors, and combs evincing far-reaching trade and plunder. Still encased in his or her limb bones, one nomad's trousers had been tailored from pieces of a fine ornamental wool tapestry woven with flowers, birds, griffins, and other designs. One pants leg was decorated with a Centaur blowing a salpinx, a war trumpet used by Scythians and Amazons in Greek art. An image of a beardless blue-eyed steppe warrior holding a spear adorned the other pants leg. The archaeologists surmise that the large pictorial wall hanging had been looted during a Saka assault on a settlement in Sogdiana/Baktria, then cut up and sewn into garments.[26]

The Sampula mass grave also yielded many short skirts with multicolored bands and motifs. Long, wide skirts have been recovered from many women's burials in Scythian lands. As we saw, the sari, worn since antiquity in India, was a large rectangle of cloth that could be easily transformed into riding breeches and battle wear. Archaeologist Polosmak described a similar versatility for the long woolen skirt worn by the Ice Princess (chapter 6). Xenophon advised a variation of this same draping and tucking arrangement to prevent chafing for Greek male horse riders, above. We can assume that nomad women on the steppes used the method of hiking a long skirt between their legs, and securing it with a belt, to make a trouser-like garment for riding and strenuous activities.

A wide variety of leather belts and buckles found in Scythian burials confirms that the belts and baldrics were accurately depicted in Greek vase paintings of Amazons. Archaeologists describe numerous broad belts with attachments, clasps, and hooks for carrying weapons and quivers, as well as narrow belts for pendants and light items such as knives and whetstones. Buckles, plates, and plaques in various shapes and sizes of iron, bronze, bone, wood, and gold, decorated with animal and abstract motifs, also occur in profusion in male and female burials, confirming the passages in Herodotus and Strabo describing the golden

FIG. 12.3. Artist's reconstruction of girl warrior and horse in the Ak-Alakha burial, based on her preserved clothing and grave goods. Painting by Verena Kälin, Zurich, reproduced with permission.

belts and baldrics of the Scythian and Saka (Massagetae) warriors. The animal and abstract geometric motifs that decorate Amazon and Scythian clothing in Greek art closely resemble the designs and shapes on artifacts found in Scythian and Thracian graves. The tombs of armed women also yield a great array of personal adornments such as earrings, necklaces, bracelets, pendants, beads, pins, animal teeth and claws, cowries (from the Indian Ocean) and other fossil and replica shells, and leather and gold appliqués. Notably, many Greek vase painters included "feminine" jewelry—earrings, necklaces, and bracelets—in their illustrations of Amazons, even those shown in the thick of battle. Leopard and other animal pelts were another accurate detail (first appearing on a black-figure vase of 575–550 BC), since furs of spotted wildcats, martens, and other animals are among the grave goods of women of ancient Scythia.[27]

Amazons' shoes and boots in vase paintings and sculpture also match the kinds of footwear found in the graves of steppe nomads. Well-made moccasins, ankle boots, and tall boots of felt and leather, often richly decorated with golden plaques, beads, scallops, and embroi-

FIG. 12.4. Examples of clothing preserved in ancient graves: pointed felt hat from Tarim Basin; leather hat with earflaps, Pazyryk Kurgan 3; trousers from Pazyryk frozen grave, fifth century BC. Collage by Michele Angel, after images in *Siberian Times* and other sites.

dery, have been recovered from numerous ancient burials of women in Ukraine, Kazakhstan, the Altai, ancient Baktria, and other sites in Central Asia (chapter 4).

The headgear of Amazons and Scythians in Greek art falls into two basic types: stiff, pointed hats and soft ("Phrygian") caps with earflaps (lappets) and/or back panel or ties. Some of the soft caps resemble pointed hoods or have curled-over tops, and some are elaborately decorated (plates 7, 11–13, figs. 7.2, 7.3, 7.5, 11.2–4, 12.2, 13.1, 13.6, 15.1, 16.1, 16.2, 18.3). These Phrygian caps with lappets or ties appear in ancient Scythian reliefs and on ancient Armenian coins. Examples of this style of cap in leather, cloth, wool, felt, and fur have been found in ancient warriors' graves on the steppes. The tall, stiff, pointed hats worn by the Saka-Scythians, known to the Persians as the *Sakā tigraxaudā* ("Pointed Hat Saka") of the Caspian-Aral region, were described by Herodotus. These high conical hats appear in the earliest Greek images of Scythians (e.g., the famous François vase and fig. 11.1), and they are also depicted in ancient Hittite and Persian reliefs and seals. Archaeologists have unearthed several examples of these pointed hats (likened to "witch-hats")—some very tall—made of leather, wool, and felt, often studded with elaborate golden ornaments, from many graves in Central Asia.

Tall pointed hats were worn by the frozen Ice Princess of the Altai, the Golden Warrior of Issyk, the skeleton of a woman in the Chertomlyk burial, the sumptuously dressed woman in Arzhan 2, and several female Tarim Basin mummies.[28]

Archaeological and literary evidence shows that the depictions of Amazon dress and equipment developed more realistic details in classical art as the Greeks discovered more about the lifestyles of real horsewomen and -men of Eurasia. The changes demonstrate that Greek artists and their audiences had access to information about nomad dress or had observed examples firsthand. The Greeks soon came to understand that the mythic warrior women they called Amazons would not have been outfitted like Greek hoplites but were mounted archers dressed and armed like contemporary nomads of the steppes. As the next chapter, on weaponry, reveals, trousers and horse riding were not the only inventions attributed to warrior queens in antiquity.

ARMED AND DANGEROUS: WEAPONS AND WARFARE

W HO WERE THE FIRST PEOPLE TO MAKE IRON weapons? According to the ancient Greeks, it was the Amazons—and this advantage gave them great power over their enemies. Ironworking originated in Anatolia and/or the Caucasus around 1600–1300 BC. Hittite inscriptions record a demand for their iron objects in the fourteenth century BC. An ancient oral tradition of the Caucasus explains how a wise and practical mythic heroine invented the anvil, hammer, and tongs for ironworking. Her name was Satanaya, Iranian-Circassian for "Mother of a War Band of a Hundred Brothers." Perhaps this tale and other oral traditions about iron from the Black Sea–Anatolian region were transmitted to the Greeks. The Greeks were probably aware of the extensive fortified ironworking site for making weapons on the Dnieper River (fifth century BC), in the heart of Amazon territory. Iron knives, lances, swords, battle-axes, and belt armor belonged to the real warrior women of their day; hundreds of examples have been recovered from Scythian kurgans (chapter 4).[1]

A battle-axe, a bow, a quiver full of arrows, a pair of light spears, a crescent shield, and a sword. These were the essential Amazon weapons portrayed in Greek art by the end of the sixth century BC. Casting off their inappropriate Greek hoplite gear (helmet, cuirass, and large shield), the warrior women were beginning to be perceived and presented more accurately as Scythian archers and horsewomen. The Amazonian arsenal included a full panoply of projectile, thrusting, slashing, hacking, and entanglement weapons for long-distance and close-range combat. Like their special clothing, Scythians' weapons, especially bows, were not only well suited for mounted hunting and warfare, but they could be handled skillfully by women as well as men on horseback. Using these weapons in battle required flexibility, dexterity, and mastery of horses gained through training since childhood.[2]

Ancient artistic and literary evidence, supported by archaeological discoveries of iron and bronze weapons, demonstrates that the Greek vase painters drew on surprisingly detailed knowledge of the kinds of arms and armor that real women warriors would have used, and they represented Amazons wielding Scythian weapons in lifelike battle scenes.

BOWS, ARROWS, QUIVERS

The deadly accuracy of Scythian archers inspired awe in antiquity. (Terror was enhanced because they poisoned their arrows.) Modern parallels suggest that a Scythian archer could shoot about 15–20 arrows a minute, probably averaging a distance of about 500–600 feet and achieving accuracy at about 200 feet. There was an ancient trick, requiring honed skills, to shooting a great many arrows per minute, recently rediscovered by modern archers. Instead of pulling each arrow from the quiver, one holds several arrows in the hand drawing the bow. A striking image on a Greek perfume jar depicts an Amazon doing exactly that. Kneeling and twisting backward, she shoots one arrow while holding two more at the ready (fig. 13.1). Some archery experts note that her bow appears to be shown in a braced position, with little grip setback, whereas the string is stretched in the drawn position, perhaps indicating that the artist knew about the Scythians' speed archery technique but was not drawing from life. On the other hand, instinctive expert archers use no fixed anchor point and may not draw the string back fully (see chapter 5).[3]

In the hands of expert archers, Scythian bows were capable of shooting arrows extraordinary distances. A fourth-century BC inscription at Olbia (northern Black Sea) honors an archer for shooting an arrow nearly 1,700 feet (521.6 m). This may seem incredible, but a "flight archery" re-

FIG. 13.1. Amazon archer using speed-shooting technique. Black-figure alabastron (perfume jar), Emporion Painter, ca. 500–480 BC, inv. B-5218, State Hermitage Museum, St. Petersburg. Photo by Vladimir Terebenin, Leonard Kheifets, Yuri Molodkovets. Photograph © The State Hermitage Museum.

cord set in 2010 was just under 1,600 feet, achieved by a 14-year-old boy using a recurve bow of modern materials. In a comparable "primitive flight" record in 1995, an archer using a composite bow of natural materials (horn, sinew, and wood) with a linen string achieved a distance of about 1,800 feet. Flight archery does not depend solely on muscular strength, so some female archers in antiquity could shoot arrows very long distances. Modern art historians have described an Amazon archer on a vase painting (by Nikosthenes, 550–510 BC) as collapsing in death, or taking "negligent aim" at the heavens. She stands bending backward and aims at the sky. But in fact she is assuming the correct position for shooting a long-distance arrow. The two mounted onlookers, a Greek and a Scythian, suggest a contest scene (rather than a bird hunt).[4]

According to ancient lore from Pontus recounted by Herodotus, archery was introduced to the steppe nomads by the mythic first king of Scythia, Scythes, a son of Heracles. Arrows are an extremely ancient prehistoric technology but about twenty-eight hundred years ago an ingenious type of bow appeared on the steppes: this historic invention was responsible for the Scythians' vaunted reputation as archers. Scythian recurve bows of composite materials differed from the large, straight bows made from a single piece of wood used by Greeks and other ancient cultures. When strung (with horsehair or sinew), the recurve bow's tips curl away from the archer, like the classic Cupid's bow. "Most bows are made of flexible branches" in a continuous arc, wrote Ammianus Marcellinus, "but Scythian bows have curved ends." The form was likened to the Greek letter sigma (Σ). The recurve bow was so characteristic of the nomads around the Black Sea that the Greeks liked to compare its coastline to the shape of a Scythian bow (with the Crimea as the belly of the bow and the coast of Turkey as the string).[5]

The recurve composite bow was smaller and stored much more energy under compression, giving Scythian arrows more force, accuracy, distance, and velocity. The highly skilled, laborious bow-making process involved fitting pieces of horn (ibex, goat, ram) wrapped with horsehair, birch bark, or sinew (deer, elk, ox) and glue (animal or fish) around a wood core. Seasoning at each stage meant that the process took several years. The result was the archer's most precious possession, perhaps even more prized than his or her horse (see below). The Scythian composite bow was compact and light, ideal for use on horseback by both men and women, and it was well suited for the deadly backward Parthian shot. Judging from ancient artistic depictions (and remnants in graves) the bow was about thirty inches long, and it was held out from the chest (breasts were no hindrance; see chapter 5). Ancient writers noted that Saka-Scythian "women along with the men shoot backward as they pretend to flee."[6]

It is very difficult to string a powerful recurve composite bow unless one knows how; it requires a special technique more than brute force. There are two ancient Greek allusions to this special knowledge. According to the Scythian origin myth, above, Heracles demonstrated the knack of stringing his bow and buckling his belt to the Viper-Woman of Scythia with whom he had three sons, and he set these feats as a test to determine which son should rule. Only Scythes was able to accomplish the tasks. Parallel tales appear in the Central Asian epics, such as *Forty Maidens* (chapter 24), in a Persian tale recounted by Herodotus, and in Homer's *Odyssey*. Many failed to string the special bow of the skilled archer Odysseus. Only he knew the trick. This passage has been taken as evidence that in Homer's time (ca. 700 BC) the Greeks were just becoming familiar with the nomads' recurve bows.[7]

Homer says that Odysseus strung his bow while seated. A Scythian bow was usually strung in a sitting or kneeling position with the belly of the bow held firmly under one's knee. The method is illustrated in Scythian artifacts. A well-known example is the golden beaker from Kul Oba Kurgan (Kerch, fourth century BC) depicting a Scythian archer, in trousers, pointed cap, and boots, stringing a recurve bow braced under his outstretched leg (while his companions nurse their injuries from failing to string the bow).[8]

Some exceptionally detailed silver coins from Soloi, Cilicia (southern Anatolia, issued 480–386 BC), depict a kneeling Amazon who has just finished stringing her bow and is adjusting the top hook, to make sure the string and limbs are properly aligned (fig. 13.2). The city of Soloi also issued coins showing the head of an Amazon. (Who was this woman warrior commemorated on the coins of Soloi? Her identity is revealed in chapter 16.) Another significant image painted on a sixth-century BC wine pitcher shows an Amazon dressed in trousers with a quiver and a dagger in a sheath. She is standing on one leg, stringing her Scythian bow by bracing it under her other bent knee (fig. 13.3; compare fig. 25.3, Mulan stringing her bow). Modern experts point out that this "step through" method might work, but only if she braces the bent leg on a rock (possibly she has braced her foot on her helmet on

FIG. 13.2. Amazon stringing her bow. Silver coins minted in Soloi, Cilicia, fifth century BC.
Top: courtesy of Michel Prieur, www.cgb.fr. Bottom: private collection; Museum of Fine Arts,
Boston Henry Lillie Pierce Fund, 041144, photograph © 2014 Museum of Fine Arts, Boston.

the ground). Her bow is correctly placed the same position used by the
seated Scythian warrior on the beaker, mentioned above. This Greek
artist apparently had heard how the task of stringing a recurve bow was
done but failed to understand the body mechanics.[9]

In Greek vase paintings, small recurve bows and sizable quivers were
standard issue for Scythian and Amazon archers (with a few exceptions). In two vase paintings (Oltos, 525–500 BC) depicting the abduction of the Amazon Antiope by Theseus, for example, she is holding a
Scythian bow. Two more Oltos vases show the Amazon Lykopis ("Wolf
Eyes") with a Scythian bow and the Amazon Andromache shooting an
arrow. Several Amazon archers appear in a violent battle scene by Euphronios; one of them, labeled Teisipyle, is taking careful aim with her
Scythian bow, which she holds well away from her chest. Numerous
vase paintings show Amazons with recurve bows visible in their quivers
or hanging from their forearms; others are testing, aiming, and shooting their bows. Steppe nomads (and modern mounted archers) used

FIG. 13.3. Amazon stringing her bow under her knee (at left) as her companion (right) holds two spears and shield. Attic Greek black-figure olpe (pitcher), sixth/fifth century BC, Smithsonian Natural History Museum, Department of Anthropology catalog no. A378476–0.

the "Mongolian" thumb draw release, and this ethnographic detail is depicted in some Greek vase paintings.[10]

Scythian archers used a combination bow case and quiver called a *gorytos* (possibly a Scythian loanword) that hung from a shoulder belt at the archer's left hip (right hip if a sword was worn too; figs. 8.1, 8.2, 12.1, 13.2, 18.3). This case, nearly two feet long, was fashioned of leather, often reinforced with *gorytos* covers, thick gold plates decorated with scales, spirals, griffins, stags, rams, boars, and horses in Scythian animal style. The *gorytos* had two compartments: one held the bow and the other was a pocket for arrows that could be closed with a flap. The unique design meant that as many as a hundred arrows of different sizes, shapes, and materials were at hand for any type of hunting or battle situation. A great many golden *gorytos* covers with stunning reliefs have been recovered from Scythian burials. In some instances, such as Arzhan 2, the leather parts of the quiver–bow case were also preserved. The *gorytos* with Scythian-style designs appears on many ancient coins and in Greek paintings featuring Scythians and Amazons; it is also illustrated in Scythian reliefs. On a fifth-century BC vase, for example, griffins decorate an Amazon's quiver.[11]

Arrowheads, sometimes vast stores of them, are found in most male burials, in about one-third of women's burials, and also in children's graves (chapter 4). Arrowheads of different shapes and materials (bone, wood, iron, and bronze with two or three flanges) had differing piercing powers and were used for different types of hunting and battle situations. The elegantly aerodynamic trilobate arrowheads, used for warfare and found in great quantities across the steppes, display superb craftsmanship. Arrow shafts, approximately twenty inches long, were made of reed or wood (willow, birch, poplar) and fletched with feathers. Wood is perishable, but many shafts have been preserved in dry or frozen burial conditions. In Pazyryk kurgans, large caches of wooden shafts were painted with red and black wavy lines and zigzags, possibly to mimic the patterns on steppe vipers, whose venom was used to make arrow poison.[12]

Every nomad boy and girl, man and woman, owned a bow and arrows. Very few bows have been recovered from steppe burials that contain a great many arrowheads, quivers, and other weapons. Bows were made of perishable organic materials. But there is another reason for their rarity in graves. Each composite bow was the result of years of fine workmanship and extremely valuable to the tribe. (Unlike horses, which were sacrificed at funerals, fine bows were hard to replace.) Bows were apparently passed down over generations of Scythians. Some votive or toy miniature bows and broken parts of Scythian bows have been recovered. For example, handgrips and recurve bow ends were excavated from kurgans at Kul Oba (Kerch) and Voronezh (near the Don). Parts of a recurve bow and a *gorytos*, containing many red-and-black-painted wooden arrow shafts and three-flanged arrowheads with gold and silver inlays of animals and spirals, were in the grave of the Scythian couple at Arzhan 2, burial 5 (Tuva; above and chapter 4). The museum at Urumchi (northwest China) has a collection of composite Scythian-style and longer Xiongnu bows and at least one *gorytos*, preserved in nomad burials of the fifth to third centuries BC in the arid deserts along the Silk Route.[13]

Dramatic evidence of archery warfare includes bronze arrowheads still embedded in the bones of women interred with their weapons on the steppes. The young Amazon buried with her weapons at Tyras, on the northern Black Sea coast, and the warrior woman in Kurgan 7 at Chertomlyk are just two examples (chapter 4).[14]

SHIELDS AND ARMOR

The shield commonly associated with Amazons and Scythians was a *pelta*, the half-moon or oval shield like that carried by Thracian *peltasts* (light-armed skirmishers who hurled javelins) who were recruited into Greek armies from the western Black Sea region. Made of wicker, leather, wood, or bronze, the pelta was held by leather handgrips or slung on a diagonal strap (plates 11 and 12, figs. 7.3, 11.3, 12.2, 15.1, 18.1, 18.3). This shield was so strongly identified with Amazons that the ancient memorial honoring a fallen Amazon queen in Megara (west of Athens) was shaped like her crescent shield.[15]

After shedding their Greek armor in early art, Amazons don soft Scythian-style caps instead of helmets and sometimes wear corselets of linen or chest armor with scale patterns. Padded linen armor was often used by hunters because it could break the fangs of lions and leopards, commented the travel writer Pausanias, but it was less effective against iron projectiles or spears. Pausanias admired a Sarmatian scaled breastplate displayed in Athens and described how the Sarmatians used horsehair to sew scales cut from horse's hooves into overlapping rows on leather to create armor that was both attractive and strong. Archaeologists have discovered examples of magnificent golden scaled armor in Scythian male and female warrior burials. Thousands of small golden plaques that were once sewn onto leather tunics recall the Persian breastplates of golden scales described by Herodotus.[16]

BELTS, BUCKLES, AND BLOOD OATHS

Just as the mythic Greek archer Heracles girded himself with a massive belt and buckle, his Amazon adversary Queen Hippolyte also possessed a fabulous war belt, and so did her sister, Melanippe. Observations of barbarian women archers' beautifully wrought belts and buckles may well have influenced the myth about Hippolyte's belt (chapter 15, plate 7 and fig. 15.1). The graves of armed women of the steppes have yielded a wide variety of leather belts and baldrics (diagonal shoulder straps) with hooks for carrying weapons and gear, as well as numerous worked gold and bronze buckles of different sizes and shapes. Fighting belts were reinforced with plaques of iron, bronze, and gold (chapter 12). Another influence on the myth may have been the magnificent bronze belts worn by mounted archers of Urartu, a mysterious nomad culture (ninth to sixth centuries BC) of eastern Turkey and Armenia (traditional Amazon territory). Urartu was known for spectacular metalwork. Their archers wore very wide (five- to six-inch) belts made of thin sheets of bronze with fabric backing and hooks for lacing, decorated with plain bands or fine repoussé reliefs of rows of archers in trousers and pointed helmets with quivers, shields, and bows, riding galloping horses. The Urartu belts come in large and small waist sizes to fit men and women, and some have been found in women's graves. The topless Amazon stringing her bow on the coin in figure 13.2 appears to wear a wide, banded belt similar to those of Urartu.[17]

A recent archaeological find may be related to a curious detail in Herodotus's description of Scythian belts. A tiny gold cup was attached to the tongue of the buckle of Heracles's belt inherited by Scythes. According to Herodotus, "This explains why to this very day Scythian archers suspend small golden cups on their belt buckles." Since male and female Scythian archers dressed alike, presumably women's belts were similarly equipped. No artistic representations of this little cup are known, but an intriguing item appears in the excavation report (2004) of the richest Scythian grave ever excavated in Siberia (Arzhan 2, burial 5, 650–600 BC), which held a couple and their arrows, quivers, and daggers. On the woman's belt was a gold-encrusted dagger (chapter 4) and a "miniature golden cauldron." This apparent link to Herodotus's description of a little gold cup on Scythians' belts had gone unnoticed by the archaeologists. What was the purpose of the miniature golden vessel? We know that Scythian archers (again, presumably both male and female) were reputed to dip their arrows in a nasty poison concocted from viper venom. To avoid self-injury with pretreated arrows, a prudent archer might poison the points just before shooting. Could the tiny vial or cup have contained the arrow drug?[18]

An alternative potential use for the miniature cup might be related to another Scythian custom described by Herodotus: blood oaths. To make a binding pact, the Scythians "stab themselves with their awls or make a small cut with their knives." They stir the blood, using the tips of their dagger or *sagaris* (battle-axe), and drink it together. An ancient Chinese source (Han Dynasty) described the Xiongnu nomads sealing a treaty by ceremonially dipping a sword tip in wine drunk from an enemy's skull. Herodotus, interviewing settled Royal Scythians, said that they used a "large earthenware cup" and mixed the blood with wine. The Roman writer Lucian, in his "Scythian Dialogue," related several examples of the deep bonds of brotherhood forged by this blood ritual. A famous gold plaque from Kul Oba Kurgan shows two "blood brothers" sharing a drinking horn. Awls, knives, and earthenware cups are among the grave goods of both men and women in many Scythian burials. A mounted nomad archer on the steppes would be likely to carry an awl, a knife, and a battle-axe, but not a large clay cup (or skull or wine, for that matter). The need to seal a blood pact might arise anytime, anywhere. A small golden cup attached to one's belt would be handy for blood oaths.[19]

Strong bonds of sisterhood are emphasized in Greek myths and historical accounts of Amazons, who were perceived as Scythian women. Their devotion to one another on the battlefield is evident in many vase paintings showing Amazons carrying their fallen companions. Ancient women warriors were tattooed, wore trousers, wielded "manly weapons," and went to war like men. Did ancient women warriors also participate in blood oath rituals? It is worth contemplating, in view of the new discovery of the tiny gold cup on the Scythian woman's belt.

BATTLE-AXES

Hoards of large, broad single-blade bronze axe heads have been unearthed in archaeological sites (ca. 1250–650 BC) of ancient Colchis (Georgia). These were once called "Amazon axes" by scholars, but by the seventh century BC these heavy axes were replaced by smaller bronze axes much like those carried by Amazons shown in Greek vase paintings.[20]

In a legend preserved by Plutarch, when Heracles took Hippolyte's golden belt, he also carried away her battle-axe, which he presented to another powerful mythical queen, Omphale of Lydia. (To atone for a murder, Heracles served as Omphale's sex slave for a year, but that's another story.) Queen Hippolyte's axe, says Plutarch, was handed down from Omphale to the kings of Lydia. That is, until King Candaules (d. 718 BC) disrespected the Amazon's axe and carelessly gave it away. Hippolyte's precious axe ultimately ended up in the Temple of Zeus at Labranda in Caria. The original axe shape was not specified in the tale, but by the time it was placed in Zeus's temple it was described as a solid gold *labrys*, the symmetrical double-headed ritual axe traditionally associated with Zeus and Minoan goddesses (see fig. 6.4 for an example in the hands of a Thracian woman). The *labrys* has been adopted as a symbol by modern "matriarchy-goddess" feminists and lesbians who admire Amazons. Ironically, however, the *labrys* does not resemble a *sagaris*, a differently shaped pointed battle-axe more typically carried by Amazons and Scythians in ancient art and literature and found buried with armed women in Scythian kurgans.[21]

The *sagaris* (a Scythian word) was a small but lethal iron or bronze battle-axe, asymmetrical, usually with a rounded cutting blade or a blunt butt on one end and an ice pick–like point on the other end. Sharp and top-heavy on a long wooden handle, the battle-axe did not require great forearm strength to inflict serious injury. Once the weapon is swung or even thrown, the weight of the axe head does the rest.

Long before Heracles left his bow to Scythes, Scythian lore claimed that a golden cup and a golden *sagaris* were among the objects that magically fell from the sky and were taken up by the first Scythians. This tale comes from Herodotus, who noted that the Massagetae and the Pointed Hat Saka also used pointed battle-axes of bronze and gold. Strabo described the weapons of the Amazons as the bow, javelin, and *sagaris*. That the Greeks strongly associated the *sagaris* with Amazons is evident in Xenophon's firsthand description of a Persian captive's "bow and quiver and *sagaris* of the same sort that Amazons carry."[22]

Archaeological evidence confirms that pointed axes similar to those depicted in ancient art were used by Scythian female and male warriors who were contemporaries of the ancient Greeks. Many bronze pointed axe heads, some with butts in the form of boars, griffins, and other animals, have been recovered from Scythian burials (figs. 4.2, 13.4). Several pointed axes were found in Arzhan Kurgan, including a slim iron *sagaris* covered with intricate swirls of inlaid gold next to the couple in Arzahn 2. Pointed axes were also recovered from fifth-century BC Pazyryk burials in the Altai in 2006–7; and a *sagaris* was buried with one of the young women warriors at Tillya Tepe (chapter 4).[23]

Graphic physical evidence testifies to this weapon's dire effect. Analysis of the punctured skulls of the sacrificed horses in Pazyryk kurgans *and* the traumatic head injuries in a number of Scythian warriors' skulls shows that they were struck down with pointed battle-axes. "The occurrence of pointed axe injuries" suggests "the widespread use of the pointed battle-axe amongst the tribes of the Scythian World," notes bioarchaeologist Eileen Murphy. In the oldest known "Amazon" burial (Semo Awtschala, near Tbilisi, Georgia, ca. 1000 BC; fig. 4.1), for example, the skull of the warrior woman with her sword on her knees and lance at her feet had been pierced by a pointed axe. Twelve Scythian warriors (Tuva, southern Siberia) have holes in their skulls consistent with pointed axes (see fig. 4.3). One was a woman between the ages of twenty-five and thirty-five; the position of her wound (left parietal, as with several of the males) indicates that she was "directly facing [her] opponent during an episode of violence," probably combat.[24]

The first appearance of Amazons carrying battle-axes in vase paintings occurred in the mid-sixth century BC, in works by the Painter of Munich. Along with the bow, the *sagaris* became a classic Amazon weapon (plate 12, figs. 8.1, 11.4, 13.8, 15.1, 16.2). Many red-figure vase paintings depict Amazons poised to whack Greek warriors with the pointed ends of their battle-axes, like those found in armed women's graves. An example is a vase by Euphronios (ca. 510 BC) showing an Amazon in a woven, striped jumpsuit and Scythian cap with a decorated quiver, holding a small recurve bow and a pointed battle-axe. Another vase (ca. 450 BC, by Polygnotus) shows Achilles dueling with Queen Penthesilea. Clad in striped trousers, belted tunic, and soft cap, Penthesilea has dropped her bow for intense hand-to-hand combat and is swinging her pointed battle-axe with both hands. A woman's perfume vase (fig. 8.2) features Penthesilea carrying a Scythian bow, two arrows, and her trusty pointed battle-axe.[25]

Who invented this quintessential weapon wielded by Scythian male and female warriors with devastating skill? The European compiler of a sixteenth-century compendium of the history of weapons was astounded to learn from an earlier medieval treatise that such a "manly weapon" as the pointed battle-axe "was invented by a tribe of women." What was the source of this idea that Amazons invented the *sagaris*? It must have come from Pliny the Elder (first century AD), who listed the mythic and historical inventors of various technologies, gathered from even older texts. Pliny names the legendary inventor of the pointed battle-axe: it was none other than Queen Penthesilea.[26]

SWORDS, DAGGERS, KNIVES, SPEARS

Amazon weapons maximize the wielder's strengths and compensate for weakness or smaller size. Like bows, lightweight spears have the advantage of long-range lethality. Many Amazons on foot and on horses in vase paintings are equipped with two light spears (for thrusting) or javelins (for hurling, see figs. 13.3 and 16.3). Amazons are often depicted in the act of spearing Greek warriors (figs. 11.3, 13.6, 18.1). An unusual spear with a sickle attached appears in a vase painting of the early fifth century BC; such sickles were used by Phrygians, Carians, and Lydians. Many Amazons in Greek art wear swords in scabbards, and others are shown wielding swords, often with both hands. Powerful leg muscles and agile hands maximize the use of small and medium-size swords, while large swords require more arm strength. Spears and swords of iron and bronze are represented in real warrior women's grave goods; some weapons at Pokrova had smaller handles suited to women's hands (chapter 4).[27]

Hoards of large bronze swords (more than two feet long) engraved with geometric designs (Kakheti type, Bronze Age, ca. 1250 BC, same time period as the so-called Amazon axes, above) have come to light in eastern Georgia (fig. 13.4). In antiquity this region of ancient Colchis was strongly associated with women warriors. Strabo located several tribes of Amazons here, and this is where Pompey's Roman army fought (and captured) women identified as Amazons in the first century BC (chapter 21). Local Georgian folklore claimed that these hoards of ancient swords must have belonged to Amazons. Indeed, it was a bronze sword of this type that lay in the lap of the warrior woman of ancient Colchis whose skull had a pointed axe wound (above, fig. 4.1).[28]

In addition to swords, archaeological excavations have unearthed many different types of bronze and iron spear and javelin points, swords, and considerable numbers of knives and daggers, with handles decorated with animals and geometric designs. Two very large iron lance points (about twenty inches long) accompanied the warrior woman buried with her knives and forty-seven bronze arrowheads on the bank of the Tyasmin River; two lances and two spears were interred with the woman in the kurgan at Tyras. Chapter 4 gives examples of the array of blades and spear/lance/javelin points in women's burials across Scythia and discusses skeletons, some of them female, that display evidence of battle injuries inflicted by swords and daggers. One striking example discovered in 2006–7 in the Altai is a young woman whose ribs were slashed by a double-edged weapon more than two thousand years ago (fig. 4.3; see also fig. 25.2).[29]

The congruence between artistic images of Amazons' weapons and those actual weapons excavated from armed women's graves, along with the skeletal evidence of combat wounds, demonstrates that by the late sixth century BC Greek artists and their customers were very familiar with the typical weapons used by genuine women warriors: archery sets, pointed battle-axes, swords, and spears. How true to life were the ancient artistic depictions of Amazons actually wielding their weapons in battle? Two fascinating examples of artistic acuity survive in a pair of quirky fifth-century BC vase paintings. Each artist chose to portray an Amazon using an unusual weapon, not yet discussed here. The two images are surprising and unparalleled in Greek art. Yet each weapon is well documented in the ancient literary sources and artistic/archaeological evidence.

SLINGS AND LASSOS

On the first vase (plate 10), an Amazon wearing high boots, a short dress, and a broad belt with a wide shoulder strap has thrust her two spears into the ground and set down her bow. We see her placing a pebble in the leather pouch of her sling, which would have been braided hemp or wool. This robust, graceful Amazon slinger appears on an oil flask made in about 440 BC. It is one of several engaging images of women in action

attributed to the artist once known as the Amazon Painter (now sadly rebranded as the Klügmann Painter). This painter was obviously familiar with proper slinging form and technique. The Amazon's weight is on her right leg, which will shift upon release of the pebble. The painter

FIG. 13.4. Facing page: three bronze swords from "Amazon" hoard, ancient Caucasian Iberia, ca. 1150–850 BC, Melaani (Kakheti) shrine complex 1, eastern Georgia. Above: bronze axe head with animal figure, from ancient Colchis, ca. 580 BC, Ozhora cemetery, Georgia. Photos courtesy of Nino Kalandadze, Georgian National Museum.

has caught her just as she begins to tense the sling's cords before the spin, aim, and release of the stone.[30]

Homer, Xenophon, Thucydides, and Strabo mention slingers, and Pliny described the deadly aim of Scythian slingers (chapter 2). Male slingers appear on Greek vases and on coins but this is the only known ancient representation of a female slinger. Like Scythian archers and Thracian peltasts who hurled javelins, slingers were elusive, highly mobile skirmishers who harassed the enemy from afar. Sling bullets of clay and lead have been recovered from many archaeological sites. Notably, piles of sling pebbles have been discovered in the arsenals of several women warriors in Scythian graves; for example, the well-armed Amazon from the Tyasmin River had five "pebble missiles" (above and chapter 4).

The other unique scene is on the lid of a pyxis (women's cosmetic box) attributed to the Sotheby Painter, about 460 BC. The delicately painted frieze shows two Amazons attacking two Greek warriors. One fighting pair is poorly preserved: a Greek hoplite is about to heave a rock at an Amazon with a spear. The other Amazon is mounted on a galloping horse, looking back over her shoulder at the lasso she is swinging (fig. 13.5). Her target is in front of her, a Greek hoplite crouching under his shield with his spear. The rest of her rope, painted purple like her shoes, is coiled around her waist, and she correctly holds the lariat's loop near the knot. Her technique is accurate for roping something straight ahead. If she intends to lasso her victim instead of snaring him by dropping the noose over his head as she rides past, she will need to "build" her loop by twirling and letting out more rope. When she is ready to throw the lasso, she will need to turn to look directly at her target (experienced ropers do not usually look back at their lariat). She has her battle-axe ready to dispatch her victim.[31]

The subject suggests that the painter and his audience were familiar with oral and written descriptions of horse nomads who used lariats. Herodotus, for example, reported that a force of eight thousand Persian-speaking mounted nomads called Sagartians joined Darius's army in 480 BC. Armed with only daggers and lassos, they cast their looped ropes of braided leather at enemy horses and riders, then dragged them in, easily "killing the victim entangled in the coils of the noose." The Sarmatians, who traced their origins to Amazons and Scythians, were also said to throw ropes around their enemies and then wheel their horses around to entangle the victim. Pomponius Mela reported that Maeotian horsewomen around the Sea of Azov used lassos. Arrian told of Libyan nomads lassoing wild asses running at full speed. (The tech-

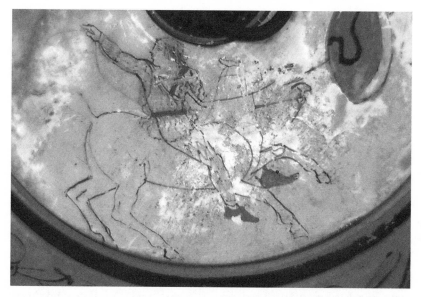

FIG. 13.5. Mounted Amazon about to lasso a Greek warrior (out of sight, cowering behind his shield on the right). Attic red-figure, white-ground pyxis (cosmetic box), Sotheby Painter, ca. 460 BC. University of Mississippi Museum and Historic Houses, David M. Robinson Memorial Collection 1977.003.0243.

nique for roping a moving target is different from roping a stationary one; modern ropers secure the lasso to the saddle to absorb the shock when a running victim is brought up short.) Other ancient Greek and Latin authors describe lasso use in battle by several Scythian tribes around the Don River: Alans, Goths, and Parthians, among others. A Scythian roper is shown on a silver vase from a fourth-century BC burial in Ukraine. Lariats are standard gear of ancient mounted warriors in the Persian epic poem *Shahnama* (chapter 23).[32]

The animated scene on the pyxis is not only unique for showing an Amazon twirling a lasso; it is also a reversal of expected outcomes. The two Amazons clearly have the upper hand over the weaker Greek warriors, the one cowering under his shield hoping to impale the Amazon's horse on his spear and the other warrior compelled to defend himself with a rock against the Amazon's spear.[33] The suspenseful scene raises intriguing questions about the attitudes of the painter and the woman who possessed this vase.

FIGHTING TECHNIQUES

Scythians were known as fearsome fighters on foot and on horses, crack archers who aimed long-distance arrows with awesome accuracy or let fly a rain of deadly arrows, even while fleeing. The mounted nomads did not use Greek battle formations but attacked from positions of strength, lured foes to chase them, and sped away when outnumbered. As classical writers often remarked, Scythian fighting women could be as skilled as the men in the same arts of war. Greek artists not only showed Amazons shooting Scythian bows but pictured them carrying out difficult archery feats (stringing recurve bows, speed shooting, Parthian shots, and flight archery) and using a full arsenal of weapons: bows, axes, spears, swords, even slings and lassos.

Many Greek vase paintings show Amazons arming and fighting in hand-to-hand duels and tumultuous mêlées involving pairs, trios, or large bands of women pitted against Greek male hoplites. Did Amazons ever fight other Amazons? Some scenes on Greek vases appear to depict Amazons attacking Amazons. The continual raiding, plunder, and warfare among tribes meant that it was likely that real women warriors came into conflict. The only case of face-to-face combat between two historical women warriors was reported by the military historian Polyaenus. In the fourth century BC, the Illyrian half sister of Alexander the Great, Cynna, personally led an army against an Illyrian force and killed their queen, Caeria, in a duel (chapter 4). The only literary examples of Amazon-on-Amazon violence are Penthesilea and Molpadia, who were said to have killed sisters in hunting accidents, and Antiope, who fought the Amazons who attacked Athens (some say Molpadia killed Antiope then).[34]

Artists usually depicted the heroes Heracles, Theseus, and Achilles overpowering and killing Amazons. There are a lot of fallen, bleeding, dying, and dead Amazons in Greek art. Yet more evenly balanced battle scenes with well-matched antagonists also occur in which Amazons—the equals of men—are shown threatening, wounding, or slaying Greek warriors.[35]

Whether the women are wining or losing, realistic action and gory details characterize Amazonomachy scenes. A complex scene on a fragmentary vase (Syleus Painter, 480–470 BC) is a good example. It shows

Greeks winning two battles and Amazons winning the other two. In one scene, Andromache wears a scale-patterned cuirass with star-embossed shoulder flaps, and a scabbard hangs from her chest strap. Heracles grabs her throat and raises his sword to strike the death blow. She has lost her helmet and holds up her sword, but she is losing her grip, her eyes roll up, and her mouth opens. Limp fingers, gasping mouth, and rolling eyes are common indications of vulnerability, defeat, and death in red-figure battle scenes. But the Syleus Painter added a unique touch to evoke the violent action of the duel: one of the epaulette flaps of Andromache's cuirass has come unfastened. This same detail recurs on her collapsing companion (Lykopis), who has just been speared in the chest. (Lykopis, "Wolf Eyes," also appears on the Oltos vase, above.) [36]

Another grim naturalistic element, unparalleled in black-figure vases, appears on a sixth-century BC cup showing an Amazon carrying a dead companion from the battlefield. Her skin is painted white, according to convention, but the flesh of her dead friend is painted a ghastly gray tone.[37]

An exceptional Amazonomachy on a large red-figure vase (Eretria Painter, ca. 420 BC) is crammed with lifelike, energetic details. Ten Amazons are pitted against eight Greeks. The painter illustrates a variety of Amazon costumes, weapons, and fighting stances, and many of the combatants' names are inscribed. Many of the metal weapons are picked out with gold paint. Two Amazon archers, Mimnousa and Charope, shoot Scythian bows. Eumache hefts a stone, while a wounded Amazon holding a *sagaris* clutches at a spear in her back. Klymene is unsheathing her sword, while her friend falls to her knees, stabbed in the chest by Theseus. Hippolyte thrusts her spear at a Greek raising his sword. Echephyle, armed with a wicker pelta and two spears, swings her sword overhead. Amynomene raises her pointed battle-axe with both hands, while Doris wields her spear with both hands (fig. 13.6). The stance—sword or axe lifted high overhead for a downward slashing strike—is called the "Harmodios blow." The Greek threatened by Hippolyte's spear takes the same stance. This position is very dangerous in most combat situations unless one is very sure of having the upper hand over a helpless victim (see plate 12, figs. 6.4, 13.8 for examples). The pose leaves the attacker's own body exposed while the victim's metal breast-plate, helmet, and shield, or even a padded linen corselet, could resist

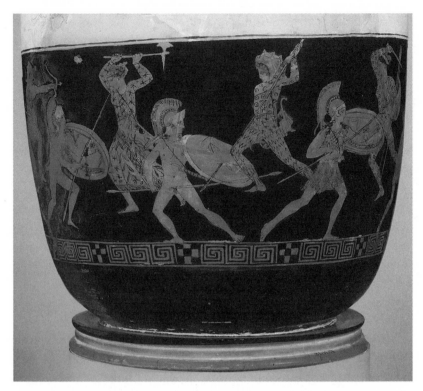

FIG 13.6. Amazonomachy. Greek, Attic lekythos (oil flask), Eretria Painter, ca. 420 BC. Metropolitan Museum, Rogers Fund, 1931, 31.11.13. Image © The Metropolitan Museum of Art/Art Resource, NY.

the blow. The move is usually a coup de grâce to finish off a fallen or vulnerable foe, but it could also be used in desperation to try to hack off the end of an opponent's spear. Perhaps that is the hope of the Greek facing Hippolyte and Echephyle.[38]

Did some vase painters depict Amazons as skillful fighters who used "feminine" or ninja-like combat techniques, as suggested by martial arts scholar N. Nemytov? He analyzed three of five duels on an Amazonomachy masterpiece painted by Aison (fifth century BC), which features several of the same named fighters as the Athenian battle scene above. In the first vignette, Antianeira ("Man's Match") steps back, turning her right side toward Theseus while raising her sword high behind her head—the classic Harmodios blow—thus exposing her torso to Theseus, who is ready to thrust his sword underhand (fig. 13.7). But

Nemytov suggests that Antianeira is only feigning desperate vulnerability, enticing Theseus into making a direct thrust, which she could deflect by suddenly shifting her center of gravity to her back leg and whirling 180 degrees, moving toward him and blocking his sword with the bow held in her left hand, bringing her chest against his right shoulder, and plunging her sword into his exposed belly. Meanwhile, Theseus seems unaware that the Amazon Laodoke is approaching him from behind, their limbs overlapping. As Antianeira can see, her companion seems about to block his sword arm and drive her spear into his leg.

In the second duel analyzed by Nemytov, the Amazon Kreousa is in a deep crouch under her shield, with her spear pointing away from the Greek warrior Phylakos, who is about to deliver the Harmodios blow, his torso completely vulnerable. He appears to have the superior position. But Nemytov suggests that Kreousa might not be so defenseless—she is coiled like a spring. What if she suddenly pushed up with her right leg, shifted her weight to the left leg, and swung her spear around to cut the vein of his exposed inner thigh or his abdomen before he could bring his shield around?

Behind Kreousa, a kneeling Amazon archer has just shot an arrow from her Scythian bow. If we walk around or turn the vase, her arrow appears to have wounded the weaponless and profusely bleeding Greek named Teithras, slumped on a rock with his shield (far right, fig. 13.7). Between them, a Greek lunges with his spear at another Amazon archer, Okyale, who aims a straight bow. Above this pair, the Amazon

FIG. 13.7. Amazonomachy. Red-figure vase (attributed to Aison), fifth century BC, drawing by A. Baumeister in *Denkmaler des klassischen altertums* (Munich, 1888) original in Naples, Museo Archaeologico Nazionale RC 239.

FIG. 13.8. A pair of Amazons overcoming two Greek warriors pinned against dead trees. Red-figure neck amphora with twisted handles, Suessula Painter, ca. 400 BC, Metropolitan Museum of Art, Fletcher Fund, 1944, Amazon attacking with battle-axe, side A, 44.11.12, image © The Metropolitan Museum of Art/Art Resource, NY; Amazon attacking with sword, side B, 44.11.13, photo by Marie-Lan Nguyen, 2011.

spearwoman Aristomache is on higher ground, battling the Greek hoplite Mounichos below; she wraps a leopard skin around her left arm as a makeshift shield.

In the third duel discussed by Nemytov, the Amazon Klymene appears to be in a very weak sitting pose, slipping downhill with her back to Phaleros, who is about to attack from above (center, fig. 13.7). She is shielding her upper body from his impending overhead spear thrust. Yet her body might also be in a springing position. Could she suddenly stand up on her outstretched leg, and turn to press her shield against his upper body, using his forward momentum to push him to the left while spearing his torso or thigh?

Theseus is involved in this scene, and we know that the mythic Greek hero will be victorious over the Amazons, yet, as Nemytov points out, there is a great deal of delicious suspense in each single combat.

Nemytov concludes that the vase painter cleverly has it both ways. He can appear to show the Greek warriors triumphant, but at the same time he has created "excellent snapshots" of the exciting action. To the eye of an experienced combat veteran, these freeze-frame moments contain the potential for split-second reversals, which could allow each Amazon to seize victory, if only in the viewer's imagination.[39]

Analysis of typical attack and defensive postures in vase paintings and sculpture involving swords, battle-axes, and spears leads some scholars to propose that the artists and their models (and viewers) were familiar with standard combat stances and typical movements. Many battle scenes were "presumably intended to convey continuous action," producing a stop-action effect that captures tiny shifts of balance and anticipates the combatants' next body positions to evoke the give-and-take of the fight. The viewer can appreciate this effect in the scenes of the Amazon roper and slinger, above.[40]

The fates of two Greek hoplites hang in the balance on a pair of red-figure vases with natural details by the Suessula Painter (ca. 400 BC; fig. 13.8). In one scene, we see a Greek hoplite pinned against a dead tree trunk (indicating barren steppes or desert). He is beset by two rampaging Amazons. The Amazon on the left raises her sword above her head, and his assailant on the right raises her pointed battle-axe with both hands. Both Amazons, in wildly patterned leggings and whirling dresses, are caught in motion, just as they are leaping up in the air to give extra force to their downward blows. The trapped Greek holds up his sword and shield as he tries to escape to the left, desperately turning his head to the right. The companion vase shows another doomed Greek warrior, viewed from the back. He is under his shield crawling around the trunk of another dead tree, as the Amazon prepares to deliver the fatal Harmodios blow.[41]

Many artists obviously relished adding exquisite small details to enhance the naturalism of their Amazon battle scenes. Another way of bestowing authenticity was to inscribe the names of the individual Amazons on the vases. The sheer number of Amazons' personal names that survive from ancient literature and art is astonishing.

14

AMAZON LANGUAGES AND NAMES

IN THE REALM OF MYTH, OF COURSE, GREEK HEROES, Olympian gods and goddesses, Trojans, Persians, and Amazons all communicated with magical ease. For example, in the myth of Heracles's Ninth Labor, winning the belt of Hippolyte, Heracles and the Amazon queen converse with no difficulty—until violence breaks out. But, since classical Greeks also wrote about Amazons as real people of Scythia, dwelling in the lands around the Black Sea, Caucasus, and beyond, what languages did they believe Amazons spoke?

Many other linguistic questions swirl around the mythic and historical Amazons. What languages were actually spoken by the peoples of the Black Sea and steppes? What might the personal names of Amazons and Amazon-like warrior women reveal? Did the Greeks suppose that Amazons could read and write? The extensive literary, artistic, and archaeological evidence from ancient Greece demonstrates what a rich imaginary realm was created for Amazons. Embedded in that evidence are strong hints that the ethnonym "Amazon" was originally a name the archaic Greeks used to designate little-known steppe peoples (chapter 1). Moreover, some individual names of Amazons inscribed on Greek vases and preserved in non-Greek sources reflect the languages of Amazons' real-life counterparts, the women of nomadic cultures in western Asia.

Greeks applied the label "barbarian" to anyone who did not speak Greek. When Greeks began exploring and colonizing the Black Sea coast in the eighth and seventh centuries BC, their contact with exotic "barbarians" resulted in exchanges of goods, folklore, and languages. Foreign words and names—such as *Amazon*—and stories about faraway lands entered Greek parlance through traders, colonists, sailors, mercenaries, allies, and travelers. Foreigners came to live and work in Athens as slaves, soldiers, merchants, and artisans. Scythian characters began to appear in Greek plays, and their languages were heard in households and marketplaces. Some names from the Black Sea region are preserved in Greek mythology, such as the sorceress Medea of Colchis (modern Georgia; her name is Iranian) and Medea's brother Apsyrtos (whose name is Abkhazian).[1]

Herodotus visited the Black Sea–Azov region in the mid-fifth century BC and preserved several authentic words from Scythian groups. Some have ancient Iranian roots and others derive from Caucasian languages. For example, Herodotus reported the folk etymology "man-killer" for the Scythian word for "Amazons," *Oiorpata*. Linguists suggest that it probably meant something like "ruler/preeminent warrior" (presumably the top "man-killer") in an Iranian language. Other Scythian words of Iranian (Indo-European) origin recorded by Herodotus include *sagaris* ("pointed battle-axe"), *akinakes* ("dagger"), *Massagetai* ("great clan"), *Arimaspi* ("owners of horses"), *Sarmatia* (Ossetian, "free people"), and *Issedones* ("people of the icy river"). A number of words preserved by Herodotus and other classical writers derive from Caucasian languages, which, unlike Iranian and Greek (and English), are mostly non-Indo-European. Examples are *Colchis* (Circassian, "mountains"), *Gargaria* (Georgian, "apricot"), *Maeotis* (Circassian, "lake not dammed up," for the Kerch Strait/Azov Sea), and *aschu* ("wild cherry juice").[2] These Iranian and Caucasian vocabulary words came from the languages spoken by the indigenous nomadic and seminomadic men and women of Scythia encountered by those Greeks who ventured north and east of the Aegean.

WHAT LANGUAGES DID AMAZONS SPEAK?

Modern classicists and historians tend to assume that all "Scythians" (and therefore the women known as Amazons) spoke a single North Iranian language. This is true of some but not all peoples of the immense territory known to the Greeks as "Scythia." In his ethnographic descriptions Herodotus commented knowledgeably about the many different languages spoken from the Black Sea to the Altai Mountains, a region of incredible linguistic diversity. He famously remarked that some information about the far eastern reaches of Scythia had been transmitted by a chain of translators. Herodotus also stated that some Scythians from the northern Black Sea area taught their language to Iranian-speaking Persians and Medes. Eurasia, especially the Caucasus region, was (and still is) a cauldron of a great many linguistic families. Some of the tribes within the Scythian cultural zone of the Black Sea–Caucasus area spoke Iranian-influenced languages, but others would have spoken non-Indo-European Caucasian languages, such as Circassian, Georgian, Abkhazian, and Ubykh. Some nomadic groups in Central and Inner Asia also spoke non-Iranian tongues.[3]

A fascinating linguistic discovery of 2011 in Pontus, one of the traditional Amazon homelands, suggests that people in that region may not have spoken a "pure" form of any single language. Real women warriors in this rugged landscape in antiquity might have spoken ancient Pontic or South Caucasian Laz, but another possibility is a recently rediscovered dialect known as Romeyka. This unique, nearly extinct dialect is being studied by Ioanna Sitaridou, a philologist at Cambridge University. Today only a few thousand people, living in a cluster of isolated villages clinging to the mountains above the Black Sea, speak Romeyka (it has no written form). Preserved chiefly by elderly but robust blue-eyed, fair-haired women who still remain in the remote villages, Romeyka has some remarkable grammatical and vocabulary similarities to ancient Greek as it was spoken in classical times. The villagers, who play lyres like those depicted in ancient Greek vase paintings, are believed to be the direct descendants of ancient Greek speakers in Pontus. The Greeks from Miletus who first colonized Trabzon in 756 BC intermarried with indigenous people of Pontus, who learned the language of the colonizers. Sitaridou and her colleagues are recording the speech of the women to learn how language structures change and persist over generations. Spoken over millennia, the mixed Greek/non-Greek hybrid dialect used by the old women of Pontus might shed light on linguistic questions about ancient Amazons of Greek mytho-history.[4]

Herodotus mentions hybrid languages spoken by peoples of the steppes and Caucasus. The Budini, a large nomadic group in what is now

Ukraine, for example, spoke an Iranian dialect, but within their territory was a city with wooden walls and temples to Greek gods. It had been established "long ago" by Greeks who left the coastal colonies on the Black Sea and settled among the Budini. Called the Geloni, this mixed group spoke a language that Herodotus called "half Greek, half Scythian."[5]

Amazons had a facility with languages, according to Herodotus in his account of the women of Pontus who intermarried with the Scythians of the Don River to become the Sarmatians (chapter 3). The women took the lead in conversing with gestures and body language with the strangers, and Herodotus makes the point that the men were "incapable" of learning the Amazons' tongue, while the women "easily picked up" the men's. The women's hybrid form of the men's language predominated in the new tribe. The result, noted Herodotus, was a Sarmatian "dialect distinct from pure Scythian," analogous to the process that created Romeyka and the hybrid language of the Geloni.

The two Oxford classical scholars who wrote the authoritative commentary on Herodotus in 1912 scoffed at Herodotus's "delightful" details. The Amazons' grasp of the unfamiliar language, the classicists asserted, was "inaccurate—as lady linguists often are." The scholars' gratuitous remark was intended to denigrate the Amazons for their "impure" version of Scythian while at the same time insulting linguists of their day who happened to be female. Herodotus, who had a strong interest in languages, was showing off his knowledge of Scythian tribes and their various dialects. But Herodotus's linguistic insights were quite perceptive. His details anticipate, by more than twenty-five hundred years, modern knowledge about how language structures evolve. Moreover, the women's initiative and success in communicating with the men is supported by scientific studies demonstrating that, compared to men, women do initiate communication and enjoy relative advantages in language acquisition and verbal abilities.[6]

PERSONAL NAMES OF AMAZONS

Did some of the names of individual Amazons who populated Greek mythology and Greco-Roman historical accounts originate from Caucasian and other languages of the steppes? In view of the non-Greek origin of the name *Amazon* and the wealth of vocabulary words and proper names from Iranian, Caucasian, and other languages preserved in Greek literature, interesting questions arise about the personal names of women warriors.

A remarkable number of personal names of Amazons are preserved in Greco-Roman literature and art. The plethora of Amazon names evidences their immense popularity and hints that a great many lively stories about individual warrior women have not survived. Besides signing their pots, vase painters often included names and phrases, in the manner of a comic strip, to identify people or actions. More than thirteen hundred Greek vases depicting Amazons are stored in museum collections around the world; about seventy figures identifiable as Amazons are accompanied by inscriptions. A few of those names, such as Hippolyte, Antiope, and Penthesilea, are very well known from myths, poems, plays, and other written works. But the majority of the Amazon names inscribed on the vases are unique and a few are non-Greek. (We will return to these below.)[7] Because we possess only a small fraction of the art and literature that existed in antiquity, many mythic scenes in ancient artworks are puzzling to us today. Countless alternative versions of familiar stories once circulated orally but are lost to us because they did not survive in writing. Since vase paintings of people and events usually illustrated well-known characters and incidents, we can guess that the adventures of some of the Amazons labeled with unknown names were recognized by people in classical antiquity. Other names may have been spontaneously made up by artists to match typical warrior women names from well-known traditions.[8]

Most of the names assigned to Amazons are Greek. A great many contain the root *hipp* (horse), reflecting the women's love of riding and equestrian skills, and pointing to the centrality of horses among Scythian peoples. It is likely that some Amazon and warrior women names given in Greek sources were translations of barbarian names. Naming customs are conservative. In steppe nomad epics, names were traditionally bestowed when one became old enough to own a horse. Warriors' names often alluded to a special horse, such as "X of the Yellow Piebald" or "Yellow Piebald."[9] Some examples of horse-related Amazon names are Melanippe (Black Horse), Alkippe (Powerful Horse), Hippomache (Horse Warrior), Ainippe (Swift Horse), Hippothoe (Mighty Mare), Hippolyte (Releases the Horses), Lysippe (Lets Loose the Horses),

Xanthippe (Palomino), Philippis (Loves Horses), and Hipponike (Victory Steed).

Amazons were archers par excellence and a great number of their names refer to archery: Toxis (Arrow), Toxaris (Archer), Toxoanassa (Archer Queen), Toxophone (Whizzing Arrow), Toxophile (Loves Arrows), Iodoke (Holding Arrows), Ioxeia (Delighting in Arrows), Oistrophe (Twisting Arrow), and Pharetre (Quiver Girl). Many Amazon names describe warlike attributes, such as Aella (Whirlwind), Charope (Fierce Gaze), Andromache (Manly Fighter), Polemusa (War Woman), and Aristomache (Best Warrior), while others call out weapons or armor, such as Chalkaor (Bronze Sword) and Thoreke (Breastplate).

Some Amazon names suggest character or virtues: Thraso (Confident), Areto (Virtue), Pisto (Trustworthy). A few were feminine versions of masculine names, such as Glauke and Alexandre; others were conventional Greek women's names that seemed appropriate for Amazons because of their connotations, such as Deianeira (Man Destroyer). Other names allude to towns or tribes associated with warrior women, such as Pitana and Asbyte (chapter 23). Significantly, a number of Amazon names allude to equality with men, such as Antianeira (Man's Match), Antibrote (Equal of Man), and Isocrateia (Equal Power). These bring to mind the meaning of Atalanta's name, "Equal Balance," and the earliest Greek connotation of *Amazones* as a barbarian tribe of "equals" (chapter 1).

Some non-Greek names of warrior women from steppe tribes were recorded in Greek literature and art. For example, the name of the historical warrior queen who attacked Greek colonies in the northern Black Sea region, Tirgatao, means "Arrow Power" in ancient Iranian (see chapter 22). Her name is in harmony with all of the archery-related Amazon names in Greek, above. The name of Sparethra, the Saka warrior woman who battled the Persians, means "Heroic Army" (her story is told in chapter 23). Many more names of historical and legendary Amazon-like women can be gleaned from epics, chronicles, and accounts in Caucasian, Egyptian, Central Asian, and Chinese sources, raising the number of warrior women names that survive from antiquity to more than two hundred (see appendix). For example, the Turkic name of a daredevil warrior woman of Central Asian legend, Harman Dali, means "Crazy-Brave," yet another perfect name for an Amazon.

RECOVERING AMAZON NAMES IN FOREIGN LANGUAGES
FROM "NONSENSE" INSCRIPTIONS

Since the word *Amazones* is not Greek, and Amazons were understood to be barbarian women from western Asia, it should not be surprising that some Amazon names in Greek art and literature were given in their original language, like Tirgatao ("Arrow Power," above). It is plausible that some Amazon names were translated into Greek from Saka-Scythian, Iranian, Caucasian, or any of the more than two dozen languages of Eurasia. There are many examples of barbarian names in Greek art and literature that reflect their original, foreign language.[10]

Taking this approach a step further, what can we say about the curious "nonsense" words that accompany the images of warriors in Amazon and Scythian-style attire on a number of Greek vases? Scholars usually interpret these so-called meaningless inscriptions, with peculiar clusters of hard-to-pronounce consonants, as gibberish scribbled by illiterate vase painters or jokes intended to mock the speech of non-Greek-speaking barbarians. But an alternative possibility occurred to me in 2010 when I examined the fragmentary sixth-century BC vase in the Getty Museum collection with unknown words inscribed above the heads of a pair of Amazons. The Amazons are shown setting out on foot, carrying quivers, swords, and spears. Trotting along beside them is a dog with a red collar. The first Amazon turns to her friend—they appear to be engaged in conversation. The apparently random letters could simply be a way of indicating the incomprehensible, silly-sounding language of barbarians. But, I wondered, instead of parody, might the strange words be the vase painter's serious attempt to indicate dialogue or names in an exotic tongue, transliterated into Greek letters? Could these letters and some of the other "nonsense" labels associated with figures of Amazons and Scythians spell out the sounds (phonemes) of genuine foreign languages from the Black Sea–Caucasus region using the Greek alphabet? Would a historical linguist of those languages be able to decipher the meanings from the phonemes? According to classicist Josine Blok, "original, non-Greek names . . . were apparently not transmitted" for Amazons on vases.[11] But in fact some were.

It turns out that in a significant sample of "nonsense" inscriptions associated with Amazons and Scythians on vases, the unfamiliar strings of letters are not so meaningless after all. I enlisted a vase expert and a linguist to investigate whether the phonemes of apparently meaningless inscriptions next to figures of Amazons and Scythians represent or capture the sounds of words, phrases, and names in ancient forms of Indo-Iranian, Circassian, Abkhazian, and other language families of the steppes and Caucasus region—tongues spoken by ethnic groups whose women joined men in hunting and battle in antiquity. According to historical linguists, the phonology (pronunciation) of isolated Caucasian languages, such as Circassian, has changed very little over more than two millennia. Non-Indo-European Caucasian languages have extraordinarily complex chains of "harsh" consonants and only one or two vowels. A nonspeaker trying to render the sounds with Greek letters would produce bizarre-looking letter strings, like those classified as "nonsense" by modern vase experts.[12]

What appeared to be incomprehensible or non-Greek words on thirteen vases are actually suitable names for male and female Scythian warriors *in their own languages*, translated for the first time after more than twenty-five hundred years. Examples of newly discovered Amazon names in ancient forms of Circassian deciphered on sixth-century BC Greek vases include *Pkpupes*, "Worthy of Armor"; *Kheuke*, "One of the Heroes/Heroines"; *Serague*, "Wearing/Armed with a Dagger/Sword"; *Kepes*, "Hot Flanks/Eager Sex"; and *Khasa*, "One Who Heads a Council." *Barkida*, "Princess," appears to derive from an eastern Iranian or Indo-Aryan loanword in Circassian. *Gugamis*, the name of an Amazon on a fifth-century BC vase found in Susa, ancient Persia, means "Iron" in Circassian with the Iranian suffix *-mis*. Her companion, labeled *Oigme*, is a nickname meaning "Don't Fail!" in Ubykh. The letter strings associated with the two Amazons setting out with their dog, above, appear to be archaic forms of Abkhazian meaning "We are helping each other" and "Set the dog loose" (as in siccing a dog).[13]

The unexpected discovery of meaningful, appropriate names (and words and phrases) in Caucasian and Iranian languages accompanying Amazon and Scythian warriors on Athenian vase paintings is startling and raises many questions for further study. How did vase painters in Greece come to paint these foreign names on their pots? One can imagine several possibilities. First, not all vase painters were Greek—some of their signatures hint at foreign origins. Second, the painters only had to hear the names to spell them out phonetically—they need not have understood their foreign meanings. Third, vase painters usually illustrated familiar stories. Accordingly, the foreign-named Amazons who are known only from their labeled portraits on vases may once have starred in popular oral traditions like those that coalesced around Antiope and Hippolyte. Vase painters may have asked resident or visiting foreigners to pronounce the names of Amazons depicted on their pots. Finally, Thracians and Scythians were present in Athens from an early date. Storytellers among them could have recounted the exploits of Amazons with non-Greek names. Household slaves in Athens were commonly from Thrace and the Black Sea region; perhaps they regaled Greek children with tales of celebrated women warriors from their homelands.

The preliminary linguistic study of just thirteen vases with non-Greek inscriptions for Amazons and Scythians resulted in the translation of about dozen names of Scythian and Amazon warriors from "nonsense" letters, names that have been obscure for more than two millennia. The recovery of this set of names in ancient Scythian languages offers further compelling evidence that the ancient Greeks understood Amazons as real fighting women from the lands around and beyond the Black Sea.

READING AND WRITING

In the second century AD, Pausanias viewed several ancient inscribed monuments in Greece that were related to the great mythic war against the invading Amazons (Battle for Athens; chapter 17), but those inscriptions were engraved by the Greeks.[14] No inscriptions attributed to Amazons or to historical women warriors of the steppes were reported by ancient writers or known to modern archaeologists.

The Scythians left no written literature. If real Amazons within tribes of the steppes or Caucasus ever left inscriptions on wood, clay, or stone, the markings would most likely have been *tamgas*, or runes, symbolic seals used to mark property. Each tribe or clan of Eurasian nomads was identified by a particular tamga emblem and their particular *uran*, battle cry. Tamgas are found on ancient petroglyphs, textiles, artifacts, and coins, and the old symbols are still used to brand livestock among pastoralists on the steppes. If warrior women known as Amazons branded their horses, it would have been with tamgas (chapter 11).

Tamgas are inscribed on nearly 1,000 ancient stone monoliths, called "deer stones," scattered over the eastern Scythian steppes. The flat stones, 3 to 15 feet high, are 2,500–3,000 years old and associated with the kurgans of Siberia, Altai, Mongolia, and Inner Asia. The granite megaliths are commonly inscribed with Scythian-style "flying" deer with fantastic antlers similar to the tattoos of the frozen Pazyryk mummies. The chevrons, dots, circles, and cross-hatching patterns call to mind the patterned attire of Amazons and the tattoos of Thracian women on Greek vase paintings. Other motifs carved on the stones include daggers, axes, bows, arrows, horses, tigers, birds, and human faces. The stones' purpose is a mystery. They do not appear to mark human burials and usually occur in groups. Were they territorial markers? Were they religious-shamanistic sites? Did they commemorate significant events or people? The images on the stones do not represent spoken language, but they were certainly signs intended to convey meaningful information to observers within the same culture zone. In this way, tamgas and deer stones resemble Scythian tattoos.[15]

Extraordinary archaeological evidence of Scythian men and women frozen in permafrost has emerged in the Altai region. Many of the naturally mummified human remains, preserved for more than two thousand years, still bear detailed tattoos of animals. As archaeologist Svetlana Pankova observed in 2012, the Scythian peoples did not leave written texts, but one might consider their heavily tattooed bodies as a kind of "writing" that conveyed significant information with individual, tribal, and cultural relevance. Like the similar motifs carved on the deer-stone megaliths, the vivid tattoos of tigers, deer, birds, and fantastic creatures, twisting, pouncing, fighting, and dying, created an "animated" panorama on human skin, with the figures appearing to breathe and jump into motion as one flexed muscles and moved. Beyond their obvious decorative power, Pankova suggests that the lively images on the skin were ways of narrating stories. Like the carved deer-stone monoliths, the tattoos functioned as "texts" passing along individual tales and cultural knowledge within each tribe and among related nomadic groups.[16]

FIG. 14.1. Deer stones, inscriptions, and tamgas on the northern steppes. Collage by Michele Angel.

Another extraordinary discovery in ancient Scythia holds a hint of writing by nomads. The Saka-Scythian kurgan at Issyk (southeastern Kazakhstan) where several tombs of women buried with weapons have been found, yielded a skeleton clad in magnificent golden armor, possibly a young warrior woman of the fifth to third centuries BC (chapter

4). Among the grave goods of the Golden Warrior is a silver cup bearing an inscription, still undeciphered, in what may be a variant of Kharosthi script, an ancient "alphasyllabary" used in Central Asia. This very rare epigraphic trace of a Scythian dialect, perhaps Khotanese Saka, offers unique evidence of writing by the nomad tribes of the steppes (other examples have been found at Tillya Tepe and the Tarim Basin on leather, wood, and birch bark). In Inner Asia, among the steppe tribes known to the Chinese as the Xiongnu, ancient Chinese chronicles reported that the nomads sent messages by "making marks in a strange script on pieces of wood." Later, in the second century BC, a renegade eunuch from China who joined the Xiongnu taught the nomads "how to write official letters to the Chinese court" on wooden tablets.[17]

In the imagination of Greek and Roman mythographers and historians, could the Amazons read and write? Amazons receive and send messages to enemies and allies in the mythic narratives. For example, in the legendary Trojan War, King Priam dispatched a message to the Amazon queen Penthesilea, requesting her help in defending Troy. Such communications could be delivered verbally. But the military historian Polyaenus specifically stated that the Scythian warrior queen Tirgatao of the Maeotians (Sea of Asov) exchanged written diplomatic letters with the king of the Bosporus in the fifth century BC (chapter 24). We do not know the language of their missives or whether translators read them, but the clear implication is that Tirgatao was literate.[18]

According to Ctesias, the Greek who served as the royal physician in Persia (fifth century BC), the Saka-Scythian warrior queen Zarina (chapter 23) was very well educated. In his fragmentary history of Persia, Ctesias told of Zarina's reaction to a letter from a Medean warrior, evidence of her literacy.[19] In a later collection of legends known as the *Alexander Romance* by Pseudo-Callisthenes, Alexander the Great exchanges a series of diplomatic communiqués with some Amazon leaders during his eastern conquests. Both the Greek version (fourth century AD) and the Armenian version (fifth century AD) "quote" the correspondence in detail. These legends even portray the Amazons holding an Athenian-style democratic assembly to decide how to respond to Alexander's letters. It is striking that the Greek mythographers imagined that Amazon society would have mirrored the strong relationship between Greek democracy and literacy.[20]

Now that we have surveyed the historical realities of Scythia and Scythians that influenced Greek ideas about women as warriors in parts 1 and 2, we can better understand the ancient myths and legends that the ancient Greeks told themselves about Amazons. Each myth, legend, story, and historical account and their many alternative versions were woven from tangled threads of facts, half-truths, plausibilities, possibilities, speculations, and fantasies. Armed with the background material in this and the previous chapters, we can sift through the layers of classical stories to see how the curious details and specific elements might have arisen from authentic knowledge encrusted with centuries of lore, misunderstood customs, rumors, imagination, and romance.

PART 3

AMAZONS IN GREEK AND ROMAN MYTH, LEGEND, AND HISTORY

HIPPOLYTE AND HERACLES

I N THE MISTS OF THE STORIED PAST, ONE GLORIOUS event stood out for the Athenians. Their founding hero, Theseus, had led the Greeks to triumph, defeating an Amazon army that swept across the Aegean, invaded Attica, and even besieged the sacred Acropolis, threatening to overrun Athens's religious center and stronghold. The hard-won victory over the Amazonian juggernaut was Athens's proudest moment in mytho-history (that battle is recounted in chapter 17). But why did the Amazons decide to make war on Greece in the first place? A covetous princess and a vengeful goddess set the chain of fateful events in motion, dispatching Heracles and his companions on a mission of aggressive plunder into the heart of Amazonia.

THE QUEST FOR HIPPOLYTE'S BELT

The myth begins in Tiryns (one of the three greatest Bronze Age citadels of the Argolid, along with Mycenae and Argos in southeastern Greece). King Eurystheus orders Heracles to retrieve Hippolyte's golden Girdle of Ares for his daughter, Admete, who yearns to own this glittering possession of the queen of the Amazons. The Amazons are awesome adversaries, daunting matches for the most mighty Greek heroes. Heracles's task, to bring back the armor of the champion Amazon fighter, is fraught with danger because, as everyone knows, these women are *antianeirai*, the equivalents of male warriors in courage and ferocity.[1]

The homeland of the Amazons lay far beyond the Aegean, beyond the Hellespont and the plain of Troy, at the edges of the known Greek world. Hippolyte and her band of Amazons dwelled along the banks of the Thermodon River in Pontus on the southeastern shore of the Black Sea. The Greeks set sail (in one, three, or nine ships, depending on the version) and followed the route taken by Jason and the Argonauts when they sought the Golden Fleece of far Colchis under the shadow of the Caucasus Mountains. In that myth, as the ship *Argo* sailed on toward the sunrise, Jason and his crew glimpsed beautiful women arming themselves in the rocky coves of the southern Black Sea coast.[2]

But now Heracles and his men are the first Greeks to drop anchor at Themiscyra, the Amazons' stronghold. The men pitch their tents on the beach. Soon Queen Hippolyte herself (her name means "Releases the Horses") rides into their camp with her retainers, greeting the strangers in a friendly manner and welcoming them with gifts. Hippolyte graciously asks Heracles the reason for his expedition. He explains that a bitter contest between the eternally squabbling divine couple, Zeus and Hera, has compelled him to accomplish a series of impossible, perilous tasks for King Eurystheus of Tiryns. Heracles tells Hippolyte that he has been commanded to present her great Belt of Ares to the king's daughter, Admete.

Up to this point, the myth makes it clear that these two great champions, male and female, regard themselves as equals. Heracles and Hippolyte converse easily and negotiate diplomatically (fig. 15.1). Keenly aware of each other's athletic physique, military bearing, and confidence, each sizes up the other's weapons, splendid armor, and impressive contingent of bodyguards. Quite unexpectedly, Hippolyte promises to make a gift of her belt to Heracles (plate 7). In some versions of the myth, Heracles and Hippolyte are attracted to each other.

But such a placid resolution seems out of place in Heracles's thrilling and violent adventures. The mutual respect of the two champions is all very fine, but Hippolyte and her Amazons are the fearsome female counterparts of the most powerful male warriors led by the greatest Greek hero. Let's see them clash!

FIG. 15.1. Heracles conversing peacefully with a bevy of Amazons and Queen Hippolyte (wearing the Belt of Ares and carrying a pelta and battle-axe, next to her white horse). Red-figure volute krater fragment, South Italian, Apulian, Baltimore Painter, ca. 330 BC, Metropolitan Museum of Art, Rogers Fund, 1919, 19.192.81.1, .7, 42, .46, .55, image © The Metropolitan Museum of Art/Art Resource, NY.

Hippolyte and Heracles scarcely have time to embrace and kiss before disaster strikes. The goddess Hera, Heracles's relentless nemesis, wrenches what began as a peaceful negotiation into a raging battle with far-reaching results. Disguising herself as an Amazon, Hera descends to Themiscyra in a cloud. Pretending to be one of Hippolyte's own guards, the goddess darts among the multitude of milling Amazons, shouting that the Greek strangers are kidnapping their queen, a hostile act of war. Grabbing their bows, spears, and battle-axes, leaping on their horses, the women storm to the beach to rescue Hippolyte.

Startled by the charging Amazons' banshee war cries, Heracles reacts impulsively to what appears to be Hippolyte's treachery. She must have promised to give him the belt, he assumes, so that her Amazons could catch him off guard and slaughter the Greeks in the harbor. Before Hippolyte can express her own surprise and stop her sisters from attacking, Heracles stabs (or clubs) her to death. The queen of the Amazons lies

FIG. 15.2. Heracles killing Hippolyte for her belt. Metope sculpture, Temple E, Selinus, Sicily, fifth century BC. Archaeological Museum, Palermo. Photo: Gianni Dagli Orti/The Art Archive at Art Resource, NY.

bleeding at his feet in the sand. Heracles rips the precious belt and her battle-axe from her lifeless body and dashes for his ships. Mission accomplished.

Other versions of the myth savor the Greek victory after a long-drawn-out battle. In Orosius's telling, the Amazon queen Orithyia was away at war, leaving her sisters, Hippolyte, Antiope, and Melanippe, with only a small force to defend Pontus. But Heracles was so daunted by the idea of confronting Amazons face-to-face that he prepared a surprise attack. "After estimating his forces, Heracles decided to suddenly surround the Amazons when they had no suspicion of attack," wrote Orosius. The Greeks ambushed the women when they were "unarmed and indolent in the care-free existence of peaceful times."[3]

Yet another version of the myth allows Queen Hippolyte enough time to react to Heracles's sudden attack. In that variant, the two warriors are so well matched that the outcome of their fight to the death is filled with suspense. But at last Heracles manages to gain the upper hand and kills Hippolyte. He snatches up her trophy belt and rushes to join the vigorous fighting that has broken out on the shore between the Amazons and the Greeks.

The Greek mythographers relished recounting the bloody details as Heracles, Theseus, Alcaeus, Telemon, Sthenelus, Timiades, and their Greek companions grapple with Hippolyte's courageous Amazon warriors, who were also well known by name. This great battle of the sexes was a wildly popular subject for Greek vase painters, many of whom inscribed the names of the male and female combatants in their scenes. A blow-by-blow account of the battle comes from Diodorus of Sicily, writing in about 50 BC. He consulted many earlier historians, now known only in fragments, such as Ctesias, who lived in Persia in the late fifth century BC, and Megasthenes, born in Anatolia in about 350 BC.[4]

Diodorus provides the following feverish description of the hand-to-hand fighting, in which Heracles single-handedly dispatches a dozen Amazons. One by one, Hippolyte's best and brightest Amazons challenge the mightiest hero, whose magical Nemean Lion–skin cloak makes him invincible. First to lunge at Heracles is Aella ("Whirlwind"), named for her deadly speed and agility. Now Philippis ("Loves Horses") leaps in—she is a valiant fighter but inexperienced. Behind her comes Prothoe ("First in Might"), a proud seven-time victor in single combat. All three of these bold Amazons are mortally wounded. Then Eriboea is cut down too, despite her ferocious attack. Marching shoulder to shoulder, three glowering huntress warriors, Celaeno, Eurybia, and Phoebe, advance on Heracles. But their spears snap in two against his lion-skin cape, and they too bite the dust. Another trio of Amazons jumps into the fray, but Deianeira, Asteria, and Marpe are also felled by Heracles. He slays grim Tekmessa and the virgin warrior Alkippe too. Then he whirls around to face the final contender. She is Hippolyte's steadfast general, Melanippe, the "Black Mare." She is also defeated, but only after a savage struggle. At the point of Heracles's sword, Melanippe offers her own beautiful fighting belt as ransom for her life and goes free. (Other tales vary the story by saying that Hippolyte gave Heracles her belt in order to save Melanippe.)

Meanwhile, the Greeks and Amazons remain locked in brutal combat on the beach, with many casualties on both sides. The tide finally turns in the Greeks' favor, and the surviving Amazons retreat, with Heracles slashing and clubbing them in mad pursuit. In some versions of the myth, Theseus defeats Antiope in a duel and Heracles gives him permission to keep the young Amazon captive for himself.

Many of Antiope's sister warriors are also taken alive—Herodotus mentioned that the Greeks captured as many Amazon prisoners as they killed in the battle. After decimating the Amazons of Pontus, Heracles and the Greeks board their ships and sail away with their prizes: the Amazon queen's belt, her battle-axe, and many Amazons, including Antiope, Theseus's prize.[5]

HIPPOLYTE'S WAR BELT IN ANCIENT LITERATURE, ART, AND ARCHAEOLOGY

Hippolyte's girdle was said to have been awarded by the war god Ares to the Amazons' champion fighter. The common English translation "girdle" for Hippolyte's Belt of Ares, with its connotations of women's intimate underwear, is "grossly misleading," as several scholars point out. Hippolyte's *zoster* (the Homeric term for war belt) would have been a heavy, richly ornamented piece of armor (something like a massive concho belt) worn over her clothing. Herodotus included descriptions of warriors' special war belts in his catalog of the golden treasures of Scythia. Archaeologists have unearthed heaps of golden plaques and buckles and leather fighting belts reinforced with gold and bronze plates, some of which belonged to real women who lived and fought in the time of Herodotus and earlier. Hippolyte's prized belt would have resembled the protective gear worn by real female warriors, like those buried in the kurgans at Ternovoye, Ukraine (chapters 4, 12, 13).

The genuine Scythian armored and gold-ornamented belts allow us to imagine how the Greeks would have visualized Hippolyte's *zoster*, and help to explain the high value and symbolic meaning of the prize that Heracles was seeking for Princess Admete. In antiquity, an article of clothing or equipment was believed to magically transfer the owner's personal qualities to the wearer. The fabled war belt and other accoutrements possessed by the Best of the Amazons would be powerful trophies indeed.[6]

Surviving ancient texts and artworks show that there were countless variations of the myth of Hippolyte's Belt, the Ninth Labor imposed on Heracles. (The Twelve Labors were penalties for murdering his own family when he was driven mad by the goddess Hera.) The Amazon queen's name also varies, and in some versions the Athenian hero Theseus was among the two dozen or so noble Greek adventurers who joined Heracles's quest. It is not possible to trace all the twists and turns in the conflicting traditions that explored this earliest "what if" scenario imagining Greeks encountering Amazons for the first time. But the kernel of the tale was always Heracles's killing of the Amazons' queen, which set the stage for the Battle for Athens.

Heracles's exciting battle with the Amazons was the second most popular theme in archaic Greek art (after his struggle with the Nemean Lion). This mythic conflict burst into the artistic repertoire of vase painters in the mid-sixth century BC, but the various oral stories had begun circulating much earlier. Some vase painters labeled dozens of individual Amazons and Greeks by name, providing more clues about alternative traditions. For example, in some scenes painted on pots Andromache ("Manly Fighter") is the name of the Amazon queen, instead of Hippolyte, whose name ultimately came to be attached to the best-known myth of the fabulous belt won by Heracles. To add to the confusion, some ancient writers call the Amazon leader Antiope or Melanippe.[7]

In many literary accounts, the encounter between Heracles and Hippolyte began amicably, then turned brutal through a misunderstanding. Some versions even promise love between equals before the battle erupts. Most of the surviving artistic representations are violent. Yet at least eight red-figure vases seem to explore alternative "what if" scenarios (fig. 15.1, pl. 7). The painters illustrate a peaceful parley between Hippolyte and a relaxed, youthful Heracles, with several Amazon guards at ease and the Amazon's horse calmly grazing. Some idyllic vase scenes even show the pair in the classic courtship iconography: the Amazon queen presenting her belt as a kind of love gift to Heracles, who leans casually on his club in the typical stance of a young lover.[8] It seems plausible that the dramatically different versions of their encounter—friendly and hostile—might have reflected peaceable and bellicose early encounters between Greek colonists and Scythians around the Black Sea.

Several monumental marble reliefs depicted Heracles brutally overpowering Hippolyte. The famous relief from the Greek Temple of Hera at Selinus (Sicily), for example, shows him grabbing her head and stepping on her foot, about to deliver a fatal sword blow (fig. 15.2). Other statues of Amazons clashing with Heracles were described by ancient Greek and Roman authors. Miraculously, fragments of these ancient statues have survived and can be identified by modern archaeologists. At the Temple of Zeus at Olympia, for example, in about AD 170, the Greek travel writer Pausanias viewed ancient sculptures of Heracles's Twelve Labors. One showed the hero stripping the Belt of Ares from the fallen Hippolyte. Pieces of those marbles were recovered by French archaeologists in 1829 and now reside in the Louvre. In Pausanias's time, the sumptuous chryselephantine (gold and ivory) statue of Zeus created by the famous sculptor Phidias in the fifth century BC still dominated the interior of the temple. Zeus was seated on a cedar-wood throne inlaid with gold, ebony, ivory, and gems. Pausanias examined the colorful paintings and reliefs on the great throne: one panel depicted twenty-nine Greeks led by Heracles and Theseus in hand-to-hand combat with twenty-nine Amazons. Pausanias also marveled at a very ancient statue of Heracles reaching out to grasp the belt of an Amazon on horseback, created by Aristocles the Elder of Kydonia in the sixth century BC. Archaeologists discovered the pedestal of this lost statue in the temple ruins in 1876.[9]

The earliest recognizable image of an Amazon in Greek art appears on a small painted terra-cotta shield made in about 700 BC. Heinrich Schliemann excavated pieces of this shattered object in 1884–85 from the ruins of the citadel at Tiryns. More painted fragments came to light in 1926. The puzzle was finally pieced together about ten years later. The crude geometric-style painting features five warriors. The two central combatants are male and female. The bearded Greek warrior holds a sword and grasps the plumed helmet of the woman warrior, who brandishes a spear. On a smaller scale, a pair of male and female warriors face off beside a dying male warrior prone on the ground with a spear in his back. The women are identifiable by their smooth cheeks, breasts, and long skirts (a convention for distinguishing women from men before white skin was used by black-figure vase painters). In keeping with the belief that Amazons were the equals of men, this archaic Amazonomachy from Tiryns shows the two Amazons holding their own, even winning. The only mortally wounded figure is the Greek warrior.

Tiryns, where this artifact came to light, was the mythic home of Heracles, and of King Eurystheus and Princess Admete who demanded Hippolyte's belt. Does this oldest picture of Amazons illustrate the myth of Heracles's expedition against the Amazons? Mythic, literary, and archaeological evidence suggests that it might. The votive shield of local clay was found among other dedications to Hera at Tiryns, which was the center of her ancient cult in the Argolid. Hera was the goddess who opposed Heracles, and Princess Admete was a priestess of Hera. One late version of the Hippolyte myth even claims that Admete sailed to Themiscyra with Heracles to make sure he obtained the prize. Was there once a tale in which it was Admete, the priestess of Hera, rather than the goddess herself, who disguised herself as an Amazon and goaded Hippolyte's women into attacking Heracles?

According to the mythographers, Heracles returned to Tiryns and dedicated Hippolyte's belt in Hera's temple. The Athenian playwright Euripides stated that in his day (420 BC) Hippolyte's golden belt *and* her gold-spangled cape could still be admired in the majestic Temple of Hera near Tiryns. That temple was first built in about 700 BC, the same time that the votive shield was made in Tiryns. A relic displayed as Hippolyte's belt in the fifth century BC might have been a real Scythian-made war belt embellished with gold plates, or a facsimile of one. Hippolyte's "gold-spangled cape" calls to mind the tunics and cloaks decorated with thousands of golden appliqués found in Scythian burials.[10]

At Tiryns, where the archaic votive shield showing Greeks fighting Amazons was found, other archaeological artifacts are thought to point to initiation rites in which young Greek boys overcame terrifying opponents, perhaps masked Gorgons or other alien adversaries, to prove their bravery. Art historian Susan Langdon proposes that ritual contests at Tiryns may have featured stories or performances of battles with Amazons to mark graduation to adulthood. According to Langdon, this theory explains Hera's involvement in the myth of Heracles and the rites of passage. Perhaps her harassment of Heracles was a guise for the goddess's religious role as a strict helper of young Greek "heroes" who proved their mettle and worthiness by ritual contests with menacing figures.[11]

That theory is speculative. But Amazonomachy narratives like the battle for Hippolyte's belt certainly demonstrated the ancient Greek belief that truly noble victories could be attained only when true equals were pitted against one another in single combat. The many artistic depictions of suspenseful conflicts between well-matched Greek warriors and foreign female fighters reinforced the idea that Amazon heroines were worthy adversaries for Greek heroes.

The myth did not end with the death of Hippolyte at the hands of Heracles and his men, of course. A host of questions arose, inspiring more mythic episodes. We already know that Heracles presented Hippolyte's battle-axe to Queen Omphale of Lydia (chapter 13). We also learned what became of the Amazons who were taken prisoner—they were marooned on the northern Black Sea coast, fell in with some Scythian youths, and founded the Sarmatians (chapter 3). The myth's sequels focus on the other Amazon survivors of the Greek attack. How would Antiope fare in Athens? And how would the furious Amazons take revenge?

16

ANTIOPE AND THESEUS

THE ONLY AMAZON OF MYTH TO LOSE HER FREEDOM through marriage to a Greek was Antiope ("Opposing Gaze"), the sister of Hippolyte, Melanippe, and Orithyia of Pontus. But exactly how was Antiope the warrior transformed into the domesticated wife of Theseus, legendary king of Athens? Was she a prisoner of war? Was Antiope abducted, tricked, seduced, or swept away by love? Should we imagine a combination of abduction and seduction, with Antiope falling victim to an ancient version of Stockholm syndrome, the "capture bonding" emotional effect sometimes experienced by hostages? Perhaps she began to identify with her Greek captors when she realized there was no hope of returning to her homeland. Amazingly enough, each of these scenarios was explored in the competing ancient versions of the Antiope myth.

ABDUCTION OR SEDUCTION?

In his biography of Theseus, the historian Plutarch (first century AD) discussed conflicting stories about Antiope, told by more than a half dozen classical Greek authors whose works have not survived. Some said that Theseus was with Heracles in the battle for Hippolyte's belt, and that Theseus carried Antiope away as his prize for valor. But Plutarch, whose stated goal was to tease out scraps of what he deemed "credible history" embedded in the old legends about Theseus, thought other versions were more convincing, that Theseus must have commanded his own expedition to the Amazon heartland on the Thermodon River.[1]

In Plutarch's telling, Theseus's quest began peacefully, just like the myth of Heracles and Hippolyte. The Amazons, "who were well disposed toward men," send a welcoming party to meet the strangers on their shore. In the version by a historian named Bion, Antiope is the leader of the Amazons and she presents gifts to Theseus. He slyly invites her onto his ship. Antiope willingly comes on board. Is she attracted to the handsome stranger? Or is she naive, off guard? Suddenly Theseus raises anchor and sails off, to the outrage of the rest of the Amazons onshore. Abduction and rape would be in character for Theseus, who was a serial sexual predator. Indeed, Plutarch recounts several "dishonorable and indecent" episodes in Theseus's life. In various myths, Theseus ravished and abandoned other women, including underage maidens. Long before Theseus abducted the Amazon Antiope, for example, he had abducted Helen of Troy when she was just a girl of ten.[2]

Plutarch clearly disapproved of such acts. But, writing about four hundred years before Plutarch, Herodotus had expressed a different view. He listed a series of abductions of foreign women by, for example, the Phoenicians, Greeks, and Trojans. "In my opinion," remarked Herodotus, "abducting young women is wrong, but it is stupid to make a fuss about it after the event. It is obvious that no young woman allows herself to be abducted if she does not wish to be." Was Herodotus perhaps thinking of marriage customs among nomadic raiding cultures, in which "abductions" of women were the norm, but usually agreed upon by the interested parties in advance? At any rate, these differing views expressed by Herodotus and Plutarch might help account for the conflicting versions in art and literature about the nature of Theseus and Antiope's relationship.[3]

For the Greeks, the Amazons' unyielding aversion to traditional patriarchal marriage was one of their defining attributes, a corollary of their parity with men. The Antiope stories could be seen as variations on the theme "What if a Greek were to marry an Amazon?" Just as scores of tales entertained different angles on the nature of the very brief encounter of Hippolyte and Heracles (chapter 15), so too the unique coupling of a Greek hero and an Amazon spun off many threads in literature and art. The profusion of alternative tales about Antiope reveals the Greeks' fascination with Antiope's plight and the choices she faced. Moreover, the existence of multiple story lines is a hallmark of heroic stature. Competing narratives about Antiope, Hippolyte, Penthesilea, and the Amazons are strong evidence that interest in these heroines was on par with that in Heracles, Theseus, Achilles, Odysseus, and other male heroes whose mythic adventures spawned so many different stories.

Ancient sculptors and painters preferred violent scenes depicting Antiope's defeat and capture by Theseus. The Athenian Treasury at Delphi, built in 510–490 BC and decorated with Theseus's exploits, shows the hero overcoming Antiope. Another marble statue of Theseus seizing Antiope graced the Temple of Apollo in Eretria, Greece (500 BC). A dramatic scene on the lid of a fine Etruscan bronze urn (480 BC) shows four mounted Amazon archers surrounding a bearded man forcefully carrying off a woman—perhaps the couple represents Theseus and Antiope (fig. 16.1). Like all heroic figures in archaic sculptures, Antiope and Theseus wear calm, austere smiles at odds with the traumatic situation, and early vase paintings also feature emotionless facial expressions. But at least two fine red-figure vases (490 BC) clearly portray a violent abduction, with Theseus roughly carrying a struggling, desperate Antiope off to his ship (fig. 16.2).[4]

ANTIOPE AND SOLOIS

Theseus did not immediately return to Athens after capturing Antiope, according to an Anatolian tradition preserved in the fourth century BC by Menecrates (a historian of the city of Nicaea in Bithynia, northwest Turkey). Instead Theseus meandered "around those parts for some time," engaged in other adventures and perhaps getting to know his new Amazon wife. Unfortunately, Menecrates's account is lost. Plutarch provides a maddeningly sketchy summary. Antiope's state of mind was not described in this curious tale, but it reveals something of her character.

In Menecrates's story, three young Athenian brothers—Euneos, Thoas, and Solois—were members of Theseus's expedition to Pontus.

FIG. 16.1. Right, Greek male (Theseus?) seizing a woman (Antiope?), surrounded by mounted Amazon archers executing Parthian shots. Detail of Etruscan bronze cinerary urn (lebes), Campua, ca. 480 BC, inv. 1855,0816.1, British Museum. © The Trustees of the British Museum/Art Resource, NY.

FIG. 16.2. The abduction of Antiope by Theseus. Red-figure Attic amphora by Myson, Athens, ca. 500–490 BC. Inv. G197, Musée de Louvre, Paris. Photo: Hervé Lewandowski. © RMN-Grand Palais/Art Resource, NY.

During the long return voyage, the youth Solois fell in love with the Amazon Antiope, who was understood to belong to Theseus. Solois confided his forbidden love to a trusted friend. Without Solois's knowledge, his friend approached Antiope on Solois's behalf. Antiope rejected the young suitor firmly but gracefully, "handling the situation with gentleness and discretion." Poor Solois in anguish drowned himself in a river. Antiope tried to keep the young man's secret love from Theseus. When Theseus did finally learn the reason for Solois's suicide, he was filled with sorrow. He named the river Solois in the Athenian youth's honor and founded the city of Pythopolis there, to be governed by Solois's two brothers, Euneos and Thoas.

We have only hints of what must have been a well-known, detailed oral tradition of Bithynia, one of the many myths about Antiope and Theseus. But with some digging, we can gather a few more pieces of the puzzle. The names Euneos (a son of Jason of the Argonauts) and Thoas appear in other myths. Thoas was the name of a son of Theseus; it was also the name of the son of the Borysthenes (Dnieper) River who ruled the Tauri tribe of the Crimea. But the name Solois is unique to Menecrates's story. The Solois (now Kocadere) River of ancient Bithynia flows into Ascania (now Iznik) Lake at the modern village of Sölöz, Turkey, where the ancient ruins of Pythopolis have been discovered. According to Homer's *Iliad*, the people of Lake Ascania sent warriors to aid the Trojans, who were also allied with the Amazons. Menecrates, as a historian of Bithynia, apparently recounted a local legend that explained how the river Solois and the city of Pythopolis were named to commemorate a tragic incident during Theseus and Antiope's "honeymoon." Today's Turkish residents tell of a different tradition. Their version does not mention Antiope or Theseus, but it does refer to the Greek myth of Jason and the Argonauts. According to the official history of Sölöz, the name of the town commemorates "the hopeless love of one of the Greek Argonauts named Solois who drowned in the Kocadere river."[5]

Menecrates's romantic tale of Antiope and Solois sheds new light on some interesting coins issued by Soloi, a port in Cilicia (later called Pompeiopolis, near modern Mersin). The town was founded in about 700 BC and came under Persian rule. As we saw in chapter 13 (fig. 13.2), in the fifth century BC Soloi issued a series of silver coins featuring the profile of an Amazon in a pointed cap and an Amazon stringing her Scythian bow. Scholars did not realize that the archer on the coins was actually an Amazon until 1923, noting that she is topless, wearing a wide belt and the same cap as the Amazon on the other coins.

But the reason why ancient Soloi associated itself with Amazons has remained a mystery until now. One ancient link between Amazons and the territory of Cilicia was mentioned by Diodorus. When the Amazons were making conquests in Asia Minor, the Cilicians welcomed the Amazons instead of resisting and were thereafter known as the "Eleuthero (Free) Cilicians." This story explains how the rugged, autonomous mountain folk of Cilicia came by that name and maintained their independence. But the city of Soloi was not named for an Amazon founder. Piecing together the clues from Plutarch and Menecrates, we can guess that ancient Soloi claimed to be named after the Athenian youth Solois, the companion of Theseus. In this way, the inhabitants of Soloi could associate their mytho-history with that of the powerful city-state of Athens, whose friendship they sought in the fifth century BC after the Greeks defeated the Persians. The Amazon portrayed on their coins must be Antiope, the Amazon who married Theseus.[6]

ANTIOPE IN LOVE AND WAR

In the second century AD, the Greek traveler Pausanias recounted yet another story, narrated in a lost poem by Hegias of Troezen. During the Greek war on Pontus, Antiope betrayed her homeland because she fell in love with Theseus. The tale apparently evolved from a version of the myth favored (and perhaps created by) patriotic Athenians in the fourth century BC. It first appears in a speech by the orator Isocrates in 380 BC, praising Athenian and Panhellenic war victories. Alluding to a story already familiar to his audience, Isocrates portrayed Antiope as a kind of stalker. Antiope "became enamored of Theseus and broke the Amazons' laws [against marriage] by following him home to Athens and living with him as his consort." By the time of Pausanias, some four hundred years later, this Athenian story had developed into more of a romance. As Pausanias tells it, Theseus was welcomed as an honored guest in the land of the Amazons. During his long sojourn along the

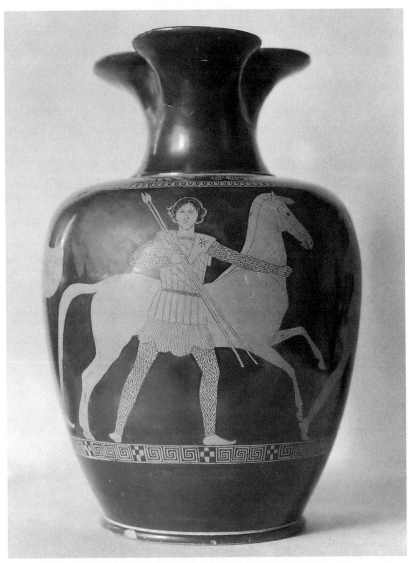

FIG. 16.3. Antiope in corselet and patterned sleeves and leggings, with two spears and white horse. Red-figure oinochoe (pitcher), Attic Greek, Mannheim Painter, ca. 440 BC. Metropolitan Museum of Art, Rogers Fund, 1906, 06.1021.189, image © The Metropolitan Museum of Art/Art Resource, NY.

banks of the Thermodon River, Theseus hunted and took part in other pleasurable sports with the warrior women, who treated him as their equal. Antiope fell in love with the handsome hero. With devotion so deep that it eclipsed her love for her sister warriors, she agreed to elope with Theseus back to Athens. In this version, Antiope willingly forfeited her independence by agreeing to become Theseus's bride.[7]

Modern interest in the myth of Antiope burst into popular consciousness in the 1920s. The ancient Athenian account of Antiope's rejection of the Amazons' "unnatural" autonomy was echoed in a racy comedy that became a hit on Broadway in 1932. Written in 1924, in the era of women's rising confidence and independence, *The Warrior's Husband* satirized male and female role reversal. The play is set in 800 BC in Pontus, during Heracles and Theseus's quest for Hippolyte's girdle. The Amazons, who dominate their sissy husbands with iron-fisted authority, are thrown into confusion by the sudden appearance of dashing, musclebound Greek men on their shores. The starring role of Antiope was played by the young, athletic Katharine Hepburn. The American audience went wild at Hepburn's entrance on stage. Dressed in a metallic tunic, a silver helmet, and leather greaves, she leaped down a flight of stairs with a dead stag on her shoulders. Antiope at first resists Theseus's

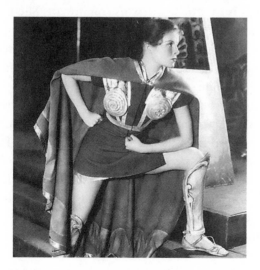

FIG. 16.4. Katharine Hepburn, aged twenty-four, as Antiope in *The Warrior's Husband*, publicity photo for the Broadway play of 1932.

advances, passionately declaring her independence. The role of the sure-footed, sexy "boy-woman" had a "tremendous influence on my career and so-called personality," Hepburn recalled in her memoir. In the 1930s and '40s, the actress cut a dashing figure in her signature trousers, at once shocking and fabulous, which also fueled her Amazonian image.[8]

Just as in ancient Athens, the idea of liberated women was both exhilarating and disturbing for modern audiences. By the 1920s in Europe and America, the word *amazon*, like *virago* (which originally meant "heroic female warrior") and even "battle-axe," was used to label self-sufficient, strong women as bad-tempered and domineering. The last act of the Broadway play resorted to saccharine romantic love to sweeten the same sour aftertaste as that left by the official Athenian message delivered by Isocrates and Pausanias more than two thousand years before: the roles of warrior and proper wife are mutually exclusive. Antiope-Hepburn falls in love, and Theseus, her "love conquest," becomes the former warrior's dominant husband. In the American play, the Amazons finally realize the "value" of masculine leadership and concede control to the "real" men.

In every version of the story of Antiope, the Amazon ends up as the wife of Theseus, king of Athens. But there is no happily ever after. The killing of Queen Hippolyte by Heracles outrages the Amazons, and Antiope's downfall is the Amazons' worst nightmare. She is no longer a headstrong warrior huntress, whether she was kidnapped, captured, or went of her own free will. Confined to the shuttered existence of other Greek wives, never to ride, hunt, and shoot with her companions, Antiope in her wedded life stands in stark contrast to the notorious sexual independence of Amazons. Antiope's domestication is the opposite of the alliances with Scythian men freely chosen by the other Amazon captives, who escaped from the clutches of Heracles and Theseus.

Some strands of the ancient Antiope myth revolve around intrigues in Athens's royal household. In these twisted domestic plots, Theseus and Antiope have a son and name him Hippolytus (the masculine version of Hippolyte), but Theseus then abandons Antiope to marry his new paramour, Phaedra. Enraged, Antiope swears to kill everyone at Phaedra's wedding. An oracle had once warned Theseus that he would be compelled to slay his Amazon bride to avert disaster—and that awful prophecy is fulfilled, in this bleak version of Antiope's fate. Compounding the

FIG. 16.5. Fantasy scene of Antiope, Theseus, and their son, Hippolytus. Impression of neoclassical eighteenth-century cornelian gem, *Catalogue des pierres gravees antiques de S.A. le Prince Poniatowski*, 1830–33. Photo by Claudia Wagner, Classical Art Research Centre and Beazley Archive, Oxford.

tragedy, Hippolytus, who has vowed to remain a virgin, is killed for rejecting the advances of his stepmother, Phaedra.[9]

In the illustrious myth of Athens's monumental War with the Amazons, however, a different, even more complex destiny lay in store for Antiope. In the great Battle for Athens, would Antiope remain loyal to Theseus and to her adopted homeland? Will she set aside women's work and take up weapons again to defend her loved ones and city from a terrible enemy? But her city is now Athens and her own people, the Amazons, are the enemy. Historical women warriors faced this same dilemma. One example, noted earlier, was Cynna, the Illyrian-Macedonian princess who killed the Illyrian warrior queen Caeria (chapters 4 and 20; and see chapter 25 for examples in China). The Greeks (and Romans) could approve of wives and mothers fiercely defending family and home in desperate straits, even though it was thought to go against women's true "nature."[10] It would be thrilling to see the "tamed" Amazon suddenly recover her long-suppressed warrior soul, even though such a turn of events evoked ambivalence for the Greeks.

Antiope's dilemma created many levels of suspense for the Greek men and women who listened to storytellers narrate the sequel to the myth of Antiope's abduction—the War with the Amazons. This great Amazonomachy would test the power of the young city-state and challenge the conflicting loyalties of the former Amazon Antiope. Could Antiope's martial skills help Athens win the war? Would the city survive the onslaught of an army of bloodthirsty warrior women? And what would happen to Antiope?

Meanwhile, back in Amazon territory, crucial decisions were being made. Provoked by the aggression of Heracles and Theseus, the Amazons vow revenge. Queen Orithyia gathers a great army and forges an alliance with the Scythian nomads of the steppes. Her mission is threefold: to avenge the death of Queen Hippolyte, to recover the Belt of Ares, and to rescue Antiope from Athens.

I 7

BATTLE FOR ATHENS

NEVER CONTENT TO STAY IN THEIR OWN TERRITORY, in their heyday the mythic Amazons had swept west and south, cutting great swaths around the Black Sea and into Asia Minor, just as the historical Scythians had done. The Greeks imagined a great battle in which Athens itself was the target of the Amazons' wrath and imperial designs. This terrifying attack, turned back after a desperate stand by Theseus and the Athenians, was "anything but a trivial or womanish affair," wrote Plutarch in his biography of Theseus. Queen Orithyia's Amazon invading army overran northern Greece and even laid siege to the sacred Acropolis, according to the Greek story. An Amazon victory would have meant utter humiliation and the extinction of the young city of Athens.[1]

The course of the mythic battle was described in minute detail by Cleidemus, a historian of Attica (fifth or fourth century BC). Sadly, his work vanished; we have only some quotations in Plutarch, who consulted many other lost works about the war, such as the history by Hellanikos.[2] Writing in the first century AD, Plutarch accepted that the Amazon invasion of Attica really had occurred in the remote past. He based his opinion on three points of evidence: the place-names, the many graves of fallen Greeks and Amazons, and the fact that the Athenians still made traditional sacrifices to the spirits of the Amazons before the annual festival for Theseus. As befitting such a momentous conflict, the details of the traditions vary—"hardly surprising," commented Plutarch, "for events so remote in time as these."[3]

THE WAR WITH THE AMAZONS

It was Theseus's kidnapping of Antiope that ignited the war. When Queen Orithyia returned to Pontus from her war campaigns, Melanippe described the murder of Hippolyte by Heracles and Antiope's abduction. Enraged by these acts of aggression, Orithyia requested aid from Sagylus, a Scythian chieftain north of the Black Sea. She told Sagylus that the Amazons of Pontus "were of Scythian origin," that long ago, "after their husbands had been massacred, the women had taken up arms and proved by their valor that Scythian women were as spirited as their men." She explained her reasons for waging war on Athens. "Stirred by national pride," Sagylus agreed to help his long-lost countrywomen. He designated his son Panasagoras to head a large contingent of mounted Scythian warriors to join Orithyia's forces. Diodorus's account is briefer but essentially the same: "The Scythians joined forces with the Amazons and thus an impressive army was assembled, led by the Amazons." This story, preserved by Justin and Diodorus (and Isocrates, below), shows that the Greeks identified Amazons as Scythians and that another Scythian tribe joined the Amazons' war on Athens.[4]

One route to Greece from Pontus would have the Amazons traveling west across Anatolia, crossing the Sea of Marmara into Thrace, and then heading south to Attica. (An alternative route, discussed below, had the Amazons invading from the north.) As they set off, their leaders would have stopped at tiny Amazon Island, the site of the massive black boulder and the altar to Cybele, sacred to the Amazons. It was the custom of the Amazon queens to sacrifice horses here before going to war. Several Greek vase paintings of Amazons at altars may have illustrated the women's preparations for invading Athens (chapter 10).

From Thrace, the Amazons advanced south through Thessaly, Boeotia, and Attica. In some accounts, the Amazons sent a message from a camp in Attica outside Athens to Theseus, requesting that he return Hippolyte's Belt of Ares and release Antiope. He refused. Breaching Athens's walls, the Amazons surrounded the city and prevented anyone inside from leaving or receiving supplies. Seizing the high ground, the women's army swarmed over the rocky crag directly across from the Acropolis, Athens's citadel. Here they pitched their tents and sacrificed to Ares. Their campsite later came to be called the Amazoneum ("Shrine of the Amazons"), and the craggy hill is still called the Areopagus, "Rock of Ares." The tragedian Aeschylus even pictured the Amazons erecting "lofty towers on their new citadel to rival those built by Theseus." That presents an unrealistic image for nomads, but Aeschylus intended to evoke the grave danger their siege posed to Athens.[5]

For seven days there was a standoff. In this emergency, Theseus consulted an oracle. The oracle's advice was to sacrifice to Phobus, a detail that further underscores the Athenians' desperate situation. The god Phobus was the personification of fear, terror, and military rout. We can imagine Theseus, like the Seven Against Thebes sacrificing to Fear in Aeschylus's tragedy, cutting the throat of a bull over a black shield and plunging his hands into the gore, asking the god to lift the paralysis that gripped the Athenians, and to sow panic among the Amazon army.[6]

The next morning, Theseus ordered the first assault on the entrenched Amazons. It was late summer, the beginning of the new year for the Greeks. Plutarch points out that the Athenians later commemorated the day of this attack with an annual festival in the month they named Boedromion, which means "Running in answer to a cry for help." This is a realistic seasonal detail, indicating that the Amazons began their march in winter, setting out for a four-month summer campaign in Greece and intending to return home before next winter. (The month of Boedromion and the god of fear Phobus converge again, in a later historical battle pitting outnumbered Greeks against a powerful barbarian army. In 331 BC, Alexander the Great may well have had Theseus's desperation in mind when, in the month of Boedromion, the Macedonian army faced Darius's imposing Persian forces at Gaugamela. On the eve of that battle, Alexander sacrificed to Phobus, praying to rout the Persians. Against all odds, Alexander won and King Darius fled in terror from the battlefield.)[7]

The detailed plan of the four-month-long Battle for Athens provided by the historian Cleidemus was imaginary. But it does tell us that the Athenians pictured the furious fighting and the crucial turning points taking place around many familiar landmarks in their city. According to the story, the Amazon forces extended from the Areopagus to the vicinity of the Pnyx. Meanwhile, Theseus gathered a contingent of Athenian warriors on the Hill of the Muses (Philopappus Hill) south of the Pnyx. From here they attacked the Amazon flank near the Pnyx. In the savage fighting the Greeks suffered very heavy casualties. The Amazons routed the Greeks, forcing them into the narrow space between the Acropolis and the Areopagus, and killing many Athenians near the Cave of the Furies at the base of the Areopagus.

The difficult topography of the battle differed markedly from the classic Greek hoplite battles, which took place on level ground. The rough terrain was a disadvantage to the Greeks, who were accustomed to facing an opposing army of hoplite warriors with exactly the same armor and arms and in the same close order formations possible on a level plain. The copies of the great shield of Athena in the Parthenon show the Greeks and Amazons fighting in a rocky, steep landscape around the Acropolis and Areopagus. Many vase painters also took care

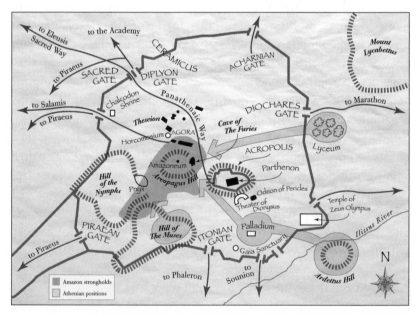

MAP 17.1. The mythic Battle for Athens. The Amazons took positions on the Areopagus and Hill of the Nymphs. The Athenians attacked from their positions at the Lyceum, Ardettus Hill, Palladium, and Hill of the Muses. Walls and structures are added for orientation in the topography of Athens. Map © Michele Angel.

to depict the uneven ground with stony outcrops, hills, and trees in their illustrations of the combat (see fig. 13.7). Several spectacular vase paintings bring the tumult to life, showing numerous named combatants embroiled in battle and duels, with gushing blood, staggering wounded, contorted corpses, broken spears, abandoned equipment, and even arrows whizzing overhead. Notably, in these Athenian battle scenes the Greeks are often outnumbered by the Amazons.[8]

The Amazons held the upper hand in the intense fighting that raged on the hillsides and the fields around the Pnyx and Areopagus. Theseus's men still held three strongholds east of the Acropolis: the military training grounds at the Lyceum outside the Diochares Gate; the Ardettus Hill beyond the Ilissus stream; and the Palladium (a sanctuary of Athena) southeast of the Acropolis. The tide began to turn in favor of the Athenians as the Greeks rushed out from these three points to clash with the Amazons. The Greeks drove them back to their camp, killing great numbers of the women warriors. After three more months of violent struggle, the Athenians finally gained the advantage and the Amazons capitulated.

ANTIOPE'S ROLE

Where was Theseus's captive bride, Antiope? Most ancient accounts say that Antiope fought bravely at Theseus's side. Some vase paintings appear to depict this. A vase attributed to the Geneva Painter, for example, shows seventeen combatants, five Greeks versus twelve Amazons. One side shows Theseus in the midst of battle, and on the other side "Antiope" rushes to the aid of a Greek warrior threatened by an Amazon ready to thrust a spear. On the other hand, at least six vases illustrate an alternative version of the myth, in which Antiope/Hippolyte fought with the Amazons *against* Theseus. In the main myth, when the tide turned against the Amazons, it was Antiope who arranged a truce. The Amazons agreed to a treaty of withdrawal at a spot north of the Areopagus that became known as the Horcomosium ("Oath Shrine"). Both sides retrieved their dead. The tombs of Athens's war heroes were said to be along both sides of the road leading to Piraeus, near the ancient shrine of the mythic hero Chalcodon. This area actually contains Dark

Age burials from 1050–900 BC (below), which the Athenians recognized as extremely ancient.[9]

The Amazons buried their dead around the Amazoneum, their camp. Several Attic vase paintings show Amazons carrying fallen companions; some may allude to the aftermath of the battle. A possible illustration of an Amazon burial appears on a vase painting depicting a "pensive-looking Amazon" leading her horse away from "a shaft or stele . . . perhaps the tomb of an Amazon."[10]

According to Plutarch's sources, Antiope secretly arranged to transport some wounded Amazons to Chalcis, western Euboea. Some of them were nursed back to health, while others died and were buried there. Like the supposed heroes' graves on the road to Piraeus (above), the "Amazon" graves at Chalcis may have been Mycenaean tombs, perceived as extremely ancient by the classical Greeks. In antiquity, Chalcis honored these fallen Amazons with an Amazoneum shrine and cult like that of Athens. Were there perhaps political advantages to the city's participation in Athens's great legend? We know that Chalcis had been forcibly allied with Athens and then became part of the Delian League to counter Persia.[11]

Antiope distinguished herself in battle and died fighting heroically. One tradition claims that Antiope was accidentally killed, while fighting beside Theseus, by a javelin thrown by the Amazon Molpadia. Molpadia was aiming at Theseus; there are hints that Antiope died shielding her husband. Molpadia was then slain by Theseus. By some accounts Antiope's tomb was marked by a single column or stele near the prehistoric Sanctuary of Mother Earth (Gaia) and the Palladium by the Itonian Gate. Molpadia was buried beside her. Some scholars have suggested that Molpadia was one of the figures in the scene on Athena's great shield. It is likely that Antiope's role in defending Athens was featured in the public wall paintings.[12]

AN ATHENIAN MYTH

The Athenian myth of the War with the Amazons appears to flow from an elaborate "what if" scenario (set out in chapter 1), imagining the Amazons as the vanguard of an invading Scythian confederation. Scythian armies really did once sweep across parts of Eurasia, including Thrace and Anatolia, but there is no evidence that Scythians ever really threatened or invaded mainland Greece. A fear of barbarian (Scythian) invaders in the past combined with *historical* Greek skirmishes with Thracians and nationalistic pride in Athens's *recent* triumph over the Persian invaders contributed to the mythic scenario of the Battle for Athens. The myth imagined how, at the height of their power, bent on revenge and conquest, the seemingly invincible Amazon army penetrated the very heart of Athenian territory in the golden era of heroes and heroines. Here in an epic battle the future of Greece would be decided.[13]

In about 900 BC, Athens had emerged as a unified center of settlements on the Attic peninsula and was periodically threatened by outside invaders, giving rise to the mixture of history and myth describing Theseus as Athens's founder and later as the victor over the Amazons. Most other Hellenic mythology about Amazons—for example, the tales of Hippolyte and Heracles and Penthesilea at Troy—was preserved in archaic oral lore and depicted in early vase paintings. But this uniquely Athenian story seems to have arisen in the classical era of the fifth century BC as self-conscious mythmaking on the part of the Athenians.

The great war with the Amazons in Athens is one of a series of tales describing Theseus's accomplishments, many of which parallel and borrow from the earlier accounts of the feats of Heracles. Plutarch rejected as "fable" an older epic called *The Rise of the Amazons* (sixth century BC), in which it was Heracles, not Theseus, who killed the Amazon invaders of Athens. Besides this lost epic, were there other earlier tales of Amazons in Attica that no longer survive? The earliest surviving literary description of the Battle for Athens occurs in a play by Aeschylus, 458 BC. Archaeological evidence of Athens's prehistory, such as massive walls on the Acropolis and rich Mycenaean tombs of 1300–1200 BC, provides hints of how the mythological Amazon invasion was elaborated and linked to antiquities in the fifth century BC. For example, a burial ground from Protogeometric times (1050–900 BC) lay along the road toward what would later become Piraeus, Athens's port. As noted above, this cemetery was believed to hold the graves of heroic Athenians killed by the Amazons.[14]

THE AMAZON INVASION ROUTE

An alternative Amazon invasion route from the northern Black Sea was first proposed by Hellanikos (fifth century BC). It was repeated by Diodorus and Lycophron, who wrote that the Amazons drove their Scythian mares across the Danube and sacked and burned the Attic countryside. Plutarch, however, doubted this route; he assumed that the Amazon army originated in Pontus on the southern Black Sea coast. If so, why would they have traversed the frozen Cimmerian Bosporus (between the Sea of Azov and the Black Sea), crossing the Danube and descending south into Thrace and Greece? But this northern route indicates how Amazons and Scythians were merged in Greek thinking: it was probably the path taken by historical Scythian armies into Thrace.[15] Hellanikos's treatise is no longer extant, but perhaps he described how the Scythian cavalry led by Panasagoras, son of Sagylus, took the northerly route and met up with their Amazon allies from Pontus as they entered Thrace over the Bosporus strait at the Sea of Marmara (map 2.2).

The northerly invasion route also suggests another logical scenario, which may have been clear in the missing sources but left out of the surviving accounts. As we know, the Amazons were described as ceaselessly moving around the Black Sea, back and forth between their northern and southern strongholds (chapters 2 and 3). Several writers stated that after the depredations of the Greeks, represented by the myths of Heracles and Theseus, the Amazons of Pontus were vulnerable to the attacks of neighboring barbarians and lost their power in the region. It would make sense for Greeks to imagine that the remaining Amazons led by Orithyia left Pontus to return to their original Scythian homeland on the steppes, where they personally enlisted the aid of King Sagylus. Pausanias knew of another story that some of the Amazon survivors of Heracles's attack fled to Ephesus (the site of their ancient sanctuary) and settled in the countryside there.[16] This dispersal scenario also suggests that the Amazons under Queen Orithyia might have been only a small contingent, perhaps the advance shock troops, of a larger army of steppe Scythians allegedly recruited and "led by the Amazons." This Amazon-Scythian alliance brings up another lapse in the myth as we have it. Whatever became of the Scythian portion of the invasion force? Why is there no mention of Panasagoras and his Scythian cavalry in the actual fighting in Athens?

The Scythian allies are missing from the action in Athens in all the surviving sources. What happened? The historian Justin explains. "A disagreement arose before the battle" and the Scythians did not continue on to Athens. "Abandoned by their Scythian allies, the Amazons were defeated in the field by the Athenians."[17] The Scythians apparently remained in Thrace. This story suggests a possible historical influence on the myth of an Amazon assault on Athens. As noted above, the Greeks were aware that Scythians did in fact conquer parts of Thrace, although Scythians never invaded Greece itself. Greek artists began to depict Scythians in vase paintings and sculpture in the sixth century BC.[18] The Greeks also knew that Scythian women rode with the men and were capable of raiding or waging war on their own, like Amazons. Ancient graves of real armed females contemporary with the Greeks are scattered across Ukraine and eastern Thrace (chapter 4). It was not an irrational notion that some female warriors, allied with Scythian forces, *could* have made incursions into northern Greece from Thrace, and the myth of the invasion of Athens could have coalesced around these grains of plausibility.

THE BATTLE FOR ATHENS IN ART

The Athenians' hard-won triumph over the army of barbarian women was presented as a key episode in the city's legendary origins and its self-image. After the Greeks defeated the Persians (490–478 BC), the Athenian story of the Battle for Athens could hark back to a much earlier time when the city had repulsed another terrifying foreign invader from the East. Beginning in the fifth century BC, the Mother of all Amazonomachies was extolled in colorful murals by renowned artists, modeled in monumental sculptures on the Acropolis and other buildings, and featured on Athena's massive shield, part of her stupendous gold and ivory statue inside the Parthenon. Phidias completed that colossal Athena sculpture in 438 BC. On her shield (about twelve feet high, lost except for fragmentary ancient copies) was a grand relief of about thirty struggling figures, Amazons versus Greeks, against the backdrop of Athens's city walls on a rocky slope. In the chaos of the battle on the shield, the male and female combatants appear evenly matched, the outcome hangs in suspense, and a further impression of symmetry is evoked by the corpses of a Greek and an Amazon at the base.[19]

Vivid images of Greeks pitted against Amazons survive on hundreds of vase paintings from the seventh century BC on. Whenever Heracles is included, the setting is recognized as his conflict with the Amazons of Pontus; other Amazonomachies clearly involve Achilles and Penthesilea at Troy. Around 450 BC, for little-understood reasons, the number of Amazon scenes on vases more than doubled. There are no certain illustrations of the Battle for Athens before about 460 BC, suggesting that the myth as we have it may have evolved in the fifth century. Some scenes on vases can be identified as the Athenian battle thanks to inscriptions, others because some of the vignettes and warriors' poses and the rocky terrain appear to be copied from Athena's great shield and other famous civic murals and public statues of 460–438 BC, details of which are known from ancient descriptions and copies. Theseus is named in thirteen such scenes. More than sixty different Amazon names are given on these vases, and Antiope is named four times.[20]

Many classical scholars believe that images of Amazons in art, especially in the fifth century BC, were not intended to represent women warriors of legend or reality but were symbolic stand-ins for Persians. In this view, Amazonomachies were really veiled "Persianomachies," a way of demeaning Persians as "feminized men." The claim that Amazons were covert symbols for Persians is a very old notion, going back to the nineteenth century. It is "arguable but impossible to prove" that the Battle for Athens myth and related art alluded directly to the Persian Wars. Several paradoxical aspects seem to detract from the merits of the oft-repeated assumption that Amazons in art were a symbolic way of denigrating Persians.[21]

After the Persian Wars, the Persians were by no means an "unspoken" topic in Greece, a group that had to be slyly represented by encoded imagery in art. Greek artists clearly depicted Persians *as* Persians in post–Persian War paintings and artworks; some are shown being defeated or humiliated by Greeks.[22] An emblematic reading in art is also at odds with contemporary Greek historians' accounts of warlike female barbarians of Scythia, often called Amazons. Greek authors were capable of using symbols and drawing attention to symbolic meanings in artworks, yet no writers ever conflated Amazons with Persians. Plentiful literary evidence suggests that the Greeks perceived the Amazons as offshoots of a real people, namely, Scythians; both groups were consistently distinguished from the Persians. Saka-Scythians were historical enemies of the Persians; the Persians tried and failed to defeat them: facts well known to the Greeks. Why have members of a nomad culture that had resisted the Persians stand in for Persians?[23]

Herodotus mentioned that the Greeks had once defeated Amazons in Pontus, and he also chronicled in great detail the rise of the Persian Empire and the Persians' dramatic downfall in Greece. Since he was writing at the height of the popularity of Battle for Athens artwork in the mid-fifth century, one might expect Herodotus to draw a parallel if one existed in his day. But his sole allusion to the Athenian myth of the Battle for Athens occurs in a speech attributed to an Athenian envoy, listing Athens's major victories over three separate entities, the Amazons, the Trojans, and the Persians. "We did well against the Amazons from Pontus who invaded Attica a long time ago," and "we were inferior to none at Troy," but "those were deeds performed long ago. . . . More remarkable was our triumph over the forty-six nations in the Persian Army." Writing four centuries after Herodotus, Strabo (a native of Pontus) did not deny the existence of Amazons in remote antiquity, but he was skeptical about recent "marvelous" tales about Amazons "sending an expedition as far as Attica." Strabo never associated Amazons with Persians, even in his descriptions of Persian attire and weapons.[24]

Can similarities between Amazon and Persian "Eastern" clothing in vase paintings support the notion that Amazons were intended to symbolize Persians? The attire of male Scythians resembles that worn by Amazons and Persians in Greek art, yet no one argues that Scythian males stood for Persians. In fact, Scythians, Thracians, Amazons, and Persians shared elements of a recognizable ensemble (patterned tunics, trousers, hats, armor, and weapons) typical of mounted foreign archers; Greek vase painters delighted in mixing up the sheer variety of these exotic styles. Artists began to portray Amazons in more realistic clothing and arms once they became knowledgeable about the weapons and dress of northern and eastern steppe cultures (chapter 12). After the

Persian Wars, some vase painters began to include elements of Persian dress too, as "new decorative possibilities" to supplement the already eclectic Amazon-Scythian repertoire. If Amazons were read as Persians in disguise, who were the Amazons in art before the Persian threat? *Before* the Greeks had become familiar with foreign warriors' garments and weapons, Greek artists had dressed and armed Amazons as *Greek hoplites*, yet it would be odd to argue that in that time the Amazons somehow "stood in" for Greeks because of their attire. In fact, Greek hoplite attire for Amazons did not entirely disappear in Amazonomachies after the Persian Wars. Even in some battle scenes obviously set in Athens, a few Amazons were depicted in Greek hoplite gear and wearing Attic helmets, and at least one of the Amazons is blonde—obvious attributes that would seem to undermine their symbolic value as "Persians." Moreover, some vases show Amazons wounding or killing Greeks, activities denied to Persians in Greek art. Many of the Amazons fighting Athenians on fifth-century BC vase paintings are inscribed with good Greek names—yet another factor that jars the illusion that the Amazons were meant to stand for Persians.[25]

If all Amazonomachies after 480 BC were triumphal propaganda representing the annihilation of the Persian threat, it is notable that so many artistic compositions continued to show suspenseful contests with slight, if any, indication of victory. Finally, if Amazonomachies were generally accepted as symbolic of violent and successful Greek resistance to Persia, then it is striking that scenes widely understood to celebrate the defeat of the Persians would have been selected, along with other episodes from Greek myth as well as historical and non-Greek scenes, to adorn monuments in Persian-controlled cities of western Asia Minor, such as the hero shrine at Gjölbaschi-Trysa, Lycia (ca. 370 BC), and the great Mausoleum at Halicarnassus, Caria (353 BC).[26]

It seems that Amazonomachies and Amazons could evoke many layers of meanings for ancient observers. As one scholar remarks, "Far from simply reinforcing the . . . cliché of the craven barbarian and the heroic Greek victor," Amazons "help question and problematize it." The Athenian Amazonomachy was a "mythic prototype for certain historical events long before" the Persian Wars, influenced by earlier Scythian conquests in Thrace. Myths and history were fluid, comments another scholar, and their flexibility allowed them to be "modified and elaborated to reflect recent events." In the unique case of the myth of the Battle for Athens, which apparently emerged as national propaganda around the time of the Persian Wars, the Amazons who invaded Attica were understood not as Persians but as a *first wave* of aggressive barbarians from the East, as another real people, hostile to the young Athens in its mythic origins. Thus the "Scythian army led by Amazons" bearing down on Greece was presented as an ancient precursor of the Persian Empire. In that sense, then, the Battle with the Amazons could be seen as a retroactive "mythic counterpart" or fictional "analogue of the Persian invasion." The myth allowed the Athenians to self-consciously retroject themselves and their hometown hero Theseus into a glorious defense of Greece from another powerful foreign enemy at the very beginning of their city's history, "when Greece was still insignificant."[27]

AMAZON MEMORIES AND MONUMENTS IN GREECE

According to ancient Greek writers, traces of the Amazons' warpath and their occupation of Athens—such as the hill where the women were said to have encamped and the graves of the war dead on both sides—were treated with respect and pride by Athenians and other Greeks. On the day before the Theseia (the Athenian festival of Theseus formally established in 475 BC), the Athenians made sacrifices to honor the bravery of the Amazons. This Amazon cult also served to stir the patriotic emotions surrounding the Athenian success against such imposing foes.

Athenian orators boasted about the magnificent defeat of the Amazons in speeches to allies and citizen assemblies. Isocrates praised the victory as a coup for the forces of civilization. In a passage demonstrating that he and his audience considered the Amazons to be allies of the Scythians, distinct from contemporary Persians, Isocrates singled out the "three most aggressive races with hostile designs on Athens": the Persians, the Thracians, and "the Scythians led by the Amazons." Isocrates declared that Athenians had won decisive wars against *all three* of these enemies. In the past, the Amazons "thought they would gain mastery over all Greece by taking our city. They did not succeed . . . they were destroyed . . . just as if they had waged war against all mankind."

The orator Lysias repeatedly referred to Athens's victory in his speeches; he declared that the Amazons "ruled many lands and enslaved their neighbors" and then marched against Athens seeking glory. Instead, "They perished and made the memory of our city imperishable because of our bravery. Because of their disaster here, the Amazons rendered their own country nameless." But, of course, because they dared to challenge not only Athens and but also the Greeks at Troy, the "glory of the Amazons" (Pausanias's words, more than five hundred years later) was never forgotten.[28]

When Pausanias visited Megara, west of Athens, in the second century AD, his guides showed him the Amazon cemetery on the road to Rhous (north of Megara, where a stream came down from the mountains). The Megarians told Pausanias that most of the Amazons had died fighting in Athens, but their leader (Orithyia, but here called Hippolyte), Antiope's sister, escaped with a few others to Rhous. In despair about the failure of their expedition and hopeless about ever returning home safely to Themiscyra, she died of grief and was buried by her companions. Pausanias noted that her memorial was shaped like a crescent Amazon shield. Pausanias also visited a shrine of Ares at Kelenderis, near Troezen, Theseus's birthplace and yet another region where it was said that Amazons had died after their defeat in Athens. To the north, in central Thessaly, graves of Amazons who had perished on the retreat were still pointed out in Plutarch's day near Scotussa and the Dogs' Head Hills (Cynoscephalae, near modern Volos); these places marked their advance and retreat across Thrace.[29]

More Amazon graves were shown in Boeotia at Chaeronea, Plutarch's hometown, along the banks of a little stream. In antiquity, the stream may have been nicknamed Thermodon (like the river in the Amazonian homeland), but Plutarch knew it as Haemon ("Bloody"). This was the site of a catastrophic event in Greek history, when Philip of Macedon defeated the Greeks at the Battle of Chaeronea in 338 BC. Before that battle, the Greek army had encamped along this stream. Some soldiers digging a trench around their tent happened to unearth a small stone carving of a figure carrying a wounded Amazon. This incident was reported by the Macedonian War historian Duris (fourth century BC, now lost). Plutarch, who may have viewed the little carved figure in Chaeronea, stated that it was inscribed with the word "Thermodon." He took the inscription to mean that the figure holding the dying Amazon was the god or personification of the Thermodon River in the Amazons' homeland.[30]

What is the meaning of this curious discovery? While it might be poignant to picture an Amazon placing this object in the grave of her fallen comrade on the retreat after their defeat, that is impossible: the War with the Amazons was a myth created by Greeks, the inscription was in Greek, and "Thermodon" was the Greeks' name for the river in Pontus, not the native name. The facts—a small stone carving of a wounded Amazon excavated in the vicinity of archaic tombs identified as those of Amazons—bring to mind the cult of wounded Amazons at Chalcis, above. In antiquity, extremely ancient Mycenaean tombs were commonly revered as those of heroes, heroines, and other figures from mythology. A similar process might account for graves recognized as extremely old and identified as those of Amazons in Athens, Thessaly, Troezen, Megara, and Chalcis, as well as the grave mounds in Anatolia associated with Amazons since Homeric times. The little stone figure of a wounded Amazon in the bosom of the River Thermodon was most likely an ancient Greek dedication or offering to a Boeotian Amazoneum at Chaeronea, similar to the Amazon heroine cults in Athens and Chalcis.

The most unexpected Amazon memorials described by Pausanias were sanctuaries at Pyrrhichos, Laconia, in the southern tip of Greece. There he viewed two very old *xoana*, crudely shaped wooden statues. These idols were called "Peaceful" Artemis and "Amazonian" Apollo. The ancient statues were said to have been dedicated by the "women from the Thermodon"—by the Amazons themselves—to mark the point where they had finally halted their invasion of Greece. Notably, *Pyrrhichos* means "rustic war dance." The Amazons were said to have danced the pyrrhic war dance around a *bretas* (small wooden idol) of Artemis at Ephesus (chapter 9).

Pausanias's account is mysterious on many levels. No other sources speak of an Amazon army penetrating this far south in Greece. This is the only ancient reference to "Apollo Amazonius" and "Peaceful Artemis." Moreover, Apollo was rarely worshipped in Greece in tandem with his twin sister Artemis, the Amazonian huntress goddess. Some scholars speculate that this idol was not the Olympian Apollo, but some non-Greek, Asiatic god, worshipped by the very early people of southern Greece, long before Greek colonization. Wooden statues indicate that this cult was indeed extremely ancient. Very few rustic *xoana* have survived, except as copies in stone, although a wooden *xoanon* of Artemis was discovered at Brauron.[31] Pausanias does not say how the idols were identified—did local people tell him the names and the old story behind them? Is it possible that they were inscribed, like the small stone carving of a wounded Amazon in the arms of "Thermodon" found at Chaeronea?

The quarrel between the Amazons and the Scythians, mentioned above, was not a complete breakdown in their military alliance. "Despite the dispute," Justin reported, the retreating Amazons "found shelter in the encampment of their allies. With the help of the Scythians they returned to their land without being attacked by other tribes." Diodorus agreed that the Scythians gave the ragtag Amazon survivors refuge after their defeat. The Amazon veterans had given up their "ancestral soil" in Pontus, explains Diodorus, because it had been overrun by neighboring tribes. Instead, the Amazons "returned with the Scythians into Scythia and made their homes among those people."[32]

But there were a few renegades. Small, scattered groups of wandering Amazons kept to their warlike ways, seeking adventure and glory. One such band was led by a legendary warrior queen whose name would strike terror into the hearts of the Greeks besieging Troy: Penthesilea, "She Who Brings Grief."

18

PENTHESILEA AND ACHILLES AT TROY

N O MATTER HOW MANY BAD THINGS WOMEN SUFFER,
nothing can take away their appetite for trouble,"
marveled Pausanias. "The Amazons of Themiscyra
fell to Heracles and the fighting force the Amazons sent against Athens
was wiped out—and yet the Amazons still went to Troy and fought
there against the whole of Greece."[1]

The myth of Penthesilea and her duel with Achilles in the Trojan
War is very old, as ancient as the myth of Hippolyte and Heracles.[2] (The
Athenians, as we saw, had inserted their own epic battle with the Ama-
zons into this chronology, locating it in mythic time before the Trojan
War.) The origins of the Trojan War myth, famously recounted by the
Greek epic poet Homer, remain cloudy, but the clues are fascinating to
contemplate. The legend of Amazon warriors arriving to help King
Priam defend the walled city of Troy against invaders from Greece: could
this have been based on ancient memories of wars with the Hittites?

The Hittites were a chariot-driving warrior society that dominated
Anatolia in the Bronze Age. Troy, in northwestern Anatolia, was a great
Bronze Age city from about 3000 to 950 BC, and archaeology shows that
it was associated with the Hittite Kingdom. The still-imposing remains
of the citadel of Troy and the great Hittite capital, Hattusa in central
Anatolia, would have been even more impressive in antiquity.[3] Troy and
the Hittites were contemporary with Bronze Age Mycenae, a major city
in southern Greece. The idea of Hittite–Trojan War connections was first

proposed in the early twentieth century. The Trojan War epics were written in Greek, but scholars agree that the names of the Trojan king Priam and several of his relatives were not originally Greek. Some believe that they derive from Luwian, the language related to Hittite that was probably spoken by the Trojans. The complex ruins of Troy reveal waves of different peoples, great wealth, and destructions by fire and warfare. Most scholars today agree that the legendary Trojan War was based on historical small-scale conflicts between the Mycenaean Greeks and the Hittite Kingdom and its outposts around the thirteenth and twelfth centuries BC.[4]

TROJAN WAR EPICS

The great events of the Trojan War were recited by bards for centuries before some versions were written down in the eighth/seventh century BC. Of the several Greek texts concerning this epic cycle, two complete versions survive. The *Iliad* and the *Odyssey* attributed to Homer describe events near the end of the war and its aftermath. The other texts are lost, except for quotations and summaries in other authors. The *Cypria* (650 BC?) covered the outbreak and first nine years of the war. The *Aethiopis* by Arctinos (775 BC?) told how the Amazons and Ethiopeans came to Troy's aid. The Homeric scholar M. L. West recently suggested that two separate epic poems, one about Queen Penthesilea of the Amazons and one about King Memnon of the Ethiopians, were combined in the *Aethiopis*. The *Little Iliad* (700 BC?) recounted the story of the Trojan Horse; the *Sack of Ilium* (seventh century BC?) described the destruction of Troy; and the *Nostoi* and the *Telegony* (seventh century BC?) covered the homecomings of the Greek heroes.[5]

In Homer's *Iliad*, the Greeks had been besieging Troy for nearly ten years, with sporadic duels outside the city walls. In one of these contests, the Greek champion Achilles killed the Trojans' last hope, Hector, son of old King Priam. Troy's survival now depended upon Priam's allies, the Amazons. The *Iliad* ends with Hector's burial, anticipating the arrival of Penthesilea. One manuscript tradition of the *Iliad* concludes, "Such were the funeral games of Hector. And now there came the Amazon, the great-hearted daughter of man-slaying Ares."[6]

What happened next was detailed in the lost *Aethiopis*. A spare out-line by a later author named Proclus survives: "Thracian-born Penthe-silea comes to the aid of the Trojans and after showing great prowess is killed by Achilles and buried by the Trojans." The *Aethiopis* was retold and elaborated in the post-Homeric epic *The Fall of Troy* by Quintus in the third century AD. Like the *Aethiopis*, Quintus's narrative takes up the story from the last line in the *Iliad*, drawing upon oral and written lore from many other vanished ancient sources. To his picture of Pen-thesilea we can add more details from many other extant poems and fragmentary works from antiquity. The daughter of the war god Ares and the Amazon Otrera, and the sister of Antiope and Hippolyte, Pen-thesilea ruled "after the reign of Orithyia and accounts of her courage have come down to us": so wrote Orosius about fifteen hundred years after the time frame of the legendary Trojan War.[7]

AMAZONS AND TROJANS AS ALLIES

What motivated Penthesilea to fight for Troy? Amazons were certainly enemies of the Greeks. But were the Amazons friends of the Trojans? It is commonly asserted that Amazons and Trojans were old enemies in the past, but for some unknown reason the Amazons changed their minds and became Troy's allies in the Trojan War.[8]

But a close reading of the relevant passage in the *Iliad* suggests—contrary to most ancient and modern scholars' assumptions—that the Amazons and Trojans might have been allies well *before* the Trojan War. Many ancient and modern readers have wondered why the Amazons came to the aid of Troy when they had supposedly clashed with Trojans two generations earlier. But this seeming inconsistency arises because of an unexamined assumption about the meaning of a famous episode in book 3 of the *Iliad*, the conversation between Helen and Priam on the walls of Troy (the "teichoscopy" scene). Old King Priam marvels at the magnitude of King Agamemnon's army of Greeks and allies massed on the Trojan plain, the largest army he's ever seen. Priam reminisces about the biggest army he had ever beheld before this day, when he was just a boy. It was when the Trojans and Phrygians and their allies, led by kings Otreus and Mygdon, had gathered at the Sangarius River. Priam remembers, "I was a young helper in the camp on the day when the Amazons came."[9]

Since antiquity, this statement has been interpreted to mean that a vast army of Trojans and Phrygians fought against an equally huge host of Amazons. Yet modern commentators agree that it is odd for Priam to bring up the Amazons here when the wording makes it clear that he is not comparing the size of the Greek force outside his walls to the size of the Amazon force he saw as a boy. As one scholar remarks, this "illogical passage" threatens the coherence of the narrative—everything "would become clearer if line 189 were missing." The solution has been to force the "awkward" inconsistency in the text to mean that Priam once took part in a battle against Amazons but now calls on Amazons for aid.[10]

But Priam's words could be taken in another way, one that makes good narrative sense without raising contradictions. The Greek wording of Homer's text simply reads "on that day when the Amazons came." The scene Priam recalls from his youth was the arrival of friendly Amazons, "the peers of men," who were *allied with* the Trojans and Phrygians against an unnamed enemy in the past. Such an alliance would have been natural: the Phrygians had Thracian origins and the Amazons were associated with Thrace; Priam himself summons both Thracians and Amazons to help defend Troy against the Greeks. The poetic context of Priam's boyhood memory is his admiration for leaders who command great allied armies of many diverse lands. His point is unambiguous: he is comparing the massed army of many nations at the Sangarius in his boyhood to his own massed multinational army at Troy.

Priam's memory of that long-ago day also serves to foreshadow the day when his own Amazon allies will come, the Thracian-born Penthesilea and her band of women warriors. The arrival of Priam's Amazon friends is also prefigured at the outbreak of the Trojan War in the *Iliad*, when Priam assembles his own great army of allies from many different lands around the grave mound of the Amazon queen Myrine. With these logical and literary considerations in mind, Priam's reminiscence—"I was there on the day when the Amazons came"—now can be seen in a new light, harking back to another time in the past when Amazons had been allies of the Trojans.[11]

On the day that Penthesilea and her cadre of mercenary Amazons arrived, Priam presented her with costly gifts and promised more rewards. So there is no doubt that Penthesilea—like her Greek counterpart Achilles—came to Troy seeking renown and recompense.[12]

But there was another reason. Penthesilea had accidentally killed a relative, and she came to Troy to be purified of blood-guilt by serving Priam. The mythic detail strongly suggests a long-standing friendship between Amazons and Trojans. In this narrative arc, Penthesilea resembles many mythic Greek heroes who fled into exile from their homelands and served various trusted kings, seeking to sacrifice themselves honorably in battle or to carry out dangerous quests to appease the gods. The hero Bellerophon, for example, fled after killing his brother to do the bidding of King Proteus. The Twelve Labors imposed by King Eurystheus were penance for Heracles's murder of his own sons. Achilles would later seek purification for killing one of his fellow Greeks.[13]

Hunting one day with her sister Hippolyte, Penthesilea had hurled her javelin at a stag and killed Hippolyte instead. To escape her despair and the reproach of the other Amazons, she came to Priam to be absolved, vowing to kill Achilles and bring victory to Troy or die trying. Penthesilea's name combines the Greek words for "grief, misery, suffering, mourning" with "the people or army." But the exact meaning is ambiguous: grief for whom? Various mythic details add layers of significance. Penthesilea's name could allude to her own grief and that of her people. In the myth, Penthesilea and Achilles are presented as a matched pair of handsome, merciless young war heroes. Perhaps it is no coincidence that Achilles's name also carries an ambiguous connotation of "pain, grief, suffering." And like Penthesilea, Achilles also experienced personal grief *and* caused great mourning.[14]

TWO WOULD-BE AMAZONS?

Were there any other "Amazons" involved in Trojan War? A shadowy account (second century AD) claimed that a maiden named Epipole ("Outsider"), daughter of Trachion of Karystos in Euboea, disguised herself as a young man and infiltrated the Greek forces going to Troy. She may have been Thracian, since the Thracian Abantes of Karystos were allies of the Greeks. But Epipole's ruse was discovered by the hero Palamedes, in charge of the preparations for war. Like the insecure

Greek men who feared the mythic Atalanta's independence (prologue), the Greek warriors reacted with violent rage. Epipole was stoned to death. Another obscure story in the same lost work tells of a Greek warrior woman named Helen, the daughter of Tityrus of Aetolia, another ally of the Greeks at Troy. At some point, this feisty Helen provoked Achilles to single combat and dealt him a glancing head wound before she killed her.[15]

Notably, these two heroines, Epipole and Helen, were identified by their father's names and cities, exactly like all the male Greek and Trojan heroes at Troy. Frustrating fragments like these hint that many other tales of women warriors once circulated in antiquity and have now disappeared except for tantalizing scraps. The two stories of would-be Amazons, one apparently Thracian and one Greek, and their deaths at the hands of Greek warriors appear to be part of the ancient debate about whether it was ever right for women to go to war. That question is a prominent theme in the myth of Penthesilea.

PENTHESILEA AND HER AMAZON WARRIORS

Twelve Amazons from Pontus accompanied Penthesilea to Troy, the entourage resembling a resplendent goddess surrounded by her noble escort. Quintus gives their names: Klonie, Polemusa, Derinoe, Antandre, Evandre, Bremusa, Hippothoe, "dark-eyed" Harmothoe, Alkibie, Antibrote, Derimachea, and Thermodosa. The spectacle of the proud Amazons with their bows and spears astride horses glittering with finery lifted the Trojans' spirits. A large group of Greek black-figure vase paintings depict Amazons and their horses, with many male warriors at their side or looking on. Some show an Amazon leading her horse before a seated man, taken to be King Priam. These scenes are thought to represent the arrival of Penthesilea and her band in Troy.[16]

The next morning, Penthesilea's heart is filled with confidence because her father, Ares, had encouraged her in a dream. Quintus tells how she puts on her gleaming gold breastplate and crested helmet and buckles on a massive sword in a silver and ivory scabbard. She takes up her half-moon shield and two spears, and in her right hand she grips her battle-axe (Penthesilea's own invention; chapter 13). Her handsome, dashing horse carries her quiver and bow. This steed had been a "gift from the North Wind's wife Orithyia when Penthesilea was her guest in Thrace." (Thrace was Penthesilea's birthplace; interestingly, Orithyia was also the name of the Amazon queen who invaded Athens.) Penthesilea's weapons are typically Thracian-Scythian, like those discovered in the graves of real fighting women (chapter 4). Her arming scene is recounted with all the loving details usually lavished on Greek male heroes.

The Greeks in their camp are surprised to see the Trojans rallying and charging onto the field with an advance guard of thirteen unfamiliar mounted warriors. The two armies clash and the slaughter commences. Penthesilea slashes through the Greek line, slaying eight warriors one right after another. Klonie kills her first opponent but is felled soon after. In fury Penthesilea slices off the arm of the Greek who disemboweled Klonie. Her comrades Bremusa, Evandre, and Thermodosa fight with valor, but at last they are cut down by Greek warriors. Derinoe battles on but she too is slain, by a spear in the neck. Alkibie and Derimachea are both beheaded by their opponents.

The mayhem rages on, the gruesome details provided by Quintus: "Many a heart was stilled in the dust that day." He likens Penthesilea to a bloodthirsty lioness or a howling gale at sea, as she destroys ever more Greeks with her axe and spear. "No one escapes my power!" she shouts, "Where is Achilles, where is Ajax? They dare not face me!" Those two Greek champions are still in their tents, mourning Achilles's beloved friend Patroclus.

The Trojan warriors exult in Penthesilea's fearless onslaught. Watching the battle from the towers, the Trojan women are amazed. One young woman, Hippodamia ("Horse Tamer," an Amazonian name), is seized with an impulse to join the Amazons. She jumps up and urges the other young women to take up arms: "Let us fill our hearts with courage and take an equal share of the fighting. Our bodies are as vigorous as men's; we have the same light in our eyes and we breathe the same air! See how bold Penthesilea overpowers the men in close combat? That foreign woman fights this ferociously even though she is far from her home," declares Hippodamia, "but we have even more urgent reasons to fight—this is our city and we have lost husbands, fathers, brothers, sons. We stand to lose everything—far better to die fighting than be enslaved!" Her rousing words inspire the women to cast aside their wool baskets and rush out with weapons, ready to die alongside their men and the Amazons. But an older Trojan woman, Theano, stops them, pointing out that even though men and women share human nature and potential for action, the Trojan girls have had no training or experience in warfare, unlike the Amazons. Those women warriors, reasons Theano, are the peers of men because they have spent their lives doing men's work, riding horses and delighting in battle since childhood. The long speeches of Hippodamia and Theano express the ancient belief that, with the right training and practice, women do possess the spirit and physical capacity to become warriors.

Meanwhile, on the field of battle, the "earth is drenched with blood and men lay writhing and grasping fistfuls of dust." Penthesilea continues her relentless attack, killing all who face her and those who flee in terror. The Greeks are being pushed back to their ships. At last the din of the battle reaches Ajax and Achilles in the camp, and they rush out to join the battle. Ajax and Achilles stride through the Trojan forces, dealing death left and right. Achilles kills Penthesilea's four remaining warrior companions: Antandre, Polemusa, Hippothoe, and Harmothoe.

PENTHESILEA AND ACHILLES

As Ajax and Achilles continue their rampage, Penthesilea suddenly spies the pair across the blood-soaked field. She hurls her javelin at Achilles, but it shatters against his indestructible shield. Urging her horse to gallop toward them, she taunts the men to come closer if they dare, and casts her second spear at Ajax. But it cannot penetrate his solid silver armor and Ajax leaps away, leaving Achilles and Penthesilea to their fate.

Mocking Penthesilea for presuming that a mere woman could take on the "two greatest warriors in the world," Achilles throws his spear at the charging Amazon. The point pierces her chest, dark-red blood gushes, and in agony she drops her battle-axe. As the "mist of darkness veils her

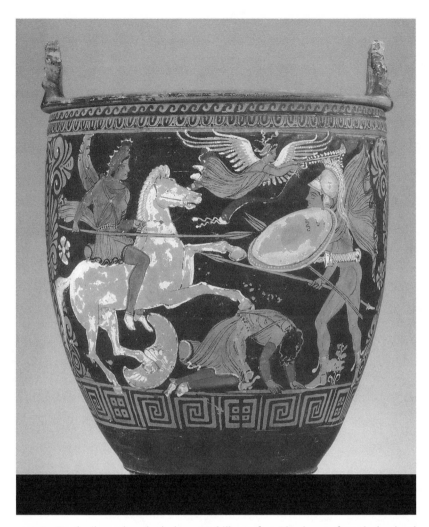

FIG. 18.1. Penthesilea on horseback charges Achilles on foot. Blood pours from the head and side of the dying Amazon between them. Red-figure Apulian vase, Group of Copenhagen 2443, ca. 340–330 BC, height 30.5 cm. Museum of Fine Arts, Boston, Gift of Dr. and Mrs. Jerome Eisenberg, 1991.242. Photograph © 2014 Museum of Fine Arts, Boston.

eyes," Penthesilea has two options as Achilles runs up to drag her from her horse. Should she draw her sword, or should she dismount and plead for her life? Perhaps Achilles would relent—after all, they are the same age. Detecting a slight movement of her hand, Achilles hurls his other spear with such force that it impales Penthesilea and her horse together.

FIG. 18.2. Achilles killing Penthesilea. Black-figure amphora, signed by Exekias, sixth century BC, from Vulci, Italy, Inv. 18,360,224.13, British Museum. © The Trustees of the British Museum/Art Resource, NY.

The Amazon collapses face down upon her magnificent steed. The Trojans flee the field in despair and fear. Triumphant, Achilles continues his tirade: Poor woman, you thought you would reap a bountiful reward from old King Priam! What lured you to abandon women's work to face me, the best of the Greeks? War causes even men to tremble!

As the Greeks crowd around the dying Amazon in the dust and blood, Achilles bends down to remove her brilliant helmet, suddenly revealing the young woman's face. Penthesilea's fierce beauty is "undimmed by death." With her loose hair and graceful form she seems to the Greeks to be like the "immortal goddess Artemis asleep after a day of hunting lions in the mountains." She has atoned for killing her sister, and the glorious death craved by all great heroes is now hers. A beautiful corpse was one of the conventional mythic proofs of a heroic demise. The Homeric ideal of the "beautiful death" had the power to make the corpse of the warrior noble and handsome, even sensuous, "despite the blood, wounds, and grime."[17] Many of the men gathered there wished that such a woman would be awaiting their return to Greece, declares Quintus. Achilles is struck silent.

"Suffering bitter grief as profound as he had felt at the death of his best friend Patroclus," overcome by Penthesilea's radiant beauty and valor, Achilles is filled with remorse for killing the girl warrior who might have been his lover. Scholars agree that Achilles's sexual attraction to the Amazon and the tragic theme of "love too late" seem to be deeply embedded features of the literary and artistic traditions. Many Greek artists illustrated this poignant motif, showing Achilles gently supporting the dying Penthesilea or the wrenching moment when he delivers the death blow and their eyes meet (fig. 18.2). In the temple of Zeus at Olympia, for example, Pausanias admired a celebrated ancient painting by Panainos (fifth century BC) showing Achilles holding Penthesilea as she breathes her last breath.[18] A sexually charged illustration of this moment was depicted on a carnelian gem carved in about 500 BC (fig. 7.5).

Achilles's act of tenderness excited the scorn of one of the Greeks, a lout named Thersites. Twisting Achilles's anguish into something obscene, Thersites jeered Achilles for lusting after the dead Amazon. In a flash of rage, Achilles struck Thersites, who fell dead. What Thersites homed in on was the psychological dissonance in an honorable duel with a "manly" warrior that suddenly ended with the vulnerable corpse of a desirable woman. Thersites's accusation of dishonor and Achilles's extreme reaction spawned a host of ancient and modern interpretations.[19]

Quintus says that Achilles did not strip away Penthesilea's armor and weapons as usual, and he honored Priam's request to bury her body, possessions, and horse. (Achilles had previously refused to turn over Hector's body to Priam and instead savagely abused it.) "Moved by admiration and pity" for the courageous Amazon, the Greeks gave her corpse to the grieving Trojans. Here is another layer of meaning for Penthesilea's name, which could signify "Mourned by the People." The Trojans lamented her death as they would that of a "beloved daughter." Old Priam built a funeral pyre, and the flames consumed the Amazon and her horse. The Trojan people reverently gathered the burned bones and placed them in a casket with perfumed oil and the fat of a fine heifer, following the same rituals that were described for the heroic funerals of Patroclus and Hector in the *Iliad*. But the Amazon's cremation *with her horse* brings to mind all the armed women who were interred with their horses across Scythia (chapter 4). The Trojans buried Penthesilea's casket in a place of very high honor, at the tower of the Skaian Gate—the resting place of the bones of King Laomedon, Priam's father. The Greeks allowed the Trojans to retrieve the twelve fallen Amazons too, and they were buried near their queen. The remains of a tower at the Skaian Gate have been identified by archaeologists in the ruins of the citadel of Late Bronze Age Troy.[20]

PENTHESILEA IN ANCIENT ART

Scenes showing Achilles and Penthesilea first appeared in Greek art by the late seventh century–early sixth century BC, indicating that their story was already widely diffused and familiar. Penthesilea's name is inscribed (in Argive and Doric Greek dialects) on three bronze shield-strap reliefs dedicated at Delphi and Olympia (early sixth century), showing her fighting Achilles. The first identifiable vase painting of the heroic duel of Penthesilea and Achilles is by Exekias (ca. 540 BC; fig. 18.2). Both their names are inscribed. Dressed in boots, a helmet, a richly patterned tunic, a sword belt, and a leopard skin, Penthesilea sinks down on one knee. The menacing Achilles, his face obscured by his helmet, leans in and plunges his spear into her neck. Penthesilea's face is uncovered and her right spear arm is raised defensively—she is in the protective posture responsible for so many "nightstick" fractures

FIG. 18.3. Trojan war scene, Achilles spearing Penthesilea, as her Amazon companion rushes up. Lucanian hydria (water jug), ca. 400 BC, from the tomb of the Policoro Painter, Heraclaea, Italy, Siritide National Museum of Policoro 35294. Photo by Marie-Lan Nguyen.

observed in the skeletons of real Scythian women with combat injuries (chapter 4). The star-crossed enemies seem to lock eyes.

The scene on the red-figure vase (fig 18.1) shows Penthesilea in red trousers and a belted tunic with crossed chest straps, astride a yellow palomino stallion charging toward a Greek warrior on foot. He is about to be crowned with a victory wreath by a winged Nike, indicating that he is Achilles. Both Penthesilea's and Achilles's cloaks are blowing out behind them, suggesting that they are rushing toward each other. Between them is a dying Amazon, her axe and shield on the ground beside her; she bleeds from wounds in her side and head. Perhaps she is dark-eyed Harmothoe, the last of Penthesilea's Amazons killed by Achilles. Penthesilea has the upper hand in another vase painting, which shows her shooting arrows while galloping away from Achilles on foot. Some vase scenes with no inscriptions can be identified as Achilles and Penthesilea by various clues: Achilles always uses a spear

FIG. 18.4. Achilles supports dying, nude Penthesilea; a mourning Amazon on left. Marble sarcophagus from Thessaloniki, ca. AD 180, inv. Ma 2119, Musée de Louvre, Paris. Photo I. Sh., 2013.

or sword to kill Penthesilea, and unlike Heracles he never grips his opponent. The vase in figure 18.3 shows Achilles viciously spearing Penthesilea, as her companion rushes to her defense and her horse rolls its eyes in terror or sympathy.

By the fifth century BC, it became popular to show Achilles supporting the dying or dead Penthesilea, as in the public painting in Olympia and in the temple at Aphrodisias. The tragic love angle was also featured in Roman-era sculptures and mosaics (fig. 18.4).[21]

A remarkable black-figure vase of about 510–500 BC (fig. 18.5) depicts Achilles carrying Penthesilea's body away from the battlefield. The Amazon's femininity is signaled by her white skin and her purple fillet, bracelet, and anklet. She wears a sword in a sheath decorated with a panther head. Penthesilea's hands and feet dangle helplessly, her eye is closed in death, and her hair falls forward. Images of male warriors and Amazons carrying their dead companions are common, but a Greek warrior bearing the body of an enemy is unique. The painting evokes the pathos of Achilles's sympathy and love for Penthesilea.[22]

FIG. 18.5. Achilles carrying the dead Penthesilea. Attic black-figure hydria (water jug), Leagros Group, ca. 510–500 BC, from Vulci, Italy, Inv. B323, British Museum. © The Trustees of the British Museum/Art Resource, NY.

PENTHESILEA IN LITERARY SOURCES

Contradictory stories about Penthesilea multiplied in classical antiquity, Roman and Byzantine times, and the medieval era. A lost work by Stesichorus (seventh–sixth centuries BC) contradicted Homeric myth, claiming that Penthesilea, rather than Achilles, had killed Hector. According to Lycophron (third century BC) the brutal Thersites had gouged out Penthesilea's eyes with his spear, and some said her body was dragged and thrown into the Scamander River. A commentator on Lycophron suggested that Penthesilea and Achilles had fought many times before he finally killed her at Troy. In yet another tradition, Achilles buried the Amazon's body on the banks of the Xanthus River, in Lycia. Another thread of the myth said she was slain not by Achilles but by his son Pyrrhus (Neoptolemus). Still another account asserted that Penthesilea actually killed Achilles (by stabbing her spear into his heel), but Achilles was brought back to life by Zeus. Then, in this zombie state, Achilles killed Penthesilea. Other commentaries twisted Thersites's gross insult into an accusation that Achilles had committed necrophilia with the Amazon's corpse.[23]

An alternative tale related by Philostratus, perhaps spun from events in the lost epic *Cypria* (above), told of a war in which the Greeks contended with an army of Scythians who came to aid the Mysians, "milk-drinking horse people," in the vicinity of Pergamon, south of Troy. Strabo identified the Mysians as a nomadic Thracian tribe from the Danube who settled among the Lydians, Phrygians, and Trojans. "The Mysian women fought from horses alongside the men, just as Amazons do," said Philostratus. Their cavalry contingent was led by a tall Amazon named Hiera (she was married to Heracles's son Telephus, mythic founder of Pergamon). When Hiera was killed by a Greek youth named Nireus, the Greeks were so filled with such admiration for her that no one despoiled her body; the grieving Telephus buried her. Hiera's death scene is illustrated on sculpted panels of the great Pergamon Altar; Hieropolis (modern Pamukkale, Turkey) may be named for her.[24]

By the Middle Ages, Achilles had faded into the background, and Penthesilea (now pictured in illustrated manuscripts as a medieval warrior queen) was given a new love interest—Hector. Christine de Pizan's catalog of illustrious women (1405) and John Lydgate's *Troy-book* (1420)

transformed her into the heroine of a romance. In their telling, Penthesilea (Pantysyllya) came to Troy because she had fallen in love from afar
with Hector, the most gallant and virtuous knight. Tragically, she arrived
just after Achilles killed Hector. In his sepulcher, kneeling before Hector's embalmed corpse, she promised to avenge the death of this "flower
of chivalry." Joining the Trojans, Penthesilea killed many Greeks but was
finally slain by Achilles's son; her body was taken back to the Thermodon. Multiple traditions and various burial sites are hallmarks of Penthesilea's heroic status, and the lore that bloomed around the figure of Penthesilea is evidence of the timeless emotional appeal of her story.[25]

In keeping with localities' ancient habit of claiming a relationship
with mythic figures, the mound at Troy was said to be the grave of
Myrine, the Tanais River memorialized the Amazon Lysippe's son, the
city of Soloi recalled the name of Antiope's drowned suitor, and numerous towns in Asia Minor took their names from Amazons. At least two
place-names were associated with Penthesilea. A curious tradition reported in late antiquity (ca. AD 1150, about two millennia after the
legendary Trojan War) claimed that Achilles and Penthesilea were in
love before they fought at Troy, and that they even had a son, Cayster,
who in turn fathered Ephesus. The Cayster (Little Meander) River was
named after this son, indirectly linking Penthesilea to the archaic sanctuary of Athena at Ephesus where the mythic Amazons performed war
dances (chapter 9). How old is this story? One source could be Strabo,
who mentioned the "hero-shrine of Cayster" on the Cayster River near
Ephesus. The tale gratifies the irresistible urge to see the thwarted desire
of the two mighty heroes at Troy somehow consummated.[26]

The other place that traced its origins to Penthesilea was very far
from Troy, across the sea in Italy. The poet Virgil (first century BC) re-
worked preexisting oral legends into a foundation epic for Rome. In his
Aeneid, the Romans were said to descend from Aeneas and other Trojan
refugees who sailed to Italy after the Trojan War. This particular tradition can be traced to a poem, by the Hellenistic Greek poet Lycophron
(ca. 250 BC), about the fates of those who escaped from Troy. Perhaps it
is significant that Lycophron was from Chalcis, Euboea, the site of a
shrine to wounded Amazon refugees from the mythic Battle for Athens
(chapter 17). Lycophron's poem tells of a young woman named Clete
(Klete, "Helper") who was Queen Penthesilea's page girl or attendant.

Left behind in Pontus, she grew desperate when her mistress did not return from Troy. She set out with a company of Amazons in search of Penthesilea, but their ship was swept off course by a tempest and they were shipwrecked in Bruttium, the toe of Italy. The Amazons named this place after Clete, who became their queen, and nearby Caulonia was named for Clete's son, the hero Caulon. "Many were laid low by Clete's hand" in Italy, and the Amazon queens who succeeded her were also called Clete.[27]

Penthesilea was the last Amazon heroine to win renown for valor in war, noted Diodorus, and after the Trojan War their race diminished so radically that people began to consider tales of their former glory to be mere fictions.[28] Yet some warrior women continued their warlike ways in splendid isolation, occasionally emerging from exotic lands to interact with historical celebrities such as the great Cyrus, Xerxes, Alexander, Mithradates, and Pompey. Before we turn to their tales, a special category of ancient Amazons deserves to have their stories told. Clete and her band found themselves lost at sea, driven by a storm to faraway Italy, much like the shipwrecked Amazons who founded the Sarmatian tribe. A surprising, little-known body of ancient lore describes many other seafaring Amazons.

19

AMAZONS AT SEA

An Amazon wearing a belted tunic, hat, and boots and carrying a crescent shield and battle-axe. The image on the ancient Anatolian coin seems commonplace. But what is that object in her right hand? A ship's anchor. What could be more incongruous? Amazons were horsewomen, not sailors.

Historical facts provide some clues to explain the curious image. The coin was issued by Ankyra (modern Ankara, Turkey) in the second century AD. A Hittite settlement in the Bronze Age, Ankyra was populated by Phrygians, Mysians, Persians, Greeks, and Celts before becoming the capital of the Roman province of Galatia in the first century BC. After Alexander the Great had conquered the city in 333 BC, Greek merchants from Pontus settled in Ankyra, situated in the arid plain of Anatolia hundreds of miles from the sea. They turned the city into an important trading center connecting the Black Sea with Colchis, Armenia, and Persia. The original Hittite name (*Ankuwa*) of this locality sounded like the ancient Greek word for "anchor" (*ankyra*). This coincidence may have led the maritime Greeks from Pontus to make an anchor the town's emblem, a reminder of their seafaring traditions. As with the mistaken etymology for "Amazon," this Greek-sounding name demanded a story, and several tales arose to explain why the landlocked city was called "Anchor." Anchors were dedicated in the city's temples and anchors began to appear on the city's coins. But why does an

FIG. 19.1. Amazon with anchor, coin minted in Ankyra, second century AD. Photo by Travis Markel, courtesy of Classical Numismatics Group, Inc. www.cngcoins.com.

Amazon hold the anchor? The best guess is that the Greek traders who settled Ankyra were originally from Pontus and wanted to honor the legendary homeland of the Amazons. Many cities in Anatolia issued coins honoring their mythic Amazon founders. A lost tradition in Ankyra about Amazons and the sea may once have drawn the two symbols together. At any rate, the juxtaposition of an Amazon and an anchor was an eye-catching, memorable image for the city's coinage.[1]

The deck of a ship is the last place one might expect to find the archer horsewomen of the steppes and mountains of Eurasia. Yet the coins of Ankyra are not the only evidence for the idea of seafaring Amazons.[2] The logistics and geography of several Greek myths about

Amazons require that the warrior women rowed or sailed ships and crossed not only rivers but large bodies of water. So far, we have already met two groups of mythic Amazons from Pontus who found themselves shipwrecked on foreign shores. The Amazon prisoners from Pontus took over the Greek ships, were swept by currents to the Azov Sea, and ultimately became the Sarmatians (chapter 3). According to legend, Penthesilea's page Clete and her companions set out by boat after the Trojan War and were swept by storms to the toe of Italy (chapter 18). Other mythic accounts suggest more deliberate sea crossings. Orithyia's Amazon army, according to some sources, traveled over the frozen Cimmerian Bosporus (Kerch) strait and the wide Danube to invade Greece. If, as other sources claim, her Amazon army came by the route taken by the historical Persian invasion armies of Darius and Xerxes in the sixth and fifth centuries BC, the women would have entered Thrace over the Bosporus Strait between the Black Sea and the Sea of Marmara. Historians tell us that Darius and Xerxes built bridges of boats. Such an engineering feat was never attributed to the Amazons of myth, but this narrow channel also freezes on occasion. Another

MAP 19.1. Amazon sea voyages. Map © Michele Angel.

unexplained example occurs in the myth of the Battle for Athens (chapter 17). How did Antiope transport the wounded Amazons across the narrow but treacherous Euripus Strait to Chalcis, Euboea?

AMAZON ISLANDS

The Greeks were seafaring people and took sea voyages for granted, so perhaps it was natural that ancient mythographers would imagine that Amazons might sail. Many incomplete literary accounts contain only oblique references to Amazons at sea, leaving the details to our imagination. Indirect evidence of mythic voyages comes from several Aegean islands that have Amazonian associations. For example, the main town of the Aegean island of Lesbos (known to the Hittites as *Lazpa*) is Mytilene, an Amazon name. According to a fanciful romance (by Dionysius Leather-Arm; chapter 23), the Amazon queen Myrine conquered several Anatolian cities and Aegean islands, and she named the city of Mytilene on Lesbos after her sister. During this campaign, Myrine was caught up in a storm at Lesbos and carried northward to a desert island where she set up altars to Cybele (see below).[3]

Cybele was also worshipped on the island of Lemnos. Both Lesbos and Lemnos were said to be allies of King Priam in the legendary Trojan War. Both islands have archaeological ruins linking them to ancient Troy. Lemnos was later settled by raiders or pirates from Thrace, a land often linked with Amazons. In Greek myth, Lemnos was an island of women who had murdered their husbands for taking up with slaves from Thrace. The Lemnian women were not Amazons, but they share some features with the mythic warrior women. They lived on their own, led by Queen Hypsipyle (a similar Amazon name appears on some Greek vases, and her mother was called Myrine). When Jason and the Argonauts landed on Lemnos, the women took up weapons to defend themselves. But Hypsipyle suggested that instead of fighting they should make love (and babies) with the handsome Greek seamen.[4]

Another Aegean island, Patmos (inhabited since the Bronze Age), was sacred to Artemis, the other goddess associated with Amazons. The southern promontory of Patmos was known as Amazoneum ("Amazon shrine"; see chapter 17 for other Amazon shrines in Greece). The reason is unknown. But an intriguing inscription (second century AD) discovered on Patmos calls the goddess "Artemis of *Scythia*." This goddess was also called Artemis Tauropolos (Artemis of Tauris, the Crimea). Herodotus mentioned her in the mid-fifth century BC, reporting that a savage Scythian tribe of the northern Black Sea, the Tauri of Crimea, lived by war and plunder. They sacrificed shipwrecked sailors to this virgin goddess, identified as "Iphigenia." Iphigenia was known to the Greeks as the daughter of Agamemnon in the Trojan War cycle of myths. The Greek playwright Euripides drew on Herodotus's account in his tragedy *Iphigenia in Tauris* (425–412 BC), casting Iphigenia as the priestess of Artemis who sacrificed shipwrecked sailors.

In his play, Iphigenia and her brother Orestes stole the ancient wooden statue of Artemis of Scythia from the Tauri tribe and set it up in Brauron, Greece (where young Greek girls gave up their "Amazonian" souls to Artemis; see the prologue). But the Patmos inscription appears to refer to a different, local version of the myth, in which the Tauri's wooden statue of Artemis was on Patmos. The inscription tells of a priestess named Vera, born near Ephesus, a place sacred to Amazons. Vera is said to have sailed from Ephesus to Patmos during a storm to care for the statue of Artemis of Scythia on the island. These threads—the worship of "Artemis of Scythia" in Brauron and by the Tauri tribe of Scythia, combined with the tale of a priestess of Artemis at Ephesus sailing to Patmos, and the mysterious Amazon shrine on the island's sea cliff—are tantalizing hints that a lost story may once have connected Artemis, seagoing Amazons, and Scythia.[5]

Patmos is not far from the large island of Samos, separated by a narrow channel from Ephesus on the Turkish mainland. Samos was the site of a mythic battle between the Amazons and the god Dionysus.

AMAZONS AND DIONYSUS ON SAMOS

In Greek myth, on his way to Greece from India, the god of wine Dionysus and his entourage encountered hostile Amazons dwelling around the sanctuary of Artemis at Ephesus. A battle broke out and the Amazons fled across the water to Samos with Dionysus in pursuit. The full myth is lost, but fragments of what was once a popular tale exist in several ancient sources. No details survive to reveal how the Amazons crossed over to Samos. Samos was connected to the mainland until about ten thousand years ago: today the shallow channel is only a mile wide. Geologists have traced variations in sea levels and tectonic (earthquake) shifts resulting in dramatic coastline changes in the Mediterranean–Black Sea region since antiquity. For example, ancient Troy was a port; it is now a few miles inland. Samos was first settled in about 3000 BC. Perhaps the Samos strait was shallower and narrower when the myth originated, or maybe the Amazons stole boats or swam with their horses. At any rate, Plutarch tells us that "Dionysus and his companions rigged up their ships and sailed to Samos in pursuit of the Amazons." Another terrible battle took place on the island. Dionysus slaughtered most of the Amazons at a spot forever after known as Panaema ("Blood-Soaked Field") because of the vast amount of blood shed there. Panaema has conspicuous red soil. Greek observers in antiquity explained the red earth there as the bloodstained battlefield where the god killed Amazons.[6]

The site of the mythic battle on Samos is well known to modern paleontologists as an extremely rich fossil bed from the Miocene epoch (25–5 million years ago). Very large bleached fossil bones of the extinct ancestors of elephants, rhinos, giraffes, and horses are visible as they erode out of the red sediments. Because of seismic stress, the fossils are jumbled and fractured, but recognizable individual mammalian bones of extraordinary size stand out. According to ancient Greek writers, some of these massive thighbones and shoulder blades were displayed in antiquity as the remains of the fallen Amazons. This was in keeping with the ancient belief that men and women of the mythic past were giants compared to present-day people. Other enormous fossil bones and huge tusks were believed to be from war elephants that Dionysus brought from India. Possibly some prehistoric horse bones and teeth were identified as the remains of the Amazons' horses. Travelers in antiquity marveled at these relics weathering out of the "battleground" and displayed in the local Temple of Hera. Archaeologists excavating the altar of the temple discovered a large fossilized femur from Panaema that had been dedicated in the seventh century BC. Another ancient dedication from the same era was a fragment of a terra-cotta shield depicting an Amazon wearing a helmet and a spotted leopard skin and carrying a spear. This Samos shield is among the most ancient artistic representations of an Amazon (comparable to the terra-cotta shield at Tiryns thought to depict Hippolyte and Heracles; chapter 15).[7]

The village near the Panaema fossil beds/Amazon battleground is called Mytilene, a familiar Amazon name. Across from Samos on the mainland was the ancient town of Anaea (exact location unknown), named for the Amazon who was buried there according to a lost work by Ephorus of Cyme (a town named for an Amazon). Priene, another very ancient town across from Samos, was said to have been named after one of Queen Myrine's commanders. It seems likely that Myrine, Mytilene, Priene, and Anaea were featured in the full story of the Amazons who battled Dionysus on Samos.[8] The myth of Amazons on Samos, the blood-soaked battlefield, the extraordinary bones displayed to ancient travelers, the Amazon on the terra-cotta shield dedicated in the temple, and the Amazon place-names: all are strong evidence of stories and rituals honoring Amazons on the island of Samos.

The evidence of traditions associated with Amazons' voyages to various Aegean islands is surprisingly extensive for such earthbound figures normally based in the steppes and mountains. These fragmentary tales suggest that there were numerous shrines and cults, with detailed narratives and named heroines, commemorating Amazons all around the ancient Greek world. But were the Amazons portrayed as mariners worth their salt? In the myths that describe the warrior women adrift on the "wine-dark seas," the Amazons' seacraft was not stellar. One might see this failing as a way of casting the barbarian women warriors as the opposites of the Greeks, who were mariners par excellence. On the other hand, there were many myths about shipwrecked Greek male heroes and their adventures on desert islands—Odysseus is the most famous example. The numerous scenarios describing Amazons carried away by storm-tossed seas and stranded on desert islands far from home are compelling evidence of Amazons' status as popular heroines of oft-told stories.

AMAZON ADVENTURES ON DESERT ISLES

In the tale about Myrine on Lesbos, her vessel was storm-swept to the northern Aegean and deposited on Samothrace, at that time an uninhabited island off the coast of Thrace. There Myrine set up altars to

Cybele in thanks for her survival. We know that Samothrace was first settled by Thracians and then by Greeks from Lesbos in about 700 BC.

The story of Myrine recalls the Amazon altars to Cybele on the tiny desert isle, off the coast of Pontus, known as Ares or Amazon Island (chapter 10). The rocky islet is less than a mile from the mainland. Did the Amazons sail or swim to the island to sacrifice their horses before going to war? In the *Argonautica* epic, Jason and his crew sailed along this coast on their quest for the Golden Fleece of Colchis. At a grave mound by the sea in Pontus, they met the ghost of Sthenelus, a Greek hero killed by the Amazons in the war between Heracles and Queen Hippolyte. They also rescued three Greek veterans of that same war stranded in Sinope. Then, when the *Argo* dropped anchor at Ares Island, Jason and the Argonauts chanced upon four survivors of a shipwreck stranded on the Amazons' sacred island. These sailors, who happened to be the grandsons of the king of Colchis, joined the Argonauts' expedition.[9]

Shipwrecked sailors also figure in a story told by Philostratus (chapter 8), in which Amazons in the region of Colchis-Pontus captured some marooned seamen. In Philostratus's tale, a fleet of ships engaged in commerce between the Black Sea and Greece was blown off course by a winter storm and wrecked on the coast of Colchis between the Thermodon and Phasis rivers. The bedraggled sailors, shipbuilders, and traders were captured by the Amazons, who chained them to troughs and fattened them up, with the intention of selling them to Scythian "cannibals." The plot recalls the account in Herodotus and in Euripides's play (above) about the Tauri tribe of the Crimea in Scythian territory, who sacrificed sailors cast up on their shores to "Artemis of Scythia." These broken strands of myth associate the Amazons with Artemis and with the real pirates who plied the Black Sea in antiquity, notorious for capturing peoples of Scythian lands and selling them as slaves in the Greek colonies.[10] Stories had long circulated among Greeks that some outlandish tribes in Scythia and the Caucasus practiced cannibalism, the product of sensational rumors about savage barbarians mixed with garbled reports of real Scythian funeral practices.

But these sailors were in luck. One young Amazon was attracted to the youngest seaman. She succeeded in convincing the Amazon leader to spare all the men's lives. Some scholars identify this young Amazon as Peisianassa, "She Who Persuades the Queen." Peisianassa is depicted wearing high boots, a long-sleeved patterned tunic, and a Thracian helmet, carrying a crescent shield and a spear, on a fifth-century BC vase painting (attributed to Polygnotus; the scene is thought to be based on famous wall paintings in Athens). Peisianassa's two mounted companions on the vase are also identified by inscriptions, Hippomache ("Horse Warrior") and Dolope (a Thracian tribal name).[11]

Given their freedom, the men chose to stay with their former Amazon captors, enjoying merry sex, and learning each other's languages. The mariners regaled the Amazons with nautical stories and the marvelous sights they had seen sailing around the Black Sea. The men described an eerie desert island, Leuke (White Island) in the northern Black Sea. The Thracian island of Leuke in the northern Black Sea was sacred to Achilles, according to several ancient poets and historians. Leuke is now identified as the minuscule Zmeinyi Island east of the mouth of the Danube. Archaeology on the island confirms the remains of several ancient shrines to Achilles.

After Achilles was killed at Troy, his bones were buried on White Island, according to the epic poem *Aethiopis*. In antiquity the little island of white marble was supposed to be haunted by the ghost of Achilles, who kept a herd of sacred mares. Philostratus says that the Amazons conceived an irresistible desire to sail to Leuke to obtain those special mares—they could also avenge the death of their queen Penthesilea at Troy. They ordered the shipbuilders among their new lovers to build boats suitable for transporting horses. Meanwhile the seamen gave the Amazons lessons in rowing and sailing. When the ships were ready that spring, the sailors and the Amazons sailed forth. After a long voyage they reached Leuke.

The Amazons ordered their men to chop down the forest that guarded the sanctuary where the sacred horses grazed. But the ghost of Achilles cast a magic spell on the axes, which bounced off the trees and rebounded on the men, chopping off their heads. Aghast at the mayhem, the horsewomen ran to mount the mares and tried to herd them toward the boats. But the ghost of Achilles filled the horses with wild terror. The mares began to neigh and rear, bucking off their riders. With pricked ears and bristling manes, the demonic horses trampled and bit the Amazons, tearing at their flesh and devouring the fallen bodies. The crazed herd of carnivorous mares, blood dripping from their teeth, stampeded to a high cliff and, believing they saw a wide plain before them, hurled themselves into the sea. Meanwhile, a violent wind arose and dashed the Amazon ships to pieces. The boats sank amid the wreckage "just as if there had been a great naval battle." The ghost of Achilles caused a giant wave to wash away all traces of the Amazons and their sailor-lovers, thereby purifying his sacred island.

Philostratus wove this baroque horror story from a skein of folklore, legend, myth, contemporary popular culture, authentic history, and pure imagination. For example, Achilles's wild mares of Leuke parallel the myth of Diomedes's diabolical man-eating mares of Thrace on the Black Sea. There is a ghastly irony in the horsewomen's inability to control the horses and grim poetic justice in the fate of those who had plotted to sell their captives to cannibals.[12]

The extensive yet little-studied body of ancient lore linking Amazons to cities and locales in Greece and Asia Minor, and even to Aegean islands, demonstrates that having an association with the legendary world of Amazons was highly desirable. Philostratus's lurid story of the Amazons who went to sea demonstrates that they continued to be a topic of keen popular interest in the third century AD. But their terrible destruction on the White Island drives home the impression that Amazons seem out of place messing about in boats. In the myths about seagoing Amazons, it must be said that their nautical adventures are rather haphazard, and their navigation skills range from rudimentary to ineffectual.

A PERSIAN ADMIRAL WITH AMAZON CREDENTIALS

Turning now from myth to history, we meet two genuine warrior queens of antiquity who won renown for their naval expertise and bold exploits at sea. One was the Persian admiral Artemisia, and the other a pirate queen of Illyria. The Greeks thought of Queen Artemisia I of Halicarnassus as a kind of maritime Amazon. She was said to sport attire typical of Persian men, similar to the dress of Amazons in Greek vase paintings—a long-sleeved patterned tunic and trousers—and to be armed with a dagger and sword. Herodotus, a native of her city, proudly recounted Artemisia's illustrious deeds in detail. An ally and trusted adviser of Xerxes during the Persian invasion of Greece, Artemisia was the king's only female admiral. She contributed five warships from Caria to the Persian fleet and distinguished herself in a naval encounter at Euboea and at the great sea battle at Salamis in 480 BC. Although she had wisely warned Xerxes to avoid the naval engagement at Salamis, when the battle took place Artemisa commanded her warship with outstanding shrewdness and courage, saving her own ship by sinking another. According to Plutarch, she also recovered the body of Xerxes's brother Ariamenes from the wreckage of his ship.

The Greeks offered a reward of ten thousand drachmas for her capture alive, but after the Greek victory at Salamis Artemisia escaped to Ephesus, a place with deep Amazonian connections. (Some survivors of the failed Amazon invasion of Athens took refuge in Ephesus, said to have been founded by Amazons.) The Greeks were the ultimate victors, but they admired Artemisia's fortitude and heroic seamanship.[13]

Artemisia I is sometimes confused with another powerful Persian queen of Halicarnassus, Artemisia II, who conquered the island of Rhodes and built the celebrated Mausoleum decorated with Amazons (353–350 BC). A sensational archaeological discovery of 1857 connects the two warrior queens of Caria. Archaeologists excavating the ruins of the Mausoleum of Halicarnassus discovered a vase of translucent stone (about twelve inches high) bearing the royal inscription "Xerxes, the Great King" in Egyptian hieroglyphs, in Old Persian Elamite, and in Babylonian cuneiform. This elegant alabaster perfume jar had been an intimate possession of Artemisia I, a costly gift from the grateful Xerxes to his famous female naval commander. The vase of Artemisia had been passed down in the royal Carian family, coming into the hands of her namesake, Artemisia II, more than a century after the Battle of Salamis.[14]

TEUTA, PIRATE QUEEN OF ILLYRIA

Another Amazonian terror of the high seas was Teuta, the steely pirate queen from the Ardiaei tribe of Illyria, along the eastern Adriatic seacoast. Unlike Persia, where Artemisia was unique for going to war, Illyria was known for women trained in warfare. Teuta inherited her husband's kingdom of confederated Illyrian pirates, who preyed on Roman

FIG. 19.2. Alabaster perfume jar from Halicarnassus (southwest Turkey), gift from the Persian king Xerxes to his admiral Artemesia, inscribed in Old Persian, Elamite, Babylonian, and Egyptian. Inv. AN 132114, British Museum. © The Trustees of the British Museum/Art Resource, NY.

and Greek shipping routes in the third century BC. From her secluded castle at Rhizon in the Bay of Kotor (now Montenegro) Queen Teuta commanded a large pirate navy of small, lightweight galleys with two banks of rowers, designed for speed and agility. These pirate cruisers had a rostrum (pointed beak) on the prow for ramming and sinking ships; some rams took the form of dragons. Teuta personally accompanied the pirates on their sea raids and incursions into port cities up and down the Adriatic coast. A typical method of pillaging a city was for the pirate crew to stagger ashore carrying water jugs, desperately begging for water, pretending to be dying of thirst. Once inside the city gates, the brigands pulled out the scimitars they had hidden in the water jars.

Teuta's raiders terrorized the Adriatic, looting, taking captives, and attacking cities at will. By 230 BC they were venturing into the Ionian Sea and the Mediterranean, further disrupting Roman and Greek sea trade. Roman envoys were dispatched to demand reparations, but Teuta informed them that piracy was a perfectly legitimate enterprise that provided gainful employment for her subjects. On their return journey to Italy, Teuta's pirates attacked and plundered the Romans' ship and murdered one of the envoys. This last straw compelled Rome to declare war on Teuta in 229 BC. With their superior numbers on land and sea, Rome finally prevailed over the pirates and took over their fortresses. Queen Teuta escaped to her castle, but she was forced to renounce piracy, pay tribute, surrender her prisoners, and turn over the Roman deserters who had joined her pirate navy. Still defiant, however, Teuta only apologized for acts of piracy that might have occurred during her late husband's reign, and refused to acknowledge her own crimes. Roman warships quickly adopted the design of the swift pirate galleys, called *liburnae* after the Liburnians, one of Teuta's pirate tribes.[15]

What became of all the loot amassed by Teuta's pirates? Some of the treasure has lain buried for more than two millennia in the queen's fortified hideaway at Rhizon. In 2010–12, Polish archaeologists unearthed two extremely large coin hoards from the time of Rome's wars against the Illyrian pirates. Hidden in a big ceramic pot, buried under a floor covered with debris caused by fire, was a treasure of 4,656 coins, the largest coin hoard known from the third century BC. Among the costly artifacts of a nearby house they recovered a leather pouch holding more than 100 coins. Other artifacts from Rhizon include more coins, amber, glass, mosaics, shipbuilding supplies, and pottery from Italy, Attica, and Corinth. Another sensational discovery was a heavy gold signet ring with a carved gem of crimson agate from Sicily. Like the coins in the large hoard, the agate gem carries a portrait of Artemis, the goddess worshipped by the Illyrians (and associated with Amazons). Analysis of the coins and pottery, stratigraphy, and radiocarbon dating of the charcoal indicate that the coins and the ring were probably lost during the pirates' escape from burning buildings during the Roman attack on Teuta's stronghold (plate 14).[16]

With the military exploits of Artemisia and Teuta, we are moving from mythology into history. When Artemisia II was building the Mausoleum of Halicarnassus decorated with fighting Amazons, Alexander of Macedon (b. 356 BC) was a boy just learning to ride a horse—and his Illyrian half sister Cynna was already leading an army. By age twenty-six, Alexander had defeated the mighty Persian Empire and set his sights on Central Asia and India. The young world conqueror enjoyed sexual liaisons along the way, but he would meet his match in the imperious Amazon queen Thalestris.

2 0

THALESTRIS AND ALEXANDER THE GREAT

FTER ALEXANDER HAD CONQUERED PERSIA, HE was determined to expand his empire all the way to India. In 330 BC, Alexander's Macedonian army of more than thirty thousand marched east from Ecbatana (Hamadan, Iran) following the course of the caravan route (Silk Route) through the high desert to Rhaga (Tehran). They threaded through the "Caspian Gates," a narrow defile in the Elburz Mountains, and reached fertile Hyrcania on the southern Caspian shore. Alexander encamped, about fifteen miles northwest of the ancient city of Hecatompylus, at a huge rock and cavern with a spring. From this base, Alexander and part of his army subdued Hyrcanian towns and received envoys from neighboring tribes pledging allegiance (map 20.1).

But the Mardians, tough horse archers to the west, resisted. Alexander took a contingent and followed the southern Caspian coastline west to try to defeat the nomad force of eight thousand. The Macedonians killed many Mardians, but the rest melted back into their mountain fastness.[1]

The wily Mardians had the upper hand. They withdrew into an impregnable hillside "fortress" made of intertwined living trees. Both sides continued to suffer casualties in skirmishes, and the Mardians captured some Macedonians who lost their way in the rough terrain. Frustrated, Alexander ordered his men to burn the countryside. His pages led the royal horses to a safe pasture while the Mardians observed from the heights. Suddenly a party rushed down and stole the best steed in the herd. They made off with the magnificent and beloved Bucephalus, who had carried Alexander in all his battles, the horse who kneeled to allow his master to mount him. Furious, Alexander vowed to chop down every tree and slaughter everyone in the land. This threat was delivered to the Mardians in their own language by an interpreter, probably a captive.

According to Diodorus, the Mardians were so "terrified" that they immediately returned Bucephalus with costly gifts. But Plutarch described the exchange very differently. The Mardians stole Bucephalus, Alexander threatened reprisals, and the nomads returned the horse, promising loyalty. Alexander treated the tribe kindly and even paid a generous ransom to the men who had so expertly captured his horse. The Mardians' actions conform to nomadic horse-raiding customs and their esteem for powerful leaders. Capturing Bucephalus initiated a sort of conversation and a test in which each side could express mutual respect. Similar captures of horses by Amazons are described in Indian and Asian tales (chapter 24). Alexander's response shows his growing understanding of the nomads' ways.[2]

Alexander rode Bucephalus back to his camp in Hyrcania. There he received a surprise visit: another army of tough warriors on horseback—three hundred Amazons led by Queen Thalestris.

QUEEN THALESTRIS'S QUEST

Renowned for her bravery and beauty, Thalestris had traveled from her land to meet the man who had defeated the Persians. "Marveling at the unexpected arrival and dignified spectacle of the women warriors in armor," Alexander asked Thalestris the reason for her visit. She replied that word of his conquests had reached her, and she had decided to have a child by him. Thalestris invited Alexander to have sex. "He was the greatest of all men in his achievements, and she was superior to all women in strength and courage," explains Diodorus in this earliest surviving account (first century BC), and so "presumably the offspring of

such superlative parents would surpass all other mortals in excellence."
Alexander, "delighted by her summons, eagerly granted her request."
The couple spent thirteen days and nights together. At the end of their
affair, Alexander honored her with generous farewell gifts and Thalestris rode away with her entourage.[3]

Another early version of their meeting was recounted in more vivid
detail by the historian Curtius in the first century AD. Thalestris, "fired
with a desire to visit the King" set out with a large escort from her land.
As the ruler of the Amazons approached his camp, she sent messengers
to "give notice that the queen was eager to meet and become acquainted
with him." At once Alexander gave his permission. Thalestris rode in
with a bodyguard of three hundred women, leaving the rest of her
forces behind. She would have presented Alexander with fine gifts upon
her arrival, such as golden trappings for Bucephalus or a woolen cape
with golden spangles.

Curtius offered a general description of typical Amazon attire and
noted that Thalestris wore a garment "knotted just above the knee"
(perhaps a skirt arranged for riding), with her right breast veiled and
the other exposed. Assuming that Thalestris was a real horsewoman
archer, ancient artistic images and archaeological discoveries permit us
to imagine her garments shimmering with hundreds of tiny golden
appliqués of animals: a long-sleeved silken tunic belted with an elaborate golden buckle, trousers or a riding skirt over soft leather boots, and
a leopard-skin cape, a dagger at her side, and a quiver and bow at her
back. Her horse would have elaborately embroidered saddle blankets
and dazzling golden accoutrements.

As soon as she spotted Alexander, she leaped down from her horse,
carrying two spears in her right hand. Brazenly she gazed at the king,
giving his physique the once over. Curtius tells us that Thalestris was
unimpressed with Alexander's slight stature and ordinary appearance,
which did not live up to the fame of his heroic exploits. Barbarians expected that only those endowed with superior physical form and majestic charisma were capable of glorious deeds. Yet when Alexander asked
if she had any requests, she boldly explained her intent to become pregnant with his child. She pointed out that she was a woman worthy of
giving him an heir for his kingdom.

Then she made an interesting promise: Thalestris would raise a baby girl, but if she bore a son, the boy would be returned to his father, Alexander. This detail in Curtius is a note of authenticity. It reflects the traditional child-rearing practices of the women called Amazons and the men who fathered their children, as reported by many ancient historians. The sons were returned to the fathers, who adopted them as rightful heirs. Similar fosterage arrangements, sending sons (and sometimes daughters) to be raised by allied clans or tribes, were long customary among peoples of the Caucasus and other tribes of Eurasia until modern times (chapter 10).

Curtius includes another significant detail: Alexander asked Thalestris to join his cavalry. Thalestris declined, saying she needed to defend her own country, but she persisted in her wish to bear his child. Her sexual passion was greater than Alexander's, commented Curtius, but he devoted thirteen days to satisfying her desire.[4]

In antiquity, this story immediately achieved legendary status. And it sparked controversy—not surprising when a larger-than-life hero, later worshipped as a god, makes love with a ruler identified as the "queen of the Amazons." The incident was discussed by numerous historians in antiquity. Some accepted the story; some doubted; others described different encounters with Amazons. Plutarch, in his evenhanded biography of Alexander, acknowledged that "most writers reported that the queen of the Amazons came to see him in Hyrcania." He listed fourteen sources for the story but gave a bit more weight to the skeptics. Letters attributed to Alexander in antiquity are highly suspect, but Plutarch accepted the authenticity of his letter to Antipater (Alexander's regent in Macedon). Plutarch thought it significant that the letter told of a Scythian chieftain offering his daughter in marriage but without any mention of Thalestris. This formal letter conveyed the political and military details of Alexander's campaign and justifications for pushing on to India, however, so a private sexual dalliance would have been irrelevant.[5]

Plutarch also repeated a well-known anecdote about an exchange that supposedly occurred between two old veterans of Alexander's campaigns. The story goes that Onesicritus was reading his narrative about the Amazon queen aloud to Lysimachus, who smiled gently and said, "And where was I, then?" Lysimachus was one of Alexander's officers; perhaps he remained with another part of the main army when Alexander was camped near Hecatompylus and turned west with twenty-three thousand men to subdue Hyrcania and the Mardians. The comment is enigmatic. Was Lysimachus bantering about missing out on the action, or humorously denying the whole story? Onesicritus's firsthand account of the Asian campaign, now known only from fragments, contained many valuable details, but he was sometimes accused of exaggeration.[6]

Among other surviving sources, Justin offers a few more details about the great stir that the Amazons' arrival and their wondrous appearance caused in Alexander's camp. Thalestris was "dressed strangely for a woman," says Justin. And "the purpose of her visit aroused general surprise: she came seeking sexual intercourse." Alexander decided to linger for thirteen days with his guest. "When she was sure she had conceived, Thalestris departed."[7]

How believable is the tale of Alexander and the Amazon who desired to have his child? For such a sensational topic, the story as we have it seems straightforward and unadorned with dubious or overwrought details, and it does not follow the familiar Greek mythic script of violence against Amazons. The episode is embedded in a sequence of historical events whose authenticity is generally accepted. Many ancient historians felt compelled to include this story: it seemed plausible to enough people to merit preservation and discussion. Plutarch, for example, kept an open mind, but he felt that the most trustworthy authors were skeptical. Strabo, dubious for the same reason, accepted that Amazons, fighting women living with or without men, had dwelled in lands of the Black Sea–Caucasus–Caspian region in the past. But he was not entirely convinced that renegade bands of Amazons were active in Alexander's time or in Strabo's own day three hundred years later, even though he acknowledged that many asserted this.

We cannot hope to prove or disprove the veracity of the meeting of Thalestris and Alexander. But we can analyze each feature of this and the related narratives for authenticity and plausibility in terms of what was possible for that time and place. Let's begin with the geography of the queen's origin and her journey to Hyrcania.

THALESTRIS'S HOMELAND AND ROUTE

Assuming Thalestris really existed, where was she from? Diodorus says her home was between the Thermodon and Phasis rivers, in Pontus-Colchis. Strabo places her in the Thermodon-Caucasus region. Curtius locates the extent of her rule from Pontus to the Caucasus range in Colchis (which he mistakenly assumed bordered on Hyrcania). This area corresponds to Caucasian Iberia, the foothills above the Phasis valley, and Caucasian Albania between the eastern end of the Caucasus and the Caspian Sea. According to Strabo, "Amazons were said to live in the mountains above Albania." (This is the region where the Roman commander Pompey would encounter Amazon fighters in the first century BC; chapter 21.) Justin reports that Thalestris's Amazons were "neighbors of the Albani." He reminds us that the Amazons had lost their foothold in Pontus, and many moved to the northern steppes after Queen Orithyia's defeat at the Battle for Athens. The next great warrior queen of the Pontus region was the brave Penthesilea, notes Justin, but her band was wiped out at Troy. He, like others, indicates that isolated pockets of beleaguered Pontic Amazons remained in the mountains around the southeastern corner of the Black Sea, in Pontus, Colchis, Iberia, and Albania (northeastern Turkey, Georgia, Azerbaijan, and Armenia). "They managed to survive down to the time of Alexander the Great," says Justin. "One of these was Queen Thalestris."[8]

Another geographical possibility is that Thalestris was based in the territory west of the Caspian Sea, northwest of Hyrcania (southern Azerbaijan, northern Iran, Armenia), and that the Greek writers simply assumed an Amazon queen must have originated on the Thermodon plain in Pontus or in Colchis, two lands where ancient Greek myths placed them. Notably, an Azerbaijani legend tells of a meeting between Alexander and a Saka "queen" from Caucasian Albania (chapter 22). The region between the Black and Caspian seas and beyond was inhabited by Saka-Scythian and related tribes (nomadic and seminomadic) whose numbers fluctuated, and whose men and women made war, traded, and raided other tribes for horses and gold, forming mixed and same-sex groups according to circumstances and whim. Thalestris could have belonged to a tribe that marshaled groups of men, men and some women, or just women for hunting, reconnaissance, negotiations, battle, raiding, or adventure—all options in nomad culture. All-women groups came together and disbanded on an ad hoc basis for various reasons (when a particularly strong woman leader arose, or when most men were away or had been killed in battle). If Thalestris "left the bulk of her army at the border of Hyrcania," as Diodorus and Curtius reported, these might even have been male soldiers. (Only Justin says her entire force consisted of three hundred women warriors.)[9]

The great news of Alexander's epic victory over the Persian Empire certainly resounded in all the Persian-influenced lands between the Black and Caspian seas. Alexander's historians describe numerous tribes of Scythians and others dispatching emissaries with armed escorts to meet and greet the leader of the next superpower. Such a party might be led by one of the tribe's best warriors, who could have been a woman.

What was the route taken by Thalestris? The sources are unclear. Strabo preserved a scrap of information from Cleitarchus, who was with Alexander but whose work is lost: Thalestris set out from "Thermodon" and came by way of the "Caspian Gates" to Hyrcania. As noted, "Amazons of Thermodon" was a familiar trope from myth. Adding to the uncertainty, three different passes were known as the "Caspian Gates" in antiquity. One was the narrow passage between eastern cliffs of the Caucasus range and the Caspian Sea (Dagestan), also called the Marpesian Rock after the Amazon queen. This pass was sometimes confused with the Scythian Gates over the mid-Caucasus because Greek historians were unclear about the precise locations of these two passes. Both were major migration routes from the northern steppes to the Caspian (chapter 2).[10] If we accept that Thalestris started from the southern Black Sea region of ancient Colchis, then she would not have crossed either of these Caucasus passes. But she may well have traveled through the third pass by that name, the "Caspian Gates" east of Ecbatana, the very same pass traversed by Alexander on the way to Hyrcania.

If she set out from the southeastern Black Sea/southern Caucasus, Thalestris's likely path would follow the Phasis and Cyrus river valleys through the lands of Caucasian Iberia and Albania, eastward to the Caspian Sea. There she would turn south, through the luxuriant horse pastures west of the Caspian Sea. Migrating nomads from the Black Sea, Caucasus, and steppes routinely ranged over this territory west of the Caspian (see chapter 4 for armed women's graves in this region). Justin

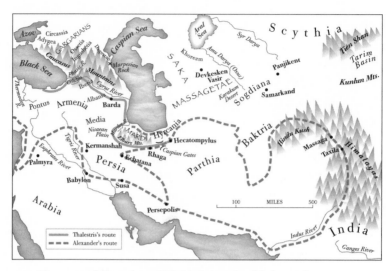

MAP 20.1. The routes of Alexander and Thalestris. Map © Michele Angel.

indicated that Thalestris's army had to avoid hostile Saka-Scythian-Sarmatian tribes on this trek. After Darius III's defeat by Alexander, nomad bands would have been attracted to the Nisaean Plain to capture fine horses from the celebrated royal Persian herds.

Because Thalestris knew only that Alexander was marching east on the main caravan route, but was unaware of his exact location, she would not travel around the southern Caspian but would continue south across the Elburz range, Mardian territory, perhaps following the Mardos (Sefid Rud) river valley. At a point near ancient Rhaga, her party would join the main caravan route. From here, she could easily retrace the path of Alexander's immense Macedonian army as it headed east through the Caspian Gates (about fifty miles from Rhaga). Thalestris would now be passing through lands recently subdued by Alexander, meeting people who could fill her in on his progress. Indeed, many of Alexander's soldiers would have been strung out along this trail.[11] Following Alexander's route made sense; sooner or later she would catch up with him. Learning the location of his headquarters at the spring north of Hecatompylus, she and her escort of three hundred female warriors would overtake Alexander after he returned from the Mardian venture, in late summer 330 BC.

Justin provides another important detail: "Thalestris traveled 35 days through hostile territories in order to have a child by king Alexander." Strabo thought that such a long journey—"more than 6,000 stadia from the Thermodon to Hyrcania"—was impractical. The distance of the trek outlined above would be about 600–700 miles (1 mile = 8.7 stadia). Depending on the terrain, weather, water, pasture, weight of her supplies, number of spare horses, and hostile encounters, Thalestris and her cohort could ride an average of 20 to 30 miles a day. Mounted nomads could easily travel 700–1,000 miles in 35 days. Strabo's geographic doubts, at least, can be laid to rest.[12]

WHO WAS THALESTRIS?

Thalestris was described in all the sources as a ruler, but "princess" and "queen" were Greek and Latin labels. Could she have been the daughter of a Scythian chieftain later promoted to "Amazon queen" by popular folklore? This possibility is suggested by Alexander's letter to Antipater cited by Plutarch, above, and other accounts discussed below. Thalestris was clearly an acclaimed warrior leader in her own right. Whether such a visitor came on her own or as a representative of her people to propose a marriage alliance or to become pregnant by the great world conqueror, a Saka-Scythian-Sarmatian woman would arrive on horseback well armed, dressed in distinctive nomad attire, and with an armed escort of women. (Curtius reported that "a troop of women on horseback attended the Persian queens" when they were captured after Darius's defeat in 333 BC.) As some modern scholars suggest, the "most likely historical explanation" is that Thalestris was a woman "of Saka stock accustomed to ride and shoot, who came with a mounted group of females also carrying weapons." It was "highly likely that there were nomadic Scythian women who practiced these customs." Many tribes sent envoys, women, gifts, and pledges of fealty to Alexander as he advanced east. Primed by mythology and travelers' tales, Alexander's men (and his later historians) might very well jump to the conclusion that such an entourage was composed of Amazons and that their leader was their queen.[13]

Thalestris had distinguished herself in battle among her own people, noted Diodorus, and now she sought a worthy mate for sex and off-spring. Whether or not Thalestris really existed, this sequence has the ring of authenticity. From Herodotus on, writers tell how Scythian "man-killers" demonstrated their mettle and then were at liberty to enjoy sex and have children with men of their own choosing, often males outside of their immediate tribe. The three hundred women who accompanied Thalestris would also have been proven warriors, and they may well have had the same idea of consorting with Alexander's soldiers. Might some of the Amazon leader's companions have remained with the Macedonian soldiers, or did they all depart after thirteen days? The usual Amazon way was to move on after mating, but Herodotus and others also refer to some lasting unions. At any rate, even though it took the Greeks by surprise, there was nothing extraordinary about a party of young warrior women inviting a group of battle-hardened men to frolic with them for a couple of weeks with the aim of going home pregnant with robust offspring. Herodotus told of a Scythian tribe that sought to reinforce their bloodlines through sex with strangers perceived to have excellent characteristics (chapter 3). More than two millennia later, Turk-oman storytellers in the vicinity of Alexander's Hyrcanian camp still tell a traditional tale of "fairy tribe of Amazon women who capture un-wary men for use as studs." A number of peoples living along Alexan-der's path of conquest across Asia claim to have descended from his soldiers. It is even said that Alexander's horse Bucephalus left equine descendants. (Bucephaus died at age thirty in Afghanistan; Alexander buried him with great honors and named a city for him.)[14]

The Amazon queen's name poses a curious riddle. In a fragment of the earliest known account, by Cleitarchus (who was with Alexander, cited by Strabo), the Amazon's name was "Thalestria"; Diodorus calls her "Thallestris." Justin added another name from an unknown source, Minythyia. We don't know her true name, of course, since both of these names are clearly Greek. "Thallestris" means "She Who Makes Bloom or Grow," while "Minythyia" means the opposite, "She Who Diminishes." Possibly Thallestria/Thallestris was a translation or Hellenization of her real barbarian name. But the pairing of this name with its opposite is suggestive. Joking names with double meanings abounded in antiquity. For a modern analogy, consider the wordplay inherent in "lady-killer" for an irresistibly attractive but ruthless cad and "man-killer" for a femme fatale. Perhaps similar wordplay surrounded "man-killer" after Herodotus introduced the Scythian word to describe Amazons to the Greeks in the fifth century. The opposition of Minythyia, "The Shrinker," and Thalestris, "The Grower," for an attractive but dangerous Amazon lover hints that there was a long-standing joke about Alexander and the Amazon queen, a sly double entendre playing on the erotic ambivalence aroused by strong women. Such a sexual innuendo might also have alluded to Curtius's claim, above, that Thalestris was unimpressed by Alexander's physique.[15]

ALEXANDER'S AMAZON SISTER

Would Alexander have agreed to a proposal to procreate with a warrior queen? Alexander (and his men) had known many Amazon-like women of intelligence, ambition, and power in the Macedonian court. Alexander's grandfather Philip I had Scythian wives, and his father, Philip II, had married Audata, the daughter of the Dardanian ruler of Illyria, in 359 BC. As noted earlier, Illyrian women were riders, hunters, and warriors like the men (and Illyrian men and women were tattooed like the Thracians; chapter 6). While young Alexander and his male companions were learning horsemanship, hunting, and fighting, Audata made sure that his half sister Cynna (or Cynnane, b. 358 BC) excelled in the very same skills. Like Alexander, Cynna became a military commander in her own right. In about 343 BC, young Cynna led an army against an Illyrian force; she personally slew many Illyrians and killed their queen Caeria with a blow to the throat. Cynna ("Little Bitch") was widowed when she was about twenty-one and never remarried. She trained her only daughter, Adea, to be a warrior too (Adea was born ca. 337 BC, when Alexander was about nineteen).[16]

Alexander and his men had also met strong-willed women in Darius's Persian court and along his route to India. Alexander dreamed of creating a vast melting-pot empire, a fusing of cultures through marriage alliances and offspring of mixed parentage. In a speech recorded by Curtius, Alexander declared that he had married Darius's Persian daughter Stateira and the Baktrian princess Roxane expressly to beget children and thereby to "abolish all distinction between vanquished and victor." We know from several sources that Alexander encouraged tens of thousands of his men to marry the barbarian women with whom they cohabited and had children on the long campaign. These mixed families traveled with his army. Alexander anticipated training their Greek-barbarian sons as soldiers to be known as "The Descendants." The independent barbarian queen Thalestris, the bravest of women (and with a sexual agenda of her own), could have been considered an ideal mother of Alexander's heir.[17]

A MOTH ON THE WALL

How would Thalestris and Alexander have communicated? The sources agree that Thalestris made her intentions very clear. It is amusing to picture the haughty queen conveying her desire with gestures and body language and Alexander agreeing in kind, conversing like the Scythian men and the Amazons in Herodotus's love story of the Sarmatians (chapter 3). But Diodorus emphasized the "dignity" of the women, and earthy gestures might have been unseemly. We don't know what language these Amazons spoke, but the queen's request was likely spelled out through interpreters, as occurred with the Mardians, above. Once alone in their royal tent, of course, there was no need for words.

What really happened more than twenty-three hundred years ago is obscured by time. As long as we recognize that we are speculating about a potentially historical event, at a certain place in time, involving a real person who later assumed mythic proportions, we might for a moment permit ourselves the perspective of a moth on the wall of the lovers' silken tent. Alexander decided to "pause here for thirteen days to fulfill Thalestris's quest," writes Justin, so we can guess that these late summer days in Hyrcania were spent in leisure, and that the Macedonian soldiers were free to enjoy the company of the queen's entourage. Alexander often relaxed by riding horses and chasing rabbits with his friends. Scythian women enjoyed the very same pursuits, so Thalestris would make a superb hunting companion.

Strabo and other Greek writers insisted that sex with Amazons invariably took place outdoors, so we might imagine Thalestris enticing Alexander in some secluded grove while their horses grazed nearby. After such pleasantly strenuous days, back in camp we might picture Thalestris setting aside her dagger and hanging up her quiver. She unpacks a small felt tent and brazier, and introduces the world conqueror to the delights of a purifying sauna enhanced with burning hemp flowers (easily obtained on her journey along the western Caspian; see chapter 9). In the intoxicating haze, the naked Alexander watches the Amazon disrobe.

Later, lounging on their bed by the light of an oil lamp, he breathes the exotic fragrance of her frankincense and cedar perfume. As they sip from their wine cups, he traces with his finger the thirteen tattoos of deer with flowing antlers, lithe panthers, and griffins curling around her arms. If only she could speak Greek, this ravishing Scheherazade of the steppes might whisper entrancing stories about each fantastic creature, one tale for each night of passion.... And here our spying moth flutters away into the starry Hyrcanian night.

DEPARTING FROM THE MYTHIC SCRIPT

What happened after Thalestris departed the Macedonian camp? After Alexander's interlude with his Amazon lover, the historians report that he began to outfit his horses with barbarian ornaments. He also began to affect Median-style robes with gold borders and fancy belts over his short Greek chiton—although he drew the line at trousers, the "barbaric" nomad attire of the Mardians and Thalestris's people. Some of Alexander's luxurious trappings were spoils; others had been presented by tribal envoys. Perhaps a few items were love gifts from Thalestris? Alexander's foreign style offended his Greek soldiers, but adopting some native customs in public appears to have been a deliberate strategy to win over Asian tribes. And by 326 BC, anyway, Alexander's men were compelled to fashion clothes out of foreign garments to replace their Greek rags.[18]

Curtius claimed that Alexander became lax and embraced barbarian attire and luxuries after consorting with Thalestris. Other historians

FIG. 20.1. Warrior huntress with bow and quiver, Baktrian-Sogdian medallion, silver chased and gilded dish, early second century BC? Inv. S-77, State Hermitage Museum, St. Petersburg. Photo by Vladimir Terebenin, Leonard Kheifets, Yuri Molodkovets. Photograph © The State Hermitage Museum.

report that Alexander now began to travel with a harem of beautiful concubines from native populations. He soon met and married Roxane (*Raoxshna*, Avestan for "Luminous Beauty"), the sixteen-year-old Baktrian princess said to be the love of his life. Roxane bore his son soon after Alexander's death (323 BC). And Thalestris? Did she give birth to Alexander's child? Justin is our only source for her fate and he is terse: "Thalestris was granted her wish to sleep with Alexander in order to have a child by him. She then returned to her kingdom and died soon afterwards, and with her all trace of the Amazonian name." We do not hear of any child born of her union with Alexander, as one might expect if their affair was a purely fictional tale.[19]

Indeed, there are other remarkable departures from the expected mythic script when real men like Alexander became involved with contemporary women warriors. In the Greek myths, when the great Greek heroes meet with Amazon queens, they oppose each other as equal enemies and engage in combat, and ultimately the mythic heroes kill the women. Yet in every one of the historical and legendary Greek accounts describing Alexander's relationships with women identified as Amazons, a fascinating new development stands out. The great hero and the warrior women meet as equals, they engage in peaceable conversations (and sex in the case of Thalestris), they refrain from fighting, they discuss the idea of joining forces, and they part on amiable terms. Instead of dominance and subservience, instead of any military contest and violence, they negotiate about sharing a child or becoming partners in war. Equality, harmony, and mutual respect are the prominent themes of the stories of Alexander and Amazons. These same peaceable features are prominent in the ancient and medieval Persian-influenced legends about Alexander (Iskander, Sekander) and a warrior queen who resembles Thalestris (Nushaba, Qaidafa; see chapters 22 and 23).

If the accounts of Alexander and the Amazons were simply mythic parallels casting Alexander as a Greek hero who must overcome a foreign Amazon queen, the irenic course of events would be unthinkable. The striking difference between the Greek myths and Alexander's friendly parleys with barbarian war leaders who happen to be female is further evidence of authenticity.

OTHER PLACES, OTHER AMAZONS

Thalestris was not the only "Amazon" linked with Alexander. Accounts by Curtius and Arrian, a respected second-century AD historian of Alexander's campaigns, might help shed some light on the identity of Thalestris. In 328 BC while in Sogdiana and Baktria (now Tajikistan, Uzbekistan, Afghanistan), Alexander received a message from a distant "European Scythian" king, who offered precious gifts and his daughter in marriage as a pledge of friendship; the king also hinted that he would send Alexander's most trusted companions Scythian wives too. According to Curtius, Alexander had sent a messenger named Derdas to this king who ruled "beyond the Bosporus." (In about 331 BC, Scythians in this area had defeated and killed Alexander's general Zopyrion.) When Derdas returned with the king's offer of a marriage alliance, Alexander declined. These accounts seem related to the marriage offer described in Alexander's letter to Antipater, above. Some modern scholars wonder whether this Scythian princess might have been the basis of the story of Thalestris.[20]

Around the same time, the "king of Khorasmia" arrived with fifteen hundred horsemen and met with Alexander. He declared that "his country shared a border with the Amazons and Colchis." Arrian says that the king offered to guide Alexander's army "should he wish to attack the Amazons and subdue all the Scythian tribes as far as the Black Sea." Khorasmia/Khorezm was located between the (now dry) Aral Sea and the Karakum (Black Sand) Desert. The ancient oral epics of this region featured many women warriors (chapter 24). By "Colchis" the king probably meant "Amazon-land," playing upon the Greeks' fantasies about mythic Amazons. From the Aral Sea west to the Black Sea would be a very long march. It is likely that by "Amazons" the king was referring to his warlike neighbors the Massagetae, Saka-Scythians, and related tribes in the Central Asia–Altai region, where numerous burials of women with weapons and tattooed frozen mummies have been discovered (chapter 4). Parts of Inner Asia were called "lands of women" in Indian and Chinese texts (chapters 24 and 25). Arrian's account underscores how little the Greeks knew about Central Asian geography. Some thought the Caspian Sea was part of the Sea of Azov, and that the Caucasus Mountains were somehow contiguous with the Hindu Kush of Afghanistan, and therefore they believed that Baktria was not so distant from the Black Sea.[21]

In 327 BC, Alexander encountered another warrior queen, Cleophis. Her name means "Famous Snake" in Greek, likely a translation of her real Sanskrit or Avestan name. Cleophis led an army of horsemen and -women (twenty thousand cavalry and thirty-eight thousand infantry) against the Macedonians at Massaga. These people were the *Ashvakas* (Sanskrit, "Horse People") of the Swat and Buner valleys in the Hindu Kush (Afghanistan–Pakistan–northern India; see chapter 24). The battle was bloody and long, and the women fought as valiantly as the men. Alexander was wounded, and Cleophis captured. The sources disagree on the details of the close fighting, the battle's outcome, and the terms of the treaty. The ancient rumor that Queen Cleophis (who was over the age of fifty) bore Alexander's son appears to have arisen because she named one of her sons—more likely, her grandson—"Alexander" in gratitude for his compassion after the battle.[22]

Six years after his liaison with Thalestris, in summer of 324 BC, Alexander was back in Media after the arduous Indian campaigns. From here Alexander made a special trip to see the famous Nisaean Plain, the pastures of grass and clover in western Iran where once as many 150,000 celebrated Nisaean horses used to graze (above, and chapter 11). Marauding nomads had captured so many after his defeat of Persia that now only a third of them remained. Then, reported Arrian, "*they say* that Atropates, satrap of Media, sent 100 horsewomen that he called Amazons to Alexander. The women were armed with battle-axes and small shields and dressed in the traditional Amazon fashion. *Some said* that their exposed right breasts appeared smaller. But *it is said* that Alexander dismissed this cavalry from his army, fearing that their presence might incite his Greek and barbarian soldiers to molest them. *They also say* that Alexander told the warrior women to inform their queen that he would later pay a visit to beget children by her." Curtius added that the horsewomen's equipment "led *some to believe* that they were survivors of the race of Amazons."[23] The frequency of phrases like "they say" and "it is said" signals the legendary nature of the incident, and Alexander's promise to impregnate their queen could allude to or reflect an alternative version of the Thalestris incident. Arrian pointed out that Aristobulus, Ptolemy, and other "reliable witnesses" failed to record this event. The location is not that far from Hyrcania. Was this story conflated in oral retellings with the account of Thalestris and her three hundred Amazons?

Arrian was a Greek native of Bithynia on the western border of Pontus, the Amazons' legendary homeland. He wrote his history in the second century AD, during the reigns of the Roman emperors Trajan and Hadrian, long after any living warrior women had been sighted in Pontus. Yet Arrian stated that he believed Amazons had existed in the past because so many distinguished ancient writers, such as Herodotus and the Athenian orators, had described them. To explain the "Amazon" cavalrywomen presented to Alexander, Arrian surmised that they "belonged to some barbarian tribe and had been taught to ride and were exhibited [by Atropates] dressed in Amazon fashion."[24]

From his vantage point during the Roman Empire, at a time when emperors dressed their girlfriends as "Amazons" and female gladiators pretending to be Amazons re-created mythic duels from the Trojan War, Arrian's explanation made sense. In 61 BC, in his triumphal parade after the Mithradatic Wars, the Roman general Pompey had displayed some genuine Scythian women warriors captured in Caucasian Albania (chapter 21). A century later, the emperor Nero surrounded himself with a personal entourage of concubines with short hair, dressed in Amazon garb and carrying battle-axes and light shields. The emperor Commodus outfitted his concubine Marcia ("Warlike," from the Roman war god Mars) as an Amazon to fight as a gladiator in the arena; Commodus also sealed letters with his signet ring depicting an Amazon, and he renamed the month of December "Amazonius." Arrian himself described mythic battle reenactments, staged for entertainment, by Roman cavalrymen wearing trousers and parade helmets with lifelike Amazon face masks. In 2000, archaeologists excavating a Roman cemetery in London announced that the remains of a gladiator appeared to be those of a female. An inscribed sculpted relief from the time of Arrian, discovered in Halicarnassus in 1846 (now in the British Museum), is even more conclusive. It shows a pair of bare-breasted gladiatrixes with greaves and shields fighting with short swords. Their noms de guerre, "Amazon" and "Achillia," suggest that they impersonated Achilles and Penthesilea, a popular mythic subject in Roman art.[25]

But these derivative "Amazon" entertainers became popular in the Roman era several centuries after Alexander, in a very different world. If a cavalry unit of armed females was shown to Alexander in the fourth century BC in what is now northern Iran, it is not out of the question that they could have been authentic women warriors from a nomadic tribe allied with the Median king.[26]

The body of legends (attributed to Pseudo-Callisthenes) dating from the third century BC (Greek version) to the fourth to sixth centuries AD (Armenian and other versions) known collectively as the *Alexander Romance* contains many spurious letters supposedly written by Alexander.

In this imaginary correspondence, Alexander exchanged letters with the warrior queen Candace of Meroe (Nubia, now Sudan, whose independent queens were called Candace/*Kandake* in antiquity; see chapter 23). Alexander also communicated with Amazons who lived on a magically large island in a wide, dangerous river at "the edge of the world." He wrote to request a meeting. The gist of their reply reads: "We are armed virgins, 270,000 strong; no male creatures dwell on our island. Once a year we sacrifice a horse and for six days we visit the men who live across the river for sex and children; we raise the girls. If an enemy invades our land we send our female cavalry force of 120,000 to the borders and our men take up the rear. We reward valor with honors, gold, and silver. If we Amazons defeat a foe, they are humiliated forever. But if men were to conquer us, they can only boast of defeating women. So beware, Alexander." Alexander "smiled" and wrote back, urging the women "and your men" to present themselves and pay tribute. He proposed that they send him a band of horsewomen to serve in his cavalry each year, to be paid in gold. In this tale, the Amazon leaders held an assembly and decided to send Alexander an annual tribute of one hundred talents of gold, one hundred fine horses, and one hundred of their bravest warrior maidens, who were to return as virgins, but "those who have sex with your soldiers may remain with you."[27]

As the Greeks expanded their worldview to include Central Asia, the vision of mythic Amazons kept receding before them, just over the horizon, behind the next mountain range, in the foothills ringing the green valleys, beyond the desert wilderness. Alexander and his men were steeped in Greek myths of illustrious heroes interacting with Amazons at the fringes of civilization. He and his army had stopped in Halicarnassus in Caria to marvel at the new, spectacular Mausoleum that Artemesia II had decorated with scenes of Amazons battling Greeks (chapter 19). They also met powerful female rulers—for example, Queen Ada (sister of Artemisia II), who became a close friend of Alexander; he made her the satrap of Caria. According to Arrian, one of Alexander's role models for his conquests was Queen Semiramis, who was said to have campaigned in Baktria and India (chapters 12, 22, 23).[28]

Reports and firsthand sightings of actual horsewomen in nomad attire with bows and battle-axes, so similar to the images of Hippolyte, Penthesilea, and all the other Amazons in ancient Greek vase paintings and sculpture, confirmed the reality of Amazons and kept alive the expectation of observing living examples. The written accounts of Alexander's encounters with Amazons were debated in antiquity and took on the trappings of legend. But the consistent realistic details in those stories and the continuing discussions about their truth in antiquity provide fascinating evidence of just how deeply embedded the prickly, enticing idea of Amazons was for the Greeks. That a bold, adventurous man might hope to find a companion in an equally strong woman of action was a perennially thrilling prospect. And just maybe, for Alexander and his men, it became a reality, at least for thirteen days and nights.

Of all the ancient historians, only Justin felt the need to wrap up the incomplete story of the Amazon queen Thalestris; he says she died not long after returning to her homeland. Alexander himself would also die in a few years' time and never returned to his homeland. The next historical figure of antiquity who enjoyed a relationship with an Amazon was King Mithradates VI of Pontus, who lived into his seventies. Not only did his Amazon lover outlive him, but her existence is not in doubt.

HYPSICRATEA, KING MITHRADATES, AND POMPEY'S AMAZONS

I N EACH ANCIENT BIOGRAPHY OF AN AMAZON QUEEN, from Hippolyte, Orithyia, and Penthesilea to Thalestris, the writers assure us that with *her* death the Amazon race perished. Yet Amazon-like women keep popping up in the traditional Amazon territories around the Black Sea, Caucasus, and Caspian Sea. Some 250 years after Alexander's idyll with Queen Thalestris of Pontus, another great monarch—himself the king of Pontus— met an Amazon who became his companion in love and battle. It sounds too good to be true. But archaeological evidence came to light in 2007 to confirm the reality of the warrior horsewoman named Hypsicratea and her relationship with King Mithradates VI of Pontus.

Mithradates Eupator (b. ca. 134 BC) inherited the kingdom of Pontus in about 120 BC. Tracing his descent from Darius I of Persia and Alexander of Macedon, Mithradates was widely respected for his intellect, fortitude, military prowess, and courage, even by his worst enemies, the Romans. As a boy he learned to ride and hunt with bow and spear. His knowledge of warlike women, both mythic and authentic, began early. Themiscyra, the Thermodon River, and the island of Ares where Amazon queens worshipped before battle—these places were all within his kingdom. Growing up in the royal palace in Sinope (named for an Amazon) in Pontus (traditional Amazon heartland) and superbly educated in Greek culture, Mithradates knew the Greek myths about heroes and

Amazons set in and around his native land: Hercules and Hippolyte, Theseus and Antiope, Achilles and Penthesilea. In addition to these tragic tales of thwarted love and missed chances for companionship with women who were the peers of men, he would have known of many romantic stories about strong women associated with his homeland: the Amazons of Pontus who founded the Sarmatian tribe, the comradeship between Xenophon's Greek soldiers and their barbarian captives as they traveled across Pontus, and Alexander's interlude with Thalestris.

As a half-Persian prince well-versed in the traditions and history of ancient Iran and Mesopotamia, Mithradates was also familiar with the lives of non-Greek warrior queens, such as Semiramis, Tomyris, and Zarina (chapters 9, 22, 23). His alliances with many Sarmatian-Saka-Scythian tribes and other peoples of the steppes and mountains from Thrace to the Caspian Sea made Mithradates well aware that real nomad women were expert archers, riders, and fighters, and he would have savored the victories of the warrior queens Tirgatao and Amage (chapter 22). The mother of his best ally, Tigranes of Armenia, came from the Alan tribe of the northern Caucasus. A Sarmatian princess from the same region married Mithradates's son Pharnaces; they named their daughter Dynamis ("Powerful Woman"), and she grew up to rule her grandfather Mithradates's Bosporan Kingdom. Queen Dynamis's portrait statue shows her wearing an Amazon's Phrygian cap. Mithradates also knew many powerful, dangerous women of Pontus during his own lifetime: his mother, sister, and aunt were notorious for plotting the deaths of several of his relatives and even tried to kill Mithradates himself. Like his Persian and Macedonian ancestors, Mithradates enjoyed a harem of concubines, as well as a series of official wives (queens), by all accounts selected not only for beauty but also for intelligence.[1] During the turbulent final years of Mithradates's wars against the Roman Republic, the horsewoman warrior Hypsicratea became his last queen.

WHO WAS HYPSICRATEA?

The personal details of Hypsicratea's life are tormentingly meager for readers keen to hear the whole story of a real Amazon and a famous historical figure. Because Mithradates was ultimately defeated (by Pom-

pey in 63 BC), the history of his lifelong resistance to Roman dominance was written by the victors, writers who lived under later Roman
rule. Only two works survive from antiquity with information about
Hypsicratea.[2] Yet we know more about Hypsicratea than we do about
the legendary Thalestris—and Hypsicratea's reality was recently confirmed by archaeology.

The earliest account of Hypsicratea comes from a collection of historical deeds compiled by the Roman moralistic writer Valerius Maximus.
Hypsicratea might have only recently died at the time of Valerius's writing in AD 14–37. In Valerius's telling, Hypsicratea and Mithradates exemplified perfect married love. "The queen Hypsicratea loved her husband
Mithradates with boundless affection," wrote Valerius. "She was happy to
trade her splendid beauty for a masculine style, for she cut her hair and
accustomed herself to riding horses and using weapons so that she could
participate in the king's toils and share his dangers. Indeed, when Mithradates was cruelly defeated by [the Roman general] Pompey and fleeing
through the lands of wild peoples, Hypsicratea was his unflagging companion in body and soul. For Mithradates, her extraordinary fidelity was
his greatest solace and most pleasant comfort in those bitter times and
hardships. He considered that even while he was wandering in adversity
he was always at home because Hypsicratea was in exile along with him."[3]

This vignette is remarkable for its celebration of ideal companionship based on "genuine parity" between a man and a woman. As one
modern scholar points out, this portrayal of unusual equality was accepted in patriarchal Rome because of the "special circumstances of
geography and ethnicity." The Romans expected barbarian women to
behave like free men. Marriages based on companionship are a strong
feature of the traditional Nart sagas of the Caucasus region; one romantic myth describes how a mythic hero and heroine couple always feel
"at home" when they are together in their wagon. Later, in the Middle
Ages, Boccaccio and Christine de Pizan took up the love story of Hypsicratea and Mithradates as an example of a companionate marriage between a king and his female squire disguised as a young man, and this
relationship became a favorite motif in medieval tales of chivalry. Numerous paintings of Queen Hypsicratea and Mithradates on horseback
leading armies appear in medieval manuscripts and medallion-coins
were struck with Hypsicratea's imagined portrait.[4]

What was the source of Valerius's touching portrait of this couple? After the Mithradatic Wars, the Romans developed admiration for their old enemy and avid curiosity about his life. Anecdotes about Hypsicratea the Amazon circulated in Rome, and her alliance with the king was likely mentioned in some of the many lost works consulted by Valerius, such as Cornelius Nepos, a biographer active during the Mithradatic Wars. Valerius was also a friend of Sextus, a son of Pompey, the Roman general who finally defeated Mithradates. Pompey captured many of Mithradates's family, followers, and allies (including women warriors, below) and brought them to Rome, along with the king's archives and personal papers—even his love letters and records of his dreams. People close to Mithradates and veterans of the wars may have imparted memories or knowledge of Hypsicratea; the king's correspondence could also have held information.[5]

Our second source is Plutarch (ca. AD 100), who consulted many sources for his biography of Pompey. Plutarch described Hypsicratea as a concubine (rather than wife) who served as the king's attendant and groom. Plutarch's picture is more accurate than that of Valerius, who suggests that she became a warrior to please Mithradates. Hypsicratea was a barbarian horsewoman who rode a "Persian steed and was dressed and armed like a Persian man. . . . She never tired of rough riding and combat," wrote Plutarch. In stamina and courage she was Mithradates's peer. Given the king's love of literature, art, history, and his respect for smart, strong-willed women, we can guess that he also considered Hypsicratea an intellectual equal.[6]

No sources explain how they met. Historical evidence suggests that Hypsicratea joined Mithradates's cavalry in 69–67 BC. In 69 BC, based in Armenia with King Tigranes, Mithradates assembled a great army to recover his kingdom of Pontus from the Romans. He gathered a force of about seventy thousand foot soldiers and thirty-five thousand cavalry from the warlike nomad tribes of Armenia, Colchis, Caucasia, and the Caspian Sea region. A flexible, light cavalry adept at lightning strikes and guerrilla tactics became the core of his new strategy to defeat the cumbersome formations of Romans hobbled by the rugged, unfamiliar terrain between the Caucasus and the Caspian. Among the nomadic peoples of these lands each man and woman was a potential warrior, raised to ride for miles on sturdy ponies and nimble horses, shooting arrows and hurling spears with deadly aim. At least some of Mithradates's cavalry recruits were female; Hypsicratea may have been one of them. Another possibility is that she was among the volunteer warriors of the hinterlands of Pontus who eagerly swelled the ranks of his large army as he surged to victory there in 67 BC. In his history of the Mithradatic Wars, Appian (b. AD 95) commented that Mithradates's allies "included those who occupy the territory around the river Thermodon, called the country of the Amazons."[7] The general timing of their meeting is secure, but many questions remain. Was she a lone freelance fighter? A member of a party of male and female riders? Did she lead a band of women warriors to join forces with King Mithradates, like a real-life Penthesilea offering her services to King Priam to defend the kingdom of Troy from invaders?

Nothing is known of Hypsicratea's tribe or homeland (in the same general territory given for Thalestris, Alexander's lover; chapter 20). An able-bodied horsewoman signing on for war duty in Mithradates's army would have been between sixteen and thirty (decades younger than Mithradates, robust in his midsixties). Hypsicratea's name is Greek, the feminine form of Hypsicrates. *Hypsi* means "high, lofty" and *krates* means "power, strength." Was this a translation of her real name? Did she receive this Greek name when she joined Mithradates's cavalry because she was tall or hailed from the mountains? Plutarch tells us that because of her "manly spirit and extravagant daring" Mithradates liked to call Hypsicratea by the masculine form of her name, "Hypsicrates." This affectionate nickname made his friend an honorary male and was a token of his esteem.[8]

COMPANIONS AND LOVERS

The new recruit's special equestrian skills led Mithradates to place Hypsicratea in charge of his own horses. As his groom, Hypsicratea manifested trustworthiness and other qualities that spurred the king to make her his personal attendant. They became friends, then lovers. We don't know Hypsicratea's original language; it may have been related to ancient Persian, or it could have been one of the myriad other dialects spoken between the Black and Caspian seas. Mithradates grew up speaking Greek and Persian, and he mastered more than twenty languages. His boast of being able to speak with all his diverse allies is generally accepted. It is likely that he and Hypsicratea conversed at first in her native tongue before she began to learn Greek.

Both had been riding horses and wielding bows and spears since childhood, so they probably took pleasure in chasing game and practicing battle skills together. She wore typical Amazon-Scythian-Persian attire, and we know that Mithradates dressed in traditional Persian style, so we can picture the couple similarly garbed in long-sleeved tunics adorned with golden animals and geometric designs, wool cloaks edged with gold, heavy leather and gold belts with golden buckles, and patterned trousers tucked into high boots. Each carried a Scythian bow and arrows in a Scythian-style quiver, a knife, dagger, and short sword of exquisite workmanship, and two light spears. Their horses, of the finest stock from the high pastures of Armenia, would have been decorated with ornaments of gold.

In 67 BC, Hypsicratea participated in Mithradates's smashing victory at Zela (central Pontus), driving the Romans out of his kingdom. And she was by his side the next year, the summer of '66, when Mithradates was dealt a devastating defeat by Pompey in eastern Pontus. The Roman general had been so frustrated by Mithradates's uncanny ability to elude him that he resorted to a sneak attack on the king's camp by moonlight (alluded to in Valerius's account, above).[9]

Plutarch provides more details of the pair's daring escape during Pompey's night strike. Mithradates and Hypsicratea were asleep, camped with their forces in a mountain stronghold near Dasteira, north of the source of the Euphrates River near the Armenian border. Without warning, Pompey attacked in the middle of the night. Leaping on their horses, Mithradates, with Hypsicratea riding at his side, led eight hundred mounted archers charging into the Roman ranks. In the chaos and darkness, however, the Romans held the advantage. The Romans killed and captured nearly ten thousand of Mithradates's soldiers, many still unarmed. Meanwhile, Hypsicratea, Mithradates, and two other riders found themselves cut off from the rest at the Roman rear. These four escaped by galloping up into the steep hills above the battlefield. They were joined later by other stragglers on horseback. Plutarch describes how the group picked their way over mountainous trails to one of the king's castles in Armenia. Here Mithradates distributed his stash of gold equally among his little renegade army and provided Hypsicratea and their two friends with poison suicide pills in case of capture.

"Never exhausted by this long journey," marveled Plutarch, "Hypsicratea kept on caring for Mithradates' person and for his horse." The king had suffered two serious wounds in the battle at Zela. With Pompey's army in pursuit, the fugitives traveled about five hundred miles north. Crossing the Phasis River in western Colchis (Georgia), they reached the point where the high wall of the Caucasus range meets the Black Sea in fall of 66 BC. Here at Dioscurius, Mithradates, Hypsicratea, and the others hid out over the winter, protected by friendly tribes.[10]

Meanwhile, searching in vain for the king, the Amazon, and their outlaw band, Pompey and his Romans wandered along the Phasis-Cyrus River valleys and Caucasus foothills. They were attacked repeatedly by determined Albanians, Iberians, Gargarians, the Scythian Gelas and Legas tribes, and other peoples of the southern Caucasus—all allies of Mithradates. These scattered tribes "assemble by the tens of thousands whenever anything alarming occurs," noted Strabo. Between the Albanians and the Legas tribe, Strabo continued, in the mountains near where the eastern Caucasus meets the Caspian Sea, dwelled the Amazons who came to consort each summer with the neighboring Gargarians (chapter 8).[11] Some of these Amazons were apparently among the tribes rallying to Mithradates's cause.

POMPEY AND THE AMAZONS

The Romans knew that Mithradates rode to battle with an Amazon at his side. They were aware that his Black Sea Empire encompassed the lands of the legendary Amazons of myth and history. Pompey's soldiers reportedly saw active combat with some women warriors aiding the rebel king. In discussing these Amazons, both Plutarch and Strabo cited Theophanes, a Greek historian from Lesbos. Strabo also cited two historians from Anatolia who lived through the Mithradatic Wars, Metrodorus of Scepsis and Hypsicrates of Pontus, well-known experts on the Amazons of the southern Caucasus area. Sadly, however, all three of these historical works are lost. They would have had much to tell us. Theophanes had accompanied his close friend Pompey during this very campaign. Metrodorus was an intimate friend of Mithradates in Pontus. And the rare name "Hypsicrates" is a curious coincidence, analyzed further below.

At one point, Pompey's Romans clashed with a huge coalition of southern Caucasus tribes numbering about sixty thousand on foot and twelve thousand on horses. "Clad in the skins of wild beasts" and leather buskins (high laced boots, like those worn by Amazons in classical art), these courageous fighters were "wretchedly armed" with javelins, wrote Plutarch. Strabo elaborated on the lives of these peoples, so diverse that they spoke twenty-six languages. Their land was good for pasturing horses and fertile, he commented, yet they neither sowed nor plowed but lived by hunting with dogs, gathering fruit, and raiding. "Unusually handsome and tall," they fought on foot and on horseback with shields, pointed axes, spears, and bows, wearing breastplates and helmets made of wild animal hides.[12]

According to Plutarch, there were Roman reports that Amazons from the mountains had indeed joined the tribes fighting Pompey. On the borderland of Iberia and Albania (near Tbilisi, Georgia) a host of hostile warriors rushed out to attack the Romans, then retreated into the thickly wooded hills. Like Alexander versus the Mardians in Hyrcania (chapter 20), Pompey set fire to the forest to drive them out. His men killed nine thousand and took many prisoners of war. After the battle, wrote Plutarch, the Roman soldiers stripping the enemy corpses came upon crescent shields, buskins, and other distinctive "Amazonian equipment." Plutarch sought to brush aside reports that women's bodies were seen on the battlefield. But some of the prisoners must have been female fighters, since Plutarch remarked that "Scythian women" from this region were among the barbarian combatants displayed in Pompey's magnificent victory parade in Rome (61 BC).[13]

Further key evidence comes from Appian's *History of the Mithradatic Wars*. According to Appian, Pompey's soldiers did discover "many women" on the battlefield and among the prisoners of war. Moreover, "the women's wounds showed that they had fought as vigorously and courageously as the men." The Romans identified these warrior women as Amazons, noted Appian, although it was unclear whether the Amazons constituted "a neighboring tribe or were warlike women" fighting alongside their menfolk. (Appian also wrote about the Bracari, "a most warlike people" of Spain, whose men and women went to battle together against the Romans.)[14] The Byzantine historian Procopius, who cited Strabo and others on the reality of Amazons, commented that in his own day (sixth century AD) the Roman soldiers found the bodies of women warriors among the powerful nomads of Scythia who swept west, perhaps neighbors of the Xiongnu of Inner Asia. Similar findings of female warriors were reported among the Avars, confederated Scythian tribes of the Caucasus steppes, who besieged Constantinople in AD 626.[15]

In chapter 4 we saw that the earliest known graves of women warriors, buried with their spears, axes, and arrows and displaying grievous war wounds, were excavated by archaeologists in the same area (near Tbilisi) where Pompey's men fought women warriors. In modern times, local people who found large hoards of bronze swords here identified them as belonging to Pompey's Amazon foes (fig. 13.4). Farther east toward the Caspian Sea, in the region of Gobustan, Azerbaijan, where there are thousands of ancient petroglyphs depicting men and women with what appear to be bows and tattoos, archaeologists have discovered graffiti left by Roman soldiers a few years after Pompey and his men were there.[16]

The Romans were excited by the surprising discovery of female barbarian fighters dressed and equipped just like Amazons depicted in Greek art and myths. Pompey, aware of the old Greek stories, Mithradates's Amazon companion, and Alexander's liaison with Thalestris, was eager to show off some live, wild Amazons in his triumph in Rome. His female captives—called "Scythian women" by Plutarch and Appian—were among the 324 illustrious prisoners paraded in Pompey's grand triumph, a lavish procession of such magnitude that it took two days to wind through Rome. Behind the carts heaped with fantastic treasures looted from Mithradates's kingdom came the king's family members and his barbarian allies all "in their native costumes"—each labeled with placards and listed in Roman archives. The "Amazons" Pompey captured in 66 BC were described as "queens of the Scythians."[17]

AMAZONS IN ROME

Those historical women warriors' adventures would make enthralling reading. Their battle with foreign invaders from the West, followed by captivity at sea bound for a faraway city, calls to mind Heracles's mythic battle with the Amazons of Pontus and Theseus's abduction of Antiope. Taken prisoner in 66 BC, these warrior women of the southern Caucasus were placed on ships laden with plunder sailing to Rome. They would have been under guard or incarcerated until Pompey's triumph, which did not take place until 61 BC. What were their lives like in those years? Did they languish in chains in a dungeon? Were they exotic involuntary "guests" in some villa? Pompey would have ordered that his captive enemy combatants be well treated in order to be impressive in his triumph. What were the women's thoughts as they were led before the Roman populace in the grand spectacle of victory over the barbarians of the East?

And what was the fate of these Amazons in Rome? It was a Roman custom to strangle enemy combatants at the end of the triumphal parade. Executing the women warriors would conform to the ancient Greek mythic pattern calling for dead Amazons. But Pompey, demonstrating mercy, did not follow the traditional script of Greek myth or of Roman triumphs. Instead, he "sent all his prisoners back to their homelands at public expense, except for the enemy kings."[18] It seems that these warrior women were treated to a second long sea voyage back to the shores of the Black Sea, where they presumably rejoined their people and resumed their lives, equipped with amazing tales to tell.

Captive Amazons soon became a popular motif on Roman sarcophagi. Two beautiful examples are displayed in the British Museum and the Capitoline Museum. The sides of the marble coffins are decorated with Amazonomachy scenes, and the lids depict rows of dejected, bound Amazons sitting by their weapons and shields. Romans battling Amazons are also depicted on the Mausoleum of the Julii, ca. 30 BC. The magnificent marble sarcophagus of a Roman commander, ca. AD 140, shows Roman soldiers fighting Amazons, with kneeling Amazon prisoners of war at each corner. "No Roman ... ever fought Amazons," claims a distinguished historian of ancient art, "but Amazon sarcophagi were commonly placed in Roman tombs." Scholars assume that all of

FIG. 21.1. Captive Amazons, sarcophagus. Photo by Adrienne Mayor.

these images were purely allegorical for the Romans, symbolizing their conquests of barbarians—just as "all Greeks knew that those depictions of the battle of Greeks and Amazons were an allusion to the clash between Greeks and Persians." Such scenes may well have held symbolic meanings, but they were also grounded in ancient Greek knowledge of Scythia and some Roman soldiers' experiences with occasional female fighters on military campaigns. Pompey and his men and other Roman soldiers discovered firsthand that women fighters existed among the Scythians, Bracari, Thracians, Gauls (Celts), Britons, and other peoples. The reality of barbarian "Amazons" like those displayed by Pompey in Rome, the powerful Queen Boudicca of the British Isles, and the pirate queen Teuta would have given a frisson of immediacy to the artistic depictions of Roman battles with Amazons.[19]

THE AMAZON QUEEN HYPSICRATEA

When he failed to capture Mithradates in 66 BC, Pompey assumed the king and his Amazon friend must have frozen to death attempting to escape over the Caucasus Mountains in winter. Hoping to retrace the steps of the great Alexander and expand his own conquests, Pompey departed for Hyrcania by the same route that Thalestris had followed southward along the Caspian Sea to Rhaga and the Caspian Gates (chapter 20).

But Pompey was mistaken. In early spring of 65 BC, Mithradates, Hypsicratea, and their band accomplished an audacious trek over the snowbound Caucasus Mountains by way of the Scythian Gates pass, braving blizzards and precipitous trails. It is reasonable to believe that among Mithradates's guides in this incredible feat was Hypsicratea herself, whose people would have known this traditional Scythian migration route.[20] The little army emerged onto the steppes east of the Sea of Azov and crossed the Don River, into the land where long ago the Amazons had joined forces with the Scythians, the land where the Amazons led by Queen Orithyia had found refuge after their defeat in the mythic Battle for Athens. The intrepid travelers were welcomed by Mithradates's Saka-Scythian-Sarmatian allies. With fresh horses, they continued northwest around the Sea of Azov and rode down to Pantikapaion (Kerch, Crimea), the capital of the Bosporan Kingdom, the northern outpost of Mithradates's Black Sea Empire, a city ruled by his son Pharnaces. Mithradates once again assumed the throne, with Hypsicratea as his wife and queen.

Two years later, in 63 BC, a revolt led by his treacherous son, secretly allied with Pompey, forced Mithradates to commit suicide by poison. He had managed to send some of his daughters to safety in Scythia, but many of the king's children and concubines were killed or captured. What happened to Hypsicratea remains a mystery. The Romans seized the corpses of the king and his family and transported the survivors to Rome: the sources report their names and fates. Dead or alive, the Amazon queen Hypsicratea would have been a prized trophy for Pompey's triumph. But she disappears from the historical record after 63 BC. Did she escape to Scythia, perhaps as the bodyguard of Mithradates's daughters?

A trail of intriguing clues hints that Hypsicratea might have survived the revolt in the Bosporan Kingdom and enjoyed a long life under the masculine version of her name bestowed by Mithradates. Only two instances of this unusual name are known in antiquity, and both were contemporaries in the same locale. One was Hypsicratea the Amazon queen who answered to the nickname Hypsicrates. The other was a shadowy person called Hypsicrates. A prisoner of war by this name was freed by Julius Caesar in Amisus, Pontus, in 47 BC. This Hypsicrates, serving as a historian, accompanied Caesar on his campaigns, reportedly lived to be ninety-two years old, and was known as an authority on two subjects: fortifications of the Borporan Kingdom and the Amazons of the Caucasus region. Could Hypsicratea and Hypsicrates be the same person?[21]

The theory that the Amazon queen of King Mithradates became the historian named Hypsicrates who specialized in Amazon history is based on circumstantial evidence. But it receives some support from an extraordinary ancient Greek inscription, recovered from the Sea of Azov by Russian archaeologists in Phanagoria, a town across the Kerch Strait (Cimmerian Bosporus) from Mithradates's Bosporan capital Pantikapaion. The inscription originally belonged to a bronze or marble statue of Hypsicratea, which has not yet been found. It reads: "Hypsicrates, wife of Mithradates Eupator. Love and Respect."

Who erected this statue of Hypsicratea inscribed with the masculine form of her name? Was it Mithradates himself? Was it Queen Dynamis, Mithradates's half-Sarmatian granddaughter born in 67 BC, who could have known Hypsicratea personally? The date of the inscription is also unknown. Was the statue a tribute to the living Hypsicratea, or did it mark her tomb? The remarkable inscription proves that the warrior woman Hypsicratea really existed. She survived the Caucasus crossing with Mithradates. She was not a concubine of Mithradates (as Plutarch suggested) but recognized as his wife and queen (as Valerius stated). She was, as Plutarch declared, called by the masculine form of her name. And that name was not just a private pet name—Hypsicratea was known publicly as Hypsicrates.[22]

THE AMAZON IN THE WOLF-SKIN CAP

Ancient coins of Pontus provide more physical evidence linking Mithradates and Amazons. His city Amisus (Samsun, on the coast between Sinope and Themiscyra) issued silver coins in about 125–100 BC showing a youthful profile with curly hair wearing a pointed leather cap with earflaps like those worn by Scythians and Amazons in Greek vase paintings. The figure could be the young Mithradates or, more likely, an Amazon. Later in his reign (sometime between 85 and 65 BC) the city of Amisus issued a large series of bronze coins, this time depicting an Amazon with very distinctive headgear. These coins, which exist in a remarkable array of different dies (versions of similar images), are cataloged as "the bust of an Amazon" wearing a cap, helmet, or hooded cape made from a wolf's head over her braided hair.[23] Wild animal skins and furs were worn by

FIG. 21.2. Amazons in wolf-skin caps, bronze coins of Amisus, Pontus, during Mithradates's reign, 85–65 BC. Top: courtesy American Numismatic Society 1944.100.41240.obv.2590 and 1944.100.41241.obv.2590, E. T. Newell Bequest; and courtesy of Michel Prieur, www.cgb.fr. Bottom: courtesy wildwinds.com; cngcoins.com; Apollo Numismatics, private collections.

Scythians and related tribes, and Strabo remarked on helmets of animal hides worn by the southern Caucasus warriors (above).

Mithradates was known to issue series of small-denomination coins with propagandistic images. The existence of so many different versions is evidence that these coins showing an Amazon in a wolf cap were widely dispersed in his empire, and that the meaning of the image was immediately recognizable to the populace. The decision to display Amazons on Mithradatic coins of Amisus might have celebrated the famous mythic warrior women of Pontus. But the unusual Amazon in the unique wolf helmet appears to represent a specific character whose identity and story were very familiar to those who used the coins. Numismatists point out that distinctive figures on coins often copied well-known statues. One possibility is that the wolf-capped Amazon portrait represented Hypsicratea, Mithradates's companion and queen. From the inscription described above we now know that at least one portrait statue of Hypsicratea did exist in antiquity. If she was known to wear a wolf-skin cap, perhaps her statue, submerged in the Sea of Azov, will someday be found. Will it match the Amisus coin portrait?

Another possibility is that the coin image referred to some well-known local story about a wolf-hunting Amazon heroine from the territory of Amisus. The wolf cap is a hunting trophy, much like Heracles's signature lion-skin cape fashioned from the Nemean Lion. In the list of Amazon names from ancient literature and vase paintings (appendix) two are wolfish: Lyke ("She-Wolf") and Lykopis ("Wolf Eyes"). Pausanias mentioned a cult of Artemis Lykeia, "Artemis of Wolves." In the epic tale of Jason and the Argonauts, one of the three tribes of Pontus known for women warriors dwelled around Lykastia ("Wolf Land"), located by ancient geographers just southeast of Amisus. Wolf names and wolf-head helmets were also associated with the wolf cult of ancient Colchis/Iberia, and wolves are featured in numerous steppe traditions. If the coins represented Hypsicratea, her wolf cap could be a clue pointing to her Lykastian or Iberian origins. The identity of the Amazon in the wolf cap remains a mystery. But the coins are striking evidence that ideas and images of Amazons were prominent in Mithradates's kingdom in the first century BC.[24]

And the story of Hypsicratea, Mithradates's stouthearted Amazon partner, whose existence is now confirmed by the newfound inscription for her honorary statue, shows that in real life it was possible to depart from the ancient Greek myths demanding defeat and death for free women who were the equals of men. Even in the myths a veiled yearning for companionship hovers in the background of the tales of Atalanta and Meleager, Heracles and Hippolyte, Theseus and Antiope, Achilles and Penthesilea. Mithradates idolized Alexander the Great and strove to copy him in many ways. With Hypsicratea, he had a chance not only to recapitulate but to improve upon Alexander's meeting with Thalestris. Thalestris declined Alexander's invitation to join his cavalry; Hypsicratea actually did join Mithradates's cavalry. Alexander and Thalestris were together for less than two weeks, but Hypsicratea became Mithradates's steadfast friend and lover for the rest of his life.

PART 4

BEYOND THE GREEK WORLD

22

CAUCASIA, CROSSROADS OF EURASIA

THE RUGGED MOUNTAINS, FORESTS, GORGES, RIVER valleys, pastures, and lonely steppes between the Black Sea and the Caspian Sea have been a cultural crossroads and a turbulent cauldron of diverse languages, ethnicities, and geopolitical conflicts for thousands of years. In antiquity, adventurous Greeks traveled to the outer fringes of this vast territory, part of ancient Scythia-Sarmatia, where they established trading colonies, met exotic peoples, and listened to their exciting tales. What the Greeks saw and heard around the Black Sea colored their ideas of barbarian life and encouraged them to imagine what might lie beyond the world they knew: war-loving tribes of Amazons, griffins, fabulous golden treasures.

Straddling the great Caucasus mountain range between Europe and Asia, these lands have long been isolated by topography and language, subject to violent conflicts, and politically atomized. Despite this history, the numerous ethnic groups of this complex terrain shared ancient traditions of nomadic and seminomadic culture centered on horses, hunting, herding, raiding, and warfare. Many of the numerous languages seem to have changed little in the past two thousand years. Outside influences arrived late, with Mongols from the east, Muslims from the south, and Christians from the west in the Byzantine-medieval periods, and Russians in the modern era. The northern Caucasus region—stretching more than one thousand miles from the Sea of Azov to the Caspian Sea—today includes parts of Russia and Ukraine, Crimea, and numerous republics declared and disputed after the collapse of the Soviet Union in 1991. Southern Caucasia or Transcaucasia (in antiquity Abkhazia, eastern Pontus, Colchis, Iberia, Albania, Armenia, and Media) today includes Abkhazia, northeastern Turkey, Georgia, Armenia, Azerbaijan, and northern Iran. Within each of these modern borders are scores of ethnic minorities, with their own dialects and histories.[1]

The staggering multiplicity of names gives a tiny glimpse into the even more impressive diversity of peoples that inhabited this region in antiquity. The peoples of these lands told their own stories about celebrated heroes and heroines, some imaginary and others based on the exploits of historical people who became legendary. Caucasus narratives are little known in the West partly because the cultures of this region were oral. In contrast to Greek myths and histories, recorded in writing more than twenty-five hundred years ago, the myths and chronicles of Caucasia were maintained in collective memories, perpetuated by spoken word. With the exception of Georgian, most Caucasian languages had no alphabets until the twentieth century. Armenian, an Indo-European language, acquired an alphabet in AD 405; the earliest Ossetian (ancient Iranian) writings are ca. AD 950–1150. Ancient Caucasian tales and epics were recounted by generations of bards in many different tongues for millennia before they were first captured in writing in the nineteenth century by European and Russian travelers and folklorists who transcribed versions they heard recited by local storytellers. Only about two hundred of nearly one thousand recorded oral traditions of Caucasia have been translated into English. The origins of the oral stories, sagas, songs, ballads, and poems of Caucasia cannot be dated with precision. But scholars agree that they contain traces of ancient Indo-European myths interwoven with local folktales. The Greek myths of Cyclops and Prometheus, for example, may have been borrowed from Caucasian traditions about a one-eyed ogre and a fire-bringing giant.

Many Caucasian sagas feature heroines who ride and do battle with men. Some ancient Caucasian traditions about independent women appear to have filtered into Greek art and literature. For example, linguistic and artistic evidence raises the possibility that an Abkhaz saga might have contributed to Greek tales and images of Atalanta (prologue). Many place-names and ethnonyms in Greek histories about this region are Hellenized versions of Caucasian names, and some names and words inscribed next to Amazons and Scythian figures on Greek vases are from Caucasian languages (chapter 14). As noted in chapter 5, the ancient Greek word for *Amazon* appears to have linguistic roots in Caucasia, perhaps linked to the name of the Circassian warrior queen Amezan, whose story is related below.[2]

Archaeological discoveries of armed women buried where the ancient Greeks located Amazons provide solid evidence that horsewomen warriors of steppe cultures really existed as contemporaries of the Greeks (chapter 4). These flesh-and-blood women were the Amazons described by Greek and Roman historians from Herodotus to Orosius. Many examples of autonomous fighting women who behaved as the equals of men can be found in ancient oral and literary traditions *beyond* the Greek world—in cultures outside Greek influence in the Caucasus, the Near East, Central Asia, and China. These facts lay to rest the Hellenocentric argument that Amazons were the exclusive creations of fantasizing Greeks.

The following narratives about women warriors are gathered from oral tales of the Caucasus translated from Circassian, Ingush, and Lak languages; legends and epic poems of Armenia and Azerbaijan; a Greco-Roman military treatise; and early European travelers' reports of oral tales they heard in the region. Some accounts are mythic. Some, like the stories of Tirgatao and Amage preserved by Polyaenus, concern historical events and peoples of special interest to the Greeks and Romans. Others describe the lives of riders, hunters, herders, raiders, fighters, lovers, and leaders who happen to be women—the steppe sisters of the women buried with their weapons and horses in archaeological sites across Scythia.

Epic stories about strong women who battle men are widely distributed among northern Caucasus groups. The tales of original "Amazons" from non-Greek cultures vary in significant ways from Amazon myths told in Greece. Unlike Hippolyte and Penthesilea and their all-women bands, the heroines of the Caucasus usually act alone or in mixed armies of women and men. This realistic feature of nomad life was captured in the earliest Greek use of the name "Amazon" to designate an ethnic group of men and women. It also corresponds with many Greek historians' accounts of Amazons as barbarian women who live or consort with men (chapters 1, 8, 10). But a crucial difference stands out in comparison with the Greek myths, in which the great heroes killed Amazons even though they found them attractive. Other cultures that had close encounters with powerful nomad women recorded more practical scenarios, and they could imagine the women as victors. The warrior women in non-Greek sagas and histories may suffer tragic setbacks in their personal lives, but, unlike the mythic queens Hippolyte, Antiope, and Penthesilea, the Amazon-like characters of Caucasus tales and histories frequently win their battles with men.

LADY AMEZAN OF CIRCASSIA

The Narts—mythic heroes and heroines of the Caucasian steppes and mountains between the Black and Caspian seas—were imagined as extraordinarily tall with superhuman strength. They were *jigits*, acrobatic riders whose skills demonstrated their noble daring and endurance. The Narts' magnificent horses were heroic (*bogatyr*) too, described in the sagas as *alyp* and *arash* ("thoroughbred"), *argamak* (Akhal Teke racing steeds from the Ferghana Valley, Central Asia), and *durdul* (*turpal, tulpar,* "winged, flying"). According the Nart sagas, it was a Nart woman who invented ironworking, and the Narts were the first to tame wild horses. The ancient Greeks apparently picked up these Caucasus traditions and credited the Amazons with these two inventions (chapters 11 and 13).

A traditional Nart saga in the Karbardian East Circassian language recounts a tragic episode in the life of the heroic warrior queen known as Lady Amezan ("Forest Mother," or "Moon Mother"). The story is set in the glorious past when the steppes rang with the "thunderous pounding of horses' hooves." It was a time when at the first sign of danger the women buckled on their daggers and swords, grabbed their bows and lances, saddled their horses, and "rode forth with their men folk to meet the enemy in battle." Women of those days were capable of deep love, but they could also "cut out an enemy's heart."[3]

One of these women was the beautiful and strong Amezan, who harbored a secret love for a handsome young man of another tribe. One day in the frenzy of mounted combat on the steppes with arrows and javelins, her "silken hair fluttering like a red flame in the wind," Amezan brought down a stranger and his horse. She bent down from her saddle over the lifeless body. Horrified, she recognized her beloved lying in a pool of blood. "Jumping down from her horse, she kissed his lips passionately and tried to warm his cold body with hers, pleading to feel his still heart begin to beat again." But the youth heard nothing, dead to the din of battle raging around them. She gently closed his unseeing eyes. "My sun has set forever!" she cried out. "With her strong arms she pulled forth her dagger and plunged it into her own heart.... They lay dead together, Amezan and the man she loved." Where their blood flowed, "their boundless courage and great love was absorbed by the earth" and a spring bubbled up. Ever after, those waters could renew lost strength and heal wounded hearts.[4]

The tale reminds us of the Greek myth of the Amazon warrior Penthesilea and the great champion Achilles, who realizes too late that the fearless young Amazon he kills is the very woman he would have cherished (chapter 18). The twist here—the victorious woman warrior discovers that she has killed her beloved—would astonish the ancient Greeks. But such a tale was natural in the context of a culture whose women were trained to make war like men.

THE INGUSH HORSE MAIDEN

The Ghalghai/Gergar of Ingushetia, northern Caucasus, are thought to be the descendants of the Gargarians, the neighbors of the Amazons described by Strabo and Pliny. Several Caucasian legends tell of young female warriors who carry out blood revenge on behalf of their families. The sad endings evoke the inescapable circle of death in cultures that practice clan vendettas. In some versions the girl succeeds but is wounded and dies later. In others she kills herself in grief afterward because her family has been wiped out. In still others she never marries, hunts alone in the forest, and lives in a tower. Many ancient stone towers of unknown dates dot the rugged eastern Caucasus landscape. One perched on a crag at Assa Gorge near Ghalghai on the border of Chechnya, Ingushetia, and Georgia is identified as the Maiden's Tower in the following Ingush saga. The tale was recorded in 1972 from a villager who heard it from his father, born in the early 1800s.[5]

A maiden's seven brothers were "all killed while out hunting and plundering" by the Nogays, a Turco-Mongolian tribe on the steppes north of the Caspian. Dressed in trousers and boots, her long braids tucked into a sheepskin cap, the nameless maiden sets off on her horse to the land of the Circassians to the west. Pretending to be a teenage boy, she makes friends with a Circassian horseman and they "ride on the steppes together." They spot a thin nag grazing apart from a herd. With her deep knowledge of horses, the girl recognizes it as a *bogatyr turpal* ("heroic flying horse") in very poor condition. (The motif of a homely foal or nag that becomes a great steed is typical of Central Asian tales.) Her Circassian friend agrees to nurse this horse back to full strength over six years.

When the horse is strong again, she and her friend "ride together across the Terek River and over sandy, stony steppes" to Nogay territory. The girl, riding the marvelous *bogatyr* horse, rounds up the entire herd of Nogay horses by herself—a feat that normally requires at least three horsemen. The Nogays mount and "dash after her in pursuit." But she kills all sixty of them with her bow and her sword. Thus the maiden avenges the death of her brothers. "In return for his companionship" she presents her Circassian friend with the heroic horse and the entire Nogay herd, pointing out the special qualities of each individual horse. After she rides away, the Circassian follows the trail of the "young hero" and discovers that she is a young woman. He begs her to marry him, but she refuses, pointing out that he was so obsessed with horses that he never bothered to find out who she really was. She threatens him with force. Dejected, he departs, and she dwells alone in her tower.

This lone female avenger of the steppes is an expert horsewoman and excellent judge of horses. Even though she acts alone, she certainly fits the ancient Greek image of beautiful, strong-willed, self-sufficient, dangerous warrior women called Amazons.

PARTU PATIMA OF THE LAKS

The tale of Partu Patima is not from classical antiquity, but it demonstrates the persistence of female fighters on horseback in a region long associated with Amazons. The Laks, indigenous mountain people of

Dagestan, have been identified as descendants of the Legas, a Scythian tribe of ancient Albania mentioned by Strabo (chapter 21). The legendary Amazon queen Marpesia campaigned here and gave her name to the narrow path between the sea and the mountain cliffs also known as the Caspian Gates at Derbent (Marpesian Rock; chapter 2). Like the Thracian and Scythian women of antiquity, the mountain women of this region traditionally tattoo their arms (chapter 6), creating "sisterhoods of blood and ink." Ancestors of these mountain people were among the diverse Caucasus tribes who united to repel the Roman invaders led by Pompey during the Mithradatic Wars in 65 BC. As we saw in the previous chapter, Pompey reportedly encountered women warriors near here.

In the fourteenth century, the Laks fought another, more terrifying invader, Timur ("Iron"; also known as Tamerlane), whose Mongol cavalry devastated the land around the Caspian Sea and then attacked the mountain villages of ancient Albania on their drive to take over Georgia. During those bloody battles, a valiant girl warrior, Partu Patima, led the Laks against Timur's cavalry. Legends arose about this heroine, and until the early 1900s the Laks, especially women, made pilgrimages to her grave in a valley known as Partuvalu. The following synopsis comes from a poetic version of her legend recited in 1938 by a Lak villager born in 1848; the tale was translated into Russian in 1954.[6]

Partu Patima sees the young men arming themselves for battle to defend the people against Timur's hordes. She demands to join them. "Give me a curved saber," a horse, an armored tunic, and a helmet—"I want to show what a girl can do!" They scoff, but she nimbly mounts her prancing black horse, winds her long black braids around her helmet, and challenges one of the youths to single combat with swords. She proves that she is a "genuine warrior," a "young lioness." She declares that all her female friends are also ready to fight. Leading the Laks in battle, she charges into the Mongol ranks and slashes off many enemy heads with her blade. Afterward, she discovers that the boy she loves was killed in the battle, and her "hawk's eyes" weep tears for the first time. But the heroine and her heroic band wend their way home proud of leaving a "mountain of corpses" for Timur. Enraged, Timur offers a reward for her capture.

Although in this version of the legend her female friends are not described as participating in the fighting, it is clear that the Lak girls could prove their mettle by challenging the boys and joining battle with foes. Stories about strong women who enter single combat with men, often to decide the outcome of a protracted war among tribes, are widely distributed among northern Caucasus groups.[7] Ancient dueling and leadership traditions from regions associated with Amazons influenced Greek historians' accounts telling how a courageous woman could emerge from time to time to head bands of barbarian warriors (chapter 2).

SEMIRAMIS AND ARA THE HANDSOME

Movses Khorenatsi (ca. AD 408–490) preserved pre-Christian Armenian legends in which Semiramis (Shamiram in Armenian, the Assyrian queen of the ninth century BC; chapter 12) was portrayed as a voluptuous, wicked sorceress. In one of these old tales, Semiramis developed a great lust for Ara Geghetsik ("Ara the Handsome") of Armenia. (Ara may have been based on the historical ninth-century BC king Arame of Ararat). When Ara scorned her advances, Semiramis led her Assyrian army into Armenia to capture him alive. After a great battle, she found Ara's body among the dead. Crazed by grief and desire, Semiramis tried to revive his corpse with black magic. Failing to bring him back to life, she chose one of her many lovers and dressed him in Ara's garments. Semiramis killed her own sons and, when she died, left her treasury to her lovers.[8]

The Armenian legend resembles some Greek accounts that portray Amazons killing their sons and having sex with many lovers. Like Lady Amezan, above, Semiramis is horrified to find her beloved dead after her attack on his army. Evidence for the persistence of women warriors in Armenia appears in the memoirs of an early European traveler in Armenia in about 1593–1600. John Cartwright's journey across the high plains of Armenia occurred about two hundred years after Timur's Mongolian depredations and during wars between the Ottomans and the Persians. He reported that the Armenian women were "very skilful and active in shooting & managing any sort of weapon, like the fierce Amazones in antique time and the women of this day which inhabit the Mountain Xatach in Persia" (Shadakh, now Çatak, Turkey).[9]

BANU CHICHAK AND BEYREK

Most of Caucasian Albania is now part of Azerbaijan between Armenia, Dagestan, Georgia, and Iran. This region is where Strabo and other historians placed Amazons, where Queen Thalestris followed the Cyrus River and turned south along the Caspian coast to catch up with Alexander (chapter 20), and where Pompey captured Amazons in 65 BC. Azerbaijani historian Fahrid Alakbarli identifies the ethnic groups mentioned in Greek and Latin works, such as Amazons, Albanians, Gelas, Legas, and Gargarians, with places and peoples of Azerbaijan. Ancient Azerbaijan was part of the Scythian conquests in the eighth–seventh centuries BC, and Saka tribes also settled this region at that time. The first century AD saw the arrival of Turkic Oghuz and Kipchak (Qipchaq) steppe nomads from Central Asia. The ancient Saka presence in western Azerbaijan is reflected in place-names such as Sakasena ("Saka land") and Shaki ("Saka") in the mountains where it was said that Amazons joined other local tribes battling Pompey. Alakbarli suggests that the "Amazons" who came to aid the Albanians against Pompey were probably Saka bands whose "women served as warriors and chiefs" like the men. There may have been separate male and female detachments of Saka-Scythian-Sarmatian mounted archers, reasons Alakbarli, leading ancient Greeks and Romans to call the men "Scythians" and the women "Amazons."[10]

Traditions arose in Azerbaijan about brave Oghuz and Kipchak horsewomen of Central Asian nomad tribes that migrated west from Kazakhstan. Oral Oghuz Turkic legends took written form in the medieval Azerbaijani epic *Kitabi-Dada Gorqud* (*Book of Dede Korkut*; Turkmen, *Gorkut-ata*). In northwestern Azerbaijan there are still *ashugs*, bards, who sing these ballads. One legend describes how the wife of Dirse Khan, an Oghuz chief, led a band of forty mounted maiden warriors (for similar tales in Central Asia, see chapter 24). Another story tells of the Oghuz prince Beyrek who declares he wants to marry "a girl who is faster than I am, who can mount a horse before I can, and who can bring me my enemy's head before I can reach him." In other words, "the kind of girl I want" is "not a wife but a companion," a daredevil heroine.[11]

That girl would be Banu Chichak ("Lady Flower") a Kipchak "princess" renowned as a skilled "rider, hunter, archer, and wrestler." But when Beyrek meets her on the steppe by chance, she pretends to be Chichak's attendant. She challenges the young man to three contests. "If you can ride faster than my horse and shoot an arrow farther than I can, then you can beat Banu Chichak; if you can defeat me in wrestling, then you'll be able to win her." They compete and with great effort the exhausted Beyrek manages to best the girl. Delighted to find a worthy mate, Chickak reveals her true identity and they agree to marry.[12]

SHIRIN AND KHOSROV

The great Azerbaijani poet Nizami Ganjavi (1141–1209) received a young Kipchak slave girl named Appaq (Afaq) from the shah of Derbent in 1173 as a gift for his first poem. Appaq ("Snow White") became Nizami's beloved wife. Nizami's next poem recounted the legend of the horsewoman Shirin ("Sweet") and Khosrov, based on real historical figures. Shirin was the wife of the Sassanid (Persian) king Khosrov II (AD 590–628). Their love story inspired poetry within a century of their deaths. Shirin's ethnic origin differs in the many versions of her tale. She has been identified as Armenian, Caucasian, Albanian, Aramaic, Kurdish, Khuzistani, Khorezmian, and Syrian, but Nizami based his romantic portrait on his Kipchak wife Appaq, who died while he was writing this poem.

Shirin inherited Armenia from her aunt, described as an Amazon-like "queen, stronger than any man, who lived a contented life with no husband." The ruins of Shirin's Castle can be seen near Kermanshah, western Iran. The Karakalpak people of ancient Khorezm (Uzbekistan) claim Shirin's grave, in Devkesken-Vasir. The courtship of Shirin and Khosrov was the subject of hundreds of exquisite miniature paintings showing them dressed alike in tunics and trousers, armed with quivers of arrows, bows, and swords, riding fine horses, chasing deer and lions together, playing polo, or conversing in a flowery meadow with their horses grazing nearby. Paintings also depict Shirin hunting on horseback with her band of armed maidens, some of whom demonstrate the notorious Parthian shot. Another favorite subject was Khosrov's first glimpse of Shirin while she was bathing, with her sword, bow, and quiver beside her on the stream bank (fig. 22.1).[13]

FIG. 22.1. Khosrov glimpses Shirin bathing. Her quiver, bow, and sword are suspended in the tree. Miniature illustration of the *Khamsa of Nizami*, ca. 1420. Inv. I. 4628, S. 231, Museum für Islamische Kunst, Staatliche Museen, Berlin, bpk, Berlin/Staatliche Museen/Art Resource, NY.

Nizami's sensuous poems are remarkable for their humanistic portrayals of women as "lovers, heroines, rulers, and even educators and challengers of men." As "equal and in some cases the superior to men," women are capable of ruling countries, fighting on the battlefield, and providing "deep insight into social and philosophical issues." The leading Persian scholar Kamran Talattof convincingly refutes other modern Iranian writers who claim that the women in Nizami's poems are not meant to be real characters but represent "symbols, codes, and secrets" with Islamic religious meanings, and that Shirin's only function "in the story [is] to exalt the . . . male character." Their perspectives bring to mind the Hellenocentric, symbolic interpretations of Amazons favored by many Western classicists.[14]

NUSHABA AND ALEXANDER

Nizami also told the story of Alexander (Iskandar), drawing on ancient Azerbaijani and Persian legends. In the *Iskandar-nameh* (1194) Alexander travels to the Caucasus seeking knowledge. He meets a warrior queen with Amazonian characteristics, Nushaba of Barda, in ancient Albania (central Azerbaijan). Nushaba is thought to have been modeled on a Saka female leader from the region of Sakasena, mentioned above. In the version of the legend related by Nizami, Nushaba develops a keen interest in Alexander, whose portrait she caused to be secretly painted. When Alexander, disguised as an envoy, visits her court of armed maidens in Barda, Nushaba recognizes him from his likeness. They converse as equals; her wisdom and bravery convince Alexander to spare her city. Many medieval illustrated manuscript paintings feature their meeting (also depicted in a beautiful 1950s mosaic in the Nizami Metro Station, Baku, and a statue group at Nizami Park, Ganja). This Azerbaijani legend appears to be a non-Greek tradition about Alexander and Queen Thalestris who came from the same region as Nushaba. In the Azerbaijani version, however, the tale is told from the point of view of the Amazon queen herself.[15]

The semihistorical accounts and legends of the Caucasus region existed apart from Greek influence, in a cultural context where it was

FIG. 22.2. Queen Nushaba of Barda and Alexander, modern statue group, Nizami Complex, Ganja, Azerbaijan. Photo by Mari Kipiani.

taken for granted that women could ride and shoot as well as men and take active roles in defending their people, making conquests, and choosing a mate for sex and love. These "mysterious Amazons were ... ordinary women," remarks Fahrid Alakbarli, and stories about them "were not just a figment of the imagination among ancient Greek and Roman historians."[16]

The following biographies of two Scythian leaders in the northern Caucasus who happened to be female, Tirgatao of Maeotia and Amage of the Roxolani, derive from the writings of the Macedonian military historian Polyaenus, and are based on historical conflicts in the fifth and second centuries BC.

TIRGATAO OF MAEOTIA

Polyaenus included the campaigns of the warrior queen Tirgatao of Maeotia in his book of war strategies (second century AD). The name *Tirgatao* has ancient Iranian origins: *tir* = arrow; *tighra tava*, "Arrow Power." Her name is appropriate for a mounted nomad archer; many Amazon names contain the "arrow" element (chapter 14 and appendix). Tirgatao behaved like the Amazons in Greek myths and resembles the Saka-Scythian-Sarmatian women warriors in the histories of Herodotus, Skymnos, and other Greek authors. Her accomplishments as a war leader would have confirmed for the Greeks that Amazons were Scythian women still active in the Black-Azov-Don region. In the late fifth century BC, Tirgatao's wars against indigenous Black Sea kingdoms allied with Athens were witnessed by Greeks living or trading in Gorgippia and other northern Black Sea colonies, and news of her conflicts circulated in Athens. Evidence of the wars among various tribes of this period, including the Sarmatian, Maeotian, and Scythian, can be found in other Greek literary sources, inscriptions in the Bosporus region, and Ossetian Nart sagas. The original account of Tirgatao's war is thought to derive from a Bosporan source consulted by Polyaenus.[17]

Tirgatao, a woman of the Ixomatae, one of the powerful Maeotian tribes, married the king of the Sinds, Hecataeus. The Maeotians, warlike Scythian tribes described as "living like Amazons" and "ruled by women," dwelled around the Sea of Azov (chapter 2). The Sinds (identified as the Adyge people) lived on the Taman Peninsula and Black Sea coast north of the Caucasus range. Their port, Sinda, was colonized by the Greeks in the sixth century BC and renamed Gorgippia after a king of the Bosporus (Crimea). In the complex, continuous wars among the various nomadic and settled groups in this region, Tirgatao's husband Hecataeus lost his throne but was restored by Satyrus, the king of the Bosporus in Pantikapaion and an enemy of the Maeotians. In return for his support, Satyrus demanded that Hecataeus kill Tirgatao and marry Satyrus's daughter. But Hecataeus was deeply in love with Tirgatao. He imprisoned her in a tower instead of killing her.[18]

Tirgatao escaped. Satyrus and Hecataeus sent men in pursuit. But Tirgatao eluded them, "traveling by deserted and difficult trails at night and hiding in the forests by day." Finally she reached the land of the

Ixomatae, her own tribe. Her father had died and she was acclaimed as their new leader. Tirgatao convinced the Ixomatae and the other Maeotian tribes to make war on the Sinds and the Bosporans. Here we can fill out Polyaenus's account from other ancient descriptions of Maeotians. The men were archers on foot, while the Maeotian women rode horses and were skilled with the bow and the lasso (chapters 2 and 13, fig. 13.5). It is reasonable to suppose that some women joined Tirgatao's army. Tirgatao and her warriors would have been dressed much like the Amazons and Scythians in Greek vase paintings, in patterned tunics and trousers, with quivers and bows.[19]

Polyaenus tells how Tirgatao's Maeotian army devastated the Sindi lands and then ravaged Satyrus's Bosporan territory. Satyrus and Hecataeus sued for peace. Tirgatao agreed to the treaty, but the two kings broke their oaths and plotted to kill Tirgatao, sending two assassins who pretended to be traitors seeking refuge with her. The conspiring kings even wrote a letter to Tirgatao, demanding that she turn over the "traitors," but she wrote back that the "laws of supplication compelled her to protect those in her care." While one assassin "distracted her about an important matter, the other struck at Tirgatao with his sword. But his blow was deflected by her girdle"—her heavily armored belt. Her guards seized the assassins and under torture they revealed the kings' plot. Tirgatao then led her army to lay waste to Satyrus's kingdom. In utter defeat, Satyrus "lost heart and died." His son pledged allegiance and sent tribute to the triumphant Tirgatao.[20]

AMAGE OF THE SARMATIANS

Polyaenus described another warrior queen, Amage, who ruled the Sarmatians north of the Black Sea. Amage had married the chieftain of the Roxolani ("Bright Alans"), a Sarmatian-Alan tribe that later allied with King Mithradates VI of Pontus (chapter 21). Amage became the leader of the Roxolani sometime in 165–140 BC, after her husband fell into a life of chronic drunkenness. As his power dissipated, Amage took charge, settling disputes, repulsing enemy raids, and making alliances with neighboring tribes. (Her name appears to derive from Persian "magus" or "meadow.")

Amage's resolve and wisdom brought her renown among the Scythians and Sarmatians. The people of Tauric Chersonesus (Crimea) were suffering attacks by another Scythian tribe at this time and requested her help. (This ancient Greek colony had a mixed population of Greeks and barbarians.) Amage sent a message to the aggressive tribe ordering them to desist. When the tribe ignored her command, she called up 120 of her strongest warriors and gave each of them three horses. She led them to the Scythian tribe's stronghold, traveling 1,200 stades (about 136 miles) in one day and one night. She and her band killed the guards and threw the Scythians into confusion and fear. Bursting into the Scythian leader's inner circle, Amage killed him and his relatives and friends, except for his son. She restored the land the Scythians had stolen to the Tauric Chersonesus and made the son of the slain chieftain the new ruler of the Scythian tribe, "encouraging him to rule justly" and to live peacefully with the neighboring Greeks and barbarians.[21]

THE AMAZONS OF GEORGIA

Early European travelers' accounts contain narratives about women warriors heard from local peoples in the crossroads of Eurasia. The Europeans were familiar with some Greco-Roman myths about Amazons, so their accounts must be used carefully.

Events reminiscent of Pompey's experiences in Iberia and Albania (chapter 21) were reported by seventeenth-century Europeans in Georgia. As with the tale of Partu Patima, above, these accounts are not from classical antiquity, but they give evidence for warlike women persisting in early modern times on the Black Sea coast of ancient Colchis, the easternmost point reached by Jason and the Argonauts, a land associated with Amazons, and the place where Hypsicratea and Mithradates hid out with friendly tribes to escape Pompey. The Italian missionary Pere Archangeli Lamberti lived in Mingrelia (western Georgia) in 1631–49. He described a three-pronged attack by Caucasus mountain tribes who descended to ravage settlements in southern Russia and on the borders of Mingrelia.

"After a long and desperate struggle with the mountaineers, they were finally repulsed and many were slain." A great many of the dead were discovered to be "women in the prime of life." These "Amazons" wore beautifully decorated, flexible scaled armor "ingeniously contrived of small iron plates laid over one another," as well as chest plates over tunics of bright red wool, and helmets and gauntlets. The women's boots were adorned with braids of brass sequins, and their arrows also showed fine craftsmanship—long gilded shafts with barbed points like "scissors." The women's armor and weapons were sent to the prince of Mingrelia, who "offered a great reward for the capture of one of these females alive." A similar incursion of mounted men and women in northwestern Georgia was reported in 1671 by Sir John Chardin, who personally observed one of the so-called Amazon's costumes and concluded that the invaders must have been nomadic Scythian men and women from the steppes.[22]

The British explorer Edmund Spencer, commenting on Lamberti's account a century later, remarked that these "Amazons were really the wives and daughters of the Circassians . . . who to this day accompany the men to the field of battle." In his travels in the Caucasus Spencer was struck by the "noble, animated, commanding features" of the beautiful Caucasian women, who "must have resembled the Amazons of old." Their fiery expressions were "very different from the feminine gentleness of our own country." Rather, Spencer fancied, they had the "character of one who could rule a kingdom, command an army, or set the world in a blaze." Perhaps he also had in mind the powerful medieval queen Tamar (1160–1213) who ruled Georgia under the masculine title *mep'e* ("king"). During her reign she subdued many mountain tribes and consolidated a Georgian empire that dominated the Caucasus, Pontus, and parts of Armenia, an empire that stood until the Mongol invasions (inspiring the tales of heroines who resisted Tamerlane, above). Although Tamar did not personally lead armies, her military successes led to a body of popular, romantic legends in Georgia, in which she was portrayed as a "beautiful Amazon."[23]

CIRCASSIAN TALES OF A TRIBE OF WOMEN

As the preceding reports show, the earliest European travelers to the remote, wild Caucasus Mountains interpreted the local warlike women in terms of ancient Greek myths about Amazons. The German adventurer Jacob Reineggs (1744–93) undertook several exploratory missions to the little-known Caucasus for the Russian court. He recorded Tcher-kessian (Circassian) tales about their ancient migrations. One story concerned a tribe of women called the *Emmetsch*. Presumably Reineggs transcribed the sounds of this name into German as he heard it pro-nounced by the storyteller and the translator. In Circassian traditions, the Emmetsch were the original inhabitants of Circassia. In Circassian the name means "those who did not leave." Reineggs's account was translated to English in 1807.[24]

"When our ancestors dwelt on the shores of the Black Sea," recited the Circassian bards, there were "frequent wars with the Emmetsch. These were women who possessed the Circassian and Soanian moun-tain regions, as well as the whole plain as far as Aghla-Kabak. They re-ceived no men among them, but, full of warlike valor," they welcomed any woman of any nation who wished to join "their heroine society and participate in their incursions." (Strabo had described the Soanes as a tribe that held the heights of the Caucasus; they gathered gold from mountain streams and used poisoned arrows.) After a long series of battles with no decisive outcome, the armies of the Circassians and the Emmetsch faced each other on the steppes.

"Suddenly, the leader of the Emmetsch, known to be a great proph-etess, requested a private meeting with Thulme, the commander of the Circassians, also a great seer himself. A tent was immediately pitched between the two armies," and the two commanders entered alone. After many hours they emerged from the tent. The leader of the women an-nounced that she was convinced by Thulme's prophecies about the fu-ture. She had "chosen to marry Thulme on condition that all hostilities should cease" and that the soldiers, women and men, of both armies "should follow their example. This took place. The women warriors immediately ended the war" and took the Circassians as husbands. The Circassians, "delighted with their wives," dispersed over the land.[25]

Alternative versions of this Circassian legend were recorded by other early travelers. In the version documented by the Polish adventurer Count John Potocki (b. 1761), the women were called *Emmetsch*, but instead of fighting Circassians on the shores of the Black Sea, they bat-tled a band of Nogays on the steppes north of the Caspian Sea (the Turkic-Mongol peoples in the Ingush story, above). The Nogay chief-tain in this version was named Tul. In 1807/8, the German agent Julius von Klaproth, sent by the Russian government on a reconnaissance mission in the Caucasus, sought to verify the tales recorded by Reineggs and Potocki. Klaproth discovered an even earlier report by the German physician Gottlob Schober. Schober had been dispatched by Peter the Great across Great Tartary (the Eurasian steppes) in 1717 to locate mineral springs. Dagestani people told Schober that a tribe of women warriors, along with other vanished tribes, had once dwelled thereabout. Schober reported that Armenian and Tartar traders sometimes met "relics of these people" in remote mountains of Great Tartary, and that they were called *Emazuhn* (his German transliteration of the name he heard). Among the Emazuhn, the men served as the women's "domestic servants and bed-fellows." According to the traders, the women of the Emazuhn no longer made war but were "passionately fond of hunting." Schober identified these women as "Amazons."[26]

In about 1722, north of the Caspian Sea, the eminent French scholar of mythology Nicholas Fréret (b. 1688) recorded a Kalmyk word for a "strong, vigorous, heroic woman," pronounced "aèmetzaine" in French. The nomadic Kalmyks (Oirats) were a Mongol people who had migrated west from the Altai and northern Kazakhstan to the old Nogay territory north of the Caspian Sea and remained there after the Mongol hordes returned to Inner Asia (see also chapter 24). *Aèmetzaine* sounds something like *Amazon*, *Amezan*, *Emmetsch*, and *Emazuhn* (see chapter 5). The word is not Mongolian. It was likely a loanword from the Caucasus, but the concept of warrior women was already familiar to the Kalmyks. Interestingly, the name *Kalmyk*, bestowed on this tribe by their neighbors ca. AD 1200, is Turkic for "remnant or to remain," recalling the etymology of *Emmetsch*, above.[27]

In 1838, during his explorations in the Caucasus, Edmund Spencer also listened to Karbardian (Circassian) bards reciting their history: "When our ancestors inhabited the shores of the Sea of Azov, the isles of Taman, and the Tanais," they warred with "the Emazuhn-ites, who lived contiguous to the mountains we now occupy." The two armies were facing each other when the Emazuhn leader "Valdusa, a famous heroine and prophetess, suddenly rushed forward on her prancing charger and requested an interview with Thulme, leader of the Circassians." Spencer's version contains other details paralleling Reineggs's older account: the leaders meet in a tent pitched between the two bands, they announce sealing the peace with their marriage, and the pairs of male and female warriors follow suit, concluding with the Circassian men admiring the women's land so much that they decide to dwell there ever after.[28]

The Circassian legend bears some striking similarities to the foundation story of the Sarmatians heard by Herodotus in the northern Black Sea area in the fifth century BC. (Another parallel appears in an Egyptian legend; chapter 23.) The tribes and locales differ in the versions preserved by the European travelers: a tribe of women battle Circassians near the Black Sea or the Nogays on the northern steppes. Spencer's version adds the woman leader's name, "Valdusa," and his use of *Emazuhn* (used in 1717 by Schober) instead of *Emmetsch* (as in Potocki and Reineggs) is noteworthy. *Emazuhn/amezan/amazon/aèmetzaine* all sound vaguely similar, as noted above. The male chieftain's name *Tul* is a variant of *Thulme*; a modern history of Circassia gives his name as *Toulmey*. Consistent names of people and places are considered signs of a legend's antiquity.[29] There is also the possibility that Spencer embroidered the legend for his European audience. Nevertheless, taken together, the reports of Reineggs, Potocki, Schober, Klaproth, Fréret, and Spencer indicate that warrior women with a name similar to the Greek word "Amazon" were featured in the historical and legendary traditions of the Caucasus in stories that resemble one that the Greek traveler Herodotus heard in the same region more than two thousand years earlier.

PERSIA, EGYPT, NORTH AFRICA, ARABIA

P ERSIA AND EGYPT, KNOWN AND RESPECTED BY THE ancient Greeks as venerable and powerful civilizations, had their own independent histories and traditions about warrior women. Ancient Iranians were more knowledgeable than the Greeks about the lives of women from Central Asian nomad tribes, since first the Medes and then the Persians fought Scythians from the north and Saka tribes on the eastern frontiers of their empires. Many Scythian groups spoke forms of ancient Iranian. Stories about Medes and Persians and their Saka-Scythian adversaries and allies fascinated the Greeks, who were curious—and apprehensive—about steppe peoples, as well as the great Persian superpower in the sixth and fifth centuries BC. The Greeks were also deeply interested in Egypt, which was taken over by Persia in the sixth century. Egyptian mytho-historical traditions were preserved by Greek writers, such as Herodotus, and recorded in Egyptian papyri.

We have already met several Amazon-like nomad queens in Persian contexts. Herodotus described the devastating battle (ca. 530 BC) between Tomyris of the Massagetae-Saka and Cyrus of Persia, and he told how Artemisia of Halicarnassus commanded a Persian warship for Xerxes in the fifth century BC (chapters 9 and 19). The captive women who became the Amazon-like companions of Xenophon's Greek soldiers (ca. 400 BC; chapter 8) were originally from Persian lands. Atossa, Rhodogyne, and Semiramis were warrior queens of Assyria and Persia (chapters 12 and 22).

The Iranian stories about Saka warrior queens that came to us via ancient Greek authors originated in Persia. These were not just rehashed Greek yarns. The Saka women in these tales display many of the same characteristics as Amazons depicted in Greek myth, art, and literature, but they make war and love with Median and Persian warriors, not Greeks. These facts, along with the evidence from the previous chapter, disprove the notion that Greeks alone invented the idea of Amazons to challenge their national heroes. We can glean traces of Persian history and popular lore from close readings of the Greek sources without accepting the Greek-centered interpretations, notes a leading historian of the Persian Empire. "It is time to liberate ourselves from the Greek view on Persian history," including Hellenocentric perspectives on "notorious women." Indeed, the existence of so many stories about warrior women's relationships with Persian heroes strongly suggests that "fighting a Scythian queen may have formed part of a conventional Iranian repertory of heroic feats, just as fighting against Amazons seems to have been a required task for many Greek heroes."[1]

The theme of valiant heroines battling male heroes as equals is widespread beyond the Hellenic world. Persia and Egypt are among many other ancient cultures besides Greece that not only could imagine warlike women but were familiar with their real counterparts within or outside their borders.

GORDAFARID AND SOHRAB

Versions of the legends of the nomad heroine Shirin and of Queen Nushaba, told in Azerbaijan by Nizami, had been recounted earlier by the Persian poet Ferdowsi (b. AD 940). In Ferdowsi's *Shahnama*, however, Shirin was cast in a negative light, in contrast to Nizami's admiring portrayal modeled on his nomad wife, Appaq (chapter 22). In the *Shahnama*, Alexander met a different queen, Qaidafa, ruler of Andalusia (Muslim-ruled Spain). Like Nushaba, however, Qaidafa commanded large armies and Alexander treated her as his equal.[2]

In Ferdowsi's time, the warlike Scythian-Sarmatian-Massagetae-Saka nomads of Central Asia—whose women still made war and ruled like the men—were known to the Persians as Turanians, and they appear in the *Shahnama*. In one of Ferdowsi's tales, for example, a powerful fighter is named Gordieh ("Woman Warrior"). In another legend, the Persian hero Sohrab is challenged to single combat by Gordafarid ("Created as a Heroine"), a champion horsewoman archer. Her long hair hidden under her helmet, she rides out to meet Sohrab. Gordafarid lets fly a hail of arrows as her swift horse weaves back and forth. Her armored belt deflects Sohrab's sword and she hacks his sword in half. Sohrab does not realize that Gordafarid is a lovely young woman until his lance knocks off her helmet. Sohrab captures her with his lasso, but she tricks him into letting her go, and she and her people escape Sohrab's army.[3]

Ferdowsi's poems were drawn from pre-Islamic oral and written tales. Iranian accounts of women warriors from the nomadic tribes of Central Asia can be traced back to pre-Islamic times in other ways. For example, Romans reported that women served in the Persian cavalry of Shapur I, the Sassanid king, ca. AD 240–270. Centuries earlier, Herodotus, Ctesias, and others recorded stories of warlike women in ancient Iran. While Herodotus knew Persian history as a native of Persian-ruled Halicarnassus in the mid-fifth century BC, Ctesias was a Greek physician in the Persian court in 413–397 BC. His history of Persia in twenty-three books drew on the rich treasury of chronicles and gossip that Ctesias heard in the Persian court, combined with royal archives, local traditions, his conversations with the Persian queen mother Parysatis, and his own personal observations and investigations. Ctesias's *Persica* was cited by more than fifty authors in antiquity. All that survives now are summaries and quotations by a few ancient historians.[4] From these fragments of Ctesias we learn of Persian tales about two Saka warrior queens, Zarina and Sparethra.

ZARINA AND STRYANGAEUS

The Saka warrior woman named Zarina ("Golden") is the star of the "Median Romance," an ancient Iranian love story set during the period of the great Median Empire (625–550 BC). Diodorus (ca. 50 BC) based part of his curt biography of Zarina on Ctesias's fuller, more romantic account; a short papyrus fragment also refers to her story. "During that time," wrote Diodorus, "the Saka were ruled by a woman named Zarina, who was devoted to warfare." In daring and prowess, Zarina was out-standing; she surpassed other Saka women in beauty and glorious ac-complishments. Considered a great hero for subduing enemy tribes and making her people happy, Zarina was honored after her death with a colossal gilded statue and a monumental pyramid tomb, six hundred feet high. We can piece together the rest of her story from fragments scattered in other sources.[5]

"Learn about the Saka whose women fight alongside the men," wrote the Byzantine scholar Tzetzes. "As Ctesias and countless others have said," he continued, "the Saka women fight from horseback, as in the story of Stryangaeus the Mede who struck a Saka woman off her horse." Zarina's story, notes a modern scholar of warrior women tales, reflects "historical reality" and belongs to ancient Persian traditions "about fictional and actual Scythian warrior women."[6]

The tale begins when the Parthians (Irano-Scythians) revolted from the Median Empire and allied with the powerful Saka, "whose women fight like Amazons." Zarina had assumed leadership of the Saka after her husband died. According to Diodorus, the Parthians "entrusted their country and city to the leader of the Saka," namely, Zarina. She became the leader of the Parthian-Saka alliance when she married Mer-merus, ruler of the Parthians.[7]

Long wars raged between the Saka and the Medes. During one of the battles, Zarina fought the Median commander Stryangaeus. Here the versions diverge. In one, the Mede knocked the young woman off her horse. Struck by her beauty, he allowed her to remount and gallop away unharmed. In another version, Zarina was wounded and fled. Stryangaeus caught her but spared her life. Soon afterward, Zarina's husband, Mermerus, captured Stryangaeus and was about to kill him. Because the Mede had saved her life, Zarina pleaded for his release. But Mermerus was unmoved. Defying her husband, Zarina freed Stryan-gaeus and other Median prisoners of war and with their help killed Mermerus.[8]

At this point the thread of the story is taken up in papyrus frag-ments of a work by Nicolas of Damascus, who wrote an influential history of the Medes and the Persians (first century BC; he was also the tutor of Antony and Cleopatra's children in Alexandria, Egypt). After peace was declared between the Medes and the Saka, Stryangaeus came to visit Zarina in Rhoxanake ("Shining City," site unknown). Zarina "greeted him with great delight, kissed him publicly, and rode in his chariot, chatting happily." Stryangaeus retired to his quarters, moaning with unbearable desire. He confided his feelings to a eunuch, who urged him to declare his love to Zarina. Hemming and hawing, groaning and blushing, he finally told Zarina that he was "burning with desire for her." But Zarina "very gently rejected him," reminding him of his beautiful wife and numerous concubines. In anguish, Stryangaeus resolved to kill himself. But first he wrote a letter reproaching Zarina.

Surviving scraps of papyrus scrolls testify to the many different versions that circulated in antiquity of the lovesick Mede's letter, filled with philosophical meditations on the torments of unrequited love. Stryangaeus's basic message was this: "I saved you. You were saved by me. And I am devastated, deprived of everything, ruined, killed because of you." The nearly complete scrap we have from Nicolas of Damascus holds its own torments for us, leaving us in suspense. The last legible sentence reads: "After writing this letter he placed the parchment on his pillow and asked for his sword to take himself off to Hades. But the eunuch . . ."[9]

The narrative seems to hold out hope that the eunuch somehow contrived a happy ending. The ancient Iranian romance of Zarina and Stryangaeus reminds some scholars of the tragic Greek myth of Penthesilea and Achilles. But the story is quite different. It presents an alternative scenario in which the male and female adversaries' lives are spared and love is at least possible.

The tales of Zarina (and Sparethra, below) are set in the period when Amazons first began to appear in Greek art and then in literature. Archaeological reports are relatively scarce in ancient Persian lands. But in 2004, archaeologists in northwest Iran carried out a DNA test of a robust skeleton in one of more than a hundred warriors' tombs from about two thousand years ago (chapter 4) The test revealed that this skeleton of a warrior buried with a sword, previously identified as male, actually belonged to a female. Further tests may identify other armed females to correlate with warrior women in Median and Persian histories.[10]

SPARETHRA AND CYRUS THE GREAT

Cyrus II of Persia conquered the Median Empire in 550 BC. Like the Medes, Cyrus also made war on the Saka tribes between the Caspian Sea and Baktria. Before hostilities broke out between Cyrus and To-myris, Cyrus battled a different army of Saka horse warriors, led by the chieftain Amorges ("Having Excellent Meadows"), in about 545 BC, in the region of Sogdiana and Baktria. These were the Amyrgioi, known to the Persians as "haoma-drinking Saka" (chapter 9). According to Cte-sias, after Cyrus captured Amorges, Amorges's wife, Sparethra ("Heroic Army"), became the leader of the tribe. Sparethra called up an immense force of male and female warriors to attack Cyrus and free her husband. Ctesias wrote that "Sparethra headed an army of 300,000 horsemen and 200,000 horsewomen." The numbers may be exaggerated, but the detail provides evidence that women and men rode to war side by side in Saka-Scythian tribes. It evokes a dramatic picture to accompany Di-odorus's comments (ca. 50 BC) about the Saka tribes: "Now, this peo-ple, in general, have courageous women who share with their men the dangers of war."[11]

Sparethra led her large force of allied tribes against Cyrus. She de-feated his Persian army and captured many of Cyrus's highest-ranking men, including three of his sons. After the battle, Sparethra negotiated a treaty with Cyrus, who released her husband, Amorges, in exchange for the Persians taken prisoner by Sparethra. Sparethra's tribe became an ally of Cyrus.[12]

Cyrus expanded the Persian Empire south to Babylon. In 525 BC, his son Cambyses conquered Egypt, marking the end of the Egyptian Saite period (Twenty-Sixth Dynasty, which began in the early seventh century BC). This was the beginning of long Persian rule in Egypt (Ach-aemenid period). Egyptians were among the myriad ethnic groups serving in Persian armies that maintained and expanded the vast Per-sian Empire, which stretched from Thrace and Anatolia to Baktria. To continue this simplified Persian-Egyptian chronology, after the reign of Darius I (521–486 BC), his son Xerxes (520–465 BC) suppressed a revolt in Egypt and invaded Greece but was defeated in 479 BC. We recall that Xerxes's gift to his female admiral Artemisia was a costly alabaster jar made in Egypt (fig. 19.2).

During the reign of Xerxes's son Artaxerxes, more anti-Persian re-
volts arose in Egypt, but in 341 BC Egypt was reconquered and held by
Persia until Alexander the Great defeated Darius III and claimed the
Persian Empire, including Egypt, in 332 BC. This began the Hellenistic
period of Macedonian Ptolemaic rule, lasting until the Romans an-
nexed Egypt after Cleopatra's suicide in 30 BC. As this history shows,
Late Period Egypt had its own traditions and was also subject to Persian
and Greek cultural influences. Most of the evidence for Persian and
Egyptian history in this time frame depends on Greek sources along
with Egyptian inscriptions and papyrus texts in both Greek and demotic Egyptian scripts.[13]

The next sections present narratives about Amazons in Egypt. The
most ancient is an Egyptian romance, discovered on papyrus fragments,
whose origins and influences are controversial. Next is a lost fantasy
about Amazons written in Hellenistic Alexandria; a summary of it was
preserved by Diodorus. We conclude with descriptions of Amazon-like
women in North Africa by two Roman poets of the first century AD.

EGYPTIANS AND AMAZONS: QUEEN SERPOT

Several Egyptian papyri contain fragments of seven related tales woven
around historical figures of the seventh century BC, when Egypt was
part of the Assyrian Empire. The tales, written in demotic (popular,
nonhieroglyphic) script, mention the current Assyrian king, Essarhad-
don (680–669 BC), and Inaros I, who led an Egyptian revolt against
Assyria, in about 665 BC. This was a period when several Egyptian
princes jockeyed for dominance. Only three of the tales have been
translated. One story, "Egyptians and Amazons," tells how Serpot, queen
of the Amazons, fought and fell in love with Pedikhons, an Egyptian
prince.[14]

Sadly, the papyrus that tells this tale "is in tatters, with less than half
of the text preserved," and it is missing the beginning and ending.[15]
Nevertheless, enough survives of this unexpected narrative of an Amazon queen in Egypt to enable us to follow the story line.

Prince Pedikhons has invaded Serpot's "land of women" in the territory of Khor. *Khor* was the old Egyptian word for Assyria or Syria (which

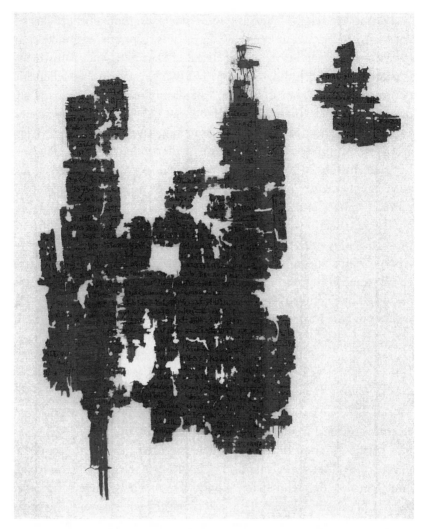

FIG. 23.1. Section of the tattered "Egyptians and Amazons" papyrus with tale of the Amazon Queen Serpot and Prince Pedikhons. Photo Austrian National Library, Vienna.

included Palestine and bordered on Egypt). Pedikhons's large army of Assyrians and Egyptians sets up camp near the stronghold of Serpot, the Amazon "pharaoh." (The title has a feminine ending.) Even though she rules a Mesopotamian land, Serpot's name is Egyptian; it means "Blue Lotus." Serpot summons her council of women to her tent and prays to the Egyptian gods Isis and Osiris for help. She sends her young aide-de-camp, Ashteshyt, to spy on the enemy camp. Ashteshyt's name is not Egyptian, but thus far the foreign origin and meaning of her name have mystified Egyptologists. (I will have more to say about her below.)

Because she is dressed as a male, Ashteshyt is able to infiltrate the army and reports back to Serpot, who devises a strategy. Serpot marshals an army of women from throughout her land. She reviews her assembled forces, exhorting them to repel the invaders. Some are mounted, and others drive chariots; all wear breastplates and some don helmets decorated with bulls' faces. (This detail recalls the helmets with bull's ears and horns worn by Amazons in Greek vase paintings of the sixth century BC, and by some tribes in Xerxes's Persian army of the fifth century BC.)[16]

Taking the offensive, Serpot leads a charge on Prince Pedikhons's army. The women "call out curses and taunts in the language of warriors" as they inflict heavy casualties. The slaughter is likened to an eagle ravaging a flock of birds. Pedikhons vows to turn the tables the next day, challenging Serpot to single combat. At daybreak, he dons his armor and takes up his scimitar and lances and appears alone on the battlefield "roaring like a lion, like a bull bursting with strength." Ashteshyt, the young spy, offers to do battle with "this evil serpent of an Egyptian," but Serpot insists on the honor. Putting on her armor and taking up her weapons, the Amazon queen goes out to meet Pedikhons. They struggle all day, "cursing and taunting each other," the blows of their weapons "resounding on their ornate shields." Rushing and feinting, they "attack like panthers; they fight as though death was greater than life itself. Neither gives way" even though the light is fading. Finally Serpot calls out to Pedikhons, "My brother, the sun has set, we can fight again tomorrow." She suggests they rest. He agrees, "One cannot fight in the dark."

Scholars can just make out sporadic words on the ragged papyrus indicating that the conversation is taking on a friendlier tone. Declaring an armistice, they sit down to talk. "My brother Pedikhons, why have you [come] here to [the land of women]? . . . fate . . . combat . . . if you wish . . . between us . . . she laughed." Settling down to rest, Pedikhons removes his armor. Serpot suddenly "did not know where she was [because of] the great desire that had entered [into her]." She removes her armor too. Looking at her, Prince Pedikhons also loses all sense of his surroundings, and says, "My sister Serpot . . ." Here the text trails off.

When it resumes, Serpot and Pedikhons are discussing their dilemma of duty versus love. They return to their own camps for the night. At dawn, they put on their armor. This time the two armies clash, but somehow peace is declared, and Serpot and Pedikhons continue their conversation. Pedikhons asks many questions about the land of women and praises Serpot's wisdom. A tent is set up for the lovers and both armies join the big celebration of their alliance. During the revelries, however, an "army from India" suddenly appears and Pedikhons's army suffers a severe blow. Serpot rushes to the rescue, taking the lead because she is experienced in combating the Indians. The fragmentary state of the papyrus cuts off the rest of the story, but the outcome is that Serpot and Pedikhons defeat the enemy together.[17]

Like Hippolyte of Greek myth, Serpot defends her land from foreign invaders. Some scholars hear echoes of the Greek myth of Penthesilea and Achilles, but the tale of Queen Serpot differs markedly and has more in common with other non-Greek stories of women warriors with happier endings. Serpot and Prince Pedikhons are so well matched that neither can win. Instead of a typical Greek zero-sum game with only one victor (the male), the ending fulfills the dream of rapprochement only gestured at in the Greek myths of Atalanta, Hippolyte, Antiope, and Penthesilea but fully realized in stories of the Caucasus, Azerbaijan, Media, Persia, and other cultures that could envision gender parity in love and war. Scholars note that the idea of female "pharaohs" was a familiar concept in Egypt, which had seen several female rulers since the Sixth Dynasty, ca. 2300 BC.[18] The story of Serpot and Pedikhons bears an uncanny resemblance to the Caucasian tale of the Amazon queen and the Circassian leader who interrupt their battle on the steppes for a tête-à-tête in a tent between their armies (chapter 22). In both of those tales, what began as a life-and-death struggle ends in mutual respect, love, and an alliance.

ORIGINS AND INFLUENCES IN THE STORY OF SERPOT

A maze of questions surrounds the tale of Serpot. She rules a "land of women" which could mean a "land ruled by women" (a phrase Greeks frequently used to describe Scythian tribes). Some scholars wonder whether Serpot might have been modeled on Semiramis, the Assyrian/ Persian queen who lived during the Assyrian rule of Egypt (ca. 1000–600 BC). How old is the tale of Serpot? It is part of a story cycle featuring documented historical figures of Egypt, Assyria, and Persia of the seventh century BC. Some scholars point out the similarities to the Persian story of Zarina preserved by Ctesias, related above. Other Egyptologists simply assume that the tale of Serpot and Pedikhons is a Hellenistic story inspired by Greek myth, and date it by the papyrus fragments to the Greco-Roman period. But other scholars point out that older Egyptian traditions could just as well have influenced Greek literature and suggest that an oral version of this tale arose in Egypt in the time period in which it is set. Indeed, the two leading authorities who translated the papyrus text itself argue that the core story of Serpot is relatively free of Greek influences; they suggest that it originated sometime between the seventh century BC and the period of Persian rule, 525 to 332 BC.[19]

Are there really no ancient parallels, histories, or traditions about Egyptians, Assyrians, and Amazon-like women to help explain the Serpot story, as many scholars maintain? Several striking coincidences may have been overlooked in which Amazons (or Scythians), Assyrians, and Egyptians come together in ancient literature. The evidence is circumstantial, but taken together it suggests that lore linking Amazon-like women with Assyria and Egypt might well have existed centuries before the Hellenistic period.

Egyptians are known to have borrowed some Persian vocabulary, and Egyptians serving in Persian armies in the east would have encountered in battle real Scythian-Saka warriors, some of whom were female. Some scholars compare Serpot with Penthesilea, whose mythic duel with Achilles appears in the *Aethiopis*, the lost ancient Trojan War epic that continued Homer's *Iliad* (chapter 18). But, as noted above, the two tales are not really similar. Egyptians could have absorbed Persian narratives about warrior women like Zarina and Sparethra, whose tales have more in common with Serpot's than with Penthesilea's.

More striking is the pairing of Amazons and Egyptians as the two allies of the Trojans in the *Aethiopis*. After Queen Penthesilea and her Amazons are killed, King Memnon of Ethiopia (south of Egypt) arrives with his army to aid Troy. Some Greek vase paintings pair Amazons and Ethiopians dressed in similar attire. In western Anatolia Herodotus viewed several statues in Egyptian and Ethiopian dress identified as Memnon (although Herodotus identified them as a legendary Egyptian king named Sesostris; see below). During his travels in Egypt, Herodotus heard many wondrous things from Egyptian guides and priests. For example, Egyptians told him a long, involved tale claiming that Helen of Troy was actually hiding in Egypt, rescued later by her husband Menelaus after the Trojan War. (Diodorus and Strabo associated this tradition with an ancient village on the Nile called "Troy.") In the second century AD, Pausanias described the remains of a colossal statue in Thebes, Egypt, broken in two during the Persian conquest in 525 BC; it was popularly identified as Memnon (probably Amenhotep). This collection of accounts, no matter how tenuous, at least suggests that Egyptian traditions about or similar to the Trojan War epic could be heard in Egypt in the fifth century BC.[20]

During the chaotic, poorly understood seventh century BC, Assyrian records mention an alliance with Scythians from the northern steppes who, according to Herodotus, were at war with, and then ruled over, the Medes. Herodotus also reported that the Scythians' southern advance was halted in Syria by the king of Egypt, Psammetichus I (664–610 BC). Here is a scrap of evidence, however tenuous, for a historical meeting between Egyptians and Scythians—whose women behaved like "Amazons"—in the "land of Khor" (Syria, as in the Serpot tale).[21]

Another coincidence is even more remarkable, for there was an ancient Egyptian tradition that Egyptians visited the Amazon homelands of Colchis and Scythia. Egyptian priests told Herodotus about a legendary Egyptian pharaoh named Sesostris. Some time before the Trojan War, it was said that Sesostris led his Egyptian army through Syria all the way north to Colchis (where he left some Egyptian colonists). Sesostris then crossed the Caucasus Mountains to the Sea of Azov and onto the steppes of Scythia. He returned to Egypt with a multitude of captives from Colchis and Scythian lands. Notably, other ancient accounts mention slaves of Thracian and other northern origins in Egypt in the sixth century BC.[22]

Versions of King Sesostris's legendary expedition to Scythia were also related by Strabo, Justin, and Diodorus (who associated Egyptians with the Maeotian tribes of the Sea of Azov and claimed that Sesostris reached "India"). Sesostris stories also appear in ancient Egyptian papyri. Modern historians believe that no Egyptian king ever traveled north of the Euphrates into Anatolia, much less to Scythia or India. The accounts of Sesostris do not specifically mention Amazons, but his legendary travels do take him into the heartland of Amazons/Scythians. The existence of these traditions, going back to at least the fifth century BC, recounted in Egypt, and attested in Egyptian papyri, might have some bearing on the "Amazons and Egyptians" tales, including the story of Serpot and Pedikhons.

One even might venture a step further. Might the ancient tradition that Sesostris brought back captives from the Caucasus region, and the historical presence of slaves from Thrace in Egypt, help explain the mysterious non-Egyptian name of Ashteshyt, the Amazon spy? To linguist John Colarusso, the phonology of her name could mean "One Who Pursues and Kills" in ancient Abkhazian, a Caucasian language. Northwest Caucasian languages, such as Abkhazian, are related to the non-Indo-European Hattic language of Anatolia in 2000–1000 BC. Another attractive theory to explain Ashteshyt's name compares it phonetically to the name of a tribe in Libya, the Asbytai, famed for warrior women, mentioned by Herodotus, Strabo, and Silius Italicus (discussed below).[23]

WARRIOR WOMEN OF NORTH AFRICA, NUBIA, AND ARABIA

Accounts of Amazon-like women emerged in North Africa after the Persian conquest of Egypt in the sixth century BC. For example, Queen Pheretime of Cyrene (Libya) led a rebel army against the Persians in Egypt in about 514 BC, as described by Herodotus. Diodorus located "a number of races of warlike women admired for their manly vigor" in Libya. Another possible influence for the Serpot tale could be powerful female rulers of the Kushite Kingdom, based in Meroe in Nubia-Ethiopia, now Sudan. The title of Kushite queens was *Kandake/Candace* in ancient inscriptions and writings of the fourth century BC to the Roman period, first century AD; Greeks and Romans mistook the title as the name Candace. The Sotades Painter's vase of 460 BC, shaped like a mounted Amazon, was found at Meroe (plate 2). The Nubians were famous archers, so "it is credible to imagine that Nubian women [were] skilled with the bow and arrow." Discoveries of "spear heads

FIG. 23.2. Amanitore, kandake of Nubia, smiting enemies with her sword, sandstone relief ca. AD 50, Naga Lower Temple, Meroe, Sudan.

and archer thumb guards" have been reported in some female burials in ancient Nubia.[24]

Several Nubian queens led armies, such as the *kandake* Shanakdakheto of Meroe (ca. 170–150 BC), who captured many prisoners and cattle in her wars. The best-known *kandake* was the one-eyed warrior queen Amanirenas the Brave (she lost an eye in battle). She is simply called "Candace" in Strabo's account of her five-year war on the Romans in Egypt in 27–22 BC. Amanirenas personally commanded the Kushites in a victory over the Roman forces at Syene (Aswan) and Philae, taking thousands of prisoners and much booty, even making off with several statues of Emperor Augustus. About ten years later (ca. 10 BC) another *kandake*, Amanikasheto, also defeated a Roman army sent by Augustus; she is represented in Egyptian art spearing enemies. The reign of her daughter Amanitore in Meroe began about 1 BC; she is portrayed smiting her foes with a sword. In 1911, British archaeologists found a beautifully preserved bronze head of Augustus that had been decapitated from a Roman statue. It was buried under the threshold of a victory shrine in Meroe—likely placed there by Amanirenas to be constantly trod on.[25]

Another possible influence on "Egyptians and Amazons" could be Arabian women warriors who commanded armies against Assyrian and Egyptian rulers between 1000 and 400 BC. Eighth-century BC Assyrian records name several queens of the Quedarites, a confederation of Arab nomads whose range extended from southern Syria to the Nile. Queen Zabibi (Arabic, "Raisin") was succeeded by Queen Samsi (Arabic, "Sun"), who allied with the king of Damascus (Syria) in a rebellion against the Assyrian king Tiglath-Pileser in 732 BC. In a battle near Mount Sa-qu-ur-ri (site unknown), Samsi's army was defeated, and according to Assyrian archives, Samsi "fled into the desert like a wild she-ass." Assyrian, Persian, and Egyptian soldiers would have fought Arabian tribes whose girls and women rode horses and used bows and javelins. Centuries later, the famous warrior queen of mixed Aramaic-Egyptian-Arabic heritage, named Bat-Zabbai but better known as Zenobia, rose to power in the third century AD in Syria and went to war against the Romans in Egypt. Later medieval Arabic romances abound in warlike heroines. The popular historical epic *Dhat al-Himma*, for example, stars the horsewoman named "Wolf" among other ruthless female warriors.[26]

THE AMAZONS OF LIBYA, A FANTASY TALE

The story of Serpot was likely already popular before the appearance of a remarkable novel about a race of mythical Amazons set in "Libya" (North Africa). In this fantasy, the queen of the Amazons forges an alliance with the king of Egypt before going on to subdue Syria—details that parallel the alliance of Serpot of Syria and Pedikhons of Egypt.[27]

The popularity of the "Amazons and Egyptians" tale, combined with the ancient links between Scythians and Egyptians and the reality of women warriors in North Africa and Nubia, may have inspired the idea of relocating the mythic Amazon queens of the Black Sea to North Africa.

Composed in Alexandria, Egypt, in about 150 BC, this tall tale sprang from the mind of Dionysius nicknamed Skytobrachion ("Leather-Arm": perhaps he had a prosthetic limb). Unfortunately, Leather-Arm's Hellenistic mash-up of Greek myths with splashes of local African color has not survived, except for a summary of the plot by Diodorus in the first century BC.[28]

Parts of Leather-Arm's tale are doublets of ancient Greek traditions about the Amazons of Scythia, and the characters and events are lifted from old myths and legends but located in Africa. For instance, his Amazons of Libya not only battle an army of Gorgons led by Queen Medusa, but they negotiate a treaty with the lost city of Atlantis. The romance also features appearances by the god Dionysus, the Egyptian deities Horus and Isis, and Jason and the Argonauts, whose quest is transposed from the Black Sea to Libya (a tradition first reported by Herodotus).

Many of the details reflect the topography and fauna of North Africa. For example, instead of the scaled armor made from hooves, horn, or gold worn by real Sarmatians of Scythia, the Amazons wear armor fashioned from the scaly hides of enormous snakes. Strabo reported that real-world Libyans made clothing and bedcovers from snakeskins. Several writers, including Aristotle, Diodorus, and Orosius, citing lost earlier works, reported snakes of remarkable size in North Africa and described a great hunt for a huge python in Egypt in the third century BC. Large pythons are depicted in Egyptian mosaics of the first century BC. Leather-Arm wove this realistic bit of local zoology into his exotic image of the Libyan Amazons' armor.[29]

ASBYTE OF THE ASBYTAI

Parallels to Leather-Arm's relocation of mythic Amazons to North Africa can be found in a later Roman epic poem, the *Punica* by Silius Italicus (AD 83–96), about Hannibal of Carthage and the Second Punic

War. Silius consulted numerous historical texts, many lost to us. His Amazons were partly inspired by Herodotus's descriptions of North African tribes. For example, Herodotus told of a festival in Libya (modern Tunisia) involving a beautiful armed maiden in a chariot, presiding over a virginity test in which girls are divided into two groups and fight with sticks and stones. Those who die of their wounds are believed to be nonvirgins. Herodotus also reported that several of the Libyan nomad tribes practiced free love, like the Amazons and the Massagetae, and noted that the women dressed in goat leather. An Amazon name, Sisyrbe (mentioned by Strabo), means "Shaggy Goatskin."[30]

In Silius's poem, one of Hannibal's allies is the fearless warrior Asbyte, princess of a people who speak both Libyan and Egyptian. Her father is a great ruler whose subjects include the Cyrenians and Nasamones of the parched desert and the Gaetulians "who ride without reins." Asbyte leads a troop of Amazon charioteers and horsewomen from Marmarica (between modern Egypt and Libya) to aid Hannibal at his siege of Saguntum, Spain. Asbyte's bodyguard, Harpe, dies defending her queen. (Harpe, "Snatcher," can also mean "sickle-shaped dagger"; another woman warrior called Harpe appeared in Valerius Flaccus's Roman retelling of the *Argonautica*, ca. AD 90.) Asbyte herself is finally killed in a duel with a male warrior named Theron ("Beast"). Hannibal avenges her death and the Numidians place Asbyte's body on a funeral pyre.[31]

Asbyte and Harpe are fictional figures who may be modeled in part on two Amazon characters already well known to Silius's readers: Penthesilea of Greek myth and Camilla, a doomed warrior woman modeled on Penthesilea dreamed up by Virgil for his patriotic Roman epic, the *Aeneid* (ca. 20 BC). Asbyte conforms to what had become a literary topos: a warrior queen brings a cohort of Amazons to aid a great commander. Her noble death follows the old Greek mythic script. However, many historical events and people also appear in the *Punica*, and Silius's description of the Amazon band includes accurate facts drawn from nomadic western Black Sea–Thracian cultures well known to the Romans.

For example, some of Asbyte's Amazons drive chariots, while others ride horses and guide them by knee and heel pressure with loose reins or none at all, realistic details of nomad horsemanship (chapter 11).

The Amazons' shields are crescent-shaped, and they wield bows and arrows, spears, and battle-axes. Asbyte is a "virgin," like many of her companions, although Silius tells us that some women in her army are married, another realistic detail. Silius compares his fictional Amazons to the warlike females of the Cicones, Getae, and Bistones, three genuine nomadic tribes of the Balkans who battled imperial Roman armies in what is now Bulgaria, Romania, and Moldova.

The name Asbyte derives from the name of a real Libyan tribe, the Asbytai, described by Herodotus and Pliny; they were known for their four-horse chariots. Ptolemy's *Geography* located this tribe in Libya south of Cyrene. Interestingly, the name "Asbyte" could sound like "Ashtyte" in Egyptian. This fact might shed light on the mysterious name of "Ashteshyt," Queen Serpot's foreign spy (above). Egyptian writing has no vowels, so exact pronunciations are unknown. The similarity of consonants in the two names raises the possibility that Serpot's scout may have belonged to the Asbytai tribe.[32]

24

AMAZONISTAN: CENTRAL ASIA

I T IS SAID THAT THE BOUNDLESS STEPPES GIVE FLIGHT to tales of heroes and heroines because the conditions of life are so harsh and extreme. The landscape itself demands human spirit on an epic scale. Scythia, for the ancient Greeks, was an immense ocean of land whose vastness paradoxically expanded as their knowledge about the world to the East increased. The exhilarating, terrifying lives of warlike archers on horseback fascinated not only the Greeks and Romans but also the Persians and Egyptians. And as we've seen, these westerners thrilled to tales of Amazons and foreign warrior queens from beyond the Black and Caspian seas, tales drawn from historical events, factual details, unwritten barbarian chronicles, hearsay, speculation, and the experiences of travelers and soldiers—and burnished by countless retellings.

Evidence for both historical and legendary Amazon-like figures in the Caucasus and the Middle East was embedded in the Nart sagas and local oral tales about strong nomad women such as Tirgatao, Tomyris, Sparethra, Zarina, Banu Chichak, and Gordafarid transmitted by Greek and Persian writers. Meanwhile, of course, the men and women of the various nomad warrior societies of Central Asia were telling their *own* war stories, adventures, and romances *about themselves and their neighbors—stories about, by, and for* real Scythians and Amazons. It turns out that women warriors were familiar characters in Middle Eastern and Central and South Asian folklore, as popular as heroes, fleet horses, and evil rulers.

Unfortunately, unlike ancient Greek, Egyptian, and Indian literature, the oral myths, ancestral lore, and folk memories of the myriad
and far-ranging ethnic groups of Central Asia were not recorded in
writing until the mid-twentieth century. What survives of this living
folklore has passed through thousands of years of turbulence, continuous migrations over vast and varied topographies, intermarriage, extinc-
tions of entire tribes, forced relocations, violent colonizations, political
oppression, and wars. In the written versions of the ancient ballads, epic
verses, and tales of lands now divided into the nations of Uzbekistan,
Kazakhstan, Kyrgyzstan, Turkmenistan, and Tajikistan, some events are
set in medieval or later times. Yet, as scholars note, many of the ethnographic and traditional details retain archaic roots.[1] The tales reverber-
ate with the small, random portions of genuine nomad lore in many
tongues that reached Greece through the writings and oral reports by
the early Greek adventurer Aristeas, who traveled across what is now
Kazakhstan, southern Siberia, and northwest China in the seventh century BC, and from Herodotus, and others. The Greek texts contain surprisingly accurate details of steppe lifestyles and histories, unavoidably
peppered with outsiders' misunderstandings and fantasy. What shines
through is the barbarians' celebration of men and women as peers in
love and war. Assimilated into Greek art and literature, this consistent
facet of nomadic life helped to shape Western ideas about Amazons.

The horse-riding heroines in this chapter seem familiar because
they strongly resemble their sisters who were kidnapped, like Antiope,
into Greek literature and art. But the Greek mythic mold produced a
crucial difference. In the stories that Scythians and Amazons told themselves, warrior women could survive battles, and their conflicts with
male warriors could end on a positive note instead of inevitable death
for the "unnatural" manly woman at the hands of a Greek mythic hero.
Significantly, the Greek historians who described real Amazons did not
hew to the mythic script, and so their accounts of barbarian women at
war, such as Tirgatao and Zarina, are more realistic. The following pages
give a sense of the kinds of Amazon tales that would have enthralled
Saka-Scythian and related peoples *and* those who lived in close proximity to nomad territories thousands of years ago, from the eastern shores
of the Caspian Sea to the Altai and Hindu Kush and the western frontier of China.

CHASE THE GIRL

The young woman on her flying horse speeds away toward the line where infinite sky meets new grass. The young man on his nimble steed hurtles after her. As the pair race, the boy manages to draw up alongside the girl for a brief moment. Now is his chance! Leaning perilously far over the side of his galloping horse, the boy tries to steal a kiss at breakneck speed. He fails. As he scrambles upright on his mount, the girl wheels around and lashes the would-be suitor with her whip to show her scorn, to the great delight of the onlookers.

The next contest begins. The haughty girl dashes off. The young man's horse chases hers in hot pursuit. The boy catches up, and as their horses run parallel, he attempts the audacious feat. The two riders' lips touch for an instant. Parting, the grinning boy and girl surge forward on their swift horses, each glowing with victory and perhaps even true love. The kiss of a *jigit* (daring, heroic rider) is said to be irresistible.

The high-spirited race is called *kesh kumay* (Turkic, *kyz kuu*, "chase the girl") and it has been played, with variations, at summer horse festivals since time immemorial by Kyrgyz, Kazakh, Azerbaijani, and other Turkic nomad groups.[2] Men and some women also compete in robust wrestling matches on horseback, archery, horse racing, and trick riding—all equestrian games that show off the *jigit* skills, strength, and endurance of both sexes. It is also a chance to display their magnificent steeds. After all, this is the heartland of the coveted Akhal Teke horses of the Ferghana Valley pastures (chapter 11).

Once part of ancient wedding rituals on the steppes, the origins of *kesh kumay* reflect an arduous selection process for companionable marriage between willing equals. In these courting games, the competition is real but cooperation is the key to success. It is difficult for a boy to "steal a kiss" at full gallop without the complicity of an equally agile and eager horsewoman.[3]

The *kesh kumay* game evokes inevitable comparisons with the life-or-death footrace devised by the Greek Amazon of myth, Atalanta, to eliminate her suitors. Atalanta also won wrestling matches against male champions and bested men in hunting with spears and arrows (prologue). Give her a horse, and Atalanta would be a full-fledged Amazon. In its ideal pairing of well-matched contestants and the girl's ability to

FIG. 24.1. A modern "Chase the Girl," *kyz kuu* (*kesh kumay*) race, near Almaty, Kazakhstan. Photo by Jeremy T. Lock, traditional games sponsored by Central Asian Battalion (Centrazbat) and US Central Command, 2000.

resist or comply, the *kesh kumay* contest also calls to mind the many single combats that led to friendship and love between worthy adversaries in antiquity, as in the stories of Zarina and Serpot. The Kyrgyz and Kazakh games recapitulate the riding, shooting, and wrestling tests set by the Kipchak warrior princess Banu Chichak for her Oghuz Turkic lover Beyrek (chapter 22).

Central Asian folklore is replete with similar contests. The prospective groom proves his worth, and the bride's combat skills are seen as an attractive feminine attribute and necessary for marriage. The loser is jokingly said to become the "slave" of the other, perhaps predicting domestic dynamics. Remarkably, the *kesh kumay* and other "mock-serious" duels confirm an ancient account by Aelian (chapter 10) about the mating "battles" of the Massagetae-Saka, Tomyris's tribe. Aelian reported that if the man lost, he became the woman's "slave." The *kesh kumay* games and the love-duels suggest, however, that the customs of premarital fighting—seriously competitive yet good-humored, symbolic yet physical—were part of wooing a compatible helpmeet and creating a flexible companionship based on mutual respect.[4]

Chinese chronicles (second century BC) and Muslim sources (seventh century AD) described the Kyrgyz as blue-eyed blondes or redheads, but millennia of migrations, conquests, and assimilation have resulted in very mixed ethnicities of Central Asia.[5] Like many of the ethnic groupings of Central Asia, the Kyrgyz (from Turkic *kyrk yz*, "forty clans or tribes") descended from a confederation of Saka-Scythian-Siberian groups from the Altai region. Some of the original clans came from the homeland of the famous Ice Princess and other men and women of the Pazyryk, Altai, Ukok, and Tuva regions buried with their arrows, battle-axes, spears, horses, hemp-burning kits, golden armor, trousers, boots, and tunics in the permafrost more than two thousand years ago (chapter 4). Opulent graves of women warriors dressed in gold and buried with their weapons have been excavated in Kazakhstan, Kyrgyztan, Uzbekistan, and Afghanistan; these were the ancient relatives of the fighting women in the tales told in this chapter.

SAIKAL, KALMYK HEROINE OF THE *MANAS* EPIC

The Kyrgyz adopted a Nogay-Kipchak form of the Turkic/Altaic language families, unwritten until 1923. The great *Manas* epic cycle (half a million verses; compare the *Iliad*, which has about fifteen thousand) is a veritable encyclopedia of Kyrgyz, Kazakh, Nogay, Uighur, and Turkic legends and songs recited by generations of bards. A Persian manuscript of 1792 is the earliest transcription of these old stories, which relate how the hero Manas and his *kyrk jigit* ("forty expert horsemen," one from each tribe) ranged over the Altai region and present-day Kyrgyzstan and Kazakhstan, interacting with Kipchaks, Oirats (Kalmyks), Uighurs, Afghans, and Chinese. Some events can be related to an inscription of AD 732, and many details are older. Scholars remark that women in the tales "are as heroic and militant as the men." Manas's wife, for example, avenges his death, killing his murderers and drinking their blood.

FIG. 24.2. Kyz Saikal, the Kalmyk warrior heroine of the Central Asian *Manas* epic, image by Teodor Gercen featured on a postage stamp, Kyrgyz Republic, 1995.

But the central "hero girl" of the *Manas* tales is a Kalmyk *aèmetzaine* named Kyz Saikal. (*Aèmetzaine* was a Kalmyk word for strong woman; chapter 22. The name *Saikal* could be related to Karakalpak *saukele*, pointed headdress.) Saikal becomes the leader of her tribe because her husband, the chieftain, is a drunkard (recalling the situation of Amage, queen of the Roxolani; chapter 22). Saikal fights in battles and horse-wrestles with the best male champions—she nearly unhorses Manas. As they prepare for single combat, Manas is filled with anxiety. "What if she dies if I strike her with force! I would [rather] marry her!" He plunges his spear into her right shoulder, but Saikal throws it off and threatens him with her spear. In the poem, Manas expresses his fear of losing the very woman he would choose as his mate, an emotion that surged after the fact in the case of the Greek hero Achilles (chapter 18).[6]

An impressive mausoleum in northwestern Kyrgyzstan near the Ka-zakh border is revered as the grave of Manas. Local legend claims that Kanikey, Manas's widow, created a false inscription on the tomb to con-fuse her husband's enemies. As with the many impressive graves incor-rectly assumed to belong to men, the mausoleum is actually that of a mystery woman. Her story has vanished except for the inscription (ca. 1334) on the ornate facade, dedicating the mausoleum "to the most glorious of women, Kenizek-Khatun" (Turkic, "Maiden-Queen").

WRESTLING WITH HERO GIRLS

The ancient Greeks knew of only one "wrestling heroine," Atalanta. But the epic tales and traditions of the nomads from the Caucasus to Mon-golia abound with girls and women, such as Lady Hero/Gunda the Beautiful, Banu Chichak, and Saikal, who challenge men to wrestling contests.[7] Wrestling is a traditional nomad sport of great antiquity; per-sonal athletic triumphs were believed to ensure heroic victories in bat-tle. Archaeologists have found wrestling images on bronze plates in Xiongnu sites. In folk wrestling matches on the steppes, adversaries were not matched by weight, age, or size. Opponents grabbed each oth-er's arms or waist and pushed and strained until some part of the rival's body was forced to touch the ground. Evenly matched competitors might be locked together for hours. The erotic nature of a man and woman wrestling was obvious in the ancient Greek vase paintings of Atalanta, and this sensuous aspect of wrestling as foreplay comes through in many of the love-contests in traditional nomad tales.

The most famous "wrestling heroine" of Central Asia was the great-great-granddaughter of Genghis Khan of the Mongols. Aijaruc (Turkish, "Bright Moon"), also known as Khutulun ("All-White") was born ca. 1260 and grew up with fourteen brothers. Her Turkish name, given in various spellings by Marco Polo, may have been a translation of her real name; "Bright Moon" was a traditional Uzbek name. A tall, powerfully muscled young woman, Khutulun excelled in horse riding, archery, and combat on the steppes around the Tien Shan range. Marco Polo described her style of warfare in terms of falconry: riding beside her father, Qaidu Khan, at the head of their army of forty thousand, she would suddenly "dash out at the enemy host, and seize some man as deftly as a hawk pounces on a bird, and carry him back to her father." Her parents were anxious to see her wed. But Khutulun declared she would marry only the man who could defeat her in wrestling. Many men tried and failed, paying ten or even a hundred horses for the chance to grapple with her. Soon she owned a herd of more than ten thousand. When she was about twenty, a worthy, strong prince came forward with one thousand fine horses. Khutulun promised her parents she would let him win. A crowd gathered. Their struggle continued for a long time in suspense. In the excitement, Khutulun forgot her promise, and with a terrific surge of energy she threw the suitor to the ground. Finally, some years later the undefeated Khutulun did choose a husband but without wrestling him first. She became the commander of the army after her father's death.[8]

An oral story cycle of Turkmenistan, also recited by Kazakhs, Uzbeks, and Karakalpaks, tells the adventures of the bandit hero Koroglu, based in the seventeenth century but drawing on earlier tales. Koroglu meets an invincible, bloodthirsty woman warrior named Harman Dali ("Crazy-Brave"). A beguiling berserker, Harman Dali thrives on killing suitors who accept her by-now-familiar challenge: "I'll only marry the man who beats me at wrestling and I chop off the heads of the losers." Their wrestling bout is described in humorously lascivious detail, until Koroglu is so enflamed with desire that he gives up. But his life is spared and his singing wins him one night of love.[9]

GULAIM AND HER FORTY AMAZONS

Forty warriors go to war in an epic tale told by another nomadic tribe, the Karakalpaks of ancient Khorezm, on the southern edge of the dry lake bed that was once the Aral Sea, now part of Uzbekistan. But the striking thing about this story is that these forty warriors were women. (Forty is a common folk motif in Central Asia: a Kyrgyz tradition also involves forty women.)

The epic song *Kyrk Kyz* (*Forty Maidens*) was "discovered" by folklorists in 1939, a few years after the Karakalpak language acquired an alphabet. It was recorded from the *zhrau* (bard) Kurbanbai Tazhibaev (b. 1883), who could name each poet who had transmitted the verses over the previous six generations. Genetic studies show that the Karakalpaks descended from a confederation of ethnic groups. Scholars believe that *Forty Maidens* has at least three layers of historicity. Medieval Turkish and eighteenth-century conquests by Kalmyks and others overlay the oldest layers, dating back to the sixth to fourth centuries BC, the heyday of the Saka-Scythian and related tribes whose kurgans are landmarks across the steppes. Historians note that the existence of female warriors led by a woman was possible in that time and place, and they wonder whether the tale explains the king of Khorezm's claim of Amazons on his border, reported in Arrian's history of Alexander's campaigns in this region in 326 BC (chapter 20).[10]

The plot of *Forty Maidens* also reminds scholars of Persian stories about the Saka warrior queen Zarina (chapter 23) and Herodotus's account of Queen Tomyris of the Massagetae-Saka who fought Cyrus of Persia (chapter 9). Tomyris is a national heroine claimed by peoples of western Turkey, Azerbaijan, Uzbekistan, and Kazakhstan, which recently issued coins in her honor. (Tomyris is a popular name in these countries.) In 1996 the Uzbek poet Halima Xudoyberdiyeva published *The Sayings of Tomyris*. Kazakh archaeologists often invoke Queen Tomyris when they describe the tombs of ancient Saka princesses buried with tall, pointed hats, arrows, and gold treasure. (Could Tomyris be the Golden Warrior of Issyk? See chapter 4.)

In *Forty Maidens*, the rebellious Gulaim ("Rose Moon"), age fifteen, rejects marriage, much like Atalanta of Greek myth, Khutulun, Harman Dali, and many other Amazonian girls. She decides to be a warrior and

FIG. 24.3. Left to right, silver coins featuring Queen Tomyris of the Massagetae, 1995; the Golden Warrior of Issyk, 2011; and the *kyz kuu* "Chase the Girl" race, 2008, courtesy of the Kazakhstan Mint.

gathers forty like-minded young horsewomen archers. Gulaim's father builds them a citadel on an island in the Aral Sea, where they live, train for war, raise crops, and ride out on raids together. This description matches ancient Greek historical accounts in which "going Amazon" is a lifestyle option, and the tales about Scythians and Amazons in which the young women prove their worth in battle and then are free to marry or remain warriors, fighting in mixed groups or in all-women cadres. In an Uzbek version of the epic, Gulaim trains an army of forty women warriors because all the men of their tribe have been killed in war. They serve as mercenaries in Timur's army, like Penthesilea's band of Amazons at Troy. If a girl falls in love and marries, she leaves the group and is replaced by another maiden. This alternative Uzbek version bears striking similarities to ancient Greek accounts of Amazon customs.

As we saw in chapter 20, Alexander campaigned in Gulaim's homeland (the region of Khorezm and Sogdiana) and he married Roxane, daughter of a nomad chieftain of these parts. It was here that the king of Khorezm told him of Amazons. It is interesting to note that the Spanish envoy to Timur in 1403 reported that Amazons still lived in the same general region. Ruy Gonzalez de Clavijo wrote that fifteen days' ride by camel east of Samarkand lay the "land inhabited by Amazons, nomadic women who travel once a year to the nearest settlements where they consort with men, each one taking the one who pleases her most, with whom they stay, eat, and drink, after which they return to their own land." They keep their daughters from these unions "but send the sons to their fathers." Surprisingly, these medieval "Amazons" had converted to Christianity.[11]

Notably, at the ruins of Panjikent, in Tajikistan near the Uzbekistan border, archaeologists have discovered fragments of ancient Sogdian paintings (ca. AD 500–700) illustrating many familiar and unknown legends. Several of the narrative friezes depict men in single combat with women warriors wearing leopard-skin leggings. The main panel is an Amazonomachy with a series of dramatic scenes culminating in the death of the women's leader. The forearm and wrist of one Amazon raising a sword is adorned with a geometric design that strongly resembles the forearm-wrist tattoos of Thracian women in Greek art (chapter 6).[12]

In *Forty Maidens*, while Gulaim and her band are away campaigning on the steppe, the Kalmyks attack the stronghold of Gulaim's tribe. Her six brothers are killed and her people taken captive. Gulaim and her Amazons rush to the rescue. They are joined by some Kalmyk rebels who hate their cruel leader, and by Aryslan, leader of a band of *jigits* from Khorezm. Gulaim challenges the evil Kalmyk chief to single combat and kills him. The captives are freed and the victorious heroes, Gulaim and Aryslan, ride home at the head of their armies. The two companions in war have fallen in love and marry with the blessings of their tribes. Meanwhile, Aryslan's sister, another warrior maiden, is chosen by the people of Khorezm as their champion in single combat with a Persian enemy. She is captured and later rescued by Gulaim and Aryslan. Gulaim and Aryslan create a confederation of the four ethnic groups of the region: Karakalpaks, Turkomans, Uzbeks, and Kazakhs. According to the Uzbeks, Kyrk Kyz Tepe, the mud-brick ruins of a fortress with towers (first to ninth centuries AD) at Termez in ancient Khorezm was the citadel of the Forty Maidens.[13]

In a fascinating Karakalpak tradition linked to *Forty Maidens*, at age fifteen girls begin to dress in a special dark-blue "girl-soldier" costume, like that worn by Gulaim. It is made of woven *torka*, hemp fibers, which are light but very strong. The costume is embroidered in the "chain-mail" pattern. Among the Kazakhs, the word *torka* designates hemp cloth suitable for armor because it is so closely woven that arrows cannot pierce it. The headgear of the girls in this region, the *saukele*, resembles the headdresses of the Golden Warrior of Issyk and the Ice Princess, as well as Amazons in Greek art. It is a pointed or rounded padded helmet of felt with earflaps, a metal nose-guard, and a metal plate with a spike on top.[14]

INDIA

Unlike the Central Asian sagas, which were recorded in writing for the first time less than a century ago, India's ancient legends about warrior women were recorded in Sanskrit epics as early as 850 BC. Before the time of Alexander, "India" in Greek literature was a vague term for the exotic Far East. On his Indian campaign, as we saw, Alexander heard rumors of Amazons and fought an army of men and women led by Queen Cleophis on the border of Baktria and "India" (chapter 20). In Greek myth, the god Dionysus meets Amazons in the same region of "India." With his train of maenads and Bacchic revelers, Dionysus takes over a mountain stronghold. According to Polyaenus's account of the myth, some Indian men and Amazons join Dionysus's bacchantes as they are about to cross a river to subdue the Baktrians hiding in the mountains. Dionysus camps on the riverbank and directs the maenads and Amazons to cross first. His strategy is to lure the Baktrians down from the mountains—he predicts they will assume that women are poor fighters. Sure enough, the Baktrians descend and enter the river on the other side. The Amazons pretend to retreat in good nomad fashion, slyly drawing the Baktrians to the other bank. Then Dionysus and the Indian men join the Amazons and kill the Baktrians.[15]

Amazon stories were among the many legends that coalesced around Alexander and his expedition to India. Popular Greek lore portrayed Alexander fighting, negotiating, and having sex with Amazons. *Digenes Akritas*, a Greek folk epic of the Byzantine era (twelfth century AD), based on older oral traditions, indicates that there was also a story about Alexander bringing Amazons from India back to Asia Minor. The star of the epic is the Greek-Syrian hero Digenes Akritas, whose palace is decorated with paintings of Alexander visiting the Brahmins and Amazons of India. This imagery alludes to earlier reports (fourth century AD) claiming that Brahmin men and women lived on opposite banks of the Ganges and met for procreation in the summertime. The arrangement is reminiscent of even more ancient Greek descriptions of Amazons and their male lovers (chapter 8).[16]

One episode describes single combat between Digenes and an Amazon named Maximou ("Daughter of the Greatest"). She was "a descendant of the Amazon women brought back from among the Brahmins of India by the emperor Alexander." Leading a band of male rebel fighters, Maximou rides a milk-white horse with red mane, tail, and hooves (dyed with henna, a Persian custom brought to India). But for the duel she arrives on a black warhorse (see chapter 11 for color choice of war horses). Wearing a green turban embroidered in gold and a breastplate over a tunic of purple silk, the Amazon carries a shield with an eagle device and an Arab spear and sword. They clash and fight strenuously. After Digenes kills Maximou's horse, they retreat to the woods where the Amazon removes her armor. Her "gossamer-thin silk shift reveals her lovely limbs and breasts," and the hero is smitten with lust. They have sex. In some versions Digenes later stalks and murders "the promiscuous creature" for seducing him. In this, Digenes seems to revert to the old Greek mythic script of killing the foreign Amazon. Some modern scholars believe that Maximou was originally the heroine of an earlier oral legend (perhaps about Amazons who returned with Alexander?), and that she was rather clumsily incorporated into this Christian moralizing epic.[17]

More ancient evidence for women warriors in India and neighboring lands in the time of Alexander comes from Greeks in India and from Indian authors. After Alexander's death, Megasthenes was the Greek ambassador to the court of Chandragupta, king of the Ganges region. Like so many missing ancient works that could have shed welcome light on our topic, Megasthenes's *Indica* (ca. 300 BC) exists only in fragments. Megasthenes described the company of trained female bodyguards who surrounded Chandragupta at all times. A large party of armed women also accompanied the king on his hunts, some shooting arrows with him from the royal platform, while others drove chariots or rode horses and elephants after game. This custom was confirmed by Chandragupta's military adviser, Kautilya, in his war manual, the *Arthashastra*. "Upon arising each morning," wrote Kautilya, "the king should be received by troops of women armed with bows and arrows

(*striganairdhenvibhih*)." Chandragupta's coruler of the Mauryan Kingdom was Queen Kumaradevi (of northeast India–Nepal); both were of
the warrior caste (*Kshatriya*), in which men and women were trained to
fight. Other ancient Indian sources refer to female spear throwers
(*saktiki*) guarding the king's palace and regiments of women soldiers.
Historians suggest that some of these women were nomads from the
Central Asian deserts beyond the mountains, the region poets called
"the land of women" (more on this below).[18]

From the *Agni Purana* (a ninth-century AD Hindu encyclopedia
based on older oral traditions) we learn that both men and women in
India practiced fencing and archery to develop body and mind. Female
warriors and bow hunters (*svaghni*) are depicted in Indian sculptures.
For example, the Bharut reliefs of the third century BC in northeastern
India show male and female mounted soldiers. Full-breasted bow-
women appear in ancient and medieval carvings on temples at Palitana
(northwestern India) and Bhatkal and Karnataka in southwestern India.
Some early European travelers in India were excited to observe a number of "one-breasted women" in ancient Indian rock art, which they
interpreted as "Amazons." But these images are now recognized as religious carvings representing half-male, half-female deities or dualistic
principles.[19]

Much earlier literary evidence for military training for girls in northwestern India is found in the *Rig Veda* and other Hindu oral traditions
originally composed in about 1700–900 BC. The *Rig Veda* legends allude to women warriors. For example, Mudgalani drove her husband's
chariot to victory on the battlefield. Vishpala ("Strong Defender of the
Village") lost her leg fighting the enemy—the gods replaced it with an
iron one. According to a late legend about Vadhrimati, when her hand
was cut off in battle the gods gave her a golden one. In the *Ramayana*
epic (fifth–fourth centuries BC) Queen Kaikeyi (from a northern land)
served as a charioteer for her husband, King Dasaratha, in a battle and
saved his life.[20]

Amazon-like women and "lands of women" apparently existed in
India's mythic imagination well before Indians had access to Greek literature. A society of warrior women is featured in an episode in the
great epic poem *Mahabharata*. The oldest Sanskrit texts were first written down in about 400 BC based on much older oral tales that origi-

nated around 850 BC (a century or so before Homer's Trojan War myths were written down). There were many regional versions of the *Mahabharata* legends. A popular Bengali version (northeastern India) describes Queen Pramila's "realm of women." Her female cavalry armed with bows captures the sacred stallion being tracked across India by the hero Arjuna. For the fearless Pramila "love or war were the same." So, clad in armor, Pramila takes her bow and sword and drives her chariot to meet Arjuna. She proposes that he become her lover. Arjuna resists and they fight a duel. But her prowess is equal to his—neither can win. Finally, heavenly voices advise Arjuna that since he cannot vanquish Pramila, he should agree to marry her.[21]

Another adventure is set in *Stri-Rajya* ("Women's Land"), a distant place located somewhere in the nomadic Saka-Scythian-Xiongnu territories of Inner Asia along the Silk Route (including parts of Kyrgyzstan, Tajikistan, the Taklamakan Desert, Tibet, and the Kunlun Mountains). Two queens ruled the land devoid of men; any man who stayed with them more than a month was killed. Several legends tell how a famous yogi traveled to a country of women and fell under its queen's spell, forgetting his spiritual vows. The yogi was allowed to stay several years and was finally rescued by his younger disciple. These women were seductresses, not warriors, however, and this legend was about sexual restraint, not armed heroines.[22]

The isolated tribes of Nagaland, northeastern India, whose languages belong to the Tibeto-Burman family, developed independent oral traditions about a land of Amazon-like women who shunned men and killed male infants. Naga folklore of the Angami and Sema collected by anthropologists in 1921 included tales about "a village of women" in the mountains farther east. The women drove men away with their war-bows, and they ate great amounts of rice and oil "to make them strong for battle." They kept their girl babies and saved one boy to raise to manhood each generation, killing all other male babies by plunging them into boiling water. Some claimed that if a man did manage to enter their village, the women were so eager for sex that "in striving to possess him they tear him to pieces utterly." The head-hunting Naga peoples had little or no contact with India or the outside world until the late nineteenth century. Was this Naga tale entirely imaginary, or did it contain specks of reality? It appears to have originated outside ancient Greek influence, but it's important to note that it was transmitted by British anthropologists familiar with classical myths.[23]

The widespread idea of women-only societies, like those associated with Amazons in some Greek accounts, can have multiple and independent origins. They could arise from the imagination, from outsiders' misunderstandings of nomads' seasonal customs, or from observations of ad hoc mixed or all-female hunting or war parties led by women. A group of girls might form to prove their hunting prowess or bravery. A group of widows might have survived the loss of a tribe's menfolk in battle. "Lands of women" could also simply mean "lands ruled by women" or even "lands known for autonomous women." Legends of "villages of maidens" circulated in Khorezm and among Turkmen, Karakalpaks, and other Turkic-speaking peoples; many medieval Muslim sources as well as Marco Polo recorded similar rumors. A number of ancient Chinese sources also refer to "lands of women" in the west. At least one "kingdom of women" really existed northeast of India and Nagaland and maintains Amazon-like traditions today (chapter 25).[24]

We have now reached the easternmost extent of the steppe nomads known collectively as "Scythians" to the ancient Greeks, and whose women were the real-life models for mythic and historical Amazons in Greek, Roman, Persian, and Egyptian accounts. This chapter shows that within the homelands of the Scythians and Amazons themselves, the customs and stories match many of the salient Greco-Roman details, confirmed by archaeology. Thus far in our journey we have been looking and moving east. Now at the frontier of China, the time has come to turn our gaze west. The next chapter assumes the vantage point of the Chinese. Far out of the range of classical Greek influence, Chinese writers described women fighters among the powerful nomad armies of the west, a relentless threat at their gates. In the fifth and fourth centuries BC—when Amazons were immensely popular subjects for Greek vase painters—Chinese emperors were recruiting warrior women for their own armies.

2 5

CHINA

T HE FORESTED MOUNTAINS WHERE THE GIRL AND
her father bow-hunted were deep and wild, sparsely
populated. Even as a child, she harbored a secret
fascination with swordplay. But there were no formal teachers. So over
the years she taught herself, at first with bamboo sticks and later with a
sword, inventing her own special techniques of lightning speed and
subtle yet powerful moves. Alone in the forest, she perfected her style of
swirling, leaping, parrying, and slashing at a host of imaginary enemies
represented by saplings and stands of bamboo. One day an old master
swordsman challenged her to a duel, using bamboo staves as swords
(some say he appeared in the guise of a monkey). The master snapped
off a branch and stripped it, but before the leaves touched the ground,
she attacked and won the upper hand. The invincible swordswoman's
reputation spread throughout the land.[1]

THE MAIDEN OF YUE

This young woman lived in the Southern Forest of the Yue State (now
Zhejiang, China) during the reign of King Goujian (496–465 BC),
nearly twenty-five hundred years ago. At that time in the fifth century
BC more than four thousand miles west of China, the Scythian queen
Tirgatao was making conquests around the Sea of Azov; Serpot, queen

of the Amazons, fought and fell in love with the Egyptian prince Pedik-hons; Artemisia of Halicarnassus commanded Persian ships at Salamis; Greek colonists were trading with Scythians around the Black Sea and beyond; and Herodotus was gathering Scythian stories about Ama-zons—who continued to be wildly popular figures in Athenian vase painting. And in Scythia itself, where the evidence gathered thus far in-dicates that at least 20–25 percent of the warriors were women, the tat-tooed Pazyryk horse people and their Saka-Scythian-Sarmatian-Sargat neighbors were roaming the steppes.

King Goujian of Yue was locked in war with his great enemy to the north, the Wu State. On the advice of his minister of war, Goujian re-cruited a champion archer from the Chu State (to the west) to train his soldiers in the art of the bow. Then the minister told Goujian about the young woman of the Southern Forest whose sword expertise was leg-endary. Intrigued, Goujian invited her to his court, where she demon-strated her marvelous skills, countering the blows of several attackers at a time. During their private audience, Goujian asked the young woman about the philosophy and methods of her martial arts. Living alone in the woods, she replied, I needed a wide array of skills, so I developed them on my own. She explained the yin-yang principles of her sword-fighting system, seemingly simple but powerful. Once these esoteric concepts were understood and mastered, she claimed, one person could subdue dozens of enemies in combat.

Deeply impressed, Goujian gave her the title Yuenü, "Maiden of Yue," and asked her to instruct his best officers and soldiers in her way of fighting so that they could in turn teach his troops. It is no surprise to learn that Goujian fell in love with the Maiden of Yue. (For this rea-son she was later banished by Goujian's jealous queen.) Her techniques became widely known as the "Sword System of the Maiden of Yue" and are considered to be the origins of Chinese martial arts theory.

The Maiden of Yue was also credited with inventing a new metal-lurgy to create untarnishable bronze swords with flexible cores and very sharp edges (called Yuenü swords). Her metal-craft innovation recalls the Caucasian legend of the Nart maiden who invented ironworking (chapter 13). In 1965, Chinese archaeologists discovered an exception-ally preserved, extremely sharp, untarnished ornate bronze sword in an ancient Yue grave with a skeleton identified as that of King Goujian, confirmed by the inscription on the blade. Analysis of the chemical composition of this weapon revealed some of the secrets of Yuenü swords. The body of the blade was mostly pliant, shatter-resistant copper (alloyed with iron, tin, and lead), while the sharp harder edges have more tin content. The brilliant sheen was preserved over two millennia by the addition of sulfur in the bronze and storage in an airtight scabbard.[2]

As we saw in chapter 11, the nomadic way of life, archery, and especially horses were the great equalizers for women. Steppe children learned to ride and handle bows at a young age; females could grow up equal to and sometimes superior to the males. A horse-centered culture permitted parity of the sexes and allowed women to participate and excel in the same activities as men. In China, the great "equalizer" for the Maiden of Yue was not the horse but what has become known as martial arts. In hand-to-hand fighting on the ground with heavy weapons, the larger, stronger opponent often has the advantage. With or without weapons, martial arts require agility, flexibility, fluid speed,

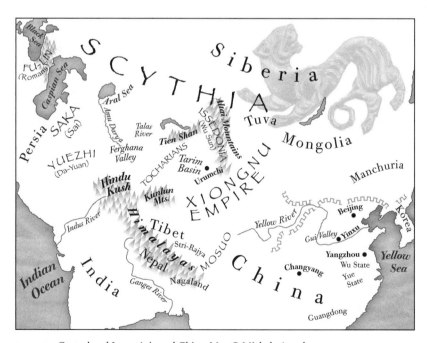

MAP 25.1. Central and Inner Asia and China. Map © Michele Angel.

strategy, balance, mental concentration, inner energy, and intense practice rather than physical strength alone. This style of fighting meant
that gender need not be so much of an issue, for a woman could become as adept as a man.

FU HAO, WARRIOR WOMAN OF THE SHANG DYNASTY

About eight hundred years before the Maiden of Yue, China's earliest
recorded female general was born. Fu Hao ("Lady Good") lived during
the Chinese Bronze Age. This was the era of the legendary Trojan War
of Greek myth, when Penthesilea and Achilles fought in single combat.
Fu Hao's father was a chieftain of an unknown northwestern tribe who
pledged loyalty to Wu Ding, king of the Shang Dynasty (1250–1192 BC,
Yellow River valley, north-central China). He sent his daughter Fu Hao,
perhaps fifteen, as a bride to seal the alliance. No record tells her people's name, much less her state of mind when she arrived in Yinxu, the
Shang capital (near modern Anyang). Fu Hao was one of scores of
young women from allied tribes in Wu Ding's large harem. As the
king's favorite, however, Fu Hao used her strong personality and intelligence to become the most powerful military leader of her time. Conscripting soldiers from her own and other tribes, she defended the
Shang borders from the hostile tribes of the northwest. With thousands
of men and important generals under her command, Fu Hao personally led an army of three thousand to win decisive battles. Many of Fu
Hao's military accomplishments were listed on two hundred tortoiseshell records excavated in 1936 in the ruins of Yinxu, some of China's
earliest written archives.[3]

Fu Hao's early origins in a warrior tribe may have been a great advantage in her new life as the emperor's wife and general. No such luck
for the coddled Chinese princesses and girls of noble families who were
married off to nomad chieftains of the powerful northwestern tribes in
later times. These palace-raised girls found themselves absurdly, sadly
unprepared for exile on the remote steppes, surrounded by rough-and-
ready men and women who spent their lives on horseback. Mournful
poems and letters express their acute disorientation and nostalgia for
court life. "My family married me off to the ends of the earth.... Alas in

a felt tent I now live . . . raw meat is my food and *koumiss* must I drink," lamented Princess Xijun (ca. 102 BC). The Han emperor Wu, who desired to obtain the wonderful Akhal Teke horses (see below), had sent her to the Altai region to be the wife of the old ruler of the Wu Sun (Issedonians). During the nomad invasions of Han territory in AD 194, the Xiongnu chieftain Liu Bao captured Cai Yan, a Chinese noblewoman. During her twelve-year captivity she bore his two sons; she also penned poetic laments. One hopes that at least some of the young Chinese women who found themselves stranded on the ocean of grass ultimately embraced the freedom of an Amazon life.[4]

Among the treasures in Fu Hao's tomb were 775 jade items (all from Khotan, southern Tarim Basin, nearly two thousand miles away on the Silk Route) and huge bronze ceremonial vessels bearing the characters of her name; her name and exploits were also inscribed on tortoiseshells used to divine oracles. She was buried with 16 sacrificed war

FIG. 25.1. Fu Hao, modern statue and one of her heavy bronze battle-axes discovered among her grave goods, Yinxi, China. Collage by Michele Angel.

captives (and 6 dogs). Among the 130 weapons in her grave were 27 knives, 2 small battle-axes and 2 very large ones (nearly 20 pounds each) inscribed with her name. As noted in chapter 4, when this rich undisturbed tomb was first excavated in 1976, the opulent goods and great cache of weapons led the archaeologists to assume the occupant was a male ruler. But the inscriptions proved that the grave belonged to Fu Hao. Until then she had been known only from records on other tortoiseshells and oracle bones. Consorts were normally buried with their husbands, but Fu Hao's military authority and war deeds were so unusual that she was honored with her own grave.[5]

Fu Hao was not the only woman warrior of Bronze Age China. Oracle shells and bones name more than a hundred women who played roles in military campaigns. Chinese archaeologists reported finding another tomb of an unnamed armed female near Beijing (dated to the Western Zhou Dynasty, 1046–771 BC). This woman was buried with a large hoard of weapons, including battle-axes, long and short swords, daggers, helmets, shields, lances, and long-range bows.[6]

SUN TZU'S AND SHANG'S ARMIES OF WOMEN

The Maiden of Yue and her patron, King Goujian, were no doubt familiar with the writings of Sun Tzu, the brilliant Chinese military strategist who had recently written *The Art of War* (ca. 544–496 BC). According to the *Shi-ji* ("Historical Records," a history of China by Sima Qian, 109–91 BC), Sun Tzu famously demonstrated how to command an army to King Helü of the Wu State, King Goujian's dire enemy. To test Sun Tzu's training techniques, the king asked him to transform 180 concubines from his palace into disciplined soldiers. Sun Tzu divided the ladies, armed with spears and battle-axes, into two companies headed by the king's two favorite consorts and drilled them in weapons use and battle formations. When the two concubine "officers" allowed their soldiers to giggle instead of obey orders, Sun Tzu beheaded them and replaced them with the emperor's next two favorites. After this, the women's army achieved perfect accuracy and precision in their drills, which convinced Helü to appoint Sun Tzu as his general. The point of the demonstration was to showcase Sun Tzu's methods, using the most unpromising recruits. Yet his success also showed that, with training, women could become soldiers.[7]

A pragmatic Chinese war treatise, *The Book of Lord Shang* (ca. 390 BC), advised commanders to divide their populations into three armies of both sexes to defend cities. Old or weak men and women would control food and supply chains for the populace and army. Strong, able-bodied women would build traps and spiked obstacles, dig pitfalls, defend fortresses, and carry out scorched earth policies. Strong, able-bodied men served in the front lines. Similar practices were used during a siege of Sparta in 272 BC, when the king's daughter Archidamis directed the women in digging ditches, bringing up weapons, and sharpening spears. But Shang went further: "Make sure these three armies never intermingle. If the robust men and women take pleasure in each other's company their emotions will focus on their own and each other's safety, and you must guard against their pity for the old and feeble. Compassion causes even brave people to be anxious and it causes fearful people to be afraid to fight."[8]

"LANDS OF WOMEN" IN THE "GREAT WILDERNESS"

Two different "lands of women" of the west were identified in ancient Chinese writings. One corresponded to the "realm of women" in the region of northern India/Tibet known as *Stri-Rajya* in Indian lore (chapter 24). The other "women-only land" was vaguely located on the eastern border of Fu-lin, a Chinese name for the Eastern Roman/Byzantine Empire. In exchange for this country's precious and rare goods, Chinese authors reported that the Byzantine emperor sent men to couple with the women each year. "If they give birth to boys, the women's custom does not permit the boys to be raised." This late report by Chan Wen-Ming and others of the seventh century AD could have been influenced by the persistent thread of classical Greek lore about Amazons living in women-only societies, having sex with male outsiders, and rejecting male babies.[9]

In the Chinese (and later Muslim) tales, there was much speculation about the sexuality and reproduction of self-contained societies of women without men. The great treasury of ancient Chinese mythology,

The Classic of Mountains and Seas (third century BC to second century AD), refers to a "country of women" in the "Great Wilderness" (Central Asian steppes). In that region dwelled mysterious entities from unknown Chinese myths, with suggestive names such as "Killer Girl," "Girl Battle-Axe," and "Long Life Hemp." Could these names be faint allusions to the Scythian women Herodotus called "man-killers" and to the favorite drug of the Scythians, hemp? Some modern scholars interpret an ambiguous passage about "pairs of women living together in one household in the country of women" as a hint of lesbianism. Unfortunately the text is obscure, garbled, and heavily edited by later Chinese scholars, who inserted contradictory commentaries over the centuries. One added that "any male babies die prematurely." Others said that the women give birth only to females. Another claimed that there are actually men in this land, but they lack beards and so appear female. Some asserted that the women became pregnant by wind or magical water. The motif of conception by water—or more often by wind—recurs in Chinese writings about lands of women. Wind as fertilizer, related to the breath of life, is thought to be an extremely ancient notion.[10]

The Chinese "lands of women" appear to have a fanciful, fairy-tale quality in the texts that survive. Although they lay in the "Great Wilderness" of the west, the women were not described as belligerent "Amazons"—except for the martial names "Killer Girl" and "Girl Battle-Axe" (above). Might a genuine women-ruled society in the remote Himalayas account for rumors of a "paradise of women" in Chinese lore (and Indian and Naga tales of Stri-Ryja and "Women's Land")? Around Lugo Lake high in the densely wooded mountains between Yunnan and Sichuan Provinces dwell the Mosuo people. Described as the "last purely matriarchal tribe in China," the Mosuo women are the decision makers; they own the property and control the economy. They practice *zuo hun*, "walking marriage," a form of polyamory (many lovers) that parallels the customs of Amazons and Saka-Scythian women described more than two thousand years ago by Greek historians. Mosuo women select lovers (called *axias*) from among the men of the tribe, inviting them to spend the night in their homes. There are no Mosuo words for "father" or "husband"; the children live with the mother and take her name.[11]

The Mosuo society is peaceful but the reality of warlike nomadic cultures of Central and Inner Asia was well documented in Chinese histories about wars, alliances, trade, and intermarriage with the steppe peoples. The earliest Chinese writings about the migrating tribes of Inner Asia appeared in the seventh century BC. Around this same time, on the other side of the steppes, the Greeks were becoming aware of Scythians and Amazons through the travels of Aristeas to Issedonian territory. The nomads left no written records, so the information in this chapter comes from ancient Chinese chronicles and modern archaeology. Both sources provide solid evidence for fighting horsewomen who match the Greek and other cultures' written descriptions of Amazons and Scythians. But as the lives of the Maiden of Yue and Fu Hao already indicate, Chinese women appear to have had opportunities to "go Amazon" during some periods of Chinese history. And foreign female warriors were admired, desired, and co-opted as allies by the Chinese, an option unthinkable to the ancient Greeks.[12]

CHINA'S MILITARY HEROINES

In the late Warring States period (246–221 BC), a woman achieved extraordinary war powers similar to those of Fu Hao. It was said that Huang Guigu possessed the physical "strength to draw a strong bow" and she "studied war manuals by night and trained by day." (*Huang* means "Yellow-Golden"; *Guigu* means from "Ghost Valley," an ancient name for the Gui Valley, Henan Province.) As the general for the first Qin emperor of unified China, Huang Guigu commanded three military units and led campaigns against the aggressive nomad tribes known as the Xiongnu and Xianbei who were encroaching on China's northern frontiers.[13]

The turbulent wars between AD 200 and 1200 brought forth a large number of real and legendary military women in China, suggesting that by this time girls were sometimes instilled with warrior values, skilled in riding horses, and trained in archery and swordplay. These Chinese heroines seem to have taken up the ways of the nomad women of the "Great Wilderness," China's erstwhile enemies. An outstanding example was the strong-willed wife of a warlord in the Eastern Han Dynasty, Lady Sun, feared for her entourage of more than a hundred swordswomen. Like other women of her day, ca. AD 210, Lady Sun came from a family of warriors and was adept with a sword. She played a strong role in power plays and conflicts, and her exploits were romanticized in many Chinese poems, novels, and operas.[14]

Xun Guan was the thirteen-year-old daughter of a warlord who rejected sewing to learn martial arts like her brothers. In a daring feat recorded in the *Historical Records of the* [Western] *Jin Dynasty* (AD 265–316), Xun Guan (b. ca. AD 303) led a small band of mounted warriors to break through strong enemy lines to save her city. Mao, wife of a warlord during the Eastern Jin Dynasty (AD 317–420), was an intrepid horsewoman archer who killed seven hundred foes with her bow before she was captured and killed for refusing to marry the enemy commander. Another horsewoman archer, Kong of the Liu Song Dynasty (AD 420–479), commanded an all-female cavalry troop. Lady Mongchi commanded her husband's fortress in AD 503 and routed the imperial army at Changyang. In AD 515, another female general, Lieouchi, defended Tsetong from imperial armies, while Queen Honchi commanded Wei forces against the emperor's assault. The widow of Hsi clan leader Feng Pao led an attack on invading nomads in Guangdong in AD 590. During the Tang Dynasty (AD 618–906), the future empress Wu Chao had learned archery as a girl and defeated several male challengers on her rise to seize the throne (AD 684). This is only a partial list of martial women in China who defied traditional gender roles.[15]

A collection of oral folktales, *The Fourteen Amazons*, coalesced around the historical Yang family of warriors active the early Northern Song Dynasty (AD 960–1127). The Yang clan defended borders against foreign invaders from Western Xia (northeastern Xinjiang and Inner Mongolia). After the last Yang man died, a dozen or so Yang widows took over the campaigns. Their Amazonian exploits became popular in Chinese fiction, drama, poetry, operas, and film. In one story, two female Yang commanders were trapped by enemy nomads in a mountain pass. Another female Yang general dispatched a fearless young "Amazon" servant named Yang Paifeng, who led a small guerrilla band in a surprise assault and rescued them.[16]

Liang Hongyu ("Red Jade"), daughter and granddaughter of generals, practiced martial arts during the transition from the Northern to the Southern Song Dynasty. At one point in her story, she was taken captive and forced to entertain the emperor's court as a wrestler—her grappling skills were admired far and wide, reminding us of other wrestling heroines from Atalanta to Chichak and Khutulun (prologue and chapters 22 and 24). Later she married a general; in helmet and armor she rode at his side in campaigns against rebel armies. When their army of 8,000 was outnumbered by 100,000 nomads (ca. AD 1130), Liang Hongyu devised a successful ambush using drum and flag signals. Pounding the great war drum, she guided the army into their positions for attack. Liang Hongyu trained an all-woman contingent that won many honors in battle. The emperor awarded her the title "Heroic and Valiant Lady of Yang," and a temple was built as a memorial to her courage.[17]

WARRIOR WOMEN AMONG THE NOMADS OF THE GREAT WILDERNESS

The Great Wall of China originated as a series of mostly symbolic defenses against aggressive coalitions of Central and Inner Asian tribes, which became known to the Chinese as Xiongnu. Like the ancient Greek collective name *Scythia*, the Chinese name *Xiongnu* implied a single ethnic group, yet both blanket terms embraced many ethnic identities with similar migratory horse-archer lifestyles, including Saka-Scythian-Sarmatian, Mongolian, Turkic, Altaian, Tocharian, Uralic, and Iranian peoples in what is now Kazakhstan, Kyrgyzstan, Altai/southern Siberia, Xinjiang, and Mongolia. The Xiongnu fought wars against the other nomadic tribes between the Tien Shan and Altai mountains, the region described in epic poems by the early Greek traveler Aristeas in the seventh century BC. The Chinese referred to some of these peoples as the Wu Sun ("Grandchildren of the Raven," thought to be the Issedonians); the Sai (Saka); the Dingling (described as "red-haired, blue-eyed giants," perhaps related to the Altai, Tuva, Pazyryk, Kyrgyz cultures); and the Yuezhi (described as fair and speaking an Indo-European tongue; perhaps related to the Tocharians driven west by the Xiongnu).[18]

From the fourth to the first century BC, a powerful confederation of nomadic tribes united as the Xiongnu Empire, which stretched from Kazakhstan and Kyrgysztan to Xinjiang and Manchuria. The Xiongnu, with their immense cavalries of as many as 300,000 mounted archers, held the advantage in this period and exerted relentless pressure on

China's western and northern frontiers. The long wars between the Xiongnu Empire and the Han Dynasty (133 BC to AD 89) entailed ferocious battles, delicate negotiations, intrigues, and ephemeral alliances. To mollify the Xiongnu, Chinese rulers sent lavish gifts as tribute, and nubile women were exchanged in "marriage treaties."[19]

After a time, the Chinese began to imitate the nomads they battled (and married), assimilating the successful triad of archery, horses, and trousers. As early as the fourth century BC, the military advantage of trousers was recognized by the Chinese king Wuling of the Zhao State (while the Greeks remained hostile to barbarian trousers; see chapter 12). The nomads' tattooing practices leaked into borderlands of western China (chapter 6), and even personal names in China were dramatically influenced by steppe culture.

The Chinese were eager to obtain warhorses to compete with the mounted nomads. In 138 BC, the Han emperor Wu's army was struggling to repel hordes of nomad archers on hardy Mongolian ponies. In 130 BC, Wu sent his agent Zhang Qian on a mission to seek an alliance with the Yuezhi in the Great Wilderness of the west. Zhang Qian traveled more than two thousand miles over deserts and mountains. On the way, he was held captive by the Xiongnu for ten years. During this time he married a Xiongnu woman and they had a son (recalling the earlier captivity of Cai Yan, above). Zhang Qian and his family managed to escape and at last reached the Ferghana Valley (*Da-yuan*). There Zhang Qian marveled at the golden Turkoman (Akhal Teke) horses, the tall, powerful desert steeds ridden by the Scythians and Amazons who traded with the Ferghana tribes (chapter 11).

Thirteen years later Zhang Qian returned to China with his Xiongnu wife and son and related information about Anxi (Persia/Parthia), Tiaozhi (Arabia), Tianzhu (India), and Da Qin (Roman Syria). He also gave thrilling descriptions of the "Celestial horses" that could save Wu's army. In 115 BC, in the vain hope of gaining some of those sublime steeds, the emperor sent Zhang Qian to another tribe in Issedonia, to deliver a royal Chinese bride to the elderly Wu Sun chieftain. (It was she who wrote the homesick poem quoted above.) Had his journey taken place five hundred years earlier, Zhang Qian might have crossed paths with the Greek adventurer Aristeas, who journeyed a comparable distance to the same general region. Wu also dispatched envoys to Ferghana with carts of gold and silk to buy Akhal Teke horses, but hostile tribes killed the envoys and kept the gold. After two long wars against the Ferghana tribes, finally in 102 BC the nomads agreed to exchange their horses for Chinese silk and other luxuries. The heavenly horses were celebrated in ceramic figures and paintings of the Han and Tang dynasties, and in poetry: "The Ferghana horse ... among nomad breeds / lean like the point of a lance, hooves born of the wind / Heading away across the endless spaces / Truly you may entrust him with your life."[20]

The grave goods of the Hunno-Sarmatian-Saka-Scythian men and women that the Chinese called Xiongnu include clothing of leather, wool, furs, and silk, caps with earflaps, horse gear, and a wealth of weapons—spears, arrows, quivers, and miniature replicas of bows. Beautiful belt plaques and buckles of gold, bronze, and iron decorated with dragons, tigers, deer, and other designs accompanied the Xiongnu horsewomen. The women's skeletons evidenced harsh lives and riding injuries, and some women's bones showed battle wounds similar to those of the males. To take just one example, in one Xiongnu cemetery two of the twelve skeletons with slashing sword cuts on the upper torso were

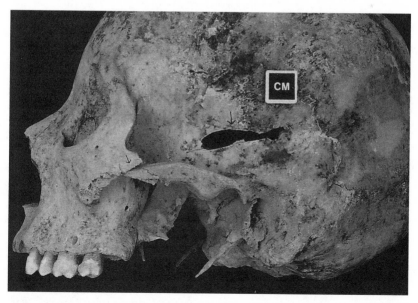

FIG. 25.2. Woman warrior's skull with sword slash, Xiongnu skeleton XXXI, 115, Han Period, Altai Region, Tuva. Photo courtesy of Eileen Murphy, from Murphy 2003, pl. 46.

female. The wounds were inflicted during "free-moving" face-to-face combat, probably on horseback.[21]

According to ancient Chinese sources, the Xiongnu were known for their highly maneuverable light cavalry armed with long composite bows. The women, noted the Chinese writers, were expert riders and archers just like the men, and the women taught the boys and girls how to ride and handle bows and arrows. The women also rode beside their men into battle and valiantly defended against attacks. For example, in 36 BC the Chinese army attacked the Xiongnu forces led by the powerful chieftain Zhizhi at his citadel on the Talas River. This is Taraz, southern Kazakhstan; the battle here marked the westernmost reach of Chinese power. Before their defeat, the Xiongnu queen and many other female archers on the fort's walls shot arrows at the Chinese invaders. The queen's name is unknown, but she was a Sogdian princess. The Xiongnu women, remarked the Chinese, remained at their posts longer than the men.[22]

LIU JINDING AND GAO JUNBAO: LOVE AND WAR ON THE NORTHERN FRONTIER

A legend set just at the inception of the Northern Song Dynasty (AD 960–1126) tells of a nomad girl who had grown up riding horses, hunting, and practicing the arts of war with her brothers. Her clan of the northern mountains is unknown but would have been part of the Golden Horde, which included Kipchak, Mongol, Turkic, Xiangbei, and other nomadic groups. The girl's real name is also lost; to the Song Dynasty she was known as Liu Jinding (Liu Chin Ting). At a young age Jinding ("Gold Ingot") led war bands (mostly young men and a few girls) out from her stronghold, "Double-Locked Mountain," and defended her people's territory from attacks. Her reputation was so intimidating that her name struck fear in the hearts of the rival tribes. Like so many young Amazons before her, Jinding rejected marriage, insisting she would consider only suitors who could defeat her. According to one version, she expressed this challenge in an inscription that she posted at the border of her clans' land. She was said to be flamboyant, wearing cosmetics, wielding a golden sword, and riding a fine red warhorse. In one story, Jinding, aged sixteen, led a revolt against the hated

Chinese emperor. The handsome young Song general Gao Junbao (Kao Chun Pao) was sent to crush the rebellion. Junbao fought courageously, but his army was easily defeated and Jinding took him prisoner, intending to behead him.[23]

While Junbao was her captive, however, they fell in love and married, vowing to become companions in war. When the Song emperor learned of General Junbao's defection, he ordered his soldiers to kill him. But Jinding negotiated for her lover's life, promising to capture the wealthy rebel city of Yangzhou for the emperor. Impressed, he placed Jinding at the head of the imperial army, and she took Yangzhou and handed it over to her former enemy. With Junbao as her second in command, Jinding led Song armies for about thirty years. There were many old illustrations of Jinding attacking the gates of Yangzhou, and many versions of Jinding's story were performed in traditional Chinese shadow theater, which originated in the Song Dynasty.

OUTSIDER HEROINES

Historical and legendary women warriors became favorite characters in folktales and were featured in shadow plays enjoyed by the lower classes and rural folk in China since at least the Qing Dynasty (1644–1911). Their popularity was due in part to the subversive themes of outsider women opposing Chinese male rulers and challenging expected gender roles. Yet these tales also played to China's vision of itself as the imperial center. As a historian of Chinese shadow theater points out, the popular women warrior characters were usually from rebel states or nomad groups that were later absorbed into China. The warrior women are portrayed as indispensable to a cause, and a typical motif is partnership or marriage with foreign women warriors as a way of subduing enemy tribes.[24]

Three thousand years ago, Fu Hao had come as a young bride from an unknown northwestern tribe and became the supreme commander of Shang Dynasty armies. The folk heroine Jinding, another girl from the northwestern tribes, became the top general of the Song Dynasty. Fu Hao's life shares some parallels with Antiope, the Amazon queen of Greek myth. Like Fu Hao (and other nomad girls sent to the Chinese emperor's harem), Antiope was uprooted from her homeland, taken to the enemy's great city, and married without her consent to the king (Theseus of Athens; see chapter 16). The historical Fu Hao and the legendary Jinding, despite their non-Chinese origins, became trusted commanders fighting foreign tribes and negotiating alliances on behalf of their adopted cities. Their stories bring to mind Cynna (half sister of Alexander the Great), who was raised as an Illyrian woman warrior to fight against other Illyrians for the Macedonians (she killed an Illyrian warrior queen; chapter 20). In the only Greek myth to bring an Amazon wife into the Greek world, the Greek mythographers did not permit the barbarian Antiope to attain personal or military power in her new home. But like Fu Hao and Jinding, the mythic Antiope did help to defend her adopted city from her own people, the Amazons who invaded Greece (chapter 17).

Far removed from classical Greek influence, the Chinese accounts of historical and legendary Amazon-like women veer away from the grim Greek mythic script in which Amazons must be killed. The Chinese tales about Xiongnu female warriors have more in common with the Greek historians' reports of steppe nomad women and the stories of the other ancient cultures who knew or met real horsewomen archers. And with good reason, since those reports and tales were either modeled upon or arose within the nomad cultures of Eurasia, Central Asia, and Inner Asia. The Chinese romance of the headstrong young "Amazon" Jinding is reminiscent of the Greek myth of Atalanta and the story of the Amazons who fell in love with their captive Greek sailors (chapters 8, 19). The tale also has parallels with other warrior women and their enemy lovers, such as the Amazons who became Sarmatians, and Zarina, Chichak, and Serpot (chapters 3 and 22–24).

China's own warrior women of antiquity were exemplified by the Maiden of Yue, Huang Guigu, and other female generals, as well as countless ordinary mothers and wives compelled to defend their besieged cities. In China it was common for female servants to learn martial arts to help defend their masters, and there are many ancient accounts of Chinese women setting aside their weaving to join their men at war in emergencies. But by far the most famous and revered woman warrior of ancient China is Hua Mulan, whose bravery in battle was celebrated in a multitude of Chinese histories, plays, poems, artworks, operas, statues, and place-names. A beloved national legend known throughout China, Mulan's tale was immortalized for modern Western audiences in popular animated Disney films in 1998 and 2005.[25] But who was Mulan? Several dynasties—Northern Wei, Han, Sui, and Tang—claim her as their heroine, and different provinces vie for her birthplace. Extraordinary new linguistic evidence reveals a secret about the quintessential Chinese heroine.

MULAN

Like the Maiden of Yue, Fu Hao, Jinding, and other women warriors, Mulan had practiced martial arts since girlhood. The many folk versions of Mulan's life story, which may have been inspired by one or more historical-legendary figures, are set in various dynasties with different names and fates for Mulan. Historians debate the dates and details of Mulan's birth and death and whether she was a real individual. The earliest mention of a version of the ballad "Song of Mulan" dates to the Wei Dynasty (AD 386–557), when northern China was ruled by a clan of nomadic invaders from the northern Xiangbei tribes—and fighting to stave off constant attacks from other northern nomads. But older non-Han Chinese folk songs had apparently circulated orally since the Han Dynasty. In the basic story, Mulan, about fourteen or fifteen, dislikes weaving and rejects marriage. The Chinese emperor is conscripting men from each family to serve in his imperial army in the eternal struggle to repel the hostile nomads beyond the Great Wall. Worried that her aged father will be drafted because her brother is too young, Mulan saves her family's honor. She sneaks off to the markets to buy a swift horse and gear. Setting aside her skirts and face powder, Mulan dresses as a young man and rides to the army camp on the Yellow River to join the soldiers.[26]

For ten or twelve years Mulan rides her "flying" horse over ten thousand miles, enduring hardships, fighting the steppe nomads with great valor, winning victories for the emperor. No one ever sees through her male disguise. In the folk song the Chinese emperor commends the gallant Mulan and grants her wish to return home. There she resumes her feminine identity, putting aside her soldier's attire, combing out

FIG 25.3. Hua Mulan, stringing her bow. Modern Chinese poster, ca. 1962.

her long white hair, and donning a skirt. She goes out to meet her old comrades at arms. The veterans are amazed to discover that their battle companion was a woman. The ballad concludes, "When a pair of rabbits, male and female, hop and skip side by side over the ground—how could they tell which is he or she?" In other versions of the legend, Mulan dies bravely in battle; or the Wei emperor offers Mulan a high post but she declines; or she commits suicide rather than become the concubine of the Sui emperor.

Mulan's name is usually translated as "magnolia" in Chinese (*hua* = flower, *mu* = wood, *lan* = orchid). But a historical and linguistic study in 2012 by the Chinese scholar Samping Chen uncovers astonishing new information about China's most celebrated war heroine. Mulan's name is not Chinese. Chen's linguistic analysis shows that her name means "deer or elk" in the ancient Altaic language of the Turkic peoples of Central Asia.

Mulan, "Deer or Elk," would be a fine name for an authentic Amazon. A non-Chinese name reveals that the warrior woman (or women) glorified in the "Song of Mulan" folktales, poems, and lore as China's ideal brave female fighter had roots in the peoples of the northwestern regions of Inner Asia. Like the historical Fu Hao and the legendary Jinding, Mulan turns out to be yet another warrior woman of nomadic origins who rose to military prominence fighting nomads for her adopted nation of China. Mulan's family apparently had nomadic Xianbei origins and fought Xianbei tribes for the ruler of northern China, whose origins were also Xianbei. While Mulan's disguise hid her gender, her ethnic identity was hidden behind a Chinese-sounding name.[27]

Not only does Mulan's name, "Elk, Deer," resemble the totemic animal clan names of Mongolia and Inner Asia, but it evokes the iconic antlered deer and elk images so common in ancient Scythian and Thracian art, artifacts, weapons, armor, belts, and clothing. The importance of the typical deer/elk image to the nomads was so well known to the ancient Greek artists that they painted stags on the clothing and accoutrements of Amazons and on the tattooed skin of armed barbarian women depicted on Athenian vases. Deer and elk with branching antlers were favorite tattoos of the Scythian men and women whose frozen mummies were discovered in the Pazyryk and Altai culture kurgans (chapter 6).

Thus with Mulan, an Amazon heroine of Chinese legend, we come full circle. Half a world away from the ancient Greeks who gazed east toward Scythia across the sea of grass, forests, mountains, and deserts, we stand on the Great Wall of China gazing west into the Great Wilderness of the Xiongnu. Between Greece and China stretched the vast homeland of nomadic horsewomen archers, the equals of men, whose heroic lives and deeds inspired awe, fear, respect, and desire in all who knew them.

APPENDIX
NAMES OF AMAZONS AND WARRIOR WOMEN IN ANCIENT LITERATURE AND ART FROM THE MEDITERRANEAN TO CHINA

S TANDARD LISTS OF AMAZONS' NAMES NUMBER ABOUT 130, compiled from ancient Greek and Latin literary sources and some inscriptions on Greek vases. This comprehensive list of more than 200 names combines all the known Amazon names from Greco-Latin literature, history, and art with new-found Amazon names deciphered from vase inscriptions in non-Greek languages, as well as the names of Amazon-like warrior women from antiquity who appear in the stories, epics, poems, histories, and other accounts in Caucasian, Persian, Egyptian, Armenian, Azerbaijan, Central Asian, and Chinese sources. This list is an ongoing project with the help of many linguists; these are the best possible translations of names in Greek and many other languages (some extinct), subject to revison. Language is Greek unless otherwise specified; sources are included. Female rulers from antiquity are not included unless they were said to have personally fought with weapons in battles.

Adea: from Greek "Abundance," "Fearless," or "Sweet"? (Illyrian-Macedonian: daughter of Alexander's half sister Cynna; Polyaenus)
Aegea: "Of the Aegean" or "Goat Woman" (Sextus Pompeius Festus)
Aella: "Storm-Gust, Whirlwind" (Diodorus)
Agave: "Illustrious" (Hyginus)

Aijaruc, Aiyurug: "Moon Light" or "Bright Moon" (Turkish: Marco Polo, another name for Khutulun)

Ainia: "Swift" or "Praise" (Greek terra-cotta relief fragment)

Ainippe: "Swift or Praiseworthy Horse" (vase)

Alexandre: fem. Alexander, "Protector" (vase)

Alkaia: "Mighty" (vase)

Alke: "Mighty" (*Latin Anthology*)

Alkibie: "Powerful" (Quintus of Smyrna)

Alkinoe, Alkinoa: "Strong-Willed" (vase)

Alkippe: "Powerful Horse" (Diodorus)

Amage: related to Iranian *mage* ("Magus") or *amarg* ("Meadow")? (Roxolani queen, Polyaenus)

Amanikasheto: from Amani, Nubian name of god Amun (Meroitic: *kandake* of Kush; Egyptian inscriptions)

Amanirenas, Amnirense: from Amani, Nubian name of god Amun (Meroitic: *kandake* of Kush; Strabo; Egyptian inscriptions)

Amanitore: from Amani, Nubian name of god Amun (Meroitic: Acts 8; Egyptian inscriptions)

Amastris: Persian princess, founder of Amastris (Strabo)

Amazo: "Amazon" (Stephanus of Byzantium)

Amezan: "Forest or Moon Mother" (Circassian: Nart sagas)

Amynomene: "Defender" (vase)

Anaea: Anatolian city (Stephanus of Byzantium)

Anaxilea: "Leader of the Host or Army" (vase)

Anchimache: "Close Fighter" (Tzetzes)

Andro: "Manly" (Tzetzes)

Androdaixa: "Man Slayer" (Tzetzes)

Androdameia: "Subdues or Tames Men" (vase)

Andromache: "Manly Fighter" (Tzetzes; vases)

Andromeda: "Thinks Like a Man" or "Measure of Man" (vase)

Antandre: "Resists Men" (Quintus of Smyrna)

Antianeira: "Man's Match" (Tzetzes; Mimnermus fr. 21a; vase)

Antibrote: "Equal of Man" (Quintus of Smyrna)

Antimache, Anchimache: "Confronting Warrior" (Tzetzes)

Antioche: "She Who Moves Against" (Hyginus)

Antiope: "Opposing Gaze" (Apollodorus; Diodorus; Plutarch; Hyginus; Pausanias; vases)

Areto: "Virtue" (vase)

Areximacha: "Defending Warrior" (vase)

Aristomache: "Best Warrior" (vase)

Artemisia: related to "Artemis" (Persian? Herodotus)

Asbyte: from the Asbytai tribe of Libya (Libyan? Silius Italicus)

Ashteshyt: "Pursues and Kills" (Abkhazian? Libyan? "Amazons and Egyptians" papyrus)

Aspidocharme: "Shield Warrior" (Tzetzes)

Asteria: "Starry" (Diodorus)

Atossa: "Well Granting" (Iranian: Hellanikos; Justin; Claudian)

Aturmuca: "Spear Battle"? (Etruscan for Andromache or Dorymache: vase)

Audata: "Lucky," "Loud," or Latin "Daring"? (Illyrian: Athenaeus)

Barkida: "Princess" (Iranian-Circassian: vase)

Bremusa: "Thunder" (Quintus of Smyrna)

Caeria, Kaeria: "She of the War Band," "Timely," or "Hill, Peak"? (Illyrian: warrior queen: Polyaenus)

Camilla: fem. Camillus, "Noble Youth" (Etruscan? Volschi warrior: Virgil)

Candace, Kandake: "Queen" (Meroitic: title of warrior queens of Kush, Nubia; Strabo; Diodorus)

Celaeno, Kelaeno: "The Dark One" (Diodorus)

Chalkaor: "Bronze Sword" (Tzetzes)

Charope: "Fierce Gaze" (vase)

Chichak: "Flower" (Turkish: *Book of Dede Korkut*)

Chrysis: "Golden" (vase)

Cleophis: "Famous Snake" (Diodorus; Curtius)

Clete, Klete: "Helper" (Tzetzes on Lycophron 995)

Cyme, Kyme: "Billowing Wave" (Diodorus; Stephanus of Byzantium; coins)

Cynna, Cynnane, Kynna: "Little Bitch" (Illyrian-Doric: Alexander's half sister; Polyaenus)

Deianeira: "Man Destroyer" (Diodorus)

Deinomache: "Terrible Warrior" (vase)

Derimachea: "Battle Fighter" (Quintus of Smyrna)

Derinoe: "Battle Minded" (Quintus of Smyrna)

Dioxippe: "Pursuing Mare" (Hyginus)

Dolope: Thracian tribe name (vase)

Doris: "Bountiful" or "Dorian" (vase)

Echephyle: "Defending the Tribe" (vase)

Enchesimargos: "Spear Mad" (Tzetzes)

Epipole: "Outsider" (Photius)

Eriboea: "Many Cows" (Diodorus)

Eumache: "Excellent Fighter" (vase)

Euope: "Fair Face or Eyes" (vase)

Euryale: "Far Roaming" (Valerius Flaccus)

Eurybia: "Far Strength" (Diodorus)

Eurylophe: "Broad Crest" (of helmet?) "Wide Hill" or "Broad Neck" (Tzetzes)

Eurypyleia, Eurypyle: "Wide Gate or Mountain Pass" (Arrian cited by Eustathius; vase)

Evandre: fem. Evandrus, "As Good as a Man" (Quintus of Smyrna)

Fu Hao: "Lady Good" (Chinese: tortoiseshell inscriptions)

Glauke, Glaukia: "Blue-Gray Eyes" (Apollodorus; Hyginus; scholia *Iliad* 3.189; Callimachus; vase)

Gogoioigi, Gogiki: "Maiden, Girl" (Georgian: vase)

Gordafarid: "Created as a Heroine" (Iranian: Ferdowsi *Shahnama*)

Gordieh: "Woman Warrior" (Iranian: Ferdowsi *Shahnama*)

Gortyessa: from Gortyn ("enclosure?") town in Crete (Tzetzes)

Gryne: Anatolian town (Servius on *Aeneid* 4.345)

Gugamis: "Metal/Iron" (Circassian with Iranian suffix: vase)

Gulaim, Gulayim: "Rose Moon" (month of June, Turkic: "Forty Maidens" epic)

Harman Dali: "Crazy-Brave" (Turkmen: "Koroglu" epic)

Harmothoe: "Sharp Spike" (Quintus of Smyrna)

Harpe: "Snatcher" or "Sickle-Dagger" (Silius Italicus)

Hegeso: "Leader, Chief" (vase)

Hekate: "Far Darting" (Tzetzes)

Hiera: "Sacred" (Philostratus)

Hippe: "Horse" (Athenaeus)

Hippo: "Horse" (Callimachus; vase)

Hippolyte: "Releases the Horses" (Euripides; Apollonius; Diodorus; Pausanias; Quintus of Smyrna; Plutarch; Hyginus; Jordanes; vases)

Hippomache: "Horse Warrior" (vase)

Hipponike: "Victory Steed" (vase)

Hippothoe: "Mighty Mare" (Quintus of Smyrna; Hyginus; Tzetzes)

Huang Guigu: "Yellow-Golden, of Ghost Valley," (Chinese: Qin commander)

Hyphopyle: "Below the Gate or Pass" (vase)

Hypsepyle: "High Gate or Mountain Pass" (vase)

Hypsicratea: "High or Mighty Power" (Valerius Maximus; Plutarch; Greek inscription)

Iodoke: "Holding Arrows" (Tzetzes)

Iole: "Violet" (vase)

Ioxeia: "Delighting in Arrows" or "Onslaught" (Tzetzes)

Iphinome: "Forceful Nature" (Hyginus)

Iphito: "Snake" (vase)

Isocrateia: "Equal Power" (Stephanus of Byzantium; Eustathius)

Jinding: "Gold Ingot" (Chinese: Northern Song Dynasty)

Kallie: "Beautiful" (vase)

Kepes: "Hot Flanks/Eager Sex" (Circassian: vase)

Khasa: "One Who Heads a Council" (Circassian: vase)

Kheuke: "One of the Heroes/Heroines" (Circassian: vase)

Khutulun: "All White" (Mongolian: alternate name for Aijaruc)

Kleptoleme: "Thief" (vase)

Klonie: "Wild Rushing" (Quintus of Smyrna)

Klymene: "Famous" (Hyginus; Pausanias; vase)

Knemis: "Greaves" (Tzetzes)

Koia: "Hollow" as in sky; "Inquisitive," fem. Koeus, a Titan (Stephanus of Byzantium)

Koinia: "Of the People" (Stephanus of Byzantium)

Kokkymo: "Howling/Battle Cry" (Callimachus fr. 693, a daughter of the queen of the Amazons)

Kong: "Glorious" (Chinese: Lio Song Dynasty)

Korone: "Crown" (vase)

Kreousa: "Princess" (vase)

Kydoime: "Din of Battle" (vase)

Kynna: town in Anatolia (Stephanus of Byzantium, see also Cynna)

Lampedo, Lampeto, Lampado: "Burning Torch" (Callimachus; Justin; Orosius; Jordanes)

Laodoke: "Receives the Host or Army" (vase)

Laomache: "Warrior of the People or Host" (Hyginus)

Latoreia: town near Ephesus (Athenaeus)

Liang Hongyu: "Red Jade" (Chinese: ca. AD 1130)

Lyke: "She-Wolf" (Valerius Flaccus; *Latin Anthology*; vases)

Lykopis: "Wolf Eyes" (vases)

Lysippe: "Lets Loose the Horses" (Pseudo-Plutarch *On Rivers*)

Maia: "Mother" (Callimachus fr. 693, a daughter of the queen of the Amazons)

Marpe: "She Seizes" (Diodorus)

Marpesia: "Snatcher or Seizer" (Justin; Orosius; Jordanes)

Maximou: "Daughter of the Greatest" (Hellenized Latin: *Digenes Akritas*)

Melanippe: "Black Mare" (scholia on Pindar)

Melo: "Song" (vase)

Melousa: "Ruler" (vase)

Menalippe: "Steadfast or Black Mare" (Jordanes)

Menippe: "Steadfast Horse" (Valerius Flaccus)

Mimnousa: "Standing in Battle" (vase)

Minythyia: "She Diminishes" (another name for Thalestris; Justin)

Molpadia: "Death or Divine Song" or "Songstress" (Plutarch *Theseus*)

Mulan: "Deer or Elk" (Xiongnu or Xianbei, Altaic: Chinese sources)

Myrine: "Myrrh" (Homer; Diodorus)

Mytilene: town, Lesbos, named for sister of Myrine (Diodorus)

Nushaba: "Water" (Iranian: Nizami)

Oas oas: "Mighty Spirit" (Ossetian: vase)

Oigme: "Don't Fail!" (Ubykh: vase)

Oistrophe: "Twisting Arrow" as in Parthian shot? (Tzetzes)

Okyale: "Swift" (Hyginus; vase)

Okypous: "Swift-Footed" (vase)

Orithyia: "Mountain Raging" (Justin; Orosius)

Otrera: "Quick, Nimble" (Apollodorus; Hyginus)

Palla: "Leaping, Bounding" (Stephanus of Byzantium; Eustathius)

Pantariste: "Best of All" (vase)

Parthenia: "Maiden, Virgin" (Callimachus fr. 693, a daughter of the queen of the Amazons)

Peisianassa: "She Who Persuades the Queen" (vase)

Pentasila: Etruscan variant of Penthesilea (vase)

Penthesilea: "She Who Brings Grief" (Apollodorus; Diodorus; Hyginus; Quintus of Smyrna; Sextus Propertius; Pausanias; Jordanes; vases)

Pharetre: "Quiver Girl" (Tzetzes)

Philippis: "Loves Horses" (Diodorus)

Phoebe: "Bright, Shining" (Diodorus)

Pisto: "Trustworthy" (vase)

Pitana: Anatolian town (Diodorus)

Pkpupes: "Worthy of Armor" (Circassian: vase)

Polemusa: "War Woman" (Quintus of Smyrna)

Polydora: "Many Gifts" (Hyginus)

Pramila: "Exhausting"? (Sanskrit: *Mahabharata*)

Priene: Anatolian town (Diodorus)

Prothoe: "First in Might, Swift" (Diodorus)

Protis: "First" (Callimachus fr. 693, a daughter of the queen of the Amazons)

Pyrgomache: "Fortress Fighter" (vase)

Rhodogyne: "Woman in Red" (Aeschines *Aspasia*; Philostratus *Imagines*, Persian warrior queen)

Saikal: "Pointed Headdress"? from *saukele*, "beautiful head" (Kalmyk: "Manas" epic of Kyrgyz)

Samsi: "Sun" (Arabic: Assyrian records)

Sanape: "From Wine Country" (Circassian: scholia on Apollonius of Rhodes, see Sinope)

Semiramis: "Exalted Name" (Iranian) or Syrian "Dove" (Ctesias; Diodorus; Justin)

Serague: "Armed with Sword" (Circassian: vase)

Serpot, Sarpot: "Blue Lotus" (Egyptian: "Amazons and Egyptians" papyrus)

Shanakdakheto: ? (Meroitic: Egyptian inscriptions)

Shirin: "Sweet" (Iranian: Nizami *Shahnama*)

Sinope: variation of Sanape; also the mythic mother of the Syrians (Diodorus; Orosius)

Sisyrbe: "Shaggy Goatskin" (Strabo; Stephanus of Byzantium)

Skyleia: "Spoiler of Enemies" (*skuleuw*? non-Greek, fem. Skyles, Scythian:vase)

Smyrna: "Myrrh" Anatolian city (Strabo; Stephanus of Byzantium)

Sosia: "Soul, Spirit" (Iranian: vase)

Sparethra, Sparethe: "Heroic Army" (Iranian: Ctesias)

Stonychia: "Sharp Point, Spear" (Callimachus fr. 693, a daughter of the queen of the Amazons)

Teisipyle: "Gate or Mountain Pass" (vase)

Tekmessa: "Reader of Marks/Signs/Tokens" (Diodorus; Homer *Iliad*)

Telepyleia: "Distant Gates or Mountain Pass" (vase)

Teuta: "Queen" (Illyrian: Appian; Polybius)

Thalestris, Thalestria: "She Makes Grow" (Diodorus; Curtius; Justin)

Thermodosa: "From Thermodon" (Quintus of Smyrna)

Thero: "Wild Beast" or "Hunter" (vase)

Theseis: "Establisher," fem. of Theseus (Hyginus)

Thiba: town in Pontus (Stephanus of Byzantium; Eustathius)

Thoe: "Quick, Nimble, Mighty" (Valerius Flaccus)

Thoreke: "Breastplate" (Tzetzes)

Thraso: "Bold, Confident, Courageous" (vase)

Tirgatao: "Arrow Power/Sharp and Strong" (Iranian: Polyaenus; Maeotian queen)

Tomyris: "Metal/Iron"? (*tomur, temur, timur,* Mongolic/Turkic with Iranian suffix? Herodotus; Strabo). Some suggest *Tahm-rayis*, "Brave Glory"

Toxaris: "Archer" (vase)

Toxis: "Arrow" (vase)

Toxoanassa: "Archer Queen" (Tzetzes)

Toxophile: "Loves Arrows" (vase)

Toxophone: "Whizzing Arrow" (Tzetzes)

Tralla: "Thracian" (Stephanus of Byzantium; Eustathius)

Valdusa (?): (Circassian-Karbardian tale)

Vishpala: "Strong Defender of the Village" (Sanskrit: *Rig Veda*)

Xanthe: "Blonde" (Hyginus)

Xanthippe: "Palomino" (vase)

Xun Guan: family name Xun plus sense of "Water, Nourish, Teach"? (Chinese: Western Jin Dynasty)

Yang Paifeng: family name Yang plus "Wind" (Chinese: *Fourteen Amazons* tales)

Zarina: "Golden" (Iranian: Ctesias, Diodorus)

Zenobia (Bat-Zabbai): "Daughter of Zabba (Wanderer)" (Aramaic: *Historia Augusta*)

NOTES

PROLOGUE
ATALANTA, THE GREEK AMAZON

1. Atalanta's story: Hesiod *Theogony* 1287–94; *Catalogue of Women*, 6th-century BC work attributed to Hesiod; Apollodorus 1.8.2–3; 1.9.16; 3.9.2; Apollonius of Rhodes *Argonautica* 1.768–73 (volunteers for the *Argo*); Hyginus *Fabula* 185; Diodorus Siculus 4.34 and 4.41–48 (hereafter Diodorus); Aelian *Historical Miscellany* 13.1 ("fiery gaze"); Ovid *Metamorphoses* 8.270; 10.560–707; and Pausanias 8.45, among others. Arcadia and Boeotia both claimed Atalanta: see Gantz 1993, 1:331–39; and Fowler 2013, 110 (gift of spear to Jason, scholiast on Apollonius *Argonautica*), and 411. Variants of Atalanta's myth in ancient Greco-Roman sources and artwork: Boardman 1983 and Barringer 1996, 2001, 2004.

2. In some versions, the youth who won the race with Atalanta is called Melanion. Xenophon *On Hunting* 1.7 (4th century BC) says he courted Atalanta by carrying out "great labors of love." Unfortunately, two ancient tragedies, *Atalanta* by Aeschylus and Sophocles's *Meleager*, are lost. Structuralist interpretation of the race: Barringer 1996, 71–75.

3. Pausanias 8.45–46, 8.35.10, 3.18.15; 3.24.2; 5.19.1 describes many ancient artworks depicting Atalanta; see Philostratus *Imagines* 15. Atalanta's "Amazonian torso" and head and the Calydonian Boar are in the National Museum, Athens: Gardner 1906, illustration 170. Atalanta's similarity to an Amazon noted by Bennett 1912, 60, 75; Tyrrell 1984, 73, 77, 83–84; and discussed in detail by Barringer 1996 (tusk dedications, 54n26) and Barringer 2001 and 2004. The immense tusks displayed at Tegea were most likely those of a prehistoric mammoth, common fossils in Greece.

4. Boardman 1983, 9–10. Barringer 1996, 51–66; Barringer 2001, 147–71.

5. Scythians in vase paintings, Vos 1963, 40–52. Dowden 1997, 104. Braund 2005; Barringer 2004, Ivantchik 2006, 219–24. Atalanta dressed as Amazon, Barringer 1996, 55–56, 59–60, 62–67. Early contact, intermarriage, and familiarity: Braund 2005; Mayor, Colarusso, and Saunders 2014.

6. Minns 1913, 53. Blok 1995, 413, 26–30, 217–19. Some argue that Scythian costumes on archaic Greek vases have nothing to do with foreign ethnicity but are

artistic conventions to indicate Greek archers of low status. But this theory deliberately sets aside the question of why Amazons, and Atalanta, are dressed in Scythian attire. The theory maintains that Scythian-costumed figures shown with Atalanta represent Meleager and other young Greek males, *ephebes* or "junior" heroes, who cross-dress in Amazonian-Scythian-style garb for ritual reasons. In this view, Atalanta herself is playing the role of a young Greek male dressed as a Scythian. But these theories fail to account for conventional heroic and ephebic Greek attire of other young men on the same vases and are hard to reconcile with other features of Atalanta's life story. See Ivantchik 2006, 198 and 206, 219–24; Osborne 2011, 143–45; Scythian-style dress = Greek ephebes, Lissarrague 1990, 125–49; Shapiro 1983, 111. For counterargument, see Cohen 2012, 471–72. The only literary evidence for the structuralist claim that Greek ephebes dressed as Scythians is a 9th-century AD Byzantine source, Photius, s.v. *sunepheboi*, saying that people of Elis called their ephebes *skuthas*. According to Barringer 1996, 61–62, Atalanta represents a Greek male ephebe, the Calydonian Boar Hunt myth describes a "perverted Greek male initiatory hunt," and even the boar itself "hunts like an ephebe." Atalanta shown with Scythians: Barringer 1996, 51–61; Barringer 2004, 16–17, 19, 23–25.

7. Atalanta as athlete, erotic scenes, Boardman 1983, 10–14; Barringer 1996, 67–70. Embroidered lion figure on red-figure cup by Oltos, 510 BC, Bologna, see Barringer 2001, 163–64 fig 90. *Perizoma*, Bonfante 1989. Euripides *Andromache* 597–600 claimed that naked Spartan girls wrestled men, but the play is considered anti-Spartan propaganda. Wrestling contests between men and women are very common in nomad traditions, see chapters 22 and 24.

8. The earliest written mention of this myth, Palaephatus 13 with Stern's commentary 44–45 (late 4th century BC), maintains that the story arose because they made love in a cave that happened to be the den of a lion and a lioness. Another early Greek account simply implies that their lust changed them into wild animals: Apollodorus 3.9.2. In the 1st century AD, Hyginus (*Fabula* 185) was the first to say lions could not mate, but his fellow poet Ovid (*Met.* 10.681–707) said they continued to have sex in the form of lions. Barringer 2001, 151–59.

9. Apollodorus 3.9.2, and see Frazer n2 in the Loeb edition for ancient and medieval explanations of the transformation to lions. Latin poets Ovid and Hyginus say that Aphrodite spitefully inflamed the lovers with passion in a sanctuary. Pliny 8.43 on lion lust, jealousy, and interbreeding. Hyginus was the first to claim that lions are "animals to whom the gods deny intercourse," but Ovid says the pair had sex frequently in the woods in the form of lions. Quotes, Barringer 1996, 76, and fig 23; Barringer 2001, on the erotic meaning of felines, 99–101, 163, 167. Some mythic sources suggest divine pity or poetic appropriateness of their transformation.

10. "The only females who hunt are those outside the bounds of civilized society, namely . . . Amazons," Barringer 1996, 59, 62; Barringer 2001, 156–57; and Barringer 2004. Outsider status of Amazons, Hardwick 1990, 17–20, and Lefkowitz 2007, 12. Aelian *Historical Miscellany* 13.1.

11. Mayor, Colarusso, and Saunders 2014.

12. Barringer 2001, 144–47; Vernant 1991, 199–200; Fantham et al. 1994, 85.

Dowden 1997, 122–23. Cf Ballesteros-Pastor 2009 for a bear cult associated with Artemis in Themiscyra, home of the Amazons.

13. Girls as "wild animals lusting after the life of Artemis," Stewart 1995, 579, citing Homer *Iliad* 21.471; Pindar *Pythian* 9.6; Xenophon *Cyropaedia* 6.13. Stewart 1998, 120. "The Amazon in her must die," Dowden 1997, 123. The mythic Amazon represents a woman's true, free soul, which must be given up or suppressed in patriarchal societies like Greece, according to the Russian poet Marina Tsvetaeva, Burgin 1995.

14. The François Vase as a wedding gift, Atalanta on perfume and unguent jars, nuptial vases, and other women's ceramics, Barringer 1996, 62–66; Barringer 2001, 143, 159–61, 171; Barringer 2004; on mirrors and jewelry boxes, Boardman 1983, 16–18. Men created vase paintings of women to teach them their place, Tyrrell 1984, 48.

15. Significantly, Amazons were also favored subjects on vases given as wedding gifts and objects used by Greek women. Outstanding examples are *epinetra* used while working wool; eg Diosphos Painter, ca 500 BC, Louvre MNC 624: one side is a scene of women weaving in their private quarters; the other side shows three Amazons. Many other examples of such images on women's objects appear in the following chapters.

16. See Woodford 2003, ch 17, on finding the keys to unlock mysteries in vase paintings. The "nonsense" inscription between Atalanta and Peleus on the vase (Berlin F 1837) by the Diosphos Painter appears to be Abkhazian for "She of the curly hair." Colarusso per corr Jan 14–15, 2012; Abkhazian and other Caucasian languages on Greek vase paintings: Mayor, Colarusso, and Saunders 2014. Colarusso 2002, Saga 83, 364–65.

17. "Befuddlement," Barringer 2001, 51–53, 157–58, 167; structuralists J.-P. Vernant and P. Vidal-Naquet, see Barringer 2004; and 1996, 61, 62, 65; Vernant 1991, 199–200. Atalanta's son was Parthenopaios, one of the Seven Against Thebes; his father is given as Meleager, Melanion, Hippomenes, or Ares. Fowler 2013, 411. Apollodorus 3.9.2.

18. Later Roman mosaics do show Atalanta hunting on horseback like an Amazon. Atalanta is unlike other mythic virgins, such as Callisto, who resist marriage and are raped and transformed into animals. That moment in Atalanta's myth would have been during the Centaurs' attempted rape, but instead Atalanta defends herself, as an Amazon would. Barringer 1996, 60, 66; Herodotus 4.116.2; Apollodorus 1.9.16; Diodorus 4.41.2, 448.5.

19. The sole exception was Palaephatus, skeptical "myth buster" of the 4th century BC. Rationalizing myths as misunderstandings of natural events, he proposed that male barbarians were mistaken for women because they shaved their beards, tied up their hair, and wore long skirts. But in real life and in Greek art, both Amazons and genuine barbarian horsemen wore trousers, not long skirts. Palaephatus 32, but he contradicted himself at 4, where he identified the Sphinx as an Amazon.

20. Long before modern archaeological discoveries in Scythia, French scholar Pierre Petit (1685) wrote an illustrated treatise arguing that Amazons of Greek myth really existed.

21. Pomponius Mela 3.34–35 (ca AD 43).

CHAPTER 1
ANCIENT PUZZLES AND MODERN MYTHS

1. The Nart sagas, myths, legends are translated from Circassian, Abaza, Ab-khaz, Ubykh, languages of the northwest Caucasus, the crossroads of numerous ethnic and language groups of antiquity. This extract is a condensed version of Saga 26, translated by Colarusso 2002, 129–31; Amezan is also known as Lady Nart Sana. See also Hunt 2012.

2. Quintus of Smyrna *Fall of Troy* 1.657–70. *Arimaspea*, Bolton 1962. Magnes of Smyrna: Nicolaus of Damascus *FGrHist* 90 F62, probably drawing on Xanthos of Sardis. Evidence for independent Amazon (*Amazonis*) epic, West 2011, 17, 21n24, 41, 69–71, 123, 147, 179, 428–30; Fowler 2013, 289–91. Scythian folklore, Ivantchik 2006, 216; Skrzhinskaya 1982; Barringer 2004; Blok 1995, 413–14. Most translations of classical sources are adapted from Loeb Classical Library (Cambridge, MA: Harvard University Press) unless otherwise noted.

3. Braund 2005; Tsetskhladze 2011.

4. Rolle 2011, 120.

5. Tyrrell 1984, 25.

6. Earliest *skyth* root words in Greek literature appear in post-Homeric Theognid lyric corpus, ca 6th century BC, *Theog.* 8.29; s.v. Liddell and Scott. Militant nomad women were the "historical core" of the Amazon myth, Tyrrell 1984, 24.

7. *Amazones antianeirai* twice in Homer *Iliad* 3.189; 6.186; *Trooiai* eg 3.384. Blok 1995, 156, 159, 164, 167, 171.

8. Amazons and men on same side, Bothmer 1957, 27, 79, 108, 113; Shapiro 1983, 111.

9. Thanks to Richard Martin for helpful discussion and the Deianeira example.

10. Risch 1974, 24e; see Blok 1995, 159, 166. Herodotus speaks, for example, of *Phoinikes andres* for the Phoenician people. Zografou 1972, 132–34: *antianeirai* and *antandros* were originally ethnonyms or toponyms.

11. Quotes, Blok 1995, 167; 155–77, on semantic ambiguities of the epic formula. Herodotus 4.

12. On the shift to "hostility" and chronology, Blok 1995, 177–85.

13. Homer *Iliad* 3.182–90; 6.171–87. Hardwick 1990, 15–18. Stewart 1995, 576–80, for the Greeks, "virginity" = unmarried, rather than a technical physical state, and did not preclude sexual activity. Aeschylus *Prometheus Bound* 415 and 720. Herodotus 4.110. Pomponius Mela 3.35. Diodorus 3.53: after virgins had served their stint in the army, they had children and served as tribal leaders while the menfolk cared for offspring. Hippocrates *Airs, Waters, Places* 17, Gera 1997, 90: married women with children usually stopped riding to war except during unusual threat to the tribe. Baumeister and Mendoza 2011.

14. Lesbian identification with Amazons began in the early 20th century, with Russian poet Marina Tsvetaeva (Burgin 1995), Natalie Clifford Barney, *Pensées d'une Amazone* (1920), and Ti-Grace Atkinson, *Amazon Odyssey* (1974). Hellanikos *FGrHist* 323a F 17c. Alcippe: Diodorus 4.16.3. Sinope: Orosius 1.15–16. Orithyia: Justin 2.4.

15. The art historian shall remain anonymous; another recent declaration of the nonexistence of Amazons is Fowler 2013, 86.

16. Amazons were first explained as vestiges of a defeated prehistoric matriarchy by Swiss anthropologist J. Bachofen in 1861, see Bennett 1912 and Eller 2011; Osborne 1997 surveys the matriarchy-patriarchy-Amazons debate. Lefkowitz 2007, 3–13, and Stewart 1995, 572–80, summarize the many meanings assigned to Amazons. Stewart's own theory relates Amazons to Greek male anxieties about "wild" unwed females, foreign brides in Athens, and the Persian threat in the 5th century BC. More interpretations of Amazons, Vernant 1991; Barringer 1996; Dowden 1997; Dubois 1991 (paired with Centaurs as enemies of civilization); Tyrrell 1984, 76–77 (refuse women's "destiny of motherhood"); Fowler 2013, 541 ("un-women"); and Hartog 1988 (inverted mirror of Greek culture).

17. Bonfante 2011, 17. Boardman 2002, 160–62.

18. Quotes, Dowden 1997, 117, 119–24, 168, on "the uses of a dead Amazon." He argues that ritual killing of mythic Amazons "reincorporated" liminal "militant" Greek virgins into "normal society." Amazons "always defeated or married or both": Barringer 1996, 60, 65. Cf Langdon 2001: early Amazons of myth embodied "warrior codes of honor" but Amazons' function was to serve, along with frightening Gorgons, in young *boys'* initiation rites. "Setting out to defeat womanish or feeble" adversaries would diminish male heroic status, notes Hardwick 1990, 32. She suggests that Greek men cleverly enhanced their own military status by portraying Amazons as powerful antagonists.

19. Amazons overcome men, Cohen 2000, 101–2. Amazons' behavior and gestures on vase paintings, McNiven 2000, 79 and nn25–26. Amazons in Greek art: Lexicon Iconographicum Mythologiae Classicae (LIMC).

20. Homeric ideal of the "beautiful death" in battle promising eternal glory for the hero, Cohen 2000, 98, 102–3, 106. Marconi 2004, 35. Blok 1995, 174–75. Nart Saga 1, Colarusso 2002, 11–12. Amazons as foreign heroines, Hardwick 1990; Vlassopoulos 2013, 167–78. Perhaps the greatest Greek "heroes" are best thought of as "antiheroes." Nudity as costume for Greek male heroes, Bonfante 1989; Cohen 2000, 9–31.

21. Hector dies heroically, but he is not Greek. Patroclus, companion of Achilles, dies heroically but is not considered a great hero of the first rank.

22. Calyx-krater from Vulci, 330 BC, Turmuca Painter, Paris, Cabinet des Médailles et Antiques, BNF no 920. Andromache: Beazley, *Etruscan Vase Painting 9*, 136, pl 31, 2. Dorymache: I. Krauskopf in *Amazonen* 2010, 46. The ghost of Patroclus, bandaged and cloaked, appears in frescoes of the Etruscan François Tomb in Vulci of the same period; Bonfante 1989, 565. Thanks to Jean Turfa and Ingrid Krauskopf for discussion of this vase. Independent Etruscan women: Theopompus of Chios *Histories* 43, *FGrHist* F 204 (Athenaeus 517d–518a).

23. Weingarten 2013.

24. Vlassopoulos 2013, 167, is the most recent reiteration of this Hellenocentric assumption; the second quote is from Hardwick 1990, 15.

25. Iranian religious scholars' claims cited and refuted by Talattof 2000, 52–54.

26. Eg Dubois 1991; Tyrell 1984; Dowden 1997; Stewart 1995 and 1998.

27. Two Amazon dolls signed by Maecius (1st–2nd centuries AD) are in the Louvre; another Amazon doll was found in Troy. Terra-cotta dolls, Merker 2000, 57, 101, see C160–C162 for other Amazon dolls. The mold-made dolls, colored with white slip, have detailed hairstyles and headdresses. Some have painted-on costumes;

others were clothed with removable garments. Many of the figurines have articulated arms and legs attached with wire. Minns 1913, 369, describes similar articulated dolls in Scythian graves.

CHAPTER 2
SCYTHIA, AMAZON HOMELAND

1. Rolle 1989 and Rolle in *Amazonen* 2010. Ivantchik 2011. Han 2008. Herodotus 4.26; 4.64. Ancient workshop for making cups from skulls in Ukraine: Rolle 1989, 82–83; Minns 1913, 81. Evidence for scalping and other war injuries to ancient Scythian skeletons, Murphy 2003, 15, 74–76, 99; Murphy 2004, 172; Baumer 2012, 186. Arrow poison, Mayor 2009, 80–85; scalping; dislodging turquoise with slings, Pliny 7.2.12; 37.33.110–12. Turquoise is found in Scythian grave goods in the Caucasus and Central Asia. Archery feats were recorded in ancient inscriptions; today archers in Mongolia practice shooting arrows at small sheep knucklebones the size of dice or at leather rings at about 80 yards. Sling pebbles and arrow shafts painted with viper-like patterns are recovered from Scythian burials (although poison residues are yet to be found): Rudenko 1970; Mayor 2009, 79–86.

2. Herodotus 4.6. Strabo 11.6.2–11.11.8. Pliny 6.19.50. Tsetskhladze 2011, 120. Extent of "Scythian" culture, including the nomads of Inner Asia known to the Chinese as Xiongnu, eg Murphy 2003, 3; Anthony 2007, 5–6; Baumer 2012, 198–269; Beckwith 2009, 58–77, 86–90. "Xiongnu" refers to a specific nomad confederation from 3rd century BC to 5th century AD; "Xirong" was a catchall term for "northern and western barbarians" in the Zhou period, ca 10th to 4th century BC. Nomads and China: Barfield 1992.

3. Lucian *Toxaris*. Quotes, Murphy 2003, 3–4. Lebedynsky 2006 and 2010; Tsetskhladze 2011; Braund 2005. Scythian triad, Baumer 2012, 179–80. Trade and shared culture: "Lost Tribe" 2013.

4. In some ways, Spartan women were an exception to most Greek women's lower status. Stewart 1998, 114–16.

5. Ivantchik 2011. Tsetskhladze 2011. Stark et al. 2012.

6. Braund 2005. Anthony 2007. Baumer 2012. Time line: Cernenko 1983, 4–5. Dating Scythian history: Tsetskhladze 2011.

7. Diodorus 2.43; Herodotus 1.104–5; 4.1–144; Scythians traverse the frozen Kerch strait, 4.28. Detailed descriptions of the routes over and around the Caucasus range, Mayor 2010, 331–38, and ancient sources, nn31–34. Maps of the Black Sea and steppes, Talbert 2000 (*Barrington Atlas*). Plutarch *Theseus* 27.1–2; Blok 1995, 90. Examples: Bosporus froze in 1954; Kerch-Cimmerian Strait between Black Sea and Sea of Azov froze in 2012. A pass south of the Caspian Sea was also called the Caspian Gates; see chapter 20.

8. List of cities founded by Amazons in ancient sources, Zografou 1972, 148–51; and Bennett 1912. Collection of coins depicting Amazons, Museum of Fine Arts, Boston.

9. Strabo 1.2.10; 7.3.6.

10. Scythian-Greek relations from the 6th to 4th centuries BC: Moreno 2007, 144–208, quotes 146; Braund 2005, 2010. Amazons were associated with Scythians, according to numerous Greco-Roman writers over a millennium, from Herodotus to Orosius: Shapiro 1983. Amazons also associated with Thrace; see chapter 6. Not easy to distinguish Thracian from Scythian attire: Thracians often have a *pelta* (crescent shield), *zeira* (long cloak with bold geometric designs), *alopekis* (soft hat with earflaps and foxtail), and animal skin boots, but these items are also depicted on Scythians, Amazons, and even some Greeks. Saunders 2014. Amazons and males fighting on the same side, Bothmer 1957, 27, 79, 108, 113; Shapiro 1983, 111. Scythians were known to the Greeks as enemies of the Persians.

11. Quote, Bonfante 2011, 17. Gera 1997, 88–90. Stewart 1995, 575–76. Blok 1995, 92–100. Hardwick 1990, 18–19. Shapiro 1983.

12. Blok 1995, 266, 273, 275–76. Cf Bennett 1912, 12. Tsetskhladze 2011, Scythians in Colchis and Anatolia, 96–120. Geography of Amazons, Dowden 1997. Strabo 12.3.21–24 discusses the various "homelands" of Amazons given by ancient sources. See discussion in Fowler 2013, 289–91.

13. Quintus *Fall of Troy* 1.18. *Aethiopis* fragments in Proclus *Chrestomathia*, cited by Stewart 1995, 576–77. Scythian *kurgans* in Sinope, thanks to Turkish archaeologist Gurkan Ergin, per corr June 14, 2013. Jason and Argonauts: Fowler 2013, 223.

14. Aristeas *Arimaspea* and Amazons: Bolton 1962, 37–75, 118, 178–81, 191. Blok 1995, 88–89. Dowden 1997, 104. Baumer 2012, 174. Justin 2.1, Curtius 5.4, Pomponius Mela 1.1, Lucan 2.

15. *Theseis*; Pindar fr. 172 Snell; Pherekydes *FGrHist* 3F15; Aeschylus *Prometheus Bound* 415–18; Strabo 11.5.1; 12.3.9; Euripides *Hercules Furens* 408–18 and *Ion* 1144–45 also locate Amazons in Pontus: Stewart 1995, 577. The histories of Ephorus (400–330 BC) survive in lengthy quotations in Diodorus and Strabo.

16. Herodotus 4.1–144. Baumer 2012, 172–75.

17. Isocrates 4.68; 12.93, 7.75. Cf Plato *Menexenus* 239B refers to the Athenian victory over the Amazons of Pontus.

18. Diodorus 2.44–45.

19. Diodorus 2.44–46; 4.28.

20. Strabo 11.5.1, citing Metrodorus and Hypsicrates, historians associated with Mithradates VI of Pontus.

21. Justin 2.1–5.

22. Justin 2.1–5. On the recurrent theme of widows who become warriors in ancient Greek texts, Gera 1997, 13–14. Herodotus 4.1–3.

23. Justin 2.1–5. We are not told whether women originally accompanied the Scythian exiles, or if the young men found wives in the new land. Had the young outcast Scythian men from the north abducted wives from the indigenous people in Pontus? That was a very common practice in antiquity. Over generations as Scythian wives, those women and their daughters would become estranged from their native tribes in Pontus, who viewed them as dangerous outsiders. Perhaps the women killed the surviving husbands because they resented their history of violent captivity—or viewed the men as cowards. Examples of each of these reactions were described by Herodotus: in western Asia, captive foreign women passed resentment of their husbands on to their daughters over many generations; in Athens, a

mob of war widows set upon and murdered a surviving veteran. Herodotus 1.146.3, 5.87.2; Schaps 1982, 196, 207.

24. Klaproth 1814, 304–5.

25. Pomponius Mela 1.11–12; 1.88–116; 3.38–39.

26. Pliny 6.6.19. Isidore of Seville 9.62; Amazons are defined as offshoots of Scythians in this compendium of classical knowledge compiled ca AD 600.

27. Orosius 1.15–16.

28. Merola 2010.

29. Jordanes 5–8.

CHAPTER 3
SARMATIANS, A LOVE STORY

1. Herodotus 4.110–17; cf 9.27, an Athenian ambassador lists his city's great victories, including the battle to defend Athens against Amazon attack. On Herodotus's sources, Dowden 1997. Sarmatians: Sulimirski 1970; Brzezinski and Mielczarek 2002; Baumer 2012, 253–69.

2. The "Cliffs" are identified as the craggy northern shore of the Sea of Azov; Talbert 2000, *Barrington Atlas*, map 84; Bryce 1878, 37. Herodotus 4.86.

3. Nightmarish inversion of this story, chapter 19. Scythian horses, Harrison 2012.

4. Hippocrates remarked that wagon-bound Royal Scythian women suffered ill health from lack of exercise. Scholars suggest that exceptional wealth from trade and agriculture had enabled the settled Royal Scythians to afford the "luxury of exempting their women from work." Minns 1913, 84.

5. The name may be just one of several names of Sauromatians/Sarmatians, which came to stand for the entire group as a xenonym in Greco-Roman ethnography, much as "Scythian" came to refer to the many tribes from the Black Sea to Central Asia. Strabo (1st century BC) named the Roxolani, Aorsi, Siraces, Iazyges as the main tribes of Sarmatia. "Sauromatian" could derive from *sauros* = "lizard" in Greek, perhaps referring to the scaled armor worn by Sarmatian warriors. Pausanias 1.21.5–6 examined Sarmatian scaled armor made of horn and hooves: "They collect hooves and clean them out and split them down to make them like snakescales" fitted together "like the notches of a pine-cone. They bore holes in these scales and sew them with horse and cattle hair to make breast plates no less good looking than Greek ones, and no weaker: they stand up to striking and shooting from close range."

6. Herodotus 4.113. Cf Homer *Iliad* 3.196, where it means "leader of the flock"; Pindar fr. 238. Aristeas: Bolton 1962, 51–52, 179–80; Dowden 1997, 104–8; and now Fowler 2013, 289, on Herodotus's "scientific" procedures and *Arimaspea*'s influence on the tale. Thanks to Richard Martin for clarifying Herodotus's word choice.

7. The Greek belief that vigorous women must be linked with emasculated men: Gera 1997, 91.

8. C. Dewald, appendix U, *Landmark Herodotus* 2007, 840. Caucasian Nart sagas emphasize women's powers and "mutual respect between husband and wife," Co-

Iarusso 2002, 3, eg Saga 27, 131–34. Possible illustration of Herodotus's story on a Thracian vessel: Marazov 2011a, 168–71.

9. On parity of women and men, Plato *Republic* 5.369e–457c and *Laws* 804e–814c. Gera 1997, 25–26.

10. Herodotus *philobarbaros*: Ctesias [Llewellen-Jones and Robson] 2010, 41–42. See Pelling 1997 for equality and Greek respect for "barbarians" of the East. Positive qualities attributed to barbarians by Herodotus and to Persians by Aeschylus, Hardwick 1990, 32; Vlassopoulos 2013, esp 195–96. Scythian tales, Skrzhinskaya 1982; 1998.

11. Brown and Tyrrell 1985; for more of the same sort of analysis, Tyrrell 1984, 41–43, 77. Cf Dewald 1981, 100: neither the Amazons nor the Scythians "dominate." Blok 1995, 86–92.

12. Pomponius Mela 3.34–45. Diodorus 2.43.

CHAPTER 4
BONES: ARCHAEOLOGY OF AMAZONS

1. Kurgan 16, at Akkermen 1, near ancient Tyras: Rolle 1989, 88; Murphy 2003, 11. Spears planted in the ground at the entrance typical of Scythian warrior tombs, Ivantchik 2011, 81. Tyragetae, Strabo 7.3.1–17; Ptolemy 3.5.25; Pliny 4.12.82.

2. Analysis of adult skull, pelvis, and teeth can establish sex with 97–98 percent accuracy; with a full skeleton, accuracy is 95–100 percent: Murphy 2003, 11; determining sex and age from skeletons, 37–40; determining sex from bones and status from grave goods, Hanks 2008, 22–29. Murphy 2004, 173.

3. As of 1991, 112 armed female graves were known, Guliaev 2003, 114. Rolle 1989; Anthony 2007, 329; Davis-Kimball 2002, 54–55. Sexing skeletons, Murphy 2003, 11 and 38–39. Lebedynsky 2010, 185; Lebedynsky 2009, 37–80; Wilde 1999, 53–56. Fialko in *Amazonen* 2010, 119–27; Fialko 2010, at Mamaj Gora cemetery 12 of 135 female burials were "Amazons" buried with weapons, female warriors of ordinary status who "formed light armed cavalry. . . . We conclude that 1 out of 10 warriors was female." Statistics, Berseneva 2008, 139; Sargat archer women, 141. Ivantchik 2011 and Stark et al. 2012, 77–80, compare Herodotus's account of Scythian funeral practices with archaeological finds. Baumer 2012, 264–65, see endpapers for precise maps of warrior women sites in Ukraine/Russia; also see maps in Aruz et al. 2000, xiv; and *Amazonen* 2010, 90, 100.

4. Eg magnificent tomb of Saka-Parthian queen Zarina, Diodorus 2.44–45. Quote, Guliaev 2003, 114.

5. Gender expectations: Jones-Bley 2008, 41, 47; Rubinson 2008, 54–55; Rolle 1989, 88; Murphy 2003, 11.

6. Guliaev 2003, 114–15. Murphy 2003, 5–8, 11, 19, 98. Rolle 1989, 79–82. Wilde 1999, 47–68. Pseudo-spindle-whorls: Davis-Kimball 2012. Mirrors in female graves in Kazakhstan led Davis-Kimball 1997a and b and 2002 to identify their owners as priestesses; but now see Hanks 2008, 24–25; Jones-Bley 2008, 41; mirrors, spindle-whorls, earrings in male graves, Berseneva 2008, 137, 141–45; Shelach 2008, 102–3. Ubiquitous mirrors: Hanks 2008, 25. Mirrors as the "seat of the soul," Baumer

2012, 187. Whetstones have magical purposes in Ossetian Nart sagas, Aruz et al. 2000, 236; Colarusso 2002, Sagas 33 and 84.

7. Bioarchaeological indications of riding, hunting, warfare, and handedness: Stark et al. 2012, 55; Hanks 2008; Rolle in *Amazonen* 2010, 116. Lebedynsky 2010, 140. Wilford 1997. Davis-Kimball 2002, 59–60; Jordana et al. 2009; Murphy 2003, 43, 50, 87, 96–97, chs 5 and 6 and plates. Ridgway 1974, 5, "a left-handed Amazon in classical times is hardly imaginable."

8. Polyaenus 8.60; Athenaeus 13.557; Romm 2011, 143–47. Carney 2000, 129–33, 239–41. A gold and ivory shield in Tomb II depicts Achilles and Penthesilea; a pair of Amazons overcome a male warrior on a mosaic in a Pella tomb. The names Kynna and Adea appear in Macedonian inscriptions; Palagia 2008. Quote, Carney 2014.

9. Farkas 1982, 37–46. Teleaga in *Amazonen* 2010, 79–85, with photos.

10. Guliaev 2003, 122–23. Herodotus 4.19.

11. Repiakhouvata Mohyla and Bobrytsia kurgans: Lebedynsky 2009, 40–42; Terzan and Hellmuth 2007. Murphy 2003, 11; Rolle 1989, 88; Wilde 1999, 47–48. Scythian burials in the northern Black Sea region, Tsetskhladze 2011, esp maps 121–26.

12. Kurgans 9, 11, 16, 30 at Chertomlyk, excavated 1983–86: Rolle in *Amazonen* 2010, 113–17; 153–59, photo of woman in Kurgan 9, burial 2, 152. Wilde 1999, 49, citing Rolle says 6 of 53 graves at Chertomlyk contained women with weapons, and that a child was with the woman in Kurgan 11. Murphy 2003, 11; Guliaev 2003, 115. Hanks 2008, 22–23.

13. Fialko in *Amazonen* 2010, 119–27; Rolle in *Amazonen* 2010, 156; Baumer 2012, 265.

14. Guliaev 2003, 116–17.

15. Guliaev 2003, 117–24, figs 1–7.

16. Ascherson 1995, 123; the Kobiakov artifacts are stored in the Rostov Museum. Baumer 2012, 258, photo 256.

17. Murphy 2003, 11. This skeleton, discovered in the 19th century, was recognized as female. Discus weapons, Colarusso 2002, 394, 398, 399–400.

18. Rolle in *Amazonen* 2010, 153–59; Amazon graves at Semo Awtschala (Zemo Avchala, Zemoavchala) near Tbilisi, Georgia, 154, color photo of her sword and necklace, 174; Wilde 1999, 48–49; Nioradze 1931. Thanks to Nino Kalandadze, Georgia National Museum. Archaeology in Georgia: Tsetskhladze 2011, 96–115, map 107. Thanks to Robert Proctor for identifying the beads.

19. Ateshi 2011.

20. *Hambastegi News* [Tehran] 2004.

21. Stark et al. 2012. Wilford 1997; Schetnikov 2001; Davis-Kimball 1997a and 2002, 57–61; Davis-Kimball 2012; Vedder 2004. Hanks 2008, 20–22.

22. Rolle 1989, 46–53; 47, Rolle dates the Issyk burial to the 5th century BC. Boardman 2012 suggests the warrior could be Yuezhi (see chapter 25). Samashev 2011 and 2013.

23. Lebedynsky 2009, 68–69. Mirrors accompany females in the Saka graves excavated by Davis-Kimball 1997b and 2002, 96–107; Wilde 1999, 66–67.

24. Lillis 2010. Gender questions: http://registan.net/2010/07/19/the-sun-lord-riseth; and http://www.express-k.kz/show_article.php?art_id=41560. Samashev 2011.

25. Scythian wealth and extensive trade: Stark et al. 2012, 107–38. Davis-Kimball 2002, 181–84; and 2012, figs 18 and 19. Tillya Tepe, Baumer 2012, 291–95; Rubinson 2008, 61; Lebedynsky 2006, 144–46; 2009, 69–71. Boardman 2012.

26. About 500 mummies have been recovered from the Tarim Basin; some are displayed in Urumchi museum. Barber 2000, 93–96; Mallory and Mair 2008; Baumer 2012, 118–34, map 118–19.

27. The pair was found in Kurgan 1, burial mound 1, Ak-Alakha. Polosmak 1994, 95, 99; Polosmak 2001; and Polosmak in *Amazonen* 2010, 129–37 with color photographs. Stark et al. 2012, 82. Jones-Bley 2008, 43; Lebedynsky 2009, 67; Baumer 2012, 193–95. The man had advanced arthritis and the young woman had early signs of the hereditary disease, suggesting kinship. On burials of couples in the northern Black Sea and Caucasus region, Ivantchik 2011, 81–82; in south Siberia; Murphy 2003, 18. Maps of Altai-Tuva sites, *Amazonen* 2010, 131; Stark et al. 2012, 12–13; Baumer 2012, endpaper map.

28. Jordana 2009.

29. Aymyrlyg cemetery complex, south Siberia, Ulug-Khemski region, Autonomous Republic of Tuva, 809 individual skeletons, Murphy 2003, 1, 3–24; Hsiung-nu (Xiongnu), 15–17; Murphy 2004, 173–84.

30. Murphy 2003, 6–8, 17, 20, 155, 171–72.

31. Arzhan 1: Rolle 1989, 38–44. Arzhan 1 and 2, burial 5: Bokovenko and Samashev 2012, 20–29, 89n9, with color photographs of the opulent couple's grave, ca 650 BC; Lebedynsky 2009, 65–67; Baumer 2012, 181–85. See also Chugunov, Nagler, and Parzinger 2001 and Deutsches Archaologisches Institut, http://www.dainst.org/en /project/russian-federation-tuva-arzhan?ft=all. Murphy 2003, 4–5, miniature weapons were found in scabbards with designs similar to Sarmatian artifacts.

32. Murphy 2003, 43–45, 57, 65–68, 78–79, 87, 95, 96–98, forensic details of female combat injuries, 213.

33. The women's partially burned bones were accompanied by horse bones, scabbard fittings, glass and silver bowls, red Samian pottery, and ivory. Cool 2004 and 2005. Cf Edmunds 1997, Greek misunderstanding of burial of maiden and horse. Notably, the Crosby Garrett Helmet, a Roman ceremonial copper helmet with a mask of an "Amazon" wearing a Phrygian cap topped with a griffin, dating to the 1st to 3rd centuries AD (the same era as the Sarmatian cremation), was discovered in Cumbria in 2010, used by Roman cavalry to reenact mythic and legendary battles.

34. Murphy 2003, 11; Guliaev 2003, 120–21; Davis-Kimball 2002, 61; Davis-Kimball quoted in Wilford 1997.

35. Guliaev 2003, 120–22; Fialko 1991, 11–13. Gera 1997, 90.

CHAPTER 5
BREASTS: ONE OR TWO?

1. Stewart 1998, 41; story of Helen's exposed breast was related by numerous authors, eg Euripides *Helen*; Aristophanes *Lysistrata* 155; *Little Iliad* fr. 13. Pliny 33.23.81.

2. Bennett 1912, 13. Not the classical ideal: Cohen 2000, McNiven 2000.

3. Rolle 1989, 91; Davis-Kimball 2002, 118. Thanks to Roberta Beene for descriptions of mounted archery techniques.

4. Other examples of "crude etymologies of names," Lefkowitz 2007, 5; Fowler 2013, 687 and n19. "Absurd" derivations, Braund 2010, 18. Hellanikos *FGrHist* 4 F 107 and Tzetzes; Tyrrell 1984, 21, suggests that Hellanikos drew on Herodotus and Hippocrates. See Fowler 2013, 291.

5. Rolle 1989, 90–91.

6. Hippocrates *Airs, Waters, Places* 17; Diodorus 2.45.3 and 3.53; Justin 2.4.5–11; Pomponius Mela 3.34–35; Orosius 1.15–16; Apollodorus *Bib* 2.5.9; Curtius 6.5.27–29. Arrian 7.13.2; Strabo 11.5.1. See Tyrrell 1984, 47–49; Dowden 1997, 97; Blok 1995, 22–36.

7. Philostratus *On Heroes* 57; Maclean and Aitken 2004, 86; Bennett 1912, 13–14. Tryphiodorus *Taking of Ilias* 35. Procopius *Gothic Wars* 6.15.16–25. Sami or Fenni, Uralic language group. Sagging breasts mocked in Greek art: Sutton 2000, 196–99; also mocked in Nart sagas, see below.

8. Amazon etymologies ancient and modern: Blok 1995, 21–37. "Husbandless," Huld 2002. Colarusso 2002, Nart Saga 26, 129–31. Mayor, Colarusso, and Saunders 2014.

9. Blok 1995, 23–24n2; "terrifying asymmetry," Yalom 1998, 23–24. Stewart 1998, 118. Tyrrell 1984, 49; Marazov 2011b, 159. Modern lesbian poet Marina Tsvetaeva rejects the ideal of symmetry and "ponders the erotic allure of the lesbian Amazons' single breast," Burgin 1995, 67. Artistic inconsistency, eg Bothmer 1957, 221; Ridgway 1974, 5.

10. A literary exception is Thersites, an ugly lout in Homer's *Iliad*. A genre of burlesque Greek vases depict gods and heroes as silly and ugly; Sutton 2000. Amazons made a rare appearance in a lost comedy by Cephisodorus, *The Amazons* (5th century BC): Bron 1996, 76.

11. Stewart 1998; Bol 1998.

12. Gidley and Rowling 2006; Hall 2013. Diodorus 3.53; Tyrrell 1984, 140n18. Pliny 7.2.15 mentions an African tribe of hermaphrodites called Androgyni ("male-female") with small nipple on one full breast, but says nothing about Amazons' breasts. The Greek queen Pheretime of Cyrene in North Africa punished her enemies' wives by cutting off their breasts, 6th century BC: Herodotus 4.202.

13. Klaproth 1814, 267. Abercromby 1891. By 1814, the Circassian corset, modified to actually boost the bust and enhance cleavage, became popular among European ladies.

14. Colarusso 2002, 37, 45n7. Bosom support in antiquity: Serwint 1993. Flattening and "cross-your-heart" effects: Sturgeon 1995, 493, 500.

15. Ancient Greek and Roman men's "muscled" cuirasses are relatively flat. Asher-Perrin 2013.

16. Padding hypothesis, Baynham 2001, 120 and n25.

17. Christy Halbert, former champion boxer, USA Boxing Women's Task Force: Levy 2012.

18. Diodorus 4.63.1–3. Ovid *Heroides* 16.149–52. Quote, Propertius 3.14.

CHAPTER 6
SKIN: TATTOOED AMAZONS

1. Harrison 1888, pl 6; white-ground cup, Pistoxenos Painter, Athens National Museum, Acropolis 439. Zimmermann 1980. Cohen 2000, 113, fig 4.4.

2. "Tattooed women in Athenian vase paintings are surely Thracian": Oakley 2000, 242. Tattoos in antiquity, Mayor 1999; Lobell and Powell 2013.

3. Thracian-Scythian shared culture: Marazov 2011a and b. Farkas 1982. Dowden 1997, 99. Homer *Iliad* 2.819. Herodotus 4.104; 4.119; 4.125; 4.48. Strabo 7.3.2–5; 11.14.14; 12.3–4.

4. Thrace and Amazons: Blok 1995, 265–76. Tsiafakis 2000. Shapiro 1983, 110, Siana cup, Berlin Antikensammlungen 3402.

5. "Thracian Amazons," Shapiro 1983, 107–14; leopard and fawn skins, 108. Blok 1995, *zeira* and Amazons, 399 (Bothmer B IX 41 and 45), 405; and trousered Amazon with *zeira*, white-ground alabastron, Athens National Museum. Red-haired Scythian, Berlin Painter, Malibu, Getty 96.AE.98.

6. Shapiro 1983, *Aethiopis*, Proklos *Chrestomathia* 2 (p 105 Allen). Hecataeus *FGrHist* 802 F 3: Vlassopoulos 2013, 183; Blok 1995, 153; and Braund 2010, 17. Strabo 7.3.2–13 11.5.1–4; Herodotus 7.73; Diodorus 3.55.10–12.

7. Thracian women's tattoos on vases discussed and illustrated in Zimmermann 1980. Tsiafakis 2000, 372–76, figs 14.4 and 14.5; Oakley 2000, 242–44, figs 9.9 and 9.10. Berard 2000, 391–92, fig 15.1. Cohen 2000, 99, figs 4.2 and 4.4. Two tattooed, running women, column krater, Pan Painter, 470 BC, Munich Staatliche Antikensammlungen 2378 (J. 777). Thracian Amazons, Blok 1995, 259–76.

8. Thracian tattoos: Saporiti 2009; Tsiafakis 2000. Thracian tattoos on silver cup: Marazov 2011b, 170–73, fig 5.24a–b; 2011a, 56–58, 78–79. Tattoos depicted on Thracian artifacts: Farkas 1982, 43, 45, In contrast, a red-figure amphora (550 BC Vienna 3722) shows an ugly foreign woman labeled "Injustice" being beaten by the Greek goddess of Justice. The barbarian hag is covered in circle tattoos that call to mind some tattoos on Thracian women as well as some designs on Amazons' form-fitting outfits. The same circles and dots mark the wings, arms, and legs of a pair of ugly barbarian woman personifying Poena (400 BC, Policoro Painter, Cleveland Museum of Art). But the same circular designs cover the unitard and sleeves of beautiful Amazons by the Eretria Painter, 420 BC, center and far right, fig 13.6.

9. Shapiro 1983, 106. Andromache's dress with griffins, birds, lions: black-figure amphora signed by Timiades Painter, ca 570–560 BC, Boston Museum of Fine Arts 98.916. Lion on Kydoime's corselet, Bothmer 1957, 136.

10. Truhelka 1896, 500; Durham 1928. Daunians of Apulia had Illyrian origins: Norman in Della Casa and Witt 2013.

11. Hippocrates *Airs, Waters, Places* A, 26. Herodotus 5.6; 4.8–13. Dio Chrysostom *Oration* 14.19. Ammianus Marcellinus 31.2; cf Pomponius Mela 2.1.10.

12. Xenophon *Anabasis* 5.4.32. Pomponius Mela 1.106. Pliny 22.2.2. Sextus Empiricus 3.202.

13. Clearchus, of Aristotle's peripatetic school, traveled as far as the Oxus (Amu Darya) River in Baktria (Afghanistan). This account from his lost multivolume

Lives is preserved by the late 2nd-century AD polymath Athenaeus, *Learned Banquet* 12.27 (524 d, e). Clearchus's story occurs in a discussion of the decadence of Scythian and other barbarian cultures. Plutarch *On the Delay of Divine Justice* 12 repeated a story that Thracian men tattooed their wives to avenge the killing of Orpheus, but this rationalization reflects the Greek notion of tattoos as punishment and conflicts with reports that Thracian men wore tattoos, and that Thracian women were depicted as already tattooed when they killed Orpheus. Tsiafakis 2000. Scythian tombs yield elaborate golden buckles, needles, and pigments. Strabo 4.6.10, 7.5.4, Iapodes and Thracians. Pliny 22.2.2. Ammianus Marcellinus 22.8; 31.2.14–17. Virgil *Aeneid* 4.136; *Georgics* 2.115. Claudian *In Rufinus* 1.313, the Geloni of Scythia tattooed their arms and legs.

14. For similar ancient tales of tattoos inflicted and then embraced with pride, and examples of tattooing prisoners of war in classical antiquity, see Mayor 1999. Stories of how tattoos originated often refer anachronistically to more recent history and reflect modern disapproval of what were once considered permanent beauty marks. According to Croatian legends in Bosnia and Herzegovina, tattooing girls began in the early Ottoman Empire (1400–1922) as protection against kidnapping by Turks. The rationale has a folkloric ring (the story in Burma, for example, is that Chin girls were tattooed to make them unattractive to would-be abductors). In other parts of the Ottoman Empire, a different version is told: Turks reportedly inflicted tattoos on abducted Christian females. Other accounts claim that tattoos began as protective "amulets" against plague in the Byzantine era. Durham 1928, Krutak 2010; plague: Meserve 1999, 175.

15. Notably, Clearchus used the positive word "decorate" for the Scythian tattoos instead of a negative verb. Shapiro 1983, on Amazons, Thracians, and Scythians.

16. Reed 2000, 7, 10–11, 17n38. Murphy 2003, 22. Lebedynsky 2010, 112. The earliest Chinese word for writing, *wén*, referred to tattoo (thanks to Victor Mair).

17. Xiongnu: Murphy 2003, 15–24; Linduff 2008, 175–81. "The Mission to the West" in the *Han Shu* 94A.3772 by Zhang Qian (Chang K'ien). Chinese ambivalence about tattoos: Reed 2000, 5–6n10, 47. Meserve 1989; Meserve 1999, 171–72. Watson 1962, 155–92.

18. Cicero *De Off.* 7.25, tattooed Thracian men. Herodian 3.14.7 on geometric and animal tattoos of Celts and Picts. Davis-Kimball 2002, 79, suggests that tattooing was a woman's art, based on mineral pigments found in women's tombs; Linduff and Rubinson 2008, 21–22, 25. But tattoo pigments and needles have been found in male burials, see below.

19. Cucuteni-Trypillian culture, Anthony 2007; tattoos, Lobell and Powell 2013. Gobustan is a UNESCO World Heritage Site. Ateshi 2011 and http://gobustan .si.edu/dating_methods_chronology.

20. Olsen and Harding 2008. Anthony 2007, 216–24. Baumer 2012, 84.

21. Stitched seam-like "ladder" designs on tattooed Thracian women, eg Nolan amphora, Oinocles Painter, ca 470 BC, British Museum E 301, Cohen 2000, p 107, fig 4.2; and hydria, Aegisthis Painter, ca 470 BC, Louvre 2587, Oakley 2000, 243, fig 9.9. Turkmenistan figures, Baumer 2012, 65, 66; tattoos, 134, 161, 186, 189.

22. Chenciner, Ismailov, and Magomedkhanov 2006. Meserve 1999, 175; Meserve 1989, 219; Field 1958; Smeaton 1937; Izady 1992. Textiles and tattoo motifs, S. Pankova in Della Casa and Witt 2013.

23. Scythian textiles: Polosmak 2003; Rolle 1989, 95–98; Barber 1991; Phoenix and Arabeth 1999; Han 2008, 50 fig 3; Murphy 2003, 5: woolen clothing in Scythian graves, four colors, rhomboid and triangle decorations; Wagner et al. 2009; Barber 2000.

24. Truhelka 1896; Krutak 2010; Field 1958, Durham 1928. Rudenko 1970, 112. Sewing with soot-laden thread: Meserve 1999, 181n2; Mayor 1999; stencils, Phoenix and Arabeth 1999. Colored tattoos in 9th-century China: Reed 2000.

25. Yablonsky 2013.

26. Scythians of the Altai steppes: Han 2008.

27. "Discovery of Tattoos" 2005. Rudenko 1970, 110–14, 247–66. Barkova and Pankova 2005. Tashtyk tattoos are evident in painted gypsum masks among grave goods, and the motifs are repeated in their textiles: Pankova in Della Casa and Witt 2013; Baumer 2012, 171; Pazyryk finds, 186–92. "Scythian" tombs compared to Herodotus: Ivantchik 2011, tattoos, 92.

28. Barkova and Pankova 2005. The Pazyryk kurgan was looted in antiquity, so no weapons were found in mounds 2 and 5. Trade items: Baumer 2012, 187–91.

29. Polosmak 1994. Bukker 2011. Ice Princess, kurgan Ak-Alakha 3, mound 1.

30. Polosmak 1994; Molodin 1995 (male tattooed mummy of Ukok). "Siberian Princess" 2012. "Fashion and Beauty Secrets" 2012. The Ice Princess was returned to the Altai Republic in 2012, where she is displayed in a glass sarcophagus in the Republican National Museum. Scythian trade with China and India, Stark et al. 2012, 121–38; "Lost Tribe" 2013.

31. Deer stones, Murphy 2003, 12; deer petroglyphs, Stark et al. 2012, 65–66.

32. Ice Princess as storyteller or shaman: "Siberian Princess" 2012; tattoos as narratives: "Tattooed Mummies" 2012 (Pankova television interview). See Marazov 2011b, 134–38, on art, and presumably tattoos, as "the principle language for recording mythological ideas" on Thracian artifacts. Abstract tattoo symbols may have been a form of "writing," with similarities to tamgas, see chapter 14 on language. Sergey Yatsenko quoted in Lobell and Powell 2013.

33. Mallory and Mair 2008; Barber 2000, 67, 130.

34. Global warming and melting ice, as well as looting and modern roads, threaten the Altai mummies still preserved in permafrost: Gheyle 2006; Han 2008.

35. Natalia Shishlina, in Della Casa and Witt 2013. Reed 2000, citing tattoo entries 285–86 of Duan Chengshi, *Youyang zazu* (ca AD 800–863), 30.

CHAPTER 7
NAKED AMAZONS

1. "Heroic nudity" of Greeks also distinguished them from clothed barbarians in art, Bonfante 1989; Berard 2000; Cohen 2000, 98–131. I use "naked" and "nude" interchangeably here, but for the differences in artistic contexts, see eg Bonfante 1989, 544–47; Cohen 2000, 98n1; and Stewart 1998. Suetonius *Tiberius* 44.2. Sexualized Amazons, Sutton 1981.

2. A 5th-century BC alabastron by the Berlin Painter Z268, Smart Museum 1967.115.339, on display in the Art Institute of Chicago, appears to show a nude Amazon from the back.

3. Cohen 2006, no 51, 196–98.

4. Neils 2000, 208; Berard 2000. Female bathers and nudes in Greek art: Sutton 2009 and Hosoi 2007, 5, see fig 5 for an unusual vase (Priam Painter, ca 510 BC) showing women identified as "nymphs" bathing in an outdoor fountain, with their clothes and accoutrements hanging on branches of trees, see also Sutton 2009, 70 (Helen, 61–62, pl 1); and Schefold 1993, 116–17; Greek women usually wash at basins or fountains in art.

5. White-ground trick party cup from Tanagra, Athens National Museum 408, Beazley 4823 (thanks to Bob Sutton). Volute krater, ca 515 BC, Karkinos Painter, NY Met 21.88.74.

6. Bathing Greek women normally use alabastra. Louvre F 203; ARV2, 4,13; Beazley 200013. Cohen 2006, 196–98.

7. Sponge: Hosoi 2007, 6, fig 6. Resemblance to Amazon-style caps, Steiner 2007, 34; Bothmer 1957, 154; Schefold 1993, 116–17. Special thanks to David Saunders, Bob Sutton, and Jody Maxmin for helpful comments on the Andokides amphora, and to Christine Walter at the Louvre for providing detailed photographs.

8. Narrative sequences and repeated images on vases: Steiner 2007, 17–39. Schefold 1993, 119, fig 138–9, Heracles and Amazons, red-figure amphora by Andokides Painter, 520–510 BC, Orvieto, Museo Civico, Coll. Faina 64—side A. Bothmer 1957, 131, 133 pl 69.1; *LIMC* 1 Amazones 61.

9. Steiner 2007, 33–34. The swimmers are Amazons: Bothmer 1957, 153–54; Schefold 1993, 116–17; Stewart 1998, 118–20; Cohen 2006, 197. Cf Sutton 2009, 70.

10. Colvin 1883, 363, 366, 367–68. I. Krauskopf in *Amazonen* 2010, 45–46.

11. Nude Amazons also appear on mirrors, lamps, and figurines of this period; eg Etruscan mirror, 3rd century BC, incised with nude Amazon in Phrygian cap, Edinburgh Museum of Science and Art, 1887. Amazons in Roman art, Leal 2010, 47–52, 47n216, *LIMC* no 546; see Leal's table 1 for all Amazon images in Roman-era art cataloged in *LIMC*. Gold relief box, J. Fornasier in *Amazonen* 2010, 34 and 57, photos. Greek roughly pulling nude Amazon from her horse, Roman blue glass gem, British Museum 1923,0401.778. Two Amazons, Metropolitan Museum, New York 10.131.4.

12. Boston MFA 27.682, from Cyprus, attributed to the Semon Master, dated by Boardman, *Archaic Greek Gems* (1968) to "around 500 BC" or early 5th century BC; Beazley, *Lewes House Gems* no 031, 25, 94–95, no 031, pls 2 and 9, "her chiton [is] drawn up so as to expose the pubes, . . . rendered by four pellets . . . very rare." Bothmer 1957, 123, pl 90.3. Depilation, Berard 2000, 392.

13. Herodotus 4.74–75. See "Fashion and Beauty Secrets" 2012 and Stewart 2012, for cosmetics residues in Scythian graves.

CHAPTER 8
SEX AND LOVE

1. Tyrrell 1984, 40. Blok 1995, 67–68, 262–63.

2. Herodotus 1.203: people of the Caucasus have sex outdoors; so did the Mossynoeci of Pontus, Xenophon *Anabasis* 5.4 and Apollonious *Argonautica* 2. Tyrrell

1984, 42, 45–49, 52–55. Sexual voracity of warrior women, Gera 1997, 82–83. "Asexual/antisexual," Fowler 2013, 541.

3. For a modern example of this pattern among Cossacks, Rothery 1910, 64–65.

4. Strabo 11.11.8; 11.9.1; 11.13.11; cf 7.3.3–5. Note that Strabo used the words for "women" and "men," which are often translated in English as "wives" and "husbands." Herodotus 2.64; 5.9, Sigynni of Thrace; Agathyrsi, 4.104. Xenophon *Anabasis* 5.4.33. Herodotus 1.216; Strabo 11.8.6. Polyandry/polyamory among the Yuezhi, Tochari, and Xiongnu: Minns 1913, 93. Colarusso 2002, 52 and 54n5. Herodotus 4.172 and 180, for similar "free love" customs among nomads of North Africa, including a staff in the ground to signal sex in progress. Companionate marriage = union based on friendship, equality, interchangeable roles, and shared responsibilities and social network.

5. Tyrrell 1984; Dowden 1997; Stewart 1995.

6. Tyrrell 1984, 45–55. Fantham et al. 1994, 68–135. Blok 1995, 272. Herodotus 4.110–17; 5.6.1.

7. Diodorus 3.53, after young women had served as fighters, they had children and served as leaders. Aelian *Historical Miscellany* 12.38.

8. Strabo 11.5.1–4. Summer, because the Caucasus is snowbound the rest of the year. Blok 1995, 91–92, compares Strabo's story to Herodotus's Sarmatian tale. Early European travelers in Abkhazia (ancient Colchis) reported liberal sexual mores but noted that decorum restricted sex to nighttime. Traditional Circassian social norms allowed married women to chose other lovers. Klaproth 1814, 207, sharing "wives" among Abasse (Abkhazians); night sex, 264–65. Jaimoukha 2001, 165–66. Etruscan women and men were promiscuous, and all children were raised without knowing who the fathers were: Theopompus of Chios (4th century BC) *FGrHist* F 204 (Athenaeus 517d–518a).

9. Strabo 11.2.15–16; 11.2.19; 12.2.3; Justin 18.5.4. Quote: Philostratus *On Heroes* 57. Dioscurias: Mayor 2010, 89–91, 335. Exogamy among Circassians: Jaimoukha 2001, 165–66. Chadwick and Zhirmunsky 2010 on bride quests.

10. Plutarch *Theseus* 26. *Traité* 1981, section 85; the Latin physiognomy treatise was based on ancient Greek sources; Rousselle in Schmitt Pantel 1992, 327–28.

11. Bothmer 1957, 152, nos 67–77. Basel, Antikenmuseum und Sammlung Ludwig KA403. Lissarrague 1990, 185, fig 107. "Kalos" inscriptions were usually associated with homosexual male eroticism. On more than 100 heterosexual courting scenes on red-figure vases, Sutton 1981, esp 276–447.

12. Athens 15002, from Delphi. Bothmer 1957, 152, 157; Lissarrague 1990, 119–20, fig 11; and 1992, 227–29, fig 63 reads "Theriachme." Erotic hunt/rabbit gifts, Barringer 2001, 89–124. The two Pasiades Painter alabastra: Cohen 2006, 211–12; Neils 2000, 221–22.

13. Tyrrell 1984, 48.

14. Tyrrell 1984, 54.

15. Philostratus *On Heroes* 57.

16. Bothmer 1957, 95–97. Woodford 2003, 100, fig 72.

17. Herodotus 4.26.2.

18. Eg Sagas 26 and 27, Colarusso 2002, 3–4, 86–87, 129–34. Klaproth 1814, 236. Davis-Kimball 2002, 43–44.

19. Studies of heterosexual behavior around the world correlate gender equality with more sexual activity and enhanced subjective sexual fulfillment for both partners. Analysis of sexual behaviors in 37 countries in 2011 demonstrated that in cultures where women and men are treated as equals, marital and casual sex was more frequent. A study of 29 countries found that self-reported physical and emotional feelings of sexual well-being of men and women were more positive in countries with gender equality compared to male-centered, patriarchal cultures. Baumeister and Mendoza 2011, "sexual economics" data on heterosexual relations. Laumann et al. 2006.

20. As in Sparta, Xenophon *Lac. Pol.* 1.3–5.

21. Xenophon *Oeconomicus* 7.4–10; *Symposium* 7–9.

22. Lee 2007, 268–75. Xenophon *Anabasis* 4.3.18–19; 6.1.11–13; the text uses both masculine and feminine forms of the Greek word for the "companions." It is not clear whether the companions actually fought, but as Lee (273) notes, the reply reveals the men's ease with and high regard for the women accompanying the army. Demetrius of Phalerum, a 4th-century BC philosopher in Athens, remarked that the Greeks' reply cast their female companions as Amazons and denigrated the Persian king at the same time. Vase paintings of women performing military dances with armor and weapons, Bron 1996.

CHAPTER 9
DRUGS, DANCE, AND MUSIC

1. Female alcoholics rare: Aelian *Historical Miscellany* 2.41. Scholiast, Apollonius *Argonautica* 2.946; Pseudo-Scymnus 986–97; Hecataeus *FGrHist* 802 F 3. Blok 1995, 153–54. Sinope's Amazon traditions, Vlassopoulos 2013, 183; Braund 2010, 16–23; procession of armed women, Aeneas Tacticus 40.4.

2. "To seize," Robinson 1906, 147. *Sanapai*, John Colarusso, per corr May 20, 2013.

3. Scythian heavy drinkers, "maenadic frenzy": Anacreon 3.43 (ca 550 BC). Herodotus 6.84; Aelian *Historical Miscellany* 2.41. Lebedynsky 2010, 167.

4. Nart saga: Colarusso 2002, Saga 55, 216–18. Archaeology of wine and amphoras in Scythian sites, Minns 1913, 49, 82; Rolle 1989, 92–93; Dugan 2009, 7 and 24–25, wine in ancient Scythia.

5. This is one of several versions of Cyrus's death. Herodotus 1.211–14; Diodorus 2.44; Strabo 11.8.5–9; Justin 1.8. See also Gera 1997, 195–203; Tomyris is thought by some to be Turkic for "iron," 187n2.

6. Murphy 2003, 10, 13.

7. Homer *Iliad* 13.5–6. The first use of "Scythian," Hesiod fragment in Strabo 7.3.7, "mare-milking milk-drinking Scythians." Hippocrates *De Morbis* 4 and Strabo 7.4.6, mare's milk and cheese. Koumiss is similar to but not the same as kefir, a fermented, less alcoholic milk drink of the Caucasus.

8. Herodotus 4.2. West 1999. Lebedynsky 2010, 165–67. Rolle 1989, 116–17. Koumiss in Caucasus legends, Hunt 2012, 25; Chadwick and Zhirmunsky 2010, 233; Lewis 1974.

9. Outram et al. 2009. Thanks to Graham Hardin, Kyrgyzstan, per corr May 13, 2013.

10. Minns 1913, 81. Dugan 2009, 21–23, 28. Wilde 1999, 67. Rolle 1989, 103–5, Chertomlyk vessel for wine. Polosmak 1994. Horse sacrifice and meat, Klaproth 1814, 316, 337.

11. Baumer 2012, 114, *Saka haumavarga*, Persian inscription.

12. Dugan 2009, 21–27. Pliny 21.95.77–78; Mayor 2010, 88–89. Klaproth 1814, 208, 244, 228 (intoxicating spring water in the Caucasus). Opium was given to horses before their riders set off on particularly arduous treks in Central Asia.

13. Olsen and Harding 2008, 86–87, hemp in Botai and other ancient sites, esp Kazakhstan. Barber 1991, 15–19 and "Archaeolinguistics of Hemp," 36–38. Cannabis, ephedra (plant stimulant), and haoma: Barber 2000, 159–61.

14. Herodotus 4.74. Greek *kannabis* has Iranian-Scytho-Sarmatian origins.

15. Herodotus 1.202.

16. Herodotus 4.73–75; and Strassler's comments *Landmark Herodotus* 2007, 311 and fig 4.73, and appendix E, 755. "Naïve," "pure hemp seeds" equated with hashish, Rolle 1989, 93–94. "Down to Seeds and Stems Again Blues," Commander Cody and the Lost Planet Airmen, 1971.

17. Rudenko 1970, 34–36, 62, 197, 199–200, 284–85, pls 35, 61c, 62, 63. Rolle 1989, 93–94. Lebedynsky 2010, 236–38. Murphy 2003, 32. Berel grave goods: Samashev 2011. Hemp seeds contain protein and essential fatty acids; coriander seeds contain linalool, thought to reduce stress when the smoke is inhaled; ephedra is a stimulant. Coriander seeds, "Siberian Princess" 2012. Opium and hashish, *Landmark Herodotus* 2007, 755. Sulimirsky 1970, 34–35 and fig 7; Hanks 2008, 25–27. Hemp tea infusions in India: Klaproth 1814, 271. Romania: Anthony 2007, 362.

18. Lebedynsky 2010, 238. Rolle 1989, 94–95. A "veritable witches' cupboard of natural" mind-altering plants were known to Scythian shamans, including *Amanita muscaria* (fly agaric) mushrooms used by Siberian tribes and by the Scythian shamans known as Agari, and *Ephedra sinica*, a stimulant found tied in bundles in Central Asian burials, Barber 2000, 159–64. Davis-Kimball 2012 believes that women buried with weapons excavated in Kazakhstan were shaman warrior priestesses who knew secrets of mushrooms and herbs. Phoenix and Arabeth 1999 citing Schultes 1976.

19. Amazons blowing trumpets, Bothmer 1957, 154, 156, 157, 181, 201, 205.

20. Xenophon *Anabasis* 6.1.1–13 described various regional military dances performed by Greek soldiers.

21. Bron 1996, figs 1, 7, 8, 9. Naples H3010, female war dancer in the Temple of Artemis. Ceccarelli 1998.

22. Bron 1996.

23. Cities founded by Amazons, Strabo 12.3.21. The Artemis temple was built upon a Bronze Age sanctuary. Pliny 34.19.53. Pausanias 7.2.7. Ridgway 1974. Bol 1998. Richter 1959. Plutarch *Greek Questions* 56. Some heads of the marble Amazon copies may have come from other statues, but all classical Amazon statues have similar expressions.

24. Pliny 34.18.48 and 34.19.82. Tzetzes *Posthomerica* 176–83 includes "Knemis" among the Amazons who fought at Troy.

25. Callimachus *Hymn to Artemis* 3.237–47, 3.270; West 2011, 123, relates this to the Amazon Myrine in the *Iliad*. Callimachus fr. 693, the seven daughters were known as the Peleiades, Fowler 2013, 416.

26. Bron 1996, 77–79, humorous pyrrhic, 76. Aelian *On Animals* 12.9. Traditional sword dances performed by women persist in the Middle East, Africa, Scotland, and Asia.

27. Rolle 1989, 95. Rudenko 1970. Music on the steppes, Chadwick and Zhirmunsky 2010, 25. The "harp" was probably bowed, see Basilov 1989, 152–59. Xie Jin 2005.

CHAPTER 10
THE AMAZON WAY

1. Diodorus 2.45–46. Justin 2.4; cf Orosius 1.15–16. Weaving and gender, Gera 1997, 20–21.

2. Mimnermus fr. 2a; Blok 1995, 31. Hippocrates *On Joints* 53. Herodotus 4.2.

3. West 1999, 78n10. Hippocrates *Airs, Waters, Places* 22. Murphy 2003, 51, 64, male and female dislocated joints at Tuva. Genetic and developmental hip dysplasia more common in some ethnic groups; Mongolia, see Wilhelm et al. 2012. Murphy 2004, esp 174.

4. Tyrrell 1984, 55. Strabo 11.5.1. Greek heroes such as Theseus and Achilles were fostered; historical examples of fosterage include Philip of Macedon, raised in Thebes; Cyrus of Persia grew up in Media; and Tigranes II of Armenia was fostered in Persia: Mayor 2010, 136. Fosterage and exogamy in the Caucasus, Abercromby 1891; Klaproth 1814, 265–66. Chadwick and Zhirmunsky 2010, 31. The idea that Scythian mothers sent boys away to fathers appears in Herodotus's account (4.9.4) of a Scythian origin tale heard in Pontus: Heracles fathered three sons with the half-woman, half-serpent mother of the Scythian race. She offered to send the boys to be raised by Heracles.

5. Jordanes 8.56–57. Philostratus *On Heroes* 57. In antiquity, daughters were thought of as "of" or "like" their mothers, while sons "belonged" to fathers. In Greek literature, the lineage of Amazons queens is usually matrilineal.

6. Pseudo-Plutarch *On Rivers* 14. See chapter 18 for late traditions claiming that Penthesilea had a son with Achilles (Cayster) and that the Amazon Clete had a son in Italy (Caulon).

7. Strabo 11.5.3. Amazons and weak men, Gera 1997, 91, 120, 147.

8. Rolle 1989, 24–25, 29, 32, Davis-Kimball 2002, 46–49. Wilde 1999, 49. Hanks 2008, 20, 22–23. Murphy 2003, 11. Guliaev 2003, 115.

9. Tyrrell 1984, 54–55.

10. Davis-Kimball 2002, 35–45. Colarusso 2002, 4–5.

11. Bothmer 1957, 91. All of these activities appear in ancient literature or art. Strabo 11.5.1–2. Klaproth 1814; Bryce 1878.

12. Herodotus 4.31; 4.8.3; 4.23–28. Ammianus Marcellinus 31.2. Pseudo-Plutarch *On Rivers* 14. Cato *On Farming* extols the virtues of cabbage.

13. Davis-Kimball 2002, 33–35, 37. Vladislav Malakhov quoted on residues in Stewart 2012.

14. Diodorus 2.44. Apollonius *Argonautica* 2.360–406. Castellani vase, Florence 3773 Museo Archeologico Etrusco; Bothmer 1957, 14; Blok 1995, 149n10, 376–77. Herodotus 4.23 (felt tents); clay wagons, see *Landmark Herodotus* 2007, fig 4.46. Nomad lifestyle: Ammianus Marcellinus 31.2. Rolle 1989 and Rolle in *Amazonen* 2010, 121–28, wagons and archaeological discovery of fortified Scythian-Greek city near Bel'sk.

15. Homer *Iliad* 3.182–90, cf 4.178–90. Priam and Hittites, Blok 1995, 100–107; 288–347. Garstang 1929.

16. Strabo 11.2.18; 12.3.29–37. Macurdy 1975, 10–11. Konstan 2002. Council of women, Jaimoukha 2001, 164–65. Jones 2000, 30.

17. Ammianus Marcellinus 31.2.

18. Davis-Kimball 2002, 35–45. Genghis Khan's dispersal of powers to women and proclamations of gender equality, Weatherford 2010, 28–29, 32–37.

19. These and the following passages about the Argonauts on Amazon Island are from Apollonius *Argonautica* 2.360–406; 2.911–29; 2.965–1001; 2.1168–78. Lykastia, Scylax *Periplus*; Stephanus of Byzantium; Pomponius Mela 1.9; Pliny 6.3, etc; *Cambridge Ancient History* 1971, 1:399–401. Apollonius uses a male eponym *Chadesios* for the Amazons. Chadesiai, Hecataeus fr. 7; see Fowler 2013, 289–91.

20. Cybele's black stone and meteors: Livy 29.11.7; Mayor 2010, 268–69. Diodorus 3.55.7–9.

21. Pliny 6.13.32; Pomponius Mela 2.7; Doksanalti and Mimiroglu 2011, 86. Aretias/Ares/Amazon Island was called Khalkeritis during the Roman Empire; also known as Kerasus Island, Island of Mars, Areos Nesos, Puga Island.

22. *Hurriyet Daily News* 2010. Doksanalti and Mimiroglu 2011. *Hamza*, "strong, steadfast."

23. Neither of the round black boulders is a meteorite. Doksanalti and Mimiroglu 2011, 95; Doksanalti, Mimiroglu, and Gulec 2011. Holes cut in bedrock similar to the offering holes for Cybele worship are found at Gobustan, Azerbaijan, south of the Marpesian Rock, a region also associated with Amazons.

24. Scythian horse sacrifices, Baumer 2012, 98–99.

25. Bothmer 1957, 109, 160.

26. Scythian religion and sacrifices, Herodotus 4.59–76. Mayor 2010, 262. Chinese accounts, Murphy 2003, 23. Sun worship and horse sacrifice, Baumer 2012, 98–99.

27. Herodotus 4.5–7 (gold and fire). Murphy 2003, 12, 14, 22.

CHAPTER 11
HORSES, DOGS, AND EAGLES

1. Lysias *Funeral Oration* 4. Abkhaz Nart saga, Colarusso 2002, 360–61. Lebedynsky 2010, 132–39. Residues of horse milk and meat on pottery by 4500 BC in western Eurasia; history of horse domestication/riding: Beckwith 2009, 60–61;

Baumer 2012, 83–86. West 1999; Anthony 2007, 193–224; thanks to Graham Harden, Kyrgyzstan, per corr May 13, 2013. Olsen and Harding 2008. Strabo 11.5.1; 12.8.6. Nomadic horse culture: Ammianus Marcellinus 31.2. Ancient horsemanship, Anderson 1961. Special thanks to Kris Ellingsen for horse knowledge and to Kent Madin and Linda Svendsen, for riding traditions of Central Asia.

2. Weatherford 2010, 120–21. Colarusso 2002, Saga 30, 169: one rider on either side and one in the middle could control a large horse herd. Baumer 2012, 86.

3. Kohanov 2001. Rolle in *Amazonen* 2010, 160–63. Gender and horses, Olsen and Harding 2008. On the far eastern steppes, grave evidence suggests that eating horse meat was a masculine activity, while horse riding and hunting were female activities: Shelach 2008, 103–105.

4. Justin 9.2–3.

5. Raiding horses in early modern times, Klaproth 1814; Bryce 1878; horse rustling in Caucasus Nart lore, Hunt 2012, 130–46; and Colarusso 2002, 169. Pausanias 1.21.5–6, each Sarmatian nomad "owns many mares." Murphy 2003, 11. Samashev and Francfort 2002. Horses' prominence in steppe cultures, Chadwick and Zhirmunsky 2010, 48, 95, 119–22.

6. Kohanov 2001, 52–56; Harrison 2012.

7. Strabo 7.4.8. Ammianus Marcellinus 17.12.2. Breaking stallions: Colarusso 2002, 360–61. Pliny 8.66.165. Pausanias 1.21.6. Rolle 1989 101–9. Cernenko 1983, 39.

8. Strabo 17.3.6–7; Arrian *Cynegeticus* 23–24 cited in Anderson 1961, 118–19. Thanks to Linda Svendsen for insight into the scene.

9. On the development of bridle bits on the steppes, Baumer 2012, 84–87; stirrups relatively late invention, spreading from Central Asia to Europe in the Middle Ages. *Jigit*, Hunt 2012.Vase from Etruria, Bothmer 1957, 111; Shapiro 1983, 112n46. Thanks to Roberta Beene for horse sense and Parthian shot techniques.

10. Herodotus 4.28.4; Strabo 7.3.18. Cernenko 1983, 39, suggests three types: scarce Akhal Teke types, small all-purpose horses, and even smaller horses used for meat. Horse pemmican was made by drying and pounding strips of meat with salt and spices, Chadwick and Zhirmunsky 2010. Surprising genetics of horses buried at Arzhan 1 and 2 (chapter 4) showed "considerable distance from Przewalski's horse, Baumer 2012, 184–85.

11. Weatherford 2010, 118–19.

12. Amazons with horses in art, Bothmer 1957, 22; 97–110, 175–84. Herodotus 4.52. Homer *Iliad* 10.423–514. Xenophon *Anabasis* 7.3.26. Strabo 11.13.7. Rolle 1989, 95–99.

13. Colvin 1883, 358, 365–66. Amazon charioteers in vase paintings, Bothmer 1957, 84–88, 106–9

14. Strabo 11.11.8; 11.14.9. Herodotus 4.189.3; 4.193; 5.9.

15. Nettos Painter, amphora, 7th century BC, NY, Metropolitan Museum 11.210.1. A vase by the Suessula Painter (fig. 11.2) depicts what appears to be an Amazon dressed in Median style driving a four-hourse chariot with a barbarian male passenger, while a similarly attired Amazon with a *sagaris* leads the way. Thanks to Michael Padgett for useful discussion of this scene; Padgett 2014.

16. Rhyton, Boston Museum of Fine Arts 21.2286. Bothmer 1957, 222; Cohen 2006, 284–87 with photos.

17. Maslow 1997. The horse breed, first registered in 1897, was named for the Akhal oasis and the Teke tribe of Turkmenistan. Harrison 2012, 307–12. Thanks to Linda Svendsen, who rode an Akhal Teke in Turkmenistan, for helpful comments.

18. Klaproth 1814, 222, 268–69—the symbol appears in the illustration of tamgas of the northwest Caucasus on p 18, bottom row, in Lebedynsky 2011. Thanks to Maya Muratov, per corr Dec 9, 2012. Other traditional brands in the Caucasus were horseshoes and triskelions.

19. Brands on horses, eg the hydria in Basel by the Archippe Painter and Vatican Painter amphora 530 BC, Minneapolis Institute of Art 57.1. Athenian cavalry brands, Kroll 1977. Amazon branded horse by the Woolly Satyr Painter, New York 07.286.84; he painted other branded horses, eg San Antonio 86.134.76. Moore 1971, 378–81.

20. Sulimirski 1970; Brzezinski and Mielczarek 2002, 10–11, 35–37, 46.

21. Rudenko 1970; Minns 1913, 46–49; 155–65; Xenophon *On Horsemanship* 7; Rolle 1989, 103–6. Herodotus 4.22; Aelian *Historical Miscellany* 12.37. Bothmer 1957, 104.

22. Herodotus 1.215. Rolle in *Amazonen* 2010, 160–63.

23. See Edmunds 1997, on an Athenian legend about a girl buried with a horse (mentioned by the orator Aeschines in 346 BC, later by Callimachus, Ovid, and Dio Chrysostom), a folk explanation for an ancient site in Athens known as the "place of the Horse and the Maiden." It was said that a maiden named Leimone had been punished by her father Hippomenes for losing her virginity. Leimone ("Meadow") is not a known Athenian name; Hippomenes ("Horse Spirit") was the name of the suitor who raced Atalanta in the myth. Leimone was locked up with a horse, which killed her; both were entombed. In later versions, the girl was intimate with her horse; her punishment was to be raped and devoured by the horse. Was an actual burial of a girl and a horse discovered in antiquity and explained by the strange, morbid tale, or did an ancient monument in Athens depicting a girl and a horse arouse speculation and storytelling? Burials with sacrificed horses are very rare in Greece (archaeologists know one archaic instance of horses buried with a man and woman at Lefkandi, Euboea). Among the Scythian nomads, sacrificed horses were typical of burials of both men and women of the steppes: Baumer 2012 and see chapter 4. In about 450 BC, Herodotus described such sacrifices of horses and their placement in graves in great detail. Was Leimone once the heroine of an old tale about another would-be Greek "Amazon"? The legend suggests that the Greeks, when confronted with evidence of a girl closely associated with a horse, resorted to their tragic mythic script of a violent death for a sexually free young woman—the same fate meted out to Amazons.

24. Lebedynsky 2010, 232–36. Ivantchik 2011; Rolle 1989. Brzezinski and Mielczarek 2002, 35–36. Genetics, Baumer 2012, 184–85.

25. Berel grave goods: Samashev and Francfort 2002; pollen in the horses' intestines indicated they were killed in autumn. Keyser-Tracqui et al. 2005.

26. Lebedynsky 2010, 255–76. Ammianus Marcellinus 23.6.31 and 50. Other theories about antlered horse masks, Baumer 2012, 187–88.

27. Herodotus 4.13; 4.27. Bolton 1962, 37–75, 181. See Marazov 2011a, 247–48. Mayor 2009, 22–33. Thanks to Linda Svendsen for horse details.

28. A dog runs alongside an Amazon, Philadelphia 4832, ca 525 BC; many other Amazons' dogs, Bothmer 1957, eg 51, 103, 109. Xenophon *On Hunting* 13.18.

29. Olsen and Harding 2008, 69. Herodotus 4.22.

30. Strabo 11.4.4–5. Hunting dogs in Scythian art, Lebedynsky 2010, 149. Hunt 2012.

31. Cybele on lion, late 5th century BC, Boston 10.187; a peculiar vase (Theseus Painter, 500 BC, Boston 99.523) shows an Amazon archer riding on a lion and confronting a monster. Shields: Bothmer 1957. Chase 1902, 97–115. Atalanta was associated with lions, see the prologue. Aelian *On Animals* 6.2, 15.14, 18.26; Aelian *Historical Miscellany*; Semiramis, 12.39, italics added; frieze, Gera 1997, 78–79.

32. Ancient history of falconry and hawking, Epstein 1943, 497–505. Weatherford 2010, 15. Ctesias cited by Aelian *Historical Miscellany* 12.39. Horse, dog, and eagles in Caucasus tales: Colarusso 2002, 57–58, 67, 72, 127, 171; Hunt 2012, 11, 191. In Kyrgyz and Kazakh epics, eg Chadwick and Zhirmunsky 2010, 48, 86.

33. The eagle is simply called a "flying bird" in the text for gold ring, Museum of Fine Arts, Boston 21.1204.

34. Hunting eagles perch on carved Y-shaped wooden supports that fit into heavy leather sheaths on the right side of the horse. Zhumatov 2012.

35. Thanks to Linda Svendsen and Kent Madin for sharing their experiences of eagle hunting on horseback in Kazakhstan. Elizabeth Barber brought the falconer's mitt at Urumchi to my attention. Tarim mummies: Mallory and Mair 2008; falconry and the woman's leather mitt: Barber 2000, 28, 196–99, fig 10.3.

36. Zhumatov 2012. Video interview: reuters.com/video/2012/03/08/female-eagle-hunter-reaches-new-heights?videoId=231446109&videoChannel=4. Falcon and eagle hunting in Nart sagas, Hunt 2012, 21.

37. Herodotus 4.134; rabbit hunting; hunting artifacts and weapons in women's burials, Shelach 2008, 104–5 and fig 5.1.

CHAPTER 12
WHO INVENTED TROUSERS?

1. Scythian clothing was clearly "tailored," often fur-lined with decorative seams, scallops, and fringe, notes Gleba 2008, 20–22; see Rubinson 1990. Recent analyses of 13th century BC nomad trousers reveal complex tailoring innovations to facilitate horseback riding: Beck et al. 2014 with detailed photographs and drawings showing trouser construction. Barber 2000, 17, 25, 27, 37–39, 108, 188, fig 2.11 and pl 1; Baumer 2012, 134, 217. Ancient textiles, Barber 1991. Neolithic leather leggings of tanned goatskin recovered from the Swiss Alps are analyzed by A. Schlumbaum et al., *Journal of Archaeological Science* 37, 6 (June 2010): 1247–51.

2. Strabo 11.13.7–10. Miller 2004, 169.

3. Atossa and Rhodogyne: Gera 1997, 8, 141–58. Rhodogyne, Aeschines *Aspasia*; Philostratus *Imagines* 2.5. Bonfante 2011, 20, erroneously states that Herodotus gave credit for trousers to Tomyris.

4. Gera 1997, 65–83; Justin 1.12; Ctesias cited by Diodorus 2.4–20. Life story of Semiramis, Ctesias [Llewellyn-Jones and Robson] 2010, 116–30.

5. Herodotus 1.71; 3.87; 5.49; 7.61–87 describes in detail the attire and weapons of the myriad eastern tribes who joined the vast army of the Persian king Xerxes in 480 BC. See also Xenophon *Anabasis* 1.5.8. Gleba 2008. Barber 2000. On barbarian dress, Bonfante 1989.

6. Hippocrates *Airs Waters Places* 22. To ride "comfortably on a horse with legs on either side of a horse, trousers are necessary," Linduff and Rubinson 2008, 125.

7. Strabo 11.13.9–10. Shapiro 1983. Miller 2004, 183–86. Ivantchik 2006; Vlasso-poulos 2013, 178–79; 186–88. Ethnicity, costume, and language, Mayor, Colarusso, and Saunders 2014.

8. Miller 2004, 184. Ovid *Trist.* 11.34. Diodorus 17.77. Xenophon *On Horseman-ship* 7 and 12. Xenophon also mentions cavalry armor "thigh pieces," Anderson 1961, 85–86. Herodotus 1.7: trousers and shirts of leather indicate a rugged life; but cf 5.49, trousers indicate easily defeated warriors. Pelling 1997, 9.

9. Miller 2004, 155–56, 183–86.

10. Aristophanes *Assemblywomen* 654; Xenophon *On Horsemanship* 7; Rolle 1989; Anderson 1961, 86.

11. Klaproth 1814, 287. Bai 1995.

12. Beckwith 2009, 71. *Zhan Guo Ce*, "Chronicles of the Warring States," ch 19, trans. G. W. Bonsall, http://lib.hku.hk/bonsall/zhanguoce/index1.html. Cultural evolution of pants: Turchin 2012.

13. Strabo 11.5.1; 11.8.7. Justin 2.2; cf Plutarch *Pompey* 35. Ammianus Marcelli-nus 31.2. Ovid cited in Rolle 1989, 58.

14. Herodotus 7.61–93. Urartu mounted archers with pointed hats and trousers, Brestian 2005–7. Lebedynsky 2006 and 2010; Baumer 2012, 184.

15. Scythian and Amazon attire, Gleba 2008. London B 210, Boardman 1983, 72. Amazons in art: Muth 2008, Bothmer 1957.

16. Bothmer 1957, 171, 104–5. Shapiro 1983, 112–14. Cohen 2012. Euripides *Ion* 1141–62.

17. Louvre G197, Bothmer 1957, 128.

18. Orvieto, Faina 64, Andokides vase, see Bothmer 1957, 133–34; 16, 28 for ex-amples of bulls' horns on Amazon helmets. London 1899.7–21.5, Polygnotus Group, 470–450 BC.

19. Bothmer 1957, 222; Cohen 2006, 284–87 with photos.

20. Eg Bothmer 1957, 163.

21. Example of painted clothing of Scythian archer from Temple at Aegina, Cohen 2006, 192, fig 5. Stewart 1995, 592.

22. Bonfante 2011, 19–22. Shapiro 1983. Lebedynsky 2009, 16–19. Bothmer 1957. Gleba 2008. Strabo 11.11.8 mentioned Tapyri nomad women's short hair and white clothing. Sturgeon 1985, 493.

23. Klaproth 1814, 287. Rothery 1910, 57; Anderson 1978, 47; Sturgeon 1995, 493. Ankle guards, Bothmer 1957, 205, 220–21, and pl 84.2. London 1899.7–21.5, Polygnotus Group. Expert riders use spurs to give horses very specific cues that could mean life or death in battle. The round "nub" shown on the heel guards in fig. 12.2 might have indicated use as spurs; thanks to Roberta Beene for this insight.

24. Minns 1913, 53–64. Lebedynsky 2009, 48, 51–75. Rolle 1989, 57–59 with photos and drawings.

25. Rolle 1989, 47–61. Rubinson 1990. Murphy 2003, 6–7, 31–32, 35–36. Polosmak 2001, 120–21. Minns 1913, 57. Polosmak and Barkova 2005, 66, 85.

26. Wagner et al. 2009 point out that the owner of the trousers could have been male or female. The tapestry pieces are in the Urumchi Museum. Thanks to John Boardman for bringing this find to my attention.

27. Murphy 2003, 6–7, 19; Rudenko 1970; Minns 1913. Herodotus 1.215. First Amazon wearing spotted pelt, on vase by Prometheus Painter, Bothmer 1957, 18.

28. Boots and hats: Herodotus 7.64. Examples of caps in art and archaeology, Aruz et al. 2000, 50–51 and fig 48; Polosmak 1994, 98; Davis-Kimball 2002, 103; Barber 2000; Mallory and Mair 2008; Murphy 2003, 6, 9, 35. Soft felt hat with lappets, like those worn by Scythians and Amazons, Pazyryk barrow 3, Hermitage 1685/16, Stark et al. 2012, 127, fig 7.21. Minns 1913, 55–57, 62, 210, 420. Rolle 1989, 47–51. Arzhan 2, burial 5: http://www.dainst.org/en/project/russian-federation -tuva-arzhan?ft=all. Examples of Amazon pointed and "Phrygian" hats on vases, Bothmer 1957, pls 64, 72, 76–78, 80–81, 84–86; and New York 10.210.19 and 07.286.84; Boston 99.524; Philadelphia 1752; Providence 34.859; Louvre K544.

CHAPTER 13
ARMED AND DANGEROUS: WEAPONS AND WARFARE

1. Lysias *Funeral Oration* 2. Colarusso 2002, Saga 49, 190–92. Ancient ironworking in Caucasus, Anthony 2007, 224–36, iron-forging site, 5th century BC, Rolle 1989, 119–22.

2. Rolle in *Amazonen* 2010, 152–59.

3. Rolle 1989, 66. Alabastron, Emporion Painter, Hermitage, St Petersburg. Thanks to ancient archery expert Jack Farrell for assessing the accuracy of the image. Scythian bows: Baumer 2012, 35–38.

4. Rolle 1989, 65–66. Zak Crawford set world record longest bow and arrow shot in 2010 with 5-foot recurve bow, pulling weight of 35 pounds. The vase: Vienna 3605 from Cervetri: Bothmer 1957, 81–82, pl 55, 5.

5. Ammianus Marcellinus 22.8.10–13 and 37. Sarmatian archery sets: Brzezinski and Mielczarek 2002, 34. Scythian weapons, Lebedynsky 2010, 188–210. Composite and recurve bows: Baumer 2012, 12, 35, 38, 84, 87, 123, 145, 195, 197, 216–17.

6. Clement of Alexandria, cited by Basilov 1989, 146.

7. Homer *Odyssey* 21.405–51. Herodotus 4.9–10; and cf 3.30, Smerdis was the only Persian able to draw a bow sent by the Kushite king of Nubia/Ethiopia; some said the bow was sent by a Scythian king.

8. Minns 1913, 66–68; Rolle 1989, 64, 66 with drawing; Aruz et al. 2000, 206–10 and pl 146. Many Persian and Parthian coins depict seated archers with recurve bows, Lebedynsky 2006, 53. A gem by Epimenes (ca 500 BC) shows a kneeling archer who has just strung his bow, New York, Richter no 42. Other vase paintings depict archers stringing Scythian bows, eg Beazley Archive 203366 and 203420.

9. Brindley 1994.Other silver staters from Soloi, Cilicia, feature an Amazon head, eg Boston MFA 04.1144. Washington DC Smithsonian Museum of Natural

History 147093 (catalog A378476–0) Keyside class, Leagros Group; Bothmer 1957, 92, pl 59, 3. Thanks to Jack Farrell and members of Asian Traditional Archery Network (ATARN.org) for information on stringing recurve composite bows, and to Roberta Beene for information on thumb release.

10. London E41, Oxford 1927.4065, Berlin 2263 (Oltos); Louvre G197 (Myson); Arezzo 1465 (Euphronios): Bothmer 1957, 124–30; 135–37.

11. Bothmer 1957, 164 (griffin-quiver vase); grave goods, Murphy 2003, 19.

12. Arrowheads, Rudenko 1970; Minns 1913; Stark et al. 2012, many photos; Murphy 2003, 5–8, 17, 19 (bronze, wood, and bone arrowheads of many shapes). Lebedynsky 2009, 40–75. Pausanias 1.21.5, bone arrowheads. Mayor 2009, 83–85. Uses for arrows of different materials, Basilov 1989.

13. Cernenko 1983, 11–13. Murphy 2003, 7–8. Anthony 2007, ch 11, esp 223–24. Thanks to Jack Farrell and ATARN; Karpowicz and Selby 2010; ancient Scythian bow from Xinjiang, http://www.atarn.org/chinese/Yanghai/Scythian_bow_ATARN .pdf. Also see http://www.atarn.org/chinese/scythian_bows.htm.

14. Murphy 2003, 104.

15. Pausanias 1.41.7.

16. Pausanias 1.21.6–7; cf Ammianus Marcellinus 17.12.2. Herodotus 9.22. Brzezinski and Mielczarek 2002, 20–22.

17. Brestian 2005–7, esp 29–30.

18. Herodotus 4.9–10. Arzhan 2, burial 5 excavation reports: Chugunov, Nagler, and Parzinger 2001 and http://www.dainst.org/en/project/russian-federation -tuva-arzhan?ft=all. Baumer 2012, 184.

19. Scythian arrows, poison, and "poison" theory of tiny golden vial: Mayor 2009, 78–85. Rolle 1989, 61–63. Herodotus 4.70. Lucian *Toxaris* 37. Minns 1913, 93, and Murphy 2003, 23, for Xiongnu versions of blood oath. Examples of Amazons carrying fallen companions, Bothmer 1957, 95–97, pl 61. Rolle in *Amazonen* 2010, 152–59.

20. Soltes 1999, 153, figs 29, 42, 43. Weapons excavated in Georgian sites, Tsetskhladze 2011, 96–115.

21. Plutarch *Greek Questions* 45, 2.302a.

22. Herodotus 4.5; 7.64; 1.215. Strabo 11.5.1; 11.8.6. Xenophon *Anabasis* 4.4.16; peltasts from Anatolian hill tribes serving in Persian army often carried light battle-axes (*sagaris*).

23. Murphy 2003, 6–7, 98, fig 6. Tillya Tepe, Lebedynsky 2006, 145; and 2010, 200.

24. Graphic photos of skull injuries from Scythian pointed battle-axes: Jordana et al. 2009. Stark et al. 2012, 26, fig 1.6. Murphy 2003, 98, 69–70, photo pl 33.

25. Bothmer 1957, 62, 187, Louvre G197; Louvre G106; British Museum London 1873,0820.368; Athens 15002.

26. Johannes Aventinus cited by Paulus Hector Mair; Pliny 7.56.201.

27. Bothmer 1957, 181; Herodotus 5.112; 7.92–93. Rolle in *Amazonen* 2010, 152–59.

28. Soltes 1999, 22, 64–65, 74–76, 154–55. Sarmatian spears and swords in burials, Brzezinski and Mielczarek 2002, 23–24, 33–34. Saka weapons, Lebedynsky 2006, 82–152.

29. Murphy 2003, 5–7, 17, 19. Jordana et al. 2009, 1325, fig 12.

30. Bothmer 1957, 202, no 153 pl 84, 1. Slingers appear on coins (eg Aspendos) and vase paintings. Similar pose by male slinger, with two spears stuck in ground, on red-figure vase by Macron (ca 490). Thanks to John Ma for assessing her slinging form.

31. Pliny 37.33.110–12. Mississippi 1997.3.243. Thanks to Linda Svendsen, Nolan Gilles, and David Meadows for roping expertise.

32. Herodotus 7.85; Pausanias 1.21.5; Pomponius Mela 1.11–12; 1.19.7; 1.88–116; 3.38–39 (the Thatae, Sirachi, Phicores, and Iaxamatae); Ammianus Marcellinus 31.2.9; Valerius Flaccus *Argonautica* 6.132; Josephus *Jewish Wars* 7.249–50; Arrian cited in Anderson 1961, 118–19. A golden lasso was the chief weapon of the modern DC comic-book Amazon heroine Wonder Woman, created by W. M. Marston in the 1940s based on Greek mythology. For a modern artist's version of an Amazon lassoing a foe: Brzezinski and Mielczarek 2002, 25, 35.

33. Amazons are shown hurling rocks in the Amazonomachy on New York Metropolitan Museum vase 31.11.13, Bothmer 1957, 162, 173–74, pl 77, 1.

34. Amazon vs Amazon, eg vases Bonn 37; Kyllenios painter, London B 322; Vatican 404; see Bothmer 1957, 11, 26–27, 88–89. Polyaenus 8.60.

35. Many examples of battles are described in detail by Bothmer 1957, 12–84.

36. Malibu 81.AE.219: see Saunders 2014.

37. Munich 2030, noted by Bothmer 1957, 95–96, pl 61, 3.

38. New York 31.11.13, see Bothmer 162, 173–74 pl 77, 1. Harmodios blow and footwork in ancient art and literature, Cook 1989, 57–61; Woodford 2003, 149–50.

39. Naples RC 239, Bothmer 1957, 162–74. Nemytov 2001. http://www.fscclub .com/history/amazon-tactics-e.shtml.

40. Cook 1989, 59, Amazon example in fig 4.

41. Suessula Painter vases, NY Metropolitan Museum 44.11.12 and 44.11.13, Bothmer 1957, 185, 191, pl 81, 3.

CHAPTER 14
AMAZON LANGUAGES AND NAMES

1. Apsyrtos (Absyrtos), Apollonius *Argonautica*, Colarusso 2002, 131.

2. Herodotus 1.215; 3.116; 4.5, 13, 22, 57–59, 62, 70 and 110; 5.4; 7.64; *Landmark Herodotus* 2007, 291–92, 307. Herodotus mistranslated *arimaspi* as "one-eyed." How and Wells 1912, 1:307, 311, 340. Minns 1913, 39. *Skyth* is thought to derive from a northern Iranian word for "archer" and *Saka* may be related to *sag*, Ossetian "deer," Baumer 2012, 198; cf Aruz et al. 2000, 19.

3. See eg Beckwith 2009, 70, and examples of scholars' assumption that all Scythians spoke Iranian in Mayor, Colarusso, and Saunders 2014, n52.

4. Connor 2011.

5. Herodotus 4.108–9.

6. Herodotus 4.110–17. How and Wells 1912, 1:340–41. Pelling 1997. "Mother-tongue" is aptly named, since babies learn language from their mothers. Cf Forster and Renfew 2011, genetic evidence suggests that if male colonists or conquerors greatly outnumber women, then the language of their children is generally pater-

nal. But perhaps this is because the women quickly take up the men's language. There is some evidence that a "women's language" was once used throughout the North Caucasus. This language is reported to have been monosyllabic and tonal. Klaproth 1814, 305.

7. Bothmer 1957, Index of Inscribed Names of Amazons. Comprehensive list of Amazon names: *LIMC*, "Amazones," 1:653; for inscribed names see http://www .avi.unibas.ch.

8. Anthony Snodgrass has written widely on alternative and lost versions of myths depicted on vase paintings; Snodgrass 1998. Thanks to Fred Porta, Richard Martin, and William Hansen for valuable help in translating the Greek names of Amazons.

9. Names and horses in steppe cultures, Chadwick and Zhirmunsky 2010, 48, 85, 119–22.

10. Mayor, Colarusso, and Saunders 2014.

11. Blok 1995, 217–19 (quote).

12. Reconstructing ancient languages from phonology, Anthony 2007, 24–82, 340–69. Lebedynsky 2009, 11–13. Mayor, Colarusso, and Saunders 2014.

13. Mayor, Colarusso, and Saunders 2014.

14. Pausanias 1.2.1; 1.41.7; 2.32.9; 3.25.2–3.

15. Klaproth 1814 described many different tamga brands in the Caucasus. Tamga-like brands appear on some animals in Attic vase paintings. Baumer 2012, 157–64. Samashev 2013. Dratchuk 1975; Lebedynsky 2011. The American-Mongolian Deer Stone Project 2006–9 (Smithsonian and the Mongolian Academy of Sciences) digitally recorded Altai stones' locations and images http://www.mnh.si.edu /Arctic/html/pdf/2009_mongolia_report_online_version.pdf.

16. Pankova's comments in "Tattooed Mummies" 2012.

17. Harmatta 1999, 421; Rolle 1989, 46–51, inscription fig 28. Murphy 2003, 23. Wooden tablets inscribed with Kharosthi script (2nd century AD) have been found in Xinjiang, China. Kharosthi inscriptions on leather, Tarim area: Barber 2000, 111–12; Baumer 2012, 206 and 291; Lebedynsky 2006, 217.

18. Polyaenus 8.55.

19. Ctesias *History of Persia*, pp 107, 158. Gera 1997, 97

20. *Greek Alexander Romance* (trans. Stoneman) 1991, 143–45, cf Armenian *Romance of Alexander* 1969 (trans. Wolohojian), 141–43, lines 251–54.

CHAPTER 15
HIPPOLYTE AND HERACLES

1. Homer *Iliad* 3.188–89, 6.186. Langdon 2001. Versions of Hippolyte myth: Apollodorus *Library* 2.5.9; Diodorus 2.46.4; 4.16; Pausanias 5.10.9; Euripides *Heracles Furens* 408ff; Apollonius *Argonautica* 2.777 and 2.966; Quintus *Fall of Troy* 1.20–25; 6.240–45; Tzetzes *Chiliades* 2.309ff and *Scholia on Lycophron* 1327; Hyginus *Fabula* 30.

2. Justin 2.4; Orosius 1.15 (nine); Herodotus 4.110 (three).

3. Justin 2.4; Orosius 1.15.

4. Diodorus 2.46.4.

5. Herodotus 4.110–17 treats the Greek mission as ancient Athenian history.

6. Gantz 1993, 1:398. Hard 2004, 263–64. Herodotus 4.10–13. Minns 1913, 253ff.

7. Bothmer 1957, 6–69, 131–43, describes more than 300 extant vase paintings featuring Heracles vs Amazons. Schefold 1993, 112–22. Shapiro 1983. Gantz 1993, 1:397–400. Langdon 2001. Blok 1995, 349–430. Diodorus 2.46.3–4 says Heracles captured Hippolyte and her belt. Plutarch, Apollodorus, Diodorus, Pausanias, Seneca, Hyginus, and Tzetses say that Theseus captured Antiope, but the orator Isocrates, the historian Cleidemus (works now lost), and the poet Simonides claimed that the Amazon captured by Theseus was called Hippolyte. Another source calls her Melanippe; yet another holds that Heracles exchanged a kidnapped Amazon for Hippolyte's belt. Still another tale describes a different death for Hippolyte— accidentally killed by her sister Amazon, Penthesilea (see chapter 18). Apollodorus *Library* 2.5.9; *Epitome* 1.15–16nn.

8. Bothmer 1957, 79. Gantz 1993, 1:399.

9. Pausanias 5.11.4–7; 5.25.11, and nn95, 97, and 249 comments by Peter Levi.

10. Langdon 2001, 1–6. The second-earliest Amazon image, with helmet, spear, and spotted leopard-skin cape, appears on a small pottery fragment of similar date in the other great Temple of Hera, on Samos. The Tiryns pair has been identified as Heracles and Hippolyte or Achilles and Penthesilea. Bothmer 1957, 1–2. Krauskopf in *Amazonen* 2010. Euripides *Hercules Furens* 408; *Ion* 1144–45. Boardman 2002, 170.

11. Langdon 2001.

CHAPTER 16
ANTIOPE AND THESEUS

1. Plutarch *Theseus* 1, 26–27, and 31; Plutarch cites competing versions by Philochorus, Pherecydes, Bion, Hellanikos, Herodorus, Menecrates, Cleidemus, and other lost historians in his discussion of Theseus and the Amazons. Orosius *History Against the Pagans* 1.15.7–9; Apollodorus *Epitome* 1.16; 4.1.16; Diodorus 4.16 and 28; Hyginus *Fabula* 30. Fowler 2013, 485–87. In some sources Antiope is called Hippolyte (Isocrates 12.193; Simonides cited by Apollodorus; Euripides *Hippolytus*) or Hippe (Athenaeus *Learned Banquet* 13.557).

2. Plutarch *Theseus* 31–34. Gantz 1993, 1:282–89.

3. Herodotus 1.1–5. On women in Herodotus, see appendix U in *Landmark Herodotus* 2007. Colarusso 2002, 32n3.

4. Antiope in art, Bothmer 1957, 124–30.

5. Plutarch *Theseus* 26. Homer *Iliad* 7.564; 2.862. Sölöz town website: www .soloz.bel.tr/index.php?md=showpage&pID=1. Thanks to Tansu Açık for translation. The Turkish story appears to retain the Argonaut link: Solois's brother Euneos was a son of Jason.

6. Talbert 2000: *Barrington Atlas*, maps 52 and 66. Soloi's silver coins of an Am-

azon profile (obols) and an Amazon and bow (staters, tetrobols) were issued ca 450–400 BC. Bothmer 1957, 223. Brindley 1994. Diodorus 3.55.4–5: Cilicians welcomed the Amazon Queen Myrina; the towns of Cyme, Pitana, and Priene were named for her top lieutenants. "Free Cilicians," eg Herodotus 1.28; Tacitus 2.78.

7. Isocrates 12.193 (he calls her Hippolyte). Pausanias 1.2.1 citing Hegias of Troizen. Fowler 2013, 486.

8. *The Warrior's Husband*, by Julian Thompson, first performed in 1924; revived in 1932 starring Hepburn, age 24; adapted as a movie (1933); and a musical, *By Jupiter* (1942), Rodgers and Hart's longest-running Broadway show. Gera 1997, 94, 200 (Sparethra was a "happily married" warrior queen of the Saka). Hepburn 1991, 119–25.

9. Euripides *Hippolytus*; Hyginus *Fabulae* 241; Ovid *Heroides* 4.117–20.

10. Thucydides 3.74.1; 2.4.2. Gera 1997, 25. Examples of women's bravery: Polyaenus bk 8; and see Schaps 1982 on Greek women in wartime.

CHAPTER 17
BATTLE FOR ATHENS

1. Plutarch *Theseus* 27. Mayor and Ober 1991. Fowler 2103, 486–87.

2. Cleidemus, Dowden 1997, 106, 114. Battle for Athens: Apollodorus *Epitome* 1. Diodorus 4.28; Aeschylus *Eumenides* 685–90; Pausanias 1.2.1, 1.15.2, 1.41.7, 2.32.9, 5.11.4–7; Justin 2.4. Plutarch *Theseus* 27–28.

3. Plutarch *Theseus* 27. Mayor and Ober 1991.

4. Justin 2.4.26–30. Diodorus 4.28.

5. Apollodorus *Epitome* 1.16; Diodorus 4.28; Aeschylus *Eumenides* 685.

6. Aeschylus *Seven Against Thebes* 39.

7. Plutarch *Theseus* 27; *Alexander* 31.

8. Rocky landscape, Harrison 1981. Bothmer 1957, shield and copies, 209–14; rocks and trees, 148, 165–73.

9. Diodorus 4.28. Plutarch *Theseus* 27. Apollodorus *Epitome* 5. All that survives of the confusing alternative version, in which Antiope/Hippolyte fought against Theseus, is that a battle broke out in Athens because of the jealous rage of Antiope/Hippolyte, who suddenly took up arms and summoned her sister Amazons to slay Theseus, his new wife Phaedra, and all their guests. In the fighting, Antiope/Hippolyte was either slain by Theseus or accidentally killed by Penthesilea.

10. Bothmer 1957, 166–68, Antiope, Geneva MF 238; 201, Amazon tomb? Ferrara T 203, Eupolis Painter. Gantz 1993, 1:285.

11. Plutarch *Theseus* 27.

12. Diodorus 4.28. Antiope's grave, Plutarch *Theseus* 27; Pausanias 1.2.1; Herodorus 31 F 25; Pseudo-Plato *Axiochos* 364–365; Harrison 1981, Molpadia, 306 and n128, Antiope, 308.

13. Amazonomachy was a "mythic prototype for certain historical events long before" the Persian Wars, Shapiro 1983, 106; Scythian conquests in Thrace influenced Amazonomachies, 113. Ammianus Marcellinus 22.8 was the only historian

to mention Amazon horses in Attica; he attributed their defeat to "unprotected flanks of their cavalry."

14. Mycenaean chamber tombs in Athens, Dowden 1997, 118. Hard 2004, 356–58. Plutarch *Theseus* 28. Gantz 1993, 1:284–85; Aeschylus *Eumenides*. Dowden 1997, 101–2. Date and sources of the myth, Fowler 2013, 486–87.

15. Plutarch *Theseus* 27; Diodorus 4.28. Lycophron *Alexandra* 1322–40. Dowden 1997, 106; Fowler 2013, 487, on the frozen straits.

16. Pausanias 7.2.7.

17. Some mounted Amazons appear in ancient murals and vase paintings of the Battle for Athens, but most are on foot, Bothmer 1957, 166–72. Justin 2.4.28–30.

18. Shapiro 2009, on Persians and Scythians in Greek art before the Persian Wars.

19. Shield of Athena, Harrison 1981, Athenian propaganda, 295. Bothmer 1957, 209–14. Stewart 1995, 585–86; 577, 582, the Battle for Athens was "concocted as an analogue for the great victories" over the Persians; 587–90, the surge in Amazon scenes after 450 BC related to rising numbers of foreign women in Athens. Stewart 1998, 75. Cf Cohen 2012, 478. Pliny 36.18; Pausanias 1.17.2. Plutarch *Pericles* 31.

20. Gantz 1993, 1:284–85. Bothmer 1957, 88–89; vases copied monumental and painted Amazonomachies by Mikon, Polygnotus, and Phidias in Athens (Theseion, Painted Porch, Parthenon metopes and Athena's shield), 144, 147, 149, 163–74, 209. Stewart 1998, 75. Antiope's alternative name "Hippolyte" appears five times.

21. Tarbell 1920, 227. Castriota 1992, 46–47, 58, 77–78, 83–85, 103, 138, 162, Stewart 1995, 583–86, 591. Harrison 1981, 307; actions of the Amazons on the shield signify the Persians at Marathon, 309. Kleiner 2010, 221, "all Greeks knew" that "Greeks and Amazons were an allusion to the clash between Greeks and Persians." Persian "nambypambiness," Pelling 1997, 2, 10. "Impossible to prove," Woodford 2003, 142–43. Cf Shapiro 1983.

22. Persians as Persians, inferior to Greeks on vases, eg Stewart 1995, 584.

23. Shapiro 2009, 338–40. Convoluted paradox of "Persian mirror reflecting the Scythian Other" and vice versa, Pelling 1997, 2.

24. Pelling 1997. Herodotus 9.27. Strabo 11.5.3; 11.13.9.

25. Gleba 2008, 14–17. Shapiro 1983, Persian clothing elements as "decorative" effects, 111, 113. Scythians and Persians in 6th- to 5th-century BC Greek art, Shapiro 2009. Blonde Amazon, and Amazons in Greek helmets, Greek names, etc, in Battle for Athens Amazonomachies, Bothmer 1957, 146, 164, 167, 187–90. Some copies of Athena's shield show male archers in boots and animal skins—are they Scythian allies? Harrison 1981, 309, 311–12. Moreover, Amazons sometimes kill Greeks on Greek vase scenes but Persians do not.

26. Tarbell 1920 makes many of these points. Trysa: Barringer 2001, 192–200. Mausolus was a Persian satrap who admired Greek culture; his memorial (one of the Wonders of the Ancient World), built by his Persian sister-wife Artemisia II, was decorated with reliefs of Centaurs vs Lapiths and Greeks battling Amazons, by the finest artists of the day. It would be hard to believe that Mausolus and Artemisia viewed the Amazons as stand-ins for defeated Persians. Amazons also appear at Alabanda, Caria. And at Pergamon, Amazonomachy scenes appeared alongside a scene of Greeks defeating Persians at Marathon. On Amazons appearing along with historical scenes, Buxton 1994, 62–64.

27. "Cliché," Stewart 1995, 584; "mythic prototype" influenced by Scythians in Thrace, Shapiro 1983, 106n9; 113–14. "flexibility," Woodford 2003, 141; "counterpart," Bothmer 1957, 118; "analogue," Harrison 1981, 309; "Athens's first brave deed against foreign attack," Pausanias 5.11.7; "insignificant," Isocrates 4.68.

28. Athenian envoy's boast, Herodotus 9.27. Dowden 1997, 120–21. Isocrates 4.67–70, 6.42, 7.75, 12.193; Ps-Lysias 2.4–6; and see Demosthenes 40.8. Pausanias 4.31.8.

29. Plutarch *Theseus* 27; Pausanias 1.2.1; 1.41.7; 2.32.8–9. Amazon tombs, Dowden 1997, 118–19.

30. Plutarch *Demosthenes* 19. Boardman 2002, 64–65.

31. Pausanias 3.25.3. Bennett 1912, 40–56. Hall 2012, 26. Brauron, see prologue.

32. Justin 2.4.28–30; Diodorus 2.46; 4.28.

CHAPTER 18
PENTHESILEA AND ACHILLES AT TROY

1. Pausanias 1.15.2.

2. Blok 1995, 195–288. Ancient sources for Penthesilea include Apollodorus *Epitome* 5.1–2; Diodorus 2.46.5–6; Justin 2.4; Hellanikos *FGrH* 4 F 149; Propertius 3.11.14; Nonnus 35.28; Ovid *Heroid.* 21.118; Hyginus *Fabulae* 112, 225; Diktys 3.15; 4.2; Tzetzes *Posthomerica* 198; and Quintus of Smyrna *Fall of Troy* bk 1 (hereafter Quintus).

3. The first archaeologists to examine the Warrior Gate at the ruins of Hattusa identified a large relief sculpture (ca 1300 BC) of a warrior with long, braided hair and "breasts" carrying a battle-axe as an "Amazon." A battle-axe was the favorite weapon of Amazons, and it is possible that some Greek observers in antiquity might have entertained the same impression that the figure was female. The ancient Egyptians called the Hittites "women" because of their long hair. But the figure on the Warrior Gate is now thought to be male. Hittite "Amazon": Garstang 1929, 85–86; *Keilschrifttexte aus Boghazköi* 1:72, 9.

4. Korfmann 2004; Strauss 2006, xix–xxii, 5–15. Hittite thesis, Blok 1995, 101–2, 289–93; West 2011, 40–41.

5. Strauss 2006. West 2011. Blok 1995, 147–54. Vase paintings on alabastra show Amazons and black Ethiopean archers: Cohen 2012, 466–68.

6. Arctinos, Aethiopis fr. 2, scholiast on *Homer's Iliad* 24.804.

7. Proclus *Chrestomathia* 2. Colvin 1872–1926. Strauss 2006, 160–62. Orosius 1.15. Quintus *Fall of Troy* bk 1. Unless otherwise noted, the descriptions of the battle are from Quintus.

8. See eg Bennett 1912, 1–2. West 2011, 132. Blok 1995, 83, 146–47, 161–62, 198n4, 293–303; see 146n3, according to the scholia on Homer *Iliad* 3.188–89 attributed to Didymus, the Amazons at the Sangarius River included Hippolyte and Melanippe; see 175 and n77, another scholiast comments that in the time of Mygdon and Otreus the Amazons "rode fire-breathing horses and plundered the neighboring districts" and later raided Phrygia. Philostratus *On Heroes* 56 also assumes that Trojans and Phyrgians fought the Amazons.

9. Homer *Iliad* 3.182–90.

10. Strabo 12.3.24 (on Apollodorus's assumption that the Amazons and Trojans were enemies) and 12.8.6, but as Strabo's Loeb translator H. L. Jones noted in 1928, this assumption does not follow the actual text in Homer *Iliad* 3.187–89. Quotes from Blok 1995, 161–62, 293–303.

11. Homer *Iliad* 2.813–14; one scholiast suggested that Myrine was the ancestor of the Trojan royal line, Bennett 1912, 2–3. Strabo 12.8.6; 13.3.6. Thanks to Richard Martin for help with this Homeric riddle.

12. Quintus *Fall of Troy* 1.91–92. Gantz 1993, 2:621–22; Diktys 4.3 and Hellanikos 4 F149, Penthesilea came "for glory."

13. The inconsistency of Penthesilea seeking purification from an enemy of her people, Priam, puzzled Blok 1995, 296–98.

14. Apollodorus *Epitome* 5.1–2; Diodorus 2.46.5; Quintus 1. 20–32. Names of Penthesilea and Achilles discussed in Blok 1995, 219–20 and n64.

15. Photius *Bibliotheca* codex 190 (9th century AD) summarizing a medley of legends and fables collected by Ptolemy Chennos (or Hephaestion) of Alexandria, *New (or Strange) History* (2nd century AD) 5.69. This Helen was one of many who lived in the time of the Trojan War; no more is known of Epipole. Palamedes was the recruiter and monitor of the Greek force going to Troy.

16. Bothmer 1957, 100.

17. Marconi 2004, 35.

18. Apollodorus *Epitome* 5.1. Cf poem 11 of Propertius *Elegies* 3.11. Pausanias 5.11.6.

19. For a full discussion of the Thersites incident, see Blok 1995, 195–210.

20. Strauss 2006, 163–64 and map.

21. Bothmer 1957, 4; 70–73 (London B210); 82 (Munich 1502 A); 148 (gazing lovers); 192–93; 200–201 (New York 06.1021.189). Shapiro 1983, 105–6. Penthesilea in art, Blok 1995, 222–38; gazing lovers, 234.

22. London B323, Leagros Group, Woodford 2003, 76–78; Bothmer 1957, 89; cf Blok 1995, 234–35.

23. Alternative versions, Lycophron 995; Hyginus *Fabula* 112; Dictys 3.15–16 (Hector sets out to meet Penthesilea and is killed by Achilles) and 4.2–3 (Penthesilea thrown in the Scamander); killed by Pyrrhus, Dares *Phryg.* 36; scholiast on *Homer's Iliad* 2.219; scholiast on Sophocles's *Philoctetes* 445 (Achilles had sex with Penthesilea's corpse); Tzetzes *on Lycophron*; Virgil *Aeneid* 1.495. Photius *Myriobiblon* 190, summary of Ptolemy Hephaestion *New History* 6; Eustathius of Thessalonike (12th century AD) commentary on Homer 1696 (*Iliad* 2.220); Benjamin Hederich, *Gründliches Lexicon Mythologicum* (1724) s.v. Penthesilea. Dictys and Dares, *The Trojan War* 1966, trans R. M. Frazer.

24. Philostratus *On Heroes* 23. Maclean and Aitken 2004, 279–80. Strabo 7.3.2. Nireus killing Hiera, sculptural panels 22–24 of the Pergamon Altar (2nd century BC) now in Berlin.

25. Christine de Pizan 1999, 43–46; perhaps inspired by Dictys 3.15–16 and 4.2–3, claiming that Hector set out to meet Penthesilea and that she was devastated by Hector's death.

26. *Etymologicum magnum* (Byzantine, ca AD 1150), 495, 40 s.v. Kaystros. Strabo 14.1.45. Pausanias 7.2.4, Ephesus founded by "Coresus son of Cayster" and by Ephesus; cf Herodotus 5.100. Bennett 1912, 9n30, 31–33.

27. Lycophron *Alexandra* 992–1007; comm. Tzetzes; comm. Servius *Aeneid* 3.553. Moscati-Castelnuovo 1999. Caulonia was founded in the 7th century BC. The location of Clete is unknown; perhaps it was a small protohistoric settlement.

28. Diodorus 2.46.

CHAPTER 19
AMAZONS AT SEA

1. Ankyra/Ancyra issued many coins featuring various figures holding anchors; different die casts show Amazons with anchors. *BMC, Catalog of Coins in the British Museum: Galatia*, p 9, coin of Ancyra, Roman Province of Galatia, reign of Antoninus Pius. *Historia Numorum* 1911, 663, 665. Pausanias 1.4 traced the name to a dream of Midas, mythic founder of Ankyra. Nero issued coins showing an Amazon holding a ball and a trident, a naval symbol: Leal 2010, 68.

2. Coins of Smyrna (2nd century AD) show an Amazon with battle-axe and the prow of a ship on the reverse.

3. Diodorus 3.55.8–10. See chapter 20, Amazons cross a dangerous river to meet Alexander.

4. Apollodorus *Bib* 1.9.17; 3.6.4; Apollonius *Argonautica* 1.609–909. Homer *Odyssey* 8.294.

5. Amazoneum, from the ancient geography *Stadiasmus Maris Magni* 283 (p 488, ed. Hoffmann); Bennett 1912, 8, 9. Herodotus 4.103. Besides Patmos, many other locales claimed to have the "true" statue of the "Scythian Artemis": Hall 2012, 142–49; Pausanias 3.16.7–8.

6. Pausanias 7.2.4–8; Plutarch *Greek Questions* 56. Dionysus and the "Amazons" of India, Polyaenus 1.1 and see chapter 24.

7. The ancient sources for this myth are Euagon, Aristotle, Euphorion, Plutarch, and Aelian; for full discussion of its paleontological meaning, see Solounias and Mayor 2005. Terra-cotta shield, Bothmer 1957, 2–3.

8. Ephorus cited by Stephanus of Byzantium. s.v. "Anaia"; Eustathius on *Dionys. Perieg.* 828.

9. Apollonius *Argonautica* 2.

10. Herodotus 4.103. Euripides *Iphigenia in Tauris*, Hall 2012. The story of the Amazons and the captive sailors is from Philostratus *On Heroes* 57.

11. Ferrara T 411, Bothmer 1957, 200. Maclean and Aitken 2004, 232–33. Castriota 1992, 44–45.

12. Philostratus 57. Leuke: Pindar *Nemean* 4.49; Euripides *Iphigenia* 436–38; Pausanias 3.19.11; Strabo 7.3.16; Pliny 4.27.1. Maclean and Aitken 2004, xxiv, 44, 146, 228–29, 232–34, 281–82, 309.

13. Castriota 1992, 44–45. Aristophanes *Lysistrata* 674–78. Herodotus 7.99; 8.68–69; 8.87–88; 8.93, 8.101–3; 8.132; and 8.185. Polyaenus 8.53. Plutarch *Themistocles* 14.3. Gera 1997, 204–18. Battle of Salamis, Strauss 2004, xix, 93–101, 180–83, 185–88.

14. Christine de Pizan 1999, 49–52, 113–14. Inscribed jar, London 1857,1220.1.

15. Teuta: Appian *Illyrian Wars* 6–8; Polybius 2.4.6–2.7.12, Cassius Dio 12 fr. 49.7.

16. Dyczek 2011a and b. www.pasthorizonspr.com/index.php/archives/09/2012 /coin-hoards-and-pottery-bring-new-insights-to-an-ancient-illyrian-stronghold. University of Warsaw, Antiquity of Southeastern Europe Research Centre, Risan (Rhizon) Excavations, Montenegro, 2007–12. www.novae.uw.edu.pl/english/coinhoard.htm.

CHAPTER 20
THALESTRIS AND ALEXANDER THE GREAT

1. Diodorus 17.76. Arrian *Anabasis* 3.20.1–3.23.1–5, hereafter cited as Arrian.

2. Diodorus 17.76; Curtius 6.5.11–21; Plutarch *Alexander* 44. Cf Arrian 3.24.1–3 and 5.19.4–6. Wood 1997, 116–23.

3. Diodorus 17.75–77. This meeting took place in Hyrcania in 330 BC, just after the Mardian venture, not later in 329/328 at the Jaxartes River as sometimes assumed.

4. Curtius 6.5.24–32. Diodorus and Curtius are believed to have consulted the same lost source, Cleitarchus, who had accompanied Alexander. Baynham 2001; Chugg 2006, 155–61; Leal 2010, 59–63.

5. Plutarch *Alexander* 46. Among the historians who accepted the story, Plutarch names Cleitarchus, Polycleitus, Antigenes, Ister, and Onesicritus; those who thought it a fiction included Aristobulus, Anticleides, Chares the royal usher, Ptolemy, Philo the Theban, Duris of Samos, Hecataeus of Eretria, Philip the Chalcidian, Philip of Theangela. Ptolemy *FGrH* 138 F28; Aristobulus *FGrH* F21. See Baynham 2001, 117–19, on the sources. Other sources for Alexander and Amazons include Strabo 11.5.3–4; Curtius 6.5.24–32; Arrian 7.13.2–3; Justin 2.4.33; 12.3.5–7; 42.3.7

6. Plutarch *Alexander* 46. For the distribution of Alexander's troops here, Arrian 3.19.5–3.25.4.

7. Justin 12.3.5–8.

8. Diodorus 17.77; Strabo 11.5.1–4; Curtius 6.5.24; Justin 2.4.33; 42.3.7.

9. Diodorus 17.77; Justin 12.3.5.

10. Diodorus 17.77; Curtius 6.5.24. Strabo 11.5.4. But Strabo may have meant Mt Kaspios = Kaukasos (11.8.9, citing Eratosthenes), see Dowden 1997, 114n55. Stoneman 2008, 77–78; in Alexander's time, geographical knowledge was inexact.

11. Arrian 3.20.1–4. Alexander was rushing to catch up with Darius; his hurried march from Ecbatana to Rhaga took only 11 days. For photos of the Caspian Gates here, see Romm, *Landmark Arrian* 2010, 133.

12. Justin 12.3.5–7; Strabo 11.5.4.

13. Curtius 3.3.22–23. Baynham 2001, 122.

14. Wood 1997, 120, 7–9; Chugg 2006, 163; Stoneman 2008, 88–90.

15. Justin 2.4.33; 12.3.5–7. Diodorus 17.77.1–3; Cleitarchus *FGrH* 137 F16. I am indebted to Richard Martin for insights about this pair of names.

16. Polyaenus 8.60. Arrian 1.5.4–5. Cynna's name is thought to derive from Macedonian for "little she-dog"; it might also be related to the Kinambroi tribe of Illyria, or to the ancient Dardanian settlement Chinna, Ptolemy 2.15; the name "Cinna" appears on Roman-era tombs in Illyria. Alexander had Cynna's husband Amyntas assassinated; after Alexander's death Cynna raised an army and led it against Antipater, Perdiccas, and Alcetas; her daughter Adea (Eurydice) wore Macedonian armor

at the head of an army to challenge a force led by Alexander's mother Olympias. Romm 2011, 143–47; Carney 2000, 58, 129–37, 239–41; and 2014. Palagia 2008.

17. Curtius 10.3.11–14; Justin 12.12; Baynham 2001, 124–26. Roxane was the daughter of Oxyartes, a Baktrian leader; she was among other captive girls who danced for Alexander at the banquet thrown by Arimazes in Sogdiana. Chugg 2006, 164–84; Alexander's melting-pot marriages, 191–95.

18. Alexander's new style: Justin 12.3; Curtius 6.6.4–5; 9.3.10; Plutarch *Alexander* 45 and *Fortune of Alexander* 1.8329–30. Baynham 2001, 123, 124, artistic image of Alexander in Eastern dress. Diodorus 17.94.

19. Curtius 6.5.1–32; Leal 2010, 61–62. Justin 2.4.33. Arrian 4.19–20; Roxane and her son, Alexander's heir, were assassinated in 316 and 310 BC.

20. Arrian 4.15.1–4. Curtius 8.1.7–9. Baynham 2001, 119–20. Chugg 2006, 158–59.

21. Arrian 4.15.4–6 and P. A. Brunt's appendix 12.3–4 and appendix 21.1–3 in his Loeb translation; and now Romm, *Landmark Arrian* 2010, appendix N. Curtius 6.4.17–20. Stoneman 2008, 78–81, 130. Baynham 2001, 117, 120. Tyrrell 1984, 24, dismisses the account of Thalestris as the result of "Amazons being on people's minds in Bactria."

22. Diodorus 17.84.1–4; Curtius 8.10.22–36; Justin 12.7.9–11; cf Arrian 4.26. Chugg 2006, 155–63.

23. Italics added. Curtius 10.4.3 and Arrian 7.13.1–6l; Arrian *Indika* 1.

24. Arrian 7.13.1–6. Leal 2010, 82–85.

25. Amazon impersonators and gladiatrixes in Rome: Suetonius *Nero* 44.1; *Domitian* 4.1. *Lives of the Later Caesars*, Commodus 10–11; *Clodius Albinus* 2; Juvenal *Satires* 6.252; Cassius Dio 59.10.1–2; 61.17.3; 67.8.4; 76.16; Tacitus *Annals* 15.32; Petronius *Satyricon* 45. Gladiatrix remains in London: Pringle and Broad 2001. Arrian *Ars Tactica* 34. Halicarnassus relief: Coleman 2000. Roman views of Amazons in art and literature, Leal 2010; Kleiner 2010, 194, Commodus's portrait bust with two kneeling Amazons.

26. Baynham 2001, 120–21 suggests these "Amazons" were prostitutes and that Alexander did not take them seriously as soldiers. See chapter 24 for female bodyguards of the Indian king Chandragupta, a contemporary of Alexander; Rothery 1910, 48–54. Numerous modern monarchs have surrounded themselves with "Amazon" escorts, from Ranjeet Singh of Lahore to Muammar Gaddafi of Libya.

27. See Armenian *Romance of Alexander* 1969 (trans. Wolohojian), 140–45, lines 250–58; 140–43; 145–46; cf variations in the *Greek Alexander Romance* 3.25–27, Stoneman trans. (1991), 143–46. Stoneman 2008, 130–31. In the Greek version, painted portraits of Alexander are featured in the stories of Candace and the Amazons.

28. Arrian 1.23.7–8.

CHAPTER 21
HYPSICRATEA, KING MITHRADATES, AND POMPEY'S AMAZONS

1. Biography of Mithradates, Mayor 2010, Hypsicratea: 114, 304, 309–10, 319–38, 328, 355–57, 362–69, 377.

2. Hypsicratea: Valerius Maximus 4.6.2; Plutarch *Pompey* 32.

3. Valerius Maximus 4.6.2.

4. Quotes, Konstan 2002, 16–18. Christine de Pizan 1999, 110–12. Colarusso 2002, Saga 13, 85–87. Boccaccio: Mayor 2010, 321–22, 356.

5. Mithradates's papers are now lost, but Pliny read them in Rome: Mayor 2010, 240–41.

6. Plutarch *Pompey* 32.8.

7. Appian *Mithradatic Wars* 12.10.69; 12.87 (hereafter cited as Appian); Cassius Dio 36.49.3. Mayor 2010, 304, 310.

8. Plutarch *Pompey* 32.8. Konstan 2002, 16–18.

9. Cassius Dio 36.6; Appian 12.88–90.

10. Plutarch *Pompey* 32.8 Eutropius 6.12 (ca AD 370): Mithradates fled "with his wife and two attendants" on horseback. For this battle and the ancient sources, Mayor 2010, 318–29.

11. Strabo 11.4–5.

12. Plutarch *Pompey* 32.8. Strabo 11.4–5.

13. Plutarch *Pompey* 35 and 45.

14. Appian 12.15.103; Appian *Spanish Wars* 6.72.

15. Procopius *Gothic Wars* 4.3.6–8. Avars: Nicephorus p 21 de Boor.

16. Ateshi 2011.

17. Appian 12.15.103 and 12.17.116–17.

18. Appian 12.17.117.

19. Kleiner 2010, 221; Amazon sarcophagi, 224, fig 15–11; Roman soldiers fighting Amazons on the Mausoleum of the Julii, 30–20 BC, 101. Magnificent sarcophagus of Romans battling Amazons and kneeling Amazon prisoners of war, Houston Museum of Fine Arts. Celtic women warriors, Freeman 2002, 53–59. Boudicca: Tacitus *Annals* 14.31–35.

20. Plutarch *Pompey* 32.8. Appian 12.101–2.

21. Mayor 2010, 355–57; 365–69.

22. Mayor 2010, 367–69; Bowersock 2008, 600–601.

23. Thanks to numismatist Ed Snible for suggesting the link to Hypsicratea and to Michel Prieur for photos of the wolf-capped Amazon coins of Amisus.

24. Pausanias 2.31.4. Apollonius *Argonautica* 2.996–1000. King Vakhtang Gorgasali (Persian, "wolf-head") of Iberia wore a wolf-head helmet, Hunt 2012, 69. Wolves in steppe tales, Beckwith 2009, 4–6.

CHAPTER 22
CAUCASIA, CROSSROADS OF EURASIA

1. For descriptions of these lands and peoples by Europeans in the 18th and 19th centuries, see Klaproth 1814; Spencer 1838; and Bryce 1878. Northern Caucasia at this writing includes Adygea, Karachay-Cherkessia, Karbardino-Balkaria, North Ossetia-Alania, South Ossetia, Ingushetia, Chechnya, Kalykia, and Dagestan.

2. Colarusso 2002, 122–24, 158–70. Hunt 2012. Mayor, Colarusso, and Saunders 2014.

3. Colarusso 2002, 48 and n1, 184; Hunt 2012, glossary.

4. Colarusso 2002, Saga 26, 128–130.
5. Klaproth 1814, 304. Hunt 2012, 166–71.
6. Hunt 2012, 77–87.
7. Hunt 2012, 171–72.
8. Khorenatsi, Moses of Khorene 1.5. Thomson 1978, 96–98. Ananikian 1925, 68–69, appendix 3. An Anatolian-Armenian version of the revival of Ara, as "Er son of Armenius" appears in Plato *Republic* 10.614–21, without Semiramis. Gera 1997, 82–83.
9. Cartwright, *The Preacher's Travels*, 1611, cited in Rothery 1910, 58.
10. Alakbarli 2005.
11. Chadwick and Zhirmunsky 2010, 308–12. Clayton 2002, 73–74. Lewis 1974, 35, 89, 117–31.
12. Alakbarli 2005. Lewis 1974.
13. Talattof 2000. Alakbarli 2005; Smith 2012, 17–22; Brend 1995; Chelkowski 1975, 23, Sassanid Castle of Shirin, 46–47. Shirin, history and legend: Baum 2004.
14. "Lovers, heroines," Chelkowski 1975, 3, 7, 47, 48. Talattof 2000, 52–54, refuting Iranian scholars Bihruz Sarvatiyan and Fatimah Alaqih.
15. Stoneman 2008, 33–5. Alakbarli 2005. Smith 2012, 37–46; Chelkowski 1975. Wisdom of warrior queens, Chadwick and Zhirmunsky 2010, 129. The Persian traditions in Nizami and Ferdowsi may have had the same ancient sources as some of the Persian tales gathered by Ctesias, 3rd century BC, Ctesias [Llewellyn-Jones and Robson] 2010, 64–65. The name Nushaba could be related to the Sumerian goddess Nisaba.
16. Alakbarli 2005.
17. Polyaenus 8.55. See Gardiner-Garden 1986 for historical evidence in literature and inscriptions for Tirgatao, her name, identities of the tribes, and Scythian wars in the northern Black Sea.
18. Strabo 11.2.11; Pomponius Mela 1.114–16; Pliny 6.7.19. Polyaenus 8.55. Modern Circassian account, Jaimoukha 2001, 44.
19. Polyaenus 8.55. Ixomatae, Iaxamatae, Exomatae, Valerius Flaccus *Argonautica* 6.144 and 569; Ammianus 22.8.31.
20. Hecataeus's fate is unknown. Minns 1913, on the name and historical context of Tirgatao, 39, 102n2, 573–78.
21. Polyaenus 8.56. Sulimirski 1970; Harmatta 1970, 15–18.
22. Pere Archangeli Lamberti, *Relazione della Colchide oggi detta Mengrellia, nella quale si tratta dell'Origine, Costumi, e cose naturali di quei Paesi* (1652) and *Relations de Thevenot*, pt i, pp 31–52, cited by Klaproth 1814, 305–6. *The Travels of Sir John Chardin* (1673–77), cited in Rothery 1910, 58–59.
23. Spencer 1838, 1:343–44; 301. Tamar, Klaproth 1814, 232; Bryce 1878, 100.
24. Rothery 1910, 56–57. John Colarusso, per corr May 22, 2013. Reineggs 1807.
25. Reineggs 1807, 264–66; Reineggs 1796, 1:238; Reineggs, *Voyages au Nord*, pt vii, p 180. Reineggs and Potocki cited in Klaproth 1814, 306. Spencer 1838, 1:22–27. Soanes, Strabo 11.2.19. See chapter 23 for a similar Egyptian tale.
26. Schober 1762; Klaproth 1814, 307.
27. Rothery 1910, 57; 61; J. Michaud and L. Michaud, *Biographie universelle, ancienne et moderne*, vol. 53 (1832): 168: *aëmetzaine*. Fréret studied classical antiquity and sought practical explanations for mythology.

28. Spencer 1938, 1:20–26.

29. Toulmey, in the retelling by Russian social historian Maxim Kovalevsky (1851–1916) cited by Jaimoukha 2001, 165.

CHAPTER 23
PERSIA, EGYPT, NORTH AFRICA, ARABIA

1. Sancisi-Weerdenburg 1993, 32; and 1985, 466.

2. Ferdowsi 2006, Shirin, 810–31; Qaidafa, 490–97. Evliya Celebi, an Ottoman Turkish traveler (1611–82), recorded local legends about Queen Kaydefa and Alexander in his *Seyahâtnâme*.

3. Ferdowsi 2006, Gordieh, 191–94. Talattof 2000, 52.

4. Zonaras 12.23.595. Ctesias, his life and sources, Ctesias [Llewellyn-Jones and Robson] 2010, 7–68; Sancisi-Weerdenburg 1993, 31–32.

5. Zarina/Zarinaia: Diodorus 2.34; P. Oxy. 2330, Ctesias fr. 5, 7, 8a and c; Ctesias [Llewellyn-Jones and Robson] 2010, 38–40.

6. Tzetzes cited in Ctesias [Llewellyn-Jones and Robson] 2010, 156. Gera 1997, 89–90.

7. Diodorus 2.34.1–5. Ctesias [Llewellyn-Jones and Robson] 2010, 156.

8. Ctesias [Llewellyn-Jones and Robson] 2010, 150–51, 156–58. Gera 1997, 6, 84–100.

9. His repetition of "I saved you" was rhetorical, ignoring the fact that Zarina also saved him. The ancient sources for Zarina: Ctesias [Llewellyn and Robson] 2010, 19–20; 36–40; 106–7; 156–58; and Gera 1997, 6; 84–100.

10. Excavations by Alireza Hejabri-Nobari (Tarbiat Modares University), reported by *Hambastegi News* [Tehran] 2004.

11. Ctesias (Photius) [Llewellyn-Jones and Robson] 2010, 171–73. Diodorus 2.34.

12. Diodorus 2.34. Gera 1997, 89, 94–95, 199–201.

13. Lichtheim 1980, 3–10.

14. The "Egyptians and Amazons" tale is contained in the Inaros-Petubastis story cycle papyri found in Dime, Fayum. Serpot tale: Vienna Demotic Papyri 6165 and 6165A. Lichtheim 1980. Almasy 2007. Agut-Labordère and Chauveau 2011, 61–62. Confusingly, Inaros II led a later revolt against the Persians, ca 460 BC. See Ryholt 2009 for historical material in Egyptian narrative papyri.

15. Lichtheim 1980, 151–52; Agut-Labordère and Chauveau 2011, 106–15. *Serpot* can also be rendered *Sarpot*.

16. Lichtheim 1980, 152–53. Bull's horn helmets, see chapters 7 and 12.

17. Translations from Lichtheim 1980, 154–56; Agut-Labordère and Chauveau 2011. Ellipses mark missing text; restored text in brackets.

18. Female pharaohs: Gera 1997, 101–5; 147; Hoffmann 2008; Jones 2000, 106–7.

19. Thanks to Justin Mansfield, Adrienn Almasy, and Ian Rutherford for bibliography and valuable discussions of the Serpot story. Hellenistic date: Lichtheim 1980, 152, and Almasy 2007, citing F. Hoffmann, *Agypter und Amazonen* (1995). But see Rutherford 1997, 206, on Egyptian influences on Greek literature. The Egyptologist-translators of the text, Hoffmann 2008 and Agut-Labordère and Chauveau 2011, argue that the Serpot tale has negligible Hellenistic influence and

took shape sometime between the Saite era (Twenty-Sixth Dynasty, 7th century BC) and the Persian era, 525–330 BC. Egyptologist Ryholt 2009 discusses reliable Egyptian ancient history embedded in the narratives on Greco-Roman papyri. Hoffmann 2008 appears in the special issue of *CRIPEL* 27 (2008) devoted to scholarly papers on "Amazons and Egypt."

20. Almasy 2007, 4. Herodotus 2.106 and 2.112–20; Euripides *Helen*. Diodorus 1.56.4; Strabo 17.1.34 and 46. Pausanias 1.42.3. Amen-hotep III's throne name "Nimmuria/Mimurria" might have sounded like Memnon to Greek ears; could Minnemei in Inaros be modeled on him? (Thanks to Ian Rutherford.)

21. Herodotus 1.103–6.

22. Herodotus 2.102–8; 2.134–35: the famous courtesan Rhodopis was a Thracian slave in Egypt, 6th century BC. Several historical pharaohs were named Sesostris (Senusret).

23. Sesoösis in Diodorus 1.53–59; Justin 2.3; Strabo 15.75.6; 17.25. Sesostris stories in demotic Egyptian, eg Papyri Carlsberg 411 and 412 (unpublished); Tebtunis Temple Library 51; O. Leipzig UB 2217; see Ryholt 2009. Rutherford 1997, 204. Thanks to Justin Mansfield and Ian Rutherford for help with Egyptian linguistics. Ashteshyt deciphered as Abkhazian, John Colarusso per corr May 27, 2013. Caucasian languages related to non-Indo-European Hattic language of Anatolia, ca 2000–1000 BC, Anthony 2007, 44.

24. Herodotus 1.103–6; 4.162–205 (Pheretime) and notes by Strassler in *Landmark Herodotus*, Herodotus 2007, 59–60. Pheretime in Herodotus, Menecles, and Polyaneus 8.47, see Gera 1997, 164–78. Diodorus 3.52–55. Fluehr-Lobban 1998. Legends about Alexander/Iskandar in late antiquity associate him with a queen named Candace, Stoneman 2008, 134–40.

25. Inscription in Meroitic hieroglyphics (Temple F, Naqa/Naga) and statues of Shanakdakheto of Meroe, in armor with a spear, Nubian Museum, Aswan, and Cairo Museum, Egypt. Cassius Dio 54.5–6. Amanirenas/Amanirense, the one-eyed Candace in Strabo 17.1.54; Fluehr-Lobban 1998, 6. Her feats are inscribed on a stele in the British Museum, EA1650. Amanitore is mentioned in Acts 8.26–40. Thanks to archaeologist of Nubian sites Stuart Tyson Smith for information about the head of Augustus; British Museum 1911,0901.1. See Cohen 2012, 466–68 for black archers (Amazons?) on vase paintings.

26. Samsi paid tribute to Tiglath and remained queen: Eph'al 1982, 82–86; 112–13. Assyrian and Egyptians vs Arabian battle queens: Jones 2000, 13–14; Zenobia, 14–18. Fluehr-Lobban 1998, 6. Zenobia: Stoneman 1994. A heroine of the Himyan tribe of Yemen fought valiantly at the head of an army at the battle of Damascus, 7th century AD, Rothery 1910, 60. Arabic heroine epics, Clayton 2002, 69–70. Islamic warrior women: Kruk 2013.

27. Diodorus 3.55.4.

28. Diodorus 3.52–55

29. Herodotus 4.179. Diodorus 3.54. Strabo 17.3.7.

30. Herodotus 4.170–80. Silius Italicus *Punica* 2. Strabo 14.1.4.

31. Silius Italicus *Punica* 2.

32. Virgil *Aeneid* 11.854–69, 11.295–96; Leal 2010, 25–34. Herodotus 7.170–80 (Asbystai); Ptolemy *Geography* 4.4 (Asbytai). Pliny 5.5.34; Strabo 2.5.33. Thanks to Egyptologists Justin Mansfield and David Salo for valuable discussion of these names.

CHAPTER 24
AMAZONISTAN: CENTRAL ASIA

1. Shoolbraid 1997; Chadwick and Zhirmunsky 2010. Alternative versions of Turkic epics are told by different ethnicities in Tajikistan, Kyrgyzstan, Kazakhstan, and Uzbekistan.

2. Kinzer 1999. *Kyz kuu*, Kazakh; *qiz-qov*, Azerbaijani. A series of *kyz kuu* races in 2012 in Kyrgyzstan can be seen here: http://www.youtube.com/watch?v=612 EegenLf8.

3. In similar but less equitable performances in Ukraine-Caucasus-Central Asian locales, parents chose the competing suitors for their daughter's hand, with or without her consent. Her public capture on horseback is said to replace older, more violent customs of forcible kidnapping to avoid paying bride-price. Thanks to Dianna Wuagneux and Linda Svendsen for firsthand accounts of *kesh kumay* and related games in Kyrgyzstan and Ukraine. Persian-ancestry Tajiks do not play *kesh kumay*, suggesting that the game is of Turkic rather than Persian origin.

4. Aelian *Historical Miscellany* 12.38; Clayton 2002.

5. See also *Xin Tang shu* (ca AD 1000).

6. Chadwick and Zhirmunsky 2010, 36–44, 82, 204–10.

7. Gunda: Colarusso 2002, Saga 83, 364–65.

8. Polo 1993, 461–65, see Yule's n1; Weatherford 2010, 116–25; her story is told by Marco Polo, Persian chronicler Rashid al Din, and the Arab traveler Ibn Battuta.

9. Clayton 2002.

10. Shoolbraid 1997, 10, 48–50 and nn53–56.

11. Gonzalez de Clavijo 1859, 174–75.

12. In Uzbek and other versions, Gulaim is Gulayim, Gaukhar, Gulsim, or Gulyaeem. Chadwick and Zhirmunsky 2010, 282–83. Amazons reported in 1403, Wilde 1999, 179; Davis-Kimball 2002, 131. Azarpay 1992, 115–16; tattoo or hennaed arm, 106 fig 46, pls 14–20.

13. Shoolbraid 1997, 10, 18, 49, 51, 83–86.

14. "Bridal Costume as a Representation of Military Armour," Karakalpaks, Russian Ethnography Museum, D. and S. Richardson, http://www.karakalpak .com.

15. Polyaenus 1.1; cf Arrian *Indika*.

16. *Digenes Akritas*: Jeffreys 1998. Brahmin men and women, reported by Palladius *de Gentibus Indiae*. Similar lore about "male and female islands" was reported by Marco Polo (3.31) who traveled to Burma and sailed up the west coast of India in about AD 1280. Rothery 1910, 41–52.

17. *Digenes Akritas* 4.397 and 6.311–798; Jeffreys 1998, 201.

18. Megasthenes cited by Strabo 15.1.55–56. McCrindle 1877, 69–73. Kautilya *Arthashastra* 1.21.1. Jones 2000, 42. Banerjee 2007, 28.

19. Rothery 1910, 45–47.

20. Banerjee 2007, 28. *Rig Veda* 1.13, 10.39 (Vadhrimati, comm. Sayana ca AD 1385); 1.112; *Rig Veda* 1.116–18 (Vispala); 10.102 (Mugdalani, trans. R.T.H. Griffith 1896). *Ramayana*, trans. W. Buck 1973).

21. *Mahabharata* and local versions composed 400 BC–AD 400. The legend of Chitrangada, *Mahabharata* 1.217 (trans. K. M. Ganguli 1883–96) was taken up by R. Tagore in 1926. For the Bengali version of Pramila: Jaimini Bharatam written in Kannada, in the Ashwamedha Parva, see Karanth 2002, 198–202. Pramila is sometimes called Parminta. Rothery 1910, 50–51.

22. Kingdoms of women, *Mahabharata* 3.51 (trans. Ganguli). The yogi Matsyendranath and Queen Mainakini: Pattanaik 2000, 72.

23. Hutton 1921, 263.

24. Chadwick and Zhirmunsky 2010, 282. Marco Polo 4.3; Chinese and Muslim sources, Zirkle 1936, 115–21. Medieval European tales of "lands of women" and Amazons, Stoneman 2008, 132–34. Chinese "Kingdom of Women": Shaltly 2010.

CHAPTER 25
CHINA

1. The story of the Maiden of Yue is told in *Spring and Autumn Annals of the Wu and Yue States* by Zhao Hua, historian of the Eastern Han Dynasty who gathered earlier lore about their conflicts in the early 5th century BC (*Wu Yue Chun Qiu* by Zhao Ye, ca AD 33). Lee, Stefanowska, and Wiles 2007, 91.

2. This is the earliest Chinese record of fencing. Other Yuenu bronze swords, found in ancient tombs, are still sharp enough to slice coins. Cohen 2010, 16–17, 182–83. Henning 2007.

3. Mair, Chen, and Wood 2013, 18–19. Details of Fu Hao's exploits, "Biographical Sketches" 2001–2, 11–13. Peterson et al. 2000, 13–16. Dong 2010, 15–16.

4. Lament of Xijun (Hsi Chun), Rolle 1989, 116; Beckwith 2009, 78. Cai Yan: Dong 2010, 112; fictionalized by Maxine Hong Kingston's *Warrior Woman* (1975). Some offspring of these diplomatic intermarriages did become powerful leaders of the Wu Sun, Peterson et al. 2000, 65–74.

5. Rubinson 2008, 63n27. Murphy 2003, 23. Jade from Khotan, Baumer 2012, 122.

6. Peterson et al. 2000, 13–16. Tomb near Beijing and accounts of numerous Chinese women warriors from Chinese sources, "Biographical Sketches" 2001–2 and http://www.colorq.org/articles/article.aspx?d=asianwomen&x=fuhao. Dong 2010, 16–30.

7. Sun Tzu *Art of War*, trans. L. Giles (1910), citing the biography by Sima Qian, *Shi-ji* ch 130.

8. Women help in defense, *Geng Zhu*, trans. W. Mei; *Book of Shang, Shang Jun Shu*, trans. J. Duyvendak, http://ctext.org/shang-jun-shu/military-defence. Sparta, Polyaenus 8.49; and see Schaps 1982, 194.

9. Zirkle 1936, 117, 119.

10. *Classic of Mountains and Seas* 1999, bk 7, 115–17; 176–77; 222–23; 269–70. Hemp (*ma*) as a drug in China, attributed to Shen-Nung, *Pen Ts'ao* (ca 300 BC based on more ancient traditions). Zirkle 1936, 97–102, 114–22, 128; see Homer *Iliad* 20.219 and Aristotle *History of Animals* 6.18.572a (echoed by Pliny and Virgil) for the belief that mares without access to stallions were impregnated by wind. At least

two nymphs conceived by wind in myth, but no Greek source suggests that Amazons conceived by any means other than intercourse with men. Medieval German chronicler Adam of Bremen 4.19 wrote that Amazons were thought to "conceive by sipping water" or by having sex with "captive men or passing merchants."

11. Mosuo: Shaltly 2010.

12. Earliest mentions of steppe nomads in Chinese texts, Minns 1913, 91–97. Lebedynsky 2006, 58–62.

13. Xiongnu: Beckwith 2009, 70–77. The Xianbei, like the Xiongnu, a confederation of northern horse archers, descendants of the Donghu described by Sima Qian in the 7th century BC; see http://www.colorq.org/articles/article.aspx?d=asian women&x=huangguigu. Linduff 2008, 177–81. Qin Shi Huang, first Qin emperor of unified China (d. 210 BC) was famously buried with an army of terra-cotta soldiers. Nomads and China, Barfield 1992.

14. Chen Shou's *Sanguozhi* ("Records of the Three Kingdoms"), vols 32, 36–37, 46–47, 50, 66; Chinese historical text of the late Han Dynasty and Three Kingdoms period (ca 184 BC to AD 280). Lee, Stefanowska, and Wiles. 2007, 348–52.

15. Perkins 1998; "Biographical Sketches" 2001–2, 19–21; Dong 2010, 17–18; Lee, Stefanowska, and Wiles 2007, 365–66. See also "Ten Ancient Chinese Women Warriors," ed. Zhao Chenxi, Xun Guan and Mao: http://history.cultural-china.com /en/48History11637.html and http://history.cultural-china.com/en/48History11638 .html. Jones 2000, 24–25.

16. Jones 2000, 26. Thanks to Victor Mair for information on the "Fourteen Amazons." The characters of Paifeng's name suggest that she and her military actions were compared to the wind (*feng*).

17. Peterson et al. 2000. Dong 2010, 21–23.

18. The meaning of Xiongnu, *Hsiung-nu*, is debated: was it a derogatory Chinese name meaning "fierce slaves"? or was it an attempt to render the nomads' own name for their confederation? Beckwith 2009, 70–73, 84–89. Ishjamts 1994. Detailed Chinese sources include the *Shi-ji* ("Historical Records," 2nd and 1st centuries BC) and other texts, see Ishjamts 1994 and Murphy 2003, 22. Chinese and the Kyrgyz and Kalmyks, Chadwick and Zhirmunsky 2010, 7–8, 18, 30–33, 38, 92, 142, 147–48, 156, 175, 266, 305. Herodotus 4.108 described the Budini as "large, red-headed, and blue-eyed."

19. Marriage treaties, Peterson et al. 2000, 66–73. China faced women warriors in the east: In the 1st century AD, the Trung sisters led a Vietnamese revolt against the Chinese. Evidence for Korean horsewomen archers, Linduff and Rubinson 2008, 111–27.

20. Steppe influences in China, Chen 2012. Zhang Qian (Chang Ch'ien), Beckwith 2009, 72n58, 77. Harrison 2012, 308–10. Peterson et al. 2000, 69. Poem by Du Fu, 8th century AD.

21. Grave goods, esp armored belts with women, Linduff 2008, 187 and fig 9.10. Murphy 2003, 15–23, 32–36, 54–67, 78–95 and pls 46–48 (female riding injuries and battle traumas). Also http://www.silk-road.com/artl/minyaev1.shtml.

22. Murphy 2003, 24; Ishjamts 1994, 164.

23. Russell 1915, 47–51. Jones 2000, 25–26. Thanks to Jenny Herdman Lando and Carla Nappi for help with the Chinese names in this tale.

24. Shadow plays about the heroine Liu Jinding and many other warrior women, Chen 2007, 6, 104–50, 227–34.

25. Maxine Hong Kingston's *The Woman Warrior* (1975), 20, 120, introduced Mulan to US readers; see discussions in Dong 2010.

26. Mulan (under different surnames—Han Mulan, Wei Mulan, Zhu Mulan, Hua Mulan, and Ren Mulan) has been associated with the Northern Wei (AD 386–557), the Sui (AD 581–618), early and late Tang (AD 618–907) dynasties, and the Yuan Dynasty (1279–1368); she starred in a popular Ming (1368–1644) novel and dramas. Lee, Stefanowska, and Wiles 2007, 323–38. Chen 2012. Dong 2010, 1–2. Kwa and Idema 2010, xiii.

27. See Lee, Stefanowska, and Wiles. 2007, 324; Chen 2012, 39–59, 76, 132; and Mair 2005.

BIBLIOGRAPHY

Ancient Greek and Latin texts are available in translation in the Loeb Classical Library or online at www.perseus.tufts.edu, unless otherwise noted.

Abercromby, J. 1891. "An Amazonian Custom in the Caucasus." *Folklore* 2, 2 (June): 171–81.

Adam of Bremen. 1959. *History of the Archbishops of Hamburg-Bremen.* Ed. F. J. Tschan. New York: Columbia University Press.

Agut-Labordère, D., and M. Chauveau. 2011. *Héros, magiciens et sages oubliés de l'Égypte Ancienne: Une anthologie de la littérature en Égyptien démotique.* Paris: Le Belles Lettres.

Alakbarli, F. 2005. "Amazons." *Azerbaijan International* 13, 1 (Spring): 74–77.

Almasy, A. 2007. "A Greek Amazon in an Egyptian Story—The Character of Queen Serpot in the Cycle of Petubastis." *Studia Aegyptiaca XVIII: Proceedings of the Fourth Central European Conference of Young Egyptologists,* 1–7.

Amazonen: Geheimnisvolle Kriegerinnen. 2010. Exhibition catalog. Historischen Museums der Pfalz Speyer. Munich: Edition Minerva.

Ananikian, M. 1925. *Armenian Mythology,* vol. 7, *Mythology of the World.* New York.

Anderson, J. K. 1961. *Ancient Greek Horsemanship.* Berkeley: University of California Press.

———. 1978. "New Evidence on the Origin of the Spur." *Antike Kunst* 21:46–48.

Anthony, D. 2007. *The Horse, the Wheel, and Language: How Bronze Age Riders from the Eurasian Steppes Shaped the Modern World.* Princeton, NJ: Princeton University Press.

Arrian. 2010. *The Campaigns of Alexander. The Landmark Arrian.* Trans. P. Mensch, ed. J. Romm. New York: Pantheon, 2010.

Arthashastra. 1992. *Kautilia's Arthashastra*. Trans. L. N. Rangarajan. Delhi: Penguin.

Aruz, J., et al., eds. 2000. *Golden Deer of Asia*. New York: Metropolitan Museum.

Ascherson, N. 1995. *Black Sea*. New York: Hill and Wang.

Asher-Perrin, E. 2013. "It's Time to Retire 'Boob Plate' Armor." May 6. http://www.tor.com/blogs/2013/05/boob-plate-armor-would-kill-you.

Ateshi, N. 2011. *The Amazons of the Caucasus*. Berlin: Ganjevi Institut.

Azarpay, G. 1992. *Sogdian Painting: The Pictorial Epic in Oriental Art*. Berkeley: University of California Press.

Bai, D. D. 1995. "Wearing the Sari Mahratta Style." *New Straits Times* (Malaysia, February 6): 36.

Ballesteros-Pastor, L. 2009. "Bears and Bees in Themiscyra: A Sanctuary for Artemis in the Land of the Amazons?" In *From Artemis to Diana*, ed. T. Fischer-Hansen and B. Poulsen, 333–40. Copenhagen: University of Copenhagen.

Banerjee, C. 2007. *Status of Daughter in Early India*. Varanasi: Divine.

Barber, E. W. 1991. *Prehistoric Textiles*. Princeton, NJ: Princeton University Press.

———. 2000. *The Mummies of Urumchi*. New York: Norton.

Barfield, T. 1992. *The Perilous Frontier: Nomadic Empires and China 221 BC to AD 1757*. Oxford: Wiley-Blackwell.

Barkova, L. L., and S. V. Pankova. 2005. "Tattooed Mummies from the Large Pazyryk Mounds: New Findings." *Archaeology, Ethnology & Anthropology of Eurasia* 2, 22:48–59.

Barringer, J. 1996. "Atalanta as Model: The Hunter and the Hunted." *Classical Antiquity* 15, 1:48–76.

———. 2001. *The Hunt in Ancient Greece*. Baltimore: Johns Hopkins University Press.

———. 2004. "Skythian Hunters on Attic Vases." In *Greek Vases, Images, Contexts, and Controversies*, ed. C. Marconi, 13–25. Columbia Studies in the Classical Tradition 25. Leiden: Brill.

Basilov, V. 1989. *Nomads of Eurasia*. Los Angeles: Natural History Museum.

Baum, W. 2004. *Shirin: A Woman of Late Antiquity—Historical Reality and Literary Effect*. Piscataway NJ: Gorgias Press.

Baumeister, R., and J. Mendoza. 2011. "Cultural Variations in the Sexual Marketplace: Gender Equality Correlates with More Sexual Activity." *Journal of Social Psychology* 151, 3:350–60.

Baumer, C. 2012. *The History of Central Asia: The Age of the Steppe Warriors*. London: Tauris.

Baynham, E. 2001. "Alexander and the Amazons." *Classical Quarterly* 51, 1:115–26.

Beck, U., et al. 2014. "The Invention of Trousers and Its Likely Affiliation with Horseback Riding and Mobility: A Case Study of Late 2nd Millennium BC Finds from Turfan in Eastern Central Asia." *Quarternary International*, in press.

Beckwith, C. 2009. *Empires of the Silk Road*. Princeton, NJ: Princeton University Press.

Bennett, F. 1912. *Religious Cults Associated with the Amazons*. New York: Columbia University Press.

Berard, C. 2000. "The Image of the Other and the Foreign Hero." In Cohen, ed., 2000, 390–412.

Berseneva, N. 2008. "Women and Children in the Sargat Culture." In Linduff and Rubinson, eds., 2008, 131–51.

"Biographical Sketches [of women who engaged in military activities in China]." 2001–2. *Chinese Studies in History* 35, 2 (Winter): 11–93.

Blok, J. H. 1995. *The Early Amazons: Modern and Ancient Perspectives on a Persistent Myth*. Leiden: Brill.

Boardman, J. 1983. "Atalanta." *Art Institute of Chicago Museum Studies* 10:2–19.

———. 2002. *The Archaeology of Nostalgia*. London: Thames & Hudson.

———. 2012. "The East Asian Relief Plaques: Central Asia and the West." *Ancient West & East* 11:123–45.

Bokovenko, N., and Z. Samashev. 2012. "The Roots of Iron Age Pastoral Nomadic Culture." In Stark et al., eds., 2012, 20–29.

Bol, R. 1998. *Amazones Volneratae* [Wounded Amazons]. Mainz: Philipp von Zabern.

Bolton, J.D.P. 1962. *Aristeas of Proconnesus*. Oxford: Oxford University Press.

Bonfante, L. 1989. "Nudity as a Costume in Classical Art." *American Journal of Archaeology* 93:543–70.

———, ed. 2011. *The Barbarians of Ancient Europe: Realities and Interactions*. Cambridge: Cambridge University Press.

Bothmer, D. von. 1957. *Amazons in Greek Art*. Oxford: Clarendon Press.

Bowersock, G. W. 2008. "In Search of Strabo, with Some New Light on Mithridates Eupator and His Concubine." *Journal of Roman Archaeology* 21:598–601.

Braund, D., ed. 2005. *Scythians and Greeks: Cultural Interaction in Scythia, Athens, and the Early Roman Empire*. Exeter: University of Exeter.

———. 2010. "Myth and Ritual at Sinope: From Diogenes the Cynic to Sanape the Amazon." *Ancient Civilizations from Scythia to Siberia* 16, 1–2:11–23.

Brend, B. 1995. *The Emperor Akbar's Khamsa of Nizami*. London: British Library.

Brestian, S. de. 2005–7. "Horsemen in Bronze: A Belt from Urartu." *MVSE* (Museum of Art and Archaeology, University of Missouri) 39–41:23–43.

Brindley, J. 1994. "A Note on the Amazon Coins of Soli in Cilicia." *Numismatic Circular* 102 (July/August): 264–65. (Footnotes are in September/October issue.)

Bron, C. 1996. "The Sword Dance for Artemis." *J. Paul Getty Museum Journal* 24:69–83.

Brown, F., and W. B. Tyrrell. 1985. "*Ektilosanto*: A Reading of Herodotus' Amazons." *Classical Journal* 80, 4:297–302.

Bryce, J. 1878. *Transcaucasia and Ararat.* London: Macmillan.

Brzezinsky, B., and M. Mielczarek. 2002. *The Sarmatians, 600 BC–AD 450.* Oxford: Osprey.

Bukker, I. 2011. "The Mysterious Tattoos of the Princess of Altai." *Pravda*, April 4.

Burgin, D. L. 1995. "Mother Nature versus the Amazons: Marina Tsvetaeva and the Female Same-Sex Love." *Journal of the History of Sexuality* 6, 1:62–88.

Buxton, R. 1994. *Imaginary Greece: The Contexts of Mythology.* Cambridge: Cambridge University Press.

Carney, E. 2000. *Women and Monarchy in Macedonia.* Norman: University of Oklahoma Press.

———. 2014. "Commemoration of a Royal Woman as a Warrior: The Burial in the Antichamber of Tomb II at Vergina." Paper delivered at the Archaeological Institute of America, Chicago, January 2.

Castriota, D. 1992. *Myth, Ethos, and Actuality: Official Art in Fifth Century B.C. Athens.* Madison: University of Wisconsin Press.

Ceccarelli, P.1998. *La pirrica nell' antichita greco romana: Studi sulla danza armata.* Rome: IEPI.

Cernenko, E. V. 1983. *The Scythians: 700–300 BC.* Oxford: Osprey.

Chadwick, N., and V. Zhirmunsky. 2010. *Oral Epics of Central Asia*. Cambridge: Cambridge University Press.

Chase, G. 1902. "The Shield Devices of the Greeks." *Harvard Studies in Classical Philology* 13:61–127.

Chelkowski, P. 1975. *Mirror of the Invisible World: Tales from the* Khamseh *of Nizami*. New York: Metropolitan Museum of Art.

Chen, F.P.L. 2007. *Chinese Shadow Theatre: History, Popular Religion, and Women Warriors.* Montreal: McGill-Queens Press.

Chen, S. 2012. *Multicultural China in the Early Middle Ages*. Philadelphia: University of Pennsylvania Press.

Chenciner, R., G. Ismailov, and M. Magomedkhanov. 2006. *Tattooed Mountain Women and Spoon Boxes of Daghestan: Magic Symbols on Silk, Stone, Wood, and Flesh.* London: Bennett and Bloom/Desert Hearts.

Christine de Pizan. 1999. *The Book of the City of Ladies*. Trans. R. Brown-Grant. London: Penguin.

Chugg, A. M. 2006. *Alexander's Lovers*. Lulu.com and www.alexanderslovers.com/main/index.html.

Chugunov, K., A. Nagler, and H. Parzinger. 2001. "The Golden Grave from Arzhan." *Minerva* 13 (1): 39–42.

Classic of Mountain and Seas. 1999. Trans. Anne Birrell. London: Penguin.

Clayton, S. P. 2002. "The Woman Warrior: Fact or Tale." *Estudio Literatura Oral* 7–8:69–84. https://sapientia.ualg.pt/bitstream/10400.1/1440/1/7_8 _Clayton.pdf.

Cohen, B. 2000. "Man-Killers and Their Victims." In Cohen, ed., 2000, 98–131.

———, ed. 2000. *Not the Classical Ideal: Athens and the Construction of the Other in Greek Art*. Leiden: Brill.

———. 2006. *The Colors of Clay: Special Techniques in Athenian Vases*. Los Angeles: Getty Museum.

———. 2012. "The Non-Greek in Greek Art." In *A Companion to Greek Art*, ed. T. J. Smith and D. Plantzos, 2:456–80. London: Wiley-Blackwell.

Cohen, P. 2010. *Speaking to History: The Story of King Goujian in 20th Century China*. Berkeley: University of California Press.

Colarusso, J. 2002. *Nart Sagas from the Caucasus: Myths and Legends from the Circassians, Abazas, Abkhaz, and Ubykhs*. Princeton, NJ: Princeton University Press.

Coleman, K. 2000. "Missio at Halicarnassus." *Studies in Classical Philology* 100:487–500.

Colvin, S. 1872–1926. "Penthesilea." Unpublished MS, 30 pp. Sidney Colvin Papers, Folder 7, no. 860682. Getty Research Institute, Los Angeles.

———. 1883. "Paintings on the Amazon Sarcophagus of Corneto." *Journal of Hellenic Studies* 4:354–69.

Connor, S. 2011. "Jason and the Argot: Land Where Greek's Ancient Language Survives." *Independent* (London), January 3.

Cook, B. 1989. "Footwork in Ancient Greek Swordsmanship." *Metropolitan Museum Journal* 24:57–64.

Cool, H. 2004. *The Roman Cemetery at Brougham, Cumbria: Excavations 1966 and 1967*. Britannia Monograph 21. London: Roman Society.

———. 2005. "Pyromania." *British Archaeology* (January–February): 30–35.

Ctesias. 2010. *History of Persia, Tales of the Orient*. Trans. and comm. L. Llewellyn-Jones and J. Robson. London: Routledge.

Davis-Kimball, J. 1997a. "Warrior Women of the Eurasian Steppes." *Archaeology* 50, 1 (January/February): 44–48.

———. 1997b. "Chieftain or Warrior Princess?" *Archaeology* 50, 5 (September/October): 40–41.

———. 2002. *Warrior Women: An Archaeologist's Search for History's Hidden Heroines*. New York: Warner Books.

———. 2012. "Among Our Earliest Amazons: Eurasian Priestesses and Warrior-Women." *Labrys, études féministes* 22 (December). http://www .tanianavarroswain.com.br/labrys/labrys22/archeo/jeannine_daviskim ball.htm.

Della Casa, P., and C. Witt, eds. 2013. *Tattoos and Body Modifications in Antiquity*. Proceedings of the European Association of Archaeologists annual meetings in The Hague and Oslo, 2010–11. *Zurich Studies in Archaeology 9*.

Dewald, C. 1981. "Women and Culture in Herodotus' *History*." In *Reflections of Women in Antiquity*, ed. Helene Foley. New York: Gordon and Breach.

"Discovery of Tattoos on Ancient Mummies from Siberia." 2005. *Hermitage News*, News Archive, Collection Highlights for 2005.

Doksanalti, E., and I. Mimiroglu. 2011. "Giresun/Aretias—Khalkeritis Island." Proceedings of International Conference, Cultural Borders and Border Cultures across the Passage of Time, Bronze Age to Late Antiquity, Trnava, Slovakia, October 22–24, 2010. *Anodos: Studies of the Ancient World* 10 (2010): 85–101.

Doksanalti, E., I. Mimiroglu, and H. Gulec. 2011. "Giresun (Aretias-Khalkeritis) Adası Kazısı Ön Rapor: 2011." *Anadolu ve Çevresinde Ortaçağ* 5 (Ankara): 163–84. English summary.

Dong, L. 2010. *Mulan's Legend and Legacy in China and the United States*. Philadelphia: Temple University Press.

Dowden, K. 1997. "The Amazons: Development and Function. *Rheinisches Museum fur Philologie* 140:97–128.

Dratchuk V. S., 1975. *Systems of Signs of the Northern Black Sea Coast (Sistemy znakov Severnogo Prichernomor'ya)*. Kiev.

Dubois, P. 1991. *Centaurs and Amazons*. Ann Arbor: University of Michigan Press.

Dugan, F. 2009. "Dregs of Our Forgotten Ancestors: Fermentative Microorganisms in the Pre-History of Europe, the Steppes, and Indo-Iranian Asia." *Fungi* 2, 4:16–39.

Durham, M. 1928. *Some Tribal Origins, Laws and Customs of the Balkans*. London: Allen & Unwin.

Dyczek, P. 2011a. *Iliria i prowincje bałkańskie w Zjednoczonej Europie/Iliria dhe provincat ballkanike në Evropën e Bashkuar/Illyria and the Balkan Provinces in United Europe*. Warsaw: University of Warsaw.

———. 2011b. "From the History of Ancient Rhizon/Risinium: Why Illyrian King Agron and Queen Teuta Came to a Bad End and Who Was Ballaios?" In *Classica Orientalia, Essays Presented to Wiktor Andrzej Daszewski*, ed. I. Zych and M. Henry, 157–74. Warsaw: University of Warsaw.

Edmunds, A. L. 1997. "The Horse and the Maiden (Aeschines 1.182 etc.): An Urban Legend in Ancient Athens (with Appendices by R. Palmer)." Paper delivered at Universities of Milan and Trieste. http://www.rci.rutgers.edu/~edmunds/HorseText.html.

Eller, C. 2011. *Gentlemen and Amazons: The Myth of Matriarchal Prehistory, 1861–1900*. Berkeley: University of California Press.

Eph'al, I. 1982. *The Ancient Arabs: Nomads on the Borders of the Fertile Crescent 9th–5th Centuries BC*. Leiden: Brill.

Epstein, H. 1943. "The Origin and Earliest History of Falconry. *Isis* 34, 6:497–509.

Fantham, E., H. Foley, N. Kampen, S. Pomeroy, and H. A. Shapiro. 1994. *Women in the Classical World: Image and Text*. New York: Oxford University Press.

Farkas, A. 1982. "Style and Subject Matter in Native Thracian Art." *Metropolitan Museum Journal* 16:33–48.

"Fashion and Beauty Secrets of a 2,500 year old Siberian 'Princess' from Her Permafrost Burial Chamber." 2012. *Siberian Times*, August 28.

Ferdowsi, A. 2006. *Shahnameh: The Persian Book of Kings*. Trans. D. Davis. London: Penguin.

Fialko, E. E. 1991. "Zhenskiye pogrebenya s orushiem v skyphskih kurganah stepnoi Skyphii (The female burials with weapons among the Scythians: Kurgans of the Scythian steppes)." *Editorial Naukova Dumka*, 4–18.

———. 2010. "Amazons' Tombs from Mamay-Gora Cemetery." *Stratum (People and Things in the Iron Age)* 3:187–96.

Field, H. 1958. *Body-Marking in Southwestern Asia*. Cambridge: Peabody Museum.

Fluehr-Lobban, C. 1998. "Nubian Queens in the Nile Valley and Afro-Asiatic Cultural History." Paper delivered at the Ninth International Conference for Nubian Studies, Museum of Fine Arts, Boston, August 20–26.

Forster, P., and C. Renfrew. 2011. "Mother Tongue and Y Chromosomes." *Science* 333 (6048):1390–91.

Fowler, R. L. 2013. *Early Greek Mythography*, vol. 2, *Commentary*. Oxford: Oxford University Press.

Freeman, P. 2002. *War, Women, and Druids: Eyewitness Reports and Early Accounts of the Ancient Celts*. Austin: University of Texas Press.

Gantz, T. 1993. *Early Greek Myth*. 2 vols. Baltimore: Johns Hopkins University Press.

Gardiner-Garden, J. 1986. "Fourth Century Conceptions of Maiotian Ethnography." *Historia* 35, 2:192–225.

Gardner, E. 1906. "The Atalanta of Tegea." *Journal of Hellenic Studies* 26: 169–75.

Garstang, J. 1929. *The Hittite Empire*. London: Constable.

Gera, D. L. 1997. *Warrior Women: The Anonymous Tractatus De Mulieribus*. Mnemosyne, Bibliotheca Classica Batava. Supplementum, No. 162. Leiden: Brill.

Gheyle, W. 2006. "Saviors from Space for Siberia's Frozen Tombs." *World of Science* (UNESCO) 4, 3:19–23.

Gidley, R., and M. Rowling. 2006. "Millions of Cameroon Girls Suffer Breast Ironing." Child Rights Information Network, July 13. http://www.crin .org/en/library/news-archive/millions-cameroon-girls-suffer-breast -ironing.

Gleba, M. 2008. "You Are What You Wear: Scythian Costume as Identity." In *Dressing the Past*, ed. M. Gleba, C. Munkholt, and M.-L. Nosch, 13–28. Oxford: Oxbow Books.

Gonzalez de Clavijo, R. 1859. *Narrative of the Embassy . . . to the Court of Timour at Samarcand 1403–6*. Trans. C. Markham. London: Hakluyt Society.

Greek Alexander Romance. 1991. Trans. Richard Stoneman. London: Penguin.

Guliaev, V. I. 2003. "Amazons in the Scythia: New Finds at the Middle Don, Southern Russia." *World Archaeology* 35, 1:112–25.

Hall, A. 2013. "Cameroon's Women Call Time on Breast Ironing." *New Internationalist* 462 (May). http://newint.org/features/2013/05/01/tales -of-taboo.

Hall, E. 2012. *Adventures with Iphigenia in Taurus: A Cultural History of Euripides' Black Sea Tragedy*. Oxford: Oxford University Press.

Hambastegi News (Tehran). 2004. "Bones Suggest Women Went to War in Ancient Iran." Reported by Reuters, December 4. "Woman Warrior Found in Iranian Tomb." MSNBC, December 6.

Han, J., ed. 2008. *Preservation of the Frozen Tombs of the Altai Mountains*. UNESCO World Heritage Centre and Flanders Funds in Trust. Paris: Ateliers Industria.

Hanks, B. 2008. "Reconsidering Warfare, Status, and Gender in the Eurasian Steppe Iron Age." In Linduff and Rubinson, eds., 2008, 15–34.

Hard, R. 2004. *The Routledge Handbook of Greek Mythology*. London: Routledge.

Hardwick, L. 1990. "Ancient Amazons—Heroes, Outsiders or Women?" *Greece and Rome*, 2nd ser., 37, 1:14–36.

Harmatta, J. 1970. "Studies in the History and Language of the Sarmatians." *Acta Universitatis de Attila József Nominatae. Acta antique et archaeologica Tomus* 13. Szeged, Hungary.

———. 1999. *History of Civilizations of Central Asia*. Vol. 2. Delhi: Motilal Banarsidass.

Harrison, E. B. 1981. "Motifs of the City-Siege on the Shield of Athena Parthenos." *American Journal of Archaeology* 85, 3:281–317.

Harrison, J. 1888. "Some Fragments of a Vase Presumably by Euphronios." *Journal of Hellenic Studies* 9:143–46.

Harrison, T. 2012. *The Horse Road*. New York: Bloomsbury.

Hartog, F. 1988. *The Mirror of Herodotus*. Berkeley: University of California Press.

Henning, S. 2007. "The Maiden of Yue: Fount of Chinese Martial Arts Theory." *Journal of Asian Martial Arts* 16, 3.

Hepburn, K. 1991. *Me: Stories of My Life*. New York: Random House.

Herodotus. 2007. *The Histories. The Landmark Herodotus*. Trans. A. Purvis, ed. R. Strassler. New York: Pantheon.

Hippocratic Writings. 1983. Ed. G.E.R. Lloyd, trans. J. Chadwick and W. N. Mann. Harmondsworth: Penguin.

Hoffmann, F. 2008. "Warlike Women in Ancient Egypt." *CRIPEL: Cahiers de Recherches de l'Institut de Papyrologie et d'Égyptologie de Lille* 27:49–57.

Hosoi, N. 2007. "Des femmes au louterion. À la croisée d'une esthétique masculine et féminine au travers des objets." *Images Re-vues* 4. http://imagesrevues.revues.org/145.

How, W. W., and J. Wells. 1912. *A Commentary on Herodotus*. 2 vols. Oxford: Clarendon.

Huld. M. 2002. "Some Thoughts on Amazons." *Journal of Indo-European Studies* 30:93–102.

Hunt, D. 2012. *Legends of the Caucasus*. London: Saqi.

Hurriyet Daily News. 2010. "4,000-Year-Old Legend about Northern Turkey." June 6, Giresun, Anatolia News Agency.

Hutton, J. H. 1921. *The Angami Nagas with Some Notes on Neighboring Tribes*. London: Macmillan.

Ishjamts, N. 1994. "Nomads in Eastern Central Asia." In *History of Civilizations of Central Asia*, vol. 3, ed. J. Harmatta, 151–69. Paris: UNESCO.

Ivantchik, A. 2006. "Scythian Archers on Archaic Attic Vases: Problems of Interpretation." *Ancient Civilizations from Scythia to Siberia* 12, 3–4: 197–271.

———. 2011. "The Funeral of Scythian Kings: The Historical Reality and the Description of Herodotus (4.7 1–72)." In Bonfante, ed., 2011, 71–106.

Izady, M. R. 1992. *The Kurds: A Concise Handbook*. London: Taylor & Francis.

Jaimoukha, A. 2001. *The Circassians: A Handbook*. London: Taylor & Francis.

Jeffreys, E., ed. and trans. 1998. *Digenis Akritas*. Cambridge: Cambridge University Press.

Jones, D. E. 2000. *Women Warriors: A History*. Washington, DC: Potomac Books.

Jones-Bley, K. 2008. "*Arma Feminamque Cano*: Warrior-Women in the Indo-European World." In Linduff and Rubinson, eds., 35–50.

Jordana, X., et al. 2009. "Warriors of the Steppes: Osteological Evidence of Warfare and Violence from Pazyryk Tumuli in the Mongolian Altai." *Journal of Archaeological Science* 36:1319–27.

Jordanes. 1915. *The Gothic History of Jordanes*. Trans. Charles C. Mierow. Princeton, NJ: Princeton University Press. Rpt. 2006, Evolution Publishing.

Justin. 1994. *Epitome of the Philippic History of Pompeius Trogus*. Trans. J. Yardley. Atlanta: Scholars Press.

Karanth, K. S. 2002. *Yaksagana.* New Delhi: Abhinav.

Karpowicz, A., and S. Selby. 2010. "Scythian Bow from Xinjiang." *Journal of the Society of Archer-Antiquaries* 53. http://www.atarn.org/chinese/Yang hai/Scythian_bow_ATARN.pdf.

Keyser-Tracqui, C. et al. 2005. "Mitochondrial DNA Analysis of Horses Recovered from a Frozen Tomb (Berel Site, Kazakhstan, 3rd Century BC)." *Animal Genetics* 36, 3:203–9.

Kinzer, S. 1999. "The Unfenced Life, under the Celestial Mountains." *New York Times International*, October 5.

Klaproth, J. von. 1814. *Travels in the Caucasus and Georgia . . . 1807 and 1808 by Command of the Russian Government.* N.p.: Henry Colburn. Rpt. 2009, General Books.

Kleiner, F. S. 2010. *A History of Roman Art: Enhanced Edition.* Boston: Wadsworth.

Kohanov, L. 2001. *The Tao of Equus.* Novato, CA: New World Library.

Konstan, D. 2002. "Women, Ethnicity and Power in the Roman Empire." *Ordia Prima* 1:11–23.

Korfmann, M. 2004. "Was There a Trojan War?" *Archaeology* (May/June): 36–41.

Kroll, J. 1977. "An Archive of the Athenian Cavalry." *Hesperia* 46, 2:83–140.

Kruk, R. 2013. *The Warrior Women of Islam.* London: Tauris.

Krutak, L. 2010. "Tattooing in North Africa, the Middle East, and Balkans." http://www.vanishingtattoo.com/north_africa_tattoo_history.htm.

Kwa, S., and W. Idema. 2010. *Mulan: Five Versions of a Classic Chinese Legend.* Indianapolis: Hackett.

Langdon, S. 2001. "Trial by Amazon: Thoughts on the First Amazons in Greek Art." *Festshrift for Eugene N. Lane.* Stoa Consortium, May 23. Lexington, KY.

Laumann, E. O., et al. 2006. "A Cross-National Study of Subjective Sexual Well-Being: Findings from the Global Study of Sexual Attitudes and Behaviors." *Archives of Sexual Behavior* 35, 2:145–61.

Leal, E. 2010. "The Empire's Muse: Roman Interpretations of the Amazons through Literature and Art." MA thesis, San Diego State University.

Lebedynsky, I. 2006. *Les Saces: Les 'Scythes' d'Asie.* Paris: Editions Errance.

———. 2009. *Les Amazones: Mythe et Realite des femmes guerrieres chez anciens nomades de la steppe.* Paris: Editions Errance.

———. 2010. *Les Scythes.* 2nd ed. Paris: Editions Errance.

———. 2011. *Les Tamgas: Une 'Heraldique' de la Steppe.* Paris: Editions Errance.

Lee, J. 2007. *A Greek Army on the March: Soldiers and Survival in Xenophon's Anabasis.* Cambridge: Cambridge University Press.

Lee, L.X.H., A. D. Stefanowska, and S. Wiles, eds. 2007. *Biographical Dictionary of Chinese Women: Antiquity through Sui.* Armonk NY: M. E. Sharpe.

Lefkowitz, M. R. 2007. *Women in Greek Myth*. 2nd ed. Baltimore: Johns Hopkins University Press.

Levy, A. 2012. "A Ring of One's Own." *New Yorker* (May 7): 38–47.

Lewis, G. 1974. *The Book of Dede Korkut*. Harmondsworth: Penguin.

Lichtheim, M. 1980. *Ancient Egyptian Literature*, vol. 3, *The Late Period*. Berkeley: University of California Press.

Lillis, J. 2010. "Kazakh Archaeologists Discover Ancient Scythian 'Sun Lord.'" Kazinform News Agency, July 16. http://www.eurasianet.org /node/61549.Linduff, K. 2008. "The Gender of Luxury and Power among the Xiongnu." In Linduff and Rubinson, eds., 175–213.

Linduff, K., and K. Rubinson, eds. 2008. *Are All Warriors Male? Gender Roles on the Eurasian Steppe*. Lanham, MD: Altamira Press.

Lissarrague, F. 1990. *L'autre guerrier: Archers, peltastes, cavaliers dans l'imagerie attique*. Paris: Ecole Français.

———. 1992. "Figures of Women." In Schmitt Pantel, ed., 1992, 139–229.

Lobell, J., and E. Powell. 2013. "Ancient Tattoos." *Archaeology* (November/ December). http://www.archaeology.org/issues/109–1311/features/1360 -cucuteni-jomon-lapita-thracian-moche-mississippian-ibaloi.

"'Lost' Tribe Linked East and West." 2013. *Shanghai Daily*, Xinhua News Agency (September 7). http://www.shanghaidaily.com/Feature/art-and -culture/Lost-tribe-linked-East-and-West/shdaily.shtml.

Maclean, J., and E. Aitken, eds. 2004. *Philostratus's* Heroikos. Atlanta: Society for Biblical Literature.

Macurdy, G. H. 1975 [1937]. *Hellenistic Queens: A Study of Woman-Power in Macedonia, Seleucid Syria, and Ptolemaic Egypt*. Westport, CT: Greenwood Press.

Mair, V. 2005. "The North(west)ern Peoples and the Recurrent Origins of the 'Chinese' State." In *Teleology of the Modern Nation-State: Japan and China*, ed. J. A. Fogel, 46–84, 205–17. Philadelphia: University of Pennsylvania Press.

Mair, V., S. Chen, and F. Wood. 2013. *Chinese Lives: The People Who Made a Civilization*. London: Thames & Hudson.

Mallory, J. P., and V. Mair. 2008. *The Tarim Mummies*. London: Thames and Hudson.

Marazov, I. 2011a. *Thrace and the Ancient World: Vassil Bojkov Collection*. Sofia: Thrace Foundation.

———. 2011b. "Philomele's Tongue: Reading the Pictorial Text of Thracian Mythology." In Bonfante, ed., 2011, 132–89.

Marconi, C. 2004. "Images for a Warrior." In *Greek Vases, Images, Contexts, and Controversies*, ed. C. Marconi, 27–40. Columbia Studies in the Classical Tradition 25. Leiden: Brill.

Maslow, J. 1997. "The Golden Horses of Turkmenistan." *Saudi Aramco World* 48 (May–June): 10–19.

Mayor, A. 1999. "People Illustrated." *Archaeology* 52, 2:54–57.

———. 2009. *Greek Fire, Poison Arrows, and Scorpion Bombs: Biological and Chemical Warfare in the Ancient World*. 2nd rev. ed. New York: Overlook/ Duckworth.

———. 2010. *The Poison King: The Life and Legend of Mithradates, Rome's Deadliest Enemy*. Princeton, NJ: Princeton University Press.

Mayor, A., J. Colarusso, and D. Saunders. 2014. "Making Sense of Nonsense Inscriptions Associated with Amazons and Scythians on Athenian Vases." *Hesperia* 83, 3 (September).

Mayor, A., and J. Ober. 1991. "Amazons." *MHQ: The Quarterly Journal of Military History*, 68–77. Rpt. in *The Experience of War*, ed. Robert Cowley, 12–23. New York: Norton, 1992.

McCrindle, J. W., trans. 1877. *Ancient India as Described by Megasthenes and Arrian*. London: Trübner.

McNiven, T. 2000. "Behaving Like an Other: Telltale Gestures in Athenian Vase Paintings." In Cohen, ed., 2000, 71–97.

Merker, G. 2000. *Sanctuary of Demeter and Kore: Terracotta Figurines of Classical, Hellenistic, and Roman Periods. Corinth*, vol. 18, pt. 4. Athens: American School of Classical Studies.

Merola, M. 2010. "Turkish Delights: Spectacular Byzantine Mosaics Revealed." *Archaeology* 53 (January/February): 35–37.

Meserve, R. I. 1989. "Tattooing in Inner Asia." In *Religious and Lay Symbolism in the Altaic World and Other Papers*, ed. K. Sagaster with H. Eimer, 206–24. Wiesbaden: Otto Harrassowitz.

———. 1999. "Writing on Man or Animal." in *Writing in the Altaic World*, ed. J. Janhunen and V. Rybatzhi. *Studia Orientalia* 87:171–86.

Miller, M. 2004. *Athens and Persia in the Fifth Century BC: A Study in Cultural Receptivity*. Cambridge: Cambridge University Press.

Minns, E. H. 1913. *Scythians and Greeks*. Cambridge: Cambridge University Press.

Molodin V. 1995. *Perspective and Preliminary Results of Archaeological Investigation of the South-Western Altai (Ukok Plateau)*, vol. 1, *Science Policy: New Mechanism for Scientific Collaboration between East and West*. Dordrecht: NATO ASI Series.

Moore, M. 1971. "Horses on Black Figured Greek Vases of the Archaic Period, ca 620–480 BC." PhD diss., New York University.

Moreno, A. 2007. *Feeding the Democracy: Athenian Grain Supply in the Fifth and Fourth Centuries BC*. Oxford: Oxford University Press.

Moscati-Castelnuovo, L. 1999. "From East to West: The Eponymous Amazon Cleta." In *Ancient Greeks West and East*, ed. G. Tsetskhladze, 163–77. Leiden: Brill.

Murphy, E. M. 2003. *Iron Age Archaeology and Trauma from Aymyrlyg, South Siberia*. BAR International Series 1152, December 31.

————. 2004. "Herodotus and the Amazons Meet the Cyclops: Philology, Osteoarchaeology, and the Eurasian Iron Age." In *Archaeology and Ancient History*, ed. E. Sauer, 169–84. London: Routledge.

Muth, S. 2008. *Gewalt im Bild.* Berlin: Walter de Gruyter.

Neils, J. 2000. "Others within the Other." In Cohen, ed., 2000, 203–26.

Nemytov, N. 2001. "Ратоборцы (Battle Fighters)." *Тайная доктрина* (Secret Doctrines) 12–13. Tavricheskiy Publishing House.

Nioradze, G. K. 1931. "Das Grab von Semoawtschala." *Bulletin du Musée de Géorgie* (Tiflis) 6 (1929–30): 221–28, and fig. p. 142.

Oakley, J. 2000. "Some 'Other' Members of the Athenian Household." In Bonfante, ed., 2011, 227–47.

Olsen, S., and D. Harding. 2008. "Women's Attire and Possible Sacred Role in 4th Millennium Northern Kazakhstan. In Linduff and Rubinson, eds., 2008, 67–92.

Osborne, L. 1998. "The Women Warriors." *Lingua Franca* (December/January): 50–57.

Osborne, R. 2011. *The History Written on the Classical Greek Body.* Cambridge: Cambridge University Press.

Outram, A. K., et al. 2009. "The Earliest Horse Harnessing and Milking." *Science* 323 (March): 1332–35.

Padgett, J. M. 2014. "Whom Are You Calling Barbarian? A Column Krater by the Suessula Painter." In *Athenian Potters and Painters III*, ed. J. Oakley. Oxford: Oxbow Books.

Palaephatus. 1996. *On Unbelievable Tales.* Trans. Jacob Stern. Wauconda, IL: Bolchazy-Carducci.

Palagia, O. 2008. "The Grave Relief of Adea, Daughter of Cassander and Cynnana." In *Macedonian Legacies . . . in Honor of Eugene Borza*, ed. T. Howe and J. Reames, 195–214. Claremont, CA.

Pattanaik, D. 2000. *The Goddess in India.* Rochester, VT: Inner Traditions.

Pausanias. 1979. *Descriptions of Greece.* Trans. Peter Levi. Harmondsworth: Penguin.

Pelling, C. 1997. "East Is East and West Is West—Or Are They? National Stereotypes in Herodotus." *Histos* (online Journal of Ancient Historiography, University of Durham) 1 (March): 1–11. http://research.ncl.ac.uk/histos/documents/1997.04PellingEastIsEast5166.pdf.

Perkins, D. 1998. *Encyclopedia of China.* New York: Facts on File.

Peterson, B. B., et al., eds. 2000. *Notable Women of China: Shang Dynasty to Early 20th Century.* New York: Sharpe.

Petit, P. 1685. *De Amazonibus dissertatio.* Paris: Andreae Cramoisy.

Philostratus. 2002. *On Heroes.* Trans. J. Maclean and E. Aitken. Atlanta: Society of Biblical Literature.

Phoenix and Arabeth. 1999. *Ancient Tattooed People of Central Asia.* Ukiah, CA.

Polo, Marco. 1993. *The Travels of Marco Polo: The Complete Yule-Cordier Edition.* Trans. H. Yule. New York: Dover.

Polosmak, N. 1994. "A Mummy Unearthed from the Pastures of Heaven." *National Geographic* 186, 4:80–103.

———. 2001. *Всадники Укока (Ukok Riders).* Novosibirsk: Infolio Press.

———. 2003. "Textiles from the 'Frozen Tombs' of Gorny Altai, Russia (400–200 BC)." Paper delivered at the Ancient Textiles Conference, Copenhagen and Lund, March 19–23.

Polosmak, N., and L. Barkova. 2005. Костюм и текстиль пазырыкцев Алтая (IV–III вв. до н.э., "Pazyryk Culture and Clothing"). Novosibirsk: Infolio Press.

Pringle, H., and J. Broad. 2001. "Gladiatrix." *Discover Magazine* 22, 12 (December):48–55.

Quintus of Smyrna. 2004. *Fall of Troy (The Trojan Epic: Posthomerica).* Trans. and ed. A. James. Baltimore: Johns Hopkins University Press.

Reed, C. 2000. "Early Chinese Tattoo." *Sino-Platonic Papers* 103:1–52.

Reineggs, J. 1796. *Beschreibung des Kaukasus.* Gotha and St. Petersburg.

———. 1807. *A General, Historical, and Topographical Description of Mount Caucasus.* London: Taylor.

Richter, G. 1959. "Pliny's Five Amazons." *Archaeology Magazine* 12, 2:111–15.

Ridgway, B. S. 1974. "A Story of Five Amazons." *American Journal of Archaeology* 78, 1:1–17.

Risch, E. 1974. *Wortbildung der homerischen Sprache.* Berlin: de Gruyter.

Robinson, D. 1906. *Ancient Sinope.* Chicago: University of Chicago. Rpt. 2010, Nabu Press.

Rolle, R. 1989. *The World of the Scythians.* Berkeley: University of California Press.

———. 2011. "The Scythians." In Bonfante, ed., 2011, 107–31.

Romance of Alexander the Great by Pseudo-Callisthenes. 1969. Armenian version, trans. A. Wolohojian. New York: Columbia University Press.

Romm, J. 2011. *Ghost on the Throne.* New York: Random House.

Rothery, G. C. 1910. *The Amazons in Antiquity and Modern Times.* London: Francis Griffiths.

Rubinson, K. 1990. "The Textiles from Pazyryk: A Study in the Transfer and Transformation of Artistic Motifs." *Expedition* 32, 1:49–61.

———. 2008. "Tillya Tepe: Aspects of Gender and Cultural Identity." In Linduff and Rubinson, eds., 51–63.

Rudenko, S. 1970 [1953]. *Frozen Tombs of Siberia: The Pazyryk Burials of Iron Age Horsemen.* Berkeley: University of California Press.

Russell, N. N. 1915. *Gleanings from Chinese Folklore.* New York: Revell.

Rutherford, I. 1997. "Kalasiris and Setne Khamwas: A Greek Novel and Some Egyptian Models. *Zeitschrift für Papyrologies und Epigraphik* 117:203–9.

Ryholt, K. 2009. "Egyptian Historical Literature from the Greco-Roman Period." In *Das Ereignis*, ed. M. Fitzenreiter, IBAES 10:231–38. London.

Samashev, Z. 2011. *Berel Kurgans*. Astana, Kazkhstan: Margulan Archaeological Institute.

———. 2013. *Ancient Art of Kazakhstan*. Almaty, Kazkhstan: Margulan Archaeological Institute.

Samashev, Z., and H.-P. Francfort. 2002. "Scythian Steeds." *Archaeology* 55, 3 (May/June): 32–35.

Sancisi-Weerdenburg, H. 1985. "The Death of Cyrus: Xenophon's *Cyropaedia* as a Source for Iranian History." *Acta Iranica* 25:459–71.

———. 1993. "Exit Atossa: Images of Women in Greek Historiography of Persia." In *Images of Women in Antiquity*, ed. A. Cameron and A. Kuhrt, 20–33. Abingdon: Routledge.

Saporiti, M. 2009. "L'Immagine Tatuata." In *Icone del Mondo Antico*, ed. M. Harari, S. Paltineri, and M. Robino, 129–38. Rome: Bretschneider.

Saunders, D. 2014. "An Amazonomachy Attributed to the Syleus Painter." In *Athenian Potters and Painters III*, ed. J. Oakley. Oxford: Oxbow Books.

Schaps, D. 1982. "The Women of Greece in Wartime." *Classical Philology* 77:193–213.

Schefold, K. 1993. *God and Heroes in Late Archaic Greek Art*. Trans. A. Griffiths. Cambridge: Cambridge University Press.

Schetnikov, A. 2001. "Amazon Graves Found in Kazakhstan." *Times of Central Asia*, April 27.

Schmitt Pantel, P., ed. 1992. *A History of Women in the West*, vol. 1, *From Ancient Goddesses to Christian Saints*. London: Belknap.

Schober, G. 1762. *Memorabilia Russico-Asiatica*. St. Petersburg.

Serwint, N. 1993. "The Female Athletic Costume at the Heraia and Prenuptial Initiation Rites." *American Journal of Archaeology* 97:403–22.

Shapiro, H. A. 1983. "Amazons, Thracians, and Scythians." *Greek, Roman and Byzantine Studies* 24, 2:105–16.

———. 2009. "A Non-Greek Rider on the Athenian Akropolis and Representations of Scythians in Attic Vase Painting." In *An Archaeology of Representations: Ancient Greek Vase-Paintings and Contemporary Methodologies*, ed. D. Yatromanolakis, 325–40. Athens: Kardamitsa.

Shelach, G. 2008. "He Who Eats the Horse, She Who Rides It?" In Linduff and Rubinson, eds., 2008, 93–109.

Shaltly, S. 2010. "Is China's Mosuo Tribe the World's Last Matriarchy?" *Guardian* (December 18).

Shoolbraid, G.M.H. 1997. *The Oral Epic of Siberia and Central Asia (Uralic and Altaic)*. Routledge.

"Siberian Princess Reveals Her 2,500 Year Old Tattoos." 2012. *Siberian Times*, August 12.

Skrzhinskaya, M. V. 1982. "Skifskije syuzhety v istoricheskikh predanijakh ol'biopolitov" (Scythian motifs in historical tales of Olbia). *Vestnik drevnei istorii* 4:87–102.

———. 1998. *Skifiya Glazami Ellinov* (Scythia through Greek eyes). St. Petersburg: Aleteiya.

Smeaton, W. 1937. "Tattooing among the Arabs of Iraq." *American Anthropologist* 39:53–61.

Smith, P., trans. 2012. *Nizami: The Treasury of Mysteries.* CreateSpace Independent Publishing.

Snodgrass, A. 1998. *Homer and the Artists.* Cambridge: Cambridge University Press.

Solounias, N., and A. Mayor. 2005. "Ancient References to the Fossils from the Land of Pythagoras." *Earth Sciences History* 23, 2:283–96.

Soltes, O. 1999. *National Treasures of Georgia.* London: Philip Wilson.

Spencer, E. 1838. *Travels in the Western Caucasus.* 2 vols. London: Colburn.

Stark, S., et al., eds. 2012. *Nomads and Networks: The Ancient Art and Culture of Kazakhstan.* Princeton, NJ: Princeton University Press.

Steiner, A. 2007. *Reading Greek Vases.* Cambridge: Cambridge University Press.

Stewart, A. 1995. "Imag(in)ing the Other: Amazons and Ethnicity in Fifth-Century Athens." *Poetics Today* 16, 4:571–97.

———. 1998. *Art, Desire and the Body in Ancient Greece.* Cambridge: Cambridge University Press.

Stewart, W. 2012. "Revealed: Fashion and Beauty Secrets of 2,500-Year-Old Tattooed Siberian Princess." *Daily Mail*, September 4.

Stoneman, R. 1994. *Palmyra and Its Empire: Zenobia's Revolt against Rome.* Ann Arbor: University of Michigan Press.

———. 2008. *Alexander the Great: A Life in Legend.* New Haven, CT: Yale University Press.

Strauss, B. 2004. *The Battle of Salamis.* New York: Simon & Schuster.

———. 2006. *The Trojan War.* New York: Simon & Schuster.

Sturgeon, M. 1995. "The Corinth Amazon." *American Journal of Archaeology* 99:483–505.

Suetonius. 1979. *The Twelve Caesars.* Trans. Robert Graves. Harmondsworth: Penguin.

Sulimirski, T. 1970. *The Sarmatians.* New York: Praeger.

Sutton, R. 1981. "The Interaction between Men and Women Portrayed on Attic Red-Figure Pottery." PhD diss., University of North Carolina, Chapel Hill.

———. 2000. "The Good, the Base, and the Ugly." In Cohen, ed., 2000, 180–202.

———. 2009. "Female Bathers and the Emergence of the Female Nude in Greek Art." In *The Nature and Function of Water, Baths, Bathing and*

Hygiene from Antiquity through the Renaissance, ed. C. Kosso and A. Scott, 61–86. Leiden: Brill.

Talattof, K. 2000. "Nizami's Unlikely Heroines: A Study of the Characterizations of Women in Classical Persian Literature." In *The Poetry of Nizami Ganjavi*, ed. K. Talattof and J. Clinton, 51–82. New York: Palgrave.

Talbert, R. 2000. *Barrington Atlas of the Greek and Roman World, and Directory*. Princeton, NJ: Princeton University Press.

Tarbell, F. B. 1920. "Centauromachy and Amazonomachy in Greek Art: The Reasons for Their Popularity." *American Journal of Archaeology* 24, 3:226–31.

"Tattooed Mummies." 2012. *Museum Secrets*, History Television (Canada), January 12.

Terzan, B., and A. Hellmuth. 2007. "Le Amazzoni, donne-arcieri e principesse della steppa" (Amazons, female archers and princesses of the steppes). In *Ori dei Cavalieri delle Steppe*. Milan: Silvana.

Thomson, R. W., trans. 1978. *History of the Armenians (Moses of Khoren)*. Cambridge, MA: Harvard University Press.

The Trojan War: The Chronicles of Dictys of Crete and Dares the Phrygian. 1966. Trans., intro., and notes R. M. Frazer. Bloomington: Indiana University Press.

Traité de Physiognomonie. 1981. Trans. and comm. J. André. Paris: Belles Lettres.

Truhelka, C. 1896. "Die Tätowirung bei den Katholiken Bosniens und der Hercegovina." *Wissenschaftliche Mittheilungen Aus Bosnien und der Hercegovina*. Sarajevo: Bosnian National Museum.

Tsetskhladze, G. 2011. "The Scythians: Three Essays." In *The Black Sea, Greece, Anatolia, and Europe in the First Millennium BC*, ed. G. Tsetskhladze. Leuven: Peeters.

Tsiafakis, D. 2000. "The Allure and Repulsion of Thracians in the Art of Classical Athens." In Cohen, ed., 2000, 364–89.

Turchin, P. 2012. "The Cultural Evolution of Pants." Social Evolution Forum (July) http://socialevolutionforum.com/2012/07/07/cultural-evolution-of-pants, and http://socialevolutionforum.com/2012/07/10/cultural-evolution-of-pants-ii.

Tyrrell, W. B. 1984. *Amazons: A Study in Athenian Mythmaking*. Baltimore: Johns Hopkins University Press.

Vedder, J. 2004. "Greeks, Amazons, and Archaeology." *Silk Road Foundation Newsletter* 2, 2:17–24.

Vernant, J.-P. 1991. *Mortals and Immortals*. Trans. and ed. F. Zeitlin. Princeton, NJ: Princeton University Press.

Vlassopoulos, K. 2013. *Greeks and Barbarians*. Cambridge: Cambridge University Press.

Vos, M. F. 1963. *Scythian Archers in Archaic Attic Vase-Painting*. Groningen: J. B. Wolters.

Wagner, M., et al. 2009. "The Ornamental Trousers from Sampula (Xinjiang)." *Antiquity* 83:1065–75.

Watson, B. 1962. *Records of the Grand Historian of China. Translated from the Shih chi of Ssu-ma Ch'ien.* New York: Columbia University Press.

Weatherford, J. 2010. *The Secret History of the Mongol Queens.* New York: Crown.

Weingarten, J. 2013, "How the Prince Became a Princess, Part II." November 3. http://judithweingarten.blogspot.com/2013/11/how-prince-became -princess-part-ii.html.

West, M. L. 2011. *The Making of the Iliad: Disquisition and Analytical Commentary.* Oxford: Oxford University Press.

West, S. 1999. "Introducing the Scythians: Herodotus on Koumiss." *Museum Helveticum* 56, 1:76–86.

Wilde, L. W. 1999. *On the Trail of the Women Warriors.* London: Constable.

Wilford, J. 1997. "Ancient Graves of Armed Women Hint at Amazons." *New York Times* (February 25).

Wilhelm, C., et al. 2012. "Hip Ultrasound Screening in Mongolia: A Swiss Mongolian Pediatric Project." *Praxis* 101, 18:1183–86.

Wood, M. 1997. *In the Footsteps of Alexander the Great.* London: BBC Books.

Woodford, S. 2003. *Images of Myths in Classical Antiquity.* Cambridge: Cambridge University Press.

Xi Jin. 2005. "Reflections upon Chinese Recently Unearthed Konghous in Xin Jiang Autonomous Region." Musicology Department, Shanghai Conservatory of Music, June 28. http://musicology.cn/news/news_299.html.

Yablonsky, L. T. 2013. "Extraordinary Kurgan Burial Shines New Light on Sarmatian Life." *Past Horizons* (September 11). http://www.pasthorizons pr.com/index.php/archives/09/2013/extraordinary-kurgan-burial-shines -new-light-on-sarmatian-life.

Yalom, M. 1998. *History of the Breast.* New York: Ballantine Books.

Zhumatov, S. 2012. "Kazakhstan's Lone Female Eagle Hunter." Reuters, March 6. http://blogs.reuters.com/photographers-blog/2012/03/06/kazakhstans -lone-female-eagle-hunter.

Zimmermann, K. 1980. "Tatowierte Thrakerinnenauf griechischenVasenbildern. *Jahrbuch des Deutschen Archaologischen Instituts* 95:163–96.

Zirkle, C. 1936. "Animals Impregnated by the Wind." *Isis* 25:95–130.

Zografou, M. 1972. *Amazons in Homer and Hesiod: A Historical Reconstruction.* Athens: n.p.

INDEX

Notes: Illustrations are indicated by page numbers in italic type. References to color plates from the insert appear in the form "**c1**" in bold type.

caps. *See* hats and caps
"Cartouche" tattoo, *113*
Cartwright, John, 364
Caspian Gates, 39, 319, 325
Caspian Sea, *42*, 48, 131, 144, 184, 186, 192, 334
Castellani Painter, 162
Caucasia, 38–39, *42*, 43, 50, 357–76; Amazons in, 43, 46, 91, 134, 322–25; archaeological finds in, 71–73, *359*; characteristics of, 357–58; family relations in, 158–60; gender equality in, 138–39; horses in, 170, 180; horsewomen warriors in, 359–76; ironworking in, 209, 360; languages of, 58, 235–36, 240–41, 346, 357–58; in Mithradatic Wars, 346; Scythians in, 38; tales from, 17–18, 28, 31, 58, 88, 358–76
Caulon, 304
Cayster, 303
Celaeno, 253
Centaurs, 1, 27
Central Asia, 395–410, *413*; archaeological finds in, 74–76; family relations in, 158–60; Greek ignorance of, 334; horses in, 175–76, 179; hunting in, 186–89; Indian tales, 406–10; intoxicants in, 143–47; Scythians in, 38; tales from, 31, 132, 134, 213, 395–96, 398–406
Chadesians, 165
Chaeronea, 284
Chandragupta (Indian king), 407–8
Chan Wen-Ming, 409
Chardin, John, 373
chariots, 123, 130, 177, *178*, 187, 287, 385, 393, 408, 409
Charope, 229
Chen, Samping, 429
Chertomlyk, *69*, 146, 182
Chertomlyk Vase, 146, 184, 204
childrearing, 55, 133, 157–60, 322, 409, 418. *See also* families
children: burials of, *69*, 70, 74, 159; feeding of, 87, 145; gender equality among, 36, 49, 159–60; horseback riding by, 173–74; relation of, to parents, 458n5; training of, for hunting and fighting, 48, 70, 74, 83, 174, 408. *See also* boys; families; fosterage
China, 411–29, *413*; burials in, 76, 412–13, 415–16, 423–24; nomads' influence on, 422; nomads near, 105–6, 169, 421–24;

outsider heroines in, 425–26; tales from, 420–21; trade with, 112; trousers in, 198, 422; warrior women in, 411–17, 419–21, 424–29; women-only societies near, 417–19
Christianity, 405, 407
Chrysostom, Dio, 104
Cicones, 394
Cilicia, 264–65
Circassian corset, 91, 450n13
Circassian language and tales, 7, 18, 58, 87, 142, 163, 209, 235–36, 241, 359–62, 373–76
Circe, 7
cities, founded by Amazons, 49, 142–43, 152, 162–63, 306, 315
The Classic of Mountains and Seas (Chinese mythology collection), 417–18
clay female figurines, 106–7, *107*, 165
Clearchus of Soli, 104–5, 451n13
Cleidemus, 271, 273
Cleitarchus, 325
Cleopatra, 380, 383
Cleophis, 334–35, 406
Clete, 303–4, 306
clothing: Amazons', 32–33, 97, 101–2, 185, 200–202, 281–82, 441n19; archaeological evidence of, 204–8, *207*; in art and literature, 199–203; of Atalanta, 3–5; in burials, 67–82, 112–13; cold-weather, 160; gender equality and, 192–94, 196–97; Greek, 191, 193–97; for horse riding, 171; in Karakalpak tradition, 405–6; magical properties of, 255; of Mithradates and Hypsicratea, 344; Scythian, 4–5, 40, 97, 160, 194–95, 199, 202, 204, 439n6; tattoos similar to, 102, 108, 109; of Thalestris, 321; Thracian, 97, 445n10; trousers, 191–208; tunics, 191, 257
coins, **c14**, 213, *214*, 264–65, 305, *306*, 317–18, 351–53, *352*, *404*
Colarusso, John, 91–92, 389
Colchis, 72, 142–43, 163, 334
cold weather, living in, 160–61, 194, 199
colewort, 161
Commodus (Roman emperor), 336
companionship, **c13**, 3, 7, 11, 25–26, 30, 31, 54, 81, 126, 131, 137–41, 151, 219, 300
contests: female-male, 440n7; for potential suitors, 2–3, 9–10, 55, 83, 131–32, 397–99, 402, 424, 480n3